GUIDE TO THE
MANUSCRIPT COLLECTIONS
OF THE
HISTORICAL SOCIETY OF
PENNSYLVANIA

Preparation and publication of this book was made possible by
generous grants from

NATIONAL ENDOWMENT FOR THE HUMANITIES
THE PEW CHARITABLE TRUSTS

GUIDE TO THE

MANUSCRIPT COLLECTIONS

OF THE

Historical Society of Pennsylvania

Historical Society of Pennsylvania
Philadelphia
1991

The Historical Society of Pennsylvania, founded in 1824, is an independent, not-for-profit research library and museum located in Center City Philadelphia. The Society is governed by a volunteer board of trustees, served by a staff of thirty-five, and aided by numerous volunteers.

SUSAN STITT
President

LINDA STANLEY
Vice President for Collections

CYNTHIA LITTLE
Vice President for Interpretation

ADAM CORSON-FINNERTY
Director of Development

GEORGE SMITH
Controller/Business Manager

Design by Carl Gross
Printing by Edwards Brothers, Inc.
Typesetting by Impressions, Inc.
Publishing by The Historical Society of Pennsylvania
1300 Locust Street
Philadelphia, Pennsylvania 19107

This book is printed on acid free paper.

ISBN 0-910732-25-6

INTRODUCTION

THE third edition of the *Guide to the Manuscript Collections of the Historical Society of Pennsylvania* is finally published, and it may be the last one to appear in print. Hardware, software, modems, databases, electronic mail, and other promises of the computer age may eliminate the need to produce such a volume. It already is a relic of another era to those who are accustomed to communicating to large audiences across great distances without committing words to paper. Yet the Historical Society is in the business of preserving the tangible evidence of history, and so it is natural that we would want to provide palpable documentation of our manuscript materials.

We are, however, willing to acknowledge our reliance on the more modern methods of sharing information. This publication had its beginnings with the manual typewriter but reached its completion with the computer and an online database.

The Society began work on the third edition in 1977. Only nine years had elapsed between publication of the first edition in 1940, under the auspices of the Works Progress Administration, and the second edition in 1949. After twenty-eight years the second edition was long out of print, and the Historical Society's own copies were reduced to shreds from constant use. Furthermore, we had added much new material to the collections since 1949, and although descriptions had been written and summaries for some were published in the *National Union Catalog of Manuscript Collections,* knowledge of these acquisitions was not generally available.

In order to redress the situation, the Society sought and received funding from the National Endowment for the Humanities. We intended to first review the collections acquired since 1949, verify the existing descriptions, and edit them for a more consistent style. In the second phase we were to turn our attention to cataloging the "backlog," collections for which no descriptions existed at all. Finally we would rework the collection entries from the 1949 *Guide.*

It was not long before we discovered that the task was much more complicated than we had originally thought. Because survey and description methods had evolved over the years, we needed to revise substantially the post-1949 descriptions. In some cases we found that the material had not

INTRODUCTION

been adequately arranged and that it first needed to be organized in order to accurately assess the contents. A two-year project stretched to four years with the continued support of the NEH. By 1981, we had resurveyed most of the newer collections, but had touched only a portion of the backlog and reviewed a small number of entries from the 1949 *Guide*.

A 1984 grant from the Pew Charitable Trusts for publication production was encouraging, but formidable hurdles remained to prevent a timely completion of the project.

The lengthy delay, while frustrating for us as well as for the many researchers who regularly asked about the status of the new edition, has, we believe, proved to be fortunate. In 1986 the Pew Charitable Trusts again provided support to the Society, through a cooperative grant with the Library Company of Philadelphia and the Rosenbach Museum and Library, that allowed us to catalog our manuscript collections into the Research Libraries Information Network (RLIN) online system. As a result, we emended all of our existing descriptions to conform to the recently established rules for cataloging manuscripts and also efficiently produced an index that adhered to these national standards.

In some respects it is still too soon to publish. We wish that each and every manuscript group could have been examined to assure complete accuracy, and we would have wanted all the holdings now at the Society to have been sufficiently arranged to be included. Nevertheless, despite some deficiencies, there is ample justification to go forward. The most compelling reason is that our public is demanding it.

A great number of individuals have contributed to the *Guide*, some of whom deserve particular mention. The project began and progressed for most of its duration under the direction of Peter J. Parker through his tenures as Chief of Manuscripts and Director of the Society. Ericka Thickman Miller, Lowell T. Young, and Rachel Dach all worked to bring sense out of confusion. Theresa R. Snyder was largely responsible for the final preparation. It is she who cataloged the collections into the RLIN database, pulled them out, fixed them up, and performed magic with the keyboard. Her enthusiastic reassurances that it was all possible carried the *Guide* into production.

The manuscript collections of the Historical Society of Pennsylvania are occasionally surprising, frequently inspiring, and always exciting. It is a pleasure and a privilege to share them with you.

LINDA STANLEY
Vice President for Collections

EXPLANATORY NOTE

THE entries are arranged according to assigned collection number. Numbers with added letters (e.g., 1792A, 1792B) indicate that the groupings of manuscripts have come to the Society from different sources or at different times, but are presumed to have once been a coherent body of papers.

Some collections have been artificially created for single volumes or small series of volumes for more efficiency (e.g., #788, Church Records). No effort has been made to correct the occasional practice in the 1949 *Guide* (collection numbers 1 through 1611) of assigning separate numbers for this type of record.

The descriptions have been prepared according to the standards established by *Archives, Personal Papers and Manuscripts* and *Anglo-American Cataloging Rules* (AACR 2). Some modifications have been made to conform to the Historical Society's own cataloging methods. An entry will consist of the main title, type of record, inclusive dates (bulk dates will be indicated with parentheses), and size of the collection. Most entries will also include biographical/historical information; descriptive notes; provenance, when known; and publication history, where relevant.

Entries that have been cancelled have either been transferred elsewhere or incorporated into other collections and are so noted. Where "no entry," is indicated the material has not yet been sufficiently processed to allow for proper description and is not available for research.

The index, following *Library of Congress Subject Headings* and AACR 2 personal and corporate name headings, refers the user to the collection number. It would be impossible to anticipate or to accommodate every point of index access for the collection descriptions. Creativity and a sense of adventure are encouraged in exploring the index.

Philadelphia and Pennsylvania are assumed to be the geographic locations unless otherwise indicated. Local designations may be given in the main title or in the descriptive notes.

The Historical Society of Pennsylvania welcomes any corrections or additions. Improving and expanding information on our holdings is a continuing interest.

1

**Van der Kemp, Francis Adrian, 1752–1829.   Collection, 1781–1829.
(ca. 150 items.)**

Francis Adrian Van der Kemp was a Dutch scholar, patriot, and
preacher who emigrated to the United States in 1788.

Letters from John Adams which convey his appraisal of political events;
his reaction to the French Revolution; comments on American foreign policy and European affairs during the Napoleonic Wars and the period of the
Holy Alliance; discussions of political philosophy, and of philosophical and
religious questions; a vivid account of Adams' confrontation with Pennsylvania Quaker leaders, 1774; scientific speculations. The letters also contain
Adams' comments on noted men (French philosophes, British political
thinkers and historians, and leaders of the American Revolution and the
early national period), on books, on the power of the press. Included are
letters, 1826–1829, from John Quincy Adams to Van der Kemp; a letter of
Marquis de Lafayette, [1788], to Benjamin Franklin introducing Van der
Kemp; a letter of George Washington, 1788, welcoming Van der Kemp to
America; letters of Abigail Adams; a letter of Van der Kemp; a certificate of
membership in the American Philosophical Society to Van der Kemp, signed
by Thomas Jefferson and others; and several miscellaneous items.

Gift of Pauline E. Henry, granddaughter of Francis Adrian Van der
Kemp.

Washington letter manuscript copy.

2

Alexander, William.   Papers, 1788–1813.   (ca. 200 items.)

William Alexander was a Revolutionary War officer and district surveyor in Carlisle, Cumberland County.

A small collection of the official papers of William Alexander including
receipts, warrants, and memoranda on the surveying of military bonus lands
in Cumberland County. Also included are correspondence and reports concerning the construction of turnpikes and canals in central Pennsylvania.

Purchased, Dreer Fund, 1926.

3

Allen, Elizabeth A.   Collection, 1699–1858.   (ca. 75 items.)

Deeds, mortgages, and other title papers for lands in Middletown,
Northampton, and Bristol townships, the borough of Bristol, and the village
of Attleborough (now Langhorne) in Bucks County. Also included are a
copy of Jeremiah Langhorne's will; a transcript of a Quaker tract, 1762, by

William Motte, on Christian pilgrimage; the constitution of the Middletown School Association, 1834; a survey plan of Washington Village, Bucks County.

Gift of Elizabeth A. Allen.

4
Allen, George, 1808–1876.   Papers, 1828–1843.   (3 v.)

George Allen, quondam lawyer and Episcopal minister in St. Albans, Vt., taught languages at Delaware College in Newark, Del., 1837–1845, and subsequently was professor of ancient languages at the University of Pennsylvania. In 1863, he published the *Life of Philidor,* a book about chess.

Included in this collection are his "Book of Extracts," begun in 1828, mostly literary; "Literary Commonplace Book," containing some notes on chess; Index Rerum, 1843 et postea.

Gift of the Estate of Gregory B. Keen, 1931.

5
Allen, James, 1742–1778.   Diary, 1770–1778.   (1 v.)

The diary of James Allen, Philadelphia lawyer, contains information on the social, political, and cultural history of the colonial and Revolutionary periods in Philadelphia, with comments on military affairs, battles, and generals and other prominent persons.

Gift of Brinton Coxe, 1881.

6
Allen, John Jasper.   "The Whippiad."   (1 v.)

A satirical poem in the classical manner on student life at Oxford University.

7
Alloway, John W.   Diary, 1863.   (1 v.)

Annual diary for 1863 of John W. Alloway, private soldier in Cooper's Battalion of the 1st Pennsylvania Artillery during the Civil War records incidents of camp life and campaigns along the Rappahannock and Radipan rivers in northern Virginia during the Chancellorsville campaign, the Gettysburg campaign, and the dispatch of troops to quell draft riots in New York City.

8
American Negro Historical Society.   **Collection, 1790–1905.**
(8 linear ft.)

The American Negro Historical Society was founded in 1897 by a group of Philadelphia blacks to study and preserve materials documenting the American black experience. Among the founders and early members were Robert Adger, W.M. Dorsey and Jacob C. White, Jr., who donated materials to the society, some of which are present in the collection.

Included are minutes of the society, 1897–1904; incoming correspondence and drafts, 1897–1905; membership lists [1897] and 1904; bills and receipts, 1900–1904; and land accession books.

Among the materials collected by the society and presented by Leon Gardiner, Philadelphia printer, are the records of several civic and philanthropic organizations: Banneker Institute, minutes kept by Jacob C. White, Jr., 1854–1859, roll books, 1854–1872, first begun as the roll of the Alexandrian Institute, receipts, 1855–1868, check book, 1867–1872, and record of lectures and debates, 1859–1861, some of which dealt with the place of the black in American society; Benezet Joint Stock Association of Philadelphia, a mutual beneficial society, minutes, 1854–1885, share records, 1871–1889, and payment orders, 1871–1885; Agricultural and Mechanics Association of Pennsylvania and New Jersey, constitution, 1839, continued as stock transfer book, 1840–1846, and stock certificate book, 1840–1844; Cultural, Social and Statistical Association of the Colored People of Philadelphia, constitution, by-laws, roll and minutes, 1860–1867, and payment orders, 1860–1867; Lebanon Cemetery, Philadelphia, letter books, Jacob C. White, Jr., secretary, 1874–1886, accounts, 1849–1867, burial vouchers, 1855–1901; Benjamin Lundy Philanthropic Society, roll book, 1830–1842; Daughters of Africa, beneficial society, minutes, 1822–1838, and payment order book, 1821–1829; Pennsylvania State Equal Rights League, executive board minutes, 1864–1872; and Frederick Douglass Memorial Hospital (Philadelphia), records, 1895–1901.

Also included are the records of several schools and churches: First African Presbyterian Church, miscellaneous correspondence and accounts, 1832–1846; Second African Presbyterian Church, correspondence, bills and receipts about its Sabbath School, 1832–1838; Zoar Sabbath School, catalogue of the library, 1844, continued as circulation record; records of the Roberts Vaux Consolidated School, 1870–1901.

Also included are correspondence and schedules of the Philadelphia Pythians, a black baseball club, 1867–1870; miscellaneous correspondence and broadsides of such organizations as the Philadelphia Library Company and the Colored People's Union League Association, and several letters and speeches of Isaiah C. Wears, 1856–1901, and Jacob C. White, Sr. and Jacob C. White, Jr., 1832–1899, some autograph material of Benjamin Banneker, 1790–1891, and Frederick Douglass, 1870–1875.

Gift of Leon Gardiner, 1934.

9

Antill, Edward, 1742–1789.   Papers, 1780.   (1 v.)

A small collection of scientific papers written or copied by Lieutenant Colonel Edward Antill while a paroled prisoner of war at Flat Bush, Long Island (New York, N.Y.) Subjects include "The principles of geology and astronomy," "elements of chronology," "elements of all the syllables within the English language," "a table of the sun's declination from 1764 to 1795," and a table showing the number of miles to each degree of longitude and latitude.

Gift of Mrs. William Stansfield, 1936.

10

Burleigh, Charles Calistus, 1810–1878.   Papers, 1844–1859. (8 items.)

Charles Calistus Burleigh was an abolitionist and reformer associated with the Garrisonian wing of the anti-slavery movement. He was editor of the *Unionists,* 1835–1837, wrote for the *Liberator,* edited the *Pennsylvania Freeman* after 1844, and served as the secretary of the American Anti-Slavery Society and editor of its annual reports.

Included in this small collection of published and unpublished manuscripts are: "Journal of the Little Things of Life," begun in 1844, including an index in another hand; the manuscript for Burleigh's *Thoughts on the Death Penalty* (1845); the texts for the Annual Reports of the American Anti-Slavery Society, 1856–1859, in several hands edited by Burleigh; incoming correspondence, 1838, 1875.

Gift of Colonel John P. Nickolson, 1909.

11

Archambault, Anna Margaretta.   Papers, 1876–1945. (2 linear ft.)

Personal correspondence of Anna Margaretta Archambault, portrait painter, miniaturist, author, and educator, is included with sketches, photos, and correspondence on her work in miniatures. Also included are correspondence and notes for *Guide Book of Art, Architecture, and Historic Interest in Pennsylvania* (Philadelphia, 1924), which she edited for the Art Committee of the State Federation of Pennsylvania Women, histories of the counties of Pennsylvania, and clippings and illustrations to accompany the histories.

Gift of Anna Margaretta Archambault, 1933–1946.

12

Longstreth, Mary Anna.   Collection, 1876–1878.   (3 v.)

A collection of biographical information gathered by Mary Anna Longstreth, Philadelphia educator, about Emma Dean Walker Armstrong, wife of Samuel Chapman Armstrong, founder of the Hampton (Va.) Normal and Agricultural Institute. The materials are assembled in letter form for the Armstrong children, Louise and Edith, and contain considerable information about the early history of the institute and the educational philosophy of its founder. Longstreth has included, as well, many letters from Emma Dean Walker Armstrong's female acquaintances, testifying to her exemplary character.

Three of the original four volumes survive in the collection.

13

Armstrong, Thomas.   Notebook, 1830.   (1 v.)

Memoranda of historical events, and on literary and scientific subjects made by Thomas Armstrong while a student at the University of Pennsylvania.

14

Armstrong, William.   Papers, 1776–1779.   (3 v.)

Quartermaster accounts of Major William Armstrong include leaves from journal, 1776; receipt book, 1778; receipt book for construction work at Fort Mifflin, near Philadelphia, 1779.

Gift of Dr. Isaac R. Walker.

15

Armstrong, William G., 1823–1900.   Diaries, 1866–1888.   (23 v.)

William G. Armstrong was a Philadelphia banknote and line engraver and portrait painter.

The annual diaries contain comment on local and national politics (demonstrating racist and anti-Republican attitudes), and on cultural, professional, and social activities.

16
Asch, Myers.   **Letters and Documents, 1876–1887.**
(ca. 50 items.)

A collection of letters from envoys of Algiers, Austria, Belgium, Italy, Japan, Russia, Spain, Turkey, expressing their government's appreciation and esteem to Colonel Myers Asch, secretary of the United States Centennial Exposition, and conferring upon him honors, titles, and decorations for his distinctive services rendered to their commissions at the Exposition.

Gift of Rebecca Asch Shoyer, David W. Shoyer, and William L. Shoyer.

17
Ashmead, Jacob.   **Papers, 1698–1794.**   **(1 v.)**

Documents of colonial and Revolutionary periods belonging to Captain Jacob Ashmead, include: surveys and indentures, 1698–1752; indenture of apprenticeship, 1762; muster and payrolls, 1776–1779; diary of western expedition, Sept. 27, 1794 to Dec. 13, 1794; will, 1794.

Gift of Samuel B. Ashmead.

18
Ashton and Roberts family papers, 1791 (1795–1841) 1890.   **(1 v.)**

Papers of the related Ashton and Roberts families of Bucks and Montgomery counties: business accounts, 1795–1810, of Robert Ashton and his daughter Margaret Ashton Roberts; commonplace book of Margaret Roberts and her son Guy Roberts, containing hymns, poems, and Quaker testimonies; inventory of the estate of Robert Ashton, 1821–1830; Quaker wedding certificate of Nathan Roberts and Margaret Ashton at Richland Friends' Meeting, 1791; the will of David Roberts, 1805; genealogical information on the Ashton, Roberts and Lancaster families of Pennsylvania.

Gift of Mrs. George Corson, 1929.

19
Ashhurst, John.   **Estate papers, 1699–1858.**   **(2 linear ft.)**

This collection contains the papers of the John Ashhurst estate. Most of the papers, primarily correspondence and receipts, pertain to the business interests of Manuel Eyre and Manuel Eyre, Jr., Philadelphia merchants. The papers give information on commodity prices, insurance rates, and real estate, biographical sketches of friends and testimonials from various meetings, 1699–1763, information on property valuation for various wards of Philadelphia; lecture notes of John Ashhurst (son) 1855, later a noted physician.

Gift of the Ashhurst family.

20

United States Continental Congress. *The Association &c.,*
1774. **(1 v.)**

In October 1774, Congress resolved to use non-importation as a political weapon against the British Government in an effort to coerce the British
into the repeal of the Intolerable Acts. The agreement was ordered printed
by William and Thomas Bradford certain of which were signed by the
delegates and sent to the colonies as official copies.

This is Maryland's copy.

21

Asylum Company. **Papers, 1786 (1793–1836) 1851.** **(350 items.)**

In April 1794 Robert Morris, John Nicholson, and others organized
the Asylum Company to develop or sell lands that they had already acquired
in Luzerne, Northampton, and Northumberland counties. French emigrés,
founders of Azilum on the North Branch of the Susquehanna River, near
present Towanda, were among their first customers. The company was reorganized twice: in 1795 Nicholson succeeded to Morris' interest, and in
1801 Nicholson's financial difficulties forced him to give up his interests.
The company frequently came into conflict with Connecticut claimants,
especially after 1801 when they expanded their operations to Bedford, Bradford, and Lycoming counties.

Included in the collection are: a draft map for lands in Bedford County,
1793; broadside notices concerning the organization of the company, 1794;
correspondence, 1795–1799, of John Keating, agent for the company, concerning improvements on the properties at Asylum, monies due to the
company, and title disputes with Connecticut claimants; deeds, 1797, for
lands in Northumberland County; correspondence, accounts, receipts, and
contracts of Samuel Baird, also agent for the company, 1802–1825; accounts
with and correspondence with shareholders, 1823–1836; copies of memorials
presented by John Astley, 1839, to the Pennsylvania Assembly for compensation for lands sold by the state but claimed by the company; miscellaneous
letters, accounts, title papers, shares of stock in the company.

Purchased by the Society.

22

Autograph Collection of the Historical Society of Pennsylvania,
1671–1939. **(80 linear ft.)**

This collection is composed of single items, groups of letters, and
miscellaneous documents acquired individually. The letters present autographs of prominent American and foreign persons.

23

Autograph Letters of the Presidents of the United States, 1788–1864.
(16 items.)

Miscellaneous letters of the Presidents of the United States from George Washington to Abraham Lincoln.

Collected by Samuel Welsh. Gift of the heirs of Samuel Welsh, 1905.

24

Bache, Franklin, 1792–1864.   Papers, 1818 (1833–1861).
(150 items.)

Franklin Bache was a Philadelphia physician, professor of chemistry, and author.

The main body of these papers is contained in Bache's letterbook and incoming correspondence, both of which consist almost entirely of letters to and from Albert Dabadie, Bache's brother-in-law and an expatriate American in Europe. The correspondence relates to Dabadie's American investments, French spoliation claims, and his appointment as American consul in Italy, as well as European political and economic conditions and family matters.

There are some letters, 1850–1852, of Bache to his son, [Thomas] Hewson Bache, who was studying medicine in Europe, with fatherly advice to the son on studies, finances, and life, and reporting on activities back home. There are also notes and a committee draft report, 1841, on the origin of the American Philosophical Society, of which Bache was an officer, and a manuscript on chemistry.

25

Balch Collection, 1699–1923.   (6 linear ft.)

A portion of the collection is made up of materials collected by Thomas Balch while he was writing *Les Français en Amérique . . .*, 1777–1783: original manuscripts of "Episodes de la Guerre maritime de l'Indépendence Américaine," by Du Petit Thouars, and "Mémoire du Marquis de Vaudreuil au Marquis de Duquesne," 1755; copies of "Mémoires du Comte de Grasse sur le combat naval, le 12 avril 1782," "Relation du voyage du Prince de Broglie, 1782," "Depuis mon depart de France, 26 mars 1781 au 18 nov. de la même année quand l'armée aux ordres de M. le Comte de Rochambeau est entrée dans le quartier d'hiver" (probably written by Cromot du Bourg, one of Rochambeau's aides), "Correspondance de M. de Kalb avec le duc de Choiseul du 20 avril 1767 du 10 février 1796." A list of names of French and British officers in the American Revolution, 1779–1783, appears in the volume with the Du Petit Thouars manuscript.

The interest of Thomas Willing Balch in international law is represented by correspondence, 1892–1918, on the use of arbitration as an instrument of international policy; papers relative to the arbitration of the Alabama Claims, 1864–1872; material on Alaskan boundaries, January 14, 1854 to May 20, 1854.

With the exception of a few incidental items, the rest of the collection contains family papers and documents on the history of colonial Pennsylvania. These include: photostats of the will, inventories of the estate, and some of the correspondence of Thomas Willing, 1776–1820; miscellaneous correspondence, invitations, 1857–1923; a group of etchings of French and American officers of the Revolution; letters and documents, 1699–1805, on social, political, and religious affairs, to the French and Indian War, and grand jury charges, miscellaneous topics are letters and documents, 1717–1923: "Journal of occurrences while in Europe," July 10, 1815-July 10, 1816, signed by H.B. Wilson; "A Theme of Verbs," by Edward Shippen, 1768; Balch family correspondence with members of the Shippen and Swift families, 1752–1830; and Swift and Willing family correspondence, 1743–1882.

Gift of Elise Willing Balch.

Will Photostatic copy.

26

Baldwin, Evelyn Briggs, 1862–1933.   Papers, 1898–1926.   (3 v.)

"Log of the Wellman Arctic Expedition to Franz-Josef Land, 1898–99," by Evelyn B. Baldwin, second in command of the expedition and "Digest of papers relating to Pensioneers of the Revolutionary War, Baldwin Family." 1926.

Gift of Evelyn B. Baldwin.

Originals on deposit. Library of Congress—Manuscript Division. Library of Congress Annex. 2nd Street and Independence Avenue, S.E.; Washington, D.C. 20540.

Genealogical data on the Baldwin, Crampton, Scranton, Beers, Hicks, Ogden, and Trist or Twiss families, compiled by Baldwin, 1926; transferred to the Genealogical Society of Pennsylvania.

27

Baldwin, Joshua, 172c/1–1800.   Ledger and Receipt Book,
1725 (1744–1796) 1847.   (1 v.)

Ledger and receipt book, kept primarily by Joshua Baldwin, Chester County, farmer and saddler, records business transactions and distribution of Baldwin's property. Also included are remarks to a Lyceum, not located; addresses to the Downingtown Temperance Society, n.d.; notes on scientific subjects, n.d.; genealogical notes, 1847, on the Clemson, Sharples, and Richardson families, all in an unknown later hand.

Formerly part of the Gilpin library.

28
Ball families.   Papers, 1676–1879.   (6 linear ft.)

This is a miscellaneous collection of papers of two contemporary Ball families of Philadelphia, sometimes confused because of common names and occupations.

The William Ball family papers: William Ball, Sr., and William Ball, Jr., were merchants who owned Hope Farm, in Northern Liberties Township (Shakamaxon): correspondence, accounts, surveys, and other papers, 1760–1771, relate to the Nova Scotia Land Company, a colonizing venture in Nova Scotia; Richmond Meadows Company account book, 1760–1762, continued with election returns book, 1763, 1766; Elizabeth Byles, wife of William Ball, Sr., letterbook, 1759–1783, and diary, 1757–1763; William Ball, Jr., rent and bond account book, 1782–1808; and miscellaneous other business, land and estate papers.

The Joseph Ball family papers: Joseph Ball was a Philadelphia merchant, industrialist, insurance executive, and bank director: business accounts and agreements for building, outfitting of several vessels including privateers, and related litigation; insurance policies; estate papers and genealogical depositions from Pennsylvania, Ohio, Indiana, and Virginia, 1855–1860, gathered in the settlement of his vast estate.

John Ball, brother of Joseph Ball, was a resident merchant at St. Eustatius, St. Thomas and St. Croix for several years, and partner of William Waddrop and Daniel Jennings (Ball, Waddrop and Jennings) business papers and correspondence, 1779–1782, including letters to William Bingham.

Henry Banks was a merchant of Richmond, Va. His business papers and correspondence relate to commercial activities, land purchases, and privateering, including correspondence with his Kentucky partner in trade and land speculation, John Fowler. Bank's financial problems are revealed in legal papers on various suits and correspondence with Philadelphia lawyer, Daniel Brodhead, in Bank's bankruptcy trial and imprisonment with Robert Morris in 1798. Joseph Ball was a trustee of his bankrupt estate.

The collection also includes, from related Richards and Dupuy families, Lewis M. Walker and John Richards, receipt book, 1817–1821; extracts of Burlington, N.J., land surveys, 1741–1833; deeds and other items.

Of uncertain origin is an unidentified Philadelphia merchant's journal, 1733–1739. Also Thomas Wotherspoon, Philadelphia merchant, receipt book, 1796–1804.

Gift of Herbert Dupuy.

29
Balliet family.   Papers, 1728 (1756–1808) 1845.   (125 items.)

Paul Balliet, an Alsatian Huguenot, settled in Whitehall Township, Northampton (now Lehigh) County. His son, Colonel Stephen Balliet, served as: Revolutionary War officer and state official; member of the Pennsylvania ratification convention, 1787; member of the Pennsylvania Assembly and House of Representatives, 1788–1797; and collector of the federal excise tax, 1797. He was also a local merchant.

The bulk of the collection consists of correspondence, business, and official papers of Stephen Balliet. The business papers include: receipts, drafts, and other business papers, 1786–1815; records of distillers' licenses issued and revenue collected, 1799–1803; daybook, 1783; miscellaneous title papers.

For Paul Balliet there are legal documents and genealogical notes.
Some of the Paul Balliet materials are in German.

30
Barber, Rhoda.   Journal of settlement at Wright's Ferry on Susquehanna River, 1830.   (1 v.)

The recollections of Rhoda Barber, Lancaster County, spinster written in 1830, describing migration and settlement, economic and domestic life, trade with the Indians, 1726–1782. Also is a narrative of the massacre of the Conestoga Indians by the Paxton Boys in 1763, and some reminiscences of incidents of the Revolution.

31
Barclay, John.   Papers, 1801–1807.   (11 items.)

Correspondence of John Barclay, Philadelphia politician and banker, with James Hamilton, judge at Carlisle, and trustee of Dickinson College, and with John B. Parker, also of Carlisle, on a tract of land involved in the settlement of an estate; letters of July 15 and July 31, 1804, discuss the Hamilton-Burr duel.

Purchased.

32
Barker, Joshua.   Docket Books, 1828–1845.   (2 v.)

Docket books maintained by Joshua Barker, Bucks County justice of the peace, and continued by Lewis Swift, also a justice of the peace, beginning 1837, and includes "Account of orders granted for the relief of poor persons," 1836–1845.

Formerly part of the Gilpin Library.

33
Barney, Joshua, 1759–1818.   **Papers, 1782–1818.**   **(150 items.)**

These papers reflect Joshua Barney's activities as an American naval officer during the Revolution, commodore in the French navy from 1796 to 1802, privateer during the War of 1812, and commander of the Chesapeake flotilla defending Washington, D.C., in 1814. The largest group of papers relate to his service in the French navy and include official papers, accounts, log of La Tribune, and related material. Some papers, possibly saved by Barney from captured ships, consist of circular letters of British postmasters, instructions and documents for the mail packet Amelia, 1793–1812, with information on intelligence-gathering, as well as a few letters for British merchants, 1812. Also commissions, naval signals, testimonials, and more.

34
Barton, Benjamin Smith, 1766–1815.   **Papers, 1778–1813.**
(ca. 200 items.)

The Barton papers contain the correspondence of Benjamin Smith Barton, professor of medicine at the College of Philadelphia, with scholars and scientists, among them: Thomas Jefferson, James Madison, Joseph Priestley, John Drayton, L. Valentine, Frederick Rush, and others; notes and observations on natural phenomena.

Also there are journals, 1789–1803. The journal for 1789 contains an interesting description of Barton's voyage on the *Apollo* from Gravesend, England, to Philadelphia; he notes talks with John Pemberton, a fellow passenger and Quaker preacher, about the early settlements in Pennsylvania; he reviews the biographies of William Penn and of Benjamin West, the painter. The later journals, 1794–1803, describe his travels through the states; his research in the fields of botany, mineralogy, anthropology, and zoology; his observations on frontier settlements, Indian tribes, and the physician condition of the land. Ten diplomas, 1790–1812 , from the College of Philadelphia and various European universities are included.

Journal of *Apollo* voyage published in *P.M.H.B.,* 9 (1885): 334–338.

35
Barton, Charles Crillon, d. 1851.   **Journals, 1827–1831.**   **(2 v.)**

Midshipman's journals kept by Charles Crillon Barton while off Brazil and Argentina aboard U.S.S. *Vandalia* and U.S.S. *Hudson,* 1828–1831, embellished by Barton's watercolors and wash drawings as well as his manuscript map of Brazil.

Gift of Edward Shippen, 1891.

36

Bartram family.   Collection, 1721 (1765–1803) 1814.
(3 linear ft.)

John and William Bartram were naturalists, both of whom undertook extensive botanizing expeditions to the Carolinas, Georgia, and Florida. John, in particular, corresponded with prominent scientists and political figures in Europe and America. John Fothergill secured for Bartram the appointment as Botanist to the King, 1765, and underwrote his expedition to the South in 1765. Moses and Isaac Bartram were Philadelphia merchants.

Included in the collection are "Journal through the Catskill mountains with Billy," 1753 by John Bartram; a portion of his observations made on his journey through the Carolinas, Georgia, and Florida, 1765; the full text of the diary, 1765–1766, transcribed by William Darlington, "with illustrative notes from his correspondence;" portions of his "Travels through the Carolinas, Georgia and East and West Floridas, 1773–1777," by William Bartram, edited for later publication by Bartram; photostats of copies of a portion of that journal made for John Fothergill now in the British Library; "Answers to Benjamin Smith Barton's queries about Indians," copied by John Howard Payne, including copies of Bartram's illustrations; commonplace Book, 1797–1803; pharmacopeia, n.d.; letterbook, 1790–1814 of Isaac Bartram; miscellaneous title papers on Bartram's Gardens, 1721–1819; fragment of ledger index, 1791 of Moses Bartram.

The collection includes letters addressed to John and William Bartram from William Byrd, Alexander Calhoun, Mark Catesby, Benjamin Franklin, Fothergill, and others; and Anthony Purvis' translation of the Bible, London, 1764, presented to John Bartram by John Fothergill.

Finding aid available.

37

Beatty-Wynkoop family.   Genealogy, [1917].   (1 v.)

Transferred to the Genealogical Society of Pennsylvania.

38

Becket, William, 1697–1743.   Letter and commonplace book,
1727–1742.   (1 v.)

Rev. William Becket was a missionary of the Society for the Propagation of the Gospel at Lewes (Sussex County, Del.) 1721–1723.

His letter and commonplace book deals with the society, his work, the parish, baptismal statistics for whites and blacks, lists of contributors, the effects of George Whitefield's preaching, and description of, and population statistics for, Sussex County.

Gift of Rev. C.H.B. Turner, 1919.

39
Beebe, Lewis.   Journals, 1776–1801.   (3 v.)

Journal, 1776–1777, is a narrative of Lewis Beebe's participation in the campaign against Canada during the Revolution, giving an account of the battles, troop movements, commanding officers, ravages of disease in camps, and the economic and social aspects of the period. Journals, 1799–1801, 1800–1801, contain notes of a journey from New England to Virginia, with details on facilities for travel, characteristics of the inhabitants of the states he traversed, their religious sentiments, education, sports, recreations, economic and social conditions. Also included is information on the political controversies agitating the period, particularly the election of Thomas Jefferson, and the contest between Democratic and Federalist factions.

Gift of Roland C. Ashbrook, 1935.

Journal, 1776–1777, published in *P.M.H.B.,* 59 (1935): 321–361.

40
**Frederick Eugene Francois, Baron de Beelen-Bertholff, 1729–1805.
Papers, (1785–1788) (1873–1913).   (50 items.)**

Copies of letters, 1785–1888, written by Baron de Beelen-Bertholff, Belgian agent to United States, to Count Barbiano di Belgiojoso, Brussels, on commercial and political affairs in the United States. They contribute information on Spain's attitude regarding United States navigation on the Mississippi, 1785; the military occupation of Forts Niagara, Oswego, and Detroit, by the British; peace treaties with the Indians negotiated at New York; John Adams' and Thomas Jefferson's diplomatic missions to France and England; Comte de Beaufort's proposal to Congress to bring 10,000 settlers to America; reports on commerce, shipping, and treaties with foreign nations; Annapolis Convention, 1786; Federal Convention in Philadelphia, 1787; and other subjects. The papers, 1873–1913, contain Joseph M. Gazzam's correspondence with John Jay and other diplomats, which relates to the diplomatic activities and ancestry of Baron de Beelen-Bertholff.

Gift of Joseph M. Gazzam, 1880.

41
DeBenneville, George, 1703–1793.   Autobiography, 1782.   (2 v.)

George de Benneville was born in England of a Huguenot family, became a convert to Universalism, studied medicine, and became an itinerant preacher among French Huguenots and in Germany and the Low Countries. He came to America in 1741, settling first in Germantown, then in Oley Valley, Berks County, where he practiced medicine and preached.

These manuscripts are incomplete and describe Dr. George de Benneville's life before coming to America and provide insight into enthusiastic religion in 18th century Europe.

Purchased, Library Fund, 1912.

Winchester, Elhanan. *Some Remarkable Passages in the Life of Dr. George De Benneville*. (Germantown, Pa.: Converse Clearves, Publisher) 1890.

Contemporary handwritten copy.

42
Duffield, Samuel W., 1843–1887.   "The Artist's Dream," 1867. (1 v.)

A manuscript poem with a pen sketch by George F. Bensell, a Philadelphia painter, dedicated to Mrs. Emma Seligman.

43
Benzinger, Mathias.   Papers, 1845.   (1 v.)

Abstract of title to twelve tracts of land in the McKean and Clearfield Counties, purchased by Benzinger from Thomas J. Stryker, cashier of the Trenton Banking Company, N.J., in 1844; the abstract recites the title from 1799 to 1844.

Gift of N.R. Ewan, 1935.

44
Berks and Montgomery Counties Papers, 1693–1869.   (ca. 250 items.)

Miscellaneous papers on to local government: petitions, laws, rules, regulations, lists of names of freeholders, assessments. There are also some letters from prominent men of the times: Thomas Mifflin, Richard Peters, John Potts, Conrad Weiser, and others, on Indian controversies, land transactions, social and economic affairs of the colonial period.

Purchased.

45
Beverly, Robert.   Papers, 1763–1852.   (ca. 800 items.)

Robert Beverly was a financier from Georgetown, D.C.

Accounts and receipts, 1763–1852, show the cost of education in 1820, prices of goods, value of slaves; also documents connected with the litigation arising out of the settling of the estate of George Washington.

Purchased, Dreer Fund, 1926.

46

Bevis, Thomas.   Genealogical records, 1737–1879.
(ca. 75 items.)

A collection of genealogical records and correspondence on the families of Bevis, Draper, Brockley, and related families, of New Jersey.
Gift of Samuel Adams Bevis, 1906.

47

Biddle, Charles, 1745–1821.   Papers, 1763–1829.   (ca. 250 items.)

Papers collected by Charles Biddle include: correspondence, 1763–1829, on politics, naval and military affairs, and the slave trade; letters of Aaron Burr, 1796–1807, including his controversy with Alexander Hamilton; letters of Benedict Arnold, 1736–1774; letter book, 1792–1806 of Charles Biddle; autobiography of Biddle, 1819.

48

Biddle, Clement, 1740–1814.   Letterbooks, 1789–1792.   (2 v.)

Clement Biddle, merchant and officer during the Revolutionary War, held several governmental offices.
His earlier letterbook, 1769–1770, documents his trade in Maryland and Virginia wheat and his trading in slaves, and contains comment on the events leading to the end of non-importation in Philadelphia. His major correspondents are: Thomas Conte, Nottingham (Md.); Andrew Leitch, Blandensburgh (Md.); James Maccubin, Annapolis (Md.); Thomas Richardson, Georgetown (D.C.); and Thomas Robinson, Newport (R.I.)
The second letterbook, 1789–1792, relates chiefly to his activities as a securities broker and reports current prices of stocks, government securities, and scrip, and contains comments on the funding of the public debt, congressional activities, and the first Bank of the United States. Major correspondents include New Yorkers Robert Gilchrist, Tobias Lear, George Lewis, William Roger. Other correspondents are William Campbell, Annapolis (Md.); Michael Heathcote & Co., Petersburg (Va.); and others in Maryland and Virginia. There are also some letters on returns for the 1790 census, and troops and supplies for the defense of the frontier.
Gift of Thomas A. Biddle and Company, 1927.

49

Biddle, Clement, 1740–1814.   Papers, 1743–1835.   (ca. 200 items.)

The papers of Clement Biddle, quartermaster general of the Pennsylvania Militia and United States marshal for Pennsylvania, are divided into two groups: one is made up of correspondence between Biddle and George Washington incident to Biddle's activities as commissary general of forage during the Revolution, and upon his subsequent business relations with Washington; the other section contains miscellaneous letters and documents from various famous men. The Washington-Biddle papers include: 9 general orders and warrants, 1778–1780, signed by Washington and issued in connection with the work of the commissary department in the Revolution; letters from Washington to Biddle, 1784–1799; letters from Tobias Lear, 1789–1791, and from Washington, 1785–1790; accounts of Washington with Biddle, 1789–1798.

The second group includes: letters and papers, 1780–1835, of John Quincy Adams, Aaron Burr, Nathanael Greene, Alexander Hamilton, Thomas Jefferson, James Monroe, Timothy Pickering, and others; Gideon Cornell's commissions of appointment as judge, 1743–1748; some colonial paper money; samples of cloth.

Correspondence of Clement Biddle, 1778–1790, published in *P.M.H.B.,* 32 (1908): 498–500; 52 (1928): 310–343; 42 (1918): 53–76, 143–162, 193–207.

50
Biddle, Thomas A.   Business Records and correspondence, 1771–1837.   (12 linear ft.)

A collection of business records and letterbooks of prominent mercantile, shipping, and banking firms of Philadelphia. They contribute valuable information on economic trends during the Revolution and the early national period. The record books, 1771–1786, contain accounts of provisions, military stores, equipment, supplied to the Revolutionary army; trade and shipping with England and other countries; privateering and distribution of prize money; goods imported and exported; current prices; financial and legal matters. The record books, 1787–1837, reflect the growth and extension of local and foreign trade; the organization of financial institutions, banks and insurance companies; accounts of municipal enterprises, erection of bridges, gas and water works; transactions in stocks and bonds.

Among the clients mentioned are Richard Bache, Horace Binney, Biddle and Wharton, John Cox, Manuel Eyre, John Keith, Edward Tilghman, John Sergeant, Taylor and Newbold, Robert Waln, Robert Willing, and others. The collection comprises: journals, 1781–1822; ledgers, 1785–1837; cashbooks, 1771–1817; daybooks, 1783–1814; blotters, 1799–1809; promissory notebook, 1798; debt book, 1785; ship book, 1784–1792; notary public registers, 1779–1786; stock book, 1817; checkbook, 1800–1801; letterbooks, 1783–1822; Upper Ferry Bridge Company, Philadelphia, minute book, 1811–1834.

Gift of Thomas A. Biddle & Company, 1927.

51

Bigler, William, 1814–1880.   Papers, 1836–1880.   (6 linear ft.)

This collection includes the correspondence, 1836–1880, of William Bigler, governor of Pennsylvania and United States senator, 1856–1861; miscellaneous papers on the Tyrone Clearfield Railway Company, and the Centennial Exposition, 1839–1876; speeches, pamphlets, and newspaper clippings, 1853–1862. The items reflect political and social trends in Pennsylvania and the United States during the period of expansion. The slavery question, the Kansas-Nebraska Bill, efforts to maintain the Union, and economic conditions after the Civil War are mentioned; miscellaneous papers on the Tyrone, Clearfield Railway Company, and the Centennial Exposition, 1839–1876; speeches, pamphlets, and newspaper clippings, 1853–1862; family papers, letters, bills, accounts.

52

Billmeyer, Mary G.   Manuscripts, 1835–1836.   (1 v.)

A collection of poetry dedicated to Mary G. Billmeyer by her friends. Gift of Mary M. Townsend, 1918.

53

Bingham, William, 1752–1804.   Letters, 1791–1803.   (2 v.)

William Bingham was a Pennsylvania delegate to the Old Congress, and a United States senator.

Letterpress copies of Bingham letters, 1791–1793, refer to many of the social, political, and financial events of the times and, incidentally, throw light on leading personalities in the political and financial affairs of the nation. The other volume, 1795–1803, contains photostats of letters and agreements about land enterprises in Maine in which William Bingham was financially interested.

54

Birch family.   Papers, (1808–1823) 1888.   (ca. 50 items.)

A miscellaneous collection of papers of the descendants of William Birch. Included is a diary, 1809–1825, of his son George Birch, career Army officer from 1808 to his death in 1837, describing the British assault upon Sackett's Harbor, Lake Ontario, 1813; army operations, Indian relations, and the purchases of land and slaves in the Louisiana Territory, 1816–1823. Also included are George Birch's commissions and other memorabilia, as well as photographs and certificates of his grandsons Thomas Russell Birch and

Carlton Birch while officers in the Pennsylvania Volunteers during the Civil War.

Gift of William R. Birch, 1888.

55
Blackmore, William.   Papers, 1873–1875.   (ca. 100 items.)

Collection of correspondence, notes, portraits, and pamphlets of William Blackmore for a sketch of William Penn.

Purchased, Dreer Fund.

56
Blackwell, John.   Letters, 1688–1690.   (1 v.)

Late 19th-century transcriptions, possibly assembled by Brinton Coxe, of letters, 1688–1690, of Lieutenant Governor John Blackwell to William Penn. Also are Coxe's notes on the sale of these and other Penn items at auction.

Originals also located at Historical Society of Pennsylvania.

Gift of Brinton Coxe.

57
Blaine, Ephraim, 1741–1804.   Receipt book, 1772–1798.   (1 v.)

Ephraim Blaine was an officer during the French and Indian War; a member of the Committee of Correspondence for Cumberland County, 1774; and a Revolutionary officer, who became a Commissary-General for the Continental Army.

The receipt book comprises mainly receipts for court judgments and lawyer's fees collected by Blaine as sheriff before the Revolution and receipts for bonds and land sales after the war; contains signatures of leading Pennsylvania political figures including George Ross, James Smith, and James Wilson, signers of the Declaration of Independence.

Purchased, 1922.

58
Blakeslee Genealogy, 1897–1929. (1 v.)

Transferred to Genealogical Society of Pennsylvania.

59
Blight, Atherton, 1834–1909.   Papers, 1849–1858.   (2 v.)

Atherton Blight attended school in Philadelphia, was graduated from Harvard and admitted to the Pennsylvania bar, and spent much of his adult life in Newport, R.I., and in Europe.

His papers comprise a book of travel expenses, 1849, 1856–1858, and a travel diary, 1855–1856, of a Grand Tour to the Continent, Egypt, Palestine, Syria, Turkey, Crimea, and Greece. In Jerusalem, he visited Warder Cresson, a former Quaker from Philadelphia who had converted to Judaism and was an early Zionist. Blight also describes the battlefields and veterans of the Crimean War.

Gift of Joseph Jackson, 1912.

60

Boinod and Gaillard.   Papers, 1777–1795.   (77 items.)

The bookselling firm of Boinod & Gaillard was composed of Daniel Boinod and Alexander Gaillard, who came to Philadelphia from the Netherlands in 1783.

The papers consist mainly of bills, receipts and other commercial paper for books bought and sold while in Leyden and later in Philadelphia. Also included are several bills for publication of their two short-lived newspapers in Philadelphia, the *American Herald*, published jointly with several other Philadelphia booksellers, and the *Courier de l'Amerique*, both 1784.

Some bills, receipts and other commercial papers in French and Dutch as well as English.

Purchased from Claude Unger, Dreer Fund, 1938.

61

Boker, Ann G.   Commonplace book, 1828–1882.   (1 v.)

A commonplace book of Ann G. Boker including verse, historical and genealogical notes, biographical essays, and some original material.

Purchased, Library Fund, 1904.

62

Boller, Eliza, b. 1799.   Musical scores, 1810.   (1 v.)

A copy book of secular and sacred Moravian music compiled by Eliza Boller while a student at the Moravian Seminary for Women, Bethlehem, 1810–1813.

Gift of Mrs. Hampton L. Carson, 1917.

63

Bollman, George.   Papers, 1784–1803.   (7 v.)

Business records of George Bollman, Pennsylvania merchant and ironmaster: letterbooks, 1795–1803; cashbook, 1784–1792; legal papers connected with a suit of attachment against a Spanish vessel, *Teresa,* in the harbor of Santiago, Cuba, 1803.

64
Bond family.   Receipt book, 1759–1810.   (1 v.)

Receipt book, 1759–1810, of Phineas Bond, Philadelphia physician, and his wife, Williamina Moore Bond, for personal and household expenses.
Gift of Mrs. Charles E. Cadwalader, 1908.

65
Bonsall, Edward H., 1794–1879.   Essays, 1814–1878.   (1 v.)

Essays by Edward H. Bonsall on literary and philosophical subjects and poetry read and discussed before the Philadelphia Literary Association.
Gift of S.H. Hudles, 1884.

66
Boone, Jeremiah, 1765–1833.   Papers, 1782–1833.   (6 linear ft.)

Jeremiah Boone and his son William R. Boone, were Philadelphia merchants and shippers. They traded in foodstuffs to the non-British West Indies with return cargoes of sugar, molasses, tobacco, leather, and hides. They owned several small ships and dealt extensively with south Jersey farmers to assemble their cargoes. To 1820 Jeremiah Boone was the principal, and afterwards William assumed that role. William Boone, in particular, entered into many partnership agreements, particularly with John B. Sartori of Trenton, N.J., yet the business never really prospered.

The collection contains correspondence, bills of lading, invoices and insurance policies relating to their trade, 1815–1833 as well as a smaller number of personal, legal, and estate papers, 1762–1831.
Gift of Howard Beacon, 1897.
Finding aid available.

67
Borton, Deborah.   Poems, 1788–1799.   (1 v.)

Poems by Deborah Borton mainly on death.
Gift of Mary O'Connell, 1936.

68
Boudinot, Elias, 1740–1821.   Papers, 1716–1828.   (ca. 500 items.)

Elias Boudinot was a lawyer and commissary of prisoners during the Revolution.

Correspondence and documents on prisoners of war; notes on the "Exchange of Prisoners of War," 1778; and parole lists. Some personal and family papers, 1716–1828, with notes on social and political affairs.

Miscellaneous items published in the *P.M.H.B.*, 15 (1891): 26–34; 16 (1892): 439–442; 34 (1900): 291–305, 453–466.

69
Boyer, John.   Diary, 1854.   (1 v.)

The diary of John Boyer, Philadelphia carpenter, contains business and personal accounts including repair work for Robert E. Peterson, bookseller and physician, and on Mary Longstreth's School.

Purchased.

70
Bradford, Thomas, 1745–1838.   Library register, 1771–1772. (1 v.)

The records of a lending library established in Philadelphia in 1769 by Thomas Bradford, printer, bookseller, and stationer, contains the names of subscribers and a list of books borrowed during the period.

71
Bradford, Thomas, 1745–1838.   Papers, 1760–1862. (3.5 linear ft.)

Thomas Bradford served as commissary general of the Revolutionary army.

The papers include: documents on British prisoners, including correspondence on prisoners from the British army and navy, 1777–1783; British prisoners' paroles, 1778–1782; a list of British prisoners, from both services, 1778–1782; returns of provisions for British prisoners, 1778–1783; American naval prisoners' paroles and bonds for their delivery, 1778–1783; miscellaneous correspondence and accounts, 1760–1862.

Gift of the Bradford family; and purchased.

72
Bradford, William.   Papers, 1682–1863.   (ca. 1,000 items.)

These papers relate to the Bradford family and to Colonel William Bradford's activities in the Revolution. There are: miscellaneous correspondence, wills, receipts, documents, and papers on shipping, law, religion, publications, and politics; memoranda of Bradford, 1757–1773; diary of Bradford, 1775; register of Bradford, 1776; letterbook and notes of Bradford, 1773–

1775; account books of Bradford, 1742–1760, 1780–1791, 1780–1792; journal of John Kidd and Bradford, 1768–1774; maritime insurance of John Kidd and Bradford, 1762; invoice book of William T. Bradford, 1767–1769; receipt book of Thomas Bradford, 1781; purchase of lottery tickets, 1753–1757; bibliography of William Bradford, 1685–1740; bibliography of Andrew Bradford, 1710–1737; list of subscribers to the *Pennsylvania Journal*, 1764–1778; list of subscribers to the *American Magazine*, 1757; newspaper and postage accounts, 1742–1775; orations at Princeton College by John Bradford Wallace, 1791–1794; Valley Forge muster roll, 1778.

A large portion of the collection gift of John William Wallace, 1878; some items purchased.

73
Braxton, Carter, 1736–1797.   Papers, 1780–1811.   (80 items.)

Papers collected by Carter Braxton, Virginia politician and Revolutionary leader, relate to litigation in the courts of Virginia, arising from a joint venture of Braxton & Willing, Morris and Company of Philadelphia to purchase military stores at Curaçao. There are letters, accounts, lengthy arguments and counter arguments, minutes and reports of the court-appointed auditors.

74
Breck, Samuel, 1771–1862.   Manuscript, 1850.   (1 v.)

Entry cancelled; see collection #1887

75
Briggs family.   Genealogical records, [1877].   (1 v.)

Transferred to the Genealogical Society of Pennsylvania.

76
Bringhurst family.   Diaries, (1777–1782) (1808–1811).   (1 v.)

A compendium compiled after 1811 of spiritual diaries of members of the Bringhurst family: an account of the death of Anna Pole Bringhurst by her husband, James Bringhurst, Philadelphia Quaker merchant, 1777; diary of the last months of Hannah Peters Bringhurst, Bringhurst's second wife, 1781–1782; diary, 1808–1810, of Elizabeth Almy of Portsmouth, R.I. recounting Bringhurst's last illness and death.

Purchased, 1927.

77
Brinton, Francis D., d. 1951.   Collection, 1789–1874.
(200 items.)

This is an artificial collection of papers of various Philadelphians. John M. Hood, Philadelphia grocer, is represented by custom house papers. Hood's son, Washington Hood, served with the United States Infantry, and Jefferson Barracks ordnance-stores requisitions and receipts, 1828–1829, are here together with a few military documents, 1839–1840, relating to his later duty as an Army topographical engineer surveying Indian boundaries. There are also Isaac H. Whyte, gentleman, personal and business correspondence and bills, 18840–1870; William Bramwell estate, letters and legal papers, 1827; miscellaneous legal papers.

Gift of Francis D. Brinton, 1935.

78
Brooke, John Rutter, 1838–1926.   Papers, 1753–1903.
(18 linear ft.)

The papers of John Rutter Brooke includes correspondence, documents, military orders, and pamphlets that primarily pertain to his career in the United States Army, 1861–1892: official reports of the battle of Fair Oaks, 1862; Civil War orders, 1862; war maps of Indian territory in Virginia, Maryland, Pennsylvania, and the Shenandoah Valley; material on suppression of mob violence in New Orleans and Baton Rouge, La.; records of Brooke's activities as commanding general in the Indian territories of Montana, Wyoming, Nevada, Utah, and Colorado, 1892–1898; list of names of outlaws, 1892; correspondence from military departments of La Platte, Dakota, Missouri, Omaha, Governors' Island, New Mexico, Texas, Minnesota; material on military expedition in Puerto Rico, 1898–1902; appointment as peace commissioner and Governor of Puerto Rico; accounts of several expeditions in Cuba, military hospitals, barracks, railroads, governor's palace, post office; letterbooks, 1888–1898; index books to correspondence; printed military regulations, 1863–1899; commissions signed by Grover Cleveland, Rutherford B. Hayes, Andrew Johnson, Abraham Lincoln, William McKinley, Elihu Root; letters of Major William Brooke on military affairs in the Philippines, 1901–1902.

79
Brooke, Robert.   Pedigree chart, 1912.   (1 item.)

Transferred to the Genealogical Society of Pennsylvania.

80

Brooke, Roger.   Patent to Land, 1684.   (1 item.)

Patent for 1,500 acres of land, "Brook Crosse," Baltimore County, Md., granted to Rodger Brooke of Calvert County, Md.

81

Brown, Alexander P.   Autograph sentiments, 1862–1913.   (4 v.)

A small collection of autographed sentiments collected by Alexander P. Brown, from foreign and American public figures.
Gift of Alexander P. Brown, 1919.

82

Brown, Andrew.   Letters, 1862–1864.   (ca. 75 items.)

The letters were written by Andrew Brown, sergeant in the Union army, to his family during the Civil War; they describe life in camp and his participation in battles.
Gift of William John Potts, 1887.

83

Brown, Carlotta Herring.   Collection, 1699–1920.
(ca. 500 items.)

Botanical and horticultural material, including copies of and notes from original manuscripts about John Bartram, 1699–1777; correspondence about mosses, 1909–1918. There are also journals and notes containing material on World War I.
Gift of Carlotta Herring Brown.

84

Brown, Charles Brockden, 1771–1810.   Manuscripts, 1715–1824.
(29 v.)

These papers of Charles Brockden Brown, early American professional man of letters, reflect the cultural trends of the period in the United States. Among the items: manuscript of "Alcuin," 1797; his miscellaneous writings, 1793–1808, on religion, morals, ethics, poetry, politics, economics.
The collection also includes: Elijah Brown journals, 1811, 1816, 1820, 1827, written while he was traveling in Europe and the United States, which describe scenes, natural phenomena, the construction of canals and dams, and philosophical and scientific subjects; Maurice Lisle memorandum books

and journals, 1715–1717, which describe domestic and commercial affairs in Philadelphia; bankbook, 1823–1824, and an obituary record, 1804–1811.

Purchased, Keim Fund, 1925.

85
Brown, David Paul, 1795–1872.   Papers, 1810–1841.   (1 v.)

Speeches and extracts delivered in court on public occasions by David Paul Brown, with an account of tribute presented to Brown at Mother Bethel A.M.E. Church, including remarks by Robert Purvis.

Gift of Eva Brown, 1903.

Speeches in *The Forensic Speeches of David Paul Brown,* Robert Eden Brown, ed. (Philadelphia : King & Baird) 1873.

86
Brown, Elias, Jr.   Diary, 1801–1805.   (1 v.)

Diaries, 1801, 1804–1805, of voyages from Philadelphia to Havana, Cuba and New Orleans, La., probably as supercargo, of Elijah Brown, Jr., later a commission merchant in Philadelphia; notes on personal expenses; list and values of cargoes; comparison of agricultural productivity of Pennsylvania and Louisiana; copybook notes.

Gift of James B. Campbell, 1916.

87
Brown, John.   Letters, 1777–1826.   (30 items.)

Letters of John Brown in which Albert Gallatin, Stephen Girard, and David Parrish are mentioned in connection with a loan made to the United States, and an account of a fire in the Treasury building in Washington, D.C.

Purchased, Dreer Fund, 1926.

88
Browne, John C., Mrs.   Lottery tickets, 1753–1866.
(ca. 200 items.)

Tickets of lotteries operated to secure funds for several national and local institutions in the United States; included is a memorandum book of Francis Gurney, 1790–1792, which records sales of City Hall and Dickinson College lottery tickets.

Gift of Mrs. John C. Browne, 1918.

89

Browne, William Hardcastle, 1840–1906.   **Correspondence,**
1890–1897.   (ca. 250 items.)

Letters about William Hardcastle Browne's pamphlet, *Divorce and Alimony.*

90

Bryan, George, 1731–1791.   Papers, 1756–1829.   (ca. 1,250 items.)

The bulk of this collection is legal opinions rendered by George Bryan, judge of the Supreme Court of Pennsylvania, which reflect judicial history in the colonial period. Among these items is his opinion in the case of *John Fitch vs. James Rumsey,* which involved claims over the introduction of steam-propelled vessels, 1789. Other papers relate to taxes, finance, shipping, sale of lands, incorporation of the city of Philadelphia in 1786, slavery, penal laws, Connecticut claims, the Constitutional Convention, Pennsylvania politics, gubernatorial nomination in 1823, election controversies, social and civic reform movements. The collection includes family correspondence.

Gift of George and S.S. Bryan, 1925.

91

Buchanan, James, 1791–1868.   Papers, 1775–1868.   (48 linear ft.)

James Buchanan graduated from Dickinson College in 1809. He moved to Lancaster where he studied law and entered into practice in 1813. After the tragic death of his fiancee, Ann Coleman, in 1819, he left law and Lancaster for a political career in Washington, D.C. He was elected to five terms as congressman, 1821–1831, running first as a Federalist but switching to the Jacksonian party in 1824. Buchanan served as minister to Russia, 1832–1833; United States senator, 1834–1845; and secretary of state for President Polk, 1845–1849 before retiring from politics in 1849. In 1853 he was appointed envoy extraordinary and minister plenipotentiary to Great Britain. Upon his return from Great Britain, 1856, he was named Democratic nominee for President and in November was elected President of the United States. He retired to his estate, Wheatland, in 1861 and remained there until his death in 1868.

These papers touch nearly every phase of Buchanan's career, legal, political, and diplomatic. They contain: autograph letters and drafts, 1813–1868; letters, reports, and documents of Buchanan's ministry to Russia, 1832–1833; material on his ministry to England, 1854–1856; correspondence while Secretary of State, 1845–1849; papers and correspondence relating to the growing differences between the North and South before the Civil War,

1857–1861; notes and articles written by Buchanan on his Administration and other topics, 1860; speeches and notes, 1827–1858; miscellaneous correspondence, 1783–1868, including letters from Simon Cameron, John W. Forney, John Slidell, Benjamin H. Brewster, Jeremiah Black, Nahum Capen, William B. Reed, John Meredith Read, Stephen Pleasonton and others; legal correspondence, 1775–1855, relating to Buchanan's early activity as a lawyer, including papers of the Koenigmacher case and the impeachment of Judge Franklin; business letters, 1828–1867, on personal investments and business transactions, including bills, receipts.

Also included: papers on the Democratic Convention, 1856; papers on the Post Office blank printing controversy, 1857–1860; biographical notes and papers on the life of Buchanan; invitations to dinners and public affairs, 1833–1868; pamphlets, 1814–1866, including speeches made in Congress, Presidential messages, pamphlets on the jubilee of the Constitution, Eve of Rebellion, trial of Judge Peck, controversy with General Winfield Scott, a scrap book, obituary notices, notes and memoranda; newspapers and clippings.

Gift of the Buchanan family; transferred to the Society, 1895–1897.

Microfilm available through inter-library loan.

Guide to the Microfilm Edition of the James Buchanan Papers at the Historical Society of Pennsylvania. Lucy West, ed. (Philadelphia) 1974.

92

Henry family.   Papers, 1770 (1826–1832) (1898–1899) 1914. (75 items.)

Family miscellany includes: Harriet Buchanan (James Buchanan's sister, later Mrs. Robert Henry) accounts, 1826–1832; and her son James Buchanan Henry, incoming letters, 1849–1914, on John Basset Moore's *The Works of James Buchanan* and other matters.

Gift of Robert E. Henry, Reginald B. Henry, and William C.A. Henry, 1937–1938.

93

Buchanan Fund.   Records, 1847–1848.   (1 v.)

Accounts, lists of subscribers, and amounts pledged and paid to a fund raised to promote the nomination of James Buchanan as presidential candidate for the election of 1848.

Gift, Fahnestock bequest, 1876.

94

Buchanan, Roberdeau, 1839–1916.   Collection, 1761–1831.   (4 v.)

General Daniel Roberdeau, merchant and Revolutionary soldier, letter book, 1764–1771; receipt book, 1761–1767, relates chiefly to his shipping interests and contains names of clients such as Henry Drinker, Benjamin Franklin, the Rev. Joseph Reed, John Rodgers, John Witherspoon, and others; Colonel Isaac Roberdeau, United States Army topographical engineer, journal of tours from George Washington with John C. Calhoun, Secretary of War, 1820–1830; Mary E. Roberdeau, poetry album, 1829–1831, contains poems written by John Quincy Adams, 1829, and another signed Abigail Adams.

Gift of Roberdeau Buchanan, 1917.

95
Buck, Charles N., 1775–1851.   Reminiscences, 1791–1841.   (1 v.)

Reminiscences of Charles N. Buck, Philadelphia merchant, consul general of Hamburg to the United States, contain records of commercial life in Philadelphia, the trade in cotton, linen, tobacco, sugar, rice, and other commodities, between the United States and Germany, and a view of the political and economic conditions of the period.

Gift of John Frederick Lewis, 1924.

96
Buck, Jacob E., 1801–1880.   Records, 1832–1840.   (2 v.)

Jacob E. Buck was a Nockamixon Township, Bucks County, tavernkeeper. His business daybook, 1834–1836, mainly records the sale of spirits. The receipt book, 1832–1840, is for his administration of the estates of Ludwig (Lewis) Afflerbach, Durham Township, Bucks County, and John Kressler (Cressler), Nockamixon Township.

Gift of Albert Cook Myers, 1904.

97
Buckingham, John Sheffield, Duke of, 1648–1720 or 21.
Manuscripts, 1688, 1708.   (1 v.)

Copies, in an unknown hand, presumably after 1723, of two of Buckingham's works: "Some Account of the Revolution," and "A Feast of the Gods in Imitation of the Cesars [sic] of the Emperor Julian written in the Year 1708."

Both works had been removed from Alexander Pope's posthumous edition of *Buckingham Works* (London, 1723), but were included in the 1726 edition. A previous owner has attributed the hand to Buckingham, but clearly it is not.

Gift of the Estate of Louise E. French, 1905.

98

Bucks County (Pa.) papers, 1682–1850. (2 v.)

Contains writs, summonses, pleas, jury returns, and other legal and governmental papers. Much of the early material originated with Phineas Pemberton, Bucks County judge, recorders of deeds, and member of the provincial assembly. There are also legal papers, 1764–1772 on litigation between James Logan, Jr., and the heirs of John Strieper over land in Bucks County, Philadelphia and Germantown. The business papers of Richard Backhouse, Bucks County ironmaster, complete the collection.

This is an artificial collection purchased and assembled by the Historical Society of Pennsylvania, ca. 1870.

Volumes indexed.

99

Buffington, Lee H. **Autograph album, 1860.** (1 v.)

Verse dedicated to Lee H. Buffington, Philadelphia gentlemen's furnishings businessman, by his friends.

Purchased, Dreer Fund, 1931.

100

Bull family. **Papers, 1799–1836.** (25 items.)

Papers of the Bull family contain deeds to land in Northumberland County; certificate of ordination of Levi Bull, priest of the Episcopal Church, signed by Bishop William White, 1805; and other items.

Gift of James H. Bull.

101

Bull, James, 1817–1904. **Journal, 1843–1844.** (1 v.)

A diary of James Bull of a journey through Mexico and lower and upper California with data on economic and social conditions, the influence of the Catholic church and Jesuits among the Indians, missions, pearl fisheries, travel, topography of the country, and incidents of the trip. Letters of introduction and a Mexican passport are also included.

Gift of Commodore James H. Bull, 1927.

102

Bunting-Nicholson papers, 1684–1850. (ca. 50 items.)

Chiefly land transactions in Burlington County, N.J., in which Samuel Bunting and George Nicholson were interested. There are patents of land, indentures, agreements, wills, surveys.

Purchased, Library Fund, 1939.

103
Burd, Edward, 1751–1833.   Partition of estate, 1834.
(41 parchment leaves.)

Deeds in partition of Edward Burd's estate.
Gift of Eli K. Price, 1934.

104
Burd, Edward Shippen, 1779–1848.   Papers, 1798–1858.   (12 v.)

Personal, business, and legal records of Edward S. Burd, Philadelphia
lawyer: receipt books, 1798–1820, 1805–1831; catalogue of Burd's law library
and copies of sample legal instruments, 1798–1800; account book of lumber
and sundries for his Pine Street, Philadelphia, building, 1820; plans and
abstracts of title of land owned by Burd, 1814–1820; receipts for taxes, water
rents, mortgage interest, wages, 1823–1833, and real estate accounts, mortgages, ground rent, 1830–1834; taxes and interest receipt book, 1813–1823;
income and investment book, 1848; Mrs. Eliza H. Burd's receipt book,
1848–1857; and grocery account books of the Burd Orphan Asylum, 1855–
1858, 1856–1858.

105
Burd, Edward Shippen, 1779–1848.   Legal Commonplace book,
1802.   (1 v.)

The legal commonplace book of Edward Shippen Burd, Philadelphia
lawyer, containing notes on definitions, forms of action, and procedures
drawn from Coke on Littleton and other British authorities; continued with
notes on admiralty practice and a summary of a decision by Richard Peters
in an admiralty case, 1802; also records several fees received by Burd, 1803,
1805.
Gift of Harold E. Gillingham, 1934.

106
Burns, James.   Collection, 1793–1860.   (15 items.)

Papers of James Burns, naval officer and Philadelphia physician: commission signed by John Adams, 1798; 3 manuscript booklets on naval signal
flags, veering and shortening sail and ships' regulations and orders on the
U.S.S. *Ganges, Congress* and *Constellation,* 1800–1802; notes certifying
Burns's medical competence, signed by Benjamin Rush, William Shippen,
Jr., and Caspar Wistar, Jr.; J.H. Gibbons class admission ticket for his medical studies in the University of Pennsylvania, 1793–1795, 1810; a broadside
of South Carolina proclamation, *The Union is Dissolved,* 1860.
Gift of Charles M. Burns, 1914.

107

Busch, Meirs.   Papers, 1838–1879.   (ca. 50 items.)

Family papers of Meirs Busch, including: an agreement to charter the ship *Susan G. Owen*, to ship merchandise to San Francisco, Cal., 1849; certificate of Spanish indemnities awarded to Joseph A. Clay, 1838, 1841; miscellaneous bills for merchandise, 1836–1860; University of Pennsylvania programs, pamphlets, correspondence.

108

Collection of Business, Professional, and Personal Accounts, 1676–1904.   (535 v.)

Records of miscellaneous business enterprises:

Allen, Nehemiah. Account book, 1698–1736. Allen was a Philadelphia merchant. (1 v.)

Andrews and Meredith. Invoice book, 1794–1795. Andrews and Meredith were merchants and shippers. (1 v.)

Archer, Isaac. Business and personal receipt book, 1795–1831. (1 v.)

Archer, Joseph. Letterbooks, 1833–1834. Joseph Archer was engaged in Canton tea, silk, and rice trade. (2 v.)

Armstrong, William. Receipt book, 1778. Armstrong was a merchant and army contractor. (1 v.)

Ashurst, William H. Receipt book, 1839–1844. Ashurst was a Philadelphia merchant. (1 v.)

Aurora. Office account books, 1822–1824. The *Aurora* was a Philadelphia newspaper. (2 v.)

Backhouse, Jones and Backhouse (Philadelphia, Pa.) Ledger, 1773–1775. Backhouse, Jones and Backhouse were Philadelphia merchants trading in raccoon and beaver skins. (1 v.)

Bailey, Robert and Francis, Records, 1794–1856. The Baileys were Philadelphia printers. Included here are a daybook, 1794–1797; Lydia Bailey waste book, 1794–1829; memorandum book, 1795–1841; and journal, 1799–1856. (4 v.)

Baily, Robert. Letterbook, 1796–1807. Baily was a Philadelphia liver oil merchant, fish and general merchandise merchant. (1 v.)

Baker, Abel and William Sill. Ledger, 1813–1815. Baker and Sill were general merchants trading in whiskey, shoes, muslin, and tobacco. (1 v.)

Baker, Charles H. Account book, 1812 and Letterbook, 1812–1813. (2 v.)

Baker, John and Samuel. Receipt book, 1824–1829. (1 v.)

Godfrey Baker and Company. Records, 1780–1805. Godfrey Baker and Company were Philadelphia merchants and shippers. Included in these records are receipt books, 1780–1782, 1786, 1796–1805 and cashbook, 1780. (4 v.)

Batho, John. Letterbook, 1765–1768. Batho was a Philadelphia-Antigua merchant and shipper. (1 v.)

Baynton, Peter. Ledger and letterbook, 1721–1726. Peter Baynton was a Hagerstown, Md. pottery merchant. (1 v.)

Benson, Alexander. Ledger, 1829. Merchant and shipper. (1 v.)

Benson, Thomas. Account book, 1748–1755 and ledger, 1809–1815. Thomas Benson was a general merchant. (1 v.)

Billmeyer, Michael. Ledger, 1809–1815. Billmeyer was a Philadelphia bookdealer. (1 v.)

Bird, James. Account book, 1777–1781. Bird was a Philadelphia cord and wood dealer. (1 v.)

Blackwell, Robert. Receipt book, 1783–1821. (1 v.)

Bonsall, James. Account book, 1722–1729. Bonsall was a Philadelphia silk and cotton merchant. (1 v.)

Booth, Louisa C. Account book, 1829–1844. This account book contains family accounts. (1 v.)

Bradford, William. Maritime insurance ledger, 1771–1775. (1 v.)

Bradywine Mills. Account book, 1815–1817, 1821–1822. (1 v.)

Brown, David S. Receipt book, 1842–1847. (1 v.)

Brown, John. Account books, 1774–1777, 1783–1787. Brown was a Philadelphia miller. (2 v.)

Brown, Peter. Account book, 1796–1849. (1 v.)

Brown, William R. Ledger, 1853–1856. Brown was a Doylestown merchant. (1 v.)

Bunting, Josiah. Ledger, 1812–1813. Bunting was a Philadelphia lumber merchant. (1 v.)

California, Philadelphia, and European Steamship Company. Subscription list, 1860. This list was for capital stock. (1 v.)

Carson, Joseph. Receipts books, 1775–1791. (4 v.)

Chalfont, Jesse. Account book, 1842–1876. Chalfont was a Wilmington, Del. merchant. (1 v.)

Chevalier, John and Peter. Journals, 1757–1761, 1770–1783. John and Peter Chevalier were Philadelphia and China merchants dealing in rugs, blankets, dry goods, and general merchandise. (2 v.)

Clark, Brainard. Receipt book, 1831–1838. Personal receipts are kept in this book. (1 v.)

Clark, Daniel. Letter and invoice book, 1759–1763. Clark was a Philadelphia furniture, china, and leather merchant. (1 v.)

Claypoole, James. Letterbook, accounts, and receipts, 1681–1683. (1 v.)

Cleaver, Ellis. Daybook, 1830–1852. Cleaver was a Philadelphia merchant. (1 v.)

Cline, Henry. Receipt book, 1800–1848. This book includes Philadelphia personal and domestic receipts. (1 v.)

Coates, Samuel. Ciphering and invoice books, 1724–1758. Coates was a Philadelphia merchant. (2 v.)

Coates, Thomas. Ledger, 1705–1726. Coates was a Philadelphia merchant. (1 v.)

Coleman, William. Ledger, 1757–1768. Coleman was the treasurer of the College of Philadelphia and merchant. (1 v.)

The Commercial Rooms Association (Philadelphia, Pa.) Records, 1767–1871. These records include: invoice book, 1767–1774; prize money ledger, 1782; tobacco and sundries account book, 1787–1789; subscription book, 1810–1812; general accounts, 1821–1823; minute book, 1837–1880; election of members, 1838–1877; roll book, 1838–1865; and journals, 1863–1871. (9 v.)

Caleb Cope and Company. Account books, 1842–1866. Caleb Cope and Company were Philadelphia general merchants. (2 v.)

Dannacker, George. Records, 1788–1795. Dannacker's records include: daybook, 1794–1795; cashbook, 1788–1795; and bankbook, 1794–1795. (3 v.)

DeKnouse and Fullmer. Bankbook, 1815–1816. DeKnouse and Fullmer were Philadelphia merchants. (1 v.)

Demuth, Jacob. Ledger, 1796–1847. Demuth was a tobacco merchant. (1 v.)

Denham, Thomas. Ledger, 1726–1729. Denham was a Philadelphia merchant. (1 v.)

Diehl, Nicholas. Ledger, legal forms, and regulations, 1796–1817. Diehl was a notary public. (2 v.)

Dilworth, Samuel. Invoice books, 1783–1792. Dilworth was a Philadelphia merchant and ironmonger. (2 v.)

Dohan and Taitt. Letterbook, 1859–1860. Dohan and Taitt were Philadelphia tobacconists. (1 v.)

Drum, Jacob. Account book, 1821–1822. Drum was a Philadelphia merchant. (1 v.)

Duvall, Henry. Records, 1821–1886. Duvall was a Greensburg merchant. Included in his records are: ledgers, 1847–1876, 1879–1886 and daybook, 1821–1822. (3 v.)

George Eckert and Company. Daybook, 1846–1861. George Eckert and Company were Philadelphia dry goods merchants. (1 v.)

Edwards, John and Hannah. Receipt book, 1841–1861. This receipt books include personal and domestic receipts for John and Hannah Edwards. (1 v.)

Egbert, Abraham. Account book, 1803–1811. Egbert was a Philadelphia merchant. (1 v.)

Ellis, Robert. Account book, 1736–1748. Ellis was a Philadelphia shipper and merchant. (1 v.)

Evans, David. Daybooks, 1774–1812. Evans was a Philadelphia carpenter. Included here are records for coffins and venetian blinds. (3 v.)

Evans, Thomas. Ledger, 1770–1795. Evans was a leather goods merchant. (1 v.)

Fassitt, Edward C. Receipt book, 1838. Fassitt was a Philadelphia attorney. Included here are both legal and personal receipts. (1 v.)

Ferris, Benjamin. Daybook, 1801–1807. Ferris was a Philadelphia clock and watchmaker. (1 v.)

Thomas, Miers, and Samuel Fisher. Account books, 1769–1795. Thomas, Miers, and Samuel Fisher were Philadelphia merchants and shippers. These records are a ledger and journal, 1769–1795. (2 v.)

Foot, John. Ledger, 1790–1841. Foot was a Susquehana County, shoe merchant. (1 v.)

Forbes, William. Account book, 1768–1787. Forbes was a Philadelphia merchant and shipper. (1 v.)

Franklin, Samuel R. and Margaret. Receipt and account books, 1814–1847. Includes both personal and domestic receipts and accounts. (4 v.)

Franks, David. Account book, 1760–1823. (1 v.)

Franks and Lewden. Daybook, 1810–1811. Franks and Lewden were Christiana, Del. merchants. (1 v.)

Franks and Wagner. Receipt book, 1824–18839. Franks and Wagner dealt in real estate. (1 v.)

Fry, John. Account book, 1795–1798. Fry was a Philadelphia hardware merchant. (1 v.)

Fuller, Benjamin. Papers, 1762–1799. These papers include letterbooks, 1762–1791; account book, 1769–1799; and receipt book, 1795–1799. (5 v.)

Gambier, Samuel. Account book, 1758–1762, 1804–1812. Gambier was a Philadelphia hatter. (1 v.)

Gardner, Sarah and Peter. Receipt book, 1761–1771. (1 v.)

Gillingham, Joseph E. Records, 1850–1879. Joseph E. Gillingham, a Philadelphia businessman, dealt in stocks, bonds, and mortgages. These records contain a personal ledger, 1850–1879, and journal, 1874–1879. (2 v.)

Gilpin, J.F. Invoice book, 1837. This invoice included records for general merchandise. (1 v.)

Gilpin, Vincent and John F. Records, 1822–1865. Vincent and John F. Gilpin were Philadelphia merchants and shippers. Their records include: daybook, 1822–1847; ledger, 1822–1847; bank account book, 1835–1838; dividend book, 1822–1847; daybook, 1828–1831; ledgers, 1838–1839; and accounts paid out, 1864–1865. (8 v.)

Gough and Caramault. Letterbook, 1757–1761. Gough and Caramault were Philadelphia merchants. (1 v.)

Graff, Jacob. Receipt and cashbook, 1776–1790. Graff was a Philadelphia dry goods, shoe, and general merchandise merchant. (1 v.)

Greeves, John. Ledger, 1753–1757. Greeves was a dry goods importer. (1 v.)

Grove, Jacob. Daybook and journal, 1838. Grove was a general merchant and shipper. (1 v.)

Habacker, George. Receipt book, 1779–1780. Habacker was a Philadelphia merchant dealing in flour, whiskey, coffee, and sugar. (1 v.)

Hamilton, John. Records, 1804–1833. Hamilton was a Philadelphia merchant. The records include: receipt books, 1804–1833; letterbook, 1809–1813; daybooks, 1804–1808, 1818–1819; ledgers, 1808–1828; and account book, 1808–1813. (9 v.)

Hamilton and Drew. Records, 1805–1810. Hamilton and Drew were Philadelphia merchants. These records include: ledger, day, and receipt books, 1805–1810. (3 v.)

Hamilton and Hood. Records, 1803–1838. Hamilton and Hood were Philadelphia merchants. These records include cashbooks, journals, ledgers, and letterbooks. (18 v.)

Harrison, John. Records, 1800–1804. These records include daybooks, 1800–1804 and ledger, 1800–1803 for a merchant dealing in drugs and sundries. (3 v.)

Harvey, Isaac. Receipt book, 1809–1838. (1 v.)

Hayes, Richard. Ledger, 1708–1740. Hayes was a merchant. (1 v.)

Henderson, Robert. Records, 1779–1823. Henderson was a Philadelphia merchant. These records include: ledgers, journals, receipts, daybooks, cash books, inventory, laundry and stockholders books. (6 linear ft.)

Hildeburn, Samuel. Letterbook, 1815–1818. Hildeburne was a Philadelphia silversmith. Continued as Hildeburn and Woolworth. (1 v.)

Hood, John M. Records, 1806–1848. John M. Hood was a Philadelphia merchant. These records include; receipts, accounts, daybooks, and ledgers. (8 v.)

Horner and Morrison. Receipt book, 1815. Joseph P. Horner and William Morrison were Philadelphia merchants. (1 v.)

Horner, Benjamin. Receipt book, 1762–1783. Benjamin Horner was a Philadelphia merchant. (1 v.)

Horner, Mary. Receipt books, 1811–1862. (2 v.)

Humphrey, Charles. Ledgers, 1739–1789. Humphrey was a Pennsylvania miller. (3 v.)

Hunt, John. Letterbook, 1747–1749. John Hunt was a London merchant and shipper dealing tobacco and general merchandise. Continued as Hunt and Greenleafe. (1 v.)

Hunter, John. Receipt book, 1784–1821. Personal and business receipts included. (1 v.)

Huron, Laurens, 1796–1803. Invoice and account book, 1796–1803. Huron was an importer of general merchandise. (1 v.)

Jackson, Isaac. Daybook and diary, 1850–1857. Jackson was a general merchant. (1 v.)

Jackson, John C. Records, 1822–1836. Jackson was a West Nottingham merchant. Included in these records are a feed daybook, 1822–1828 and account book, 1830–1836. (2 v.)

James and Drinker. Letterbooks, 1756–1762. Jones and Drinker were Philadelphia merchants. (2 v.)

Jeffries, Chalkley. Account book, 1835. (1 v.)

Jones and Wister. Invoice books, 1759–1762. Jones and Wister were importers of dry goods. (1 v.)

Jordan, Robert and Moses Lancaster. Receipt book, 1790–1833. Jordan and Lancaster were Philadelphia carpenters and builders. (1 v.)

Andrew Kennedy and Company. Receipt book, 1789–1794. (1 v.)

Kidd, John. Letterbook, 1749–1763. John Kidd was a Philadelphia merchant and shipper.

Kinloch, Bowden and Farquhar. Account book, 1751–1758. Bowden and Farquhar Kinloch were London merchants dealing in skins tobacco, and general merchandise. (1 v.)

Kite, Thomas. Daybook, 1831–1839. Kite was a bookdealer. (1 v.)

Kittell, William. Account book, 1838. Accounts of transportation between Philadelphia and Pittsburgh. (1 v.)

Lancaster, Moses and John. Records, 2809–2844. Moses and John Lancaster were Philadelphia carpenters and builders. These records include receipts, daybooks, and account books. (8 v.)

Landenberger, Matthias. Receipt book, 1784–1791. These receipts are for personal and domestic items. (1 v.)

Lawrence, William. Daybook, 1769–1798. Lawrence was a Philadelphia merchant selling hats, skins, and food products. (1 v.)

Laws, C. Account book, 1815–1818. (1 v.)

Leedom, Samuel. Ledger, 1837–1878. Leedom was a Haverford lumber merchant. (1 v.)

Lehman, Benjamin. Price book, 1786. Lehman was a Philadelphia cabinetmaker. (1 v.)

Lentz and Hood. Records, 1803–1828. Lentz and Hood were Philadelphia merchants. Their records include: receipt book, cashbook, daybook, and waste book, 1803–1838. (4 v.)

Levers, Robert. Receipt book, 1759–1776. Robert Levers worked with shipping and merchandising. (1 v.)

Lewden, Josiah. Letter and daybook, 1801–1802, 1852–1865. Lewden was a general merchant. (2 v.)

Lewis, Levi. Account books, 1769–1809. Levi Lewis was a Radnor miller. These are his flour mill accounts. (2 v.)

Litzenberg, William H. and Charles A. Journal and daybook, 1862–1878. William H. and Charles A. Litzenberg were blacksmiths and wheelwrights. (1 v.)

Lloyd and Sharpless. Ledger, 1794–1801. (1 v.)

Collins Logstreth and Company. Cashbook, 1815–1817. Collins Longstreth and Company was a Philadelphia bond and general merchant. (1 v.)

Markley, Benjamin Judge. Account book, 1779–1786. Markley was a Philadelphia blacksmith and farmer. (1 v.)

Marlow, Gregory. Account book, 1676–1703. Marlow was a Philadelphia shipbuilder. (1 v.)

Marshall, Christopher and Charles. Bills of lading and ore book, 1762–1768. (1 v.)

Marshall, John. Receipt books, 1775–1786. Marshall was a general merchant. (1 v.)

Marshall, S.J. Account book, 1853–1866. Marshall was a carriage maker. (1 v.)

Marshall and Wier. Account book, 1865–1869. Marshall and Wier were carriage makers. (1 v.)

Martin, William. Receipt book, 1821–1830. (1 v.)

Maxwell, Hugh. Daybook, 1803–1806. Maxwell was a Philadelphia bookseller and stationer. (1 v.)

McBay, William R. Account book, 1778–1781. McBay was a Philadelphia coal, wood, and iron merchant. (1 v.)

McConkey, James. Invoice books, 1834–1867. McConkey was a Peach Bottom (York County, Pa.) commission merchant, canal boat owner, and postmaster. Also in partnership with John Q.A. Mary Ann (10 v.)

McConkey, John Q.A. Invoice book, 1877–1879. McConkey was a canal boat owner and shipper on the Delaware Raritan Canal. (1 v.)

McCorkle, William. Ledger, 1804–1887. McCorkle was an advertising and periodical dealer. (1 v.)

McCurrach, James and Company. Accounts, 1790–1796. James McCurrach and Company were shipping agents. (1 v.)

Mead, George. Receipt book, 1784–1788. George Meade was a Philadelphia shipper and general merchant. (1 v.)

Mendenhall, Ellwood. Account book, 1846–1854. Mendenhall was Pennsbury School treasurer. (1 v.)

Meredith, David. Account book, 1813–1817. David Meredith was a Philadelphia merchant. (1 v.)

Meredith, Jesse. Accounts, 1795–1850. Jesse Meredith was a Downingtown merchant and shoemaker. These records include accounts, vital statistics, ledger, 1795–1850, and daybook, 1805–1850. (2 v.)

Meredith, Jonathan. Records, 1784–1800. Jonathan Meredith was a Philadelphia tanner. These records include hide accounts, wastebooks, leather, sales, and bark ledger, daybooks, and blotter book. (34 v.)

Mifflin and Massey. Ledger, 1760–1763. Mifflin and Massey were Philadelphia general merchants dealing in teas, coffee, sugar, and flour. (1 v.)

Morgan, Benjamin R. Letterbook, 1830–1840. Morgan was a Philadelphia judge. This letterbook mainly deals with land transactions. (1 v.)

Morgan, Thomas. Ledger, 1771–1803. Morgan was a clockmaker. (1 v.)

Morris, Elliston P. Journal, 1848–1849 and cashbook, 1849. Morris was a Philadelphia merchant and shipper. (1 v.)

Morris, Robert and John Nicholson. Bill book, 1795. (1 v.)

Morris, S. and Isaac L. Bartram. Receipt book, 1766–1770, 1779–1783. (1 v.)

Morris, Samuel. Records, 1848–1904. Morris was a Philadelphia merchant and wholesale grocer. These records include: journal, ledger, daybooks, accounts, cashbooks. (10 v.)

Moulder, John and William. Accounts, 1771–1776, 1794–1805. John and William Moulder were Philadelphia and Chester merchants. (1 v.)

Moulder, Margaret. Ledger, 1794–1799. Margaret Moulder was a grocer. (1 v.)

Moulder, Robert and Lydia. Accounts, 1760–1817. The Moulders were tavern keepers. (1 v.)

Moulder and Clayton. Account book, 1726–1763. Moulder and Clayton were Philadelphia merchants. (1 v.)

Mount, Joel. Ledger, 1829–1865, and daybook, 1837–1849. Mount was a Philadelphia cabinet maker. (2 v.)

Muir, James. Ledger, 1782–1795, 1786–1788. James Muir was a Philadelphia bookbinder and merchant. (2 v.)

Murdock, Samuel. Receipt book, 1765–1771. Murdock was a general merchant. (1 v.)

Neave, Richard. Account book, 1773–1774. (1 v.)

Osmond, David. Account book, 1790–1830. Osmond was a general merchant. (1 v.)

Oyster-ship owners vs. State of Virginia. Minutes, 1849. (1 v.)

Paul, Joseph M. Receipt book, 1807–1817. Paul was a Philadelphia merchant. (1 v.)

Penrose, Ella. Account book, 1888–1893. Ella Penrose was a Philadelphia seamstress. (1 v.)

Penrose, Washington H. Records, 1810–1870. Penrose was a Philadelphia merchant. The records include pattern and machine shop accounts, diaries, ledgers, and personal records. (11 v.)

Penrose Ferry Bridge Company. Receipt book, 1859–1863. (1 v.)

Peterson, Israel. Receipt book, 1852–1866. Peterson was a Philadelphia leather merchant. (1 v.)

J. Peterson and Company. Receipt book, 1866–1873. J. Peterson and Company were Philadelphia leather merchants. (1 v.)

Philadelphia Public Stock Exchange. Stock sales, 1865–1866. (1 v.)

Phillips and Cozens. Record book, 1829. Phillips and Cozens was a Philadelphia firm concerned with the navigation of canals by steam. (1 v.)

Port of Philadelphia. Exciseman's account book, 1739–1742. (1 v.)

Potter, James. Account book, 1752–1767. (1 v.)

Potts, Stacy. Daybook, 1813–1822. Stacy Potts was a Philadelphia shoe merchant. (1 v.)

Potts, W.J. Account book, 1790–1791. These accounts are for general merchandise at Valley Works. (1 v.)

Powel, Samuel. Invoice and daybook, 1748–1750. Powel was a Philadelphia merchant. (1 v.)

Randolph, Samuel and Company. Receipt book, 1836–1846. Samuel Randolph and Company were Philadelphia carpenters and builders. (1 v.)

Redwood, William. Records, 1749–1810. William Redwood was a Newport, R.I. importer of general merchandise. These records include: ledgers, 1749–1761, 1787–1790; journal, 1749–1760; journal and ledger (Antigua) 1782–1787; ledger, 1775–1809; daybooks, 1787–1790, 1792–1810; wastebook, 1775–1797; and journal, 1787–1790. (10 v.)

Redwood and Birkett. Records, 1773–1775. Redwood and Birkett were general merchants. The records include ledger, journal, and wastebook. (3 v.)

Reed, Joseph. Ledger, 1824–1829. The ledger relates to Philadelphia real estate transactions. (1 v.)

Reinhart, George V. Receipt book, 1800–1810. (1 v.)

Rhodes, Willis and Company. Journal, 1834–1836. Rhoades, Willis and Company were Philadelphia dry goods merchants. (1 v.)

Richardson, Joseph. Records, 1732–1757. Joseph Richardson was a Philadelphia silversmith. These records include: account book, 1733–2739; letterbook, 1732–1757; and daybook, 1744. (3 v.)

Riché, Thomas. Records, 1757–1792. Riché was a Philadelphia merchant and shipper. The records include: journal, 1757–1761 and letterbooks, 1757–1792. (4 v.)

Ritter, George. Receipt books, 1834–1849. Ritter was an undertaker. (2 v.)

Robeson and Paul. Letterbook, 1807–1813. Robeson and Paul were merchants dealing in iron, lumber, and general merchandise. (1 v.)

Robinson, Charles C. Daybook, 1809–1825. Robinson was a Philadelphia chair maker. (1 v.)

Roman, John. Receipt book, 1770–1780. Roman was a Philadelphia merchant. (1 v.)

Ross, James. Records, 1812–1818. Ross was a Christiana Bridge, Del. merchant. These records include a daybook, 1812–1818 and ledger, 1813–1816. (2 v.)

Ross, John. Records, 1774–1810. Records include: daybook, 1774–1783; invoice book, 1776–1779; account book, 1776–1791; ledger, 1776–1780; receipt book of the executors of John Ross' estate, 1800–1810. (9 v.)

Ross, John. Records, 1776–1791. Ross was a general merchant and shipper. The records include accounts current book, invoice book, and ledger. (3 v.)

Rutter, Thomas and Samuel Potts. Account book, 1784–1786. (1 v.)

Saltonstall, Joshua. Ledger, 1790–1794, 1803–1806. Saltonstall was a Philadelphia merchant and grocer. (1 v.)

Sarched, J. Inventory of general merchandise, 1827–1828. Sarched was a tobacco merchant. (1 v.)

Savery, Thomas. Account book, 1782. Savery was a Philadelphia carpenter and builder. (1 v.)

Scully, Thomas. Daybook, 1773–1775. Scully was a Christiana, Del. merchant. (1 v.)

Sharples, Nathan. Business records, 1774–1826. Sharples was an East Bradford (Chester County, Pa.) merchant. (4 v.)

Sharples, Joseph and Jesse. Receipt book, 1794–1819. Joseph and Jesse Sharples were Philadelphia merchants dealing lumber, shoes, tobacco and general merchandise. (1 v.)

Sharpnack, Destonet and Company. Ledger, 1818–1821. (1 v.)

Shee, Elizabeth A. Daybook, 1843–1870. This daybook lists expenses for the Rose Valley Farm. (1 v.)

Shipping accounts, 1788–1792. Accounts for the *Diana*, the *Betsy*, the *Mary*, the *Resolution*, the *Friendship*, and the *Theodore*. (1 v.)

Shreve, R.C. and A.R. Receipt book, 1840–1856. R.C. and A.R. Shreve were grain merchants. (1 v.)

Simmonds, David. Receipt book, 1813–1830. (1 v.)

Slesman, John. Receipt book, 1799–1802. Slesman was a Philadelphia merchant. (1 v.)

Smith, William. Letterbook, 1771–1775. Smith was a Philadelphia merchant and grocer. (1 v.)

Smith and Leedmon. Ledger, 1845–1846. Smith and Leedmon were grain merchants. (1 v.)

Speel, John. Receipt book, 1804–1813. Speel was a baker. Receipt book includes business and personal receipts. (1 v.)

Springfield Farm. Accounts, 1780–1782. (1 v.)

Stiles, Amos. Daybook, 1812–1821. Amos Stiles was a Moorestown, N.J. wheelwright. (1 v.)

Stites, John. Account book, 1814–1819. Stites was a Philadelphia grocer and general merchant. (1 v.)

Stuart and Welsh. Journal, 1780–1792. Stuart and Welsh were shippers. (1 v.)

Sweetman, Richard. Receipt book, 1771–1780. Sweetman was a Philadelphia grain merchant. (1 v.)

Swift, John. Letterbooks, 1747–1813. Swift was a Philadelphia merchant and executor of the estate of William Kennersley. (3 v.)

Taylor, Joseph. Ledger, 1715–1723. Taylor was a liquor dealer. (1 v.)

Taylor, Samuel. Receipt book, 1774–1789. (1 v.)

Taylor, William P. Account book and diary, 1849–1855. (1 v.)

Topliff, John. Receipt book, 1793–1794. (1 v.)

Townsend, Samuel and Solomon. Receipt book, 1810–1813. The Townsends manufactured ship anchors. (1 v.)

Trent, William. Ledger, 1703–1708. Trent was a Philadelphia merchant. (1 v.)

Trimble, James. Account book, 1726–1728. (1 v.)

Trotter, Dawson and Newbold. Accounts, 1862–1868. (1 v.)

Trotter, Joseph. Account book, 1829–1830. Trotter was a carpenter. (1 v.)

Unidentified accounts, 1694–1836. (16 v.)

United States. Accounts, 1805–1836. Accounts of foreign commerce, recording coal trade, railroads, and arrivals of vessels. (1 v)

Warder and Brothers. Account book, 1821–1835. Warder and Brothers were Philadelphia merchants and shippers. (1 v.)

Washington Mutual Insurance Company. Records, 1838–1870. These records include: letterbook, 1838–1858; minute book, 1843–1856; receipt book, 1851–1858; and ledger, 1857–1870. (4 v.)

Webb, Samuel. Receipt book, 1822. (1 v.)

Webster, Peltiah. Account and letterbook, 1773–1790. (1 v.)

Weems, James N. Records, 1810–1831. James N. Weems was a Philadelphia dry goods merchant. The records include: sales records, daybooks, letterbooks, and administration of estate records. (8 v.)

108

Weirs, Robert and Uriah S. Records, 1825–1860. The Weirs were Christiana, Del. blacksmiths. The records include ledgers and daybooks. (8 v.)

West, David. Receipt book, 1803–1869. (1 v.)

Wetherill and Budd. Records, 1807–1825. Wetherill and Budd were Philadelphia merchants dealing in drugs, chemicals, and paint. The records include a journal, 1807 and ledger, 1807–1825. (2 v.)

Wetherill family. Accounts, 1845–1917. (1 v.)

Wharton, Thomas. Receipt book, 1752–1755. (1 v.)

Whyte, Isaac H. Receipt book, 1824–1857. Whyte was a Philadelphia carpenter and builder. (1 v.)

Wilkins and Atkinson. Daybook, 1808–1809. Wilkins and Atkinson were Philadelphia tailors. (1 v.)

Williams, J.T. Receipt book, 1855–1868. Personal receipts. (1 v.)

Williams, Peter. Daybooks, 1829–1836. Peter Williams was a Newport, Del. merchant. (2 v.)

Williams, Thomas and Company. Accounts, 1791–1822. Thomas Williams and Company were dealers in skins and hides. (1 v.)

Williamson, William. Records, 1826–1844. Williamson was an attorney for West Chester Railroad. These records include accounts, wages, cashbook, for the railroad and personal accounts. (5 v.)

Willing, Charles, Thomas and Morris. Letterbook, 1754–1761. The Willings were Philadelphia merchants. (1 v.)

Willing, Edward S. Account books, 1861–1895. (2 v.)

Wilson, John. Cashbooks, 1767–1777. (12 v.)

Wistar, Caspar. Receipt book, 1747–1784. (1 v.)

Woodhouse, Hariott. Receipt book, 1854–1875. These receipts include information on Philadelphia mortgages, bonds and personal expenses. (1 v.)

Woodhouse, Samuel. Receipt book, 1812–1843. (1 v.)

Woolman, Uriah. Bills of lading, 1772–1775. (1 v.)

Wynkoop and Sieman. Receipt book, 1783–1787. Wynkoop and Sieman were truckers. (1 v.)

Physicians' records and medicinal recipes:

Birkey, William J. Daybook, 1847. Birkey was a dentist. (1 v.)

Caldwell, Charles. Records, 1798–1815. Caldwell was a Philadelphia physician. The records include ledgers and day journals. (4 v.)

Coates, Benjamin H. Ledger, 1824–1830. Coates was a Philadelphia physician. (1 v.)

Coates, Josiah. Records, 1810–1815. Coates was a Philadelphia physician. The records include daybooks and ledgers. (4 v.)

Coxe, Daniel W., Mrs. Medicinal recipes, cookbooks, receipt books, 1801–1852. (5 v.)

Elmer, Ebenezer. Daybooks, 1790–1802. Elmer was a Hopewell and Bridgeton, N.J. physician. (2 v.)

Griffith, Elijah. Receipt and daybook, 1804–1814. Griffith was a Philadelphia physician. (1 v.)

Klapp, Joseph. Daybook, 1886–1889. Klapp was a Philadelphia physician. (2 v.)

Moon, Robert C. Daybook, 1886–1889. Moon was a Philadelphia physician. (1 v.)

Estate administration accounts:

Baker, George A. Account book, 1794–1805. (1 v.)

Bartow, Thomas—estate. Receipt book, 1793–1797. (1 v.)

Bordley, John Beale estate. Account and receipt books, 1804–1813. (3 v.)

Burd, Edward. Receipt and account book, 1813, 1815–1817 Burd was executor of the John F. Mifflin estate. (1 v.)

Chalfont, Joel and James. Receipt books, 1834–1855. (2 v.)

Cox, John D. Account book, 1825–1830. (1 v.)

Gillingham, Joseph E. Account book, 1863–1900. Gillingham was the administrator of the estate of Jacob Donaldson. (1 v.)

Gratz, Michael. Administration book, 1811. (1 v.)

Haga, Godfrey—estate. Receipt book, 1825–1848. (1 v.)

Hall, John. Account books, 1807–1808, 1811–1818. Hall was executor for the estate of Levi Adams, Joseph Israel, William Mann. (2 v.)

Hanthorne, Isaac—estate. Estate inventory, 1814–1820. (1 v.)

Harris, Robert. Account book, 1796–1808. (1 v.)

Jenks, Michael H. Account book, 1837–1839. Jenks was executor for the estates of Jeremiah Bennett, Dr. W.B. Watson, and Charles Alexander. (1 v.)

Knight, Daniel. Administration account, 1836–1843. (1 v.)

McCleay, Robert. Receipt book, 1791. McCleay was executor of the estate of Joseph Garson. (1 v.)

Mechlin, Jacob—estate. Journal and ledger, 1785–1790. (1 v.)

Nagle, Rudolph—estate. Receipt book, 1807–1812. (1 v.)

Paris, Peter—estate. Receipt book, 1776–1789. (1 v.)

Powell, Elizabeth—estate. Accounts of executors, 1830–1848. The executors of the Elizabeth Powell estate includes: the Bank of North America, William White, Edward Burd, and Edward Shippen Burd. (2 v.)

Price, Eli Kirk—estate. Accounts, 1826–1830. (3 v.)

Tilghman, William. Ledgers, 1785–1835. William Tilghman kept these ledgers in account of estate with James Tilghman. (5 v.)

Ulrich, Valentine—estate. Receipt book, 1775–1820. (1 v.)

Voigt, Thomas—estate. Account books, 1840–1851. (2 v.)

Wall, George—estate. Account book, 1778–1780. (1 v.)

Wilson, Benjamin—estate. Letterbook, 1823–1824. William Meredith and William Smyth were assignees of the Benjamin Wilson estate. (1 v.)

Wilt, Abraham—estate. Receipt books, 1788–1852. (5 v.)

Worrell, Isaiah—estate. Accounts, 1749–1883. (1 v.)

109A
Butler, Pierce, 1744–1822.   **Estate papers, 1810 (1846–1891) 1894. (3 linear ft.)**

These are financial papers of trustees and agents of the Pierce Butler estate. The principal beneficiaries represented are estate of John Butler, his widow, Gabriella M. Butler, Pierce (Mease) Butler, and his daughters Sara Butler Wister and Frances Butler Leigh. Among the papers are: receipted bills and accounts 1810, 1847–1891, for the management of Philadelphia real estate; Butler's Island, Georgia, receipted bills and accounts, 1846–1860, 1881–1884, for crops, goods shipped from Philadelphia, and payroll; Gabriella M. Butler receipted bills, 1846–1861; John Butler estate letterbook, 1859–1868, journal and ledger, 1862–1870.

Gift of Owen J. Wister, 1932, 1947.

109B
Butler family.   **Papers, 1772–1888.**   **(6 linear ft.)**

Papers, 1770–1822, of Major Pierce Butler include bills and receipts, especially for the education of his son Thomas Butler in London, England, and family estate business. The miscellaneous papers of his grandson Pierce Butler (Mease) include a letterbook, 1837, on business of his Georgia plantation.

Gift of Owen J. Wister, 1961.

110
Butler, Richard.   **Diary, 1775.**   **(1 v.)**

Richard Butler was an officer in both the Continental and United States armies who was killed by Indians at Fort Recovery, 1791.

The diary recounts Butler's embassy as agent for the Continental Congress, 1775, to the Delaware, Wiyot, Mingo and Shawnee nations and reports in detail the speeches of the chiefs, describes a meeting with Cornstalk, and assesses the effects of the British-American conflict upon the frontier political situation.

Gift of Thomas Montgomery, 1898.

111
Cadwalader, John, 1742–1786.   Estate papers, 1630–1863.
(ca. 1,500 items.)

Entry cancelled; see collection #1454.

112
Colhoon, Benjamin C.   Receipts, 1800–1815.   (1 v.)

Receipt book, 1807–1812, of Benjamin C. Colhoon of Baltimore, Md., for water rent, chimney sweeping, pew rent, and other expenses. There is also manuscript music of popular melodies and national airs, including *Hail to the Chief* and a simplified version of *The Star Spangled Banner*.

113
Campbell, James Hepburn, 1820–1895.   Papers, 1861–1867.
(50 items.)

James Hepburn Campbell was a Pennsylvania lawyer, U.S. Representative, Civil War officer and American diplomat.

Campbell's letters and documents relate to his service in the Pennsylvania Volunteers, 25th Regiment, 1861, and in the Pennsylvania Militia, 39th Regiment, 1863, and as minister to Sweden, 1864–1867. There is also material on his son, Francis Duncan Campbell, who served with the United States Navy Mississippi Squadron, 1862–1864.

Gift of A. Keightley.

114
Campbell, Samuel, 1763?-1836.   Collection, 1790–1876.
(85 items.)

Miscellaneous papers of Samuel Campbell, early bookseller and printer, and John Campbell, astronomer, chiefly of personal, business, and legal content; a letter, 1793, of P. Garson relates to printing and publication of books, with details of subscription by George Washington, Alexander Hamilton, Henry Knox, and others to a new edition of the Bible; other papers include documents on land sales in Marietta, Ohio, and apprentice indentures, 1791–1793; poetry by William Riley, 1825; financial documents; a letter, 1865, that alludes to John Campbell's telescope.

Gift of Mrs. John S. Saxe, 1934.

115
Carpenter, Louis H., 1839–1916.   Papers, 1695–1903.
(6 linear ft.)

Brigadier General Louis H. Carpenter's war records of the Civil War, personal papers, family papers, and some manuscripts gathered by him:

Carpenter's letters from the field, 1861–1864; military papers on service in various departments, 1862–1903; letters and documents on personal matters, business, legal and real estate, 1695–1887; a receipt book, 1811–1816; papers on the Ware and Bateman controversy, 1843; an army account book, with tables of rations, 1759; a collection of the ledgers, daybooks, receipt books of Dr. James Stratton, 1779–1816; broadsides on raising revenue for the continuance of the Revolution, 1780; biography of Elizabeth Estaugh, 1894.

Gift of E. Carpenter.

116
Carr, Robert.   **Papers, 1811–1823.**   **(1 v.)**

Robert Carr was a Philadelphia printer and served as an officer during the War of 1812.

Diary, letterbook, and account book. The diary, interspersed with Carr's correspondence, describes recruiting, army movements, and warfare in New York State and Canada, and contains general orders and orders issued by Carr; military accounts, 1813–1815; and letters, 1813–1823, relating to political affairs in Pennsylvania and Carr's effort to obtain appointments for himself and his sons.

Gift of W. Bartram Snyder, 1866.

117
Carson, Hampton L. (Hampton Lawrence), 1852–1929.
Collection, 1690–1929.   **(30 linear ft.)**

Autograph letters and portraits, 1690–1921, of lawyers, judges, and others involved in the administration of law and justice in the courts of Pennsylvania, and of other states, from the early colonial period to the present.

Among the letters are those of governors of Pennsylvania, 1789–1920; attorneys general of Pennsylvania, 1791–1920; members of the colonial bar, 1690–1775; members of the High Court of Error, 1761–1815; lawyers of the Revolutionary period, 1776–1801; justices of the Supreme Court of Pennsylvania, 1712–1921; and others. There are also seven boxes containing approximately 400 caricatures of political leaders, members of the bar, and other prominent people, ca. 1880–1929. Other items are pamphlets, speeches, newspaper clippings, on public questions; correspondence of Hampton L. Carson about his legal practice, and his presidency of the American Bar Association and of the Historical Society of Pennsylvania; correspondence and papers on Governor Samuel W. Pennypacker of Pennsylvania.

Gift of Hampton L. Carson, 1929.

118

Cathrall, Charles E.   Papers, 1822–1835.   (3 v.)

This collection contains materials written or collected by Charles E. Cathrall, Philadelphia merchant, as a young man. They include: a sentiment book, 1822–1826, containing verse and prose passages written by his friends; a diary containing an account of a passage from Philadelphia to Liverpool aboard the Cope packet *Pocohontas*, 1834, and continued as a series of letters, 1834–1835, describing travel through England, Ireland, France, and Italy; also a sentiment book, 1831–1833(?), with a continuation of the description of Cathrall's trip through Italy, 1835.

Two volumes purchased, Dreer Fund, 1934, 1974; one volume gift of Harold E. Gillingham, 1935.

119

Centennial Exposition (1876: Philadelphia, Pa.) Collection, 1876. (11 linear ft.)

This is a collection of miscellaneous souvenirs, printed form letters, invitations, relating to the Centennial Exposition held in Philadelphia, 1876.

Gift of Samuel J. Castner, 1934.

120

Chaloner and White.   Records, 1744 (1777–1792) 1836. (5 linear ft.)

John Chaloner and James White, Philadelphia merchants, were appointed assistant commissaries of Purchase for the Middle Department of the Continental Army in 1777.

The papers consist of letter books, 1778–1784; accounts of purchases for the army, 1777–1778; accounts of provisions bought, 1778–1785; a daybook, 1777; receipt books, 1778–1784; and extensive correspondence revealing the operations and problems of army provisioning. Post-war papers, mostly correspondence, relate primarily to Chaloner's commercial activities.

Purchased, 1913.

121

Chase, Salmon Portland, 1808–1873.   Collection, 1824–1881. (12 linear ft.)

Papers, correspondence, letterbooks, diaries, and miscellaneous documents on political trends, economic situations, and social history in the United States, before, during, and after the Civil War. Incoming correspondence from noted men, on national politics, the Civil War, financial policies,

1833–1871; outgoing correspondence, 1824–1863; diaries, journals, and memoranda, 1855–1872; letterpress books, 1862–1867; copies of "Special Letters," 1861–1865; speeches, notes and lectures, 1845–1865; legal opinions and decrees; miscellaneous documents that pertain to the Treasury, financing of the Civil War, religious questions and slavery, 1831–1881; biographical notes by J.W. Schulker, editor and writer on the life of Chase; and other miscellaneous papers.

Finding aid available.

122
Brooke, Robert.   Survey notes, 1791–1812.   (2 v.)

Robert Brooke was a Philadelphia surveyor and a regulator of the Northern Liberties.

This collection comprises notes of the construction of the turnpike, surveys, calculations, names of landholders, and items pertaining to the maintenance and management of the roadway in Norther Liberties, 1791–1812, and of the Willow Grove Turnpike Road, 1803–1810.

Purchased, Library Fund.

123
Chester County (Pa.) papers, (1684–1800) 1847.   (ca. 600 items.)

Miscellaneous papers relate to domestic affairs, local government, land transaction; correspondence of prominent men, illustrative of social, economic, legal, and political affairs during the colonial period; a volume of documents deals with the British army in Chester County, 1777.

124
Weather diary, 1818–1833.   (1 v.)

Daily record of weather conditions in Chester County.
Purchased, Dreer Fund, 1937.

125
Chew, Benjamin, 1722–1810.   Estate papers, 1776–1904.
(1 linear ft.)

A collection of land office warrants, patents, surveys, indentures, agreements, and land transactions in Fayette, Somerset and Westmoreland counties, in which Benjamin Chew was financially interested. Some of the early legal instruments contain the signatures of John Penn, 1776; John Dickinson, 1783; Edward Shippen, 1787; Thomas Mifflin, 1793; Thomas McKean, 1803; William Tilghman, 1813; and others.

Gift of Fannie M. Ewing.

126
Chew, David S.B.   Papers, 1828–1898.   (350 items.)

A collection of miscellaneous papers including: correspondence of David S.B. Chew on politics and public affairs, 1893–1898; David S. Browne's correspondence on legal and commercial transactions, 1853–1885; Anaconda Printing Company, accounts and statistics, 1872–1878; cashbook, 1857–1861; account books, 1828, 1831–1836; school exercise books, 1857–1879.

Gift of David S.B. Chew, 1935.

127
Childs, Cephas Grier, 1792–1871. Documents, 1793–1871.
(3 linear ft.)

Cephas Grier Childs was a Philadelphia publisher, editor, engraver, and lithographer.

Papers collected by Childs include statistics on railroads, canals, iron, coal, agriculture, and population.

128
Christ Church Hospital.   Papers, 1708–1895.   (ca. 100 items.)

A collection of papers reflecting the history and management of Christ Church Hospital, Philadelphia. Included are deeds, 1732–1835, abstracts of wills, leases, mortgages, letters of bequest, expense accounts, correspondence bearing the names of prominent citizens and clergymen, photographs, and other items.

129
Church and meeting collection, 1682–1910.   (ca. 120 v.)

A group of miscellaneous materials for church history:
Addison, Alexander. Sermons, 1794.
"Annals of the Moravian Church in America," 1734–1857. (1 v.)
Ashbury M.E. Church. (Philadelphia, Pa.) Minutes, 1829–1837. Minutes of the quarterly conference meetings held at the Ashbury and Haddington M.E. Churches; miscellaneous items include shares of stock in the Ashbury M.E. Church Corporation. Purchased, Gratz Fund, 1956.
Brinkle, S.C. Diary, 1834–1844. Kept as rector of St. James (Kingsessing, Philadelphia, Pa.) (1 v.)
Bruce, David. Shecomeko journal, 1746. (1 v.)
Campbell, Colin. Sermons, 1766. (1 v.)
Chalkley, Thomas, 1675–1741. Journal, 1675–1724. (1 v.)

"Christian Advice," 1682–1762. Directed at the Pennsylvania Yearly Meeting of Friends. (1 v.)

Christ Church and St. Peters (Philadelphia, Pa.) Records, 1758–1819. The records include: subscription list, 1758–1761; charter, 1765; and register, 1782–1819. (2 v.)

Churchmen's Missionary Association for Seamen of Port of Philadelphia. Papers, 1849–1875.

Clarke, [John]. Commonplace book, 1824–1836. Contains memorials, addresses, and letters on religious education, and temperance, and poems written for young ladies' albums; list of questions for Zane Street School, 1852, and Northwestern Grammar School, 1854. Purchased, 1979. (1 v.)

Conyngham, ? "History of the Mennonites and Aymenists (or Amish)," 1830. (1 v.)

Doane, George Washington, 1799–1859. Writings, 1841–1856. Writings appearing in *Banner of the Cross,* 1841–1842, and sermons, 1853–1856 at St. Mary's. (1 v.)

Evangelical Society. Minutes, 1808–1817. (1 v.)

Evans, Evan. "A Memorial of the State of the Church in Pennsylvania," 1707. (1 v.)

Fifth Presbyterian Church of Philadelphia. Minutes, 1821–1834. Association minutes of the Fifth Presbyterian Church of Philadelphia (Arch above 10th Street), including articles of association, about construction of the building and subsequent management of the Church. Purchased, Dreer Fund, 1962. (1 v.)

First Reformed Presbyterian Church of Philadelphia. Minutes, 1906–1914. With child's school copybook. Gift of the Genealogical Society of Pennsylvania, 1975. (1 v.)

Fortieth Street Church (Philadelphia, Pa.) Subscription book, [1871]. This pocket subscription book was for completion of the Methodist Episcopal church building completion, with miscellaneous memoranda. Gift of Bart Anderson. (1 v.)

Frankford Presbyterian Church (Philadelphia, Pa.) Cashbook, 1818–1819. Cashbook kept by George Castor, treasurer. (1 v.)

Grant, James, 1829–1905. "The Flag and the Cross : a History of the United States Christian Commission," 1894. Lecture delivered at the Tioga Presbyterian Church by James Grant who had been a Commission delegate. Typescript. Gift of Kent Packard, 1946. (1 v.)

Hiellern, Michael. "Pastilla über die Evangellien," 1752.

Huntington County Bible Society. Minutes and accounts, 1827–1847. (1 v.)

Jordan, John W. "Historical notes in regards to Wyoming Valley," 1883. Depicting Moravian missionary enterprises among the Indians also containing biographical sketches of leaders of the Moravian Church.

Knipp, L.O. Diary, 1892–1904. Kept while pastor of Christian Church (Pennypack, Pa.) (1 v.)

Kollock, Henry, 1778–1819. "First Sketch of the Life of [John] Calvin," [1819]. Continued with a brief sketch of Theodore de Beze. Removed from the Gratz Collection. (1 v.)

Konkle, Burton Alva, 1861–1944. "A History of the Presbyterian Minister's Fund, 1717–1928," 1928. Gift of Burton Alva Konkle, 1930. (1 v.)

Linville Creek Baptist Church (Rockingham County, Va.) Minutes, 1756–1818. Continued as Brock's Gap Church, 1842–1844. Gift of Henry W. Scarborough, 1923; courtesy of the Genealogical Society of Pennsylvania. Abstract published in *Virginia Valley Records*, by John W. Wayland (Strasburg, Va.) 1930. (1 v.)

"The Lutheran Church," 1733–1741. (1 v.)

Marriage records, 1684–1869. (ca. 1,000 items.)

McCullogh, William Wallace, Jr. "Faggs Manor Presbyterian Church in Chester County, Pennsylvania," 1944–1946. Contains materials used in sketch recreations of the three early meeting houses; mostly H.F.C. Heagey letters. Typescripts. Gift of William W. McCollough, Jr., 1944, 1946. (2 v.)

Mercer, Alexander G. Commonplace book, [1842–1849]. Contains notes on theological, philosophical, and ethical subjects. Gift of Lily M. Boyd, 1947. (1 v.)

Methodist Episcopal Church (Rossville Circuit, N.Y.) Register, 1831–1859. Includes information on members, baptisms, marriages, in a New York (State) Circuit which included Orange, Ulster, and Dutchess counties. Purchased, Mifflin Fund, 1946. (1 v.)

Moore, Ann Herbert. Report, 1756–1778. Report of Ann Herbert Moore, Quaker minister travelling to Pennsylvania, New York, New Jersey, Connecticut, and England; with testimonies concerning Ann Moore and other miscellany. Xerox; original in possession of family. (1 v.)

"The Moravian Church in Philadelphia," 1745–1748. (1 v.)

"Moravian Church in West Jersey," 1745. (1 v.)

Moravian Church (York, Pa.) Papers, 1780–1791. (1 v.)

"Moravian Emigration to America," 1734–1800. A register of members of the Moravian Church who emigrated from Europe to America, includes biographical sketches by John W. Jordan. (1 v.)

Newton, Richard. Sermons, 1865. (1 v.)

Oxford Presbyterian Church. Ladies Dorcas Society. (Philadelphia, Pa.) Minute book, 1888–1899. This organization sewed for charity. (1 v.)

Parliament Court Chapel. Records, 1791–1804. Contains records of the Universalist ministry of Elhanan Winchester and William Vidler. Recorded by Thomas A. Teulon to 1802. Purchased, John T. Morris Fund, 1950. (1 v.)

Philadelphia Moravian records, 1743–1761. (1 v.)

Pennsylvania Baptist Education Society (Philadelphia, Pa.) Account book, 1851–1870. This society was formed to provide financial aid for the education of young men for the ministry and young women for missionary work. Purchased, Mifflin Fund, 1972. (1 v.)

[Prayers], n.d. Portions in shorthand. (1 v.)

Protestant Episcopal Church of Pennsylvania. Invoice of stores, 1867–1868. (1 v.)

Quintard, Charles Todd. "Bishopric of Virginia," 1872. (1 v.o

Register of Inhabitants of Nazareth," 1745–1752. (1 v.)

[Religious discourse on the 73rd Psalm, verses 12–13], 1780. Transferred from the Meredith Papers. (1 v.)

St. James Church. Vestry book and register, 1799. (1 v.)

St. Michael and Zion Lutheran Church of Philadelphia. Records, 1796–1800. Records relating to John Stock.

Salem Lutheran Church (Logan's Valley, Blair County, Pa.) Records, 1805–1877. (1 v.)

Scot's Presbyterian Church of Philadelphia. Session minutes, 1768–1791. Recorded by William Marshall; William Marshall's "State of the Case of the Scots Presbyterian Church," [1790], reviewing the church dispute over joining the Reformed Presbyterians in 1786. [Gift of John McAllister.] (2 v.)

Society of Friends. Burlington (N.J.) Yearly Meeting. Advice, 1719–1763.

Society of Friends. Chesterfield Meeting. Minute books, 1685–1712, 1756–1760. (2 v.)

Society of Friends. Darby Monthly Meeting, 1743–1749, 1796–1798, 1799–1801. (1 v.)

Society of Friends. Discipline, 1719. (1 v.)

Society of Friends. Epistle, 1755. (1 v.)

Society of Friends. Exter Monthly Meeting (Berks County, Pa.) Minutes, 1875 (1877–1880) 1882. (1 v.)

Society of Friends. First day school, 1880–1887. (1 v.)

Society of Friends marriages for city and county of Philadelphia, 1682–1762. Copied by Samuel Morris Lynn. (1 v.)

Society of Friends. Nantucket (Mass.) Meeting, 1698–1848. (1 v.)

Society of Friends. Port Elizabeth (N.J.) visiting Friends, 1753–1844. (1 v.)

Society of Friends. Radnor Meeting. Papers, 1714–1766. Kept by Thomas Thomas on building and assessments from members.

Society of Friends. "Reunion of Orthodox and Hicksite," 1916. (1 v.)

Society of Friends. Testimonials, 1703–1780. (1 v.)

Synod of Philadelphia. Committee on marriage and divorce. Minutes, 1684–1689.

Stoever, John. Ministerial records, 1730–1779. (1 v.)

Taylor, Henry P. "Early Recollections of Grace Church," 1877. (1 v.)
Trinity Protestant Episcopal Church. Register, 1839–1849. (1 v.)
Young Men's Christian Association (Philadelphia, Pa.) "Historical Sketch of the Fifth St. M.E. Church, Philadelphia, [1832–1869]." Continued by J. Thorton Seaver to 1882. With photographs and engravings. (1 v.)
Yearly Meeting of Friends for Pennsylvania and New Jersey. A Collection of Christian and Brotherly Advices, 1681–1765. Gift of Frank M. Etting, 1887, and of the Elizabeth S. Allen estate, 1923. (2 v.)

130
Churchman Papers of Kirk Brown, 1716–1835.   (2,000 items.)

John Churchman and his son, George Churchman, were deputy surveyors of Pennsylvania.
This is a collection of Maryland and Pennsylvania surveys, 1716–1835, covering a wide field of information on the early settlements and subdivisions of land. It includes land warrants as issued by the province, petitions for road building, drafts, indentures, agreements, showing the land holdings and the names of pioneer settlers; a volume *A Book containing the Records of the Surveys made by John and George Churchman*, ca. 1744–1777. There are also records of the Quaker Monthly meetings held at East Nottingham, and other places, 1743–1805.
Collected by Kirk Brown; gift of J. Clemson Brown.

131
Churchman, George.   Papers, 1720–1850.   (2.75 linear ft.)

George Churchman was deputy surveyor of Pennsylvania.
Land warrants issued by the provincial government, surveys, drafts, agreements, indentures, signed by James Hamilton, Nicholas Scull, George Churchman, and others, with information on early settlements in Pennsylvania counties, land holdings, names of settlers.

132
Clark, William, Jr.   Docket book, 1844–1848.   (1 v.)

William Clark, Jr. was a justice of the peace for Dauphin County.
Gift of William Bell Clark, 1924

133
Claypoole, James, 1634–1687.   Letter book, 1681–1683.   (2 v.)

James Claypoole, a London Quaker merchant, emigrated to Philadelphia in 1683.

Business letters and transcripts.

The transcriptions, in an unknown 19th-century hand, provide only extracts of the letters about Pennsylvania written from London, but contain the full text of letters written from Philadelphia.

Gift of Deborah Bringhurst, 1852.

134

Clement, John C.   Papers, 1681–1871.   (ca. 500 items.)

Entry cancelled; see collection #791

135

Clemson, Elizabeth C.   Autograph album, 1824–1828.   (2 v.)

Verse dedicated to Elizabeth C. Clemson by her friends.
Gift of Mrs. T.H. Neilson, 1918.

136

Clifford family.   Papers, 1722–1832.   (6 linear ft.)

World-wide trade conducted by several generations of the Clifford family, a prominent Philadelphia merchant family, is documented in this voluminous collection of papers and correspondence. The papers fall in two periods: 1722–1776 and 1777–1832. There is information on the commerce with China, Russia, England, Holland, France, Spain, Italy, Portugal, West Indies, United States territories; lands; world markets, flow of goods, transportation, and fluctuation of prices, influenced by political trends. The invoices, receipts, bills, legal instruments, insurance policies, charters of vessels, give an account of the hazards of the enterprises, the economic factors involved, and the commodities exchanged such as cotton, tea, silks, rum, salt, sugar, wheat, beef, and cloth.

A letter from Harper and Hartshorn, 1765, Antigua, gives an account of the feeling of resentment and rebellion aroused against the Stamp Act; letters, 1763, describe the outfitting of privateers; diary, 1778–1779, relates events of the Revolution, as seen by a Tory; charter for building canals, 1791; duties imposed by England on American grain, 1791; and captures of English vessels by French frigates are described in letters, 1792. Trade expansion to the South and West is shown in letters, 1805, to Kentucky and New Orleans, La. merchants; sale of cotton is discussed in a letter, 1804, from Stathart and Bell to Andrew Jackson.

Included are letterbooks of Thomas and John Clifford, 1759–1789; Thomas Clifford receipt book, 1750–1751; diary of a trip to Ohio from Philadelphia, 1804; *Clifford Estate vs. Stephen Girard Papers,* 1822; pocket almanacs with marginal notes, Poor Will's, 1791, Gaines, 1791, Bioren, 1819, Agricultural, 1821, Astronomical Calculations, 1792; printed catalogue of 350 cases of china goods to be sold at auction, Philadelphia, 1828.

There are items of literary interest: manuscript of a dialogue between Dr. Samuel Johnson and Mrs. Knowles, n.d.; *An Epistle from the Celebrated Abbe de Rance at the Abbey of La Trappe,* n.d.; Quaker sermons, 1787; poetry, 1822.

Gift of Henry Pemberton, Jr.

137
Cliffton, William, 1772–1799.   Selected works, 1791–1798.   (1 v.)

A selection of unpublished works of William Cliffton. Includes several obituaries, pastoral poems and odes on the deaths of Samuel Hollowell, Dr. [Matthew] Clarkson, William Waring; prose essays on painting, *Ideas,* innate principles. Some of the fragments at the end of the volume may have appeared in revised form in the *Fenno* (New York, 1800) edition of Cliffton's works.

Collected and transcribed by J. Cliffton, presumably after 1800.

Purchased, Dreer Fund.

138
Clymer, Daniel Cunyngham, 1748–1810.   Papers, (1766–1809) 1899. (60 items.)

Daniel Cunyngham Clymer was an officer of the Philadelphia Military Associators, 5th Rifle Battalion, 1776, a deputy commissary general of prisoners in the Continental Army, 1777–1781, and then a lawyer in Berks County.

His papers include: Philadelphia volunteer lists, 1775; circulars, delegate election reports, and minutes of the Associators of the Colony of Pennsylvania meeting to elect brigadier generals, 1776; miscellaneous letters and documents of his military and civilian career; Cunyngham family genealogical notes.

Gift of William Hiester Clymer descendants, 1908.

139
Coates, William M., 1845–1937.   Papers, 1731–1860.   (25 items.)

These papers contain the Yearly Meeting treasury book of Beulah Coates, 1731–1741; broadside addressed to the president and council of Pennsylvania by prominent Quakers protesting against religious and political persecution, and reply to accusations of Quaker opposition to the cause of the American Revolution, 1776; Quaker broadside issued by John Pemberton, 1776; pamphlet, *Address to the Inhabitants of the British Colonies in America*, 1776; Nancy Gregory, indenture to Benjamin Hornor, 1803; letter of Frederick Douglass, African American orator and author, to Benjamin Coates, in behalf of abolition of slavery, and against colonization of Liberia, 1856; facsimile of a testimonial by members of the medical profession in Philadelphia, addressed to Dr. T.G. Morton, reputed discoverer of ether as an anesthetic, 1860.

Gift of William Coates, 1930.

140A
Coates and Reynell. **Papers, 1702–1843.** **(15 linear ft.)**

For the most part, these are commercial papers, records of prices, business correspondence, ledgers and daybooks. In addition to strictly mercantile papers, there are other items relating to Indian affairs, the development of frontier lands, medicine, finance, and family matters.

The papers of Samuel Coates and John Reynell include: correspondence, 1722–1838; bills receipts, orders, and accounts, 1702–1838; statements of prices current, 1790–1816, mostly of Liverpool; letterbook of John Reynell, 1734–1774; his daybooks, 1728–1738; ledger, 1734–1736; invoice book, 1731–1738; account books, 1735–1736, 1738–1767; receipt books, 1763–1791; records of Pennsylvania and New Jersey meetings accounts with John Reynell, 1762–1783.

Samuel Coates papers include: letterbooks, 1763–1781, 1795–1802; letterbook of Josiah and Samuel Coates, 1784–1790; daybooks, 1796–1804; daybooks of Josiah and Samuel Coates, 17830791; ledger pertaining to sugar business, 1768–1775; memoranda of wages and similar items, 1784–1806; sales book, 1795–1817; journal, 1791–1798; journal of Josiah and Samuel Coates, 1785–1789; bankbooks of Samuel Coates, 1791–1794; bankbooks of Josiah and Samuel Coates, 1778–1787, 1812–1824; receipt book of Josiah and Samuel Coates, 1778–1791; their bill of lading book, 1786–1791; letterbooks of George M. Coates, 1803–1821, 1831–1843; daybook, 1729–1737, of Samuel Coates, Sr.; Mary Coates receipt book, 1748–1759; Josiah L. Coates receipt book, 1795–1809; and the papers of Benjamin H. Coates which include social and professional correspondence, 1806–1843; his notes and essays on medical subjects, 1830–1847; his cashbook, 1839–1845. There are papers on the settlement of various family estates, 1745–1839; record of Joseph Stansbury's account with Samuel Coates and Ezekiel Edwards, 1773–1775; and the daybook of the estate of Captain John Vicary, 1784–1795.

The papers from the Deborah Morris estate, which form a part of this collection include: correspondence of Deborah Morris on land transactions and social affairs, 1724, 1763–1793; wills, inventories, 1774–1787; bonds and agreements, 1785–1813; ledgers relating to the estate, 1752–1768, 1760–1789; account book, 1760–1769; rent account, 1777–1793; daybook, 1782–1785; receipt book, 1788–1793; Benjamin Morris ledger, 1747–1755; his memorandum book, 1755–1758.

Since Samuel Coates was the executor of Isaac Zane's estate, many of the Zane papers are found in this collection: correspondence of members of the Zane family, 1761–1825; accounts, receipts, bills, 1731–1824; deeds, leases, lands, 1752–1824; papers on the Marlboro Iron Works, 1772–1808; catalogues of the books belonging to Isaac Zane, 1791; inventory of Zane's possessions, 1794; daybook of Zane, 1759–1780; account book of Zane, 1761–1793; receipt book of Sarah Zane, 1796–1814; receipt books of Samuel Coates, executor of the estate of Isaac Zane, 1821–1824; receipt books of Charles Meredith, 1753–1772, 1773–1791.

Purchased, Library Fund, 1914.

Wyoming journal of Isaac Zane published in *P.M.H.B.*, 30 (1906): 417–426.

140B
Coates and Reynell family papers, 1677–1930.   (300 items.)

This is a collection of accounts and other papers of the Coates and Reynell families of Philadelphia. John Reynell, shipping merchant, business and household cashbook, 1737–1738; business invoice book, 1758–1772; Overseers of Publick School account and receipt book, 1758–1770; estate waste book, 1784- 1789. The rest of the account books are personal: Thomas Coates, nephew of Reynell, receipt book, 1768–1772; estate account book, 1773–1795. Josiah Langdale Coates, brother of Thomas, also a shipping merchant, pocket ledger, 1788–1803. Josiah Coates, son of Josiah L., receipt book, 1810–1814, 1843–1850; bank account, 1813–1814. George Morrison Coates, brother of Josiah and hardware merchant, receipt book, 1839–1868.

There is some miscellaneous incoming personal correspondence, 1711–1930, to family members among whom are Hannah Pemberton, Amy Hornor and later as Mrs. Samuel Coates, and Amy and Samuel's son Dr. Reynell Coates; also family deeds, wills, and other legal papers. Additionally, the family came into possession of a few manuscripts relating to colonial Pennsylvania, including a bundle of Benjamin Franklin papers, 1761–1764, concerning Market Street property.

Gift of Estelle L. Sharp and May B. Sharp, 1966.

140C
Reynell, John, 1708–1784.   Papers, (1729–1761) 1783.
(6 linear ft.)

The papers of John Reynell, Philadelphia shipping and commission merchant, consist of incoming business correspondence, invoices, bills of exchange, with a small amount of personal material. Merchants and factors writing to Reynell include: Elias Bland, London; Nathaniel Booth, Antiqua; Michael Lee Dicker, Exon; Daniel Flexney, London; David Fogo, Antiqua; John Moffatt, Portsmouth, N.H., largely concerning mercantile insurance; Henry Sherborne, Portsmouth, N.H.

141
Cochran, Henry C.   Lecture notes, 1845–1848.   (3 v.)

Notes of Henry C. Cochran for lectures delivered in 1845 on the history of Philadelphia hospitals and public utilities (the Pennsylvania Hospital, the Pennsylvania Hospital for the Insane, Will's Hospital; the Philadelphia Gas Works, the Northern Liberties Gas Works and the Water Works), and for lectures delivered in 1848 on the history of Pennsylvania and the history, organization, finances, teachers, and curriculum of the public schools of Philadelphia.
Gift of Daniel E. Pennypacker, 1903.

142
Earle, Morris, 1859–1924.   Collection, 1776–1838.   (1 v.)

Accounts of Isaac Collins for the printing of New Jersey resolutions, ordinances, and acts of assembly of the American Revolutionary period; genealogical records of the Collins family; and an almanac, 1838.
Gift of Morris Earle estate, 1924.

143
Collins, Matthew.   Surveys, 1771.   (1 v.)

Contemporary extracts from records of the surveyor general's office in Burlington, N.J., relate to a survey of land in Egg Harbor, N.J.
Gift of William John Potts, 1857.

144
Colonial-Revolutionary period manuscripts, 1738–1808.
(ca. 150 items.)

A collection of papers relating chiefly to Berks County colonial legal cases, and political and economic matters. Among the papers are: John Prinz letter from Reading, 1757, to James Read, depicting Indian depredations; Conrad Weiser, letters and writs, 1754–1760; Frederick Weiser, letter, 1762, on the collection and adjustment of county debts; bonds for the observance of the laws of the province, 1773; marriage contracts; tavern license signed by Robert Hunter Morris; James Read commission, signed by William Plumsted, 1752; receipts for military equipment from members of the Reading militia, 1776; Captain John Patton letter to James Read, on the refusal of battalions to obey orders to march, 1776; oaths and affirmations of justices of Berks County, 1776–1778; Thomas McKean communication to Congress on his controversy with Brigadier General Thompson, 1778; report of the council of censors that Timothy Matlack is "unworthy of public trust and confidence," 1783; records of admiralty cases, 1766–1779, on prizes of war, adjustments of shares of prize money, libels, surveys, adjudicated before Francis Hopkinson, George Ross, Edward Shippen, and others; John Adams letter, Paris, France, 1780, to Samuel Huntington, President of Congress, containing Russia's declaration of principles adopted by her as neutral during the war between England and the United States; Peter Collinson letter, 1738, John Ross, 1762, Edward Biddle, 1764, John Morris, 1762.

145
Commonplace book, 1775–1780.   (1 v.)

These manuscripts contain accounts of the theatrical and carnival performances produced by the Tories for the entertainment of British soldiers during the Revolution. Included is a prologue to the *Tragedy of Zara,* spoken at the opening of the theatre at Boston, written by General John Burgoyne; prologue spoken by Major Robert Chew, at the opening of the theatre in Philadelphia, written by Rev. Jonathan Odell; an account of the Meschianza, held at Philadelphia in 1778, by one of the company; miscellaneous verse by Philadelphia writers.

Gift of I.T. Sharpless, 1868.

146
Conarroe, George M. Autograph collection, 1643–1882.
(3 linear ft.)

Alphabetically arranged.

This collection includes letters and documents of the signers of the Declaration of Independence and of members of Congress, 1758–1811; of generals and prominent civilians of the Revolutionary period, 1770–1820; of signers of the Constitution, senators, congressmen, governors of states, 1754–1853; of presidents, vice-presidents, and cabinet officers, 1777–1882; letters from authors, 1778–1869; foreign generals and statesmen connected with the Revolution, scientists, physicians, and philanthropists, 1759–1873; English and American lawyers, 1676–1854; American lawyers and judges, 1753–1859; officers in the American navy; clergymen, 1779–1871; other celebrities, 1643–1870. There are about 200 portraits, 1836; and a few papers of Robert Morris, Thomas McKean, and George Read, 1757–1788.

Gift of Nannie Dunlap Conarroe in memory of George M. Conarroe, 1899.

147
Conner-Powell Genealogies, 1775–1893.   (ca. 250 items.)

Transferred to the Genealogical Society of Pennsylvania.

148
Cooke, Jay, 1821–1905.   Papers, 1842–1901.   (60 linear ft.)

This extensive collection of papers relates to many aspects of the career of Jay Cooke, financier of the Civil War and the great period of American expansion: correspondence with influential men of the time, 1842–1880, contain information on the conduct and financing of the Civil War, nationalization of banks, westward expansion, railway building, especially the Northern Pacific Railroad episode which was a factor in the financial crisis of 1873.

There are also some letters of Henry D. Cooke, relating to his enterprises in western mines, lands, and shipping; letter books of Jay Cooke, 1870–1873; newspaper clippings, scrapbooks, pamphlets, receipts, bills, 1863–1901, which contain interesting material on political and economic trends. Many family letters contain, in addition to personal affairs, indications of Cooke's interest in church and civic affairs.

Purchased.

149
Cooper, James Fenimore, 1789–1851.   *Home as Found,* 1838.
(1 v.)

Original manuscript of the latter part of James Fenimore Cooper's *Home as Found.*

Cooper requested the manuscript be left with Lea and Blanchard, Philadelphia publishers, October 25, 1838. Gift of Lea Brothers and Company, 1887.

150
Cope, Gilbert, 1840–1928.   Collection, 1682–1877.
(ca. 500 items.)

Quakeriana: Falls Monthly Meeting (Fallsington, Bucks County), papers, 1697–1877, include certificates of removal, memoranda of discipline of members and some financial records; contemporary copies, Friend's Discipline, 1719, 1755; notes on the Gurney Crisis in London Yearly Meeting, 1846; Bradford Monthly Meeting, papers, ca. 1760–1805; Cope's notes on the history of Pennsylvania Meetings of Friends.

Pennsylvania legal papers: Supreme Court bail book, 1760–1763; list of jurors, 1847; Supreme Court, docket book, 1857; Philadelphia County, Court of Quarter Sessions, bail book, 1798–99; Green County, Court of Nisi Prius, docket, 1798–1799.

Miscellaneous papers: Cope's transcription of "An Account of the Disturbances in America," by John Ettwein, a Moravian minister; a modern transcription of letters, 1768–1775, to the Society for the Propagation of the Gospel from the parish of St. David's, Radnor; professional and business papers of Jesse Conard, 1820–1837; anonymous contemporary manuscript of "Some Account of the Visit of the Friendly Indians to Philadelphia," 1760; depositions and other legal papers in *Levett Harris v. William D. Lewis,* the Riga consulate case, 1820.

Purchased, 1921.

In 1952, the greater part of the materials listed as part of this collection in the 1949 Guide to Manuscripts were transferred to the Chester County Historical Society, West Chester, Pa.

151
Coryell, Lewis S., 1788–1865.   Correspondence, 1806–1867.
(700 items.)

Papers of Lewis S. Coryell, lumber dealer and political leader in Pennsylvania: correspondence relates to state and national politics, and includes letters of A. Beaumont, Nicholas Biddle, John C. Calhoun, Simon Cameron, Stephen A. Douglas, George Mifflin Dallas, John M. Forney, John Forsyth, Samuel D. Ingham, Sam Houston, Dixon H. Lewis, F.R. Shunk, J.D. Stiles, George Wolf, W.S. Woodward, and others; letters of James Buchanan, containing comments on the outcome of the Civil War and criticism of the Lincoln administration; Coryell's business letters relate to construction of canals, railroads, roads and to his lumber business at New Hope.

Gift of Lewis S. Coryell.

152
Pennsylvania Militia.   Accounts, ca. 1797.   (1 v.)

Names of military officers and soldiers in various Pennsylvania counties, and records of their certificates for the funded debt.

153
Lewis, Joseph J.   Memorial of Henry Hamilton Cox, 1881.
(1 v.)

Biographical sketch of Henry Hamilton Cox who came to the United States in 1799, from Dunmanway, County Cork, Ireland. He leased a farm in Chester County, 1813–1817, became a member of the Society of Friends, ca. 1813 and returned to Ireland in 1817.
Gift of Joseph J. Lewis, 1881.

154
Cox-Parrish-Wharton family.   Papers, 1600–1900.   (9 linear ft.)

This collection of papers and correspondence contains information on the religious, humanitarian, social, and economic influence of the Quakers in American life. A large portion of the collection consists of letters, 1785–1845, from John and Ann Cox of Burlington, N.J., to Dr. Joseph and Susannah Parrish of Philadelphia. There are also letters of William Penn, Israel Pemberton, James Pemberton, John Pemberton, John Rodman, Benjamin Lightfoot, John Bringhurst, Hannah Lloyd, George Mifflin, William Logan, David Barclay, John Fothergill, Roberts Vaux, Dolley Madison, and numerous others, 1700–1840.

There are monthly meeting reports, broadsheets, and papers, 1700–1847, pertaining to religious doctrine, discipline, moral precepts, humane treatment of the Indians, abolition of slavery, and economic affairs. Also copies of William Penn's letter to the Indians, 1681, and of a Quaker Address to King William III, 1703; "An Indian's Answer to a Swedish Missionary," 1704; list of the number of slaves in the United States, 1779; printed list of the Company of Merchants Trading to Africa, 1755; Isaac Parrish's receipt book, 1780–1807; his invoice book, 1762–1767; Samuel Parrish and Job Bacon, account book, consignment from Calcutta, 1806–7; John Parrish, Friends discipline, 1719; minutes of the Society for the Relief of Negroes, 1775–1787; "Divine Odes," by Thomas Wilkinson, 1787; reports of Quaker meetings, 1801–1806; genealogical notes of the Parrish family, 1600–1862; records of the Cox, Dillwyn, Mitchel, and other families; letters addressed to Samuel Emlen, 1826; *Expressions of dying sayings,* Hannah Hill, 1714;

poetry of Susannah Parrish, 1820; moral impressions and observations, 1800; John Cox, weather reports and memoranda book, 1830–1833; schedules of *Bills before House of Commons,* 1879; portraits and biographical sketches of prominent Quakers.

Gift of Mrs. Rodman Wharton, 1914 and Miss Susan Wharton.

155
Crispin, M. Jackson, 1875–1953.   Collection, 1665–1814.
(ca. 25 items.)

Colonial documents of the Crispin family, which settled in New Jersey and Pennsylvania in 1687: deed of land granted by William Penn to James, Joseph and Benjamin Cripsin in 1687; an inventory of the estate of James Holmes, 1690; correspondence relating to British shipping, signed by the duke of Albemarle, 1665; Quaker marriage certificate of Benjamin Crispin and Margaret Owen, 1722; writ issued by Thomas Hopkinson, 1747.

Gift of M. Jackson Crispin, 1931.

156
Cunyngham family.   Genealogy.   (1 v.)

Account of ancestry of a Scottish family, Stephen de Cunyngham, Earl of Glencairne, and his descendants, and of Isaac Roberdeau family of Rochelle, France, 1057–1799.

Gift of R. Buchanan.

157
Custom House Papers, 1704–1789.   (12 linear ft.)

Papers of the United States customs service of the Port of Philadelphia illustrating commercial and shipping interests, as well as foreign trade relations, of colonial America and the United States. The records include: account book, 1704–1713, duties imposed on tobacco, and data on merchandise exported; Custom House papers, 1750–1774, including letters, clearance papers, bonds, entries, cargo manifests, names of vessels, reports of seizures, accounts of contraband and smuggled merchandise, complaints, and other official records of the Port of Philadelphia; Custom House records, outward entries, 1784–1787, 1789–1791; inward entries, 1786–1787, 1789–1793, 1792–1794; and an inward index, 1789–1817.

Papers after 1789 were transferred to the National Archives.

158

Dallas, George Mifflin, 1792–1864.   Diary, 1848–1849.   (1 v.)

Photostat of Vice President George M. Dallas' diary of the last few months of James K. Polk's administration, including an account of Senate politics, tariff controversy, territorial expansion, gold discovery in California.

Original in the possession of Robert D. Abrahams, Philadelphia; copy purchased, 1936.

159

Dallas, Alexander J.   Dallas Family History, 1894.   (2 v.)

Transferred to the Genealogical Society of Pennsylvania.

160

Darrach, Charles Gobrecht, b. 1846.   Papers, 1906–1918.   (7 v.)

Correspondence and miscellaneous writings of Charles G. Darrach, Philadelphia civil and consulting engineer: *Topography of the Earth*, 1906, contains maps and essays on the formation of the universe; *Obligation, a Compilation*, 1919, a metaphysical treatise on evolution; *Folly of Philadelphia*, 1918, criticism of politics, transit problems, concentration of business; *The World War*, 1917, correspondence on conscription in the United States Army; *Port of Philadelphia, Public Utilities*, 1913; *National transportation and a discussion of the report on Atlantic Intracoastal Canals*, 1917; *Water Supply, Philadelphia*, 1914–1917, a history of the water system, plans of dams and pumping plants.

Gift of Charles G. Darrach.

161

Darrach, William, 1796–1865.   Diaries, 1830–1838.   (2 v.)

Diary, 1830–1838, contains William Darrach's notes on pharmacology and his professional activities; diary, 1832–1837, reflects his interest in Presbyterian Church affairs, prayer meetings, religious revival, and doctrinal controversies.

Gift of Alfred Darrach, 1926.

162

Davidson, William B.   Journal and Sketchbook, 1824–1825. (2 v.)

Journal of William B. Davidson, 1824–1825, member of the Philadelphia bar, details activities in law college, daily local events, his observations on sermons preached in local churches, politics, tours through Pennsylvania, travel by coach and canal, and describes a reception tendered Marquis de Lafayette on the occasion of his visit to Philadelphia, 1824. Davidson's sketchbook, 1825, contains drawings of Mauch Chunk, Berwick, Pa., Harpers Ferry, W.Va. and other places.

Purchased, 1902.

163
Davis, John, d. 1827.   Diaries, (1781–1782) 1800.   (2 v.)

John Davis was captain of the 1st Pennsylvania Battalion, Continental Army, under General Anthony Wayne.

His diary covers the Virginia campaign, Yorktown, and the march to North and South Carolina to join Nathanael Greene. Also a short diary of a Pennsylvania trip, 1800.

Gift of Mrs. David Lewis Fultz, 1946.
Revolutionary diary published in the *P.M.H.B.*, 15 (1881): 290–310.

164
Davis, William Morris, 1815–1891.   Letters, 1853–1879.
(181 items.)

William Morris Davis was a Philadelphia sugar refiner, abolitionist, and member of Congress, 1861–1863.

This small collection consists primarily of letters from William Morris Davis to Henry Kirke Brown, a New York sculptor. Also included are letters to and from Davis' wife, Elizabeth, and their friends Catherine Brooks Yale and her husband, Linus Yale, developer of the Yale lock. The correspondents discuss Brown's sculptures, fly fishing, forging and casting, religion, machine tools, the Panic of 1857, and Republican politics. Davis also reports Passmore Williamson's imprisonment for contempt of court during a fugitive slave case, 1857, sending his daughter to Theodore Weld's school, his support for John C. Frémont's presidential candidacy, and his criticism of both James Buchanan and Abraham Lincoln. An 1861 letter gives an account of a confrontation between Jessie Benton Frémont and Francis Preston Blair in St. Louis.

Gift of H.K. Bush-Brown, 1933.

165
Decatur, Stephen, 1779–1820.   Papers, (1801–1805) 1820.
(75 items.)

The papers of Stephen Decatur, American naval officer, contain copies of orders and letters, 1801–1805, on his service with the United States Navy in the Mediterranean before and during the Tripolitan War, a letter of Decatur's about his fatal duel with Captain James Barron, and articles of agreement.

Gift of Mrs. F.H. Getchell, 1896.

166
Delaware.   Papers, 1710–1822.   (ca. 30 items.)

Miscellaneous legal papers including papers on justice of the peace courts; addresses of the Delaware assembly to the proprietors and the king, 1726, 1760; application for tavern license, and other items.

167
Delaware and Schuylkill Canal Company.   Papers, 1796–1797. (ca. 35 items.)

Statements of account, surveys, and correspondence on the construction and maintenance of the canal.

Purchased, Library Fund.

168
Devereux, B.H.   Letterbook, 1837–1843.   (1 v.)

Copies of letters written by B.H. Devereux, merchant and shipper in Pernambuco, Brazil, to his brother John Devereux, Philadelphia merchant, and to other clients in South America, the United States, and London, England. Letters concern his extensive commercial enterprises in sugar, coffee, sperm oil, spices, flour, and other commodities.

Gift of Langdon Williams, 1924.

169
Dewitt, Peter.   Letterbook, 1794–1822.   (1 v.)

Letterbook of Peter Dewitt, Philadelphia merchant, reflects his trade in lumber and other commodities, 1794–1813, continued as accounts current of an unidentified Philadelphia shipping line, 1818–1833, and domestic memoranda.

170
R.G. Kennedy and Company.   Charles Dickens, Rare Print Collection, 1900.   (1 v.)

A small collection of prints and facsimiles of autographs, manuscripts and caricatures relating to the life and work of Charles Dickens, edited by

Seymour Eaton and published "for private circulation" in Philadelphia, 1900.

Purchased, Dreer Fund, 1934.

171
Dickinson, John, 1732–1808.   Papers, 1760–1772.   (8 v.)

Dickinson's copies of Samson Euer's *Doctrina Pacitandi, ou L'Art et Science de Bon Pleading* (London, 1677), with interleavings and marginal notes in Dickinson's hand; his notes on legal practice; a continuance docket, 1760–1772; and a commonplace book. There is also a memorandum book of the Rev. James Sayre, 1765–1772, who was admitted to practice before the Pennsylvania Supreme Court in 1765.

Purchased, 1912.

173
Diller, William S.   Papers, 1861–1899.   (125 items.)

William S. Diller of Hanover, was an officer in the 76th Pennsylvania Volunteers, 1861–1864.

These are mainly military papers: muster rolls, supply documents, reports and correspondence. Also included are a few later documents on his pension, and his activities in the Masons and Loyal Legion.

Gift of Leroy Diller, 1910.

175
**Dreer, Ferdinand Julius, 1812–1902.   Collection, 1492–1925.
(84 linear ft.)**

The Dreer Collection consists of four sections: specimen autographs arranged by Dreer in categories; additions to the collection after 1890, largely alphabetically arranged; individual letterbooks, journals, literary manuscripts, and small collections assembled by others; and a collection of English and continental literary figures of the mid-19th century, assembled by Samuel Carter Hall, editor of the British *Art Journal*. The collection includes: political and military figures; European political and military figures; fine and performing artists; American and European literary figures; clergymen; scientists and explorers; and British and continental literary figures of the nineteenth century.

Autographs of political and military figures, 1497–1922: Colonial Conventions, including the Albany and the Stamp Act Congresses; members of the Old Congress; signers of the Declaration, with the state seals; members of the Federal Convention; Presidents Washington to Harding and their cabinets; governors of the states; mayors of Philadelphia to 1893; American statesmen; officers in America before the Revolution; generals of the Revolution; soldiers of the Revolution; officers in the War of 1812 and the Mexican War; American naval officers; Union generals; Confederate generals; and Union officers.

Autographs of European political and military figures, 1571–1917: Statesmen of continental Europe; British statesmen; French Revolution; royal personages; British military; British navy; officers of the French army and navy; miscellaneous military figures.

Autographs of fine and performing artists, 1492–1921: Actors, singers, and dancers; painters and engravers; architects and sculptors; musicians and composers.

American prose writers; American poets; British prose writers; British poets; German prose writers; French prose writers; European writers; continental poets.

Autographs of clergymen, 1492–1921: American Protestant Episcopal bishops; American clergy; popes and cardinals; figures of the Protestant Reformation; British clergy.

Autographs of scientists and explorers, 1492–1921: Inventors; travelers and explorers; physicians, surgeons, and chemists; astronomers; scientists.

Miscellaneous manuscripts, 1730–1892: Letters of Nicholas Biddle; Bank of the United States; American lawyers; British lawyers; philanthropists; and famous merchants.

Literary and scientific autographs and manuscripts, 1703–1900: Letters, literary manuscripts, and journals organized around individuals, institutions, or events. Of American interest are: letters of the Penn family, 1666–1786; letter of Evan Evans, Rector of Christ Church, Philadelphia, to the Society for the Propagation of the Gospel, 1707; Franklin's "Queries to be asked the Junto;" letters from Patrick Henry to George Washington, 1777–1778, concerning the Conway cabal; papers of George Washington, 1744–1799; letters of Thomas Jefferson, 1774–1825; letters of Robert Morris, 1777–1799; Jacob Rush's letters to John Hancock, 1777; letters to Philadelphia naturalist Humphrey Marshall from Thomas Parke, John Abell, and other naturalists in America and Europe, 1772–1796; John Heckewelder's journal, 1793; and letters, papers, and prints illustrating Marquis de Lafayette's life, 1784–1830.

Dreer also collected a comprehensive group of papers relating to the publication of John Marshall's *Life of George Washington,* including the holograph manuscript for volumes 4 and 5 (the first three volumes were destroyed in a printing office fire), subscription lists, and letters between Caleb P. Wayne, the publisher, and Mason Locke Weems and William Poyntell, his agents, as well as letters from Bushrod Washington and John Marshall.

From his friend Robert Dale Owen, Dreer received holograph copies of "The Future of the North West in connection with the scheme of Reconstruction without New England," 1863; Owen's examination of spiritualism, "Footfalls on the Boundary of Another World," 1860; and a letter addressed to President Lincoln in 1863, "The Pardoning Power in its Relation to Reconstruction."

Other literary manuscripts include: Edgar Allan Poe, holograph copies of verse and a book review; letters of Jared Sparks, 1835–1843, to Edward Ingraham; Leigh Hunt, manuscript for *About Ben Adhem;* William Duane's book of humorous anecdotes; John Fanning Watson, "Historical Incidents of Germantown," 1823, "Annals of Philadelphia" and supplement, and genealogical material concerning the Fanning family; Francis Hopkinson's transcription, 1776, of Chronological Tables of Europe;" John Redman's annotated copy of Emanuel Swedenborg's *Delights of Wisdom concerning Conjugal Love* (London, 1794); and John Penn's copy of *Les Vrais Principes de la langue française* (Amsterdam, 1747).

Scientific and miscellaneous manuscripts complete this section of the collection: Benjamin Rush manuscripts, 1786–1813; materials relating to the polar expedition of John Ross, 1832–1836; letters to Alfred L. Elwyn, Treasurer of the American Association for the Advancement of Science, 1848–1856; and Elisha Kent Kane's journal, 1853–1855, of the 2nd Grinnel Expedition and correspondence with George W. Childs concerning its publication. Also present: Thomas Rush, memorandum book, 1711–1749; surveys of land of Richard Peters, 1742–1765; miscellaneous manuscripts of Friends Meetings, Middletown, Bucks County, and elsewhere, 1731–1832; records of the Homony Club, Annapolis, Md., 1770–1773; Chester County, bail books, 1768–1785, and special bail book, 1805–1830; Bucks County, militia brigade inspector's reports, 1800–1818; Philadelphia Fire Company, constitution and minutes, 1818–1837; dockets of justices of the peace, Adams County, 1830–1832, 1858–1860; subscription list for mezzotint engraving after Athenaeum portrait of George Washington, published by George W. Childs, 1852, with testimonial letters from U.S. senators; diaries and accounts of Mrs. Scott Siddons, 1881–1890; Robert Proud, accounts for his Philadelphia school, 1751–1790, with a list of students; and Thomas Sully's *Register of Portraits.*

Political and military history papers, 1518–1864,: Dreer collected Civil War materials extensively, including: William G. Brownlow, "History of the Rise, Progress and Decline of the Great Rebellion, 1861–1862," published in 1862; letterpress book of Brevet Brigadier General James A. Ekin; papers relating to John Brown's raid on Harper's Ferry, W.Va. his trial and subsequent execution; letters of Confederate General Gideon J. Pillow to his wife

Mary; scrapbooks of "Rebellion Relics," including ephemera, songsheets, broadsides, photograph of John Wilkes Booth, and Confederate and United States fractional currency; diary, 1862–1863, of John H. Markley, a sergeant in the Pennsylvania Volunteers; and Francis Janvier's manuscript of his Civil War poem, "The Sleeping Sentinel," 1863.

Present, too, are a number of political and military figures from other periods: documents relating to the history of Holland, 1518–1673, including several of William the Silent and William III, in Dutch, and a summary account of the Estates General; letter of James VI of Scotland to Queen Anne of Denmark, 1593; documents relating to Admiral Sir William Penn, 1650–1651, including minutes of several Councils of War off Spain and of the Admiralty Board, 1655–1667; holograph and typescript of William Darlington's "Memoirs and Correspondence of John Lacey, Esq.;" Jacob Vandel's "Notes on the Mexican War," 1846, revised 1874; returns of Daniel Wier, Commissary to His Majesty's Troops in America, 1777; log of the U.S. brig *Argus,* 1808–1811; account with sloop *Sally,* 1763–1764; and letters of Edward Rutledge of South Carolina.

Miscellaneous letters, 1703–1883: Miscellaneous letters and papers of Americans and Europeans including correspondence of John Fothergill, Yorkshire Quaker merchant, and his son, Dr. John Fothergill, 1703–1798; letters collected by the family of John Franklin, pioneer settler in the Wyoming Valley; and papers of Edwin Greble, Philadelphia politician, 1853–1883. Also included is ephemeral Americana removed from a volume labeled by Dreer "Historical and Literary Curiosities."

Samuel Carter Hall letters, ca. 1850–1880,: Letters addressed to Samuel Carter Hall, editor of the Art Journal, and his wife, Anna Maria Fielding Hall. Correspondents include: W. C. Aitken, William Cullen Bryant, Fredrika Bremer, Samuel Taylor Coleridge, Edward Robert Bulwer Lytton, and Walter Savage Landor, 1850–1880s.

Dreer formed this collection of "letters written by the hands of persons of different nationalities and distinguished in almost every arena of intellectual activity" between 1848 and 1890. To these holograph items Dreer added engravings, lithographs, and other ephemera illustrative of the careers of the individuals whose autographs he collected. With funds provided by Dreer at the time of his gift and by his estate, the Historical Society of Pennsylvania has continued to add to the collection.

The Dreer Collection was formed by gifts, purchases, and exchanges. Dreer's most important early purchase was part of the Robert Gilmor Collection in 1851, a collection particularly rich in the papers of the Penn family, George Washington, and British and European artists and literary figures. In 1863 Dreer retired from the jewelry business to devote himself entirely to "my favorite employment and recreation of collecting, repairing, and arranging autograph letters." The collection he formed is rather idiosyncratic and personal and reveals his interest in the arts and sciences, exploration, spiritualism, and the Civil War. Until 1870 Dreer dealt exclusively with American dealers and collectors, but thereafter he began to buy extensively in Europe. Throughout his collecting career Dreer received significant gifts from individuals whose papers he was collecting as well as from other collectors. Such gifts included an important group from Robert Dale Owen, and the Hall Collection from George W. Childs, editor of the Public Ledger.

After Dreer's death, Simon Gratz bought extensively for the collection. The purchases recorded in the accession book reveal Gratz' taste for political Americana more than they reflect Dreer's interests.

176
Drinker, Henry, 1734–1809.   Business papers, 1756–1869.
(5 linear ft.)

Henry Drinker was a Philadelphia merchant and Quaker. Drinker was the partner of Abel James in the firm of James and Drinker, which traded extensively with London, England, Dublin, Ireland, and other American cities. The partnership appears to have dissolved in 1786 although both partners remained involved in the operation of the Atsion Iron Works and the Union Saw Mill in New Jersey, and speculated jointly and separately in lands in Pennsylvania, New Jersey, and New York.

The collection contains voluminous documentation of the efforts of Drinker and his executors to develop and keep track of Drinker's interests in lands in Beaver, Bradford, Cambria, Clearfield, Cumberland, Jefferson, Luzerne, Lycoming, Northampton, Northumberland, McKean and Tioga counties.

Included are James & Drinker letterbooks, 1756–1786; a volume of the firm's "foreign letters," 1772–1784; Henry Drinker's own letterbooks, 1762–1809; his journals, 1776–1809; his ledgers, 1786–1809; and the ledger of the Atsion Iron Works, 1786–1801. Included, too, are the more fragmentary records of the executors of Drinker's estate, Thomas Stewardson, Henry S. Drinker and William Drinker: William Drinker's journal of estate accounts, 1816–1841; Henry S. Drinker's estate letterbook, 1816–1828; Thomas Stewardson's letter books, 1821–1841; the cashbook of Stewardson's estate, 1844–1854; and a ledger of the estate of Henry Drinker, 1809–1824.

There are other miscellaneous records and accounts of the Drinker land-holdings including a volume of surveys, 1794–1804; ledgers for the "Beech Lands" in Luzerne and Northampton counties, 1788–1805, and for "Stockport," 1789–1807; a compendium of tax information for Pennsylvania counties and townships, probably begun for Henry Drinker in the 1780s; a narrative of the settlement of the estate of Samuel Wallis, 1798–1807; and accounts of the sales of Drinker estate lands, 1844–1869. Also included are bonds, deeds, mortgages, and surveys of Drinker lands.

177
Drum, Augustus, 1815–1858.   Papers, (1794–1795) (1832–1856).
(55 items.)

Augustus Drum was a lawyer and congressman from Greensburg.

Letters from clients and lawyers on legal matters and land transactions; surveyor's returns and warrants, 1794–1795, 1832–1854; letters to Congressman Drum on veteran's claims from the Revolutionary War, the War of 1812, and the Mexican War, and civilian claims against the government.

178
Duane, William, 1808–1882.   "Canada and the Continental Congress," 1850.   (1 v.)

An address, 1850, delivered before the Historical Society of Pennsylvania by William Duane, Philadelphia lawyer, and Librarian and Vice President of the Society, concerning the efforts of the Continental Congress to enlist the aid of Canadians in the revolt against Great Britain.

Gift of William Duane, 1901.

179
Dulles, Joseph, d. 1829.   Diary, 1808–1810.   (1 v.)

Travel diary to New York on the ship *Minerva* and to England and Ireland, 1808–1810, aboard the ship *Princess Augusta,* compiled by Joseph Dulles, merchant of Charleston, S.C., who settled in Philadelphia in 1812. Describes British institutions, debates in the House of Commons, social events, food and drink, business transactions, and visits to several manufacturing plants.

Typescript.

Gift of Charles W. Dulles, 1906.

180
Dunlap, John, 1747–1812.   Estate papers, 1812.   (2 v.)

Photostats of surveys of land in Philadelphia, Kentucky, and Virginia as well as copies of letters, inventories, and other accounts created to settle the estate of John Dunlap, Philadelphia printer.

Gift of the Genealogical Society of Pennsylvania, 1929.

181
**Du Ponceau, Peter Stephen, 1760–1844.   Papers, 1663 (1781–1844).
(6 linear ft.)**

Du Ponceau was a Philadelphia lawyer who arrived in Portsmouth, N.H., from France in 1777, achieved early prominence as an aide to von Steuben, and as secretary to Robert Livingston, Secretary of Foreign Affairs for the Congress in 1781. Du Ponceau was admitted to the Philadelphia Bar in 1785 where his familiarity with both American and European law brought him an important practice. His intellectual interests included both history and linguistics and he published extensively in both fields. He was a member and officer of both the American Philosophical Society and the Historical Society of Pennsylvania.

A group of incoming letters relate to law, linguistics, and, less importantly, history, 1781–1827. Among the correspondents are James Fenimore Cooper and John Sergeant on law, George W. Featherstonhaugh, Albert Gallatin, and John Pickering on linguistics, and Jared Sparks on history. The second group consists of Du Ponceau's correspondence and notes, including notes on silk culture, 1820s, copies of the legal opinions of Bushrod Washington, and papers dealing with constitutional questions in Alabama, 1831–1833. Also present in this group are autobiographical letters, 1836–1844, addressed to Robert Walsh and others. The third group contains Du Ponceau's letter books, 1792–1801, 1803–1814, 1820–1842; legal precedents, 1784–1798, 1801–1830; letters, 1818–1843, from John Pickering, the Boston lawyer and judge who shared Du Ponceau's interest in linguistics.

Du Ponceau's notes and abstracts concerning the origin of the American Philosophical Society, taken from the minutes of the Junto, the American Society for Promoting Useful Knowledge, the American Philosophical Society, and from the Jared Sparks edition of the *Works of Benjamin Franklin*.

The transcriptions of letters sent to Du Ponceau, prepared by Job R. Tyson, a Vice-President of the Historical Society of Pennsylvania, were to be used for a memorial biography of Du Ponceau, prepared after his death in 1844. Tyson's selection reflects a strong bias toward military and political figures including DeWitt Clinton, James Kent, John Marshall, James Madison, and James Monroe.

182
Dupuy, Herbert.   Collection, 1770–1879.   (25 items.)

Collection of deeds and patents to lands in which the Ball and Dupuy families were interested.

Gift of Herbert Dupuy.

183
Dutch West India Company.   Papers, 1626–1834.
(ca. 500 items.)

Minutes, legal documents, letters, resolutions, agreements, instructions to shipmasters, and other business records of the Dutch West India Company on ventures in South Africa, Brazil, and other parts of the world. Among the minutes for 1660 is an item about the claims of Cecil Calvert, proprietor of Maryland, to the land at New Amstel, Del.; *Extract de Heeren Staten von Hollandt, Ende West Vrieslant in Haer Groot Mog,* 1674; legal documents on a suit in Saint Eustatius over sale of a mulatto servant from Philadelphia, 1786.

There papers are part of a lot, sold at auction in Amsterdam, Holland, 1867, known as the Bantemantel papers because most of the papers are in the handwriting of Hans Bantemantel, one of the directors of the Amsterdam Chamber. The other portion of the collection is now in the possession of the New York Public Library.

Gift of Charles R. Hildeburn.

184
Dutilh and Wachsmuth Papers, 1704 (1780–1810) 1846.
(3 linear ft.)

Etienne Dutilh, French merchant, emigrated to Philadelphia in 1783 and established several commercial firms including E. Dutilh & Company, 1783–1789, Dutilh & Wachsmuth, with John Godfried Wachsmuth, 1790–1797, and Dutilh, Soullier & Company, with John Soullier, 1793–ca. 1797, largely engaged in the West Indies and northern European trade, with sugar, coffee, cocoa, and logwood being the major commodities mentioned.

The collection contains: business correspondence, mainly in French; accounts, bills of lading, invoices and cargo manifests for several vessels; and legal papers relating to commercial and maritime litigation, including a prize case of Nottnagel, Montmollin & Company. Also accounts, bills, receipts, notes of: Frederick Schinkles (several variant spellings), a Philadelphia grocer, 1755–1777; [Daniel] Boinod & [Alexander] Gaillard, booksellers, 1783–1785; Charles Graff, Philadelphia merchant, supercargo on a Canton voyage, 1809–1810.

Purchased, Dreer Fund, 1928.

185
Dyer family.   Genealogies, [1895].

Transferred to the Genealogical Society of Pennsylvania.

186
Dyers journal, 1763–1805.   (1 v.)

Journal of Dyers, a Bucks County Quaker, contains records of daily events, family and domestic affairs, and transactions.
Purchased, 1892.

187
Eberheart, Allen M.   Papers, 1913–1921.   (3 linear ft.)

Allen M. Eberheart was secretary of Local Draft Board No. 19, Philadelphia.
These papers relate chiefly to the Selective Draft Service, 1917–1918, and contain reports, correspondence, and memorabilia from the draft board of the 19th district, Philadelphia. Included are statistics on enlisted and drafted men, deserters, persons seeking exemption for various reasons, mobilization forms and receipts, pamphlets issued by the federal government, rules and regulations prescribed by the President, and other items pertaining to the army and to the World War.
Gift of A.M. Eberhart.

188
Edmunds, Albert J., 1857–1941.   Manuscripts, 1908–1918.
(1 v. and 1 folder.)

Religious poem, *Soteriology,* by Elliot Robinson, 1910; a collection of lyric poems by Albert J. Edmunds, 1908–1911; Edmunds' diary notes portending events of the World War.
Gift of Albert J. Edmunds.

189A
Edwards, Howard, 1833–1925?   Collection, 1778–1842.
(66 items.)

Small collection of Anglican clergymen and other British public figures. Included are letters, 1778–1801, of Rev. John Newton, curate of Olney, Buckinghamshire, and friend of Cowper; Rev. John Berridge, 1781; Rev. Thomas Scott, 1793; William Wilberforce, 1800–1833; Hannah More, 1801–1825; Thomas Folwell Buxton, 1827–1842; Elizabeth Fry, 1830.
Gift of Howard Edwards.

189B
Edwards, Howard, 1833–1925?.   Memoirs, 1837–1922.   (4 v.)

"Memoirs and Reminiscences of Society, Individuals, and Events in the City of Philadelphia and its adjacent neighborhoods, Commencing A.D.

1837" was written by Howard Edwards, Philadelphia Quaker, from 1887 to 1922. Edwards provided detailed recollections, especially of his physical surroundings and expressed himself strongly on contemporary events and society, which did not meet the standards of his past. Accompanying the narrative are related newspaper clippings and memoranda.

Gift of Howard Edwards Estate, 1925.

190

Elliott, Isaac.   Genealogical notes, [1897].   (1 v.)

Transferred to the Genealogical Society of Pennsylvania.

191

Elliott, Jesse D. (Jesse Duncan) 1782–1845.   Papers, 1826–1828. (11 items.)

Correspondence of Commodore Jesse Duncan Elliott, naval officer, includes comments on the election of 1828 and a letter from Sir John Phillimore.

Purchased, Dreer Fund, 1926.

192

Paul, Joseph M.   Papers, 1810–1829.   (ca. 50 items.)

Joseph M. Paul was a Philadelphia merchant, vice-president of the Pennsylvania Abolition Society, and a prominent Friend.

There is incoming correspondence and accounts current, 1817–1825, from and with the Embree brothers of Jonesboro, Tenn., proprietors of the Pactolus Iron Works there. Elihu Embree also published the short-lived *Emancipator,* 1820, of which there is some mention. Paul acted as agent for the Elihu Embree estate in Philadelphia and collector for subscriptions for the support of the Philadelphia Monthly Meeting, 1810–1820. Included, too, are Paul's journal, 1800–1820, his letter book, 1812–1829, and a small diary of his trips through western Pennsylvania, 1815, 1820.

Gift of William John Potts, 1886.

Collection formerly described as the Embree Papers, collection #192, and now incorporates materials formerly included in the Joseph M. Paul Records, collection #479.

193

Etting, Frank M.   Collection, 1558–1917.   (15 linear ft.)

Frank M. Etting's connection with the Historical Society began in 1855 when he was elected recording secretary at age 22. After a decade in the army, 1861–1870, he returned to Philadelphia to begin a career of public service. He became director of the city's public schools, chairman of the committee to restore Independence Hall, and director of the Historical Department of the Centennial, 1876.

The collection represents both Etting's personal interests and his professional concerns. It consists of three distinct groups of papers: an autograph collection containing materials of distinguished Americans and Europeans, 1558–1887; family papers, 1739–1847, which document the efforts of the Gratz, Frank, Etting, and Hart families and their associates in the settlement and development of trade in early Pennsylvania and contain some information on the domestic affairs of these families; and, finally, a group of papers on the public and professional career of Frank M. Etting.

The autograph section includes: letters of early Quakers and the Penn family, 1650–1815; colonial governors, 1675–1776; governors of states, 1768–1852; members of the Provincial Council of Pennsylvania, 1685–1762, with letters of members of the Stamp Act Congress, 1762–1763, with orders of the Council of Safety of Maryland, 1776–1782; autographs, prints, and documents relating to the Washington family with autograph letters of signers of the Constitution; signers of the Declaration of Independence; material connected with colonial and Revolutionary wars, 1719–1782, including lists of pay for the army and navy, 1774, lists of general officers, n.d., minutes of the Continental Congress' Commission on Claims, 1775–1776; return of British prisoners of war, 1780–1782; correspondence of Generals Amherst and Forbes, and Sir William Pepperill; officers in the American and British navies, 1740–1865; officers in the American and British armies, 1757–1887; generals of the Revolution, 1755–1809.

Also in this section are: letters of John Quincy Adams, James Buchanan, Jonathan Dayton, Alexander Hamilton, Robert Harper, Thomas Jefferson, Robert Morris, Timothy Pickering, William Tilghman, William Wirt, and others, 1738–1887; letters of George Bancroft, William Cobbett, James Fenimore Cooper, Joseph Drake, Salma Hale, John Heckwelder, Oliver Wendell Holmes, Washington Irving, Henry W. Longfellow, John T. Morse, Thomas Paine, Timothy Pitkin, Noah Webster, and others, 1707–1889; Lord Byron, Charles Dickens, Alexander Dumas, Baron de la Motte Fouque, Benjamin Disraeli, John Keats, W. Roscoe, Madam de Stal, and others, 1762–1885; Thomas Birch, Thomas Cole, John Singleton Copely, Pierre Eugene du Simitieire, Charles Willson Peale, Jacques Louis David, Thomas Sully, Benjamin West, and others, 1767–1889; letters of James Abercrombie, Jacob Duché, Jonathan Edwards, Cotton Mather, Henry Muhlenberg, Henry W. Onderdonk, William Smith, William White, George Whitefield, and others, 1761–1880; George Bryan, John Growdon, Robert H. Harrison, John Marshall, Jonathan D. Sergeant, Robert B. Taney, John Tyler, Bushrod Washington, and others, 1769–1887; Eric Bollman, Jacob M. DaCosta, Samuel P. Grffith, John Morgan, Joseph Parrish, Caspar Wistar, and others, 1766–1887; letters of William Bartram, Peter Collinson, John Fothergill, Robert Fulton, Joseph Priestly, John Ramsey, John Tyndall, and others, 1762–1876; French autograph letters, 1559–1850; royalty, generals, statesmen, scholars. Also Pennsylvania papers, acts of Assembly, 1732–1750; letters of persons prominent in the Stamp Act Congress, Federal Convention, Old Congress, 1734–1823; Maryland Council of Safety, 1776–1786; letters of presidents, vice presidents, and members of cabinets, George Washington to James Buchanan, 1789–1861.

The group of family papers, with additions, includes papers of some of the important merchants and shippers of the early period, Croghan, Pemberton, Gratz, and others, influential in the economic affairs of Pennsylvania. The group comprises: Pemberton papers, 1654–1806; miscellaneous manuscripts, 1658–1889; Phineas Pemberton, account book, 1670–1690, ledger, 1674; miscellaneous correspondence, legal papers, documents, powers of attorney, agreements, bills of lading, commercial transactions, policies accounts, 1685–1872; Pentecost Teague, receipt book, ledger, account book, bills of lading, 1700–1752; Miller Cooper, account book, 1704–1705; Anthony Morris and Elizabeth Janney, ledger, 1705–1708; Abraham Scott Laudin, account book, 1706–1707; parchment deeds, patents, leases, exemplifications of wills, 1726–1835; receipt books of John Pemberton, 1748–1880; William Fisher receipt book, 1752–1757; David Franks, account book, 1757–1762; Stephen Collins, receipt book, 1773–1783; letters of John Fothergill to Israel Pemberton, 1757; Etting family correspondence, 1794–1927, including various commissions issued to members of the family. Papers in which the Gratz family was specifically interested: Gratz family miscellaneous correspondence, 1695–1917; Gratz-Croghan papers, 1733–1830; George Croghan estate, 1747–1816; Ohio Company, 1753–1817; Michael Gratz, ledger, 1759–1784, account book, 1759–1762, receipt book, 1762–1767, letterbooks, 1768–1772; Gratz ledger, receipts, commercial correspondence, 1760–1796; Miriam Gratz, market and household accounts, 1765, memorandum book, 1807; drafts and surveys, 1762–1785; census of York County, 1762; treaty with Indians at Fort Stanwix, 1768; Michael and Bernard Gratz, papers, deeds, conveyances of land, trade with Indians, an account of the French and Indian War, 1769–1786; Bernard Gratz, George Croghan, estate papers, 1780–1816; Revolutionary pension receipts, 1792; papers of various land companies on the sale of lands, 1794–1819; pamphlets on Philadelphia Water Works, 1792–1872; papers and agreements on Philadelphia and Boston Water Works, 1817–1834. Financial affairs are dealt with in "A Historical Sketch of Paper Money Emitted by Pennsylvania," 1722–1785; bills of exchange, 1755–1806; papers on the Bank of North America and both Banks of the United

States, 1787–1848; acts of Congress, incorporation papers, letters of secretaries of the Treasury; papers on the Bank of Pennsylvania, 1793–1859 include minutes, accounts, correspondence; miscellaneous correspondence of early banks in the United States, 1793–1859.

Civic affairs in Philadelphia, social and professional activities in which Etting was interested, are shown in his voluminous correspondence, 1856–1890. A large portion of the letters relate to the Centennial Exposition; papers and photographs on Independence Hall and its restoration, 1871–1876; papers on the historical department of the Centennial Exposition, 1875–1878; American members of the American Philosophical Society, and subscription list for carrying on the building in the State House Yard, for that Society, 1876; biographical sketches of members of the Old Congress.

There are also printed books, some inscribed with the names of prominent persons, and other containing marginal notes; portraits of the signers of the Declaration of Independence and some other eminent men; pamphlets petitioning against the stage and other public amusements, 1754–1811; pamphlets on politics, law, religion, colonial affairs, 1759–1783; miscellaneous papers, Masonic degrees, 1734–1884.

Gift of Frank M. Etting estate, 1891; later items acquired by purchase.

194
Evans, Griffith.   Papers, 1786–1848.   (ca. 125 items.)

Miscellaneous business and personal papers of Griffith Evans, deputy surveyor of Pennsylvania: letters from Captain William Stuart of New York, with comments on national and state politics, congressional activities, economic depression in New York, United States relations with England and France; papers on John Nicholson's land sales, David Rutter's Pine Forge enterprise, and other of Evans' interests.

Gift of G.E. Abbot, 1923.

195
Evans, Robert T., 1780–1858.   Papers, 1803–1863.
(ca. 250 items.)

Papers about real estate in Cumberland County and in West New Jersey, 1803–1865; correspondence, 1840–1862; bills and receipts, 1844–1859; also wills, indentures, bonds and other legal papers.

Gift of the heirs of Eliza F.E. Frazer, 1926.

196
Ewing, Jasper, 1753–1800.   Papers, 1776–1778.   (3 items.)

The papers of Jasper Ewing are his commissions, 1776, from the Continental Congress to serve in Colonel Edward Hand's rifle regiment as a second lieutenant and later as adjutant; and his declaration of allegiance to the United States, 1778, with the signature of Brigadier General Edward Hand.

Gift of John W. Jordan, 1915.

197
Williams, J. Fletcher (John Fletcher) 1834–1895.   "Memoir of George W. Fahnestock," 1868.   (1 v.)

Fahnestock was a prominent Philadelphia writer, antiquarian and book collector who died in the burning steamer *United States* on the Ohio River.

Paper read at a regular meeting of the Minnesota Historical Society on December 14, 1868.

Gift of J. Fletcher Williams, 1902.

198
Faires, John Wylie, 1803–1901.   Papers, 1830–1888. (ca. 400 items.)

Papers of John Faires Wylie, prominent educator and founder of the Classical Institute, Philadelphia. There are account books, essays, catalogues, lists of names of pupils, and other items.

Gift of Elizabeth Faires.

199
Fallon, S.L.   Collection, 1684–1860.   (ca. 70 items.)

Letters of Henry Ward Beecher, James Buchanan, Henry Clay, John Hancock, Marquis de Lafayette, John Marshall, George Peabody, Victorien Sardou, Edward Shippen, George Washington, and others.

Purchased, Library Fund, 1914.

200
Farmer, Eliza.   Letterbook, (1774–1777) (1783–1789).   (1 v.)

Eliza Farmer's letters to her nephew, Jack Halroyd, clerk in the East India Company, London. The letters, written from Philadelphia, are mainly personal, but they contain comments on embargo on tea, the non-importation act, secret session of Congress, rumors of bombardment of Boston, military preparedness, commercial activities. Included are medical recipes written at a later date.

Purchased by the Library Fund, 1883.

201
Fearon, Joseph.   **Waste book, 1783–1809.**   (1 v.)

Memoranda of personal and domestic expenses and purchases of provisions of Joseph Fearon, Philadelphia merchant and tallow chandler.

202
Feltus, William W., 1797–1814.   **Journal, 1812–1814.**   (1 v.)

Journal of W.W. Feltus, midshipman on board the U.S.S. *Essex,* under command of Commodore David Porter, a narrative of daily occurrences on board, sea battles with British warships, chase and capture of pirates, privateers, and merchant vessels, and accounts of encounter with savage tribes on the Marquesas Islands in the Pacific.

203
Fennell, James, 1766–1816.   *The Force of Nature or The Errors of Concealment: a Tragedy in five parts.*   (1 v.)

Purchased, Dreer Fund.

204
Fergusson, Elizabeth Graeme, 1737–1801.   **Collection, (1766–1768) (1797–1799).**   (2 v.)

Commonplace books of religious poetry and prose written or copied by Elizabeth Graeme Fergusson, including several original translations of Psalms.

One volume gift of S.F. Smith; the other purchased, Charles Morton Smith Fund.

205
Fire Companies of Philadelphia record books, 1742–1872.   (170 v.)

A collection of record books of Philadelphia fire companies, contributing information on their organization, personnel, activities, equipments. The records are:

American Hose Company. Roll book of members, 1828–1856; directors' minutes, 1853–1865; contributing members, 1864–1870. (3 v.)

Consolidated Insurance Company. Register of fire risks, alarms, list of firemen and equipment. (1 v.)

Delaware Fire Company. Minutes, 1786–1801, 1812–1823, 1826–1830, 1834–1849, 1952–1966; roll book, 1782–1785, 1858–1871; journal, 1802–1815; ledgers, 1789–1801, 1802–1818; engineers' minutes, 1811–1823; standing committee, 1813–1816, 1819–1821; members' accounts, 1812, 1861–1874; engineers' account book, 1812–1816; constitution, 18832, 1869–1870; roll book, 1860–1879; mementoes, pamphlets, invitations, badges, Confederate money, n.d. (23 v.)

Diligent Hose Company. Minutes, 1791–1820; board of directors' minutes, 1839–1841; record of fires, 1862–1865, 1867–1870. (5 v.)

Fellowship Fire Company. Minutes, 1798–1840; ledger, 1816–1839; cashbook, 1816–1840. (7 v.)

Franklin Fire Company. Minutes, 1838–1876; directors' minutes, 1839–1842. (4 v.)

Fame Fire Hose Company. Minutes, 1818, 1819–1828, 1840–1855; constitution, 1864–1867. (4 v.)

Hope Fire Company. Minutes, 1843–1871; ledger, 1850–1858; constitution, 1856–1879; daybook, 1859–1871; roll book, 1864–1872; receipt book, 1872. (9 v.)

Humane Fire Engine Company. Minutes, 1794–1843, 1852–1866; board of engineers' minutes, 1836–1838. (3 v.)

Hibernia Fire Company. Minutes, 1792–1857; treasurer's accounts, 1758–1797; engineers' minutes, 1815–1817; treasury books, 1818–1834, 1850–1856; constitution, 1818–1868; record of fires, 1838–1866; directors' minutes, 1857–1871; ledger, 1857–1871. (22 v.)

Lillie Yacht Club. Minutes, 1863–1865; collection of pictures of fire engines and fire extinguishing implements; *The Chronicle Fire Tables,* 1875–1891; list of stockholders. (200 items.)

Neptune Hose Company. Minutes, 1818–1870. (6 v.)

Pennsylvania Fire Company. Minutes, 1806–1857; record of fires, 1809–1865; roll book, 1828–1851; board of engineers' minutes, 1833–18836; checkbook, 1852–1857; address by Caleb Cope, president, 1835. (16 v.)

Perseverance Hose Company. Minutes, 1806–1861; treasurer's ledger, 1828–1830. (4 v.)

Phoenix Hose Company. Minutes, 1818–1832. (1 v.)

Philadelphia (Pa.). Fire Department. Minutes, 1853–1870; roll book and board of directors, 1868–1870. (4 v.)

Philadelphia Fire Company. Minutes, 1811–1821, 1842–1847, 1859–1864, 1865–1872; record of fires, 1838–1842. (5 v.)

Philadelphia Hose Company. List of contributing and active members, 1837–1857. (1 v.)

Reliance Fire Company. Constitution, 1786–1841; minutes, 1796–1821; ledger, 1800–1821; roll book, 1820–1871. (5 v.)

Ringgold Hose Company. Minutes and treasurers' reports, 1847–1871. (1 v.)

Robert Morris Hose Company. Minutes, 1843–1853, 1847–1858. (2 v.)

South Penn Hose Company. Constitution, 1846. (1 v.)

United States Escort Association. Minute book, 1866; receipts, 1845–1871; proposition book, 1868; account book of ball at National Guard Hall, 1868. (5 v.)

United States Hose Company. Minutes, 1826–1871; constitution, 1826–1870, 1830–1845; monthly dues, 1828–1831, 1835–1838; membership, 1838–1847; directors' minutes, 1842–1876; treasurers' accounts, 1830–1851, 1869–1885; roll book, 1860–1904; fire records, 1854–1858; order book, 1862–1869. (22 v.)

Washington Fire Company. Minutes, 1799, 1839; constitution, 1796–1852; ledgers, 1824–1833; board of directors, 1833–1846; treasurers' receipt book and reports, 1802–1868. (11 v.)

206

Fisher, Howell Tracy, Mrs.   Collection, 1783–1911.
(ca. 50 items.)

A collection of family papers comprised of: cooking, health, household, and recipe book, ca. 1800; deed, 1783, for property in Gloucester County, N.J., to Aaron Hewes; Samson Sheafe of Crambrook (England), genealogy, 1393–1817; Michael C. Fisher's commission as master in chancery of New Jersey, 1821; and other items.

Gift of Mrs. Howell Tracy Fisher

207

Fisher, Miers, 1748–1819.   Papers, 1775–1814.   (ca. 60 items.)

Papers of Miers Fisher, Philadelphia lawyer and member of the Common Council, include miscellaneous letters and documents chiefly about the city government of Philadelphia, 1789–1791. They include the first ordinances, laws, minutes, and regulations of the city; the plans for the accommodation of Congress and the president; and a few miscellaneous letters written by Benjamin Franklin, Edmund Randolph, Lord North, Elias Boudinot, Tobias Lear, and others.

208

Fitch, John, 1743–1798.   Papers, 1763–1828.   (50 items.)

The papers of John Fitch, surveyor, clockmaker, silversmith, and inventor from Bucks County contain letters, agreements, and other legal papers relating to surveys and sale of lands in Ohio, and to the building of his steamboat. Fitch's ledger and daybook, 1773–1776 include accounts for button and silverware manufacture and for worker's wages. Also in the papers are Jonathan Delaney ledger, 1799–1828, for weaving; Warminster Township,

Montgomery County, tax list, 1763; a summary of tax receipts and tax debt of the Province of Pennsylvania, 1770.

Gift of John L. Longstreth.

209
Fitz Randolph-Snowden Genealogy, 1695–1832. (1 v.)

Genealogical data on the Nathaniel Fitz Randolph family of Princeton, N.J., and Philadelphia; also a fragmentary history of the College of New Jersey, 1725–1757, by Nathaniel Fitz Randolph.

Gift of Mrs. William Stansfield, 1936.

210
Forbes, Thomas. **Letterbook, (1722–1723) (1729–1732).** (1 v.)

Letters of Thomas Forbes, London wine merchant, chiefly on wine trade.

Gift of the Mary I. Gozzaldi estate, 1936.

211
Ford, Paul Leicester, 1865–1902. **Papers, 1891–1893.** **(1,000 items.)**

Papers of Paul Leicester Ford include correspondence, notes, and proof sheets prepared by Ford when writing *The Life of John Dickinson*.

212
Forges and Furnaces records, 1726 (1760–1840) 1921. **(100 linear ft.)**

Business records of several Pennsylvania forges and furnaces, many of which were active during the Revolutionary War. The records include:

Berkshire Furnace. Records, 1767–1793. Berkshire Furnace, southwest of Wernersville, was founded by William Bird, ca. 1750. The records include: daybooks, 1767–1789; journals, 1767–1781; ledgers, 1768–1781; hauling ledger, 1784–1785; time book, 1790–1793; hauling men's book, 1777–1780. (21 v.)

Richard Blackhouse & Company. Records, 1779–1780. These records cover the Chelsea, Greenwich, and Durham Forges. (2 v.)

Bird, William. Ledgers, 1741–1765. Ledgers from New Pine and Hopewell Forges. (3 v.)

Birdsborough Forge (Berks County, Pa.) Journal, 1798–1800 and daybooks, 1800–1803. Birdsborough Forge was founded by William Bird in 1740.

Caroline Furnace. Daybook, 1855. (1 v.)

Castle Fin Furnace. Records, 1826–1863. Castle Fin Furnace was founded by Robert Coleman. The records include: daybooks, 1826–1846; journals, 1846–1863; ledgers, 1833–1863; cashbooks, 1826–1850; receipt books, 1841–1863; time books, 1826–1863; anchonies, bloom, and barr books, 1828–1863; coal and cordwood books, 1826–1860; provision books, 1836–1863; grain books, n.d. (45 v.)

Charming Forge. Records, 1763–1819. Charming Forge was owned by Henry William Stiegel. It was originally called Tulpehocken Eisenhammer, which was built in 1749 by John George Nickoll. The records include: daybooks, 1763–1791; journals, 1763–1798; ledgers, 1772–1819; cashbooks, 1793–1812. (20 v.)

Chestnut Hill Ore Bank. Records, 1756–1870. The records include: daybooks, 1756–1870; time book, 1864–1870; bank reports, 1851–1865. (4 v. and 1 box.)

Cordorus Forge and Ore Bank. Records, 1802–1861. Cordorus Forge was founded in 1765 by William Bennett. The records include: daybooks, 1802–1809; journals, 1802–1867; cashbooks, 1805–1812; provision book, 1804–1808; miscellaneous papers, 1738–1861. (10 v. and 1 box.)

Colebrook Furnace (Berks County, Pa.) Records, 1791–1891. Colebrook Furnace was founded by Robert Coleman, 1791. The records include: daybooks, 1791–1865; journals, 1791–1863; ledgers, 1791–1863; cashbooks, 1791–1891; time books, 1791–1884; coal books, 1808–1857; casting books, 1824–1853; coal and cordwood book, 1822–1834; cordwood books, 1792–1882; farm books, 1857–1887; grain books, 1837–1862; letter and account book, 1855–1879; ore books, 1794–1848; mill books, 1837–1861; pig iron books, 1749–1858; provision books, 1811–1879; receipt books, 1838–1859; estate settlement book, 1857–1879; store order book, 1846–1848; memorandum book, 1800–1815; blast book, 1848–1857. (109 v.)

Colebrookdale Furnace (Berks County, Pa.) Records, 1735–1801. Colebrookdale Furnace was founded by Thomas Rutter, Thomas Potts, Anthony Morris, James Lewis, and others. The records include: daybooks, 1746–1766; journal, 1735–1742; ledgers, 1736–1757; production/rental book, 1729–1752; Dale Furnace ledger, 1799–1801; Dale Furnace journal, 1799–1801. (8 v.)

Coleman, Robert H. Journal, 1885–1895 and Mount Gretna time book, 1888–1895. (2 v.)

Conestoga Furnace. Store daybooks, 1830–1833. (3 v.)

Cornwall Furnace. Records, 1764–1911. Cornwall Furnace was founded by Peter Grubb in 1742. The records include: daybooks, 1764–1833; journals, 1764–1847; ledgers, 1764–1871; provision books, 1820–1881; mill books, 1842–1881; grain books, 1826–1872; grain order book, 1768–1774; ore book, 1804–1822; coal and cordwood book, 1776–1860; coal book, 1833–1848; coal and pig iron book, 1877–1897; blast and pig iron book, 1776–1867; cordwood book, 1880–1881; blast book, 1867–1883; bar book, 1803–1809; time books, 1776–1881; time and payroll book, 1902–1911; store daybooks, 1852–1876; store beef and pork book, 1870–1879; store journal; 1847–1848; settlement ledgers, 1846–1875; memorandum books, 1868, 1877; sales book, 1882–1884; cashbooks, 1779–1871; miscellaneous indices, n.d.; miscellaneous receipt book, n.d. (136 v.)

Coventry Iron Works (Chester County, Pa.) Records, 1727–1796. Coventry Iron Works was founded by Samuel Nutt in 1718. The records include: daybook, 1753–1763; journal, 1747–1796; ledgers, 1727–1796; index, n.d. (16 v.)

Durham Forge. Ledger, 1744–1749. Durham Forge was founded by fourteen people, including James Logan, in 1727.

Elizabeth Furnace (Lancaster County, Pa.) Records, 1762–1832. Elizabeth Furnace was founded by Jacob Huber in 1750. The records include: daybooks, 1767–1802; journals, 1766–1832; ledgers, 1762–1832; cashbook, 1825–1832. (16 v.)

Elk Furnace. Records, 1775–1792. The records include: journals, 1777–1792; ledger, 1789–1790; cashbooks, 1775–1781. (6 v.)

Grubb family. Papers, 1814–1869. Business accounts of Peter and Henry Bates Grubb, early iron masters of Pennsylvania. Among others, they controlled Hopewell Forge, Mount Vernon Furnace, Mount Hope Furnace, Cordorus Forge, and Manada Forge. The papers include: Cornwall weight and ore accounts, 1849–1851; Grubb account books, 1836–1862; passbooks containing David Hughes accounts; account books; Henry Clay Furnace statements of working, 1852–1853; Manada Furnace business papers, 1827–1862, records of castings, 1840–1848, and ore shipments, 1853, 1863; miscellaneous surveys, n.d.; Union Canal permits for boats, 1849–1850; Grubb correspondence, 1834–1868; Columbia Furnace, 1853–1860; miscellaneous receipts, 1850–1860; circular letters and miscellaneous; Mannheim and Lebanon Plank Road correspondence, 1852–1862, tonnage and tolls; and miscellaneous business papers, 1814–1869. (2.5 linear ft.)

Hopewell Furnace (Berks County, Pa.) Records, 1765–1817. Hopewell Furnace was founded by William Bird as a forge in 1744 and as a furnace in 1771. The records include: daybooks, 1769–1817; journals, 1765–1817; ledgers, 1765–1802; cashbooks, 1803–1817; coal, iron, and time books, 1803–1816; bar iron book, 1803–1816; bar iron book, 1803–1816; coal and cordwood book, 1803–1816; anchonies book, 1811–1816; canal book, 1841; moulding account book, 1831–1832; Birdsborough Forge daybook, 1804–1807; pig iron and time book, 1803–1816. (50 v.)

Isabella Furnace. Records, 1871–1921. The records include: daybooks, 1871–1893; ledgers, 1871–1893; vouchers, 1880–1921; letters, 1880–1896; notes of William Potts, 1888–1891; pig iron data book, n.d.; cashbook, 1887–1890;

memorandum book, n.d.; record book, 1894–1897; docket, 1877–1878; record book of real estate negotiations, 1886–1892; analyses book, 1884; bills, 1882–1897; exercise book, n.d.; checkbooks, 1895–1896. (12 linear ft.)

Joanna Forge. Ledger, 1791–1799. (1 v.)

Manada Furnace. Records, 1836–1856, n.d. The records include: cashbook, 1836–1841; pig iron book, 1856; surveys and deeds record book, n.d. (3 v.)

Manheim Glassworks. Records, 1763–1773. The Manheim Glassworks was founded by William Stiegal in 1764. The records include: daybooks, 1770–1773; ledgers, 1764–1774; rent book, 1763–1767. (3 v.)

Martick Furnace. Records, 1818–1832. Martick Furnace was founded by Thomas and William Smith in 1751. The records include: journal, 1828–1833; ledgers, 18288–1833; store ledger, 1830–1833; provision daybook, 1830–1833; cashbook, 1828–1835; iron book, 1828–1832; time book, 1818–1830; anchonies book, 1830–1832; pig iron received book, 1830–1832; coal and cordwood book, 1830–1831. (11 v.)

Mary Ann Furnace (York County, Pa.) Records, 1734–1838. Mary Ann Furnace was founded by George Ross & Company in 1761. The records include: daybooks, 1762–1838; journals, 1764–1779; ledgers, 1765–1838; account book, 1837; Tough Creek provision book, 1838–1834; record book, 1836–1838; settlement books, 1836–1838; receipt books, 1734–1836; time books, 1765–1771, 1836; blast and pig iron book, 1837; pig iron book, 1833–1835; cordwood book, 1836; provision book, 1837–1838. (47 v.)

May, Thomas. Papers, 1762–1800. Papers of Thomas May include ledger for Pottsgrove, 1762–1764, Pine Forge, 1770–1773, and Elk Forge, 1774–1777; Wilmington ledger, 1781–1800; and journal, 1781–1794. (3 v.)

Middleton Forge. Surveys, letterbook, journal, 1849–1861. (1 v.)

Mount Hope Furnace. Miscellaneous papers, n.d. (1 folder.)

Mount Pleasant Furnace (Berks County, Pa.) Records, 1737–1796. Mount Pleasant Furnace was built by Thomas Potts, Jr., before 1737, on the west branch of the Perkiomen. The records include: daybook, 1737–1740; daybooks/ledgers, 1740–1796; ledger, 1738–1740. (4 v.)

Mount Vernon. Records, 1742–1824, n.d. The records include: daybooks, 1742–1812; journal, 1800–1805; ledgers, 1805–1815; provision book, 1809–1824; coal book, 1800–1801; and miscellaneous papers, n.d. (10 v. and 1 folder.)

Pequea Furnace. Records, 1736–1833. The records include: journal, 1830–1833; ledger/daybook, 1736–1741; ledger, 1829–1832; bar iron book, 1829–1832; time book, 1828–1832; cashbook, 1828–1832; coal and iron book, 1828–1832. (7 v.)

Philadelphia Forge. Records, 1749–1807. The records include: daybooks, 1749–1775 (one for Pottsgrove); journal, 1805–1807; and ledgers, 1753–1775. (11 v.)

Pine Forge (Berks County, Pa.) Records, 1730–1800. Pine Forge was built by Thomas Rutter in 1724. The records include: daybooks, 1759–1785; journals, 1760–1783; ledgers, 1730–1781; ledger/journal, 1770,1800; daybook/flour accounts, 1757–1767; receipt books, 1752–1790; bar iron book, 1787–1790; coal book, 1744–1766; time book, 1762–1763. (23 v.)

Popadickon Furnace (Berks County, Pa.) Records, 1744–1764. Popadickon Furnace was founded by Thomas Rutter and others in 1726. The records include: daybooks, 1744–1755; ledger, 1744–1755; promises for money, 1755–1764. (5 v.)

Potts family. Papers, 1738–1888. The papers for the Potts family include: William J. Potts miscellaneous book with notes and genealogical material; ledger, 1806; list of employees at West Jersey, 1869; stock blanks for Copper Mine Company, 1806; Pottsgrove daybook, 1816; Pottsgrove store daybooks, 1765–1770; Pottsgrove journals, 1758–1765; Pottsgrove daybook, 1772–1773; Pottsgrove journal, 1789–1795; Pottsgrove ledgers, 1757–1777; Mount Joy daybooks, 1757–1772; Mount Joy ledgers, 1757–1766; Philadelphia ledger, 2738–2748; journal, 1824–1825; ledgers, 1769–1830; Pine Forge journal, 1774–1781; Potts lawbook, 1770; cashbook/estate book, 1772–1783; surveying notes, 1799–1801; miscellaneous, 1757, n.d.; checkbooks, 1884–1895; pig iron data book, [1883–1888]. (40 v.)

Reading Furnace. Records, 1793–1857. Reading Furnace was founded by Samuel Nutt in 1720/1736/1737. The records include: daybooks, 1793–1814; journals, 1793–1829; ledgers, 1792–1816; cashbooks, 1793–1850; time books, 1794–1829; receipt book, 1845–1851; pig iron book, 1828–1856; blast book, 1852–1857. (31 v.)

Robesonia Furnace. Pig iron orders, 1875–1883. (1 v.)

Roxborough Furnace. Daybook, 1756–1760. (1 v.)

St. Charles Furnace. Records, 1854–1880. The records include: daybook, 1857–1877; journal, 1858–1860; ledger, 1855–1880; statement of working, 1854–1857; draft of erection invoices, 1856–1863; Chestnut Hill ore bank labor reports, 1857–1861; pig iron orders, 1859–1862. (2.5 linear ft.)

Schuylkill Furnace. Records, 1790–1826. The records include: daybooks, 1797–1837; journals, 1796–1811; ledgers, 1790–1800; cashbooks, 1801–1826; time/coal and cordwood books, 1799–1826; provision book, 1797–1801. (15 v.)

Seram Forge (Chester County, Pa.) Daybook, 1767–1771 and ledger, 1767–1771. (2 v.)

Smith, Robert. Inventory, 1795. (1 v.)

Speedwell Furnace. Records, 1784–1882. Speedwell Furnace was founded by James Old in 1760. The records include: daybooks, 1784–1870; journals, 1784–1849; ledgers, 1784–1869; cashbooks, 1788–1869; time books, 1806–1878; record books, 1819–1860; mill books, 1809–1842; provision book,

1814–1829; bar iron books, 1822–1849; bar iron and anchonies books, 1784–1848; anchonies and blooms book, 1832–1848; bar, pig iron, and bloom book, 1848–1853; cordwood and coal books, 1812–1861; atlas, 1864; memorandum book, 1851–1868; and miscellaneous book, 1863–1882. (55 v.)

Spring Furnace. Records, 1765–1852. The records include: daybooks, 1815–1850; journals, 1765–1852; ledgers, 1767–1852; cashbooks, 1773–1852; time books, 1805–1852; provision books, 1814–1862; cordwood and coal book, 1818–1838; bar iron books, 1818–18850; pig iron books, 1818–1848; bars and blooms book, 1843–1852; grain books, 1834–1852; supplies book, 1818–1848. (39 v.)

Springwell Forge. Ledger, 1804–1805. (1 v.)

Schocken Furnace. Ledger, 1757–1760. (1 v.)

Tulpehocken Furnace. Journal, 1754–1756 and ledger, 1744–1749. (2 v.)

Union Forge. Records, 1783–1795. The records include: daybooks, 1783–1792; journals, 1783–1795; ledgers, 1783–1795; time book, 1783–1795; pig and bar iron/coal and cordwood book, 1784–1795.

Warwick Furnace (Chester County, Pa.) Records, 1747–1773. Warwick Furnace was founded by Samuel Nutt's heirs in 1739. The records include: daybooks, 1747–1773; ledger, 1759–1762; receipt books, 1752–1765. (13 v.)

Unidentified records include: daybook, 1795–1797; ledgers, 1800–1859; anchonies book, 1796–1799; memo book, 1827–1834; index books, n.d. (14 v.)

213
Foster-Clement Collection, ca. 1676–1875.   **(4 linear ft.)**

Josiah Foster served as justice of the peace for Burlington County, N.J., in 1788 and 1798 and for Gloucester County, N.J., in 1812; as a judge for the Common Pleas Court of Burlington County in 1798 and of Gloucester County in 1812; and, as deputy surveyor of New Jersey in 1773 and 1781.

William Foster, ca. 1775, served as one of the King's judges of the Common Pleas Court of Burlington County, N.J. Samuel Clement served as a Justice of the Peace for Gloucester County, N.J. in 1748, 1812, and 1822; as a judge in 1755, as deputy surveyor appointed to establish township boundaries in Gloucester County; as a member of the Assembly from the Western Division of New Jersey in 1761; as a trustee of the poor in 1807; and as an incorporator of the Salem National Banking Company.

Papers on early settlements in and largely by the Clement and Foster families of Burlington and Gloucester counties, New Jersey: deeds, 1677–1875; wills, 1681–1867; family papers, 1761–1819, which includes papers and receipts of Josiah Foster and William Foster, draft of William Foster's land, will of William Foster, will of Josiah Foster, Clement and Foster genealogies, long book (account book) of Benjamin Robinson, 1784 and surveying note-books of Josiah Foster, 1778–1779, 1794–1795, Account of Sleepcreek Mill book, of which Josiah Foster was director, 1785–1786, and correspondence largely of Josiah Foster and Samuel Clement; Indian papers, 1777–1819 and pamphlets, 1778–1819, in which the former section includes papers on In-dians and the sale of lands in New Jersey and Charles Mooles' Vandeu[?] (sale) book, and the latter section contains pamphlets pertaining to legisla-tive bills; New Jersey Land Society, ca. 1788, which was involved in the Burr Conspiracy; abolition societies; friends meetings; New Jersey elections; *New Jersey State Gazette*; and religious tracts.

Miscellaneous legal papers, 1762–1873, which includes judgments, bonds, agreements, papers on the *Albertson v. Norcross case,* involving Josiah Albertson, ca. 1753–1833 and Isaiah Norcross, and other legal documents concerning Gloucester and Burlington counties; cashbook, 1781–1783 and dockets, 1790–1794, 1798–1801 of Josiah Foster; and, land surveys, 1687–1801, which includes an undated volume entitled *Penn's Survey in New Jersey* copies from the surveyor general's books at Burlington, N.J., 1712–1784, and road maps in and around Burlington County, ca. 1802–1846, which show detailed maps of surrounding tracts, and Atsion Company (of Josiah Foster) papers, 1764–1799.

Gift of John Clement, ca. 1904.

214
Fox, Benjamin Franklin, 1805–1869.   **Papers, ca. 1838–1913.** (5 v.)

Scrapbooks, poetry satirizing Philadelphia politics, fictional narratives, newspaper clippings, and other matter of literary character.

Gift of William J. Fox.

215
Franklin, Benjamin, 1706–1790.   **Papers, 1747–1794.** (3 linear ft.)

The papers of Benjamin Franklin in this collection include: accounts, 1747–1766, of the firm of Franklin and Hall; miscellaneous accounts, 1750–1781; receipt book, 1764–1766; bill book, 1777–1781; letters and papers, 1750–1783; of notes on the Franklin family, 1561–1794, with a genealogical chart; photostat of Franklin's will, 1790. The official part of Franklin's career is represented by papers and correspondence on his activity as agent of the colony of Pennsylvania, 1757–1771; correspondence with Congress while he was minister to France, 1776–1783; and miscellaneous papers, from his French ministry, 1776–1785.

Purchased by the Historical Society.

216
Franklin, Walter, b. 1727.   Letterbook, 1772–1773.   (1 v.)

Letters of Walter Franklin, New York (N.Y.) merchant, to John Pemberton and Thomas Lightfoot, Philadelphia, refer to his financial difficulties, business and land transactions, and efforts to adjust the controversies between them in a legal and equitable manner.

217
Freeman, Corinne Keen, b. 1868.   Liberty Loan papers, 1918–1819.
(3 linear ft.)

Corinne Keen Freeman was chairperson of the Women's Committee of the South Philadelphia, Liberty Loan Committees, 1918–1919.

The collection contains correspondence, account books, lists of names of subscribers, committee reports, pamphlets, books, and memorabilia of the Fourth Liberty Loan Campaign of 1917.

Gift of Mrs. Duncan Graham Foster, 1933.

218
French, B.F. (Benjamin Franklin) 1799–1877.   Manuscripts, 1884.
(1 folder.)

Papers of Benjamin Franklin French on Indian ethnology: "Among the Natchez, by a Mississippian"; "Push-Ma-Ta-Ha" concerns a distinguished chief of the Choctaws, who served under Andrew Jackson in the Seminole War; included also is his pseudo-scientific narrative, "Voyage Round the Moon."

Gift of Louis E. French, 1905.

219
French West India Company.   Papers, 1712, 1744–1747, 1757.
(50 items.)

Miscellaneous personal and business correspondence; copy of "Essai de Géographie Physique," by Philippe Bauche, French royal geographer, 1752, with maps; "Mémoires touchant la Martinque," n.d.

220
Freneau, Philip Morin, 1752–1832.   Verses, 1770.   (1 v.)

"Father Bombos' Pilgrimage to Mecca in Arabia," by Philip Morin Freneau and Hugh Henry Brackenridge and others of their satiric pieces, together with several by James Madison, written while they were students at Princeton. Contemporary copy, probably by William Bradford, another Princetonian, in whose papers it was found.

Gift of John William Wallace, 1881.

"Father Bombos' . . . " published in the *P.M.H.B.*, 66 (1942): 461–478.

James Madison verse published in *The Papers of James Madison*, edited by William T. Hutchinson and William M.E. Racheal (Chicago : University of Chicago Press, 1963), 1: 61–65.

221

Der Freund in der Noth, ca. 1752.   (1 v.)

A booklet on the prevailing superstition and witchcraft, with magic formulas and recipes for the cure of diseases and protection against evil.

In German script.

222

Confederacy (ship).   Papers, 1776–1779.   (ca. 525 items.)

Papers of Major Joshua Huntington, Norwich, Conn., a soldier in the Revolutionary army. The papers deal with the construction of the *Confederacy,* which was build by Huntington under the direction of the Governor and Council of Safety of Connecticut and launched in 1788. Included are accounts, payrolls, reports, 1777–1779, which present details of construction and outfitting of the frigate.

Purchased.

Accession note published in the *P.M.H.B.*, 63 (1939): 494.

223

Fry and Rambo papers, 1843–1859.   (ca. 200 items.)

The papers include receipts and bills of Jacob Fry and James F. Rambo, Montgomery County merchants, for merchandise.

224

Furness, Horace Howard, 1833–1912.   Papers, 1861–1865. (6 linear ft.)

A collection of papers on the Sanitary Fair held in Philadelphia in 1864. Among the items are letters, pamphlets, and broadsides on sanitation in the United States; badges, photographs, committee reports, vouchers, bills, receipts, and account books containing the names of the prominent citizens of Philadelphia active in civic and social life during the Civil War.

Gift of Fairman Rogers Furness and Mrs. Wirt L. Thompson.

225
Galloway, Grace Growden, d. 1782.   Papers, 1778–1781.   (1 v.)

Grace Growden Galloway was the daughter of Lawrence Growden, whose family controlled Durham iron furnaces; she married Joseph Galloway in 1753. Joseph Galloway, prominent in the social and political circles of Philadelphia sided with the British during the Revolution. Eventually, he was forced to flee with his daughter, Elizabeth, to England. Grace Galloway remained behind in America in an attempt to salvage the family's estate.

These diaries and letters detail the difficulties Grace Galloway had in securing the property once owned by her family. Social life among prominent Philadelphians is also described.

Purchased, Dreer Fund.

Seven additional volumes of photostatic letters and diaries are available for the same time period.

Diary, June 17, 1778 to July 1, 1779 published in *P.M.H.B.*, 55 (1931): 35–94.

Diary, July 1 to September 30, 1779 published in *P.M.H.B.*, 58 (1934): 152–189.

226
Gamble, William, 1823–1850.   Papers, (1839–1845) 1914.
(45 items.)

A small collection of papers reflecting William Gamble's travels to California and the West in search of birds and flora. Included are letters from family and friends especially Thomas Nuttall, Anglo-American botanist.

Gift of William J. Middleton, nephew of William Gamble, 1914.

227A
Gardiner, Edward Carey, ca. 1879–1945.   Collection, 1632–1939.
(32 linear ft.)

A collection of the papers of the Baird, Carey, Gardiner, and Penington families, prominent in political, economic, and cultural affairs. The papers are rich in material on literary trends of the country, its authors and writers, publication and distribution of books, the art of printing, bookbinding, copyrights, and other subjects pertaining to the publishing business.

The Carey family group of papers includes those of Mathew Carey, and Henry Carey editors, writers, and civic leaders who established one of the largest publishing houses of the period in America. The papers are: Carey genealogical records, 1632–1938; Mathew Carey, correspondence, 1784–1839;

his own letters, 1791–1834; biographical sketch of Mathew Carey, by Michael Hennessey, 1860; Henry C. Carey, correspondence, 1825–1879, relating to politics, political economy, and the Civil War; Carey and Hart, and Carey and Lea, publishers, correspondence, 1830–1850; Carey and Hart, and Henry C. Baird, copyright papers, 1837–1852; their record books, 1830–1886; Edward L. Carey, journals, 1822–1839; correspondence, 1841–1845; St. Clair Tract papers, concerning collieries in Schuylkill County, 1835–1892.

Papers of the Penington family include letters of: Isaac Penington, a distinguished Quaker and author; Edward Penington, author, who accompanied William Penn to Pennsylvania in 1698 and later became surveyor general of the province; Edward Penington, Quaker, merchant, member of the Provincial Council; John Penington, physician; John Penington, author and a leading bookseller; Henry Penington, lawyer, author; and others. These papers comprise: Penington family genealogical notes, 1667–1873; Isaac and John Penington (several of that name) letters and documents, 1844–1867; journal, 1790–1791; Edward Penington, journal, 1749–1751; letters, 1812–1850; a later Edward Penington daybook, 1799–1806; Henry Penington correspondence, 1829–1858; legal journal, 1829; legal notebook, 1829–1840; account book, 1829–1841; receipt book, 1832–1839; ground rents, 1829–1838; Edward Penington, journal, 1860–1867; and other items.

The Gardiner papers, 1636–1936, are chiefly genealogical notes of a prominent New England family; Sylvester Gardiner, physician, merchant, philanthropist, who founded the town of Gardiner, Maine; John Gardiner, lawyer, statesman; John Gardiner; and others.

The Baird family papers contain letters of Henry Carey Baird, author, political writer, publisher, leader in the Whig, Republican, and Greenback parties. The papers consist of: documents and papers on the Baird family, 1794–1916; Henry Carey Baird correspondence, 1845–1911; record of his tour through England and Europe, 1847; miscellaneous documents, 1856–1870; letters and journal concerning Rear Admiral Louis M. Goldsborough's naval career in the Civil War, 1862–1922; Thomas J. Baird military papers, 1813–28, on his military career, frontier life, Indian wars; letters 1817–1842, pertain to his domestic and personal affairs.

In addition, there is a miscellaneous section containing letters, documents, 1682–1939, contributing information on domestic, legal, political, commercial affairs; Martha Powell Bowen estate papers, 1830–1856, include material on Jamaica plantations, economic affairs in the West Indies, sugar, rum, commerce; Thomas Coates estate in Philadelphia, 1828–1850; Maybin estate, New Orleans, papers, 1827–1843; the Fitz-John Porter papers, 1862–1886, relating to his court martial and military charges brought against him during the Civil War.

Gift of Edward Carey Gardiner.

227B
Lea and Febiger.   **Records, 1785 (1788–1871) 1941.**
(100 linear ft.)

These papers comprise a fairly comprehensive record of the business operations of Mathew Carey & Co. and successor firms. Carey began as printer and publisher of the Pennsylvania Evening Herald in 1785, but soon abandoned the Herald for book, magazine, and Bible publishing. The firm, which still exists as a limited partnership specializing in medical publishing, has changed its name a number of times. Until 1817, it was Mathew Carey & Co., when Mathew's son, Henry C. Carey, joined the firm to form M. Carey & Son. In 1821, Carey's son-in-law, Isaac Lea joined the firm and it became M. Carey & Sons. The senior Carey retired in 1824, and shortly thereafter the partnership became Carey, Lea & Carey, when younger son Edward L. Carey joined the firm. In 1829, Edward Carey withdrew to form a bookselling partnership with Abraham Hart. In 1833, William A. Blanchard became a partner and the firm became, briefly, Carey, Lea & Blanchard. In 1836, Henry C. Carey retired and the firm was known as Lea & Blanchard until 1851. That year Isaac Lea withdrew in favor of his son, Henry Charles Lea, and the firm became Blanchard & Lea, which it remained until Blanchard's retirement in 1865. Thereafter, the firm bore only the Lea name until 1907 when Lea's sons joined with Christian Febiger to form the partnership which still retains the name of Lea & Febiger, despite changes in principals. In its early years, the firm successfully published a wide variety of American and English literature, including Scott's Waverly novels and Cooper. In the late 1830s, however, at the urging of Isaac Lea, a well-known naturalist and conchologist, the firm increasingly specialized in scientific and medical publication, specialization clearly shown in the cost books and contract records, but for which there are no correspondence files present.

The collection is rich in materials from the period of Mathew Carey's active participation. Present are three series of letterbooks, 1789–1822, and incoming correspondence, 1785–1822. Although the correspondence is mostly about business, there is a sizeable representation of American literary and political figures. There are also ledgers, 1817–1824.

The firm's records after Carey's retirement are less complete but no less rich. Henry C. Carey is represented by three letterbooks, 1822–1823, and two ledgers, 1822–1825. The period of the partnerships with Isaac Lea and William A. Blanchard are reflected in a letterbook, 1834–1835; ledgers, 1827–1834 and 1850–1851; copies of accounts, 1826–1846; incoming correspondence, 1850–1860; cost books, 1825–1837, 1840–1878; and a volume of contracts and copyright assignments, 1847–1890.

After Blanchard's retirement in 1865, the firm's operations are documented by the cost and contract books, above, a well as two additional cost books, 1878–1910; copies of contracts, 1885–1912; index to incoming correspondence, n.d.; and a volume of retained copies of letters sent, 1925–1941.

Gift of Lea and Febiger, 1930.

228
Gardner, John.   Papers, 1785–1791.   (150 items.)

John Gardner was an officer in the Chester County militia during the Revolution and sheriff of the county from 1780 to 1783.

The collection contains personal and business papers (bonds, notes, bills, receipts, and letters) and official documents including sheriff's accounts and receipts, lists of fees collected, tax duplicates, court judgments, a "Routh Continuous Docquet," 1780–1783, and papers related to the settlement of his official accounts and estate. Also included are some papers of William Gibbons, a Revolutionary officer, innkeeper, and friend and successor of Gardner as sheriff.

229
Gardom, George, d. ca. 1890.   Papers, 1840–1890.
(ca. 200 items.)

George Gardom was a Philadelphia pharmacist.

A collection of family and personal correspondence, contributing information on domestic and economic conditions prevailing in the period and incidentally presenting a picture of Philadelphia life.

Gift of J. Anna Gardom.

230
Garrigues, Edward.   Diary, 1798.   (1 v.)

This copy of a diary by Edward Garrigues provides a narrative of Quaker activities, meetings, social and domestic events, and the yellow fever epidemic in Philadelphia; 1755 Yearly Meeting Epistle; essays of Thomas Garrigues for *The Experiment,* publication of the Darby First-Day School Association, [1882]; Chester County arbitrations, 1704–1705; Garrigues and Bonsall family genealogical data.

Edward Garrigues diary copied by Thomas Garrigues.

Gift of Sarah C. Pennypacker and Matilda Garrigues, 1914.

231
Baum, Irwin, Graff, and Sterett families.   Genealogical notes,
1700–1885.   (5 v.)

232
Gernon and Keating.   Papers, 1805–1829.   (ca. 150 items.)

This business and social correspondence between John Keating, Philadelphia importer, and Richard Gernon, French merchant, reflects economic, social, and political developments in Europe and America.

233
Gesellschaft der Unterstutzung.   Cashbook, 1790–1794.   (1 v.)

Cashbook of the German Relief Association of the Evangelical-Lutheran Society of Philadelphia: expense accounts and relief disbursements.
In German.

234
Gibbes, William.   Genealogy, 1841–1908.   (1 v.)

Genealogical data on the families of: William Gibbes, Robert Wilson, Thomas Allston, Thomas Hasell of South Carolina, Patrick Miller of Pennsylvania, and others.
Gift of William Gibbes, 1937.

235
Gibbons, James.   Journal, 1804.   (1 v.)

The journals of James Gibbons provide a narrative of a tour through the western part of Pennsylvania and part of Ohio, describes topography, immigration, settlements, abundance of game, travel facilities, and Quaker families and their meeting places.
Gift of Dr. A.S.W. Rosenbach, 1939.

236
Gibson, James.   Papers, 1712–1846.   (2.5 linear ft.)

The collection relates to the colonial and early national periods: it contains land claims and deeds of Maryland, 1712–1716; French and Spanish passports for trade and shipping; agreements of Philadelphia merchants to decline acceptances of notes of credit in lieu of specie, 1766; correspondence on local affairs and general politics.

Included are accounts of money paid out on warrants by the auditor general, 1777; minutes of proceedings in charges brought against the Board of the Treasury by Francis Hopkinson, treasurer of loans, 1780; a statement of Treasury accounts of Francis Hopkinson, 1780; contract between Robert Morris and Daniel Parker to supply rations to the Revolutionary Army; register of accounts and claims against the United States, and a review of the business transacted by the Chamber of Accounts, 1779–1780; legal papers and subpoenas issued by the Supreme Court of Pennsylvania against Robert Morris and John Nicholson relate to unsatisfied judgments.

The formation of land companies in Pennsylvania in which Robert Morris, John Nicholson, and James Gibson were interested, is shown in the papers of the Pennsylvania Population Company, Asylum Company, Erie County, lands, and Donation lands, 1792–1828: the correspondence of their agents, Judah Colt and James Gibson, mortgages, agreements of sales, surveys, deeds, powers of attorney, claims, court proceedings, minutes of the board of managers, and plats. There is also a copy of the map and exemplification of the grant of the Erie triangle from the United States to Pennsylvania, 1792.

In addition there is a group of letters, 1824–1846, addressed to Carey & Lea; Carey, Lea, & Carey; Lea & Blanchard, booksellers and publishers. Among the names of the correspondents are: William Bainbridge, John C. Breckinridge, Horace Binney, C.C. Bonaparte, Thomas Cooper, Joseph Drayton, Millard Fillmore, C.J. Ingersoll, John Marshall, Joel R. Poinsett, Peter S. Du Ponceau, Joseph Quincy, R. Randolph, J. Reed, Thomas Riche, Richard Rush, Andrew Stevenson, Bushrod Washington, Hamilton Washington, Noah Webster.

237
Gillingham, Harrold Edgar, 1864–1954.   **Collection, 1792–1855.**
(ca. 200 items)

Chiefly United States Custom House documents, with some papers of other departments. Among the items are: shipping manifests for the importance of liquors, 1792–1805; lists of alien passenger arrivals, 1798–1829; distillery inspection permits, 1792; data on importation of spool cotton by Bates and Coates, 1855; and other items.

Gift of Harrold E. Gillingham.

238
Gilpin family.   **Papers, 1727–1872.**   **(15 linear ft.)**

A collection of papers emanating from a family distinguished in scholarship, commerce, and political leadership. Most of the papers are those of

Henry D. Gilpin, whose long and varied career makes his papers particularly informative on many aspects of national history. His correspondence includes letters from Martin Van Buren, 1836–1862; James Buchanan, 1839–1856; George M. Dallas, 1831–1859; Edward Everett, 1831–1861; T.F. Bayard, George Peabody, Edward Livingston, Henry Clay, Richard Rush, Charles Gallagher, George Bancroft, Gouverneur Kemble, John W. Forney, J. B. Francis, Benjamin Chew, Joseph Reed Ingersoll, General Winfield Scott, and others, 1819–1872. In addition to Gilpin family items, the collection includes groups of papers of the following: Joel R. Poinsett, James Wilkinson, Daniel Clark, William Short, James Brown, and David Porter.

Joel R. Poinsett's correspondence, 1794–1850 forms a notable group in this collection. It reveals the many roles played by him in a long and active career of diplomacy and national leadership. They contain vivid descriptions of incidents, travel, home, and social life of that period, as seen through the eyes of an impressionable youth. Glimpses of Russia and travel through Europe are seen in his letters of 1807–1808, his participation in the revolutionary movements of the South American countries against European dominion are shown in his letters of 1811–1812. His interest and activities in the Mexican Revolution and its internal strife, while he was minister of the United States to Mexico, are depicted in the letters of 1821–1829. Interesting is his description of the origin and causes of those conflicts and the important parts played by the Scottish Rites Masons on one side and the York Rite Masons on the other.

Poinsett's letters between 1829 and 1850 deal mainly with the turbulent political questions and economic affairs affecting the United States. The topics discussed are the nullification and secession movements in South Carolina; the split and strife in the Democratic party; abolition and slavery issues; the political influence of John C. Calhoun; the machinations and intrigues in the Baltimore convention; Indian affairs and Indian warfare in the Floridas; the United States war with Mexico; western expansion; the statehood of California; the gold discovery; his interests in organization of the Smithsonian Institution in Washington, D.C.; the agitation aroused over his army reorganization bill while secretary of war; controversies and the danger of war with England; and the building and financing of railroads through the South. The letters tell of his interest in agricultural innovations, arts and sciences.

Another group of papers are letters of Commodore David Porter, on his naval service as commander-in-chief of the Mexican naval forces in the was against Spain, 1825–1827. The letters are chiefly to Joel R. Poinsett, U.S. minister to Mexico, and are full of complaints about the humiliations experienced and indignities suffered by him because of the intrigue and jealousies prevailing among the various Mexican political leaders.

General *James Wilkinson vs. Daniel Clark* papers, 1788–1808, in a legal controversy present a vivid picture of the life and character of James Wilkinson; the papers depict him as an adventurer, a secret agent for the Spanish government, a conspirator with Aaron Burr plots to separate the western countries from the United States, and an instigator of the rebellion in Louisiana and the Floridas; incidentally, the papers throw light on Wilkinson and Clark's commercial enterprise, commodities traded, extension of frontiers, south and west, navigation of the Mississippi, and life in New Orleans, La., in that period.

William Short, United States chargé d'affaires in Paris and secretary to Thomas Jefferson while minister to France, present in his group of papers, 1786–1801, a graphic picture of the violent throes of the French Revolution, European politics, and United States diplomacy; the letters are addressed to Jefferson, John Jay, John Rutledge, Gouverneur Morris, Marquis de Lafayette, Edmund Randolph, James Monroe, Thomas Pinckney, David Humphreys, William Nelson, and others.

James Brown, statesman and minister to France, his letters, 1824–1835, addressed chiefly to Edward Livingston, deal with politics in France and Spain. Brown's commercial interests in Louisiana, and American politics.

Biographical sketches and letters, 1727–1824, relating to the lives and character of the signers of the Declaration of Independence, written by the descendants of Benjamin Harrison, Samuel Adams, Eldridge Gerry, Charles Carrol of Carrolton, Richard Henry Lee, Thomas Nelson, William Paca, C. Rodney, and George Taylor are included.

Henry D. Gilpin's papers: letters to his father, Joshua Gilpin, 1822–1841; correspondence with his family, 1824–1843; letter books, 1831–1833, 1846–1849; diaries, 1822–1859; docket book, United States district attorney, 1828–1833; United States district attorney, letters and correspondence, 1832–1838; United States Bank papers, 1833, 1836–1837, contains correspondence of Henry D. Gilpin, director and examiner of the Bank, with Andrew Jackson, Edward Livingston, Louis McLane, George M. Dallas, R.M. Whitney, William J. Duane, Roger B. Taney, Nicholas Biddle, Levi Woodbury, John M. Sullivan, and others, on illegal transactions of the institution, misuses of Bank funds, diversion of funds for propaganda purposes, withdrawal of public deposits from the Bank.

Henry D. Gilpin's letters written during his tour through Europe, 1853–1854; his journals of that tour, 1853–1854; correspondence while in Florence, Italy, which discloses his interest in art, 1853–1854; correspondence, 1856–1858; scrapbook, Henry D. Gilpin, "Governor of Michigan," 1834, Gilpin's journalistic and literary talents are shown in his manuscripts of biographical sketches of the lives of signers of the Declaration of Independence, 1826; literary reviews of current and contemporaneous publications, 1829–1830;

notes on current topics and literature, 1828–1831; memoranda, catalogue references on bibliography and literature, n.d.; miscellaneous printed matter pertaining to the University of Pennsylvania, and kindred subjects, 1825–1864; his magazine, *The Atlantic Souvenir, Christmas and New Year's Offering,* 1828, Philadelphia, and other publications; letters of condolence, tributes, eulogies received by Mrs. Henry D. Gilpin upon the death of her husband, 1860; Mrs. Gilpin's publication, *A Memorial of Henry D. Gilpin,* 1860; letters from prominent persons acknowledging receipt of her book, 1861.

The papers of Joshua and Thomas Gilpin pertain to domestic, commercial, and industrial affairs: Joshua Gilpin correspondence, 1795–1841; 1797–1815; general correspondence, 1800–1822; family letters from England, 1824–1830; Bainbridge and Brown, London, legal correspondence with Joshua Gilpin, 1809–1834; John Bainbridge vs. Benjamin Chew of Philadelphia, papers in a legal suit, 1809–1831; Thomas Gilpin correspondence, 1769–1817; contracts and agreements for sales of lands in Virginia, 1769–1811; Alexander Taylor field notes of surveys for Joshua and Thomas Gilpin, 1802–1812; papers on western lands, 1770–1780; contracts and agreements for sales of land in Pennsylvania, 1800–1817; Luzurne lands, 1808–1852; letter book of Joshua and Thomas Gilpin containing the accounts of Gilpin and Fisher, 1800–1818; Thomas Gilpin journals, eastern states, 1805; New England, 1805; West, 1809; Chester and Duck Creek surveys, estimates, maps, on building canals, 1772; pamphlets on the construction of canals, railroads, tunnels, maps, printed in England, 1789–1835; maps of projected English railroads and canals, London, 1832–1835; collection of specimens of bank-note paper and of engraved currency, manufactured at Brandywine Mills, Del., n.d.

Richard Gilpin's manuscripts include material on papermaking machinery, 1815; his philosophical and literary essays, n.d.; notes on history, theatre, astrology, religion, literature, transportation, canals, agriculture, travel, 1813–1828; poetic notes, 1799–1818; *Pieces in Verse and Prose,* by Joshua Gilpin, essays on medical science, hygiene, politics, history, 1796–1806; Joshua Gilpin's history of the colonies and the State of Delaware, n.d.; essays on the manufacture of woolen goods, n.d.; *Wool and Cotton Manufacture, Sheep and Other Subjects Connected,* 1815; *Report on the Manufacturers of the State of Delaware, and a Report of the History and Principles of Tariff and Public Labor,* n.d.; *Report on the Economic Condition of Philadelphia and Other Subjects,* 1809; *History of the Colonization of America and of the Charter and Grant of Pennsylvania and Delaware,* n.d.; copies of letters of Thomas Fisher, and some additional notes, 1840; journals and diary notes of travel, unidentified, 1836–1858; manuscript copy of *Barremore,* a novelette by Bernard Gilpin, anecdotes, n.d.; maps of ancient Greece, engraved by Barbie du Bocage, 1781–1788.

In addition, there are parchments of the marriage settlement between the Gilpin and the Dilworth families, patents of lands, deeds, 1776–1834; the genealogical records and notes of the Gilpins consist of: *Memoir of the Life of Thomas Gilpin,*: 1769; *Family in England,* 1795; *Memories in England,* n.d.; genealogical memoranda, 1206–1811; *Memories in America,* 1800; and some other items.

Gift of the Henry D. Gilpin estate.

Joshua Gilpin's "Journal of a Tour from Philadelphia through the Western Counties of Pennsylvania" published in the *P.M.H.B.,* 30 (1906): 64–78, 163–178, 380–382; 51 (1927): 172–190, 351–375; 52 (1928): 29–58.

Extracts from the commonplace book of Henry D. Gilpin, 1819 published in the *P.M.H.B.,* 45 (1921): 224–242.

Memoir of Thomas Gilpin published in the *P.M.H.B.,* 49 (1925): 289–328.

Finding aid available for Poinsett papers.

239
Gilpin family.   Poetic and Prose Selections, 1793–1833.   (3 v.)

Essays, verse, historical narratives, and other literary compositions in the handwriting of Joshua Gilpin, Thomas Gilpin, and other members of the Gilpin family.

Gift of Thomas Lynch Montgomery, 1935.

240
Maria and Elizabeth Gilpin.   Collection, 1739–1878.
(125 items.)

A miscellany of correspondence and legal documents of the Gilpin family of Philadelphia, concerned largely with the land and property affairs of Richard and Mary Penn and Mary's sister, Sarah Masters; of Joshua Gilpin, his sons, William and Henry Dilworth, and his brother, Thomas, a paper manufacturer. Tench Francis was agent for many of these transactions. Correspondents include Richard Penn, Edward Livingston, John Forsyth, and Senator John Dix (Democrat, N.Y.) Also letters, author unidentified, seeking a consular appointment; Continental loan certificates, and maps of the Brandywine Manufacturing Company of Wilmington, Del., n.d., and of Indiana County, Gilpin land tracts, 1838.

Gift of Maria and Elizabeth Gilpin, 1923.

241
Gobrecht, Christian F., 1785–1844.   Papers, 1795–1844.
(ca. 100 items.)

Miscellaneous correspondence of Christian Gobrecht, engraver in the United States Mint, about his inventions and improvements in the art of engraving, and about other activities in the field of his profession; a few items of personal and domestic character are included.

242
Godfrey, John W.   Journal, 1795–1796.   (1 v.)

Journal by John W. Godfrey of a journey from Philadelphia, on the brig *Diana,* to London, and a tour through England, Holland, Brabant, Flanders, and France, in the service of an American land company. The narrative gives some account of European cultural and social life and describes economic conditions.
Gift of Eliza Heale, 1876.

243
Goodfellow, Edward, 1828–1899.   Journal, 1860.   (1 v.)

Journal of a tour to Labrador on board the steamer *Bibb,* 1860, by Edward Goodfellow, United States Coast Survey, member of the Labrador Eclipse Expedition, which was in the charge of Professor Stephen Alexander, of Princeton College; describes hazards of the journey, collisions with icebergs and submerged rocks, fishing industry off Nova Scotia, life of the Eskimos and Indians, magnetic and other scientific observations.
Gift of Mrs. Edward Goodfellow.

244
Goodfellow family.   Papers, 1823–1881.   (ca. 125 items.)

Miscellaneous letters, accounts, documents, and memorabilia of the Goodfellow and related families: James Goodfellow, Jr., conducted an academy in Philadelphia, and his personal account book, 1834–1840, 1853–1857, includes some student accounts, 1836–1839; Edward Goodfellow, son of James and an officer with the Coast and Geodetic Survey, 1866–1899; Thomas Smiley, Edward's father-in-law and a Philadelphia and Civil War doctor; 1823–1864; Stephen Coulter, Edward's brother-in-law and a mariner, 1833–1855; Thomas Loud, Edward's wife's grandfather and Baptist preacher, religious poem, n.d.
Gift of Mrs. Edward Goodfellow.

245
Hubbard, Edwin, 1811–1891.   Goodrich and Cocke genealogy, ca. 1861.   (2 v.)

Genealogies of the William Goodrich family, which settled in Wethersfield, Conn., about 1635, and of the Abraham Cocke family, early pioneers and settlers in Virginia and Kentucky, about 1748. These notes, compiled by Edwin Hubbard, contain data on the derivation of family names, coats of arms, biographical sketches.

Gift of the Helen G. Goodrich estate, 1935.

246
Goodson and Cart.   **Papers, 1681–1761.**   **(75 items.)**

Deeds, agreements, wills, and accounts; also some correspondence relating to commercial and legal transactions of John Goodson, surgeon, and Samuel Cart, merchant.

247
Gordon, Thomas F.   **Papers, ca. 1813.**   **(ca. 100 items.)**

Collection of notes, biographical data, and essays prepared by Thomas F. Gordon in connection with his research in United States history. Topics include: Pierre DuSimitiere, George Keith, James Hamilton, and the history of: Maryland, New England, New Jersey, New York, Pennsylvania, South Carolina, and Virginia.

248
Graff Papers, 1860–1909.   **(ca. 150 items.)**

Diaries, 1882–1893, 1897, of Paul Graff; and account book, 1905–1909, of Edgar P. Graff.

Gift of Annie A. Graff, 1921.

249
Granvill, Bernard.   **Family history, [1880].**   **(1 v.)**

Transferred to the Genealogical Society of Pennsylvania.

250A
Gratz, Simon.   **Collection, 1343–1928.**   **(350 linear ft.)**

The collection is arranged by category of achievement.

The collection was assembled by Simon Gratz, Philadelphia lawyer, school board member, and trustee of the Free Library. He began collecting at age 17 and, by the time he died, amassed about 175,000 manuscripts and portrait engravings and lithographs. Many of the latter he personally commissioned. He was a long-time member of the Historical Society of Pennsylvania and, by the time he joined the Council in 1901, he established an international reputation as a collector which brought him into contact with dealers and collectors throughout the United States and Europe. In 1916 he became a vice-president of the Historical Society.

Gratz continued until the end of his life to deal with such notable American collectors as George Brinley, Louis J. Cist, Adrien Joline, Charles J. Jones, E.H. Leffingwell, and Joseph J. Mickley. The dealers with whom he dealt included Charavay in Paris, Naylor and Maggs in London, Cohn in Berlin, Benjamin in New York, and A.S.W. Rosenbach in Philadelphia. The records of his transactions survive from 1861 to 1925 in his "Autograph Journals." On January 1, 1925, Gratz noted that his collection had, because of astute sales and exchanges, "cost less than nothing."

Gratz acquired his collection by exchange with and purchase from a great number of collectors and dealers. Perhaps as many as 350,000 items passed through his hands. Perhaps his most important purchase came in 1881 when he bought a collection of 90,000 items assembled by William B. Sprague, author of Annals of the Pulpit, for $20,000, a sum which Gratz noted was "probably twice as much as it was worth." Despite his misgivings about the Sprague collection, assimilation of the material left its mark upon the Gratz Collection: Sprague's system of arrangement by category survives almost intact in the first section. In 1917 Gratz deeded his manuscripts and portraits to the Historical Society and began transferring parts of the collection to the Society, a process that was not completed until after his death.

Topics included in the collection are: American politics; American wars; jurists; church and clergymen; arts and sciences; miscellaneous personal papers; Indian affairs; territorial expansion and settlement in Pennsylvania; Pennsylvania politics and legal affairs; commercial records; correspondence of U.S. government officials; miscellaneous American papers; European letters and papers; and Protestant American clergy.

American wars autographs, 1676–1906: American navy in the Revolution, 1742–1843; Board of War and Navy Board, 1776–1799; British officers in War of 1812, 1803–1866; colonial wars, 1657–1815; American officers in the Revolution, 1747–1842; French and Indian War, 1756; French officers in the Revolution, 1764–1836; foreign officers in British army in the Revolution, and American loyalists, 1747–1827; generals in the Revolution, 1691–1863; Indians and Indian wars, 1676–1858; Mexican War, 1819–1894; United States naval officers, 1795–1906; War of 1812, 1793–1844; Civil War colonels, 1857–1890; Civil War brevet brigadier generals, 1803–1904; Civil War Confederate generals, 1841–1901; Civil War Union generals, 1777–1901; Confederate army, 1834–1895; Confederate navy, 1836–1883; Confederate Congress and miscellaneous, 1832–1886; constitution of the Confederate States, 1832–1889; governors of the Confederate States, 1837–1884.

Jurists autographs, 1668–1924: American judges, 1668–1925; American lawyers, 1699–1913; attorneys general of Pennsylvania, 1702–1922; High

Court of Errors and Appeals of Pennsylvania, 1758–1808; judges, Supreme Court, 1778–1924; Supreme Court of Pennsylvania, 1679–1923.

Church and clergymen autographs, 1647–1921: American clergy, 1683–1920; American colonial clergy, 1647–1803; chaplains in the French and Indian wars, 1732–1812; Methodist bishops, 1790- 1902; Moravian bishops, 1738–1880; Presbyterian moderators, 1788–1900; Protestant Episcopal bishops, 1768–1921; Protestant Episcopal ministers, 1813–1893; Roman Catholic prelates, 1795–1921; sermons, 1650–1788; sermons of early New England clergy, 1654–1805; and miscellaneous church papers, 1745–1815.

Participants in cultural life, arts, and sciences autographs, 1647–1923: American actors and actresses, 1794–1928; American authors, 1782–1879; American historians, 1684–1915; American literary men, 1670–1890; American poets, 1728–1907; American prose writers, 1700–1921; hymn writers, 1753–1793; prose and poetry of American authors, 1780–1915; literary miscellaneous, 1790–1912; notable American women, 1724–1894; inventors, 1733–1876; explorers, discoverers, mathematicians, and astronomers, 1776–1911; painters, sculptors, and engravers, 1790–1921; physicians, 1682–1923; philanthropists, international, 1761–1902; scientists, 1740–1909; university and college presidents, 1647–1921.

Miscellaneous personal autographs, 1754–1824: John Dickinson correspondence, 1775–1798, includes Congressional acts signed by Charles Thomson, Benjamin Franklin, and John Hancock; George Washington letters, 1781–1782; Marquis de Lafayette, 1789; George Latimer, 1788; Robert Morris, 1797–1798; Charles Lee, 1775; Tadeusz KAsciuszko and others; Albert Gallatin correspondence, 1801–1811; Stephen Girard papers, 1794–1811; Charles Thomson correspondence, 1754–1824, includes his memorandum book, 1754–1774, with notes on the Revolutionary Convention; Baron von Steuben, letters and correspondence, 1782–1793.

Indian affairs autographs, 1758–1807: Papers of John Reynell, commissioner for Indian affairs, relate to Indians at Fort Augusta, Fort Pitt, 1758–1765; copy of Cornplanter's speech to the Quakers, 1790; letters relating to trade and shipping; Deborah Morris' letters, 1788; school funds, 1765; taxes, 1735; Indian affairs, 1756–1763, including commissioners' accounts, cash and receipt books; Pennsylvania-Pittsburgh invoice books, 1760–1761; daybook, Pittsburgh, 1760–1765; daybooks, Shamokin, 1759–1761; daybook, Fort Allen, 1759–1760; John Willington correspondence, 1786–1807, relates to frontier activities, Indian fighting, and United States army operations.

Territorial expansion and settlements in Pennsylvania, 1712–1895: Asylum Company, 1794–1839; list of stockholders, notes, correspondence, agreements of sales of lands in Bradford, Columbia, Lycoming, Northumberland, and other counties; Avon-by-the-Sea Land and Improvement Company, 1892–1895; deeds, 1712–1845, documents of properties in various counties; John Nicholson's land transactions, 1781–1832; Northumberland County, 1773–1794, land transactions, surveys, trade, legal, politics; Pennsylvania Population Company, 1792–1794; North American Land Company, 1800–1880; early Pennsylvania and New Jersey, 1684–1853, contain correspondence of colonial settlers, surveys, trade, military, and domestic records; surveys, 1688–1829; York County, 1768–1847, land transactions, legal, domestic, and political records.

Pennsylvania politics and legal affairs, 1800–1879: Benjamin S. Bonsall correspondence, 1830–1836; Thomas Bradford correspondence, 1800–1846; Charles Gilpin correspondence, 1864–1868; A. Boyd Hamilton correspondence, 1806–1840, contains Jackson and anti-Jackson material, Simon Cameron letters, and Buck Shot War papers; Samuel D. Patterson correspondence, 1839; Thomas Lamborn docket books, 1813–1859.

Commercial records, 1699–1835: John Astley, 1799–1819; Thomas Astley, Philadelphia merchant, 1813–1835, correspondence on trade and land transactions; Andrew Clow and David Cay, Philadelphia merchants, papers, 1730–1816, relate to trade with England, West Indies, Newburyport, Mass., Wilmington, Del., and other places; Samuel Coates receipt books, 1740–1756, 1781–1818, and memorandum book, 1813–1818; William Manington accounts, 1699–1703; Cramond, Phillips and Company, Philadelphia merchants, correspondence, 1789–1801; Hamilton-Hood papers, 1813–1835, relate to commerce, finance, accounts, receipts; Thomas Barn day and receipt books, 1827–1835; William Clarkson and George Morrison ledger, 1767–1779; Isaac Zane ledger, 1748–1759; bonds, 1749–1775, miscellaneous agreements and obligations signed by men of the colonial period.

Correspondence of officials of the United States Government departments, 1795–1868: Department of Internal Revenue, 1849–1868; Navy Department, 1862–1868; Treasury Department, 1821–1868; United States Attorney General's office, 1850–1865; War Department, 1851–1868; Custom House revenue inspector certificates, 1795–1807; revenue documents, 1806–1808.

Miscellaneous American papers, 1570–1919: John Williams and family papers, 1706–1811; Elizabeth Graeme Ferguson correspondence, 1737–1794; Loganian Library and Library Company papers, 1767–1824; Benjamin Lightfoot letters from Reading, 1770; Philadelphia Almshouse poor daybook, 1739; Philadelphia Monthly Meeting and Free School Corporation accounts, 1743–1778; Wistar papers, 1773–1815; Martha Lees poetry and miscellaneous papers, 1775–1800, includes sketches of the State House, 1800; William Maclay drafts and family papers, 1767–1792; Nathan Arnaut ciphering book, 1775; "Americana," 1787–1802, miscellaneous manuscripts of diaries, poetry, religious writings; Benjamin West correspondence, 1789–1824; criminals and their victims, 1791–1868; J.H. Walmouth account of the yellow fever epidemic in Philadelphia, 1798; Penn-Gaskill-Hall correspondence, 1816–1899; Dr. Joseph Chamberlain correspondence, 1828–1845, relating to the medical profession; Sallie Knowles diaries, 1845–1850, and journal concerning the building of the Annapolis and Elk Ridge Railroad, 1838.

Loyalist Poetry of the Revolution by Winthrop Sargent (Philadelphia, 1857) interleaved with autograph letters, portraits, and newspaper clippings, 1767–1857; Winthrop Sargent notes and poetry, ca. 1847; Art Union of Philadelphia papers, 1849–1851; Cohocksink Presbyterian Church, Philadelphia, papers, 1877–1911; Simon Gratz manuscript of "A Book About Autographs," 1919; Simon Gratz correspondence, 1860–1919, on civil affairs, education, autographs; miscellaneous letters, 1570–1879; American and European celebrities, royalty, diplomats, statesmen, authors, military and naval officers; miscellaneous papers, 1686–1880, relate to national and local politics, trade with Indians, land transactions, religion, penal law; lottery tickets, 1699–1860; Continental, New England, Middle Atlantic, Southern, and Confederate paper money and stamps; playbills, 1821–1847; portraits of American and European celebrities.

European letters and papers, 1383–1916: European actresses and actors, 1712–1900; European clergy, 1568- 1870; European critics and orientalists, 1568–1892; European military and naval, 1459–1893; European miscellaneous, 1557–1906; European painters and sculptors, 1508–1903; European physicians, 1559–1900; European scientists, 1635–1899; European statesmen, 1504–1910; British authors, 1590–1912; British bishops, 1600–1903; British clergy, 1568–1871; British dramatists, 1648–1898; British historians and essayists, 1697–1909; British jurists, 1557–1911; British literary, 1600–1912; British poets, 1600–1912; British prime ministers, 1563–1903; British statesmen, 1572–1890; Canadians, 1711–1916; French authors, 1443–1904; French generals, 1680–1847; French Revolution, 1768–1812; foreign hymn writers, 1566–1888; German miscellaneous, 1735–1868; Italian authors, 1407–1908; Luther and the Reformation, 1515–1603; musicians and composers, 1616–1913; Napoleon and his marshals, 1792–1832.

Northern and central European literary, 1559–1887; northern and central European historians and novelists, 1525–1920; northern and central European poets and dramatists, 1525–1920; notable European women, 1573–1872; popes, 1586–1831; Portuguese, Italian, Belgian, Spanish authors, 1471–1893; royalty of England, 1479–1870; royalty of Denmark, Norway, Sweden, Russia, 1587–1872; royalty of France, 1383–1890; royalty miscellaneous, 1461–1866; royalty of Prussia, Austria, Germany, 1509–1883; royalty of Spain, Portugal, 1402–1870; Swiss authors, 1650–1859; Thirty Years' War, 1583–1699.

250B
Gratz, Simon. **Collection, 1677–1910.** **(150 linear ft.)**

Alphabetically arranged.

This collection is particularly rich in papers of Protestant American clergymen. Letters, 1795–1820, of American Presbyterian clergy addressed to William Wallace Woodward, a Philadelphia bookseller. Manuscript sermons of such clergymen as Abiel Abbot, Lyman Beecher, Nathaniel Chauncey, Timothy Edwards, Ashbel Green, Levi Hart, Alexander Murray, James Muir, William B. Sprague, Solomon Stoddard, Samuel Willard, and others.

The collection includes letters and portraits of many other prominent Americans and Europeans: Theodosia Burr Alston; Governor Edmund Andros, 1677; General John Armstrong, 1769; Susanna Anthony, 1770; John Jacob Astor, 1842; John Bradford, 1720; Governor Jonathan Belcher; George Bryan; George Clinton; George Clymer; DeWitt Clinton, 1822; John Dickinson; William Dearborn, 1808; William Duer, 1786; Edward Everett, 1827; Benjamin Eastburn, 1734; William Eaton, 1805; Albert Gallatin, 1801–1811; Joseph Galloway, 1769; Adolphus W. Greely; Jonathan Greenleaf, 1843; Alexander Hamilton; Samuel Hopkins, 1770; William Harrison, 1786; Patrick Henry; Jared Ingersoll; John Jay, 1822; Washington Irving; Dyre Kearney, 1787; James Kent; Francis Scott Key; John Laurens, 1778; Gouverneur Morris, 1806; John P. Montgomery, 1776; Thomas Mifflin, 1791; John Nicholson, 1795; Isaac Morris; Samuel Otis, 1789; Richard and Thomas Penn, 1755; Edmund Pendleton; James Parker, 1793; Colonel James Rodney, 1764; Joseph Reed, 1812; Peyton Randolph; J. Bayard Smith, 1778; Jonathan D. Sergeant, 1784; Henry De Saussure, 1787; Theodore Sedgwick, 1799; William Tweed, 1871; John Tyler, Jr., 1842; James Wadsworth, 1780; John F. Zubley, 1767; and others.

Other miscellaneous items are: manuscripts of James Monroe, 1794–1828, on the French Revolution; instructions to James Monroe by Edmund Randolph, 1794–1796; Aaron Burr letters, 1775–1811; Erick Bollmann, 1810; William Eaton, 1802; Joseph Bonaparte correspondence, 1815–1827; parchment deeds, 1691–1786, of Pennsylvania and New Jersey; Judge John Cleves Symmes to Captain Dayton on settlements west of Ohio and on the Miami, 1789; papers relating to Indian affairs, 1789–1806; Irish Revolution papers, 1806–1813; Mexico and South America, 1785–1843; United States Bank, 1805; Bank of North America, 1813–1814; Canadian Rebellion, 1837–1838; political relations between France and America, 1783–1793; letters of writers, artists, scholars, scientists, physicians, apothecaries, penologists, reformers, ca. 1711–1910, including Joseph Lancaster's correspondence on education, James Rumsey's manuscripts and printed material, 1788, concerning his invention of the first steam vessel, and other papers bearing on intellectual trends.

251

Gratz, Henry M.   **Papers, 1762–1921.**   **(50 items.)**

A collection of miscellaneous papers from members of the Gratz family. Among the items are: copy of the will of William Trent, 1796; legal documents of Simon and Hyman Gratz, 1805; Simon Gratz stock certificates in various transportation enterprises, 1811–1831; scrip paper money, 1837–1839; French assignats, 1792; Simon Gratz certificate to practice before the Supreme Court, 1860; stock accounts, 1864–1864; Alfred Gratz, patent certificate for an attachment to a talking machine, 1903; and other items.

Gift of Henry M. Gratz.

252

Grotjan, Peter Adolph, 1774–1850.   **Memoirs, 1844–1846.**   **(2 v.)**

Peter Adolph Grotjan, German merchant, emigrated to Philadelphia in 1796 where he engaged in trade with Hamburg, Germany, New York (N.Y.), Baltimore, Md., Alexandria, Va., and the West Indies. He operated a commercial house in Reading in 1797, and then returned to his Philadelphia business. In 1812, he began publishing *Grotjan's Philadelphia Public Sale Reports,* a commercial newspaper which he continued until 1822. He then became interested in politics as a Jacksonian and founded the Philadelphia Hickory Club in 1822. He served as Philadelphia County auditor, 1828–1836, 1841–1844.

The first volume, begun in 1844, consists of "preparatory notes and memoranda" for the second, the autobiography itself, which is a detailed account of Grotjan's life to 1817. It gives a detailed description of the cholera and yellow fever epidemics in Philadelphia, journeys to the west, the upper south, and to the West Indies, Albert Gallatin's visit to Reading and the ensuing riot, 1798, as well as his encounters with other political figures including Jefferson, Burr, and Buchanan. The last chapter of the autobiography was completed posthumously from the notes.

Gift of Pedro G. Salom, 1936.

253

Grubb family.   **Furnace and forge papers.**

Entry cancelled; see collection #212.

254

Hall, Abraham Oakley, 1826–1898.   **Manuscripts, ca. 1860–1890.** (1 v.)

Abraham Oakley Hall was a lawyer, politician, New York City mayor, newspaperman, and author.

This is a collection of lore, tales, narratives of old New York, romance of Broadway, stories of prominent men, crimes, and celebrated legal cases; also contains poetry and essays on religion, politics, history, and other items of journalistic and literary character. Among Hall's writings are: "Old and Young Broadway," "Crimes of Broadway," "The Birth of Central Park," "A Memorable New York Summer," "New York Murder Sensation," "New York, City of Inventors," "Evolution of Olden Manhattan Christmas," "The Past Glories of Saratoga Springs," "Why Fulton and Clinton Deserve New York Statues," "The Loves of Queen Elizabeth," "Catholicism," "Degeneracy of Protestantism," "Victoria's Recollections," "The Prodigal."

Gift of Mrs. Skinner.

255
Hall, John Elihu, 1783–1829.   Translation of Anarcreon, ca. 1822.
(1 v.)

Translation of "Memoirs of Anarcreon, from the version of Thomas Moore," written about 1822 for *Port Folio*, by its editor, John Elihu Hall, of Philadelphia.

Gift of Gregory B. Kean.

256
Hall, Edward S.   Papers, 1861–1889.   (ca. 100 items.)

Edward S. Hall was active in two Civil War organizations: the Cooper Shop Volunteer Refreshment Saloon, which was organized in 1861 to care for Union soldiers passing through Philadelphia, and the Soldier' Home of Philadelphia, which was a successor organization to the Saloon. The home incorporated in 1864 to care for disabled veterans, turned to supporting and educating veterans' children at the Educational Home in 1873, and dissolved in 1889.

The papers include a letterpress book, 1863–1865, receipts and election returns. There are some letters, minutes, and reports concerning the Home's activities and dissolution.

Gift of Mrs. Reynold T. Hall, 1934.

257
Hallowell, Susan Morris, b. 1845.   Collection, 1849–1884.
(ca. 200 items.)

Anna Hallowell, daughter of Philadelphia merchant and banker Morris Longstreth Hallowell, was active in philanthropic and educational work. She was the first woman member of the Philadelphia Board of Public Education, 1887-1896.

A collection of family papers preserved by Susan M. Hallowell. The papers for her father, Morris Longstreth Hallowell, Philadelphia merchant and banker include: incoming correspondence, bills, receipts, orders and telegrams of Morris L. Hallowell & Co., importers of India and China goods; as well as papers of successor firms, including Hallowell & Co., bankers. There are also Anna Hallowell's notes on Greek mythology and literature are also present.

258
Hamilton, James.   **Collection, (1713–1771) (1834–1905).**
(1 v. and 25 items.)

Official documents, petitions, instructions, commissions, and reports of James Hamilton, governor general of Pennsylvania, 1713–1771; and papers on Hamilton heirs' litigation, 1834–1905.
Gift of H. Hamilton Palairet and Lena Cadwalader Evans.

259
Hamilton, Hance.   **Papers, 1739–1779.**   **(ca. 225 items.)**

These papers of Hance Hamilton, first sheriff of York County, 1749, and officer in the French and Indian War, pertain to official, legal, and commercial transactions and include bonds, receipts, accounts, mostly relating to York County, during the colonial period.
Gift of Donald McPherson, 1927.

260
Hamilton, James.   **Docket book, 1739–1740.**   **(1 v.)**

James Hamilton was a prothonotary in Philadelphia.
Gift of Frank M. Etting, 1876.

261
Hand, Edward, 1744–1802.   **Papers, 1771–1807.**   **(1.5 linear ft.)**

Edward Hand served as a Major-General during the Revolutionary War.
Correspondence, accounts, and military orders, including: papers and correspondence, 1771–1803; orderly books, 1776; revenue account books, 1792–1807, 1797–1801; miscellaneous letters written by Hand, 1775–1801; and letters to his wife.
Correspondence, 1779–1781, published in the *P.M.H.B.*, 33 (1909): 353.
Orderly book, 1776, published in the *P.M.H.B.*, 41 (1917): 198–223, 257–273, 458–467.

262
Cromie, Robert James, b. 1887.   Harding in Canada letters, 1924.
(1 v.)

Letters of eminent statesmen of Canada and the United States, addressed to R.J. Cromie, publisher of the *Vancouver Sun,* Vancouver, B.C., commends him for presenting to the National Press Galleries at Washington, John Innes' painting in commemoration of President Harding's visit to Canada in 1923.
Gift of Frederick R. Kirkland, 1937.

263
Hare-Powel and related families.   Genealogy, 1807–1907.   (1 v.)

Transferred to the Genealogical Society of Pennsylvania.

264
Harley, Lewis Reifsneider, b. 1866.   Papers, ca. 1891–1918.
(2 linear ft.)

Collection of Lewis R. Harley's essays and addresses on historical and biographical subjects. Among his writings are "The English Idea of Government at the Close of the Sixteenth Century," "Abraham Lincoln," "Baron von Steuben," "America and the Star Spangled Banner," "Reflections on the Uses of History," "Henry Ford and History."

265
Harper, S. Bell.   Recipes and fact book, 1809.   (1 v.)

Recipes for cooking and baking; also memoranda of populations of several cities in Europe and America, and notes on academic studies.
Purchased, Charles Morton Smith Fund, 1939.

266
Harris, John.   Collection, 1687–1915.   (500 items.)

Correspondence, accounts, and other papers of John Harris, founder of Harrisburg, and some of his descendants; a group of autograph letters and documents signed by governors of the colony and state of Pennsylvania and by some members of the supreme executive council. The signatures of William Penn, John Penn, William Markham, Thomas Wharton, James Logan, Edward Shippen, James Hamilton, Simon Cameron, John Quincy Adams, James Buchanan are included. In addition, the collection contains:

the ledger books of John Harris, 1748–1775, 1770–1791; correspondence, accounts, documents, relating to commercial, legal and land transactions, and to family affairs, 1734–1915; autograph letters and documents, 1687–1915; and two pamphlets, Companion for the Counting House or, Duties payable on Goods Imported into America, 1789, and the *Patriot Hymn Book,* 1862.

Manuscripts in this collection were assembled by Colonel William C. Armor.

Purchased, Library Fund.

267

Harrison, George. Papers, 1812–1832. (150 items.)

Correspondence of George Harrison, United States Navy agent at Philadelphia, with Benjamin W. Crowinshield and Levi Woodbury, secretaries of the Navy; Robert T. Patterson, director of the United States Mint; and others and copies of resolutions of Congress, on the manufacture of medals, emblems, swords, for presentation to distinguished officers in recognition of gallantry in service against British vessels. The officers so honored include Isaac Hull of the *Constitution,* Stephen Decatur of the *United States,* Jacob Jones of the *Wasp,* William Bainbridge, Oliver H. Perry, and others.

268

Todd, Charles S., 1791–1871. Vindication of William H. Harrison, 1854. (1 v.)

A defense of the military character of General William Henry Harrison, whose merits and soldierly ability had been severely criticized by Joel T. Headley in *The Second War With England* (2 v., New York, 1853). The papers deal particularly with the campaigns in the Northwest during the War of 1812. Todd's work was published in the *National Intelligencer,* October 19, 1854.

269

Harrison Oil Company. Papers, 1864–1866. (100 items.)

The Harrison Oil Company was organized in 1864 by a group of Philadelphians to drill for oil on French Creek in Venango County. Philadelphians involved with the company were: George W. Anderson, George Williams, James W. Packer, M. Spiegle, Charles D. Colladay, and Amos Ellis.

The collection includes agreements for purchase of land and drilling rights, a drilling contract with Charles Gibson, and correspondence of

George W. Anderson and other company agents with officials in Philadelphia concerning problems and progress of drilling operations, as well as bills, receipts, and a receipt book, 1865–1866.

Gift of Charles B. Harding, 1918.

270

Hart family.   Genealogy, 1735–1920.   (1 v.)

Transferred to the Genealogical Society of Pennsylvania.

271

Hatkinson, John.   Ledger, 1748–1758.   (1 v.)

Ledger of John Hatkinson, Philadelphia merchant, partner of Robert Morris, contains accounts of general business transactions, names of clients, and prices of commodities.

Purchased, 1902.

272

Haupt, Herman, 1817–1905.   Letterbook, 1852.   (1 v.)

Letterpress copies of letters of General Herman Haupt, written during his employment as chief engineer of the Georgia, Mississippi and Southern Railroad. They relate to his managerial activities and contribute information on the growth and extension of transportation facilities in the South.

Purchased, Library Fund, 1913.

273

Hawkins, John H.   Journal, 1779–1781.   (1 v.)

Military campaigns in New England during the American Revolution are described by Hawkins, sergeant major in one of the Revolutionary brigades, operating in the northern colonies. The journal furnishes details of troop movements, battles, military and economic conditions, espionage, and courts-martial.

274

Hayley, William, 1745–1820.   Manuscript, ca. 1800.   (1 v.)

Entry cancelled; see collection #299.

275
Heckewelder, John Gottlieb Ernestus, 1743–1823.
Papers, 1755–1822.   (150 items.)

The correspondence and papers on John Gottlieb Ernestus Heckewelder's life, and his work among the Indians, with notes on Indian vocabulary, folklore, and traditions, include: correspondence, biographical and historical narratives of the Indians, 1755–1822; "Iroquois Vocables," by J.C. Pyrlaeus, 1749; and Heckewelder's account of his journey to Ohio, 1797.
Gift of John W. Jordan.
Account of journey published in the *P.M.H.B.*, 10 (1886): 125–157.

276
Hele, James E.   Letterbook, 1825–1828.   (3 v.)

Copies of James E. Hele's letters to relatives and friends, written from Puerto Cabello, Colombia. The letters describe living conditions, Hele's business and shipping enterprises, local affairs, and military and political events.
Gift of Daniel R. Pennepacker, 1903.

277
Henderson-Wertmüller papers, 1779–1822.   (ca. 150 items.)

Miscellaneous correspondence, accounts, and documents on the settlement of the estates of John Henderson and Elizabeth Wertmüller; data on labor costs, commodity prices; correspondence of Lydia Henderson and John Nicholson, 1790–1795; list of the subscribers for the purchase of an organ for St. Paul's Church, 1783.
Gift of Charles Henry Hart, 1917.

278
Henry, Alexander, 1823–1883.   Papers, 1858–1876.   (350 items.)

Alexander Henry was mayor of Philadelphia from 1858 to 1865.
Most of the correspondence reflects the impact of the Civil War and concerns the defense of the city and the state: the recruiting of troops, the draft, the Philadelphia Bounty Fund, the use of "colored" troops raised in Philadelphia, and relations with the federal government and the military. Telegrams of Governor Andrew G. Curtin chronicle the advance of Lee into Pennsylvania. Several items, including Secretary of State William H. Seward telegrams, concern a rumored plot to burn Northern cities. Other letters

concern security investigations, police and crime matters, and aid for persons in need. The papers also include Mayor Henry's list of marriages solemnized, 1858–1861, and letters about the use of police at the International Exposition, 1876.

Gift of Mrs. Bayard Henry.

279
Betsy and Eliza Henry.   **Music books, 1796–1823.**   **(6 v.)**

Secular music in manuscript in vogue in Pennsylvania during the 18th century.

Some songs in german.
Gift of Laura Bell.

280
Henry, William.   **Papers, 1759–1826.**   **(7 v.)**

Correspondence and other documents relating to William Henry's political interests in Lancaster County and his activities during the Revolution. Included are: letters, documents, and accounts, 1759–1812; ledger, 1777–1779; a record of the "disbursements of the Hide Department," 1779–1783; Lancaster County docket, 1774–1781; J. J. Henry's journal of the campaign against Quebec, 1775; his notes on Indian names of rivers and streams, Indian vocabulary, and notes for a history of the Indian nations, with maps of Pennsylvania counties.

Gift of John W. Jordan, 1889.
Sixteen letters to William Henry, 1777, 1783 published in the *P.M.H.B.,* 22 (1898): 106–113.

281
Hicks, Isaac.   **Docket books, 1772–1832.**   **(2 v.)**

Isaac Hicks was justice of the peace in Bucks County.
Docket book containing lists of cases to be heard in his court, records of marriages performed, judgements, and writs issued.

282
Hiester, Daniel, 1747–1804.   **Papers, 1739–1822.**   **(65 items.)**

Daniel Hiester was a farmer, businessman, and political leader of Pennsylvania and Maryland, as well as U.S. Representative from both states.

Miscellaneous correspondence, land warrants, indentures, and plans mainly of colonial Pennsylvania.

Gift of the descendants of William Hiester Clymer.

283
Hildal, Martin.   Commonplace book, 1764.   (1 v.)

Commonplace book containing lessons in arithmetic, English composition, and poetry.

Purchased, Library Fund, 1926.

284
Hildeburn, Charles Swift Riché 1855–1901.   Collection, (1770–1792) 1900.   (132 items.)

This is a collection of letters to Mary ("Polly") Riché, Hildeburn's great grandmother. Many of the letters are from Christian Amiel and Sarah Bard primarily on family, personal, and social matters with only occasional comments on contemporary events. There are also some Alice Swift (later married to Robert Cambridge Livingston) letters, largely from Charleston to her parents in Philadelphia, 1771.

In addition, there are Hildeburn's transcripts of the letters with drafts and notes for an intended publication *A Trunkful of Old Letters from Loyalist Ladies in Revolutionary Times.*

Purchased, Library Fund, 1926.

285
**Hildeburn, Charles Swift Riché, 1855–1901.
Obituaries, 1728–1791.   (1 v.)**

Obituary notices copied from the *Pennsylvania Gazette.*
Gift of Charles Riché Hildeburn.

286
**Hildeburn, Charles Swift Riché, 1855–1901.   Papers, 1738–1894.
(9 linear ft.)**

Papers of Charles Swift Riché Hildeburn include: miscellaneous correspondence, records of commercial transactions, and notes, 1738–1885; correspondence on reprinting of Bradford, *Laws of New York,* 1893–1895; papers

on the Isaac Harvey estate, 1891; miscellaneous printed pamphlets, 1790; correspondence relating to the Swift, Riché, and Inman families, 1740–1885.
Gift of Charles Riché Hildeburn, 1896.

287
Hillegas, Michael, 1729–1804.   Letterbooks, 1757–1760.   (2 v.)

Michael Hillegas was a prominent Philadelphia merchant and treasurer of the United States, 1775–1789.

The letterbooks relate to his business affairs and administrative activities reflecting his extensive trade in paper, spices, calico, musical instruments, and records of the sale of loan certificates and other financial transactions for the United States government.
Gift of Charles Lockrey, 1905–1907.

288
Hinrichs, John.   Diary, 1778–1780.   (1 v.)

John Hinrichs was staff captain in the Hessian Hunters Corps operating with the British army in the American Revolution.

Contemporary copies of letters addressed to Hinrichs' relatives and friends, describe the war from a British point of view, economic condition of the country, lack of supplies in the Revolutionary army, the political motives involved in the struggle, the course of the military campaigns from Philadelphia, Flushing, New York, South Carolina, and other places, French and Russian interests in the war, and the strategies of commanding officers in both armies.

289
Hollingsworth family.   Papers, 1748–1887.   (ca. 195 linear ft.)

Zebulon Hollingsworth, flour manufacturer in Elkton, Levi Hollingsworth, and their descendants were distinguished merchants. The name of the family business establishment was changed in the course of its history: in 1759 it was "Adams and Hollingsworth"; in 1770, "Hollingsworth and Rudulph"; in 1772, "Levi Hollingsworth"; in 1793, "Levi Hollingsworth and Son"; in 1824, "Paschall Hollingsworth and Company"; and in 1837, "Morris, Tasker and Morris."

The papers relate to trade in America, the West Indies, and Europe, prices of commodities, finance, shipping, political and economic conditions, leading personalities, and local, domestic and social affairs. The collection includes: correspondence, 1761–1887; checks, drafts, bills of exchange, 1760-

1858; orders, 1765–1863; invoices, 1764–1849; promissory notes, 1769–1830; legal papers, 1734–1851; bills and receipts, 1751–1863; market reports, 1770–1839; and miscellaneous, 1761–1890.

Also included are: ledgers, 1748–1863; order books, 1748–1859; cash books, 1758–1864; flour books, 1765–1774; bank journals, 1794–1853; daybooks, 1755–1865; journals, 1755–1861; memorandum books, 1760–1853; waste books, 1762–1844; disbursement books, 1765–1847; ship frieght books, 1766–1859; sales books, 1772–1860; receipt books, 1772–1859; property docket book, 1849; machinery repair record book, 1779–1863; weight books, 1783–1792; delivery books, 1792–1861; bundle books, 1779–1859; letterbooks, 1780–1846; and purchase books, 1786–1847.

Among the miscellaneous papers are items dealing with domestic affairs, commercial enterprises, land transactions, legal controversies, politics. There are broadsides, travel diaries, accounts of the yellow fever epidemics, sale of lottery tickets, prices current, an account of the construction of the Ohio Canal, sheep raising, deeds and patents of lands, insurance policies, vendues, reports on military ordnance, introduction of steam heating, surveys, and other subjects.

"Descriptive Report of the Hollingsworth Collection" / by Works Progress Administration, 1938.

290
Hoopes, Daniel.   Practical arithmetic, 1802.   (1 v.)

Examples in arithmetic, simple and compound interest, permutation, and bookkeeping of David Hoopes.

Purchased, Dreer Fund, 1938.

291
Hopkins, Gerard T.   Journal, 1803–1804.   (1 v.)

Journal by Gerard T. Hopkins of a tour from Baltimore, Md. to Fort Wayne, Ind., in which Hopkins traveled as a member of a deputation of the Society of Friends to the Western Indians, for the purpose of "instructing them in agriculture and useful knowledge"; there are comments on topography, agriculture, economic conditions, and customs and life of the Indians.

Gift of Howard B. French, 1899.

292
Hopkins, Thomas.   Journal, 1780.   (1 v.)

Journal of accounts describing working conditions at the Friendship Salt Works in New Jersey.

293

Hopkinson, Joseph, 1770–1842.   Lecture notes, 1791.   (1 v.)

A collection of notes taken by Joseph Hopkinson during a course of lectures on law, delivered by James Wilson, University of Pennsylvania.
Gift of Charles R. Hildeburn, 1885.

295

Hornor, Joseph R.   Commonplace books, 1798–1818.   (4 v.)

Literary and cultural trends of the early part of the 19th century are shown in Joseph P. Hornor's commonplace book, containing "Miscellaneous tracts, poetical effusions and copies of letters signed Junius Americanus and addressed to Thomas Jefferson," 1801; also lyric poetry written by Rosalie N. Hornor, including free translations of several odes of Horace, 1798–1818.
Gift of Rosalie N. Hornor estate, 1932.

296

Horsfield, Timothy.   Letterbook, 1754–1755.   (1 v.)

Contemporary copies of correspondence between Robert Hunter Morris, governor of Pennsylvania, and Timothy Horsfield, justice of the peace in Northampton County on Indian disturbances and massacres; includes testimony of Moravians who witnessed atrocities at Gnädenhutten, Gabriels Creek, Wyoming.
Gift of Jacob Wolle, 1845.

297

Horsfield, Timothy.   Receipt book, 1763.   (1 v.)

Timothy Horsfield was justice of the peace for Northampton County. Receipts for money paid to officers and men in the service of the Province of Pennsylvania, and for powder, guns, stores, in the defense of the frontiers of Northampton County.

298

Hough, Oliver family.   Papers, 1721–1857.   (ca. 75 items.)

A collection of papers of several generations of the Oliver Hough family, members of the Society of Friends in Philadelphia. They relate to personal and domestic affairs, social conditions, religious activities, and business transactions.

299
Edwards, Howard, 1833–1925?   Collection, 1760–1919.   (3 v.)

Autograph letters, portraits, and pamphlets, gathered by Howard Edwards, on the life of John Howard, distinguished British philanthropist and humanitarian; "Anecdotes on the life of John Howard," by Rev. W.L. Brown, Aberdeen, Scotland, 1817, contains accounts of adventures in travel and other events in the life of John Howard; "Eulogies of Howard," by William Hayley, ca. 1800, a memoir.

Gift of Howard Edwards estate, 1926.

300
Hubley, Adam, ca. 1744–1793.   Journals, 1778–1780.   (2 v.)

The first volume contains rules and regulations passed by Congress on the establishment of the Revolutionary army, lists of officers, muster rolls, and instructions from Baron von Steuben. The second volume, July, 1779 to Oct. 7, 1779, is an account of the Western Expedition commanded by Major General Sullivan, and contains drawings, maps, plans of the territory traversed, a narrative of the hardships experienced and of the final success and victorious return of the expedition.

Volume two published in *P.M.H.B.,* 33 (1909): 129–146, 279–302, 409–422.

301
Hugh, John.   Account book, 1714–1762.   (1 v.)

Accounts of John Hugh, for milling grain, receipts for provisions and services, expense account of a trip to Burlington, Elizabethtown, and Trenton, N.J.; also a record of speeches made at an Indian conference held at Easton in 1756, attended by Tedyuskung and representatives of the Six Nations.

Gift of Mrs. A. Morris Harkness, 1900.

302
Hughes, John.   Papers, 1725–1818.   (ca. 400 items.)

Among these papers are several on the history of the Stamp Act, including a letter from Benjamin Franklin to John Hughes, Indian agent and distributor of stamps in Pennsylvania, 1765; a pamphlet, *Instructions for the Distributors of Stamped Parchment and Paper in America,* 1765; the manifest of the ship *Royal Charlotte* carrying three cases and seven packages of stamps for America, 1765; the account book of Hughes with Franklin, 1755–1757; letters from Anthony Wayne to Hughes on survey of land in Nova Scotia,

1765; a folder of the correspondence of Hughes on the land project in Nova Scotia in which Franklin was interested, 1763–1769; bonds, mortgages, and agreements, 1753–1782; letters from John Hughes to Isaac Hughes, relating his journey to Charles Town, 1769–1771; a pamphlet, *The Bill for Better Raising of Money on the Inhabitants of Philadelphia for Public Use,* 1739; the commission to John Hughes and Edward Shippen to build a fort and houses in Indian territory in connection with the Tedyuskung treaty signed by William Denny and Richard Peters, 1757; the daybook of John Hughes, 1761–1818; a record of bills introduced in the House of Representatives of Pennsylvania, 1814–1815; and patents and deeds, mostly pertaining to land in Upper Merion, Montgomery County, 1730–1802.

303
Huidekoper, Harm Jan, 1776–1854.   Papers, 1796–1854. (ca. 500 items.)

The papers of Harm Jan Huidekoper include: letters describing a journey to and arrival in America, 1796; others give a description of the physical, social, and economic conditions in Pennsylvania, particularly the western part, 1796–1854; manuscripts on Unitarian doctrines; sermons, essays, and interpretations of the Bible; papers on Meadville Theological School, 1847–1850; correspondence and other papers on the construction of the canal from Pittsburgh to Lake Erie, 1828; pamphlet on the proceedings of the Nicholson commissioners, relating to the Pennsylvania Population Land Company, 1842.

Gift of Mrs. H.P. Kidder, 1929.

304
Humphreys, A.A. (Andrew Atkinson), 1810–1883. Papers, 1827–1901.   (15 linear ft.)

The papers of General Andrew Atkinson Humphrey pertain to his military career, especially to his activities during the Civil War, and to his work as a civil engineer with the United States Topographical Engineers, as head of the coast survey, and similar projects. There are correspondence and documents, 1827–1901; a large group of military papers, 1862–1867; field dispatches, 1863–1864; telegrams, 1862–1865; special and general orders, 1862–1878; reports, returns, and casualty records, 1862–1865; and reports and other miscellaneous documents, 1865.

Other papers connected with the history of the Civil War are: papers on sieges and battles, 1862–1866; manuscript of Humphreys', *From Gettysburg to the Rapidan;* notes and papers on the Virginia campaign, 1864–1865; correspondence between Grant and Lee relating to Lee's surrender, 1865;

campaign maps, 1864–1865; topographical maps, 1861; lake and coastal surveys, 1862–1869; miscellaneous items including newspaper clippings and newspapers, 1838–1889; a scrapbook, 1800, on the U.S.S. *Constitution;* reprint of *Who Built the United States Navy,* 1793; pamphlets dealing with the case of Fitz-John Porter, 1869; and pamphlets on the Battle of Gettysburg, 1866. Also included letters forming part of the correspondence of N.N. Humphreys, 1867–1901.

Presented by members of the Humphreys family; some items purchased by the Historical Society.

305
Humphreys, Clement, 1777–1803.   Papers, 1798–1801.
(ca. 250 items.)

The papers of Clement Humphreys, agent to France during the John Adams administration, include: Humphreys' letter book, 1798, containing material on his official missions, with detailed accounts of events; "list of Staple Articles of Commerce between the United States and Foreign Ports," 1798; official instructions and correspondence, 1798–1801; manuscript maps of ports in the West Indies, 1798.

Letterbook, 1798 published in *P.M.H.B.,* 32 (1908): 34–53.

306
Humphreys, Joshua, 1751–1838.   Papers, 1682–1835.   (20 v.)

Business records of Joshua Humphreys, naval constructor for the United States government: letterbooks, 1793–1835; account books, 1784–1813, 1792–1806; ledgers, 1766–1777, 1772–1773, 1784–1805; roll call book, 1794–1799; a daybook, 1791–1823; navy yard mast book, 1797–1806; records of the building of the *United States,* 1798–1801; Wharton and Humphreys notebook with plans for construction of warships, drawings, and details of the building of the *Constitution, Franklin,* and other ships. In addition to these papers there are Humphrey's correspondence, 1775–1831; miscellaneous papers, accounts, agreements, 1738–1823; deeds and marriage contracts 1682–1758; account book, 1747–1748; notebook of Daniel Humphreys, 1638–1716; ciphering book of Joshua Humphreys, 1800–1802; his "Journal of a Voyage from Philadelphia to Lisbon," 1809; journal of Clement Humphreys, 1798; and 2 copies of the *American Repository,* 1796, 1798.

Gift of the Humphreys family.

307
Huntly, John C.   Diary, 1863.   (1 v.)

Diary of John C. Huntly, assistant engineer in the United States Navy, of the *Pensacola,* off New Orleans, contains eyewitness account of war conditions and operations against the Confederate forces, rumors of battles, troop movements, military and naval affairs, and personal notes.

Purchased, Dreer Fund, 1932.

308
Hutchins, Thomas, 1730–1789.   Papers, 1759–1788.
(ca. 300 items.)

Correspondence and papers of Thomas Hutchins, geographer general of the United States, on the topography of the United States, observations on the coast of Florida, navigability of rivers; journals of surveying parties, describing the land surveyed, and contact with Indian, French and Spanish settlements.

Journal, 1760, published in the *P.M.H.B.*, 2 (1878): 149–153.

309
Hutchinson, Francis M..   Pedigrees, genealogies, family histories,
1891.   (1 v.)

Genealogical data, records from parish registers, and descriptions of coats of arms relate to the ancestry and history of several British families.

Gift of the Francis M. Hutchinson estate, 1927.

310
Indian papers, 1716–1856.   (16 v. and 62 items.)

Miscellaneous materials on the American Indian:

Aupaumut, Hendrick. "Narratives of his mission to the Western tribes of Indians who were carrying on a distressing war against the frontier settlements of the United States in the North Western Territory," n.d. Gives details on various tribes, origin of their names, speeches delivered in councils, names of Indian chiefs participating, and the war conditions of the period.

Bonaduci, Lorenzo Botourini. *The History of the Indians of North America . . .*, 1746. Translated from Spanish by W.W. Handlin, [1850]. (1 v.)

Chew, Benjamin, 1722–1810. Journal, 1758. Contains an account of a journey to Easton with Andrew Allen, John Mifflin, and James Peters. Contemporary copy. (1 v.)

Delaware and Iroquis Indians manuscripts, 1746–1749. The manuscripts include: 19th century copies of Conrad Weiser's letters to Christopher Sauer on the customs and religion of the Iroquois and Delaware Indians. This Compilation was prepared by Abraham H. Cassel. English translation published in *P.M.H.B.*, 2 (1878): 407–410.

Foulke, William Parker. "Notes respecting the Indians of Lancaster County." Foulke's account of the Indian tribes inhabiting the Chesapeake Bay, Susquehanna Valley, New York, and other regions. (1 v.)

Friends' Indian Aid Association. Minutes, 1869–1874. (3 v.)

Friendly Association. Minutes, 1755–1757. (1 v.)

Henry, Mathew. Indian vocabularies, 1835–1859. Vocabularies of the Witchita, Caddo, and Comanche in Texas, 1854; Santeau in British Columbia, 1835; Delaware; Klikitat and Kalapooyah, lower bank of the Columbia River, 1836. (4 v.)

Jones, David. Journal, 1772–1773. David Jones, minister of Freehold, N.J., describes his journeys among Indians of the Ohio valley. Published by Isaac Collins, 1774.

Minutes of a council held at Easton, 1756. Present at this council were Benjamin Chew, William Denny, James Hamilton, Lynford Lardner, William Logan, John Mifflin, Richard Peters, Teedyuscung, Conrad Weiser, and others. Published in *Colonial Records,* v. 8, p. 649 ff. (1 v.)

Minutes of Indian conference at Lancaster, n.d. (1 v.)

Miscellaneous papers on Indian losses, 1766–1770. Mainly letters and documents to and from Captain William Trent, Carlisle, on losses sustained from Indian depredations in 1763. (1 v.)

Narrative of the massacres of the Connestoga Indians by the Paxton Boys, 1763. With an appeal for punishment of the murderers. (1 v.)

"Some short remarks on the Indian trade in the Charikees," 1717. Journal describing trade between white traders in North Carolina and Indians, and particularly the conflict between Virginia and Carolina traders over Indian trade. Photostat. (1 v.)

311
Inkson, John.   Example book, 1791.   (1 v.)

Specimens of calligraphy, arithmetic problems, calculations, computing of interest, and bookkeeping.

Gift of the Free Library of Philadelphia, 1916.

312
Irvine, William.   Papers, 1768–1834.   (4 linear ft.)

Papers of William Irvine primarily relate to his service as a brigadier general in the Revolutionary army. They include: letters, muster rolls, records of courts martial, petitions, orders, and resolutions of Congress, 1768–1834; letters, 1780–1811, of John Rose (Baron Rosenthal), Irvine's adjutant; letterbook, 1781–1782; Irvine's order book while commanding the Western

Department, 1781–1783; receipt book, 1776–1777; account and cashbook, 1783.

Gift of Henry Carey Baird.

313
Jackson, Caroline H., 1824–1851.   Memoir, 1824–1851.   (1 v.)

Memoir of Caroline H. Jackson, daughter of Thomas and Eliza Hoopes, members of the Society of Friends, West Goshen Township, West Chester. These volumes furnish information on prevailing religious sentiments, economic and social standards, education, and home life of a prominent Quaker family in the first half of the 19th century.

Purchased, John T. Norris Fund and Dreer Fund, 1936–1937.

314
Jackson, Joseph, 1867–1946.   Manuscripts (for publication), 1923–1926.   (9 linear ft.)

Manuscripts of Joseph Jackson, Philadelphia historian and writer: "Bibliography of Works of Charles Godfrey Leland," 1840–1903; "Early Architecture, Architects and Engineers," on colonial architecture and early Philadelphia architects and engineers, 1923; "Development of American Architecture," 1926, chapters on early national period, early New England architects, the building of Washington, D.C., New York, N.Y., Philadelphia, Charleston, Va., and New Orleans, La., beginning of national architecture, early monuments, interior plans and decorations.

Gift of Joseph Jackson.
Finding aid available.

315
Jackson, Samuel.   Letters, 1862–1863.   (20 items.)

Letters written by Samuel Jackson, medical officer in the United States Navy, to his wife, while he was on board the U.S.S. *Brooklyn* during the blockade of Southern ports during the Civil War.

Gift of Robert C. Rathbone.

316
Jacobs family.   Papers, 1681–1838.   (500 items.)

The papers of John Jacobs, member of Assembly for Chester County; Joseph Jacobs, saddler; Israel Jacobs, weaver, member of Congress, 1791; Isaac Jacobs, mayor of Philadelphia, 1767–1768; Benjamin Jacobs, surveyor, appointed by the Continental Congress to sign and number bills of credit, 1776.

Among the papers are patents of land granted to early pioneers, one issued to Clement Dungan, Bucks County, 1684, signed by William Penn; another to Joseph Tanner, 1681, signed by William Parr; and a map of land on Delaware Bay, N.J., laid out and surveyed by John Woolidge and John Budd, 1691, containing a list of names of settlers. There are also records of the names of the first purchasers of land within the extended boundaries of Bedford, Sussex, Cumberland, Northumberland, Westmoreland, Philadelphia, and Bucks counties, on the Allegheny and Susquehanna rivers, on the Perkiomen, Yellow and Briar creeks, and other localities, 1729–1770, and an agreement pertaining to purchase of land in Nova Scotia, 1766.

There are letters and documents of William Maclay, David Rittenhouse, Michael Hillegas, Edward Shippen, H. Vanderslice, John Robinson, Robert H. Morris, James Hamilton, Thomas Lawrence, Owen Biddle, Jacob Duché, Robert Bass, Nicholas Scull, John Lukens, Joseph Hilbon, treasurer of Pennsylvania Hospital, and many others, 1744–1769.

Commerce and prices of commodities are shown in Joseph Jacobs ledger, 1760–1765; Joseph Jacobs and Samuel Wallis ledger, 1762–1766; Israel Jacobs ledger, 1776–1810; John Jacobs ledger, 1784–1818; Benjamin Jacobs ledger, 1765–1775; Juanita Iron Company stock books, 1766; bills of exchange, bills of lading, bonds, receipts, accounts.

A large portion of the papers pertain to incidents during the period of the Revolution: Sargent Chambers, London merchant, letter, 1766, gives an account of Benjamin Franklin's efforts before Parliament for repeal of the Stamp Act; other letters are from John Galloway, R. Strettel Jones, Francis Johnston, commissioner to negotiate with the Indians, Benjamin Lightfoot, mobbed as a Tory, Jacob Richardson, who conducted the British army into Philadelphia, and others.

Gift of John F. Lewis, 1920.

317
James, Abel, d. 1790.   Diary, 1766–1769.   (1 v.)

Diary and memoranda of Abel James's land and commercial transactions near Bethlehem and Nazareth, relate to the clearing of swamps and creeks and building of canoes.

Gift of the Thomas Stewardson estate, 1932.

318
Jefferson Committee.   Papers, 1826–1828.   (2 v.)

The Jefferson Committee was a committee of citizens of the city and county of Philadelphia organized for the purpose of establishing a fund for the relief of Thomas Jefferson, with a resolution of the committee "to transmit on the 10th day of January next [1828] to the trustees under the will of Thomas Jefferson, for the exclusive use and benefit of his daughter [Martha Randolph] whatever balance may at that time exist."

Papers, correspondence, and subscription lists.

319
Jenkins family.   Papers, 1702–1902.   (ca. 500 items.)

Collection of the family papers of Charles F. and Howard M. Jenkins, with information on some of the Welsh families settled in Montgomery County and adjacent territory in Pennsylvania. There are abstracts of titles, and deeds to lands in Chester, Berks, Northampton, Lancaster, Philadelphia counties, 1702–1785; drafts and surveys of lands in Gwynedd, Carnarvon, Salisbury, Honeybrook townships and other places in which Robert Jenkins, ironmaster, was interested, 1745–1847; papers on the Spring House and Sumneytown Turnpike Road Company, 1847–1872.

There is a record of marriages solemnized by Algernon S. Jenkins, justice of the peace in Montgomery County, 1851–1869; road construction in Gwynedd Township, 1800–1848; list of members organizing the Gwynedd Invincibles, 1864; genealogical notes on the Jenkins, Evans, Griffith, Foulke, and Roberts families; also correspondence on local affairs, commerce, shipping, indentures, licenses, commissions of appointments, 1794–1812; papers relating to Lieutenant Colonel Isaac Franks, 1794–1819.

There are a group of autograph letters of eminent Pennsylvanians, 1794–1892, collected by Charles F. Jenkins; Howard Jenkins' political correspondence, 1858–1902; his notes on the Hanks-Lincoln families, 1883–1894; his articles and material pertaining to local history of Pennsylvania, Anthony Wayne, battle of Brandywine, Swedish Pilgrims, French and Indian War, 1744–1764, rebel invasion of Pennsylvania, burial grounds, the Schwenkfelders, Welsh memoranda.

Gift of Charles F. Jenkins, 1937–1939.

320
Jenkins, Charles Francis, 1865–1951.   Correspondence, 1924–1938.
(ca 1,000 items.)

Correspondence, 1925–1938, of Charles F. Jenkins, relates chiefly to his research on the life, history, and genealogy of Button Gwinnett, and contains information on the early history of Georgia. A large portion of the correspondence relates to the sale and collection of autographs.

Gift of Charles F. Jenkins, 1930, 1938.

321

Jennings, Francis.   Index to Authors of Hymns, 1870.   (1 v.)

A collection of data on the authorship and dates of hymns of various denominations.

Gift of Francis Jennings.

322

Jervis and Sandwith families.   Genealogies.

Transferred to the Genealogical Society of Pennsylvania.

323

Johnson, Anna G.   Autograph album and diary, (1826–1830) (1843–1844).   (1 v.)

Verse dedicated to Anna G. Johnson by her friends, 1826–1830; diary contains a description of a tour through Pennsylvania and New York, and other personal entries, 1843–1844.

324

Johnston, Josiah Stoddard, 1784–1833.   Papers, 1821–1839. (6 linear ft.)

Josiah Stoddard was raised in Kentucky and moved to the Louisiana Territory in 1805. He was a lawyer, member of the territorial legislature, state judge, Congressman, 1821–1823; and United States senator until his accidental death in 1833. His widow, Eliza Sibley Johnston, subsequently married Henry D. Gilpin.

The collection contains correspondence and papers containing information on the contest for the presidential nomination of John Quincy Adams, William H. Crawford, Henry Clay, and Andrew Jackson.

Among the numerous correspondents are James Brown, United States Minister to France, Judge A. Porter, Edward Everett, Matthew S. Quay, R.W. Stoddard, William Shaler, Henry D. Gilpin, Nicholas Biddle, John H. Johnston, and others. Some of the topics and issues discussed in these papers are: the Antimasonic movement, the recharter of the United States Bank, Judge Peck's impeachment, French spoliation claims, tariff, sugar, expansion of territory, legislation before Congress. A large portion of the material relates to political affairs in Louisiana, the building of roads and canals, land claims, memorials to Congress, cotton, slavery, requests for governmental positions, election to office. Henry Clay's letters, 1824–1833, deal with his personal aspirations and his bitterness against Andrew Jackson; letter of Thomas Jefferson, 1825; Dr. John Sibley letters, 1821–1832; invitation to a reception tendered to Marquis de Lafayette, 1824; family letters disclosing Senator Johnston's personal affairs and financial transactions; there are also some personal items of William S. Johnston.

Gift of Gilpin family.

325
Jones, Blathwaite.   Docket book, 1780–1784.   (1 v.)

Docket book of Blathwaite Jones, a Burlington County, N.J. justice of the peace.

326
Jones, David.   Estate papers, 1813 (1847–1849).   (1 v.)

Copy of the will of David Jones and inventory of estate in Darby, Delaware County; the volume also contains receipts and accounts of G.E. Sellers, 1847–1849.

Gift of Charles C. Sellers, 1935.

327
**Jones, David, 1736–1820.   Memorandum book, 1786–1816.
(1 v.)**

A collection of miscellaneous texts from the Bible from which the Rev. David Jones, Baptist minister in Great Valley, Chester County, preached his sermons; there are also records of marriages performed by him, medicinal remedies, financial accounts, and details of his botanical experiments.

328
**Jones, Horatio Gates.   Sketch of the Rittenhouse Paper Mill, 1863.
(1 v.)**

Historical sketch by Horatio Gates Jones of the early manufacture of paper in America, particularly of the Rittenhouse Paper Mill, the earliest in the British colonies in America, erected in Roxborough, Philadelphia County, in 1690. This mill was founded by William Ryttenghuison a Dutch settler, who later changed the name to Rittenhouse. William Bradford and Samuel Carpenter figure in the narrative. The paper on which the sketch was written was made at the Rittenhouse mill before 1699.

Gift of the H.G. Jones estate, 1896.

Published in the *P.M.H.B.*, 20 (1896): 315–333.

329
Jones, Owen, 1711–1793.   Papers, 1696–1867.   (3 linear ft.)

The papers of the Jones family throw light on the mercantile and political affairs of colonial Pennsylvania and of later periods. There are deeds and patents to land, 1705–1809; a copy of a memorial presented to George III, concerning purchase of land from the Indians in New York and on the Ohio River, 1774; treasurer's book of the province of Pennsylvania, 1768–1776; Owen Jones daybook, 1759–1761; his waste book, 1767–1772; his ledger, 1767–1773; his invoice book, 1767–1774; daybooks, 1775–1776, 1783–1784, 1783–1790; accounts in the estate of Mary Howell, 1785–1791; letter book 1785–1793; rent book, 1793- 1824; invoice book, 1796–1797; market book, 1786–1787; geometrical problems, surveys, 1761; Jones and Wister invoice book, 1759–1762; their account book, 1762–1769; Owen Jones, Jr., waste book for estate of Thomas Wharton, 1786–1807; his daybook, 1789–1791; Owen Jones and Company invoice book, 1789–1795; their daybook, 1793–1796; letter book of Jones and Foulke, 1783–1845; their daybook, 1796–1819; their order book, 1789–1802; Jones and Wister letter book, 1759–1771; Jonathan Jones receipt book, 1796–1803.

There is also Mary Powel Potts commonplace book (poetry), 1782; her cypher book, 1782; Robert Wharton receipt book, containing city, poor, and county tax receipts, 1800–1808; Robert Lettes Hooper journal and field book of surveys in Franklin Township, Albany County, 1770; Owen Jones correspondence with congressman during the Civil War, giving an account of his military service and also a report of the skirmishes of the regiment of the First Pennsylvania Volunteer Cavalry, 1861–1863.

330

Jones, Thomas.   Piece book, 1850.   (1 v.)

A collection of verse.
Gift of R.P. Schick, 1929.

331

Jones and Clarke papers, 1784–1816.   (ca. 500 items.)

Letters, accounts, and other business records on the commercial enterprises of William Jones and Samuel Clarke of Philadelphia and Charleston, South Carolina, who were engaged in trade with the West Indies and European countries, shipping sugar, coffee, turpentine, brandy, and other commodities. The papers contain information on British and French spoliation, embargoes, privateering, shipbuilding, finance, insurance, commodity prices. The correspondence includes letters, 1808–1812, of Nathaniel Macon, member of Congress from North Carolina, concerning congressional debates on the question of war with England in 1812; also letters of Commodore Thomas Truxtun, Captain Hugh G. Campbell, Thomas Willing, Joshua Humphreys, John Binns.

332
Jordan, Edward.   Engravings, 1830.   (1 v.)

Transferred to the Graphics Department.

333
Journal of a voyage from England, 1742.   (1 v.)

An anonymous record of life on board a sailing vessel: daily activities, books read, and passengers.

334
**Keim, De B. Randolph (De Benneville Randolph), 1841–1914.
Papers, 1808–1912.   (ca. 300 items.)**

Genealogical notes of the Keim family, 1808–1912; scrapbook 1885–1893, contains correspondence on *The Tariff Record*, which Keim edited.

335
**Keith, Charles Penrose, 1854–1939.   Papers, ca. 1699–1866.
(ca. 115 items.)**

Papers of the commercial enterprises, land transactions, administrative affairs in which members of the Keith family were concerned.

Among the items: letter of William Penn to Augustine Herrman; letter of John Penn, 1799; John Pringle accounts, 1782; deeds, leases, surveys, land claims, wills, 1740–1852; genealogical notes, 1846–1932.

Gift of Charles P. Keith estate.

336
Kelpius, Johannes, 1663–1708.   Hymns, ca. 1707–1772.   (1 v.)

Hymns with German text, by Johannes Kelpius known as the hermit of the Wissahickon; included are hymns by Johann Gotfried Seelig, Bernhard Kasten, and others.

Gift of Samuel Pennypacker, 1900.

337
**Bundock, Mary.   The Testimony of Mary Bundock concerning
Elizabeth Kendall, 1722–1765.   (1 v.)**

A tribute to the memory of Elizabeth Kendall, an ardent member of the Society of Friends.

Gift of Dr. A.S.W. Rosenbach, 1934.

338
Kennedy, Anthony.   Papers, 1781–1827.   (ca. 150 items.)

Anthony Kennedy was a Philadelphia merchant.

Correspondence with clients; records of land sales; bonds, receipts, agreements, tax bills, tax receipts; stock in turnpike road company; land warrants, drafts, surveys, claims.

339
Kenny, James.   Journal to the Westward, 1758–1761.   (1 v.)

Journal of a Quaker trader describes his tours to the Ohio, Pittsburgh, Carlisle, and other places, where he carried provisions for the Indians at the behest of commissioners for Indian affairs; presents details of pioneer life, colonial warfare, trade in skins, liquor, lead, and other commodities, travel through the wilderness, military protection. George Croghan, Israel Pemberton, Samuel Lightfoot, and George Allen figure in this narrative.

Published in the *Pennsylvania Magazine of History and Biography*, 1913, p. 1–47, 152–201, 395–449.

340
Kensington register, ca. 1812.   (1 v.)

Copies of deeds, surveys, road records, list of property holders, and other items pertaining to Kensington (Philadelphia)

Purchased, Library Fund.

341
Keyser-Goverts families.   Genealogies.   (1 v.)

Transferred to the Genealogical Society of Pennsylvania.

342
Kinnersley, Ebenezer, 1711–1778.   A course of experiments on the newly discovered electrical fire, 1752.   (1 v.)

Ebenezer Kinnersley was a schoolmaster in Philadelphia.

Philosophical treatise describing the properties of electricity and experiments performed with it.

Gift of Edward Shippen descendants.

343
Kirk family.   Genealogy, n.d.   (1 v.)

Transferred to the Genealogical Society of Pennsylvania.

344
Klapp, Joseph.   Legal papers, 1800–1826.   (12 items.)

Dr. Joseph Klapp was a prominent Philadelphia physician in the 19th century.
Collection of legal papers concerning the purchase of a house by Dr. Joseph Klapp.
Gift of Langdon William, 1924.

345
Kneass, Joseph A.   Scrapbook, 1863–1891.   (1 v.)

Newspaper clippings, letters, and miscellaneous papers chiefly on the life of Joseph Allison, president judge of the Court of Common Pleas, Philadelphia.
Gift of Joseph A. Kneass, 1927.

346
De Krafft, Charles.   Surveys and plans, ca. 1791–1816.   (1 v.)

Colored plats and surveys of tracts of land in Philadelphia and other parts of Pennsylvania, made by Charles de Krafft, surveyor and draftsman. They show names of owners, boundary lines, drawings of houses, sizes of properties.

347
Krewson, George.   Collection, 1770–1878.   (ca. 500 items.)

Legal and business papers from the estates of Samuel West, 1871; Anna West, 1858; Anthony Kennedy, 1828; Jennet Risk, 1831; letters of Abraham Kintzing, 1831–1833; and Tench C. Kintzing, 1832–1836; and estate papers of Edward Shippen Burd, 1800–1857.
Gift of George Krewson.

348
Kunze, M.   Sermons, 1774–1776.   (1 v.)

M. Kunze was pastor of the Lutheran Zion Church, Philadelphia.

349
Lamberton, James Findley Peffer.   Collection, 1734–1786.
(200 items.)

Letters and documents of Scots-Irish settlements, Cumberland County. The papers give the names of the early settlers, extent of their lands, and include legal papers and memoranda which describe the conditions of frontier life.

350
Lancaster, Albert Edmund.   The Song of the Sangamon, ca. 1890.
(1 item.)

A poem by Albert E. Lancaster, dedicated to the memory of Abraham Lincoln.

Gift of Emily Lancaster, 1916.

351
Lancaster County (Pa.) docket book, 1743–1749.   (1 v.)

Docket book for a Lancaster County, justice of the peace.

352
Lancaster County (Pa.) papers, 1724–1816.   (500 items.)

The collection is contained in two volumes: "Miscellaneous papers," 1724–1772, and "Petitions for Lebanon," 1772–1816.

Miscellaneous papers on local government and economic affairs of Lancaster County: letters, 1733–1740, of Samuel Blunston to the proprietors deal with the disputes between the Maryland and Pennsylvania authorities, land transactions, Indians on the Susquehanna, politics, legal matters, etc; letters of Thomas Cookson, George Craig, William Parsons, Richard Peters, George Smith, and others, 1739–1764; material on Conrad Weiser, 1756; accounts of Indian massacres, 1755; petitions, court records, surveys, indentures, land warrants, tax returns; petitions and lists of names of tavern keepers, 1766, 1769; account of the plan of the town of York, 1749; list of books added to the Lancaster library, ca. 1770; list of subscribers for the relief of inhabitants of Boston, Mass., 1774; military accounts and muster rolls, 1776; wills, estate papers, broadsides, and other items.

Purchased.

353
Langdon, John, 1741–1819.   Papers, 1659–1824.   (ca. 600 items.)

The papers of John Langdon include: correspondence, documents, and commercial accounts. Most of the letters pertain to the Revolution, 1777–1778. Also included are: his messages as governor of New Hampshire, and related documents, 1659–1824.

Gift of Alfred E. Elwyn.

354
Languis, Joachim.   *The Medicine of the minds* ... (1 v.)

"Written by Joachim Langius, Minister of the ye word of God at Berlin, and the discovery and rejecting of learned folly, according to the principles of true philosophy, then treats the healing of sick minds, and of its use when healed, for the searching out and communicating of truth and right. Published for the sake of all such who by the help of solid learning seek after truth wisdom." A religious tract on human behavior and ethics.

The Latin original was published in three editions: Berlin, 1704 and 1708, and London, 1715.

355
Larchfield, E.H. Warder.   **Diary, 1832.**   (1 v.)

Journal of daily events in the life of Miss E.H. Warder Larchfield, Philadelphia.

Gift of Mrs. Trevanion Dallas.

356
Laurens, Henry, 1724–1792.   **Correspondence, 1762–1780.**
(ca. 1,500 items.)

Correspondence of Henry Laurens reflects American political opinion before and during the Revolution. It contains information on the proceedings of the Continental Congress, Indian treaties, and financing the Revolution, 1774–1780.

357
Laurens, John, 1754–1782.   **Commonplace book, 1779.**   (1 v.)

Commonplace book of John Laurens includes his observations on military activities in the American Revolution and on the importance of defending the Carolinas from the British; also his account of the aid rendered by the French fleet in the Chesapeake and Delaware bays, under command of Comte de Grasse and Comte d'Estaing, preventing the arrival of British reinforcements and retarding British operations.

Gift of Simon Gratz, 1881.

358
Leach, May Atherton.   **Correspondence, 1928–1930.**
(ca. 50 items.)

Correspondence on the effort of the Historical Society of Pennsylvania to trace the ownership of "the blue sash worn by William Penn on the occasion of his Treaty with the Indians," which M. Fassitt donated to the Historical Society in 1919.

Gift of May Atherton Leach, 1933.

359
Leaming, Aaron, 1715–1780.   Diaries, 1750–1777.   (4 v.)

The economic development of Cape May, N.J. and adjacent territory is shown in these diaries of Aaron Leaming, 1750–1751, 1761, 1775, 1776. They furnish an account of land transactions, surveys, early settlers, military organizations, farming, trade in timber and other commodities, acts of New Jersey assemblies, legal and domestic affairs; also contain lists of books in which Leaming was interested.

Gift of J. Granville Leach.

360
Lee, Charles, 1758–1815.   Remarks by Mr. Lee, Attorney General of the United States on the principles and reasoning contained in the notes which Mr. MacDonald has laid before the board of examination, 1798.   (1 v.)

Charles Lee's remarks relate to the interpretation of articles in the treaty of peace between Great Britain and the United States, 1794, concerning the value and recovery of debts.

361
Lee, George, Sir, 1700–1758.   Manuscripts, 1656–1753.
(ca. 1,000 items.)

Collection of opinions and interpretations of maritime laws, gathered from the writings of George Lee, British jurist, about the commercial rights of neutrals, seizure of vessels, confiscation of merchandise, prizes captured by privateers, etc; depicts hazards of shipping and commerce during the period.

362
Lehman, Christian.   Collection, 1742–1799.   (200 items.)

These papers consist chiefly of surveys, drafts, and plats of land situated in colonial Germantown and Roxborough. They show the names of landowners, their holdings, changes in titles; included are German manuscripts on astrology and bee culture, and items on Pennsylvania German political and economic interests.

Gift of the Lehman estate.

363
Leland, Charles Godfrey, 1824–1903.   Papers, 1835–1906.
(9 linear ft.)

The published and unpublished manuscripts of Charles G. Leland, prominent literary figure. Among the items are: essays, poetry, academic studies at Princeton, 1841–45; travel diaries, 1845, 1847, 1856.

Leland's interest in art education is shown in his manuscripts: "How to establish schools, classes or circles in the minor arts;" "Nature and Art Culture;" "Compendium of the Minor Arts;" "Eye Memory;" "Manual of Design;" "Profitable Work, Leather Work, Wood Carving;" "Relief Painting or Gesso, Plaster of Paris;" "One Hundred Profitable arts, drawings, designs, sketches;" and others.

Among his illustrated literary works are: proof sheets of *Meister Karl Sketch Book; Hans Breitman Ballads;* the manuscripts of "Mottoes for Every Occasion," "Travels in Shadow Land," "Witch Ballads," "The Witchcraft of Dame Darrel of York," "The Dead Alive," "Dreams," "The Goths' Mother Goose," "German Nursery Rhymes," "Children Stories and Fables," "Proverbs," "Rules of Etiquette for Men About Town," "Slaves and Contrabands," "Flaxius on Politics," "Legends of Birds," "Those Six Cabbages," "Sea Foam Fairies," "Milton and Dante," "Martin Luther," "Wayside Wanderers and Vagabonds," "Roman Lays and Legends;" epigrams, essays, poetry, narratives in German, French, and Italian; drawings and sketches from life of characters in Italy, Germany, France, and other countries; designs for book covers; playbills, ca. 1853–67; newspaper clippings; curiosa and mementoes.

A large portion of the collection is composed of Leland's correspondence with eminent persons of the period, and with his publishers: Ticknor and Fields, Sheldon and Company, R. Shelton Mackenzie, 1861; Henry W. Longfellow, 1855; Madame Anita de Barrera, 1858; and others.

Gift of Henry Morris Harrison and John Harrison, Jr.

364
Levy, Edgar M., 1822–1906.   *Memoirs of Captain John Patterson Levy (with family sketches).*   (1 v.)

John Patterson Levy was a Philadelphia shipbuilder and prominent Baptist.

Copy. Original owned by William Tumbleston.

365
Lewis, Ellis, 1798–1871.   Papers, 1810–1870.   (ca. 100 items.)

Correspondence of Ellis Lewis including letters from James Buchanan, 1841–1865; Chief Justice Roger B. Taney, 1845–1860; and Chancellor James

Kent, 1846–1847. There are family papers, 1815–1851, miscellaneous documents, and newspaper clippings.

366
Lewis, Emma.   Verses, 1853–1854.   (1 v.)

A collection of lyric and religious verse.
Gift of Dr. C.H. Vinton, 1918.

367
Lewis, Howard W., Mrs.   Collection, 1799–1866.   (36 linear ft.)

This collection is composed chiefly of business papers of early nineteenth century Philadelphia auctioneers: Weir and Fisher, 1799–1809; Silas E. Weir, 1809–1819; Lisle, Weir and Company, 1819–1821; Willing, Weir and Co., 1822–1823; Weir, Smith and Lewis, 1823–1826; Weir, Lewis and Company, 1827–1830; John E. Lewis, 1811–1866. Records of trade in silks, tea, rum, tobacco, cloth, linen, glass, for disposal at auction, with details on commercial enterprises, markets, prices, variety of goods traded, supply and demand, legal requirements.

Included are: auction accounts, 1799–1830; correspondence, 1807–1828; imported bonds, 1825–1828; notes and drafts, 1809–1839; bank checks, 1808–1818; account books, bank books, blotters, ledgers, cashbooks, receipts, 1802-1866; John F. Lewis papers, 1825–1866, on his personal and family affairs, bills, receipts, accounts; papers on Scots Presbyterian Church, St. John English Evangelical Lutheran Church, Association of Reformed Churches, 1808; papers on the Society for the Relief Association of the Poor, 1817; estate of Elizabeth Steele papers, 1801–1827; and maps of railways.
Gift of Mrs. Howard W. Lewis, 1939.

368
Lewis, John Frederick.   Papers, 1771–1931.   (1,000 items.)

A collection of pamphlets, photostats of early historical records, portraits, manuscripts, and typewritten material used in John Frederick Lewis' writing, *The History of an Old Philadelphia Land Title,* 208 S. 4th Street. Among the items are autograph letters, 1771–1796, of men prominent in Philadelphia affairs, genealogical notes on Daniel W. Coxe, John Beylard, John Bradford Wallace, and others, with information on Pennsylvania history. Other items are: Joseph H. Skelton correspondence, 1814–1817, about Somerset, N.J.; notes about the art of illuminating and illustrating; and papers about personal and civic affairs.
Gift of Anna H. R. Baker Lewis.

369
Lewis, William A.   Papers, 1760–1847.   (10 items.)

Family papers, legal documents about land in Chester County.

370
Pennsylvania.   Licenses for marriages, taverns, and peddlers, 1761–1776.   (2 v.)

Records of financial accounts of the Province of Pennsylvania, including records of money received for marriage, tavern, and peddler licenses issued in various counties, 1763–1774; lists of names of persons married, 1763–1775; letters of marque issued, 1762–1775, with names of vessels and their masters; notary public records for funds received for warrants, 1767–1776; forfeitures, 1767–1775; names of licensed tavern keepers and their locations, 1769–1776; pardons and reprieves granted, 1772–1774; expense accounts relating to Indian affairs at Fort Pitt, 1774–1775.

371
Lightfoot family.   Papers, 1733–1816.   (9 linear ft.)

Land warrants issued by provincial governors of Pennsylvania to settlers in various counties, surveys and field books, and a few miscellaneous items, the papers of a family of surveyors: survey of the boundary between Pennsylvania and Maryland, by Samuel Lightfoot, 1735–1787; manuscript notes of a survey of a line from Pottsville to Shamokin, by Benjamin Lightfoot, 1759; warrants of land and surveys, Lancaster, Chester, Berks, Philadelphia, and other counties, 1733–1775; field book, 1734–1812, and receipt book of Benjamin Lightfoot, 1751; field book of Samuel Lightfoot, 1738–1771; field books of Thomas Lightfoot, 1784–1785, 1794–1816; field book of Edward Scull, 1753–1755; field books of Mordecai Yarnall, 1749–1776, 1765–1768; field book of Henry Vanderslice, 1771–1794; field book of Andrew Lytle, 1747–1788; field book of Benjamin Parvin, 1759–1764.
    Gift of Thomas M. Lightfoot.

372
Lightfoot, Benjamin, 1726–1777.   Journals and surveys, 1770–1772. (1 v.)

Journals of a tour of Benjamin Lightfoot from Reading. to Tankhannink Creek, and of surveys of a large tract of land there containing pine timber suitable for masts; topography of the country, Indian relations, frontier life, military posts, means of travel, and adventures of the trip are described.

Photostatic copies.
Gift of Thomas M. Lightfoot, 1936.

373
Lindstrom, Peter.   Journal, 1691.   (1 v.)

Peter Lindstrom's journal account of New Sweden on the Delaware, topography of the territory, society and economic development in the settlements, war with the Dutch; contains a contemporary map of New Sweden.

374
Lippincott and Company.   Collection, 1787–1913.   (702 v.)

Lippincott and Company was a Philadelphia firm engaged in international trade in sugar, groceries, and other commodities.

Ledgers, 1797–1903; journals, 1797–1898; daybooks, 1797–1900; blotters, 1804–1865; purchase books, 1828–1910; merchandise books, 1826–1913; cashbooks, 1831–1900; sales books, 1818–1900; receipt books, 1837–1903; invoice books, 1816–1901; order books, 1834–1899; bank deposit books, 1866–1898; letterbooks, 1841–1899; letters, 1856–1898; and other items.

Gift of Lippincott and Company, 1933.

375
Lloyd, David, 1656–1731.   Manuscript, 1683.   (1 v.)

David Lloyd was attorney general, 1686 and chief justice of Pennsylvania, 1717–1731.

A manuscript volume of British statutes; formerly in the possession of David Lloyd.

Gift of William M. Tilghman, 1895.

376
Lloyd, Howard W.   Genealogical records, n.d.   (1 v.)

Transferred to the Genealogical Society of Pennsylvania.

377
Lloyd, Peter Zachary.   Journal of first session of the House of Representatives of Pennsylvania, 1790–1791.   (1 v.)

Extracts from the journal by Peter Zachary Lloyd.
Handwritten transcript of printed copy.

378

Logan family.   Business papers, 1808–1836.   (23 v.)

These records comprise: George Logan's Stenton farm diary, 1809–1813; Albanus C. Logan cashbooks, 1808–1811, 1811–1814; his Sommerville farm cashbooks, 1809–1815, 1812–1813, 1820–1821, 1824–1825, 1831–1836; Charles F. Logan's Stenton mill daybooks, 1816–1823; his ledger, 1818; his letterbook, 1818–1819; the Loganville mill journals, 1819–1822, 1822–1824; and the Loganville mill daybook, 1822–1824; the book of accounts of the team hauling, 1820–1823; Charles F. Logan's sawmill journal, 1820–1823; his cashbook, 1822–1823; his daybook, 1823–1825; his journal, 1823–1825; and a copy of John Moland's analysis of the law.

Purchased, Dreer Fund.

379

Logan family.   Papers, 1664–1871.   (30 linear ft.)

A large section of this collection comprises the papers of James Logan, scholar, secretary to William Penn, clerk of the Provincial Council, commissioner of property and receiver general for the province. These papers include: correspondence, among which are letters from William Penn, and some of Logan's scholarly, scientific, and biographical papers, 1681–1753; letterbooks, 1701–1709, 1702–1726, 1712–1715, 1716–1743, 1720–1731, 1748–1750; correspondence, copied by Deborah Logan, 1700–1747; letters on political and business affairs, 1698–1769; documents relating to Indian affairs, 1701–1802; archives of the Provincial Council, 1694–1755; James Logan's "Justification" before the assembly, 1709; his receipt book, 1702–1709; account book, 1712–1720; ledger, 1720–1727; and daybook, 1722–1723.

The large body of official papers in this collection includes: records of the court held at Upland, under Edmund Andros, 1676–1681; extracts from the record book of the county court at Upland, 1676–1681; early Pennsylvania laws, 1693–1699; New Castle court records, 1677–1682; appeals, petitions, and grievances presented to the provincial council, 1700–1713; accounts of the quitrents collected by Governor John Blackwell, 1689, listing the names of the first settlers of Philadelphia; quitrents for the three lower counties, 1701–1713; the receipt book for quitrents of Lynford Lardner, receiver-general, 1739, 1743–1750; and Penticost Teague's receipt book, 1700–1717.

Among the Logan family papers are: William Logan's journal of a trip to Georgia, 1745; correspondence of Dr. George Logan, 1784–1820; his letter book and journal of a trip to England while he was a student at the University of Edinburgh, 1775–1779; notes from Dr. Hunter's lectures on the physiology of the alimentary tube (Dr. James Hutchinson to Logan), 1775; letters and printed pamphlets on the political activities of Dr. George Logan, and to his foreign missions, 1809–1822; correspondence of Mrs. Deborah Logan, with a few miscellaneous additions, 1730–1836; an anatomy chart, some literary and biographical sketches by Deborah Logan, 1815–1827; her transactions on the farm and memoranda on various matters, 1813–1827.

The Logan Collection includes many of the papers of John Dickinson and Dickinson family papers, 1697–1843. They include: documents expressing John Dickinson's opinion on educational, religious, and political matters; correspondence, 1764–1807; notes of arguments on Pennsylvania laws, 1760; notes on the question of the abolition of slavery; on religious, philosophical and administrative matters; on domestic and personal affairs, 1777–1803; Dickinson's Bible, 1740, with marginal notes; papers from the Dickinson estate, 1664–1806; papers on Dickinson's manor and other tracts of land; Poplar Ridge (Stephen Pleasonton) papers, 1677–1805; Kingston-on-Hull (Hunn and Asa Manlove) and Town Point (Caleb Luff and John Wethered) papers, 1671–1803; Dickinson's records pertaining to Rixom, 1747–1807, Canterbury, Rejected Valley, Wyeberry, Wyefield, 1714–1802; account of repairs at Fairhill House Chestnut St., Philadelphia, 1771–1776; records of his land and house in Wilmington, Delaware, 1754–1800, containing an account of material and labor, including records of land in the Brandywine Hundred, 1664–1797, and of a house in Jones Neck (Gideon Emery, Thomas White), 1791–1806; Dickinson's miscellaneous papers, 1750–1847, relate to land and include demand notes, indentures, and other business records; papers on land in Merion, 1710–1818; and Jonathan Dickinson's ledger, 1699–1701.

Also included are Henry W. Stiegel papers, Elizabeth Furnace in Elizabeth Township, Lancaster County, 1766–1775; papers belonging to the estate of Thomas Wilson, 1763–1776; John Moland's family, 1745–1785; and William Hicks, 1763–1792.

Other volumes in the Logan collection are the estate of Richard Hill, 1708–1758; the estate of Richard Hill Accounts, 1729–1742; papers of Thomas Griffiths estate, 1719–1788; of Richard Harrison's estate, 1744–1775; of Dr. Lloyd Zachary's estate, 1730–1774; Thomas Fisher's ledger of the estate of William Logan, 1772–1783; Thomas Fisher's letterbook, 1793–1808; inventory of goods, copies of William Logan Will, 1772–1781; miscellaneous papers relating to the Norris estate, 1700–1797; including the Shardlow-Sweetapple (Wood-Ellis) papers, 1682–1775; papers relating to land of Duck Creek, 1683–1767; Beasley's land papers, 1725–1772; Friends meeting accounts, 1707–1743; a letterbook of Isaac Norris, 1735–1755; James Steel letterbooks, 1715–1732, 1730–1741, with some James Logan letters in them; some Logan Parchments, 1734–1770; Norris Parchments, 1682–1764; Dickinson parchments, 1679–1803.

A part of the Logan Collection contains a smaller collection called the Logan-Dickinson-Norris Collection, 1675–1876, comprising contracts, testimonies, agreements, which are mainly John Dickinson's legal notes for law cases, 1675–1876; surveys, 1722–1850; accounts, list of prices of commodities, salaries, labor costs, 1729–1861, mainly Logan family accounts; deeds, bonds, leases, 1675–1839; wills, marriage certificates, 1726–1854; papers pertaining to administration of estates, 1730–1860; and "Charles Thompson's opinion of J. Dickinson and the Declaration of Independence," copied from the original by D. Logan, recopied by Sarah Miller Walker, 1845. This collection also has some miscellaneous correspondence, mostly by the Logan family, 1725–1871.

Barbara Jones's master thesis on Deborah Logan, 1964.

Gift of the Logan family, 1840.

Logan-Dickinson-Norris papers purchased, Gratz Fund, 1932.

380
Logan, Deborah Norris, 1761–1839.   Diaries, 1815–1839.   (17 v.)

The diaries of Deborah Norris Logan, wife of George Logan, eminent Philadelphian, friend of Thomas Jefferson, reflect the social life of many prominent Philadelphia families, and political, religious, and cultural developments. Because of Mrs. Logan's association with many of the prominent men of the Revolutionary and early national periods, her biographical notes on John Adams, Samuel Adams, Joseph Bonaparte, Pierce Butler, John C. Calhoun, John Dickinson, Benjamin Franklin, Stephen Girard, John Hancock, Stephen Hopkins, Thomas Jefferson, Henry Laurens, Joseph Reed, Roger Sherman, Francis Lightfoot Lee, John Randolph, Edward Rutledge, Timothy Pickering, John Penn, Thomas Penn, Richard Peters, Charles Thomson, General James Wilkinson, George Washington, are particularly interesting. Other topics include the Declaration of Independence, Revolutionary War, cholera and yellow fever epidemics, slavery, European conditions, Napoleonic Wars, national and local events, travel and transportation facilities, natural phenomena and weather conditions, Friends meetings, and literature.

Index available.

Gift of Maria Dickinson Logan, 1934.

381
Logan, James, 1674–1751.   A letter . . . , 1741 Sept. 22.   (1 v.)

Copies of James Logan's letter to the Society of Friends commenting on their opposition in the legislature to all measures for the defense of the colony as well as extracts from other letters on related subjects, petitions, and grand jury charges.

Handwritten transcript.

Published in *The Collections of the Historical Society*, 1853, p. 36–41.

382
Logan, Maria Dickinson, 1857–1939.   Collection, 1671–1890.
(3 linear ft.)

These miscellaneous papers include the letterbook of Jonathan Dickinson, 1698–1701; letterbook of James Logan, 1731–1732, 1741–1742; letters of Mary Norris, 1786–1799; biographical sketch of Dr. George Logan, 1821; a leather-bound manuscript, "Observations in a Voyage of the Low Countries," 1671; and letters and pamphlets on religion, politics, and society in Pennsylvania, 1705–1890, by people prominent in the history of Pennsylvania, including Benjamin Franklin, Thomas Jefferson, John Dickinson, Hannah Griffitts, John Hancock, Thomas Rodney, Caesar Rodney, Archibald Hamilton Rowan, Conrad Weiser.

This collection also contains letters from people in England, including Hannah and William Penn and John Fothergill. There are letters by the botanists John Bartram and John Blackburne. Most of this collection is letters by the Logan family and their relatives, the Fishers and Norrises, including a letter from Benjamin Franklin to James Logan, 1748.

Gift of Maria Dickinson Logan, 1934.

383
Logan, Robert Restalrig.   Collection, 1671–1863.   (6 linear ft.)

Correspondence, documents, business records, essays, notes, and newspaper clippings of John Dickinson, lawyer and statesman. The collection consists almost entirely of papers collected by Dickinson on his political and business activities, but there is a large quantity of miscellaneous papers by other people, mainly from the Logan family. Although the correspondence deals predominantly with Dickinson's activities in the public, governmental sphere, a significant portion concerns his private affairs, especially land and business activities. Correspondents include various statesmen and Revolutionary leaders among whom are Samuel Chase, Dickinson's brother Philemon Dickinson, poet and political satirist Hannah Griffitts, Arthur Lee, Richard Henry Lee, Charles Lee, George Read, Caesar Rodney, Thomas Rodney, army surgeon James Tilton, and the first president of Congress Thomas McKean. There are one or two letters each from Samuel Adams, Josiah Quincy, Robert Morris, George Washington, Joshua Clayton, James

Madison and Caesar Wilson. Later letters include those of Archibald Hamilton Rowan and Tench Coxe.

Documents from the Revolutionary War period, 1776–1783, relate chiefly to Dickinson's service as an officer in the Pennsylvania militia. They include furlough recommendations, hospital reports, notes on military movements, militia returns, and information on soldiers' provisions including ammunition. Government documents extend from the early Revolutionary period and Dickinson's involvement in the Stamp Act Congress to his participation in the 1787 Constitutional Convention. Included are an original draft of Resolutions from the Stamp Act Congress, two Olive Branch Petitions, a copy of the Speech of the Earl of Chatham in the House of Lords 1775, drafts of the Articles of Confederation, the original manuscripts of the "Letters of Fabius" written in support of the Constitution by Dickinson. There are Dickinson's notes on the first Continental Congress, papers on early national land policies, foreign policy, taxation proposals, and military regulations. Also included are peace negotiation notes and drafts with Great Britain and "Urgent advise to Inhabitants of Quebec" signed by John Hancock.

Pennsylvania government documents, 1764–1784, include financial accounts, drafts of Dickinson's speeches prepared while he was president of the Supreme Executive Council of Pennsylvania, bills, court-martial records, materials on the Wyoming controversy, and miscellaneous Dickinson notes on government affairs.

Dickinson was President of the Delaware Supreme Council 1781–1782. Delaware government documents, 1772–1789, include papers on the Delaware River land dispute, 1772, militia returns, 1782, budget figures and various bill drafts and notes.

The collection includes Dickinson's land and business records, 1760–1808. Leases, agreements, memoranda, bills, receipts, center on the management of his real estate holdings, primarily in Delaware: house construction, relations with tenants, property sales, production figures. There is material relating to Dickinson's law practice which include information on cases argued before the High Court of Errors in Pennsylvania. Drafts of Dickinson's will, with codicils, are also present.

Miscellaneous notes and essays include the *Pennsylvania Pocket Almanack* with marginal notes, 1774, *Poor Will's Almanack* with marginal notes, 1776, the Manumission of John Dickinson's slaves, 1777, and Drafts for Dickinson's "Essay Towards the Religious Instruction of Youth."

Miscellaneous correspondence includes Jonathan Dickinson, Philemon Dickinson, Samuel Dickinson, Hannah Griffitts, Albanus C. Logan, Algernon S. Logan, Deborah Logan, George Logan, James Logan, James Logan, Jr., John Dickinson Logan, Maria Dickinson Logan, Isaac Norris, Isaac Norris, Jr., Isaac Norris, III, Mary Parker Norris, and George Read.

Gift of Robert Restalrig Logan, 1928.
Finding aid available.

384
Long, William Summer.   Genealogy, n.d.   (1 v.)

Transferred to the Genealogical Society of Pennsylvania.

385
L'Orrange, Louis.   Receipt book, 1797–1815.   (1 v.)

Receipt book of Louis L'Orrange of Philadelphia, containing records of payments made by him for the purchase of commodities, rent, business transactions.
Gift of John Campbell, 1898.

386
Lukens family.   Papers, 1759–1808.   (3 v.)

A collection of genealogical data of the Jan Luckens family, which, emigrated from Crefeld, Germany, to Philadelphia in 1684, compiled by Cyrus Lukens in 1906; another volume contains records of the Lukens-Ambler-Wilson families. Included in this collection is a group of papers and letters, 1759–1808, addressed to Richard Wistar, mainly Quakeriana, and domestic and business matters.
These papers were discovered in the secret drawer of a chest belonging to William Lukens.
Gift of Ms. L.D. Ellis, 1916 and Joseph Borton estate, 1929.

387
Luzerne County (Pa.) papers, 1620–1823.   (8 items.)

Miscellaneous items on the first settlements of Luzerne and adjacent counties, the disputes arising among New York, Connecticut, and Pennsylvania; charters granted; Indian traders; Moravian missionaries; Count Zinzendorf's travels, 1742; Indian chiefs; formation of the counties; other items, 1793–1823, on land claims, road building, and local affairs.
Purchased.

388
Lyman, Benjamin Smith, 1835–1920.   Papers, 1851–1918.
(ca. 1,500 items.)

Correspondence of Benjamin Smith Lyman, Pennsylvania geologist and mining engineer, on natural science, geology, and literature; letters from

Japan on Oriental culture; letters from Franklin Sanborn, notes on vegetarianism.

389
Lynch, Edward.   **Memorandum book, 1795–1797.**   (1 v.)

Memorandum book of Edward Lynch, of the firm of Lynch and Kennedy, Philadelphia merchants. The entries record financial transactions and imports of cotton and silk cloth; and include: a sketch of a phenomenon observed in the heavens, July 25, 1796; a notice that President Washington will vacate his house on Market Street, Philadelphia, in March 1797; abstract of the Stamp Act passed in Philadelphia in extraordinary session of Congress, 1797.
Gift of William John Potts, 1885.

390
MacEuen, Malcolm.   *A legend of sad loveliness,* **1869.**   (1 v.)

A translation into English of M. André Chenier's poem, *La Jeune Captive.*
Dedicated to Thomas MacEuen in 1869.
Gift of Mrs. Thomas H. Neilson, 1923.

391
MacPherson, William, ca. 1756–1813.   **Papers, 1784–1865.**
(ca. 1,000 items.)

Military papers and letters of General William MacPherson, 1784–1827, most of which are on the enforcement of the revenue laws in Pennsylvania, 1799; a list of officers' names, and other papers on "MacPherson's Blues," 1794–1798; the minutes of a meeting of the Society of the Cincinnati, 1802; some of the papers and correspondence of Joseph Wallace, treasurer of Harrisburg Bridge Company; inventories and vendue lists, 1815–1851; correspondence and other papers on the state arsenal at Harrisburg, 1836–1839; some personal correspondence and business papers of Joseph Wallace, 1788–1865; correspondence rising out of the Antimasonic agitation and efforts to form a new political party, 1831–1851.
Gift of William MacPherson Horner, 1916.

392
Madison, James, 1751–1836.   **Papers, 1794 (1801–1836).**   (2 v.)

"Report of a speech delivered in the United States House of Representatives on Jay's Treaty by James Madison," ca. 1794, his observations on the treaty making powers of the Congress. Letters, drafts of letters, 1801–1836, relate chiefly to Madison's personal and cultural interests: the establishment of a central seminary of jurisprudence, his literary criticism, opinion on the introduction of vine culture in the United States, and other subjects.

393
Magee, James, 1802–1878.   Papers, 1832–1852.   (ca. 150 items.)

Papers of James Magee chiefly on commerce and shipping. Included are the account book of Magee's ship *Commerce*, 1845; ledger book, 1832; prices current at New Orleans; and other personal and business items.
Gift of Anna J. Magee.

394
Man, William.   Music book, 1829.   (1 v.)

A collection of William Man's manuscript music for the pianoforte.
Gift of John W. Jordan, 1889.

395
Marshall, Christopher, 1709–1797.   Papers, 1773–1793.   (9 v.)

Diaries of Christopher Marshall, Philadelphia druggist, with details of events during the Revolution; also information on pharmacy. There are diaries and notes, 1774–1793; letter book, 1773–1778; and accounts with the Continental Congress, 1776.
Gift of Charles Marshall, 1903.

396
Marshall, Samuel R.   Scrapbook and correspondence, 1876–1882.
(1 v.)

Correspondence, newspaper clippings, programs, invitations, and miscellaneous mementoes relate to civic and political affairs in Philadelphia in which Samuel R. Marshall participated as a political leader in the Democratic party.

397
Martin, John Hill, 1823–1906.   Papers, 1856–1878.   (3 v.)

Journal of John Hill Martin, a prominent member of the Philadelphia bar, ca. 1856, with notes on the ancestry of his family, who settled in Pennsylvania in 1681, and on events of his lifetime, military training at West Point, 1838–1841, his resignation from the army, 1841, preparation for the bar, interest in social and cultural affairs, plays, opera, and literature. The narrative embraces also some data on national and local events such as the Mexican War, Civil War, and riots in Philadelphia between the Native American Party and the Catholic Irish. List of officials, 1878, contains the names of members of state administrations and heads of state government departments, compiled by Martin; mementoes of the Civil War, 1861–1865, cartoons, pictures, and epigrams ridiculing the leaders of the South.

Gift of John Hill Martin and Mrs. Edward S. Sayres, 1923.

398
Mason and Dixon Line papers, 1701–1768. (5 v.)

These papers include the original warrant of William Penn to Isaac Taylor and Thomas Pierson to survey the line between Chester County and New Castle County, Del., 1701–1705; diary of John Watson, assistant surveyor to the Commissioners of the Province of Pennsylvania, on the determination of the 12-mile circle at New Castle and running the east-west boundary lines from Cape Henlopen, Del., 1750–1751; and the original manuscripts of the Mason and Dixon surveys, including the one that established the boundary line between Pennsylvania and Maryland, 1763–1768.

399
Mason, Samuel.   Diary, 1827–1835. (1 v.)

Diary of Samuel Mason on his farming and domestic interests. The pages are interleaved in *Farmer's Almanac*, 1823–1831, *Agricultural Almanac*, 1827, 1829, and *Friends Almanac*, 1831–1835.

400
Massachusetts papers, 1774–1780. (ca. 1,600 items.)

Copies of letters and documents from the Archives of the State of Massachusetts, chiefly on the Revolution: resolutions, orders, appointments, adopted by the House of Representatives; details of allocation of troops, battles; accounts of the capture of Ticonderoga, the burning of Charleston; requests for medical supplies; letters of thanks from George Washington and Charles Lee; records of prisoners of war; petitions for safe conduct passes; committee of safety reports; financial records; letters from prominent generals and political leaders; correspondence, 1774–1775; resolves, 1777–1778; Board of War letters, 1777–1780; and petitions, to the General Court, 1779.

Transcripts.

401
Matlack, T. Chalkley.   **Manuscripts, 1912–1939.**   **(4 linear ft.)**

T. Chalkley Matlack was a Quaker artist and scholar interested in public education in Philadelphia.

Quakeriana include: historical sketches and pictures of Friends meeting houses in Pennsylvania, New Jersey, Delaware, Maryland, and Virginia, and the boarding homes, schools, and burial grounds associated with them; also historical notes on several Friends meeting houses.

Literary and musical manuscripts include: synopses of novels, bibliographies, biographical sketches, literary quotations, and water color sketches of maps, scenes, coats of arms, and characters in works of Sir Walter Scott, James Fenimore Cooper, and George Moritz Ebers, the Egyptian romancer; notes on the lives and works of 160 composers of music. There are: Cooper maps, 1911–1913; Cooper dictionary, 1914; Waverly maps, 1912–1923; Ebers maps, 1919; Ebers dictionary, 1919; and Aeolian records, 1916–1919, 1922.

Gift of T. Chalkley Matlack, 1921–1939.

402
McCall, Peter, 1809–1880.   **Papers, 1773–1879.**   **(500 items.)**

These papers represent a substantial part of the lecture notes of Peter McCall, professor of practice, pleading and evidence in the Law Department of the University of Pennsylvania, 1852–1860. The papers include five introductory lectures, delivered in successive years; notes on his "Course of Practice and Pleading at Law"; an almost complete set of notes on his course in "Evidence" as well as his course on the "Practice and Pleading in Equity"; eight unidentifiable lectures; a small group of miscellaneous notes; and what appears to be an 1839 docket of two moot courts. The lectures evidently followed Simon Greenleaf, *A Treatise on the Law of Evidence,* vols. I and II (Boston: 1844, 1846).

Gift of Gertrude McCall, 1926.

403
McEuen, Hale, and Davidson.   **Lands in Bradford and Tioga Counties, 1799–1830.**   **(1 v.)**

Records of land allotted to Thomas McEuen, Thomas Hale, and William Davidson by an indenture of partition, May 6, 1799; included are drafts, entries of sales of land, names of purchasers, prices, locations, and a printed copy of the original title in the names of William Buckley, William Davidson, Henry Drinker, and Thomas Paxson, Thomas M. Willing, William Waln.

Purchased, 1902.

404
MacInall, Edward.   Correspondence, 1916–1917.   (ca. 65 items.)

Letters written to Dr. Edward MacInall by leading men of the United States during the critical period of the World War and reflect the intellectual climate of America at war. Among the correspondents are: Felix Arder, William E. Borah, Charles W. Eliot, Oliver Wendell Holmes, Henry Cabot Lodge, James C. McReynolds, Janet Rankin, Theodore Roosevelt, William Howard Taft, and William B. Wilson.

Gift of Edward MacInall, 1918.

405
McKean, Thomas, 1734–1817.   Papers, 1759–1847. (ca. 650 items.)

Correspondence with prominent people of the time, on the events of the Revolution. The papers include letters from George Washington, Thomas Jefferson, John Adams, Samuel Adams, John Laurens, Caesar Rodney, and others, 1759–1847; letters to McKean's wife, 1775–1806; commissions, diplomas, and miscellaneous documents, 1777–1802; pamphlet, "Discourse of a Vacuum," 1752; book of poetry and songs; and McKean's charges to grand juries on his circuit, 1777–1779.

406
Subscription list to memorial of Morton McMichael, 1879.   (1 v.)

A list of citizen's names, subscribers to a fund for the erection of a monument to the memory of Morton McMichael, editor of *North American*.

407
McMillan, John.   Autobiography and journal, 1752–1776. (1 v.)

A copy of the autobiography and journal of the Rev. John McMillan, founder of Jefferson College, Canonsburg, with genealogical data on his family. The narrative reflects colonial life, McMillan's adventures as a young man, his travel through the province, and his studies and preachings in various Presbyterian communities.

Transcript.

408
McPherson, Robert.   Papers, 1749–1856.   (1,250 items.)

The papers of Robert McPherson, sheriff and treasurer of York County, and of several other members of the McPherson family, with information on local and state politics, legislation, taxation, commercial enterprises, land sales, law suits, and the general history of York and Adam counties.

409
McShane, Mary.   Autograph Album, 1836–1840.   (1 v.)

Autographs with prose and verse sentiments dedicated to Mary McShane by her friends.
Gift of Mrs. William C. Lawrence, 1922.

410
Meade, George Gordon, 1815–1872.   Collection, 1793–1896. (12 linear ft.)

The letters of General George Gordon Meade, to his wife, 1845–1847, relate to political issues in the Mexican War, battles and campaigns of the American military forces, accounts of the exploits of the commanding officers, and other incidents of that war. The Civil War in all its aspects, military and political, is reflected in Meade's later letters, 1861–1872, leadership, plans of campaigns, strategies of the Army of the Potomac, accounts of the battle of Gettysburg, controversies among commanding officers, and issues before the American public.

Other items are: copies of reports to Brigadier General Lorenzo Thomas, 1863; field reports on the battle of Gettysburg, 1863; list of casualties, 1863; minutes of council held at Gettysburg, July 2, 1863; official dispatches, 1864; official letters, 1835–1865, relate to Meade's assignments, duties as a topographical engineer, including his surveys in Florida, Texas, Mexican territory, and other places; letters, 1861–1868, describing his efforts to gain promotion in the army; a group of miscellaneous letters of Meade and other commanding officers addressed to Mrs. Meade; official letters to and from Mead, 1863–1881; Meade's military commissions, certificates of membership in societies, tributes, 1836–1871; official war maps of the Army of the Potomac and Southern States, 1861–1865; surveys, accounts of reconnaissances, astronomical observations, maps of Mexico, Indian territories, Texas, coastal surveys, lake surveys, 1793–1881; letters of condolence on Meade's sickness and death, 1872.

Colonel George Meade's papers include: letters on Meade and Gettysburg, 1870–1896; "Life of General Meade," 1815–1872; letters of condolence, visiting cards, newspaper clippings on the death of Colonel George Meade, 1897.

Gift of George Meade.

411
Mead, David. *Journal of the town of [blank] laid by David Mead at Cussewaga, and commenced the sale of lots . . . , 1793–1798.* (1 v.)

Record of land transaction at Cussewaga, lots sold, and names of purchasers. Includes ledger accounts of David Mead. Includes accounts of Mead's trade in beef, flour, furs, and other commodities.

Purchased, Dreer Fund, 1938 from James D. Gill.

412
"Memoire sur le commerce entre la France et les Etats Unis, 1783." (1 v.)

A treatise on economic conditions and international trade, advocating closer commercial relations between the United States and France.

Gift of Wilson King, 1880.

413
Menzies, John. *A brief narrative of the adventures of John Menzies alias John Little in the year 1793 and 4, 1831.* (1 v.)

Narrative by John Menzies of the adventures of his youth in Scotland, his experiences as a sailor, and travel to Portugal, Africa, China, and other places, 1793–1794, written in Philadelphia, 1831. The volume includes a diary of a trip from Philadelphia to Scotland; also Scottish verse.

Gift of R. Ball Dodson, 1931.

414
Merriam, Cyrus L. **Collection, 1937.** (1 v.)

Collection of autobiographical sketches of miniature paintings of members of the Macpherson and related families with photographs.

415
Merrian, Richard. **Estate ledger, 1774–1795.** (1 v.)

Accounts in the liquidation of the Richard Merrian estate: payments made, sale of certificates, and other transactions are recorded.

416
Meyers, Oscar R.   Legal papers, 1865–1905.   (ca. 500 items.)

Legal papers of Oscar R. Meyers on real estate and settlement of estates. Gift of Josephine V. Meyers.

417
Mickle-Nichol Family.   Papers, 1766–1817.   (10 items.)

Family papers, including the Bible of Sophia Brown Mickle, 1766; marriage certificate of Samuel Mickle and Ann Lord, 1775; marriage certificate of Richard Rawson Hitchcock and Mary Stead, 1817; and other items.
Gift of Caroline Marshall Nichol and James Hitchcock Nichol.

418
Middleton, Arthur H.   Manuscripts, 1903–1909.
(1 v. and 100 items.)

Genealogical data, letters, copies of records, and charts about the family of Arthur H. Middleton, manufacturer of machinery and supplies in Philadelphia.
Gift of the executors of the Arthur Middleton estate, 1910.

419
Mifflin, John.   Genealogy, n.d.   (1 v.)

Transferred to the Genealogical Society of Pennsylvania.

420
Mifflin, Lemuel.   Papers, 1784–1837.   (ca. 50 items.)

Accounts of settlement of the estate of Lemuel Mifflin; copy of his will, 1824; tax receipts; and miscellaneous related items.

421
Mifflin, Thomas, 1744–1800.   Abridgement of Metaphysics, 1759.
(1 v.)

Manuscript schoolbook used by Thomas Mifflin contains essays entitled "Mente Humana," "Ontology," and "Of God and His Perfections."

422
Miles, George K.   Papers, 1775–1910.   (ca. 250 items.)

Genealogical papers and notes about the Miles family and related families, 1775–1910.
Gift of Sarah E. Miles, 1927.

423
Milliman, Francis A.   **Text books, 1833–1835.**   **(8 v.)**

Educational methods used in Philadelphia are reflected in these lessons in arithmetic, penmanship, English composition; one of the arithmetic books contains a daybook account, illustrating bookkeeping methods.
Gift of Mary E.W. Milliman, 1933.

424
Mills, Charles K. (Charles Karsner), 1845–1931.   **Papers, 1864–1941.**
(1 v.)

Scrapbooks of Dr. Charles K. Mills, containing his correspondence, lectures, pamphlets, programs, invitations to professional and social affairs. They present a view of the progress of medical science, treatment of insanity, and other diseases, institutional work, and contain information on many men in the medical profession.
Gift of Andrew Weisenburg.

425
Historical Society of Pennsylvania.   **Miscellaneous manuscripts,**
1661–1931.   **(200 linear ft.)**

Collection of petitions, accounts, and other miscellaneous material, much of which relates to the political and military history of the colonial period. The collection include: military accounts, payrolls, of Virginia, pertaining to protection of the frontier, 1729–1798; accounts of the paymaster general of the Pennsylvania Militia in the Whiskey Insurrection, 1794–1795; acts of the Jamaica assembly about prisoners of war, 1706; affidavits and court-martial, 1778–1805; Alabama letters, 1870–1885; apprenticeship indentures, 1677–1849; arbitrations and boat cargoes, 1682–1838; British depredations, 1778–1783; boundary disputes between Pennsylvania and Maryland, 1736; military certificates and discharges, 1776–1817; Civil War, Pennsylvania volunteers, 1862–1868; Clarke and Lockry expedition papers, 1781; Council of Safety papers, 1775–1778; county petitions, 1726–1848; paper on petitions about church deeds and letters patent, 1691–1891; Doylestown stageway bills, 1848; miscellaneous estimates, bills of goods, importations, accounts, 1690–1856; Federal Congress papers, 1789–1811; muster rolls of French officers who served in the Revolution, 1778–1783; account of Fries's insurrection, written, 1839; George Croghan, petitions about western boundary of Pennsylvania and Indian affairs, 1749; Georgia, New York, and Virginia Assembly papers, 1698–1759; Harrisburg Bridge Company, 1814; Indian affairs papers, on land, trade, and legal matters, 1661–1930; intercepted letters, Revolution, 1775–

1780; legal papers on land transactions, servants, 1678–1931; letters on Revolutionary activities, 1774–1814; miscellaneous list of names, 1682–1864; list of surveys, 1692; Mexican War items, 1848; muster rolls, 1757, 1863; naturalization certificates, 1724–1917; act of New Jersey Assembly, 1777; oaths of allegiance and recruiting papers, 1776–1782; Old Congress, 1777–1787; Palatine and redemptioners, 1768–1803, containing passenger lists of immigrants and their bonds; paroles and prisoners, 1776–1781; passes and passports, 1776–1908; payrolls, pertaining to the Revolution, 1776–1798; Provincial Council of Pennsylvania, 1688–1769; proclamations, 1686–1816, including one signed by William Penn, 1686; Philadelphia poor records, 1750–1767; property returns, 1798; tavern petitions on railroads, 1818–1902; yellow fever epidemic records, 1793; and numerous other items.

426
Mitchell, John.   Papers, 1812–1814.   (ca. 100 items.)

These papers contain letters and other documents addressed to John Mitchell, agent for American prisoners of war at Halifax, Nova Scotia, from American seamen captured by the British in the War of 1812.

Gift of Ida C. Wilcox.

427
Monroe, James, 1758–1831.   Bankbook, 1812–1818.   (1 v.)

James Monroe's account with the Bank of Columbia, showing cash deposits, discounts of notes, and balances.

Gift of Ferdinand J. Dreer, 1878.

429
Moore, John, 1659–1732.   Commission of Attorney General, 1701. (1 item.)

Original parchment commission of Moore's appointment as attorney general of Pennsylvania, 1701 signed by William Penn.

430
Moore, John.   Collection, 1903.   (2 v.)

A collection of biographical notes, pictures of landmarks, and newspaper clippings compiled by James W. Moore, Lafayette College, 1903, tracing the origin and history of the family of Rev. John Moore; *General Index* containing names of families.

431
Morgan, John, 1735–1789.   Journals, 1764 (1781–1784).   (2 v.)

The journal for 1764 is a narrative by Dr. John Morgan, surgeon general in the Revolutionary Army in 1776, of his tour from Rome to London in 1764, with details on important persons he met, his visit to Voltaire, universities and academies of learning, palaces, cities, travel, and social life in Europe.

Journal of 1781–1784 contains Dr. Morgan's accounts of his professional activities, services rendered and medical supplies sold to his patients, with data on 18th century pharmacology. This volume includes a list of members of the American Philosophical Society.

1764 journal handwritten copy made by George Appold, 1847.
Purchased, Library Fund.

432
Morris, Deborah, 1723/4–1793.   Account book, 1759–1786. (1 v.)

Account book of Deborah Morris, with entries on Sarah Powel's board, clothing, and schooling expenses, 1759–1769; included are Deborah Morris' accounts as executrix of the estate of John Morris Potts, 1782–1786.
Gift of S. Davis Wilson.

433
"Greek address to Edward Joy Morris," 1870.   (1 item.)

An address in Greek bearing the signatures of many prominent persons, and a letter to Edward Joy Morris, United States minister to Turkey, expressing sentiments of gratitude for his humanitarian activity in behalf of the Greek nation.
Letter in french.

434
Morris, Effingham Buckley, 1856–1937.   Photoprints, 1933. (ca. 50 items.)

Transferred to the Graphics Department.

435
Morris, Henry, 1802–1881.   Papers, 1822–1825.   (4 v.)

Letterbook, 1822–1825, correspondence of Henry Morris and Stephen P. Morris with clients, on the manufacture of iron and brass forgings, coal shipments; cashbook, 1823, his expense account and journal of a trip to Spain; daybooks, 1825–1826, about the manufacture of umbrella frames.

Journal of trip to Spain in Spanish.
Gift of Harold E. Gillingham and others.

436
Morris, Levi.   Papers, 1836–1845.   (250 items.)

Correspondence, orders, bills, receipts, of Levi Morris' iron and casting business.
Gift of C.S. Brigham.

437
Morris, Robert, 1734–1806.   Business records, 1769–1836.
(ca. 250 items.)

These papers relate chiefly to Robert Morris' large-scale speculation in western lands. They include: bill book, 1795–1798; journals, 1791–1801; ledger, 1794–1801; wastebook, 1792–1797, 1794–1801; correspondence, agreements, and notes, 1769–1803; abstract, "In the Case of Robert Morris a bankrupt, extract from the examination before the commission, 1790–1798;" abstract of a deed to land in Northumberland County, executed between Robert Morris and Charles Maurice de Talleyrand-Périgord, 1796; and miscellaneous correspondence, accounts, bonds, of John Nixon and others, 1791–1836.
Bill book gift of William S. Lewis, 1883.
Journal, ledger, and wastebook gift of George W. Childs, 1875.
Remaining materials gift of Charles Henry Hart, 1915.

438
Morris, Samuel, 1734–1812.   Business records, 1740–1811.   (3 v.)

Miscellaneous business records of Samuel Morris, prominent Philadelphian: ledger, 1740–1765, contains farm and trading accounts; receipt book, 1806–1807, includes ledger accounts of Samuel Morris as executor of the estate of Israel Morris, Jr., 1806–1811; Effingham Lawrence in account with Samuel Morris, 1788–1799, relates to Pennsylvania Loan Office certificates deposited as collateral by Charles and Andrew Pettit.
Gift of Alfred Cope, 1925.

439
Morris, Samuel Buckley, 1791–1859.   Diaries and bank checking
accounts, 1845–1868.   (4 v.)

Diary, 1845, of Samuel B. Morris describes a trip from Flat Rock Bridge to Towanda; diaries 1849–1851, contain his farm and domestic expense accounts; checkbook stubs, 1864–1868, drawn on the Bank of Germantown, show his business and private financial transactions.

Purchased, Charles Morton Smith Fund.

440
Morris, Susanna, d. 1755. *An Account of part of the travels of Susanna Morris,* **1729–1754.** (1 v.)

Journal of a Quaker traveler in the American colonies; describes dangers encountered and shipwreck; Friends meetings visited in Virginia, the Carolinas, Maryland, Pennsylvania, New Jersey, Great Britain, Ireland, and The Netherlands.

Gift of Mrs. William H. Nicholson.

441
Mucklé, John Seiser, 1862–1929. **Papers, 1898–1915.** (4,000 items.)

John S. Mucklé was commander of the state naval forces of Pennsylvania and later president of the Pennsylvania Red Cross Society.

The papers for 1898–1905 deal with the Pennsylvania State Naval Militia and contain Mucklé's correspondence on the organization and discipline of the naval and military forces, annual reports, records of equipment, ordnance, inspection of vessels, with information on activities during the Spanish-American War. The papers for 1907–1915 contain papers of the Pennsylvania Red Cross Society which relate to activities of the Society in combating tuberculosis and other diseases, and include data on its personnel, and rules for enrollment of volunteers and paid nurses.

Gift of John S. Mucklé.

442
Mucklé, Mark Richard, 1825–1915. **Memorial album, 1915.** (1 v.)

Obituary notices, letters of condolence, visiting cards, and testimonials of several organizations to the memory of Mark Richard Mucklé, a prominent citizen of Philadelphia.

Gift of John S. Mucklé.

443
Muhlenberg, Henry, 1753–1815. **Papers, 1781–1815.** (ca. 400 items.)

The correspondence of a prominent clergyman and botanist, relating chiefly to herbs and plants.

444
Butler, Thomas, 1871–1945.   *Chapters from the life of John Murray.*
(1 v.)

Manuscript of the Rev. Thomas Butler, used by him in his illustrated lectures on the life of John Murray, father of Universalism in America. Thomas Potter's home and church on the shores of New Jersey and Murray's first preaching there in 1770 are described. There is a full account of Murray's missionary work and travel through the colonies.
Gift of Thomas Butler, 1929.

445
United States Flotilla.   **Muster books, 1813–1815.**   (2 v.)

Muster roll and enlistment records of personnel of the Chesapeake Flotilla, United States Navy.

446
Myers, Leonard.   **Collection 1854–1905.**   (ca. 150 items.)

Chiefly letters to Leonard Myers from presidents, senators, representatives, cabinet members, officers in the army and navy, and prominent citizens, on legislative matters, politics, appointments to offices, military and personal affairs. Included are two volumes of autographs of members of Congress, 1865–1875, gathered by Leonard Myers during his term as a representative in Washington, D.C.
Gift of George de B. Myers, 1921.

447
Nead, Frank B.   **Collection, 1663–1866.**   (ca. 150 items.)

Autograph letters and documents primarily about Pennsylvania colonial history; patent of land on the Delaware granted to Erick Nichelsen by Governor Richard Nicholls, 1663; original deed from Indian chiefs to William Penn for a portion of land in Pennsylvania, 1683; letter of instruction about legal and provincial matters, signed by William Penn, 1700; instruction to Governor Patrick Gordon about duties on English importation, signed by George II, 1732; papers, 1728–1777, on Indian affairs in which Robert Orme, William Johnson, Governor Robert H. Morris, Governor William Denny, Conrad Weiser, the Council of Safety, and others, were interested; petitions about extension of county boundary lines, iron industry, construction of roads, Connecticut affair, 1728–1814; letters signed by George Washington, 1777–1783; certificates of enlistment, discharges, papers of the Committee of Safety of Pennsylvania, 1775–1783; plans of the Asylum

Company and of the North American Land Company, 1795; letters of James Buchanan, John C. Calhoun, Alexander J. Dallas, General Edward Braddock, Alexander Hamilton, James Madison, John Nicholson, Louis Marie de Noailles, James Hamilton, Timothy Pickering, Edmund Randolph, Joseph Reed; and other items.

Purchased, Henry D. Gilpin Fund.

448
Neagle, John, 1796–1865.   Commonplace book, 1839.   (1 v.)

Notes on the art of painting by John Neagle, Philadelphia portrait painter, describe the media and technique used by master painters and his own experience in the mixing of colors and the use of oils, canvases, varnish.

Gift of Charles Henry Hart.

449
Nelson, George.   Diary, 1780–1781, 1790–1792.   (1 v.)

Diary of George Nelson, Philadelphia merchant. Entries for 1780- 1781 contain data on the Revolution, accounts of battles, mutiny and dissatisfaction in the Pennsylvania Line of Continental troops acts of Assembly and of Continental Congress, city affairs, trading conditions, and church activities; entries for 1790–1802 describe Nelson's commercial enterprises, church interests.

Purchased.

450
New Jersey papers, 1664–1853.   (ca. 600 items.)

Miscellaneous papers, which include patents, charters, surveys, laws, papers on property transfers and provincial boundaries; correspondence on social and political matters; Burlington County, N.J., materials, oaths of officials.

Purchased.

451
Nice, John, d. 1806.   Papers, 1776–1864.   (ca. 100 items.)

Military papers about the Revolutionary War; miscellaneous legal and domestic correspondence. Most of these papers relate to the military career of Captain John Nice and include: muster and pay rolls of the 13th Pennsylvania Regiment, at Valley Forge, 1779; receipt book of noncommissioned officers and soldiers for pay and extras granted by Congress, 1778; military instructions, 1778; orderly book, 1777; diary and notes describing military affairs in New York and Long Island, 1776; diary begun at Valley Forge, June to August 1778; lists of names of prisoners, and of enlistments, 1776. In addition, there are some family papers including correspondence, accounts, 1788–1836; and the receipt book of Levi Nice, 1819–1863.

Gift of Mary Adelaide Jacoby and Anne C. Cooper, 1915.

452
Nicholson, John, 1757–1800.   Letterbooks, 1795–1798.   (7 v.)

These letterbooks contain copies of John Nicholson's correspondence with prominent men pertaining to real estate, and financial and legal matters; some of the letters relate to financial difficulties of Nicholson and Robert Morris occasioned by their speculations in land in Washington, D.C.

Gift of the Hood Gilpin estate, 1918.

453
Nixon, John, 1733–1808.   Papers, 1707–1845.   (6 linear ft.)

The collection includes correspondence on the estate of John Nixon, merchant and first president of the Bank of North America; financial papers; receipts, accounts and settlements, 1771–1845; deeds, 1707–1811; and marine insurance policies, 1806.

454
Norris family.   Papers, 1742–1860.   (30 linear ft.)

The papers of Isaac Norris (1671–1735), merchant, mayor of Philadelphia; Isaac Norris (1701–1766), merchant, alderman, speaker of the Assembly; Charles Norris (1712–1766), trustee of the General Loan Office of Pennsylvania. These papers include letterbooks of the two Isaac Norris', 1699–1766; account books, 1705–1761; the second Isaac Norris' account with the estate of Thomas Griffith, 1723–1766; Norris and Griffith papers, 1753; documents relating to real estate in Chester and Delaware counties, 1682–1762, in Philadelphia, Bucks, and Berks counties, 1685–1768, in Montgomery, Lancaster and Mifflin counties, 1728–1789; family accounts, 1740–1790, and 1748–1816; miscellaneous correspondence, 1740–1765; family letters and other papers, 1684–1814, including some of the papers of Thomas Lloyd, 1664–1698, among which are documents relating to the controversy between Lloyd and the Bishops of St. Asaph, 1681; a box of deeds and wedding certificates, 1687–1790; architect's plan for a house; and some correspondence dealing with the affairs of the Pennsylvania Fire Company, 1850–1860.

Among the Norris miscellany are genealogical notes and extracts from the letterbooks of Isaac Norris on the Norris-Lloyd families; extracts from the letterbooks of Isaac Norris, 1699–1734; scrapbook containing letters from Thomas Lloyd, 1642–1779; extracts of letters from Thomas Penn to Richard Peters, 1752–1772; papers relating to the Library Company of Philadelphia, 1773–1812; pamphlets, 1746–1804; *The Examiner, Student's Gazette*, 1777–1778, *Theatre Critic Universal*, 1759; almanacs: *Bailey's*, 1883, *Poor Will's*, 1834, *Philadelphia*, 1835; 12 school exercise books, 1774; some mathematics problems; a box of poetry, with notes, 1750–1835.

Many of Charles Norris' papers preserved in this collection deal with the administration of the General Loan Office of Pennsylvania: list of subscribers to a loan, 1758; Edmund Wooley's account with the Province of Pennsylvania, 1750–1758; an alphabetical list of the mortgages in the General Loan Office, n.d.; list of mortgages in Chester County, 1755; undated list of mortgages in Philadelphia; mortgage list for Bucks County, 1755–1756; list of payments due or discharged, 1753–1758; an account with the Province of Pennsylvania, 1742–1756; General Loan Office account books, 1750–1768; settlements of the General Loan Office, 1751–1765; General Loan Office accounts of quota and interest money, 1751–1766; General Loan Office entry books, 1753–1757; General Loan Office records of orders of commissioners, soldier's certificates, and account books, 1755–1760; warrants from the commissioners to Charles Norris to make payments to militia and the French who remained neutral, and to discharge bills of various sorts, 1755–1765; certificates, 1758–1760; Loan Office accounts of Indian charges, 1753–1764, and assemblymen's wages, 1750–1751; a box of pay vouchers issued by the commissioners of the General Loan Office, 1762.

Also included are expense accounts of James Burd's road to the Ohio, and the road cutters' accounts, 1755; Charles Norris letterbook, 1733–1734; cashbook, 1748–1750; cashbooks and account books, 1733–1766, among which are the cashbooks of Joseph Sermon, 1751–1759, Hugh Robert, 1747–1755, and a cashbook for 1717; Norris' receipt book, 1758–1762; tax receipt book of C.S. Norris, 1744–1747; letterbook of William Griffith, 1748–1752; cashbook of Charles Norris, Jr., 1809–1812; bill of lading book, 1765; undated sheriff's subpoena book, notes of the House of Representatives, 1734–1735; minutes of the Pythonian Society, 1779; minutes of the Board of Education, 1845–1847.

Gift of the Norris family.

Isaac Norris journal of trip to Albany, N.Y. published in the *P.M.H.B.*, 27 (1903): 20–28.

455
North Carolina papers.   (ca. 300 items.)

The participation of North Carolina troops in the Revolution is described in letters of General Robert Howe, Stephen Moore, R. Rutherford, Allen Jones, John Armstrong, Thomas Burke, William Davidson, Richard Caswell, John Penn, and others, 1777–1783; and in orders of the Assembly, 1777. The letters discuss the resolutions of the Assembly on the ratification of the Constitution, 1787–1788; the question of imposts by North Carolina, 1788; paper currency, 1785; treaties and sales of Indian lands, 1827; slavery, laws, finances, freemasonry, religion, local affairs, political and military appointments.

Also included are: manuscript map of the dividing line between Virginia and Carolina, 1728; printed copy of the amendment to the Constitution of North Carolina and of the Declaration of Rights, 1788; "Orderly Book, North Carolina Line," 1777; muster roll of British troops in Charleston, S.C., 1782.

Gift of the Lanier bequest, 1908–1918.

456
Northampton County (Pa.) papers, ca. 1682–1887.   (27 linear ft.)

The collection deals with the founding and early settlement of Northampton County. It reflects the character and nationality of the settlers, religion, commercial and land enterprises, Indian warfare, and includes letters and documents of men who were prominent in the economic development of the country.

There are: land warrants, 1734–1887; surveys, 1705–1886; deeds, 1689–1867; correspondence, 1743–1804; field notes of surveys, 1768–1865; minutes of the Board of Property, 1776–1779; wills, administration accounts, 1682–1860; accounts, 1775–1855; bonds and agreements, 1742–1880; pleas and prosecutions, 1753–1848; tax list, 1816; and miscellaneous papers on land transactions, and municipal, legal, political and domestic affairs, 1706–1880.

The collection also contains: commissioners minutes and accounts, 1755–1782; provincial tax assessments, 1767–1782; Northampton County, assessments, 1768–1793; tax rates, 1762–1789; funding tax, 1789; state tax, 1782; supplementary tax, 1781; county treasurer's accounts, 1754–1770; miscellaneous assessments, 1808–1815; indentures, land warrants, petitions for roads, taverns, creation of new townships, oaths of allegiance, indictments, criminal proceedings, details of Indian warfare, military defenses, requests for provisions, arms, ammunition for forts and garrisons, letters on the Moravians in Bethlehem, the Nazareth community, 1727–1858. Among the letters are those of: Edward Biddle, William Bradford, Henry Engel, James Hamilton, Timothy Horsfield, Robert Levers, Thomas Mifflin, Thomas McKean, Jacob Orndt, William Parsons, Richard Peters, Nicholas Scull, Jonathan Sergeant, William Shippen, Bishop Spangenberg, Daniel Stroud, Edward Tilghman, Conrad Weiser, and others.

Included in the collection are: provincial tax receipts, 1776; duplicates for county tax, 1770; tax and assessment book, 1779; county tax, 1786; duplicates of provincial tax, 1789; duplicates of county tax, 1766, 1788; letters and documents on the Revolutionary War, transportation, litigations, commerce, politics, grand jury, indictments, marriage contracts, domestic affairs, 1749–1783; surveys, surveyors' returns to the general office, 1776–1865; tax lists, papers on the Continental Army, Connecticut claimants, muster rolls, bonds, legal instruments, list of constables, 1765–1859; Bethlehem materials, letters about the number of people killed by the Indians, 1755–1757, Indian accounts, Quakers and their conduct at Easton, Nazareth community affairs, drafts, bills of sale, 1765–1859.

Other papers are: surveys and deeds, 1689–1867; Bethlehem and vicinity papers, 1741–1886, containing letters and documents on the settling of Bethlehem and adjacent areas, surveys and drafts of lands, details of Indian warfare military protection, means of defense of Forts Norris, Allen and Hamilton; petitions for new roads and tavern licenses, constables' returns, records of prices of food; minutes of the Committee of Observation and Inspection of Northampton County, 1774–1777, with Major Robert Traill's report of the proceedings of the Committee of Safety, on the execution of measures adopted by the Continental Congress; manuscript histories of Northampton County, by Matthew S. Henry, 1851, with notes on development of townships, education, religion, witchcraft, trade, Revolutionary War, Indian affairs, court cases, names of taxables, assembly proceedings.

Gift of Jacob Fatzing, Ethan Allan Weaver, and John Jordan.

Documents on the founding of Easton published in the *P.M.H.B.*, 38 (1914): 110–114.

457
Northern, Interior, and Western counties (Pa.) papers, 1744–1859. (ca. 250 items.)

Miscellaneous papers concerning domestic and political affairs, land transactions, laws, petitions, rules and regulations, and including correspondence reflecting social and economic conditions.

Purchased.

458
Northumberland County (Pa.) papers, 1767–1899.   (15 linear ft.)

Papers and documents, chiefly of Charles G. Donnel and Charles W. Hegins, jurists and political leaders of Sunbury, Northumberland County:

land warrants, deeds, surveys, field notes, 1767–1859, show the subdivisions of land in townships and names of purchasers and settlers; agreements, mortgages, indentures, relate to iron mines, coal lands, dams, canals, railroads, 1768–1857; letters of men in politics, judiciary, and commercial enterprises relate to court trials, settlement of estates, land transactions, commercial accounts, 1793–1853; receipts and bills for the supply of provisions of the Continental army and to the army in the War of 1812; names of holders of Continental certificates of the unfunded debt issues and redeemed, 1790–1793. Surveys and calculations, 1767–1899; correspondence, 1793–1853; Continental certificates, 1780–1864; miscellaneous, 1768–1871; field notes, 67 booklets, 1786–1824; deeds, 1774–1859; legal cases, 1794–1864; commissary papers, 1809–1820; canals, railroads, coal, telegraph, 1831–1858, complete the collection.

Purchased, 1937.

459
Notes of Trials in Colombia, 1822. (1 v.)

These papers relate to legal controversies in South American countries. Among the items are: notes of a law suit brought by E.W. Robinson against J.G. Williamson, United States consul at Columbia from 1827–1829; other cases relate to shipping, moral transgressions, and other matters.

460
Oberholtzer, Ellis Paxson, 1868–1936. **Collection, 1735–1931.** (24 linear ft.)

Correspondence and miscellaneous papers of Ellis Paxson Oberholtzer, Philadelphia historian, include material on: the thrift movement, establishment of school savings banks and thrift savings banks in the United States, 1886–1928; Historical Pageant of Philadelphia, 1912, data on its organization, administration, finance, and executive committee meetings, with water color drawings of costumes and pageantry, posters, names of subscribers and of members, souvenirs; Indian Welfare in Oklahoma; Civil War; abolition of slavery; Temperance Union; Valley Forge Commission; education; motion picture censorship; League for Better Moving Pictures; Sesqui-Centennial Exposition. A portion of correspondence relates to publications, essays, lectures, and biographies of Robert Morris, Jay Cooke, Salmon P. Chase, Charles B. Brown, and others; included in this group of papers are Sarah Louisa Oberholtzer's letters, poems and essays. Papers of an earlier period include: deeds of grants of land in Uwchlan Township, Chester County, 1735–1809; inventory of the estate of Thomas Potts, 1762; Uwchlan Society of Friends, notes and minutes of meetings, 1806; John and Paxson

Vicker correspondence, 1823–1844; papers relating to the Pickering Valley Railroad, 1869–1870; and other items of social and political character.

Gift of Ellis Paxson Oberholtzer.

461
O'Bryen, Richard. *Remarks and observations in Algiers,* 1789–1791. (1 v.)

Richard O'Bryen was consul general of the United States to the Regency of Algiers.

The position held by the Barbary States in the Mediterranean and the state of their political and domestic affairs are described in this journal. It contains some account of the humiliating conditions imposed upon American and European citizens, the Bey's haughty attitude toward foreign ambassadors and their agents, payment of tribute and ransom exacted for the redemption of prisoners, and the cruel treatment of Christian slaves. The conflicting interests of England, Spain, France, Genoa, Portugal, Russia, Turkey, and other countries are shown in the narrative of their diplomatic activities, wars, naval battles, and the capture of vessels.

462
Orr, Dunlap, and Glenholme. **Letterbook,** 1767–1769. (1 v.)

Commercial and shipping activities of the colonial period are reflected in this letterbook of Orr, Dunlap, and Glenholme, the Philadelphia firm. The letters, addressed to clients in Europe, West Indies, and the colonies, show business trends, commodities traded, prices, hazards of, shipping.

Gift of George C. Lewis, 1896.

463
Oxley, Joseph, 1714–1775. *Joseph's offering to his children : His life travels and labors of love in the fellowship of the Gospel of our Lord Jesus Christ.* (1 v.)

"Joseph's Offering to his Children" is an account of an English Quaker's travels through England, Scotland, Ireland, and the American colonies, 1770–1772, in the service of his religion. Joseph Oxley's record of his American tour presents a picture of life and religion in Virginia, the Carolinas, Maryland, Pennsylvania, New Jersey, New York, and New England. He describes means of travel, accommodations, meetings attended, prominent Quakers he met.

Gift of Sally F. Lewis, 1909.

464

Page, Anne F.   Journal, 1839.   (1 v.)

Journal of Anne F. Page of a trip through France and Italy, describes cities visited, historical monuments, manners and customs of inhabitants.
Gift of Maria P. Ryan.

465

Page, William.   Diary, 1808–1812.   (1 v.)

Diary of William Page, Philadelphia merchant; records family matters, travels, and business.
Gift of the William J. Potts Estate, 1921.

466

Parker, Daniel, 1782–1846.   Papers, 1800–1846.   (9 linear ft.)

A large portion of the papers is official correspondence of the War Department in which Daniel Parker was adjutant and inspector general, 1810–1845. There are letters of: Thomas Jefferson, 1803–1808; James Madison, 1808–1814; James Monroe, 1811–1819; Andrew Jackson, 1803–1818; William Henry Harrison, 1802–1813; General John Armstrong, 1812–1842; H. Dearborn, 1803–1819; William Eustis, 1809–1822; George Izard, 1813–1817; Thomas Johnson, 1808; Winfield Scott, 1807–1821; James Wilkinson, 1801–1820; and others. Included are: Governor John Drayton to Thomas Jefferson, 1802, on the landing of French blacks on the southern coasts of the Union; petitions of Indian tribes to Thomas Jefferson, 1804–1808; Jefferson's letters to Indian chiefs, 1805–1808; Andrew Jackson letters, 1804–1818, on Indian depredations on the Tennessee River, Mobile Creek warfare; Captain Meriwether Lewis' report to Jefferson on western territories, 1803; letters of W.C.C. Claireborne and of other noted persons concerned in the affairs of Louisiana, the Floridas, Alabama, Georgia, Mississippi, Kentucky, Tennessee, 1801–1821; survey of the head of Muscle Shoals, Tennessee River, east of the Chickasaw nation, 1818; letter of James Wilkinson to Thomas Jefferson, 1806, denouncing Aaron Burr as a conspirator and a traitor, and discussing means of defense of New Orleans; Stephen Decatur's reports on the condition of the *Chesapeake* after the battle with the *Leopard,* 1807; papers on war agitation, embargoes, and military preparedness against England, 1806–1812.

Material on the War of 1812 in the voluminous official papers, 1812–1815; letters of William Eustis, James Madison, James Monroe, and of commanding officers, deal with mobilization plans, military campaigns, movement of troops, battles, General William Hull's disaster at Detroit,

1812, his subsequent trial for treason in 1814, and other important incidents of the war.

Official papers, 1816–1841, include letters of Colonel J.J. Abert, John C. Calhoun, John Henry Eaton, H. Leavenworth, David Porter, T. Ringgold, Winfield Scott, John Tyler, and others, on military, administrative, political, and economic affairs, courts-martial, claims against the government, regulations of settlers, 1818–1820, Mexican War, Cherokee and Dakota treaties, West Point regulations.

Daniel Parker correspondence, 1811–1845, relates to his official and financial activities: letters of Amos Binney, James Byers, William Duane, D. Gadsden, C. Irvine, W. Rawle, Parker family, and others.

Additional items include: numerous pamphlets, army and navy registers; books on medicine; map of West Genesco, N.Y., 1800; view of Cincinnati, Ohio, 1807; map of a route from Kansas to the Pacific, 18843.

467
Parker-Franklin correspondence, 1747–1773.   (ca. 150 items.)

Correspondence between Benjamin Franklin and James Parker, printer and later comptroller of the Post Office.

Letterpress copies made by Sarah Cresson.

Gift of Sarah Cresson.

468
Parrish, John, 1729–1807.   Diaries, 1773–1793.   (3 v.)

These diaries pertain to Indian customs, life, and habitations, with an account of "John Parrish's visit to the Indians at Muskingon," 1773; treaty at Newton Point, 1791; record of a trip to Lower Sandusky to conclude a treaty with the Indians, 1793.

Diaries copied by Richard Eddy, 1882.

Gift of Richard Eddy, 1882.

Journal, 1773, published in *P.M.H.B.,* 16 (1892): 443–448.

469
Parry, George T.   Diaries, 1858–1886.   (13 v.)

Diaries, 1853, 1857, 1861, 1864–1867, 1869–1870, 1879–1880, 1886, of George T. Parry, Philadelphia engineer, contain his narrative of daily events, family affairs, and his professional and business activities.

Purchased by the Wendell P. Bowman Fund, 1935.

470
Parsons, William, 1701–1757.   Papers, 1723–1751.   (7 v.)

Miscellaneous business papers of William Parsons, shoemaker, scrivener, dyer, surveyor, sheriff and founder of Easton, include: ledger of accounts, 1723–1726; field book of surveys, 1734–1736; list of property owners and the surveys of their land; commonplace book, 1741–1747; receipt books, 1736–1737, 1738–1751.
Gift of Jacob Wolle, 1845.

471
Paschall papers, 1734–1875.   (ca. 100 items.)

Miscellaneous family papers of the Paschall and Sellers families, 1747–1871, include: receipt book of Dr. John Paschall, 1747–1776; account book of Thomas G. Paschall, 1811; poetry albums of George and Ann Sellers, and Mary Francis Paschall, 1830; family correspondence, 1813–1815; deeds and patents to land, 1750–1871; and wills, deeds, and other papers concerning the estates of the Paschall and related families.
Gift of Ann Paschall.

472
Paschall, Mary Frances.   Autograph albums, 1853–1861.   (2 v.)

Bits of verse dedicated to Mary Frances Paschall by her friends.
Gift of Anne Paschall.

473
Paschall, Sarah.   Poetry, 1786.   (1 v.)

Collection of Sarah Paschall's poetry.
Gift of the John T. Morris Estate.

474
**Paschall and Hollingsworth.   Papers, 1660–1665, 1711–1861.
(24 v. and ca. 100 items.)**

Economic trends, trade conditions, commodity prices are shown in the business record books of this leading mercantile firm. Thomas Paschall: ledgers, 1660–1665, 1711–1722, 1713–1766, 1718–1733; Stephen Paschall: ledgers, 1735–1744, 1737–1759, 1752–1776, 1758–1789, 1764–1765, 1778–1800; daybooks, 1756–1796, 1758–1782; Paschall and Hollingsworth: bankbooks, 1825–1830; receipt book, 1825–1827; cash books, 1825–1837; blotters, 1830–1839; correspondence on political and domestic affairs, 1772–1844; Dr. Caspar Morris, receipt book, 1832–1861.
Gift of Herbert Morris, 1935.

475
Pastorius, Francis Daniel, 1651–1719.   **Papers, 1683–1721.**
(3 linear ft.)

Papers of Francis Daniel Pastorius on theological, medical, legal, philosophical subjects, including "Liber Intimissimus Omnium Semper Mecum," 1697–1701; "Artzney und Kunst ist all umsunst ohne Gottes Gunst," 1695; commonplace book, 1683–1716; "The Great Law of Pennsylvania" including a copy of the Germantown charter, 1693; papers on the Frankfort Company, 1683–1709; marriage certificate of Henry Pastorius, 1721.

Some materials in German.

Purchased, Library Fund; some items presented by Harry C. Kessler, Charles M. Wayne, and others.

476
Patterson, Robert, 1802–1876.   **Diaries, 1835.**   **(2 v.)**

These are copies of Robert Patterson's journals of a trip from Philadelphia to Iowa, Wisconsin, Kentucky, Tennessee, and other states. He describes historical landmarks visited, stopping places, means of travel, social events, dinner with President Andrew Jackson at the White House, scenes and topography of the country. Included are his notes on European history, English literature, and Biblical events.

Handwritten transcript.

Purchased, Dreer Fund, 1934.

477
Patterson, Robert, 1743–1824.   **Notes on navigation, 1789.**   **(1 v.)**

A treatise on navigation and methods of calculating latitude and longitude, written by Robert Patterson, professor of mathematics in the University of Pennsylvania.

Gift of A.C. Vaute.

478
Patton, William Augustus, 1849–1927.   **Letters, 1899–1918.**
(2 v.)

These volumes, chiefly composed of congratulatory letters, telegrams, and newspaper clippings, relate to William A. Patton's service with the Pennsylvania Railroad and to his elevation to the presidency of the New York, Philadelphia and Norfolk Railroad Company.

Gift of Mrs. Martha A. Patton.

479
Paul, Joseph M.   Records, 1800–1829.   (3 v.)

Entry cancelled; see collection #192.

480
Payne, John Howard.   "Historical account of the Indians in the southern states," [1835].   (1 v.)

An account of the Muscogee, Chickasaw, Cherokee, Creek, and other Indian tribes living in the souther states; information on their origins, traditions, customs, character traits, social and domestic life, language, government, religion.

This book was formerly in the possession of John Howard Payne. It was found among his effects at Tunis after his death, by the United States consul there, who sent it to the Department of State, Washington, D.C.

481
Peale family.   Papers, 1794–1854.   (ca. 250 items.)

Papers of Charles Wilson Peale, Rembrandt Peale, and Titian R. Peale, mainly relate to Peale's Museum, and include: C. W. Peale, "A walk through the Philadelphia Museum;" records of subscriptions for tickets in Peale's Museum, 1794–1833; records and memoranda of the Philadelphia Museum, 1803–1837; minutes of the Philadelphia Museum, 1841–1845; a rough minute book of the Philadelphia Museum, 1841–1845; extracts of letters from C. W. Peale, 1821–1823; copies of letters from Rembrandt Peale to his wife, 1830; correspondence of Titian R. Peale with George Ord, 1827–1854; ornithological journal, with a catalogue of birds, collected in United States Exploring Expedition by Titian R. Peale, 1843; 10 drawings by T.R. Peale.

Presented in part by members of the Peale family; some items purchased by the Historical Society.

482
Pearce, Cromwell, b. 1771.   Memoir, 1855.   (1 v.)

A memoir of Colonel Cromwell Pearce, of Chester County, with an account of his ancestry. The volume contains a sketch of the distinguished services rendered by him as a colonel of the 16th Regiment of the United States Infantry in the War of 1812; a detailed description of the military campaign against Canada, the attack on Sackets Harbor and Little York, N.Y., the explosion of a powder magazine causing the death of General Zebulon M. Pike, sickness and lack of discipline among the soldiers, Commodore Isaac Chauncey's naval activities on the Great Lakes.

Gift of Gilbert Cope, 1884.

483
Pearsall, Mary.   Journal, 1873.   (1 v.)

This journal of Mary Pearsall of a trip from Philadelphia to Montreal describes the topography of the country, hotel accommodations, means of travel.

Gift of Mrs. Trevanion B. Dallas, 1937.

484A
Pemberton family.   Papers, 1641–1880.   (33 linear ft.)

Papers of Phineas Pemberton, Israel Pemberton, Sr., Israel Pemberton, Jr., James Pemberton, John Pemberton, and their descendants, distinguished Quakers, prominent in the colonial affairs of Pennsylvania. The extensive correspondence maintained by the Pembertons with Friends in America, England, and other parts of the world, contains valuable material on the history of the Society of Friends.

Papers for 1641–1702, relate chiefly to events during the lifetime of Phineas Pemberton, colonial social and economic conditions, religious intolerance and persecution, Quaker meetings, prominent personalities. Papers, 1702–1774, include among others letters from Richard Partridge, agent in England for the Pennsylvania Assembly, to Chief Justice Kinsey of Pennsylvania; material on England's colonial policies; petitions addressed to the king; a memorial and protest against Parliament's strangulations of the iron industry in America; letters on the Scottish rebellion and the Spanish and French wars; data on commerce and shipping, London earthquakes; list of Friends' monthly meetings; information on the growing tension between England and the colonies. Papers, 1775–1783, record incidents of the Revolutionary period; war conditions in Providence, R.I.; Patrick Henry's insurrection in Williamsburg, Va.; the arrest of Quakers accused of disloyalty in Philadelphia; orders of the General Assembly; the occupation of Philadelphia by Howe's troops; prevailing economic conditions; a group of John Fothergill letters, 1740–1780, relates to political, social, and moral trends. Papers, 1783–1808, relate to Quaker monthly meetings; abolition of slavery; Indian peace measures; the Constitutional Assembly; presidential elections; United States controversies with France.

Additional papers, 1681–1880, contain: memorandum book, 1768–1771; Pemberton receipt books, 1792–1798, 1807–1830; Thomas Parke diary of a journey from Philadelphia to London, 1771–1772; Thomas Clifford account book of cargoes at Bristol, 1789; John Pemberton's religious essays, n.d.; essays on religion and politics, 1814–1838; genealogical notes, 1880; commissions, parchment deeds, legal documents, 1656–1831, some of which bear the signatures of James Monroe, John Q. Adams, Andrew Jackson, Thomas

Jefferson, Martin Van Buren; Philadelphia estates papers, 1684–1797, contain miscellaneous deeds, documents, and plats; New Jersey estates papers, 1683–1803, surveys, plats, indentures; Chester County estates papers, 1681–1795, surveys, deeds; Bucks County estates papers, 1689–1700; Maryland estates papers, 1657–1795, land patents, correspondence; biographical sketch of James Pemberton, and one of Phineas Pemberton, by James Pemberton, 1778; Shoemaker and Rawle letters, 1780–1821, family correspondence.

Miscellaneous items completing the collection include: letters of John Hunt to Israel Pemberton, 1758–1764; miscellaneous papers of Thomas Clifford, 1764–1789; journals and diaries of John Pemberton, 1750–1795; "Notes of a journey through Scotland with John Pemberton and David Dusat," by Thomas Wilkinson, 1787; *Some account of Last Journey of John Pemberton to the Highland and other parts of Scotland,* by Thomas Wilkinson, 1811; *A Testimony of the monthly meeting of Friends at Pyrmont, in Westphalia, Germany, concerning John Pemberton,* 1798; 12 Poor Will's Pocket Almanacks, with manuscript marginal notes, 1782–1813; Joseph Pemberton memorandum book, 1798–1803; his receipts, rules and memoranda, 1801–1805; *An Appeal to the Society of Friends on the Primitive Simplicity of the Christian Principles,* 1801; *Early Christian Instruction in the form of a dialogue between Mother and Child,* 1807; *An Epistle to the Members of the Religious Society of Friends,* 1827; *Plan of the Philadelphia Dispensary for the Medical Relief of the Poor,* contains list of names of contributors, 1787; the Philadelphia *Directory,* 1800; "An Exact Copy of James Pemberton's Diary, 1777–1778."

Additional miscellaneous items are: Rebecca Warner Rawle's diary, 1813; Excerpts of letters, sequel to the Friendly Association, 1872, containing marginal notes; *Some chapters in the History of the Friendly Association, for Regaining and Preserving Peace with Indians, by Pacific Measures,* by Samuel Parrish, 1877; and some additional items.

Gift of Henry Pemberton, Jr., 1892.

484B
Pemberton family.   Papers, (1800–1910) 1948.   (15 linear ft.)

The papers of three generations of the Pemberton family include correspondence, diaries, and personal, family, and business records.

John Pemberton, naval officer of the Port of Philadelphia under President Jackson, is represented by correspondence, 1807–1847, which offers some documentation of the spoils system. There are letters of Pemberton to Andrew Jackson, mostly letters of recommendation, but there are only 5 of Jackson's letters to Pemberton. There is material of John's wife Rebecca Clifford Pemberton, including correspondence, 1806–1869, some accounts, and papers dealing with the administration of her estate.

The bulk of the collection consists of the papers of the children of John and Rebecca Pemberton. Their eldest son, Israel, was a civil engineer who surveyed for railroads in Delaware, Ohio, Pennsylvania, and Tennessee. His surveying work as well as his travels in Cuba and Europe are well documented in correspondence, 1822–1885, and diaries. Particularly interesting are the many letters from John Swaby and William Stewart, revealing their mutual familiarity with Philadelphia's demimonde. Included, too, are materials detailing Israel Pemberton's patronage of and friendship with the Spanish artist Mariano Fortuny y Carbo. John Clifford Pemberton, the Confederate commander at Vicksburg, is represented by correspondence, 1829–1881, but no Civil War letters are present. Andrew Jackson Pemberton is represented by correspondence, 1862–1900, much of it concerning his estate held in trust. The greater part of Henry Pemberton's correspondence, 1837–1910, reflect his career as chemist and businessman with the Pennsylvania Salt Manufacturing Company. There are also personal and business letterbooks, 1859–1911, bills and receipts, 1853–1856, and miscellaneous chemical notes, contracts, patents, and clippings.

Many other members of the family tree are represented by small groups of correspondence, financial papers, legal papers, genealogical notes, photographs, and other miscellany. Related families that appear are Cowgill, Corbit, Lovering, and Clifford.

Gift of Henry R. Pemberton, 1952.

485A
Penn family   Papers, 1629–1834.   (40 linear ft.)

Sir William Penn, 1621–1670. Papers, 1644–1710: journal of Sir William Penn, 1644–1647; letters, 1650–1660; Forbes collection, 1653–1710; "The Duty of the Principal Officers of his Majesties Navy Joyntly Considered," 1646; "The Office of the Admiralty of England," n.d.

William Penn, 1644–1718. Papers, 1654–1735: correspondence, 1654–1855, includes family letters, official correspondence with Admiral William Penn, Hannah Penn, James Logan, Harbert Springett, Thomas Bishop Vickris, John Barclay, J. Freame, and others; letters to and from John, Thomas, and Richard Penn, on Irish immigration, books, ducation, epidemics; printing account with Benjamin Franklin; drafts, naval accounts, household accounts, land records. William Penn letterbooks, 1667–1675, 1699–1701, contain conciliatory letter to his father; diary of a journey through Kent, Sussex, and Surrey, 1672; narratives of his trial and committal to the Tower; letters to the King, Friends, governors, Lords of the Admiralty, Lords of Trade and Plantations. Domestic and miscellaneous letters, 1682–1794, contains letters of William Penn to Hannah Callowhill, and members of Pennsylvania Council, 1684–1694; letters of James Logan, to William Aubrey, 1703–1735.

Penn manuscripts, 1680–1715, contains last will and testament of William Penn, with codicil in his hand, 1705, 1706; original draft of grant of Province of Pennsylvania, with corrections in his hand, 1680; William Penn to Archbishop Tillotson, 1691; to Robert Turner, 1693; to Lord Romney, 1701; to Samuel Pepys, 1670; commission to William Markham, 1697; "The Case of William Penn," "State of efforts of Crown to regain control of Pennsylvania in Queen Anne's reign," "Act of Pennsylvania vesting proprietary estates in Commonwealth," and other items. Penn's letter to the Free Society of Traders, 1683; Irish journal, 1669–1670; "An account of My Journey into Holland and Germany," 1677, includes letters to the King of Poland, Anna Maria de Horn (Countess of Horn), essay; William Penn receipt book, interest on loans, 1710–1728; William and Hannah Penn journal, 1710–1726; Hannah Penn cash book, 1712–1720.

Records of the proprietary government, 1629–1828: papers on the three lower counties, 1629–1774; Penn's deeds, 1639–1759, 1760–1801; leases and mortgages, 1670–1771; governor's proclamations, 1670–1775; county court records, town and county of Deale, 1681–1709; autograph petitions, 1681–1716; receipts for beaver skins for tenure, 1752–1780; addresses to William Penn by Trade Society; petition to Lord Baltimore; petitions from Berks, Bucks, and Chester counties in favor of proprietary government; Pennsylvania land grants, 1681–1806; Assembly of Provincial Council of Pennsylvania, 1682–1874; the laws of Pennsylvania, 1682–1688; Pennsylvania charters, Frame of Government, with revised forms, 1683–1696, and marriage settlement and will of Thomas Penn, 1751–1774.

Official correspondence, 1683–1817: letters from James Logan to John Penn and Hannah Penn, Lord Baltimore, William Penn, Governor Andrew Hamilton, Isaac Norris, W. Popple, Colonel Benjamin Fletcher, on Pennsylvania boundaries, acts for regulating trade, efforts to make Pennsylvania a crown colony, piracy and smuggling, decline in public morals, copper mine beyond Susquehanna, Keith-Logan controversy, Indian treaties, Conrad Weiser's address to the Germans, factions in politics, paper money, yellow fever, Ohio Company, Nicholas Scull, Edward Shippen, George Croghan, Connecticut intrusion, battle of Lexington.

Philadelphia land grants, Episcopal church, Society of Friends, University Island in Delaware, 1684–1772; warrants and surveys, 1684–1776; Connecticut claims, 1684–1799; *Planter's Speech to his Neighbors and Countrymen of Pennsylvania, East and West Jersey;* Indian affairs, 1687–1801, contain information to Thomas Dongan, governor and vice admiral of New York, on invasion of Indians of the Five Nations, 1787; Governor Logan's speech to Sassoonan, 1731; negotiations with Six Nations; data on German Palatines, Conrad Weiser, Richard Peters, Sir William Johnson, Albany Congress, Connecticut purchase, Delaware controversy; George Croghan's account of Indian affairs, 1748–1749, to Braddock's defeat; maps and documents on Indian Walk; Governor John Blackwell manuscripts, 1689–1690; and acts of assembly, 1700–1763.

Pennsylvania cash accounts, 1701–1778: Pennsylvania journals, 1701–1779, contain accounts of lands, quitrents; James Logan receipt book, 1702–1709, papers relating to iron, peltries, trade, 1712–1817; bonds and powers of attorney, 1714–1828; "Supplementary Saunders Coates," 1720–1766, chiefly Thomas Penn letters to Richard Peters, on administrative affairs; Pennsylvania Assembly messages, 1727–1771; Wyoming controversy papers, 1731–1775, and William Smith and William Moore v. Assembly, 1758–1759; account of quitrents, 1742; accounts of land in Chester County called "William Penn's Manor," 1747–1750; warrants to affix the great seal, 1749–1775; accounts, provincial tax for Philadelphia, 1759–1768; William Baker letterbook, 1769–1789; John Mifflin letterbook, 1788–1802; receipt book (of Philip Syng), provincial tax, 1759–1770; proprietary manors and lands in Pennsylvania, n.d.

Penn family. Papers, 1606–1834: Pennsylvania miscellaneous papers, *Penn v. Baltimore*, Penn family, 1606–1834; wills of Harbert Springett and Anthony Springett, 1682–1721; letters of the Penn family to James Logan, 1701–1730; additional miscellaneous letters and Penn-Engert-Lewis papers, 1683–1872; letters of the Penn family, 1654–1775; papers relating to Penn family title, 1712–1726; "Family Deeds," 1718–1787, contain items relating to Hannah Penn, agreements of Thomas and Richard Penn; Thomas Penn private letters, 1738–1741; Penn-Hamilton correspondence, 1748–1770; letters from Thomas and Richard Penn to James Hamilton; marriage settlement of Thomas Penn, 1751; account book of money due Thomas Penn from T. Asheton, Joseph Yeates, W. Peters, Sir William Johnson, et al., 1758–1769; Penn-Justice manuscripts, 1769–1804, relate to land warrants, surveys, financial accounts with the Penns, political and domestic affairs; John Penn's commonplace book, ca. 1785–1787; Penn letter books, 1789–1834, proprietaries' correspondence relating to Pennsylvania political and domestic affairs; litigation papers, 1672–1764; Penn-Physick papers, 1676–1804; Sir William Penn papers, 1644–1710; and records of the proprietary government.

Penn-Baltimore boundary dispute papers, 1606–1775: *Penn vs. Baltimore*, 1606–1774; New York records, 1664–1679; Kent County records, 1675–1683. "Boundaries Pennsylvania and Maryland, 1680–1768, Boundaries Virginia and Pennsylvania," 1773–1775, contains the answer of William Penn to Lord Baltimore, 1683; George Talbot to all persons on West of Delaware between Schuylkill and Whorekill; petition of Lord Baltimore to George II, 1753; letters to Charles Mason and Jeremiah Dixon, 1765; petition of all proprietors concerning southern and western boundaries, 1775; "Lands on Delaware Bay," 1683; controversy between Lord Baltimore and Penn, 1683;

address to the King from Penn about Charter, 1693; accounts miscellaneous, 1723–1760; boundaries of Delaware and Maryland, 1732–1733; report of commissioners, 1733–1734; "Drafting the new bill," 1735; petition, 1735; decree, 1735, 1750; Lord Baltimore's answer, 1737, 1740; drafts of interrogatories, 1739; depositions, Philadelphia, 1740; "Relating to particular points in case," 1743; brief for the plaintiff, 1747; brief for the amended bill, 1749; brief of the original bill against Frederick, Lord Baltimore, 1754; bill of revivor, brief for plaintiff, 1754; draft of bill of revivor, 1754; acts of assembly, 1756, 1759, 1760; drafts of the agreement with Lord Baltimore, 1757–1760; bill of revivor and supplemental bill, 1764.

Penn-Physick papers, 1676–1804: land grants and surveys, 1676–1801; extracts from patent books and list of land warrants; bonds, surveys, powers of attorney, 1681–1806; correspondence, 1682–1803; Penn accounts, 1683–1770; accounts of quitrents, 1701; accounts, 1701–1804; extracts from ledgers and journals, 1701, 1763; returns of warrants and surveys, 1732–1804; journal, 1742–1772; warrants to affix the great seal, 1767–1776; account books, 1769–1800; letterbook, 1769–1804; journal, 1779–1801; and additional warrants to affix the great seal to certificates of land patents, sheriff's commission, pardons.

Miscellaneous litigations and papers, 1672–1764:?xAmiscellaneous litigations: *Ford vs. Penn* accounts, 1672–1694, plea of the defendants, 1682–1727; *Ford vs. Penn, Penn vs. Beranger,* 1674–1716; *Ford vs. Penn,* 1705–1707; law suits, 1713–1869; *Penn vs. Penn,* 1722–1727, contains bill of complaint of Hannah Penn, et al., against Aubrey Thomas and Gulielma Maria, his wife, answer of Springett Penn, interrogations, depositions.

Other items: letters of William Penn, 1681–1692; records of Sussex County, 1681–1710; an act of Parliament, 1697; maps and surveys, Mason and Dixon Line, 1701–1705; Eastburn map of Indian Walk, 1757; original warrant signed by William Penn ordering Isaac Taylor and Thomas Pierson to survey line between County of Chester and County of New Castle, 1701; certificate signed by Isaac Taylor and Thomas Pierson, with map, "The Figure of the Circular Line Dividing between the County of New Castle and County of Chester, 1701;" merchants account books (Bristol, Eng.), 1717; map of part of the estate of William Penn in the Barony of Imokilly, 1764; proprietary manors and lands in Pennsylvania of John Penn, Jr., and John Penn, including maps; and other material.

Letters of William Penn, 1681–1692 manuscript copies by J. Francis Fisher, 1840.

485B
Tempsford Hall papers, 1669–1916.   (ca. 350 items.)

The collection contains the will of Admiral Sir William Penn, 1669; William Penn's instructions, 1689, to William Blackwell concerning the Proprietor's estate at Pennsbury; the marriage certificate of William and Hannah Penn, 1695; an inventory of Pennsylvania title papers and administrative records in the Proprietors' Philadelphia office, 1741, prepared by Richard Peters and Lyndford Lardner for Thomas Penn; letters, memoranda, and copies of wills of several Penn family members, 1682–1875, concerning family lands and forfeited estates in Pennsylvania.

The collection also includes letters and personal financial papers, 1774–1830, of Archbishop Stuart, containing family, political, and ecclesiastical news, as well as letters to and from his grandson, William Stuart, 1870–1888, about the latter's Irish estates.

Present, too, is a group of letters, 1805–1837, addressed to William Granville, natural son of Granville Penn, Sophia's brother. Most were sent to Granville by members of the Penn family and discuss Granville's career as a merchant in Ceylon and other family news.

This is a miscellaneous group of Penn and related family papers gathered or retained by the Stuart family, descendants of William Penn through Thomas Penn's youngest daughter, Sophia Margaretta Juliana Penn, who married William Stuart, Archbishop of Armagh, Anglican Primate of Ireland. For a number of years the collection was kept at Tempsford Hall, Bedfordshire, one of the Stuart family houses. The collection was purchased from a Stuart family descendant in 1968 with the Gratz fund.

485C
Penn-Forbes papers, 1644–1744.   (203 items.)

The papers of Admiral Sir William Penn include the journal of his service with the Irish Fleet, 1644–1647; sailing instructions for the fleet, 1653; an inventory of his property, 1670; letters to his son William, 1666–1670; letters to the Admiral. A larger group reflects the efforts of William Penn, the Founder, to administer his province, his intention to surrender the government to the Crown, 1710/11, and the conflict over the Penn inheritance among the children of his two marriages. There are several letters from English political figures, 1674–1710, as well as from prominent early Friends, including George Fox, 1674–1689, and John Gratton, 1689–1693. This small group of manuscripts was purchased by the Society from Stewart Forbes, administrator of the estate of Thomas Gordon Penn in 1882.

Published inventory available in the *P.M.H.B.*, 28 (1904): 155–168.

486
Penn, Granville, 1761–1844.   Book of poems, 1808–1838.   (1 v.)

A collection of poetry in the handwriting of Granville Penn.
Gift of A.L. Smith, 1934.

487

Penn, William, 1644–1718.   Commemoration papers, 1931–1932.
(200 items.)

Records of the general committee of William Penn's commemoration, the 250th anniversary of the founding of Pennsylvania. The papers include correspondence, financial reports, minutes of committees, programs of exercises in schools and colleges, lists of patriotic societies, and other matter pertaining to the event.
Gift of Harold E. Gillingham.

488

Pennsylvania Counties papers, 1708–1882.   (1,500 items.)

Miscellaneous papers of several Pennsylvania counties: Allegheny, 1790–1849; Armstrong, ca. 1785–1816; Bedford, 1782–1794; Berks, 1772–1795; Bucks, 1708–1863; Carbon, ca. 1789–1823; Chester, 1729–1818; Centre, 1785–1816; Clearfield, 1785–1816; Crawford, 1772–1823; Cumberland, 1782; Delaware, 1786–1811; Dauphin, 1790–1813; Fayette, 1790–1796; Franklin, 1788–1812; Indiana, 1823; Lancaster, 1743–1876; Lehigh, 1757; Lebanon, ca. 1789–1823; Lycoming, ca. 1789; Luzerne, 1793–1823; Mifflin, ca. 1789–1823; Monroe, 1846; Montgomery, 1728–1882; McKean, ca. 1789; Perry, ca. 1789; Snyder, ca. 1789–1823; Susquehanna, ca. 1789; Tioga, 1847; Washington, 1781–1784; Wayne, 1790–1802; Westmoreland, 1774–1823.

Among the items is a narrative by C. Van Horn describing the Connecticut invasion, pioneering, colonial warfare, and incidents during the Revolution, 1772–1837, in Crawford County; a history of Monroe County and of the Indian Walk, 1746; a history of Luzerne County, 1793–1823; a history of Lehigh County townships, n.d., and the journal, 1757, of Lieutenant A. Engel, stationed at Leckley Township; letters and accounts of David Franks, Bernard Gratz, L. Andrew Levy, Joseph Simon, and others, of Lancaster, relating to provisioning of British and American soldiers and prisoners during the Revolution, 1777–1778; taxable property, Chester County, 1783–1788; petitions to assemblies and legislatures relating to changes of county seats, road building, dam construction; indentures; surveys; court records of indictments; penal records; deeds and land patents; jury lists; muster rolls; and other items.
Purchased.

489

Pennsylvania Population Land Company.   Papers, 1792–1834.
(1,000 items.)

Papers of John Nicholson, president, and Tench Francis, treasurer, of this land company, active in Allegheny, Beaver and Mercer counties. Among the papers are patents for land in Allegheny County, signed by Governor Thomas Mifflin, 1792–1800; records of transfers of land by Aaron Burr to John Nicholson, 1795; stock transfer book, containing the names of Aaron Burr, Theophilus Casenove, Walter Stewart, James Wilson, and others, 1794–1806; deeds to Aaron Levy, 1792–1794; stock certificate signed by John Nicholson, and Tench Francis, 1795–1797; stock transfers by John Nicholson, 1794–1801; a colored map of land owned by John Ashley, n.d.: correspondence of Enoch Marvin and Thomas Ashley, 1798–1825; miscellaneous accounts, agreements, contracts, and correspondence, 1796–1834.

Gift of James Gibson.

490
Pennsylvania Abolition Society.   **Papers, 1748–1979.**
(12 linear ft.)

Organized in five series as described.

Growing out of egalitarian concerns of members of the Society of Friends, the Pennsylvania Abolition Society, as it is now known, was founded in 1775 as the Society for the Relief of Free Negroes Unlawfully Held in Bondage, but the Revolution caused its early Quaker members to suspend operations until 1784, when it reorganized with a broader base. From the beginning, the Abolition Society's programs were devoted not only to the abolition of slavery, but to the social and economic improvement of Black Americans as well. As early as 1794, the Society helped to found the American Convention, a loose affiliation of anti-slavery societies everywhere, founded a school for Black males, and conducted the first census of Philadelphia's Black community. The Society operated through an Acting Committee of officers and through its Board of Education.

Series I: Minutes and reports, containing minutes of the General Meetings, 1775, 1784–1979; minutes of the Acting Committee, 1784–1842; minutes of the Electing Committee, 1790–1826; Committee for Improving the condition of free Blacks, minutes, 1790–1803; Committee of Guardians, 1790–1802; Board of Education, minutes and reports, 1797–1865; Committee on the African Slave Trade, minutes, 1805–1807. Also present in the first series are loose and draft minutes and committee reports.

Series II: Correspondence, 1789–1979. It contains letters on a variety of political, social, and personal subjects. Correspondents include most of the anti-slavery organization in the United States as well as a number of anti-slavery advocates including Jacques-Pierre Brissott de Warville, Condorcet, William Wilberforce, Benjamin Lundy, Lucretia Mott, and others.

Series III: Financial Records, 1792–1979. Treasurer's accounts, 1792–1840, 1937–1949; Board of Education (Committee of 24), 1793–1812, Subscription books, 1813–1821, 1813–1825, 1835–1837, Clarkson School tuition accounts, 1819–1822, 1838; miscellaneous bills, receipts, audits, 1795–1972.

Series IV: Manumission and indentures, 1785–1865. The majority of these materials have their origins with two committees of the Society: the Committee of Guardians, 1790–1803, recorded manumissions and indentures as they occurred under the Pennsylvania law for the gradual abolition of slavery (1780); the Committee of Inspection safeguarded the legal rights of Blacks, 1790–1803. After 1803, the Acting Committee assumed both roles. The manumission are contained in eight volumes, 1780–1853. Other records present in this series includes indentures for manumitted slaves, legal papers concerning efforts of the several committees to secure the release of Blacks brought into Pennsylvania, transcriptions of the laws regarding slavery in Pennsylvania, Virginia, New York, New Jersey, Rhode Island, and Georgia, 1750s to 1790s.

Series V: Miscellaneous papers. Lists of officers and members, 1784–1819; memorials to both houses of Congress and several state legislatures regarding slavery, 1788–1860; records of related institutions, including: Lombard Street Infant School, roll book, 1849–1850; Clarkson Institute, Constitution, 1832, minutes, accounts, and reports, 1829–1837; Committee to Visit Colored People, Census Facts collected by Benjamin Bacon and Charles Gardner, 1838; Facts on Beneficial Societies, 1823–1838. Present, too, are extensive materials on the American Convention, which met irregularly in Philadelphia, 1794–1836, arranged by year: minutes, credentials, lists of members, committee reports, treasurer's accounts.

Also present in this series are the papers of organizations to which Abolition Society members belonged: Philadelphia Female Anti-Slavery Society, minutes, 1833–1870, incoming correspondence 1834–1853; Young Men's Anti-Slavery Society, committee reports, 1836–1837, incoming correspondence, 1834–1837, treasurer's accounts, 1835–1838; South Mulberry Ward (Philadelphia) Anti-Slavery Society, minutes, 1837; Junior Anti-Slavery Society of Philadelphia, constitution and minutes, 1836–1846; Bache Institute, accounts, 1851–1852; Philadelphia Yearly Meeting, Committee on Requited Labor, minutes and correspondence, 1837–1839; American Free Produce Association, correspondence and circulars, 1838–1840; Philadelphia Anti-Slavery Society, constitution, 1839; Pennsylvania Anti-Slavery Society, minutes, 1838–1846, executive committee minutes, 1846–1870, accounts, 1847–1849, Vigilance Committee of Philadelphia, accounts, 1854–1857, "Journal C of Station No. 2 of the Underground Railroad," William Still, agent, 1852–1857; 13th Ward Republican Club of Philadelphia, constitution and minutes, 1856–1859.

The Society's records were originally maintained by its officers and members, but were then gathered together at Clarkson Hall in 1839, where they remained until the building was sold in 1863. Ten years later they were placed with the Friends' Historical Association where they remained until the 1920s, when they began to come to the Historical Society. Because the officers and members of the Abolition Society frequently held positions with other meliorative organizations, fragmentary records of other organizations are frequently found among the Abolition Society's records. The Society's records were reorganized on archival principles in 1976, in preparation for the comprehensive microfilm of the records completed that year.

Microfilm edition available through the inter-library loan from the Historical Society.

491
Pennsylvania Constitutional Convention. Autographs, 1837–1838. (ca. 200 items.)

Autograph letters and biographical sketches of members of the convention that framed the Constitution of Pennsylvania in 1837; also autographs on visiting cards and newspaper clippings and other printed matter relating to the activities of the convention.

Gift of Francis Shunk Brown and George R. Bedford.

492
Penrose, Washington H. Arithmetic books and scrapbook, 1824–1829, 1859. (3 v.)

Arithmetic exercise books, 1824–1829 and scrapbook, 1859, containing newspaper clippings of poetry.

Gift of James H. Lord.

493
Percy, William. Journal and commonplace book, 1774–1776. (1 v.)

The Rev. William Percy's account of his activities in behalf of the religions revival, his travel and preaching in various towns of Pennsylvania, New Jersey, Maryland, Delaware, and his views on the moral influence of the Church; also aphorisms, epigrams, and Biblical excerpts.

Purchased.

494
Perkins, Samuel C. Papers, 1669–1899. (6 linear ft.)

These papers of a Philadelphia lawyer relate to real estate, legal business, and social matters. They include deeds and mortgages, 1669–1861; miscellaneous correspondence and documents, 1869–1899; correspondence of Samuel H. Perkins, relating to the academic and economic affairs of Girard College, 1847–1849; "Private Docket, Naval General Court Martial, Navy Yard, Philadelphia, Samuel G. Perkins, Judge Advocate," 1864; letter book of Frederick A. Packard, editor of the American Sunday School Union, 1832–1842.

495
Perkins, Samuel C.   Incoming letters, 1829–1885.
(ca. 600 items.)

Letters from Frederick A. Packard, editor of the *American Sunday School Union,* Philadelphia. They mainly relate to publications, missionary work, subscriptions, church activities.
Gift of Samuel C. Perkins.

496
Perkins, Samuel H.   Journals, 1818–1832.   (2 v.)

Journals of a Philadelphia teacher and lawyer, recount his travel and sojourn in Mattamuskett, N.C., 1818, legal apprenticeship and admittance to the Philadelphia bar, his professional struggles, and reflect the social and religious life of the city.
Gift of A. Rogenburger.

497
Peters, Anna M.   Papers, 1856–1899.   (ca. 50 items.)

Family papers including letters, accounts, wills, drafts, and surveys of land in Delaware County.

498
Peters, Richard, 1704–1776.   Papers, 1697–1845.   (3 linear ft.)

The papers of Richard Peters comprise correspondence and documents, including accounts of negotiations and treaties with the Indians and some notes of General Timothy Pickering on the battle at Brandywine. They are of special interest for the colonial history of Pennsylvania because of Peters' official connection with the proprietary government. There are: minutes of council, 1756–1757; letters of Thomas Penn to Richard Peters, 1752–1772; letter book, 1737–1750; Governor James Hamilton accounts, records of marriage licenses, public house permits, 1748–1751; commonplace book, 1725; Richard Peters' drafts of Pennsylvania lands, 1795–1813; letters of the Rev.

Richard Peters to the proprietors of Pennsylvania, 1755–1757; diaries, 1750, 1758, 1762; Episcopal license of the Rev. R. Peters, 1725.

Letters of Rev. Richard Peters to the proprietors of Pennsylvania are photostatic copies.

Gift of the Peters family.

499
Peters family.   Papers, 1687–1871.   (3 linear ft.)

Organized into three sections: Rev. Richard Peters papers, Judge Richard Peters papers, and Richard Peters estate papers.

Rev. Richard Peters (1704–1776) was pastor of Christ Church, Philadelphia, and secretary of the proprietaries of Pennsylvania, 1749–1755.

Judge Richard Peters (1744–1828) was an eminent legal authority and agricultural scientist, 1772–1827.

Richard Peters (1780–1848) was a lawyer and a merchant.

The papers for Rev. Richard Peters include: correspondence, legal documents, that deal with domestic affairs, land transactions, legal cases, Thomas Cookson estate, in Lancaster, of which Peters was an executor; also some items, 1776, pertaining to Christ Church.

Papers for Judge Richard Peters chiefly pertain to his experiments in agricultural science, including professional and personal correspondence, daybooks, 1792–1828; bills and receipts, 1803–1828, "City Lots," 1786–1790; accounts with Joseph Kennedy relating to an island and fishery in the Schuylkill River, 1804–1813; accounts with Isaiah Kirk for William Peters' board and clothing, 1808–1819; York County, lands (correspondence between Richard Peters and D. Cassat), 1816–1821; Mantua Farm, 1815–1849; promissory notes and bank checks, 1811–1819.

The estate papers for Richard Peters (1780–1848) include papers on western lands of Pennsylvania, 1798–1871; correspondence, 1824–1834; Venango County lands, 1810–1841; General Robinson estate, 1808–1843; account with James Kay, Jr., for printing supreme court reports, 1829–1840; bankruptcy case of Peters, Campion, and Linder, 1841–1847; land papers, 1846–1862; J.W. Howe letters, 1849–1853; account book, 1807–1849; receipt book, 1812–1819; Willing estate papers, 1687–1806; Schuylkill Permanent Bridge papers, 1797–1828; Sarah Peters correspondence with Thomas Cowperthwaite and Company, 1850–1853; and miscellaneous items.

Gift of Captain Richard Peters.

Twelve letters to Judge Richard Peters, 1793–1807 published in the *P.M.H.B.*, 44 (1920): 325–342.

500
**Philadelphia Assemblies.   Collection, 1879–1929.
(ca. 250 items.)**

The social world of Philadelphia is reflected in this collection of invitations, announcements, and newspaper clippings relating to the Philadelphia Assemblies.
Gift of the Edward S. Sayres Estate.

502
**Philadelphia Committee of Defense.   Minutes, 1814–1815.
(3 v.)**

The records of the Philadelphia Committee of Defense relate to: fortification of the Delaware River approach, organization of volunteers, preparation of ammunition, erection of forts, floating of loans, August 26, 1814 to August 16, 1815.
Gift of John Goodman.

503
Philadelphia surveys, 1784–1831.   (35 items.)

A collection of petitions and surveys on the opening of streets in various parts of Philadelphia. Purchased, Library Fund, 1914.

504
**Philanthropic Burial Ground Association.
Account books, 1834–1880.   (2 v.)**

Treasurer's accounts of the Philanthropic Burial Ground Association including records of receipts and disbursements.
Purchased, Library Fund.

505
Physick, Edmund, 1727–1804.   Receipt book, 1773–1779.   (1 v.)

Edmund Physick was an agent of the proprietaries of Pennsylvania.
Accounts of funds returned by the proprietaries to settlers who had paid for lands that were found to have been previously distributed; also disbursements for services rendered in surveying, advertising, judiciary affairs, and general public expenses.
Gift of Dr. Emlen Physick, 1916.

506
Pike, Zebulon Montgomery, 1779–1813.   Journal, 1805–1806.
(1 v.)

General Zebulon Montgomery Pike's "Journal of a Military Expedition to the Western Territory," a detailed description of his expedition to trace the Mississippi to its head, with data on the topography of the territory, hardships encountered, life and adventures among numerous Indian tribes, French trading interests, hunting deer and elk for food, and notes on Pike's surveys of rivers and streams.

507
Pilmore, Joseph, 1734?-1825.   Sermons, 1816.   (1 v.)

Sermons delivered at St. Paul's Church, by Dr. Joseph Pilmore; also includes his notes on the Bible.

508
Plan for the general government of America, 1780.   (1 v.)

A plan for the government of the American provinces, advocating allegiance to England.
Gift of Samuel N. Lewis, 1907.

509
Des Plantations de L'Amérique, 1714.   (1 v.)

A treatise on the British settlements in America; a plan for their economic improvement; recommends enactments for the administration of their affairs.
Purchased, De la Roche Fund, 1935.

510
Pleasants, Thomas Franklin.   Journals, 1814–1817.   (4 v.)

Journals of Thomas Franklin Pleasants, Philadelphia lawyer and merchant, describes professional activities, daily social events, travel through southern states, and cotton enterprises in New Orleans, and discusses military training in the War of 1812, and other events of the time.
Gift of Henry Pleasants, 1914.

511
Pleasonton, Augustus James, 1808–1894.   **Diary, 1838–1844.**
(1 v.)

Diary of General Augustus Pleasonton, a prominent Philadelphian, describes events of 1838, 1841, and 1844; the "Buckshot War," military activities in Harrisburg, abolitionists and African American riots in Philadelphia, the Maine boundary controversy, incidents in the Canadian insurrection, Nicholas Biddle and the Bank of the United States, presidential elections, destruction of the steamer *Erie,* and other incidents of local and national importance. Included are accounts of Pleasonton's literary and musical interests, social activities, a description of a trip to Washington, D.C., and Alexandria, Va., a tour through West Point, N.Y., and other personal matters.
Gift of Mrs. John T. Dohan, 1915.

512
Poinsett, Joel Roberts, 1779–1851.   **Papers, 1785–1851.**
(8 linear ft.)

The papers of Joel Roberts Poinsett, American agent to Latin America and secretary of war in the Van Buren administration.

The papers of Poinsett's education period, 1797–1809 include: data on his studies; journals of travel in American and Europe; letters of introduction to important persons, by J. Allen Smith, 1806; letters describing Poinsett's sojourn in Russia, friendship with Czar Alexander I, tour through the Caucasus, Caspian Sea region, Baku, and Persia; comments on European political affairs, and impending war between Russia and Sweden.

Papers from Poinsett's term as United States agent and consul general in Buenos Aires and other South American capitals, 1810–1815: data on the revolutionary movements against Spain and Portugal; letters from R. Smith, James Monroe, and James Madison, from José M. De Carrera, I.X. Elio, and other South American political and military leaders; also Spanish and Portuguese pamphlets, broadsides, proclamations, general orders.

Papers primarily on political and economic conditions in South Carolina, 1815–1825: on factional party strife, public questions, tariff, transportation, territorial expansion, the Greek issue before Congress; letters of John C. Calhoun, Edward Everett, William Johnson, Peter S. Du Ponceau, Commodore David Porter, Richard Rush, Robert Walsh.

Letters and documents of the period during which Poinsett was minister plenipotentiary of the United States to Mexico: data on Mexican politics and economic conditions, revolutionary movements, civil wars, the influence of free-masonry on national affairs, United States commercial and political interests in Mexico, and Poinsett's treaty negotiations; letters of John Forsyth, Rufus King, Commodore David Porter, Samuel L. Southard, General Guerrero, Antonio Lopez Santa Anna, and Juan de Canedo, and general orders, proclamations, pamphlets; also a memorandum by Joel R. Poinsett to John Quincy Adams, 1827.

Letters reflecting American politics, the rise of the secession movement in South Carolina, and the organization of the Union Party, 1830–1836; letters of Andrew Jackson, 1830–1833, on his toast to the Union, opposition to nullification, and his plans for suppressing that movement by armed force; papers on tariff, economic issues, Cherokees in Georgia; letters of Dr. Joseph Johnson, James Brown, A. Butler, William Drayton, Lewis Cass, Henry Rutledge, Louis McLane, and others; also memorials and pamphlets.

Papers of Poinsett's War Department administration, 1837–1841: material on plans for the reorganization of the army, fortifications, introduction of new ordnance, and administration of West Point; letters of General Winfield Scott relate to the defense of the Northwestern boundary and the Canadian controversy; Nicholas Biddle papers on United States Bank affairs; Cherokee, Creek, Winnebago Indians; letters from Andrew Jackson on the Seminole War in Florida; miscellaneous letters on Texas boundary, state banks, claims against Mexico, requests for military and government positions; letters of Martin Van Buren, John C. Calhoun, Gouverneur Kemble, James Buchanan, Levi Woodbury, Dennis H. Mahan, Richard Rush, James Gadsden, Alfred Huger, James K. Polk, John C. Frémont, Stephen W. Kearny, Felix Huston, J.K. Paulding, William J. Worth, Silas Wright, Millard Fillmore, Amos Kendall, Edward Everett, George Bancroft, Francis Markoe, and others; also papers on the promotion of science, the National Institution, exploring expeditions, horticulture, and historical research.

Letters and documents, mainly personal, 1841–1851: comments on the Mexican War, secession movement, Union party, agriculture, European political conditions, and other topics; Poinsett essays, drafts of speeches and letters, autobiographical notes; sketch of Poinsett's life by Dr. Joseph Johnson.

Gift of Mrs. John Julius Alston Pringle, 1885.

513
Pollard, William.   Letterbook, 1772–1774.   (1 v.)

Letterbook of William Pollard, Philadelphia merchant and shipper, containing his copies of letters to clients in many parts of the American colonies, West Indies, and England. They reflect his extensive shipping and commercial interests, and throw light on prevailing economic conditions.

514

Port of Philadelphia.   Papers, 1789–1855.   (ca. 300 items.)

Entry cancelled; see collection #237.

515

**Port of Philadelphia.   Bills of Lading, 1716–1772.
(ca. 350 items.)**

Material on merchandise shipped by William Bishop, Richard Poor, Oswald Peel, Thomas Riché, and others, to the West Indies, especially Barbados.

516

Port of Philadelphia.   Record books, 1796–1804.   (2 v.)

Bonds of importers to guarantee payment of custom duties at the Port of Philadelphia, 1796–1797; debenture book, containing stubs of certificates issued, 1804.

517

**Porter, William W. (William Wagener), 1856–1928.   Collection,
1770–1880.   (ca. 350 items.)**

This collection contains the papers of several members of a Pennsylvania family, distinguished in the Revolutionary War, political leadership, jurisprudence, and administrative affairs.

Andrew Porter papers, 1773–1813, deal chiefly with land transactions in which he was officially and personally interested, in Allegheny, Mercer, Northumberland, Westmoreland and other Pennsylvania counties. Included are several items on his military career, 1776, 1778; his astronomical observation, 1786–1787; the Pennsylvania western boundary line, 1784–1786.

The correspondence, 1829–1867, of David R. Porter, governor of Pennsylvania, 1839–1845, includes: letters, 1838–1867, of James Buchanan; letters of Sam Houston, 1858; copy of an address to John C. Calhoun; and other items on state and national political affairs. There are also papers of George B. Porter, Robert Porter, James Madison Porter, and other members of the Porter family, 1770–1880.

Gift of W.W. Porter.

518

Puerto Rico.   Papers, 1806–1885.   (ca. 300 items.)

Licenses to masters of vessels, passports, and similar legal documents issued by the Puerto Rican government; copies of government rules and regulations regarding ports.

Gift of J. Madison Taylor, 1917.

519

Post, Christian Frederick, 1710?-1785.   Journal, 1758.   (1 v.)

"Journey from Philadelphia to the Ohio on a Message from Government of Pennsylvania to the Delaware, Shawanesse and Mingo Indians," by Christian Frederick Post, Moravian missionary, describes the hazards of travel through the wilderness, Indian hostilities and massacres, the desolate condition of the country, conflicting French and British interests, peace councils held with Indian chiefs, and the military protection afforded by posts and forts.

520

Potts family.   Papers, 1733–1874.   (ca. 600 items.)

Papers, notes, proofs, and original manuscripts gathered by Mrs. Thomas Potts James, and her correspondence with various members of the Thomas Potts family, on the compilation of "The Potts Memorial."

Gift of Mary I. Gozzaldi.

521

Potts, Jonathan, 1745–1781.   Papers, 1766–1780.   (ca. 500 items.)

Dr. Jonathan Potts was medical director-general of the Northern Department of the Revolutionary Army.

Papers of Jonathan Potts, include: letters, muster rolls, and other documents relating to medical supplies and hospital service in the Revolution; also essays on the controversies between England and the colonies.

522

Potts, Thomas.   Genealogy, 1747–1867.   (7 v.)

Genealogical data on the Thomas Potts family of Pottstown.

Gift of Mary I. Gozzaldi, 1936.

523
Potts, William John.   Notes, 1887.   (1 v.)

William John Potts' notes taken from the Pennsylvania Gazette, 1758, on scientific experiments and discussions, literary subjects, local social events, and affairs of general interest.

524
Powel, Samuel, 1704–1759.   Letterbooks, 1724–1747.   (3 v.)

Samuel Powel, Jr., was a Philadelphia merchant and shipper.
Letterbooks beginning with his arrival in Philadelphia in 1727, illustrating Powel's dependence upon British Friends such as Thomas Plumstead and David Barclay to develop trans-Atlantic trade with England, Portugal, and the West Indies.
Purchased.

525
Powell, Howell.   Notes, 1704–1706.   (1 v.)

Excerpts from Latin and Greek histories and philosophies, astronomical calculations, and miscellaneous memoranda, written by a scholar at Kingsland, Herefordshire, England, interleaved in *Merlinus Liberatus: being an Almanack for the Year of our blessed Saviour's Incarnation,* 1704, and in *The London Almanack,* 1706, bound in one volume.

526
Lowrie, Sarah Dickson, 1870–1957.   Biography of Eli Kirk Price, 1936.   (1 v.)

Eli Kirk Price was a distinguished citizen of Philadelphia.
Gift of Sarah D. Lowrie.

527
Price, John.   Diary, 1831–1847.   (1 v.)

Diary of John Price, a Chester County farmer, recording farm economy, sowing, harvesting, prices, and building information.
Purchased.

528
Proceedings of the tribunal of the inquisition at Barcelona. Transcript, 1624.   (1 v.)

Record of judicial proceedings in the Spanish Inquisition.
Gift of George Read, 1861.

529

Proud, Robert, 1728–1813.   Collection, 1681–1811.   (3 linear ft.)

The collection includes original manuscripts of histories of Pennsylvania and Philadelphia, and other literary works by Robert Proud; official papers and letters gathered from various sources on the colonial government of Pennsylvania; and some of Proud's papers; "The History of Pennsylvania in North America from the original Institutions and Settlement of that Province in 1681–1742"; "The History of the original Institution and Settlement of the Province of Pennsylvania in North America under the First Proprietor, and Governor William Penn, between 1760–1770"; "The History of Pennsylvania, 1680–1708"; "A View of the Province of Pennsylvania, between 1760–1770"; "Observation on the Increase of the Population, Commerce and Improvements of Pennsylvania before the Revolution," 1776; Proud's notes on the history of Pennsylvania, 1800–1807; "Historical memoranda of the rise and progress of the city of Philadelphia, 1682–1789"; The Municipal Rights and Privileges of Philadelphia," 1801.

Also included are notes, including list of names of Quaker preachers in Pennsylvania, and a list of marriages, 1681–1772; a collection of indentures, 1681–1706; miscellaneous documents, letters, petitions, addresses to council, warrants, memorials, and proclamations, bearing the signatures of Thomas Lloyd, William Markham, John Holme, and others, 1684–1775; account book of Robert Proud's school, with a list of names of his pupils, 1759–1792; letters of John Proud to Robert Proud, 1775–1811; Robert Proud letterbook, 1770–1811; subscription book, 1799–1806; "Short notes on the Life of Robert Proud written by himself," 1806; "Strictures on Theatrical Entertainments, both ancient and modern, and an Ironical defense of the State," 1767; "Proud's memoranda on Experimental Philosophy," 1750; memoranda, essays, and poetry written by Proud, 1750–1803; copy in the hand of Robert Proud, of Thomas Makin's poem, "Landis Pensilvaniae," and some other poetry, 1774; translations from Greek and Latin, miscellaneous sketches and essays, 1778, 1785; translation of Colvius' treatise on the end of life, and other memoranda, 1774–1804; a translation of Boethius, and other memoranda, 1776; "Commentatorium de Vita," and other essays and observations, 1806.

Purchased.

530

Bernard, Richard.   Diary, 1774–1792.   (1 v.)

Diary of Richard Bernard recording accounts of Quaker meetings, names of Quaker families, record of personal and domestic events, prices of farm products and commodities; notes on British army in Philadelphia, Captain Henry Lee.

Gift of C.N. Barnard.

531
Queen, James W.   Journals and letters, 1849 (1864–1865).   (2 v.)

These journals and letters contain James W. Queen's accounts of his journeys in various parts of Europe, cultural conditions, religious sentiments, facilities for travel, palaces and art museums visited, hotel accommodations. Also included are plans and maps of cities, time tables, and related items.
Gift of James W. Queen.

532
Quick, Lavington, 1819–1876.   Papers, 1847–1876.
(ca. 400 items.)

This collection of papers and correspondence relates mainly to the medical activities of Dr. Lavington Quick, brigadier surgeon in the United States Army during the Civil War.
Gift of Mrs. William C. Quick, 1917.

533
Raesly, Harry E.   Autographs, 1871–1874.   (1 v.)

A collection of verse and poetry dedicated to Harry E. Raesly by friends and classmates from Lafayette College.
Gift of F.H. Price, 1938.

534
Raguet, Condy, 1784–1842.   Official letters, 1824–1827.   (2 v.)

Condy Raguet's copies of his official letters as United States chargé d'affaires at the Court of Brazil, addressed to John Quincy Adams and Henry Clay, secretaries of state. They concern United States foreign policy, relations with the Brazilian Government, revolutionary developments, commercial and shipping conditions, British and French interests in South America. Included is a broadside, 1828, presenting the case of the seizure of the American vessel *Spark* by the Brazilian government and the resignation of Condy Raguet from his post.
Gift of Mrs. William L. Mactier, 1895.

535
Ramsay, David, 1745–1815.   *History of the United States*.   (1 v.)

David Ramsay's proof copy of a portion of the first edition of his *History of the United States,* published by M. Carey, Philadelphia, in 3 vols., 1816–1817, with notations in his hand.
Gift of Brinton Coxe, 1887.

536

Rawle family.   Papers, 1683–1915.   (12 linear ft.)

Among these papers are Francis Rawle's ledger book, 1720–1726; waste book, 1735–1737; William Rawle's journals, 1782–1830; letters, 1778–1834; his official correspondence as United States attorney for Pennsylvania, 1791–1800; papers on the Whiskey Rebellion, 1791–1796; papers concerned with the insurrection in Northampton County, 1798–1800; Penn letters and records of the Penn estate of Springettsbury Manor, 1683–1825; William Rawle's essays on philosophical, scientific, historical, political, and social subjects, 1775–1835; papers on the Pennsylvania boundary question and to the abolition of slavery, 1794–1834; correspondence on the "Cavalry Fight of the Right Flank at Gettysburg," 1863–1912; adjutants regimental journal of the third Pennsylvania Cavalry, 1862–1865; notes on family history, 1619–1884; Junior Legal Club papers, 1870–1915; manuscript of Horace Binney's "Leaders of the Old Bar of Philadelphia"; printed account of the trial of John Peter Zenger, 1738; copy of Francis Rawle's manuscript, "A Just Rebuke," 1726; and James Logan's "Dialogue Showing What's Therein," 1726; and diary of Rebecca Warner Rawle Shoemaker, 1804, at Clifford Farm.

Gift of the Rawle family.

Extracts from William Rawle's journal published in *P.M.H.B.,* 25 (1901): 114–117, 220–227.

537

Read family.   Correspondence, 1716–1872.   (ca. 200 items.)

Correspondence of George Read, member of the Continental Congress and President of Delaware; George Read, Jr., district attorney of Delaware, and William Thompson Read, senator from Delaware. The letters contain material on the development of the state of Delaware, in which the Reads played an important part, socially and politically. Letters from prominent men of the period, John Dickinson, Benjamin Franklin, William Thompson, Caesar Rodney, George Ross, and many others are included.

538

Read, William Thompson, 1792–1873.   Papers, 1776–1869. (2.5 linear ft.)

This collection includes: "Historical Notes on the Life of George Read," 1827; "Life and Correspondence of George Read, a signer of the Declaration of Independence, with notes of some of his contemporaries," 1855–1858; "Some Leaves of the Early History of New Castle, Delaware, and Maryland," 1868; "From Brooklyn to Brandywine, a sketch of the Campaign of General Washington from Sept. 1776-Sept. 1777," 1869; "Notes and Essays," 1814–1819; "Notices of Captain John Barey, and Captain David Ross," 1867; biographical sketch of C.A. Rodney, 1853; biographical sketch and some letters on the life of Bishop George W. Freeman, 1871; pamphlets, addresses delivered by William T. Read, 1816–1870; excerpts from newspapers, 1858–1860, 1865–1866; copy of the proceedings of the state convention of Delaware, Aug. 27, 1776; *The Biographical History of Dionysius Tyrant of Delaware addressed to the people of the United States of America by Timolean,* a political satire, 1788; Review of "Historical Inquiry concerning Henry Hudson, his early life and connection with the Muscovy Company, and Discovery of the Hudson," by John Meredith Read.

539
Records from family bibles, 1739–1927.   (ca. 51 items.)

Collection of miscellaneous notes on births, deaths, and genealogical data.

Gift of C.H.B. Turner, R. Ball Dodson, and others.

540
Redwood, Francis T., Mrs.   Collection, 1762–1835.   (69 items.)

Letters of the Rev. Thomas and Mary Hopkinson, of colonial Philadelphia, on social and religious subjects. Included are letters of Benjamin Franklin, 1765; Thomas McKean, 1767; John Morgan, 1776; Mary Hopkinson; Mary Morgan; Esther Duché; Jacob Duché; Joseph Hopkinson; John Quincy Adams, 1835.

Gift of Mrs. Francis T. Redwood.

541
Reed and Forde.   Papers, 1759–1823.   (12 linear ft.)

The papers and correspondence of John Reed and Standish Forde, Philadelphia merchants, relate mainly to foreign commerce, and include accounts, receipts, invoices of goods, bills of lading, insurance policies, charters of vessels, with a detailed account of business transacted with England, France, Spain, Holland, Portugal, the West Indies, French and Spanish America. The hazards of American shipping due to European wars, French and Spanish embargoes, capture by privateers and war vessels, litigations, and the prices and variety of goods traded, including grain, salt, furs, cloth, tea, metals, powder, rum, and wine, are described in detail.

Letters, 1789–1792, from James Wilkinson, Daniel Clark, Daniel Cox, Captain Abner Dunn, Clement Biddle, Robert Morris, John Nicholson, J.

Ball, Thomas Morgan, and numerous other merchants show the business transactions and land ventures in the Floridas, New Orleans, Kentucky, Virginia, west of the Ohio, Mississippi, and other territories. Included are land records, indentures, warrants for land in various estates, 1764–1816; James Wilkinson's letter to Captain Dunn, on trade with Florida by Kentuckians, 1789; an agreement with James Wilkinson to ship goods to the Mississippi and the Spanish country, 1790; French legal papers concerning goods shipped to St. Pierre, Martinique and other places; Reed and Forde letterbooks, 1787, 1788–1790, 1793–1794, 1801–1803; ledgers, 1776–1779, 1779–1780; daybook, 1785–1791; account books, 1766–1784; daybook of Reed and Forde estates, 1808–1815; John Reed letterbook, 1808–1814; Joseph Boggs waste book, 1791–1792; Samuel Israel letterbook, 1804–1807; Joseph Graisbury (tailor) ledger, 1759–1773; Reed and Forde commonplace book, 1782–1790, in which is a list of invalids belonging to the Pennsylvania Line; memo. booklets, 1777–1819.

Also included among the business papers are: Forde and Reed bankbooks, Bank of Pennsylvania, 1793–1805; Bank of North America, 1782–1791; Bank of the United States, 1792–1796; Andrew Summers' bankbook of North America, 1790–1791; apprentice indentures, 1784–1795; bonds and notes, 1782–1801; lottery sale records, 1773–1802; Forde journal of a trip to New Madrid, Tenn., 1790, and one from New Madrid to New Orleans, 1790–1792; his certificate of membership in the Hibernian Society, 1793; John Reed bankruptcy papers, 1801–1814; will of Rebecca Cappers, 1793; and other items.

There is a group of Robert Morris letters and papers, 1795–1802 which deal with his financial difficulties and assignment of his property; also papers and letters, 1814–1823, of John Reed, Jr., describing his service in the Navy, his active duty in the West Indian waters on the U.S.S. *Congress, Guerriére, Constitution, Independence,* and *Macedonian.*

542
Port of Philadelphia.   Register, 1741–1742.   (1 v.)

Names of vessels, cargoes, points of sailing, ports of call, listed in this register of ships entering the Port of Philadelphia.

543
Reliques of broad toppe : being a collection of anciente mss. discovered in the summer of 1865.   (1 v.)

Allegorical poetry, narrative, and satire, composed by an unnamed writer in 1865.

Gift of Joseph F.A. Jackson, 1910.

544
Remey, George Collier, 1841–1928.   Reminiscences.   (3 v.)

The reminiscences of George Collier Remey, rear admiral, U.S.N., contain genealogical data, records of his travels and service, information on American naval activities in the Civil War, Spanish-American War, Philippine Insurrection, and Boxer Rebellion in China. Included are the reminiscences of his wife, Mary Josephine Mason Remey, 1845–1919, which present a picture of social life and of many notable persons of the period. There are also photographs, newspaper clippings, and coats of arms.
Gift of Charles Mason Remey, 1932.

545
Richards, Joseph T.   Genealogical papers1841–1928.
(ca. 100 items.)

Transferred to the Genealogical Society of Pennsylvania.

546
Richards, Joseph T., 1845–1915.   Papers, 1857–1929.   (2 v.)

Letters, notes, charts, maps, and other genealogical material on the Richards family, which settled in Delaware County in 1682; also United States maps drawn by Joseph T. Richards (chief engineer, Pennsylvania Railroad, 1903–1913) in his school days in Cecil County, Md.
Gift of Joseph T. Richards, 1917.

547
Richards, Samuel, 1769–1842.   Papers, 1787–1845.
(ca. 400 items.)

Contracts, bonds, receipts, legal papers on the settlement of the estate of William I. Smith; accounts of sales of land, timber, shipping.
Gift of J. Bartram Richards, 1924.

548
Riché, Charles Swift, 1787–1877.   Subscription book, 1844.
(1 v.)

Record of subscription for the aid and support of families of citizen soldiers killed in riots in Southwark, 1844, showing names of subscribers and amounts of subscriptions.

549
Riché, Thomas.   Street lottery book, 1760–1761.   (1 v.)

The records of Thomas Riché's street lottery drawings, names of his clients, prizes, and tickets sold.
Gift of C.R. Hildeburn, 1899.

550
Richmond, George Chalmers, b. 1870.   Papers, 1915–1917.
(2.5 linear ft.)

Typewritten notes and papers of the ecclesiastical court of the diocese of Pennsylvania, held in Philadelphia, in the trial of the Rev. George Chalmers Richmond, rector of St. John's Episcopal Church, Philadelphia.
Gift of Henry Budd.

551
Ridgway, John.   Fieldbook, 1782–1786.   (1 v.)

Field book of surveys of land in Burlington County, N.J., and adjacent territory, showing names of early settlers, their land holdings, locations.
Gift of George Krewson.

552
Rittenhouse, David, 1732–1796.   Papers, ca. 1755–1802.   (3 v.)

Photostats of David Rittenhouse's miscellaneous documents, correspondence, and scientific writings: "Mss. Notes of Rittenhouse's Observations at Wilmington for determining the Longitude," 1784; "Commonplace Book, Rittenhouse letters, etc.," 1755–1780, containing extracts from the Rev. Thomas Barton's letter on Indian warfare, massacres; "Letters, Documents," 1793–1802, including Thomas Jefferson letters, 1791–1793, letters from Dr. William Smith concerning University of Pennsylvania, 1793, and others.
Original of "Mss. Notes of Rittenhouse's Observations at Wilmington . . . " owned by the American Philosophical Society; original of "Commonplace book . . . " owned by Fanny D. Abbot; original of "Letters, Documents" owned by George M. Abbot.

553
Ritter, Jacob, b.1784.   Autobiography, 1836.   (1 v.)

Autobiography of Jacob Ritter, Philadelphia merchant and shipper, descendant of early German settlers, covering the period 1784–1836. Topics treated are: economic conditions, religion, education, trade, yellow fever epidemics, political trends, travel. Ritter describes his adventures as a super-cargo in the trade with the West Indies, South America, Cape of Good Hope, Java, Sumatra, Batam Islands, giving a detailed account of his commercial enterprises, commodities traded, the hazards of shipping, naval battles between the British and French fleets, running of blockades, and customs of nations visited.

Gift of John C. Trautwine, Jr., 1924.

554
New Castle Hundred.   Minutes, 1844–1858.   (1 v.)

Minutes of the road commissioners recording extension of roads and road surveys for New Castle, Del.

Purchased, Dreer Fund, 1935.

555
Road and travel notes collection, 1699–1885.   (100 items.)

Among the papers are petitions to state and county governments concerning construction of new roads; surveys and drafts of projected turnpikes between cities and extensions of border lines. Included is a manuscript of "Pack Horse and Horseback Transportation in Pennsylvania," by J.L. Ringwalt, 1885, a description of transportation in Indian trade in the colonial period.

556
Roberts, Algernon Sydney, 1828–1868.   Papers, 1580–1865.
(ca. 200 items.)

This collection consists mainly of papers on the Roberts family of Pencoyd, Merion, 1580–1865. It includes booklets, memoranda, and journal books, 1826, 1829, 1834, and the minutes of trustees of Girard College, 1833–1838.

557
Roberts, Jonathan, 1771–1834.   Memoirs, 1799–1830.   (2 v.)

Memoirs of Jonathan Roberts, Quaker, political leader in Pennsylvania, congressman, and United States senator. Besides genealogical data on the Roberts family, who settled in Merion Township in 1682, and moral precepts, these volumes contain information on political trends, 1799–1830, and on the social and economic development of the nation. The reminiscences present scenes of Roberts' domestic life, early school days, apprenticeship, intellectual development, and his activities as an ardent Jeffersonian Democrat in state and national politics. John Quincy Adams, Simon Cameron, Henry Clay, William H. Crawford, Albert Gallatin, Andrew Jackson, James Madison, James Monroe, Martin Van Buren, and others are discussed. Roberts' participation in the debates on the War of 1812, financial problems, and other national issues are described.

Purchased, Library Fund.

558
Roberts, Jonathan, 1771–1834.   Papers, 1780–1930.   (6 linear ft.)

These papers relate particularly to state and national political history during the Jefferson, Madison, and Monroe administrations. Among the subjects dealt with in the papers, 1780–1848, are: Pennsylvania legislation, political affairs at Lancaster, Republican and Adamite factions, promotion of manufacture, controversies over the charter of the United States Bank, embargoes, the British orders in council, agitation for war with England, opposition of the Federalists to government war loan; French decrees affecting American ships and commerce, foreign trade, New England political factions, land claims, Jackson's conduct in Florida and New Orleans, restoration of the Capitol, political appointments, the Missouri question, ratification of the Spanish treaty, Marquis de Lafayette's reception at Harrisburg, presidential elections, religion, Texas slavery contest, California, Roberts' appointment as collector of the Port of Philadelphia, his dismissal by President Taylor, and various other subjects. Roberts' letters to his wife, 1814–1847, describe economic conditions, domestic and cultural life, travel, and agricultural and industrial development.

Other letters, 1852–1930, are from various members of the Roberts family. There are also genealogical notes of the Roberts family, poetry, speeches, proclamations, indentures, newspaper clippings.

Purchase, Gratz Fund, 1938.

559
Roberts, Sarah.   Cookbook, 1840.   (1 v.)

A small collection of Sarah Roberts' cooking recipes of the early part of the 19th century.

Gift of E.E. Wright.

560
Rodney, Thomas, 1744–1811.   Journal, 1796–1797.   (1 v.)

The journal of Thomas Rodney reflects the cultural and social history of Delaware at the end of the 18th century. Included are philosophical reflections on daily events, memoranda of personal affairs, comments on the Revolution, George Washington, Thomas Jefferson, Horatio Gates, John Adams, Benjamin Franklin, Caesar Rodney, and others, on the Constitutional government, congressional activities, political affairs, and financial and economic problems.

Purchased, Library Fund.

561
Rose, Cropley.   Letterbook, 1779–1781.   (1 v.)

Letters of Cropley Rose, a British wine merchant, relate chiefly to his business affairs in Madiera and the West Indies.

562
Ross, John, 1714–1776.   Docket book for Kent County, Del., 1736–1738.   (1 v.)

563
Ross, John, fl.1776–1780.   Orderly book of John Ross of New Jersey, Major of Brigade in the Service of the United States of America, 1780.   (1 v.)

564
Rossell, William.   Docket book, 1769–1799.   (1 v.)

Entry cancelled; see collection #572.

565
Rotch, William, 1734–1828.   Memoir, 1814.   (1 v.)

Autobiographical account of the years 1775–1794, written by William Rotch, Quaker merchant, in 1814; describes distressing economic conditions, seizure of vessels by British and American privateers, arrests, destruction of property, decline of whaling industry, and the plight of Nantucket in the Revolution. Rotch encountered hostility in England, 1785, in his efforts to reestablish the whaling industry; in France the government accepted his project to organize an American sperm oil and whaling industry in Dunkirk. Included in the volume is a copy of "The Respectful Petition of the Christian Society of Friends called Quakers, Presented to the National Assembly of France by William Rotch, 2nd month, 10th, 1791;" also extracts from letters of William Rotch, dated Dunkirk, 1792, presenting glimpses of the French Revolution.

Gift of Alfred Cope, 1874.

566
Roth, John.   **Diary, 1774.**   **(1 v.)**

Rev. John Roth's diary describes his tour from Friedenhutten through the wilderness to Indian towns and camps in the western part of Pennsylvania.
In German script.

567
Routh, Martha Winter, 1743–1817.   **Journal, 1794.**   **(1 v.)**

Journal of Martha Routh's voyage in the company of Friends, on the ship *Barcly,* from London, Eng., to Boston, Mass., presents a picture of daily life on board a ship of that period, passengers' fear of capture by privateers, supply of provisions.
Gift of Edmund Dudley, 1888.

568
Rowland, Joseph Galloway.   **Papers, 1795–1812.**   **(ca. 50 items.)**

Joseph Galloway Rowland's papers relating to the administration of William Roberts' estate and family papers.

569
Rozier, Francis C.   **Papers, 1841–1857.**   **(ca. 300 items.)**

Business correspondence, bills, and receipts from Philadelphia mercantile firms for goods purchased by Francis C. Rozier, merchant in St. Genevieve, Mo.
Gift of Henry L. Rozier.

570
Rush, Richard, 1780–1859.   **Letters, 1811–1822.**   **(50 items.)**

Richard Rush's letters to John Adams. They contain his observations on the War of 1812, American statesmen, congressional activities, Treaty of Ghent, European affairs, literature, publication of books, academic subjects, personal notes.
Purchased, General Fund.

571
Russell family.   **Papers, 1760–1869.**   **(3 linear ft.)**

A collection of papers of the William Russell and Thomas Russell families, engaged in finance, shipping, and in land enterprises in the United

States. There are letters, documents, account books, maps, and plans of lands.

The letters of George Russell to William Russell, 1794, give an account of political affairs in France and Spain, hazards to American shipping and commerce, seizure and capture of ships and goods by French war vessels, and imprisonment of crews and passengers; William Russell's letters, 1797–1798, describe his journeys and business affairs in Virginia, Maryland, Philadelphia, and New York; miscellaneous letters and statements of account, 1760–1857, to William Russell and Thomas Russell from their agents, John Philip de Gruchy, Thomas Gibbs Morgan, J.R. Priestly, Hugh Roberts, and others, relate to land enterprises conducted by them in Maryland, Connecticut, Louisiana, Virginia, Pennsylvania, and other places; legal papers of a controversy between Fulwar Skipwith, United States consul general in France, and the Russells, 1794–1830; Thomas Russell waste book, 1799–1802; journal, 1799–1802; ledger, 1799–1801; account with the Bank of the United States, 1800–1801; certificates of stock with the Bank of the United States, 1829, 1836; journal, 1823–1839; William Russell, accounts of travel, household, mercantile enterprises, 1795–1802; waste book, 1795–1802; ledger, 1794–1815; estate account, 1818–1839; record of trade in Baton Rouge, La., 1816; list of books sold at auction by order of William Russell, 1801.

Also includes sketches of towns drawn by Thomas Russell, 1792–1802; drafts of land on Loyalsoc Creek, Westmoreland, York, Lycoming, Luzerne counties, "Onions Fishery," and of lands on Lackawanna Creek, 1800–1825; family papers.

Gift of Thomas H. Russell and Mrs. Alexander Scott.

572
Russell, William.   Docket book, 1795–1799.   (1 v.)

Docket book of William Russell, justice of the peace; dockets of John Munrow, 1769–1771; list of marriages, 1796–1800; invoice book of William Russell, merchant of Mt. Holly, N.J., 1790–1791.

Purchased.

573
Ryan, William J.   Collection, 1871–1905.   (350 items.)

The William J. Ryan collection of theatrical programs, listing many of the plays and players appearing before Philadelphia audiences in the latter part of the 19th century.

574
St. Jacobs Church (Philadelphia, Pa.)   Accounts,1855–1904.
(1 v.)

St. Jacobs was later called St. James Evangelical Lutheran Church.
Purchased, Library Fund.

575
Sands family.   Genealogy, [1834].   (2 v.)

A genealogy of the James Sand family, "The House of Sands from the
Earliest Antiquity to the Present Time," with data on related families, coats
of arms, newspaper clippings, letters, notes. Members of the Sands family
sailed from Berkshire, England, to Plymouth, Mass., in 1658; the family was
prominent in the colonial period.
Gift of F. Prince.

576
Sargent, Winthrop, 1825–1870.   Papers, 1845–1868.   (5 v.)

These manuscripts include the commonplace book of Winthrop Sargent, Jr., 1845–1846; notes on literary topics, 1846; catalogue of medals from
Julius Caesar to the Emperor Heraclius, and other notes, correspondence,
1854–1868, relates to Sargent's literary interests.
Gift of Sargent family.

577
Sargent, Winthrop, 1753–1820.   Surveys, 1754–1807.
(ca. 100 items.)

Winthrop Sargent was governor of the Mississippi Territory.
Surveys, maps, and drawings of land in the Northwest Territory, and
some miscellaneous manuscripts of Winthrop Sargent.
Gift of the Sargent family.

578
Say, Benjamin, 1755–1813.   Account book, 1785–1804.   (1 v.)

The account book of Dr. Benjamin Say, as guardian of the estate of
John Bird, executor of the estate of Thomas Say, and guardian of the chil-
dren of Cornelius Barnes.
Gift of Francis Fisher Kane, 1908.

579
Schaffer, Charles.   **Meteorological record books, 1860–1903.**
(4 v.)

Meteorological observations and records, 1860–1867, 1870–1879; United States Weather Bureau, Philadelphia, invoice book, 1890–1903.
Gift of Mrs. Charles Schaffer.

580
Schell, Frank H.   **Collection, ca. 1920.**   **(1 v.)**

Manuscript by Frank H. Schell on the history of fire fighting. Included in these papers is a manuscript entitled "Old Volunteer fire laddies, the famous, fast, faithful, fistic fire fighters of bygone days" with illustrations.
Gift of F. Crusen Schell, 1920.

581
Schofield, Jonathan.   **Docket book, 1801–1806.**   **(1 v.)**

Jonathan Schofield was a justice of the peace in Philadelphia.
Gift of John F. Lewis.

582
Scott, Samuel.   **Collection, 1850–1909.**   **(3 linear ft.)**

Records of the Gloucester Manufacturing Company, a New Jersey calico manufacturing enterprise. Included are miscellaneous correspondence, blueprints, checking accounts, stock ledgers, cashbooks, sales books, with data on American cotton manufacture in the second half of the nineteenth century.
Gift of Samuel Scott.

583
Scott, Walter Quincy.   **"Robert Burns."**   **(1 v.)**

Manuscript of poem, "Robert Burns," first read at the fortieth anniversary of the Burns Club of the city of Albany, N.Y. and dedicated to Judge J.B. McPherson.
Gift of John B. McPherson.

584
Scull, Nicholas, 1686?-1761?   Field notes, 1730 (1741–1755).
(7 v.)

Scull was surveyor general of Pennsylvania.

A collection of field notes relating to Nicholas Scull's surveys mainly in Philadelphia.

Gift of Henry D. Biddle, 1888.

585
Seller, Charles.   School notebook, 1828.   (1 v.)

Notes taken by Charles Sellers during a course of lectures given by Nathaniel Chapman, professor of the practice of medicine in the University of Pennsylvania.

Gift of Dr. J.L. Rhodes, 1935.

586
Sergeant, John, 1779–1852.   Papers, 1783–1897.   (2 linear ft.)

These papers relate to activities of the United States Bank, ca. 1806–1831; the national banking situation; currency and tariff issues; the building of canals and communications facilities, 1821–1828; Indian appropriations, Cherokee memorials to Congress, 1821–1835; important legal cases; applications for governmental positions; personal and domestic affairs.

Included are: "A Slight Geographical and Political Sketch of Peru," 1823; "An Essay on the Necessity of a General Federation among the Spanish American States and a Plan for its Organization," by Colonel D. Bernardo Monteagudo, Lima, Peru, 1825; will of Samuel Rowland Fisher, 1783; agreements and correspondence on land transactions in Washington, D.C., including material on Robert Morris, John Nicholson, James Greenleaf, and General Walter Stewart; letters of William Wirt, Nicholas Biddle, Daniel Webster, James Buchanan, Sam Bayard, Horace Binney, and numerous others.

Gift of M.H. Smith, D.S. Miller, and other persons.

587
Sesqui-Centennial Exhibition, (1926 : Philadelphia, Pa.)
Papers, 1926.   (ca. 150 items.)

A collection of mementoes, programs, advertisements, correspondence, pamphlets, on the Sesqui-Centennial Exhibition of which Elizabeth F.L. Walker was an active committee member.

Gift of Elizabeth F.L. Walker.

588
Shackleton, Mary, b. 1758.   A Tour through England, 1784.
(1 v.)

Journal of Mary Shackleton, member of a prominent Quaker family describing cultural life in England, personalities, customs, palaces, museums.
Gift of Thomas Stewardson, 1897.

589
Shaler family.   Papers, 1797–1903.   (ca. 1,000 items.)

The papers of William Shaler, United States agent in Mexico, consul general to the Barbary States and Cuba, and Nathaniel Shaler, captain of a privateer during the war with England, 1812–1814, reflect American diplomatic relations in the early 19th century, particularly foreign interference with American commerce, seizure of American vessels by Algerian, Spanish, and Neapolitan ships, the part played by the United States in the Mexican, Cuban and Florida controversies, the War of 1812, naval battles, privateering, Algerian negotiations and the resulting peace treaty.

Included are: accounts; cargo and shipping papers; miscellaneous records of the Shaler family; "Journal of the Mission to Algiers," 1817, signed by the secretary of the commission, Charles O. Handy; autograph letter to William Shaler from Commodore O.H. Perry, of the *Java*, 1817; copy of an account of a naval battle with a British frigate, 1814, by Nathaniel Shaler; letter to William Shaler from Vincent Gray describing the burning of the city of Washington by the British, and the battle of New Orleans, 1815; correspondence, 1797–1833; miscellaneous papers, documents, accounts, cargo and shipping manifests, 1798–1867, including the military papers of Captain N.T. Shaler, 1862–1867, and the passport of Nathaniel S. Shaler, 1903.

590
Sharpe, John, 1680–1713.   Journal, 1703–1713.   (1 v.)

Journal of Rev. John Sharpe, Scottish clergyman, who arrived in Virginia on board the ship *Southampton* in 1701. The diary entries beginning in 1703 at "point Love, in Chesapeack bay in the province of Maryland," contains his notes of travel through Maryland, New Jersey, Pennsylvania, New York. He describes his visits to homes and churches, a military expedition to Canada in 1709, Indian warriors and names of their tribes, unrest in the colonies, and uprising and murder by African Americans in New York in 1712. Included is a list of baptisms and marriages performed by Sharpe, 1707–1712.

Journal published in the *P.M.H.B.*, 40 (1916): 257–297, 412–425.

List of baptisms and marriages published in the *P.M.H.B.*, 23 (1899): 104–105.

591

Shaw, John, 1778–1809.   Journal, 1799.   (1 v.)

Narrative by John Shaw of a trip in the Mediterranean on the ship Sophia, to ports of Algiers, Bizerte, Tunis, Tripoli, presenting details of the hazards of shipping, attempted attack on a French merchant vessel, Oriental customs and life, visits of American consuls to northern Africa, inhuman treatment of an African American held captive in Tunis. Included is a description of the "Principles of the Arabic language and the different methods of its orthography."

592

Shelley, Albertus.   Papers, 1882–1905.   (ca. 150 items.)

Family papers relate chiefly to Albertus Shelley, of Philadelphia, violinist: correspondence, newspaper clippings, programs, on Shelley's musical studies in France and Germany and his professional activities. Included are autographs of Ole Bull, Joseph Joachim, Adelina Patti, John Philip Sousa, and Pauline Viardot-García.

Gift of Mrs. Albertus Shelley Hiester, 1938.

593

Shewkirk, E.G.   Letter, 1776.   (1 item.)

Letter, December 2, 1776, addressed to the Rev. Nathaniel Sudel, Bethlehem, with details on the beginning of the Revolution, arrival of British troops, seizure and burning of homes in New York, arrests, and references to church matters and personal affairs.

594

Pennsylvania.   Ship register books, 1722–1776.   (21 v.)

Records of ownership of vessels registered by the province.
Purchased.

595A

Shippen family.   Papers, 1701–1856.   (16 linear ft.)

The papers of several generations of the Shippen and Burd families pertain to the history of colonial Pennsylvania. They include material on the westward expansion of the colonies, trade with the Indians, frontier life, and the French and Indian War, as they touched the lives of the Shippens: miscellaneous correspondence, 1701–1823; Shippen-Burd family letters, 1746–1856; legal and business papers, 1721–1855; bills, receipts, and accounts, 1721–1824; jury lists, 1784–1804; bail book, 1773; Cumberland County docket book, 1790; military papers, 1755–1795.

For Joseph Shippen: account book of his regiment at Fort Augusta, Shamokin, 1756; journal at Augusta, 1757–1758; orderly book, 1758; journal, 1758; letterbooks, 1751–1752, 1754–1755, 1760–1761; journal of the building of Fort Augusta, 1756–1757; letterbook and army statistics, 1758; commonplace book, 1750; account book, 1768–1775; estate accounts.

Henry Shippen, executor, 1810–1815; Henry Shippen daybook, 1817–1835; Edward Shippen's abstracts of Lord Raymond's reports, n.d.; notes on the law, and a letterbook, 1763; Margaret Shippen album, 1824; Shippen family account book, 1837; Mount Regale Fishing Company papers, 1762–1765; papers on the estate of Governor John Penn, 1715–1814; letters from Anne Penn to John F. Mifflin, 1795–1818; Lansdowne bills, 1793–1801; letterbook of Colonel James Burd, 1756–1758; fragments of a journal kept at Loyal Hannon, Oct. 1758; notes on the law by Edward Burd, 1766–1769; notes of a lecture on moral philosophy delivered at the University of Pennsylvania, by Edward S. Burd, 1793; Lancaster docket book of Edward S. Burd, 1785–1795; a court docket book of Westmoreland County, 1782–1801; bankbook of Edward S. Burd, 1784–1794; Sarah Burd bankbook, 1835–1839; Sarah Burd scrap and journal book, 1847–1849; Jacob Hubley's music books, n.d. "The Complete Tutor of the German Flute," 1776; school exercises, 1804; Chester County tax list, n.d.

Gift of the Shippen family.

595B
Shippen family.   Papers, 1749–1899.   (21 linear ft.)

This collection of personal and professional papers spans several generations of the Shippen and related families. Joseph Shippen [III] was a colonel in the provincial service, a merchant, and a secretary of colonial Pennsylvania and the Governor's Council. Following the Revolution, he was occupied as a gentleman farmer in Chester County. Some of Joseph Shippen's correspondence, 1749–1809, touch on his military and political career, but most of the letters are to and from his brother Edward Shippen [IV] and nephew Edward Burd on the family's extensive real estate holdings throughout Pennsylvania.

The main body of the collection is incoming correspondence, 1829, 1842–1897, to Edward Shippen, grandson of Joseph Shippen. His correspondents include his father, Joseph Galloway Shippen, his mother, Anna Maria Buckley Shippen, his siblings Anna Maria (Mrs. William) Newell, Harriet Amelia Shippen, and Joseph Shippen, his aunt, Margaret Shippen, and other relatives. These letters relate family and social news, advice to Edward as he begins his legal career, and family business. There are letters, ca. 1849-ca. 1876, to Shippen from his wife, Augusta Chauncey Twiggs, from Georgia where she lived with relatives for several winters and visited frequently. Augusta writes of her efforts in raising her children alone, her several disagreements with her husband over family problems, and the coming of the Civil War.

In 1848, Shippen began his own law practice, assuming the business of his uncle, James Gibson. Gibson's letterpress volumes, 1802–1847, and Shippen's letterpress volumes, 1848–1872, are concerned with clients' estates, properties, and stocks. Loose letters and documents also relate to legal affairs including cases involving insurance companies and estates, many on family members. Among the estates represented are those of E.B. Bordley, Daniel Buckley, Sarah Burd, Hannah and Jacob L. Florance, Francis Stockton, Twiggs family.

Edward Shippen served in several diplomatic posts from 1872 to 1898. He was an officer of the Chilean and Argentinian commissions to the Centennial Exhibition and served as Philadelphia consul for the two countries at various times, as well as for Japan and Ecuador. This collection holds miscellaneous correspondence, official papers, clippings and memorabilia concerning this aspect of his career.

Other papers of members of this extended family who are represented in the papers are incoming letters, 1799–1872 to Margaret Shippen from her brothers and sisters, nieces and nephews; letter fragments, 1852–1883, of Edward's sister Harriet Amelia to her nephews William and Edward Newell which give Harriet's observations on European society and politics, and comparisons with the United States; correspondence of (another) Edward Shippen, M.D., a career surgeon with the United States Navy, consists of family letters, 1855–1856, from his wife Mary Katharine Paul, and Dr. Shippen's letters to his wife while he was on tour to Brazil, 1859–1860, and to Europe, 1865–1868.

Josiah Harmar, related to the Shippen family through the Buckley branch, was a Revolutionary War officer, commander of the army stationed on the Ohio frontier, 1784–1791, and adjutant-general of Pennsylvania, 1793–1799. A small number of letters in this collection are to Harmar from John Cleves Symmes, which cover his post-Revolutionary military service. A larger group of letters, 1800–1813, are from Harmar's successive agents in Cincinnati, Ohio, reporting on land investments there. After Harmar's death, this correspondence is addressed to his wife Sarah and then to his son William.

William Harmar account books, 1827–1868 and loose financial records, 1807–1872, relate mostly to the Josiah Harmar estate. There is Josiah Harmar, Jr., quarry account book, 1842–1847. Also from the Buckley side of the family are 300 pages of prose and poetry for and by Elizabeth Bordley Gibson (Mrs. James).

The papers include scattered correspondence of many other Shippens. Additionally there are papers of several individuals of no (known) genetic connection: incoming letters, 1843–1859, of James Burnside, Clearfield County judge, mentions court activities, politics, and personal business; Charles D. Drake's prose and poetic inspirations, 1832–1834, from Cincinnati; Henry Huber's accounts, 1852–1865, as treasurer of the State in Schuylkill; letters and drafts, 1783–1789, of Frederick Smyth, colonial chief justice of New Jersey, mostly concerning his efforts to gain compensation from the British government for deprivations incurred as a result of his loyalist position during the Revolution.

Gift of Roland S. Morris estate per Edward S. Morris and Mr. and Mrs. William F. Machold, 1950.

595C
Shippen family.   Papers, 1749–1860.   (200 items.)

Letterbook, 1753–1770, of William Allen, colonial Pennsylvania chief justice, concerns his business interests as partner of Allen and Turner, a merchant firm which was also active in iron manufacturing and copper mining. Much of the correspondence is with David Barclay & Son, London, to whom Allen also includes reports on the French and Indian War and the Pennsylvania 1764 election. The volume continues as Edward Shippen letterbook, 1782–1806, and relates to family lands and finances. Shippen writes to his daughter Margaret Arnold, his brother Joseph Shippen, brother-in-law James Tilghman, and nephew-in-law Jasper Yeates.

A miscellany of Burd, Hubley, Shippen, and Yeates letters make up the loose correspondence. Although most of the letters refer to family activities, including the marriage of James Burd, Jr., to which his family objected. There are some references to public events including the arrival of the Indian delegation to the Mason-Dixon survey party in 1767. Some of the writers are Margaret Shippen Arnold, James Burd, and Sarah Shippen Burd and others.

Gift of Sara Burd Commmack, 1964.

596
Shippen, Edward, 1729–1806.   Docket book, 1779–1780.   (1 v.)

Chief Justice Edward Shippen's record of cases for trial in the Supreme Court of Pennsylvania.

597
Shoemaker, Annie.   Tributes, 1891, 1897.   (2 v.)

Expressions of tribute and appreciation to Annie Shoemaker, principal of Friends Central School, from her pupils and members of the joint committee of faculty and pupils, for her faithful services to the cause of education from 1853 to 1889.

598
Shoemaker family.   Diaries and letters, 1780–1786.   (5 v.)

Manuscripts of a loyalist family of Philadelphia: Samuel Shoemaker diaries, 1783–1785, written by him "For the entertainment of his wife" during his stay in London, Eng., as a loyalist refugee; copies of diaries and letters, 1780–1786, written by Rebecca Shoemaker and her daughters, Anna and Margaret Rawle; an index to the Shoemaker and Rawle papers; and a typewritten copy of Shoemaker's diaries.

Mrs. Shoemaker's diaries are typewritten copies made in 1908.

Original diaries of Mrs. Shoemaker in the possession of her descendants, Israel Pemberton and Henry Wharton.

Gift of William Brooke Rawle and T.I. Wharton.

599
Shreve, Richard Cox, 1808–1896.   Diary, 1861.   (1 v.)

Diary written by Richard Cox Shreve during a trip from Mt. Holly, N.J., to St. Paul, Minn., describing travel by boat and railroad, topography of the country traversed, stopping places, a visit to an Indian reservation on the Minnesota River, events of the Civil War, social and economic conditions.

Gift of Isaac R. Pennypacker, 1910.

600
Sill, Joseph.   Diaries, 1831–1854.   (10 v.)

Diaries of Joseph Sill, Philadelphia businessman, and artist by avocation, with personal notes, detailed comments on books, plays, art, lectures, travel, religion, political leaders and issues of the period, United States Bank affairs, railroad and canal expansion.

Gift of Edward W. Madiera.

601
Silliman, Benjamin, 1779–1864.   Correspondence, 1785–1867.
(ca. 700 items.)

Collection of the correspondence of Benjamin Silliman, chemist and inventor, on scientific matters in general, on chemistry, and his discoveries in that field. Included are letters on the historical paintings of John Trumbull, and social and domestic affairs.

602
Smiley, Sarah F.   Diary, 1868–1869.   (1 v.)

The journal of Sarah F. Smiley, written during a trip to England on the steamer *Cuba,* presents details of her philanthropic interests, religious activities, preaching, church meetings, visits to schools and benevolent institutions.
Gift of S.T. Hand.

603
Smith family.   Papers, 1757–1861.   (300 items.)

Documents in the case between the Pennsylvania Assembly and William Moore, chief justice of the Court of Common Pleas of Chester County, and Rev. William Smith, provost of the College and Academy of Philadelphia, 1757–1759. Among the papers are: statement of the case, with testimony taken before the House of Assembly; affidavits of J. Ross and William Peters; printed address of William Moore; Smith's letters to Attorney General Pratt and to Solicitor General Yorke; report of the attorney general and solicitor general; trial order of the King and Council; Smith's petition to Governor Hamilton; included are sketches of historical landmarks and of men concerned in the case, 1773–1861.
Gift of William R. Smith, 1867.

604
Smith, Charles, 1765–1836.   Casebook, 1819–1820.   (1 v.)

Legal opinions and records of legal cases adjudicated by Judge Charles Smith in the county courts of the 9th district of Pennsylvania.
Gift of Horace W. Smith, 1870.

605
Smith, Charles Morton, d. 1914.   Collection, 1685–1843.
(300 items.)

Deeds, 1685–1805, and letters, marriage licenses, 1686–1842, of genealogical and historical interest for colonial Pennsylvania; documents relate to the early settlers and the proprietors: William Penn, James Logan, George Claypoole, William Markham, Benjamin Franklin, Hugh Roberts, and others.
Correspondence between Franklin and Roberts published in The *P.M.H.B.,* 38 (1914): 287–301.
Gift of the Smith family.

606

Smith, George, 1804–1882.   Collection, 1681–1804.   (400 items.)

Deeds, patents, agreements of original settlers in Pennsylvania, New Jersey, and Maryland, 1681–1752; papers on the estate of Jasper Yeates, 1721–1723; letters of William Hamilton to Benjamin Hays Smith, 1784–1804; and a bundle of miscellaneous accounts, bills, 1782–1792.

Gift of Benjamin N. Smith.

607

Smith, John, 1722–1771.   Letters, 1740–1770.   (1 v.)

Copies of letters written to John Smith, a son-in-law of James Logan and a prominent Quaker of Philadelphia and Burlington, N.J., social and domestic life, political trends, economic conditions; many of the leading personalities of the period are mentioned.

Gift of Thomas Stewardson, 1897.

608

Smith, John.   Papers, 1801–1818.   (2 v.)

Letters of John Smith, United States marshal at Philadelphia, on the interpretation and execution of federal legal matters, claims against the government, courts-martial, finance, maritime regulations, land cases, 1801–1817; Smith's official receipt book, 1801–1818.

609

**Smith, John Frederick, 1815–1889.   Letters, 1886–1888.
(ca. 500 items.)**

Letters of managers and boards of trustees of hospitals and charitable institutions, of ministers and missionaries, expressing their appreciation to John F. Smith, Philadelphia philanthropist, for his humanitarian endeavors. One volume of letters, 1888, relates chiefly to the launching of the steamer *Elizabeth Monroe Smith*.

610

**Smith, John L., 1846–1921.   Letters and diaries, 1862–1916.
(ca. 250 items.)**

The letters of John L. Smith, corporal of the 118th regiment of Pennsylvania Volunteers, during his participation in the Civil War, 1862–1865. Diaries reflect his career as a businessman, map maker, stock dealer, 1867–1916.

Gift of Mrs. Hannah Schmitt.

611

Smith, Richard Penn, 1799–1854.   Papers, 1785–1856.   (5 v.)

Plays, poetry, narratives, essays, by Richard Penn Smith, Philadelphia dramatist and lawyer. Among the manuscripts are: "The Divorce, or Mock Cavalier"; "William Penn," a melodrama; "The Triumph at Plattsburg," a drama; "The Bombardment of Algiers;" "Quite Correct," a comedy; "The Pelican," a farce; "The Man of Mystery"; "A Wife at a Venture," comedy. Some of these plays were successfully produced at the Arch Street, Walnut Street, and Chestnut Street theatres. Included is a volume containing a list of names of subscribers to the *Political Works of the late Richard Penn Smith,* 1856, and a cashbook of William Monroe, 1785.

Gift of the Horace W. Smith estate.

612

Smith, Richard S.   Reminiscences, 1867.   (1 v.)

"Reminiscences of Seven Years of Early Life," by Richard S. Smith, and dedicated to Guillaume Aerston, narrative of his early travels, commercial and shipping activities in the Scandinavian and Baltic countries, 1808–1813, their customs, social and economic conditions. Included are his data on the contemporary wars of England, Denmark, Sweden, Russia, France; America's dominant shipping and commercial interests; British convoys; War of 1812; and personal matters.

Gift of Anna S. Folsom and Ellen M. Folsom, 1926.

613

Smith, William, 1727–1803.   Papers, 1765–1774.   (1 v.)

Abstracts of the papers of Dr. William Smith, provost of the College of Philadelphia. Among the papers copied are "Notes on the Commencement of the American Revolution," "Letters of the Lord Bishop of London," "Stamp Act," and others.

Handwritten transcripts made by J. Larson, 1869.

Purchased, Library Fund, 1888.

614

Smith, William H.L.   Papers, 1843–1869.   (2 linear ft.)

Deeds, 1843–1862; correspondence, 1858–1869; reports, agreements, bills, receipts, 1860–1861; papers on the Samuel R. Philbrick estate, 1858–1862. The collection contains much material on the development of the oil industry in Pennsylvania.

615

Snowden, Louise H.   **Papers, ca. 1910–1920.**   **(ca. 200 items.)**

A collection of papers containing lectures on the feudal system, church, political organizations in medieval Europe; includes also notes on science.
Gift of Mrs. Oliver Randolph Parry.

616

Snowden family.   **Papers, 1788–1865.**   **(16 v.)**

Papers of the Rev. Nathaniel R. Snowden, preacher and curator of Dickinson College, Carlisle, and of his son, James R. Snowden, jurist and scholar: Nathaniel R. Snowden's diaries, 1788–1789, 1791, 1795–1801, 1801–1804, 1836–1839; lectures, 1791–1826; marriage and birth records, 1793–1828; James R. Snowden's diaries, 1825, 1864–1865, and the latter containing information on the Civil War, civic and legal matters. Included is a volume of autographs of judges of the Supreme Court of Pennsylvania, an autograph album of Mrs. James R. Snowden, and genealogical records of the Snowden family.
Gift of Mrs. William Stansfield, 1936.

617

Snyder, Simon, 1759–1819.   **Letters, 1808–1817.**   **(51 items.)**

Collection of personal letters written by Simon Snyder, Governor of Pennsylvania, to Nathaniel B. Boileau, secretary of the Commonwealth of Pennsylvania, on political influences in state administration, appointments, pardons, appropriations, financial matters, policies, the management of the state's military affairs, and other public questions.

618

Songs of the Revolution.   **(ca. 250 items.)**

Correspondence and notes on the origins and traditions of war songs of the Revolutionary period. Included are photographic negatives and prints of some of the songs of the Revolution.
Gift of Fred Perry Powers.

619

Southwark commissioners.   **Papers, 1789–1842.**   **(9 linear ft.)**

Official papers of the Commissioners of Southwark: minute books, vouchers, agreements and contracts for lighting, building of markets, construction of wharves and streets, tax lists, surveys, ordinances, rules and regulations, expense accounts.

Purchased.

620

Cassel, A.H. *Sower's Newspaper,* **1885.** (1 v.)

A copy of A.H. Cassel's account of Christopher Sauer's journalistic enterprises.

Handwritten transcript, 1885.

Gift of Charles R. Hildeburn, 1885.

621

Spackman, John. Papers, 1726–1845. (25 v.)

Family papers, marriage certificates, indentures, land title records, wills, releases.

622

Leaming family. Papers, 1706–1861. (6 linear ft.)

Papers of the Leaming and related families, prominent in the history of New Jersey: West New Jersey Land Society deeds, 1716–1753; land warrants, surveys, drafts, indentures, agreements of sale of lands in Cape May, N.J., and adjacent counties, 1706–1855; bills, receipts, inventories of goods, records of commercial transactions, 1717–1840; Thomas Leaming memorandum book and survey, 1763–1785; memorandum book, 1781–1797, 1794–1795; receipt book, 1778–1796; 15 booklets of Leaming's notes and accounts, 1791–1797; accounts of red cedar posts for Seven Mile Beach, 1786–1791; Leaming's correspondence with Lieutenant Benjamin P. Griffith on Griffith's release on parole in the Revolutionary War, 1781; family papers, estate papers, 1736–1828; Rebecca Leaming's receipt book, 1797–1809; expense book, 1797; account book, 1791–1797; account book, 1797–1799; letterbook, 1808; Isaac Sharp account book and surveys, 1796–1801; Thomas Murgatroyd contracts, 1803–1817; receipt book of the Sarah P. Murgatroyd estate, 1824; wills, 1715–1833; Mary Maxwell expense and receipt book, 1837–1838; Anthony P. Morris receipt book, 1826–1854.

In addition there is a group of J. Fisher Leaming's papers and correspondence, 1810–1861: his letters to his wife (a daughter of Robert Waln) relate to travel, society, theatre, and culture in the United States in the first half of the 19th century; invoice book, China trade, 1819; memorandum book of his ship *Scattergood,* 1819; memorandum book, Canton trade, 1819–1822; daybook, 1819; invoice and ledger book, 1819; memorandum book,

1819–1844; account book, 1818; ledger books, 1819–1823; invoice book, 1817; price records, 1817–1818; bills of lading, 1816–1819; and other items of personal and business character.

623
Sprague, William Buell, 1795–1876.   Autograph collection, 1749–1814.   (60 items.)

Autograph letters of the signers of the Declaration of Independence. The letters give expression to the ideals of prominent early Americans. Bound with this collection are Sanderson's biographical sketches of the signers of the Declaration of Independence, 1865, and portraits of these men. Photocopies.

This collection was assembled by T.A. Emmet, and presented by him, as a Christmas gift, to his lifelong friend W. B. Sprague, 1872. The collection was later purchased by the Historical Society and sold in 1976.

624
Sproat, James, 1722–1793.   Journal, 1753–1786.   (1 v.)

Miscellaneous journal of James Sproat, prominent Presbyterian preacher and hospital chaplain, containing accounts of his church activities and visits to settlements throughout Pennsylvania, 1753, 1757, 1778–1780, 1782–1784, 1786.

625
Stamper, John.   Letterbook, 1751–1770.   (1 v.)

Letters of John Stamper, Philadelphia merchant, to his associates and correspondents in the West Indies mainly deal with commercial, shipping, and financial matters.

626
Steele, John, 1758–1827.   Papers, 1808–1812.   (100 items.)

Papers and accounts of John Steele, United States agent for Marine Hospital, Philadelphia.

627
Stephens, Alexander Hamilton, 1812–1883.   Letters, 1858–1882. (ca. 300 items.)

Letters written by Alexander H. Stephens to William H. Hidell, a lifelong friend, on political and social subjects.

628

Sterrett, James P.   Essays, ca. 1844.   (1 v.)

Essays by James P. Sterrett of Jefferson College on philosophy, political institutions, theology, and other academic subjects.
Gift of William E. Stokes.

629

Steuart, Charles.   Letterbooks, 1751–1763.   (92 v.)

Data on shipping, prices of commodities, trading ventures, markets, and finance of the colonial period are in these letters of Charles Steuart, merchant and shipper of Norfolk, Va.

630

Steuben, Friedrich Wilhelm Ludolf Gerhard Augustin, Baron von, 1730–1794.   Letters, (1777–1791) 1835, 1837.   (15 items.)

Letters of Friedrich Wilhelm von Steuben relating to his military service in the Revolutionary Army; 2 letters of Peter S. Duponceau, 1835, 1837.

631

Stewardson, Thomas, 1829–1902.   Collection, 1759–1844.   (1 v.)

Abstracts and copies of letters of prominent Quakers, such as Sarah Dillwyn, Margaret Morris, Hannah Griffitt, Milcah Martha Moore, Dr. Richard Hill, Benjamin Marshall. The letters concern the purchase of land from the Indians, the Quakers, social work, epidemics, travel facilities, marriages, incidents of the Revolution.
Handwritten transcripts.
Many originals in the possession of the Library Company of Philadelphia. 1314 Locust Street; Philadelphia, PA 19107.
Gift of Thomas Stewardson, 1903.

632

Stewardson, Thomas, 1762–1841.   Papers, 1716–1900.
(9 linear ft.)

Thomas Stewardson, Sr., Philadelphia Quaker, identified himself as a merchant, but his primary occupation was as agent for local and British concerns and estate administrator. His agency was carried on by successive generations, by his son George, also a merchant, and his grandson, Thomas, an attorney.

Records of commercial activities, shipping, land speculation, legal matters, and Quaker affairs, of the colonial and early national periods, and additional family papers of a later date.

A large portion of the correspondence, 1770–1792, is with Frederick Pigou, of London, England, pertaining to the disposal of iron foundries and land holdings in the colonies, in which Henry Drinker and Abel James were interested. Among the papers are miscellaneous land patents, 1716–1820; bonds, indentures, receipts, tax records for Pigou lands, 1798–1831; leases on Philadelphia properties, 1719; fire insurance policies for Philadelphia estates, 1784; tax lists of Washington and Bedford counties, 1789; an account of the Pennamites, 1770; miscellaneous broadsides, 1775; Quaker boarding school receipts, 1795; lottery tickets for the construction of the Schuylkill, Susquehanna, and Delaware canals, 1795; price reports, 1802; turnpike road construction papers, 1807; personal account book, 1777–1786; records of estate settlements, family correspondence, genealogical notes on various families, and other items.

Gift of Eleanor Stewardson, 1929.

632A
Stewardson family.   Papers, 1718–1900.   (300 items.)

A diverse and miscellaneous group of papers with early deeds, indentures, powers of attorney, and other documents, as well as letters between Morrises, Dillwyns, and other Quakers reporting on spiritual and physical conditions of Friends in America and England. Beginning about 1790, material becomes increasingly related to the Stewardson family business interests.

Gift of Eleanor Stewardson, 1929.

632B
Stewardson family.   Papers, 1750–1857.   (220 items.)

Largely letters to Rachel Smith Stewardson, 1811–1839, from her family on spiritual and family matters; also her letters to her husband, George, 1825–1839. There are Thomas Stewardson, Sr., diaries, n.d. of journeys to S.W. New York state with a report on land management negotiations with Indians.

Gift of Eleanor Stewardson and Mary Morton Stewardson, 1938.

632C
Stewardson family.   Papers, 1702, 1783 (1787–1839) 1868. (500 items.)

Correspondence, mainly between Frederick Pigou, Henry Drinker, and Thomas Stewardson, Sr., on Pigou's business and land dealings. Also deeds, leases, powers of attorney, miscellaneous legal, real estate, and commercial papers.

632D
Stewardson family.   Papers, 1768–1902.   (6 linear ft.)

Primarily Thomas Stewardson, Jr., incoming correspondence, 1847–1871, on land and estate business. Other members are represented by miscellaneous business and family letters and receipted bills: Thomas Stewardson, Sr., 1773–1841; George Stewardson, 1820–1867; Stewardson executor related papers; Margaret Haines Stewardson, 1859–1871. Also included is: Morris Smith incoming correspondence, 1822, 1827 while he was conducting business at the Charleston end of the merchant firm Smith and Stewardson, with account book, 1825–1827, of their ship *Florian;* Henry J. Williams, 1828–1879; Alexander W. and Anne McKennan Biddle, 1856–1918, especially letters from Sara O. Fell while cruising in the Mediterranean.

633
Stiles, Amos.   Daybook, 1812–1821.   (1 v.)

Daybook of Amos Stiles, wheelwright of Moorestown, N.J., reflects the commercial activities of the community and adjacent territory.

The names entered in the book contribute data on early families of Moorestown.

634
Stillé, Charles J. (Charles Janeway), 1819–1899.   Papers, 1845–1893. (ca. 500 items.)

Charles Janeway Stillé was a historian and provost of the University of Pennsylvania.

Among these papers are letters, written to Stillé, 1862–1864, which reflect the effect of the Civil War on writers; correspondence on personal and family matters, and letters and papers on University of Pennsylvania, 1853–1900; letter from Abraham Lincoln concerning Stillé's pamphlet, How a Free People Conduct a Long War, 1862–1863; manuscript of Stillé's historical writings: "Logan and Wayne," "American Colonial History," "Anthony Wayne," "Proprietary Government under the Successors of William Penn," "English History," "Silas Deane," "International Law," "Medieval History," "Modern History," "Maximilian in Mexico," "Madame de Stael," and others.

Gift of Charles Janeway Stillé, 1893.

635
Stocker, Anthony Eugene, 1819–1897.   Papers, 1826–1888.
(50 items.)

Papers on Anthony E. Stocker's appointments and commissions in the Civil War. They include a letter of Abraham Lincoln, and correspondence on personal and family matters.

636
Stockton, William S., Mrs.   Cashbook, 1823.   (1 v.)

Cash account book of Mrs. W.S. Stockton of Philadelphia shows business transactions with prominent people of the period.

637
Stokes, Elwood Redman.   Papers, 1840–1843.   (1 v.)

A volume containing the roll, minutes, and a brief history of the West Philadelphia Lyceum; included are notes on geology and poems.
Gift of William E. Stokes, 1936.

638
Strahan, William, 1715–1785.   Letters, 1751–1776.   (40 items.)

Letters of William Strahan, London printer, bookseller, and associate of Benjamin Franklin, addressed to David Hall, printer and merchant of Philadelphia, and to his son, William Hall. The letters describe the British political scene, activities of Parliament in the crucial years before the American Revolution, East Indian Company affairs, colonial legislation, elections, the question of quartering troops in the colonies, disturbances in Boston, and other incidents leading to the War for Independence. There are references to Franklin's travels, his friendship with Strahan, and his examination before the House of Commons.

639
Strawbridge, James.   Correspondence, 1772–1802.
(ca. 1,000 items.)

Miscellaneous business correspondence on James Strawbridge's mercantile interests and to land transactions; bills, orders, receipts, indentures.
Gift of George S. Cullen, 1930.

640
Strettell family.   Papers, 1686–1820.   (ca. 500 items.)

Legal documents and correspondence on trade, land transactions, politics, and personal affairs, 1737–1820; deeds and patents to land in New

Jersey, 1686–1810, involving the interests of Robert and Amos Strettell, shippers and landowners in Pennsylvania and New Jersey.

641
Strettell, Amos.   Jane Hassell Trust Account, 1757–1778.   (1 v.)

Accounts of funds left by Jane Hassell for charitable purposes.

642
Stuart, Gilbert, 1755–1828.   Catalogue, 1828.   (1 v.)

A catalog of an exhibition of 182 portraits painted by Gilbert Stuart, exhibited in Boston after his death, 1828.

643
Sullivan, William A.   Autograph album, ca. 1876.   (1 v.)

Collections of autographs of William Sullivan's friends in various parts of the United States.
Gift of Mrs. William A. Sullivan.

644
Susquehanna and Delaware Navigation Company.
Papers, 1796–1797.   (1 v.)

Surveys, calculations, accounts, statements and correspondence relating to the construction and maintenance of the canal.
Purchased, Library Fund.

645
Swank, James Moore, 1836–1914.   Papers, 1785 (1871–1898).
(ca. 250 items.)

Correspondence of James M. Swank, secretary of the American Iron and Steel Association, with industrialists, political leaders, and others, on tariff and to the development of the iron industry in the United States. Among the correspondents are: George Bancroft, 1885; William Belknap, 1871; Simon Cameron, 1876; H.C. Carey, 1871; Andrew Carnegie, 1898; S.P. Chase, 1872; A.G. Curtin, 1878; John Dallzell, 1896; Hamilton Fish, 1871; H.C. Frick, 1893; A. Gorman, 1894; Benjamin Harrison, 1888; Marcus A. Hanna, 1902; William McKinley, 1891; Justin S. Morrill, 1893; O.H. Platt, 1884; M.S. Quay, 1884; Samuel J. Randall, 1884; Carl Schurz, 1872; General W.T. Sherman, 1871; J.W. Forney, and others.
There are also letters of an earlier period contributing information on political and economic trends; Hugh H. Brackenridge, 1808; John Binns,

1812; Abner Lacock, draft of a letter, 1832, to President Andrew Jackson on the Seminole and Florida War, and revealing J.C. Calhoun's attitude toward Jackson in 1818; Henry C. Clay, 1849; John C. Breckinridge, 1860; James Monroe, 1822; deeds of John Penn, Jr., and John Penn, 1785, conveying land in Westmoreland County; and other items.

Gift of Mrs. James Swank.

646
Swayne, W. Marshall.   Collection, 1701–1812.   (ca. 200 items.)

Collection of legal papers and surveys relating to land in Chester County.

Gift of A. Casanova Swayne, 1922.

647
Mickley, Joseph J., 1799–1878.   Collection, 1636–1811. (ca. 500 items.)

Copies of letters and miscellaneous manuscripts, containing material on the Swedish settlement on the Delaware River.

Gift of John J. Mickley.

648
Sypher, Josiah Rhinehart, b. 1832.   *History of Pennsylvania,* 1868.   (1 v.)

The manuscript of J.R. Sypher's *History of Pennsylvania published* in 1868, also related historical notes.

Purchased, Charles Morton Smith Fund.

649
Philadelphia and Montgomery Counties (Pa.)   Tax and assessment books, 1762–1855.   (ca. 725 v.)

Entry cancelled; returned to Philadelphia Department of Records, August 28, 1953.

650
Taylor, Bayard, 1825–1878.   Sketchbook, 1845–1846.   (1 v.)

Sketches of views in Italy and France, made during a walking tour in Europe, 1844–1846, by Bayard Taylor.

651
Jacob and Isaac Taylor papers, 1672–1775. (4 linear ft.)

Correspondence, 1683–1750; miscellaneous documents and letters, 1672–1775; Chester County warrants, 1682–1748; Chester County surveys, 1701–1740; Delaware County surveys, 1682–1740; Lancaster County warrants, 1710–1742; Lancaster County surveys, 1701–1740; New Castle County, Del., warrants and surveys, 1679–1740; field notes, 1736–1741.
Purchased.

652
Thomas, Lawrence Buckley. **Genealogical notes, 1877.**
(ca. 200 items.)

Pedigrees of the Lawrence Buckley Thomas family and related Maryland families, illustrated with views and coats of arms.

653
Thomas, Lydia and Mary. **Commonplace book, 1826–1832.**
(2 v.)

Literary compositions in prose and verse, with miniature drawings in watercolor.

654
Thompson family. **Papers, 1607–1903.** (16 linear ft.)

This collection comprises the papers of Jonah Thompson and his descendants, Philadelphia Quakers, humanitarians, merchants, ironmasters, and landowners.

The papers of the period, 1745–1850, pertain to commerce, land transactions, and manufacture. They include Jonah Thompson's manuscript books on the manufacture of iron, nails, machinery, 1783–1829, and journals while abroad, 1812; George Thompson papers, 1769–1876, relate to land holdings at Fort Pitt, legal controversies, administration of estates, Thompson's business interests in the Pennsylvania Salt Company, in iron, coal, copper, potash, 1831–1876, and to Eastern Penitentiary, 1839–1850; among the papers of John Thompson, 1793–1803, are his accounts with Robert Morris.

John J. Thompson papers, 1803–1903, relate to the iron industry, manufacture of steam engines, machinery, and his other interests; papers of estates in which the Thompsons were interested.

Joseph Trotter's papers, 1725–1868, include items on literature, ethics, commerce; Newbold family papers, 1755–1838, letter and daybooks, material on Mexico; Abel James, merchant, account with Lawrence Growdon, 1765–1868; John Harper papers, 1776–1779; Thomas Pleasant's papers, 1776–1793; Henry Drinker papers, 1771–1783; Joseph Galloway papers, 1782–1792; accounts, legal papers, bonds, deeds, surveys, 1607–1851; Quakeriana, monthly meeting reports, 1661–1802; copies of deeds, 1676–1789; Sir William Johnson letter to Tedyuskung, 1760; New England colonists' petition against the Sugar Act, 1763; petition for a road from Philadelphia to Chester, 1764; North Carolina land warrants, surveys, leases, 1796–1838; Deaf and Dumb Institution, papers, 1813–1817; Thaddeus Stevens letters, 1813; William C. Poultney, journal on board the brig *Washington*, 1805; journal of a trip to Europe on the *Montyuma*, 1827; James Gallagher journal, Easton through New Jersey, 1831; Hanover Furnace records, 1793–1838; Bridgewater, N.J., copper mine records, 1831; broadsides on fire extinguisher, 1848.

Purchased, Gratz Fund.

655
Thompson, Jonah.   Collection, 1683–1854.   (ca. 350 items.)

These papers relate particularly to colonial Pennsylvania: correspondence on agreements between Lord Baltimore and William Penn; letters from Benjamin Franklin, Robert Morris, Thomas Penn, and other noted men, on political and social matters; an account of Indian religious beliefs, by Conrad Weiser; some pamphlets, broadsides, portraits, and early views of Philadelphia.

656
Thompson, Rebecca.   Manuscript, 1827.   (2 v.)

Lyrical composition in prose and verse.

657
Thomson, Hannah, d. 1807.   Household memorandum book, 1792–1793.   (1 v.)

Memoranda of accounts, household goods, farm products, personal and domestic affairs. Included in the volume is *Poulson's Town and Country Almanack*, 1793.

658
Thomson, Charles, 1729–1824.   Papers, 1774–1811.   (9 v.)

The papers of Charles Thomson, secretary of the Continental Congress, include records of the Continental Congress, other documents on the Revolutionary period; secret journals of Congress, 1774–1780; Charles Thomson's defense in Congress against charges of Henry Laurens, 1779; account of official ceremony on the occasion of the French minister's appearance before Congress, 1782; Charles Thomson letterbook, 1784; scrapbook, 1782–1811; account book, 1815–1816; original manuscript of Thomson's translation from the Greek of "The New Covenant commonly called The New Testament," n.d. (one volume marked "not a correct copy"), "Synopsis of the Four Evangelists," n.d.; interpretations of Biblical words and their translation from Greek into English.

659
Tilghman, William, 1756–1827.   Correspondence, 1772–1827.
(24 linear ft.)

Letters to William Tilghman, Philadelphia lawyer and jurist, from clients, friends, and members of his family. The main portion of the collection pertains to claims, controversies, collections of debts, land settlements, suits in court, politics and other legal matters; bills and accounts of money spent for wearing apparel and similar commodities; receipts for pew rents in Christ Church; accounts and correspondence relating to the purchase, sale, condition and eventual manumission of slaves, and traveling expense accounts.

Some of the correspondents include: John Barclay, James Cheston, Stephen Collins, James Earle, Samuel Earle, the Philadelphia firm of Thomas, Samuel, and Miers Fisher, John Galloway, Daniel Charles Heath, Richard Hynson, Thomas Jones, James Pearse, P. Bond, Henry Drinker, Henry Pearse, James Carey, William Cooke, Tench Coxe, James Earle, Jr., Joshua Gilpin, Thomas W. Francis, Nicholas Hammond, John M.D. Laurence, Robert Milligan, Maria Lloyd Hemsley, William Hemsley, Mary Livingston, James Lloyd, Anna Maria Tilghman, Ann C. Tilghman, Elizabeth Tilghman, Ann Allen, Ann Greenleaf, Thomas Hemsley, Henry W. Livingston, Charles C. Tilghman, Tench Tilghman, Benjamin Chew, Jr., John McDowell, Samuel Hanson, Elizabeth Wistar, Richard Wistar, and others.

Gift of William M. Tilghman, 1889.

Finding aid available.

660
Till, William.   Letters, 1735–1745.   (1 v.)

Letters of William Till, a Philadelphia merchant, to merchants in England (especially Lawrence Williams), West Indies, and other places. They relate to trade, shipping, prices of commodities, insurance, cargoes, legal matters.

Typescript copies.

661
Tilly, Matilda Bingham de.   Letters, 1799.   (1 v.)

Letters concerning Matilda Bingham de Tilly's divorce from Comte de Tille April 11 to June 17, 1799.

662
Tirowen, Terence.   Papers, n.d.   (1 v.)

"His posthumous papers : being for the most part, familiar letters in rhyme written in youth, from the country of his adoption, to kindred in his native land." Each letter of rhyme is preceded by an introduction. The topics include: a Fourth of July celebration in Philadelphia; the death of his aunt, Mrs. Jane Hamilton; gratitude for a gift of slippers; a visit paid to New York; the politics of Ireland; a reception of the Pennsylvania Volunteers by the citizens of Philadelphia following the soldier's return from the Mexican War; hymns written for Trinity Church (Philadelphia) at Christmas; New York politics; and other family sentiments.

Handwritten transcript "compiled by one who knew him for the possible entertainment in after years of his daughters, Anna W. and Mary Caroline."

663
Todd, Michael.   Genealogical records, 1698.   (1 v.)

Copy of a record of the ancestry of Michael Todd, an early settler in Dorchester and Caroline counties, Md.

Gift of John R. Witcraft, 1911.

664
Tousard, Ann Louis de, 1749–1817.   Military papers, 1765–1837.
(50 items.)

These papers relate to the service in the American army of Ann Louis de Tousard, lieutenant colonel attached to George Washington's staff; congressional citations; his commissions, bearing the signatures of Washington, John Adams, James Madison, Thomas Jefferson, Lafayette, and others.

665
Towers, Robert, 1726–1790.   Papers, 1694–1808.   (ca. 150 items.)

The family papers of Robert Towers, Sarah Evans, Issachar Evans, Elizabeth Gostelowe, and Robert Towers, Jr., relate chiefly to land speculation in west New Jersey and Pennsylvania, including: deeds, 1739–1769; indentures and bonds of indebtedness; the will of Robert Towers, Jr., 1783; and some miscellaneous items.

Gift of heirs of Eliza F.E. Fraser.

666

Transportation line record books, 1798–1865. (11 v.)

The record books include:

Company for erecting a permanent bridge over the Schuylkill River at Philadelphia: stockholders' record book, 1798–1803; stock transfer book, 1799–1815; stock certificates, 1804–1805.

Philadelphia and Lancaster Stage Transportation Company: account book, 1792–1865; records, 1798–1799.

Western Stage Transportation Company: drivers' account ledger, kept by William P. Thompson, 1831–1835.

Western Transportation Line for Baltimore: shipping records for sloop *William Penn*, 1827–1828.

667

Trauthmann, Anna Maria. **Papers, 1760–1767.** (1 v.)

"Letzte Stunden," essays, poetry, and letters, describing religious revelations experienced before death.

Gift of William C. Malin, 1875.

668

Great Britain. Treaty of Amity, Commerce, and Navigation, 1795.
Records, 1799–1804. (50 items.)

Record of claims against the governments of the United States and England, made by their citizens, to be adjusted according to the Treaty of Amity, Commerce, and Navigation, 1795.

669

Trent, William, 1715–1787. **(Papers, 1765–1775.** (1 v.)

A brief history of Indian warfare, 1765, and legal opinions on the validity of William Trent's title to land on the Ohio, ceded to him by the Six Nations in 1768. Documents bear signatures of Henry Dagge, John Glynn, counsellors, and of B. Franklin and P. Henry, 1775.

Purchased.

670

Trimble, James, 1755–1837.   **Papers, 1782–1835.**   **(6 linear ft.)**

Records of James Trimble's official activities as deputy secretary of Pennsylvania, and his correspondence on personal affairs and commercial ventures. Among the papers are: the account book of the secretary of the Commonwealth, 1793–1801; account of receipts for furnishing military standards to Pennsylvania military regiments; deeds, agreements of sales of lands; advertising accounts; receipt book, 1782–1784; memorandum book, 1798–1800; expense account book, 1794; bankbooks in account with Harrisburg banks, 1812–1815, 1815–1816, 1821–1823; bankbooks in account with Lancaster banks, 1803–1808, 1808–1812; newspaper clippings, 1824; James Trimble in account with John Foster, 1834–1835; insurance policies; powers of attorney, real estate agreements, leases, and other items of official and personal character.

671

Trites, Anna Pyewell.   **Family papers, 1739–1859.**   **(25 items.)**

Transferred to the Genealogical Society of Pennsylvania.

672

Truxtun, Thomas, 1755–1822.   **Papers, 1798–1801.**   **(3 v.)**

Letterbook of Thomas Truxtun aboard the U.S.S. *Constellation,* 1798–1799; his journal, aboard the same ship, 1798–1800; his letterbook aboard the U.S.S. *President,* 1800–1801.
Purchased.

673

Turner, Charles Henry Black, b. 1852.   **Papers, 1687–1875.**
(ca. 1,500 items.)

This collection pertains chiefly to the early history of Sussex County, Del. Included are: "Minute Book C," a copy of the minutes of the commissioners for the proprietors of Pennsylvania, on surveys and grants of land to the first settlers in Sussex County, 1687–1732; returns and surveys of lands, with plats, giving names of settlers, 1725–1807; the Rev. William Becket's "Notices and Letters concerning incidents at Lewes Town," with observations on religious, social, and educational matters, 1727–1735; Thomas Rodney commonplace book, containing data on elections, names of candidates, and laws of George Town, Sussex County, 1791–1827; official records of bonds, deeds, and petitions, recorded in Sussex County; Susan Marriner accounts, with data on tailoring and prices of wearing apparel, 1784–1801; list of taxables, Sussex County, 1874–1875.

Gift of C.H.B. Turner.

674
Tyndale, Mary.   Briefs of title, 1684–1867.   (1 v.)

Transcript of the title of land from Front Street to Second Street, Philadelphia, granted by William Penn to Thomas Wynne, 1684.

Gift of the George de Benneville Keim Memorial, 1934.

675
United States Bank.   Papers, 1797–1850.   (ca. 2,200 items.)

Collection of miscellaneous papers from various sources, on the business of the Bank of the United States: letters, 1797–1859; financial reports, some signed by Nicholas Biddle, powers of attorney, bank notes, bills of exchange, loan and stock certificates, pension vouchers, 1799–1839; papers of Paschall Hollingsworth on settlement of Bank accounts after its discontinuance, 1843–1850; report of a committee of citizens of Philadelphia to present a memorial to Congress and to President Jackson for return of government deposits to the United States Bank, 1834; checks, subscribers' lists, agreements, of the Bank of Pennsylvania, 1797–1849.

Gift of Israel W. Morris, Horace W. Smith, and Mrs. John Struthers.

676
Constitutional Centennial Commission.   Papers, 1886–1887.
(3 linear ft.)

The Constitutional Centennial Commission was organized in December of 1886. Its purpose was to provide for a celebration of the "Centennial Anniversary of the Framing and Promulgation of the Constitution of the United States."

The formal celebration involved plans for: a commemorative oration and poem, a military display, an industrial processional display, and creation of a memorial within the city of Philadelphia reflecting the progress of the Nation since the signing of the Constitution. Invitations to participate in the celebration were extended to the President and his cabinet, the Federal Judiciary, Congress and all national Government agents, members of civic organizations across the country, descendants of the Signers of the Constitution, and all individuals of local prominence.

John A. Kasson was appointed Chairman of the Centennial Commission with Hampton L. Carson serving as Secretary. Commissioners were designated by the governors of the states and territories. Each commissioner was responsible for securing a list of individuals from within their respective geographical zones to whom invitations were to be sent. Committees and subcommittees were formed within the commission.

Records of the commission: list of names of guests invited, letters of acceptance, letters of refusal, and miscellaneous letters, 1887; official programs, broadsides, pamphlets, memorial to the Senate and House of Representatives, songs, tickets, 1887; correspondence of Colonel A. Loudon Snowden, marshal of Philadelphia, 1887; letterbook, guests' register book, account book of expenditures, letter copy book, acceptance book, magazines, 1886–1887.

Gift of the Constitutional Centennial Commission.

677
United States manuscript, 1733–1799.   (12 items.)

These miscellaneous items include: order in council on title of lands in Maine, 1733; letter of John Peagrum, 1737; letters on the defense of the colonies against the French, 1754; James Hamilton to General Monckton, 1760; observations on the relations of Great Britain with the United States, ca. 1785; and other items.

Purchased, 1890.

678
United States. Navy.   Papers, 1831–1877.   (ca. 150 items.)

Letters, general orders, court-martial records, regulations, addressed to officials at the Navy Yard, Philadelphia. Among the commanders mentioned are James Barron, Captain George C. Read, Charles Stewart, and others. Some of the letters and documents bear the signature of George Bancroft, John Boyle, Mahlon Dickerson, A.P. Upshur, and Levi Woodbury.

Purchased.

679
United States Sanitary Commission and Fair.   Papers, 1861–1873. (3,500 items.)

Material on humanitarian efforts made during the Civil War by the Philadelphia Association of the United States Sanitary Commission: correspondence of Mrs. Thomas P. James, on the sale of autographs during the Fair; minute book of the commission, 1861–1873, containing names of officials and members; bills, vouchers, reports, bank and check books and other items.

680

Universalist Church (Philadelphia, Pa.)   **Papers, 1810–1934.**
(9 linear ft.)

Among the records of the First Universalist Church, are: minutes of the vestry, 1810–1893; miscellaneous documents, 1812–1844; pew books, 1819–1825, 1893; ledgers, 1833–1896; accounts, 1866–1875; Sunday School Association records, 1866–1874; treasury books, 1854–1868; correspondence with Pennsylvania Universalist Convention, 1893, 1909; Fernwood Cemetery Papers, 1890–1934; Missionary Society material. Records of the Third Universalist Church, Philadelphia, 1840–1855, include: minutes, accounts, ledgers, constitution. There are also Sunday School attendance books of the First Universalist Church, 1874–1877.

Gift of Thomas Butler.

681

Vali, Louis du Pui.   **Collection, 1703–1861.**   **(ca. 300 items.)**

Collection of deeds, 1703–1814, papers and correspondence, both legal and personal, 1795–1861, chiefly from the estates of Judge John Hollowell and Judge George M. Strand of Harrisburg.

Gift of Louis du Pui Vali.

682

Van der Kemp, Francis Adrian, 1752–1829.   **Autobiography, 1817.**
(1 v.)

The autobiography of Francis Adrian Van der Kemp, Dutch patriot, intellectual, and friend of the early American government. It contains accounts of war in the Netherlands, Van der Kemp's arrival and sojourn in America, and his friendship with many political and social leaders, such as John Adams, DeWitt Clinton, Thomas Jefferson, George Washington, and others.

Gift of Pauline E. Henry, 1871.

683

Varick, Margarita van, d. ca. 1695/6.   **Inventory, 1695–1696.**
(1 v.)

Inventory of the estate of Margarita Van Varick, widow of Rudolphus Van Varick, of Flatbush, Long Island, N.Y. Included is a list of names of debtors to the estate, which contributes data on early Dutch families settled in Long Island and adjacent territory.

Photostatic copy made by the New York State Library, 1930. Court of Appeals; Albany, New York.

Gift of Harold E. Gillingham.

684

Vaux family.   Papers, 1686–1893.   (9 linear ft.)

The correspondence pertains to social and political reform, penology, the regulation of hospitals, and problems of general welfare. There are also letters of a domestic character and some pertain to local and national political events during Richard Vaux's term as mayor of Philadelphia, 1856–1857. Also included are: Richard Vaux diaries, 1779–1780, 1781–1782; typewritten copy of a journal, 1781; his account book, Bank of America, 1789; poetry and prose, 1762–1814; acts of assembly; notes on the Insane Hospital, ordinances, resolutions, receipts and accounts; autograph letters from officers in the French army, 1686–1789; minutes of the stockholders of the Bank of Northern Liberties, 1811; Richard Vaux docket book, 1856; his expense account and checkbook, 1848–1852; scrapbook, 1831–1880; visiting cards, invitations, and printed notices of social and cultural events, 1779–1878.

Gift of Mrs. Mary Vaux Buckley.

685

Wallace James W.   Collection, 1794–1862.   (9 linear ft.)

This collection contains the papers of Joseph Wallace, merchant, lawyer, and deputy secretary/treasurer of Pennsylvania. These papers cover Joseph Wallace's partnership with Joshua Elder and give information on trade (prices and commodities) between Philadelphia and Harrisburg in the early nineteenth century. Legal clients of Joseph Wallace include: his son-in-law Dr. William C. McPherson, James Emerson, several Elders, John Rhoads, James Wilson (absconding debtor), Mary Kelso, and others. A small amount of papers for Joseph Wallace relate to his business as secretary/treasurer of Pennsylvania. Personal papers finish out the remainder of the collection.

Gift of James W. Wallace.

686

Wallace, John William, 1815–1884.   Collection, 1725–1854. (3 linear ft.)

Letters from George Washington, Alexander Hamilton, James Madison, Charles C. Pinckney, Benjamin Tilghman, Daniel Webster, Benjamin Rush, Duke of Wellington, and others are in this collection. They are scattered through the volumes of William Bradford, United States Attorney

General, 1772–1796, and the volume of letters and documents of the Rev. Robert Blackwell, chaplain at Valley Forge, and of Thomas Willing, financier, 1771–1854. The bulk of the collection consists of family papers: letters of John Maddox, the Rev. W. Wallace, J. Wallace, and Joshua Maddox Wallace, 1725–1801; letters to Joshua Maddox Wallace, 1784–1819; letters to John B. Wallace and his wife, Susan Wallace, 1805–1848.

Finding aid available.

687
Waln, Robert, 1794–1825.   Papers, 1792–1823.   (ca. 500 items.)

Most of these papers relate to the commercial transactions of Robert Waln in the East India and China trade and include some of his personal correspondence, 1799–1819; miscellaneous papers, passports, accounts, and bills, 1792–1823; insurance policies, 1810–1817; protest of loss and claim to indemnity for the ship *Emila*, wrecked 1811. There are papers of some literary interest, among which are the manuscripts of Robert Waln: "Horace in Philadelphia," 1813; "The Hermit in Philadelphia," 1818–1820; "Return of Regulars to Rome," 1811; notes on religion, temples, superstitions; and a list of books in the Waln house in Frankford, 1818–1819.

Gift of Dr. Emlen Wood, 1936.

688
Walsh, Robert, 1784–1859.   Papers, 1806 (1830–1845) 1904. (35 items.)

This very miscellaneous collection contains: personal letters, 1819–1845, to Robert Walsh, Philadelphia journalist and litterateur, who settled in Paris, from Chateaubriand, Baron Dupin, Alexander von Humboldt, Sir Robert Peel, Sismondi, and others, primarily on Walsh's writings; other autograph letters and documents of noted Americans; Walsh family genealogical material; "The Fire Fly," 1842, a juvenile manuscript newspaper issued in Nantucket, Mass., by [Samuel H. Jenks, Jr.]; and memorabilia.

Gift of D. Francis Walsh, 1919.

689
Walter, Thomas U. Genealogical sketches, 1871.   (1 v.)

Transferred to the Genealogical Society of Pennsylvania.

690
War Service Committee.   Papers, 1918–1919.   (ca. 100 items.)

Entry cancelled; see collection # 1561.

691

Ward, Christopher L. 1807–1870.   Diaries, 1841–1869.   (2 v.)

Christopher L. Ward was a Towanda lawyer, land speculator, and businessman who was active in local, state, and national Democratic politics.

His business diary, 1841–1869, and personal diary, 1863, relate to legal affairs, business and land transactions, state politics in Harrisburg, and financial memoranda, primarily about lands.

Purchased, Dreer Fund, 1934, 1938.

692

Warder, Ann Head, 1758–1829.   Diaries, 1786–1789.   (14 v.)

Ann Warder was the British-born wife of John Warder, a Philadelphia shipping merchant who lived in London from 1776–1786. In 1786, she accompanied her husband to Philadelphia, where they settled.

The diaries she kept from 1786 to 1789, addressed to her sister Elizabeth Head, detail the social, domestic, and religious life of Friends in and near Philadelphia, with some comparisons with her native England. Ann Warder comments on her social circle, primarily members of the related Warder, Head, Emlen, Parker, Vaux, Morris, Fry, Capper, and Hootten families, and of the Foulke, Waln, Fisher, and Townsend families; her domestic affairs, including sewing, mending, washing, and ironing; observations on clothing styles and cuisine; Quaker meetings; and trips in Pennsylvania and New Jersey. Volume 1, 11, 12 are devoted to detailed descriptions of ship voyages between England and the United States.

Gift of the estate of Elizabeth, Sarah, and Emma Cadbury, 1923.

693

Warder, John, 1751–1828.   Letterbooks, 1776–1778.   (3 v.)

John Warder was the junior partner in the Philadelphia shipping merchant firm of Jeremiah Warder and Sons, the business of which was chiefly with London. In 1776, he was sent to England to protect the interests of the house.

These letters, written while in England are primarily to other merchant houses and to his parents. He mentions business hazards of commerce, speculation in grain and other staple commodities, news of and British opinion on the progress of the Revolution, and the commercial climate in England and America.

Gift of Henry Bond, 1894.

694
Warder and related families papers, 1747 (1810–1860) 1903.
(ca. 300 items.)

For three generations, the Warders were engaged in a family shipping merchant firm whose trade was primarily with England. The third generation, Warder and Brothers, were general commission shipping merchants from ca. 1813–1837, after which some of the business was carried on by partner John H. Warder until his death in 1843.

This is an artificial collection of the Warder and related Hoskins and Pearsall families of Philadelphia. Business papers in this collection include: Warder & Brothers account books, 1819–1837, one of which is continued as John H. Warder accounts current, 1837–1840, and as John H. Warder business letterbook, 1837–1840; business letterbook, 1834–1836, continued by John H. Warder, 1837, mentioning investments and the banking and commercial situation in Philadelphia; John H. Warder journal, 1836–1843; cash books, 1836–1865 (continued after his death); and business letterbook, 1841–1843; brother William S. Warder, Philadelphia merchant, ledger, 1829–1831; cash book, 1829–1831; and letterbook, 1830, largely on land speculation and other real estate; and notes, 1805–1834 primarily to Warder and Brothers.

The collection also contains deeds, 1747–1886, and other legal documents, 1781–1903, drafts of land, including divisions of squares in Washington, D.C., 1792–1795; letters, 1799, 1810–1830, 1903, primarily to Jeremiah Warder of Warder & Brothers, on speculative lands in Indiana; receipts and receipted household bills, 1803–1871; manuscript sermon, 1852, n.d. : "The Lord bless thee & keep thee," Numbers 6:24–6; estate papers of Ann, John H., William G., and William S. Warder, and of Henrietta Hoskins, John Hoskins, and Eleanor H. Pearsall; Warder family record book; and other miscellaneous items.

Gifts of the Misses Pearsall, 1908; Mrs. Trevanion Dallas, 1935; and Mrs. W.W. Frazier, Jr., 1936.

695
Washington Benevolent Society of Pennsylvania.
Papers, 1814–1829.   (ca. 350 items.)

A collection of papers on the activities and financial affairs of the Society. Among the items are lists of names of stockholders, legal papers, and items relating to the transfer of Penn properties.

Gift of William Brooke Rawle.

696
Washington family.   Papers, 1675 (1770–1799) 1833.   (85 items.)

This artificial collection contains miscellaneous documents on the Washington family, 1675–1831, including legal papers, surveys, correspondence, loose accounts; George Washington letters, 1770–1799; Washington pocket diary, Jan. 1–June 21, 1796, primarily weather records; Washington household journal, 1793–1797, while in Philadelphia; Martha Washington's "A Booke of Cookery" and "A Booke of Sweetmeats," a fair 17th century copy of an earlier manuscript; and subscription book to aid William A. Washington, Owensboro, Ky., grand-nephew of George Washington, 1883.

Cookbook gift, 1892.

Subscription book to aid William A. Washington gift of E.T. Stuart, 1917.

Pocket diary, 1796 published in *P.M.H.B.*, 37 (1913): 230–239 and in *The Diaries of George Washington* edited by Donald Jackson and Dorothy Twohig.

Household journal published in the *P.M.H.B.*, 29 (1905): 385–406; 30 (1906): 30–56, 159–186, 309–331, 459–478; 31 (1907): 53–82, 176–194, 320–350.

"A Booke of Cookery" and "A Booke of Sweatmeats" published in *Martha Washington's Book of Cookery*, edited and annotated by Karen Hess.

697
Watson, John Fanning, 1779–1860.   Collection, 1693–1855.
(10 v.)

These papers of a Philadelphia historian contain information on the cultural, social, and economic development of Pennsylvania. Included are autograph letters, sketches, pictures of historic landmarks, drafts, portraits of eminent men, newspaper clippings: Mason and Dixon Line material, 1750; Lucy Watson's account of new settlers, 1762; account of John F. Watson's visit to Valley Forge, 1820, to Chester, 1827, to Delaware and Chesapeake Canal, 1829; French exercises, by John F. Watson, 1803; account of the first settlement of the townships of Buckingham and Solebury, Bucks County, by Dr. John Watson, 1804; John F. Watson correspondence, 1823–1828. Notes for Watson's works: "Annals of Philadelphia," 1829; "Annals of Philadelphia, Supplement," 1846; "Visit to Tinicum," "The Workings of Covetousness," 1853; notes on Germantown, Roxborough and Valley Forge, 1855; "Visit to Graeme Park, Horsham," 1855; "Historical Notes and Maps," 1855; notes and maps of counties in Pennsylvania, n.d.; "Philadelphia Views," n.d.

698
Watson, William.   Journal, 1684–1827.   (1 v.)

The book includes: account of William Watson's voyage with his family from Nottingham, England, to Philadelphia, 1684, and to Burlington, West Jersey, where he settled; records of business transactions; medical recipes; and diary notes.

Gift of Sarah Iveston, 1871.

699
Wayne, Anthony, 1745–1796.   Papers, 1765–1890.   (15 linear ft.)

Papers on Anthony Wayne's activities in the Revolutionary War and later, his campaign against the Indians, and the peace treaties concluded with them: Wayne's correspondence with other army officers, with the secretary of war, and with other men active in colonial affairs, 1765–1779; records of courts-martial, 1776–1796; military documents, monthly returns, muster rolls, and department returns, 1777–1794; orderly books, 1781, 1792–1796; note of the itinerary of the Pennsylvania Line, 1781; journals of proceedings at treaty councils held with Indians, 1778–1795; "Instructions to Major General Anthony Wayne to be employed on the Western Frontier," 1792; copy of "Treaty of Greenville," 1795. Wayne family papers include: Chester County survey by Anthony Wayne, 1771; the Wayne farm book, 1784–1820; miscellaneous manuscripts of Isaac Wayne, 1842–1890.

Gift of Abram R. Perkins family, 1912.

700
Weiser, Conrad, 1696–1760.   Papers, (1741–1760) 1783.
(225 items.)

Conrad Weiser was a Berks County farmer, tanner and president-judge who served as a colonial Indian agent and interpreter as well as Lieutenant Colonel and commander of the First Battalion of the Pennsylvania Regiment during the French and Indian War.

These papers contain correspondence, chiefly with Richard Peters, Pennsylvania provincial secretary, 1743–1760 and Captain Christian Busse, commander of Ft. Henry, 1756–1757, memoranda, official documents, muster rolls, accounts, and receipts on Weiser's affairs as Indian agent and soldier. The collection also contains original and photostat of Conrad Weiser ledger, 1746–1760, continued by son Conrad Weiser, Berks County farmer, 1773–1783; photostat of a copy of "A Journal of the proceedings of Conrad Weiser in his journey to Ohio," 1748; and "A Journal of the proceedings of

Conrad Weiser in his journey to Onontago," 1750. In addition, the papers contain son Samuel Weiser, Berks County, correspondence, accounts, receipts, and draughts of land, 1760–1766.

Gift of Heister H. Muhlenberg, 1838; Mr. Paul T. Anderson, 1961; Thomas F. Gordon, n.d.; portion purchased by Gratz Fund, 1936.

701
Weiss family.   Papers, 1733 (1780–1835) 1862.   (130 items.)

Jacob Weiss, Assistant deputy quartermaster general for Northampton County during the Revolution, who settled in Towamensing Township, Carbon County where he was a farmer, lumberman, and a founder of the Lehigh Coal Mine Company, the first anthracite coal mining company of the Lehigh region.

The collection includes miscellaneous quartermaster accounts, ca. 1778–1781; papers relating to Jacob Weiss and Jacob Weiss, Jr. coal mining interests, 1795–1832; Weiss family correspondence, 1780–1837; and miscellaneous receipts, legal papers, loose accounts, and draughts of land. The collection also contains "Smith Book on Cookery and Cures, making sundry Wines, etc." ca. 1810, photographs, and portraits.

"Smith Book on Cookery . . . " mostly in german.

Gift of Mrs. H.M. Berlin, 1910; portion purchased, Library Fund, 1912.

702
Welsh, Herbert, 1851–1941.   Collection, 1853–1934.
(39 linear ft.)

The collection is arranged in the following categories: correspondence, 1875–1934; Philippines, 1892–1925; Indian rights, 1877–1934; international arbitration, 1896; National Civil Service Reform League, 1881–1929; Philadelphia and National Municipal League, 1893–1896; Friends of German Democracy, 1914–1919; Syrian affairs, educational, religious, foreign missionaries, 1907–1916; Armenian affairs, 1896–1924; Waldensian affairs, 1907–1923; Society for the Protection of Forests, 1890–1929; public education, 1890–1891; John Welsh correspondence on the Centennial Exhibition, 1858–1886; post office political discrimination in Philadelphia, 1898; ballot reform in Philadelphia; 1890–1891; Honest Government Party, Dr. S.C. Swallow campaign in Pennsylvania, 1898–1899; Lincoln Independent Republican Committee, Pattison for Governor, 1890; Anti-Combine Committee, Pattison for Mayor, Philadelphia, 1895, Independent Committee, W. Redwood Wright for Treasurer, Philadelphia, 1891.

The arrangement continues with pure water and sanitation, Railroad Safety Commission, 1893; personal interest cases, 1873–1933; Welsh family correspondence, 1891–1926; Welsh foreign correspondence, 1873–1935; Welsh personal correspondence, 1863–1935; Welsh essays and speeches, 1863–1934; Welsh journals, 1898–1919; shorthand notes, n.d.; cancelled checks and bills, 1886–1920; invitations, greeting cards, announcements; broadsides and miscellaneous printed material, 1880–1925; lists of names and addresses of members of various organizations, n.d.; diaries, 1883–1928; letterbooks, 1886–1931; account books, 1854–1899; photographs, views, clippings.

The correspondence of Herbert Welsh, 1875–1934, with prominent men and women, including presidents of the United States, cabinet members, members of Congress, jurists, scientists, scholars, civic reformers, local and national political leaders. It contains material on a variety of political, social and economic subjects: Indian rights, anti–imperialism, international arbitration, League of Nations, Philippine annexation, scandals involving American soldiers, Turkish atrocities, Armenian massacres, Syrian relief and education, domestic and foreign missionaries, Waldensian Society and its evangelism in Italy, civil service reform, World War, establishment of the Friends of German Democracy, Centennial Exhibition, Society for the Protection of Forests, political corruption in Pennsylvania, reform movements in Philadelphia, education, sanitation, Audubon Society, Racial problems, arts, sciences, and local charities.

Gift of Herbert Welsh, 1937.

703
Welch, Emma Finney, b. 1855.   **Collection, 1714–1921.**
(275 items.)

Emma Finney Welch was an antique pewter collector from Germantown.

"My Pewter Scrapbook," 1921, containing descriptions of individual pieces in her large pewter and Britannia ware collection, together with genealogical material on previous owners and makers, photographs of houses and gravestones of previous owners, and newspaper clippings, notes, and correspondence on pewter collecting. The papers also contain letters to Mrs. Welch, 1903–1921, on her pewter collection, loose notes regarding pewter, and collection inventories.

In addition, the collection contains Welch family papers, including: Jeremiah Bumstead, Boston mechanic, and sister, Sarah Bumstead, personal letters, 1714–1731, to their sister, Mrs. Abigail Lambert in Connecticut, providing spiritual encouragement; John Lambert, U.S. Representative and Senator from Amwell Township, Hunterdon County, N.J., family letters, 1807–1815, written from Washington, D.C., with reference to domestic affairs at his N.J. home; Lambert family papers, 1793–1837, primarily John and

Hannah Lambert estate papers, which include George Larason account books, 1823–1837, as an administrator of the estate of his father-in-law; James Seabrook, Lambertville, N.J., miscellaneous legal papers and letters received, 1809–1840; and Phinney family papers, 1798–1885, including Asa Phinney, Canterbury Township, Windham County, Conn., farmer, expense account book, 1798–1806, and family letters received by Dr. Elisha and Lucas O. Phinney.

Gift of the Emma Finney Welch estate, 1927.

704
West, Benjamin, 1730–1813.   Drawings and account books,
1790–1811.   (4 v.)

Benjamin West's drawings and sketches, ca. 1790–1807; and his accounts with his banker, Thomas Coutts, London, 1790–1804, 1810–1811.
Account book gift of Samuel P. Avery.
Drawings and sketches purchased, Gilpin Fund.

705
Westcott, Esther Montgomery.   Poetry album, 1812.   (1 v.)

Gift of Mrs. Medora P. Cockerill, 1908.

706
Westcott, Thompson, 1820–1888.   *History of Philadelphia.*
(1 linear ft.)

This manuscript of Thompson Westcott, editor of the *Philadelphia Sunday Dispatch,* is a continuation of the history of Philadelphia which appeared in that paper from 1867–1884. The published history brought the narrative to 1830; the manuscript is a detailed history of the city from 1830 to the consolidation of the city and county of Philadelphia in 1854.

707
Wetherill, Edward.   Collection, 1822–1916.   (100 items.)

Miscellaneous collection of autograph letters, newspaper clippings, and memorabilia, gathered by Edward Wetherill, Philadelphia abolitionist, and wife Anna Thorpe Wetherill. One volume relates to the anti-slavery movement and contains letters to James Miller McKim, anti-slavery leader associated with the Pennsylvania Anti-Slavery Society and the Pennsylvania Freeman, 1853–1860, and letters from Mary Grew, Philadelphia abolitionist and suffragette, 1860, 1891.
Gift of Mrs. F.M. Ives, 1923.

708A
Wharton family.   Papers, 1679–1834.   (3 linear ft.)

Papers of the Wharton family, Philadelphia merchants: Thomas, Joseph, Charles, William and James Wharton.

For Thomas Wharton there are letterbooks, 1752–1759, 1773–1784; receipt books, 1755–1763, 1758–1763; book of patents and deeds of the Indiana Company, 1776; correspondence and business papers with a few additional documents, 1679–1820; patents and deeds, 1682–1834.

James Wharton came finally to concentrate in ship chandlery and the manufacture and sale of rope. Wharton joined various partners in his several undertakings of whom Enoch Story was one. For James Wharton there are accounts relate to the chandlery and rope walk businesses, but Wharton's interests in shipping ventures occasionally surface. The records include: daybooks, 1759–1777; journal, 1756–1761, 1768; sail loft journal, 1765–1768 with Robert Smith; ship chandlery ledgers, 1753–1758, 1761–1764; general ledger, 1761–1764, 1771, mostly chandlery and rope accounts; Quebec ledger, 1760–1761; account book of invoices and sales, 1752–1756, with [?]Usher; invoice book, 1756–1760, of ship chandlery to Philadelphia from London; receipt book, 1763–1776; cashbook, 1772, 1775. There is some loose material of incoming correspondence and accounts, 1756–1781, and receipted bills of Thomas Wharton, Jr., estate, 1776–1784.

The papers for Joseph, William and Charles include: Joseph Wharton ledger book, 1736–1793; William Wharton ledger, 1761–1803; Charles Wharton cashbooks, 1765–1771, 1771–1780; daybooks, 1768–1772, 1775–1785; invoice and memorandum book, 1774–1792; Charles Wharton account with William Wharton estate, 1805–1811; and letterbook of the firm of Baynton and Wharton, 1761.

There is also a receipt book for James C. Fisher.

Gift of Miss A.H. Wharton, 1923.

708B
Baynton and Wharton.   Letterbook, 1758–1760.   (1 v.)

[John] Baynton and [Samuel] Wharton, Philadelphia merchants, letterbook, 1758–1760. Major correspondents are Robert Bulley, St. Johns, Newfoundland; Richard Neave, London; Sargent, Aufrere & Co., London; John Tillotson, Duck Creek, Cecil County, Md.; Gersham Williams, New Providence, Bahamas.

Purchased, 1956.

709
Wharton, Robert, 1757–1834.   Record book, 1793–1806.   (2 v.)

Wharfage accounts, 1793–1795; alderman's court docket, 1797–1800; and civil dockets, 1805–1806.

710

Wharton, Thomas I. (Thomas Isaac), 1791–1856.   Papers, 1664 (1812–1891).   (15 linear ft.)

Papers of Thomas Isaac Wharton chiefly on legal cases, estates, and Philadelphia properties in which Wharton was professionally interested: Franklin Fire Insurance Company, 1834–1851; *Van Dyke v. Philadelphia* (Kensington), 1857; Jay Cooke bankruptcy, 1875; Library Company of Philadelphia, 1871–1878; papers on the Wiccacoe Tract, containing abstracts of title, briefs, warrants, surveys, plans, 1664–1870; Pennsylvania Steam Ship Company, 1851; papers on the Civil Code, 1830–1836, of which Wharton was one of the commissioners; Griffith family estate papers, 1817–1847; Worth family estate papers, 1812–1891; surveys of the Delaware and Schuylkill Canal Company, 1839.

Gift of Mrs. Henry Wharton, 1937–1938.

711

White, William, 1748–1836.   Manuscripts, 1765–1865. (44 items.)

These papers of William White, first Protestant Episcopal bishop of the Diocese of Pennsylvania, include manuscript sermons: CXXVII, "Of Sinful Anger," and "Of Tribute, to Caesar and that to God," n. d.; certificates of consecration, 1770–1787; diplomas, 1765, 1781; and papers on William White lands and the administration of his estate, 1773–1865, including George W. Hunter, Philadelphia scholar, letterbook, 1856–1865, as administrator of the estate.

The collection also contains the draft and printer's copy of "Memoir of the Life of the Right Rev. William White, D.D.," 1839, with miscellaneous notes by Bird Wilson, D.D., professor of systematic divinity at the General Theological Seminary, New York.

Gift of G.H. Wiltbank, 1864, the Rev. William White Bronson, 1872, Israel W. Morris, 1905, and Dr. James H. Montgomery, 1912.

712

Whiteman family.   Papers, 1849–1856.   (49 v.)

A collection of small, handwritten, juvenile publications, the longest of which is "The Ladder," 1849–1853, of brothers John G., W[illiam] A., James G. and Horace Whiteman of Philadelphia, reflecting mid-nineteenth-century popular culture. The volumes contain articles on natural history, descriptions of exhibitions at the Franklin Institute and the Pennsylvania Museum, news items, poetry, satire, stories, puzzles, riddles, descriptions of 4th of July and Christmas holiday festivities, and illustrations in color. The papers also contain works attributed to a more mature John G. Whiteman, 1851–1856, amateur musician and leader of an orchestra that produced light operas: "Jack and the Bean Stalk: a Fairy Drama;" "The Queen of Hearts;" and operas "Blue Beard," "Lord Bateman," and "Miranda."

Gift of Dora A. Whiteman, 1935.

713
Whittier, John Greenleaf, 1807–1892.   Hymn, 1876.   (1 v.)

A hymn written by John Greenleaf Whittier to be sung at the opening of the International Exhibition of Art and Industry at the Centennial Exposition, Philadelphia, 1876. This copy is illuminated by Annie L. Wiley. There is also a letter of John G. Whittier to Mrs. Wiley, on her work in illuminating the hymn.

Gift of Mrs. W.H. Sayen.

714
Willcox family.   Papers, 1704 (1770–1850) 1895.   (6 linear ft.)

The Willcox family paper mill, Ivy Mills, established in 1729 in Concord Township, Delaware County, became a leading supplier of paper for Provincial, Continental, and Federal currency, as well as of banknote paper.

These papers of Thomas Willcox, son Mark, and grandsons, John and James M. Willcox, include: mill books, 1788–1841, which contain records of payroll and production; incoming business correspondence 1814–1842, from consumers and dealers in banknote paper, suppliers of rags and machinery, and others; miscellaneous receipts, receipted bills, bills, invoices, and legal papers, 1724–1837; samples of paper and watermarks, 1704–1858; and miscellaneous papers, 1786–1831, relating to land speculation. The collection also contains Nathan Edwards, shoemaker and tavern keeper of the Black Horse Tavern, Middletown Township, Delaware County, ledgers, 1729–1784; daybooks, 1776–1784; account book, 1774–1783; and bills, receipted bills, memoranda, and loose pages from ledgers and daybooks, 1743–1783.

Gift of Joseph Willcox, 1896, 1897, 1899.

715
Williams, Annabella, b. 1815.   Papers, 1829–1831.   (3 v.)

Schoolbook, 1829–1830, with hand-drawn maps of states and poetry; commonplace book of poetry, 1831; journal, 1831, continued as a diary, n.d., of a Williams family trip from Philadelphia through New York to Cleveland

and return through Pennsylvania, with descriptions of train and canal transport and sights en route.

Gift of Mary W. Shoemaker, 1938.

716
Williams, Richard J.   Genealogical notes, ca. 1907–1913.   (1 v.)

Transferred to the Genealogical Society of Pennsylvania.

717
Dunbar, Elizabeth.   Papers, 1808–1936.   (1 v.)

The collection consists mainly of typewritten copies of letters, testimonials, addresses, obituary notes, tributes of Africa Americans, bibliographical notes, mementoes, and sketches, gathered by Elizabeth Dunbar for a biography of Talcott Williams. Included are letters, 1933, addressed to Elizabeth Dunbar; papers on Morocco, the Muslim world, and related subjects.

Gift of Elizabeth Dunbar.

718
Jones family.   Account books, 1810–1874.   (17 v.)

Benjamin Jones and his sons, Andrew M. and Benjamin W. Jones, were Philadelphia iron merchants. Their papers relate primarily to the family-owned Hanover Furnace and Mary Ann Forge in Burlington County, N.J., as well as to Jones family real estate.

They include: Jones & Howell, Philadelphia iron merchants, receipt book, 1810–1811, continued by Benjamin Jones, 1810–1849, and by the executors of the estate of Benjamin Jones, 1849–1855; Benjamin Jones account book, 1818–1850 (continued after his death); cashbooks, 1822–1869 (continued after his death by the executors of his estate); daybook, 1821–1849; ledger, 1821–1849; letterbook, 1834–1847, including drafts by A.M. Jones, 1844–1851; A.M. Jones and A.S. Morris account book, 1849–1874, as executors of the estate of Benjamin Jones; Andrew M. Jones receipt book, 1822–1855, including receipts of Andrew M. Jones & Brother, 1837–1845, and A.M. and B.W. Jones, 1844–1849; Andrew M. Jones daybook, 1835–1854, and Andrew M. Jones & Brother daybook, 1837–1845; Andrew M. Jones ledger, 1823–1854, and Andrew M. Jones & Brother ledger, 1837–1845; Andrew M. Jones letterbook, 1823–1854, including drafts by Andrew M. Jones & Brother, 1837–1842, A.M. and B.W. Jones, 1842–1852, and Benjamin Jones; Andrew M. Jones letterbook, 1851–1861; Andrew M. Jones receipt book, 1864–1871, as administrator of the estate of William J. Taylor; Andrew M. Jones journal, 1839–1870, as executor of the estate of James Cooper.

718–722

The collection also contains Harvey Beck, Philadelphia merchant, receipt books, 1821–1843.

Gift of Mrs. Charles Willing, 1939.

719

Willis, Robert, b. ca. 1713–1791. Diary, 1770–1789. (1 v.)

The diary of Robert Willis, an itinerant Quaker, a mender of fishing nets, with daily entries giving accounts of his travels in England, Scotland, and Ireland, 1770–1774, and in the United States, 1774–1789. There is some account of Friends' meeting places Willis visited, people he met, social conditions, transportation facilities, and religious sentiments.

Purchased, Dreer Fund, 1935.

720

Wills and administration papers, 1697–1915. (25 items.)

A collection of miscellaneous wills and administration papers for Matilda Anderson, Isaac Bartram, Clarissa M. Blodget, John R. Brown, Isabella Louisa Watson Brown, Eliza C. Deery, Mary A. Eckstein, Joseph Galloway, Thomas Goleborn, Ann Amanda Hailer, Abraham Hopper, Joseph Bonaparte Howell, Sarah Hulings, Jessie Hussey, Thomas Hynes, James Franzier Jacques, Elizabeth Lee, Randal Maliu, Katherine M. Moore, John Ogden, James Roberts, Thomas A. Rogers, Lizzie Rue, Paul Solomon Schwizk, John D. Shaeff, Edward Philip Snooke, Richard Thomas, John Wilkins, Jr., and Dunk Williamson.

721

Wilson, James, 1742–1798. Papers, 1718–1857. (3 linear ft.)

Material on the early federal government and on James Wilson's business and professional activities: draft of the Constitution and a corrected copy of the same, 1787; notes of debates, resolutions, in the Constitutional Convention; drafts of treaties, memoranda on regulation of immigration, and establishment of the National Bank; business correspondence, 1773–1857, including a journal, July 9, 1794 to Aug. 26, 1794; letters and miscellaneous documents, 1770–1815; docket book, 1743–1768; commonplace book, 1767; deeds and wills, 1718–1785; surveys and maps of lands in Pennsylvania, 1737–1794; articles of agreement, bonds and accounts, 1794–1830; and letters of Mary Wilson Hollingsworth, 1801–1812.

722

Wilson, John, d. 1798. Ledger, 1794–1803. (1 v.)

This ledger contains the accounts of John Wilson's surveying and engineering work done for landholders, canal companies, farmers, in Scotland;

continued by his wife, Judith, as domestic accounts after Wilson's death in 1798.

Gift of Mrs. Walter W. Pharo, 1937.

723
Wilson, John A., d. 1896.   Diaries, 1859–1895.   (33 v.)

Diaries of John A. Wilson, chief engineer of the Pennsylvania Railroad, reflect chiefly his personal and domestic affairs, and contain accounts of his income and expenses during the period. One volume contains notes on railroad engineering, 1859–1874.

Gift of Mrs. Walter W. Pharo, 1937.

724
Wilson, William B.   Diaries, 1817–1871.   (4 v.)

The diaries of William B. Wilson, orthodox Quaker of Bendersville, Adams County, containing accounts of domestic affairs, farming, weather, Quaker meetings.

Purchased, Library Fund, 1935.

725A
Wilson, William Hasell, 1811–1902.   Papers, 1706–1900. (ca. 100 items.)

These family papers include correspondence, genealogical notes, marriage certificates, 1706–1762, school certificates, 1753–1829, portraits and records of the Wilson, Allston, Gibbes, and Simons families.

Gift of Arthur Morton Wilson, 1932.

725B
Wilson, William Hasell, 1811–1902.   Papers, 1855 (1889–1896) 1898. (11 items.)

William Hasell Wilson was a civil engineer with, and president of, various Pennsylvania railroads.

These papers include William H. Wilson correspondence, 1855–1898, mainly on the history of the South Fork Dam, Cambria County, which broke during the Johnstown Flood of 1889; "Personal Reminiscences," 1896, describing incidents in Wilson's life from 1817 to 1896, mentioning childhood in South Carolina, with references to plantation life, activities with Pennsylvania railroads, and genealogical data; "War Reminiscences," n.d., describing Wilson's participation in defending the Pennsylvania Railroad during the Civil War.

Gift of Miss S.H. Wilson, 1937; Mrs. Walter W. Pharo, 1937–1938; Miss Susan D. Wilson (through Mrs. Walter W. Pharo), 1938.

726

Wilson, William W.   Papers, ca. 1800–1840.   (ca. 100 items.)

Miscellaneous specimens of engraved banknotes, checks, commercial labels, etc; also pictures of Gloucester Iron Works.
Gift of S.B. Chew.

727

Wistar family.   Papers, 1717 (1730–1800) 1848.   (150 items.)

Caspar Wistar was a Philadelphia merchant and brass button maker who began a Salem County, N.J., glassworks in 1739.

The papers include Caspar Wistar's letterbooks, 1733–1737; letters to Wistar, 1732–1754; and glassworks account book, continued by son, Richard, 1743–1769. There is also an account book of the estate of Caspar's wife, Catherine Wistar, 1787–1789. In addition, the collection contains miscellaneous family and personal correspondence, mainly to Caspar Wistar's grandson, Thomas Wistar, Philadelphia merchant, 1783–1848, and from: Thomas' brother Dr. Caspar, Jr., while traveling in England and studying medicine in Edinburgh, 1783–1784, and concerning the yellow fever epidemic in Philadelphia, 1798; his wife Mary Waln Wister courtship letters, 1783–1787; and other relatives.

Gift of John M. Whitall, Mrs. Walter Nordhoff, John Schoberkimber, 1916; and Mrs. William P. Buffum, 1916, 1920, and 1924.

All Caspar Wistar material in german.

728

Wistar, Isaac Jones, 1827–1892.   Memoirs, 1892.   (2 v.)

These memoirs describe incidents in the life of Isaac Jones Wistar, pioneering journeys through the wilderness of the western territories before the Civil War, life of pioneers and first settlers, and enterprises in hunting, gold mining, farming, Indian trade, lumbering, shipping, transportation, canals, railroads, finance, with details on the Middle West, California, Oregon, Alaska, and Mexico. Included are Wistar's reflections on government, accounts of his participation in the Civil War, and data on the genealogy and history of the Wistar family.

Gift of Dr. Henry Winsor, 1924.

729
Wister, James W.   Family papers, 1777 (1800–1870) 1890.
(620 items.)

The Wisters and related Miercken and Whitesides kin resided in Germantown and Philadelphia. Sarah Whitesides married Charles J. Wister, a Philadelphia merchant and amateur scientist; one of the children Charles J. Wister, Jr., also had scientific interests.

Among the Wister papers are: John M. Price estate receipts, checks, and other financial and legal papers, 1796–1837, Charles J. Wister, executor; "Gems of Thought," 1833–1835, a teacher's personal tutorial letters to Susan Wister, another child; Sarah Whitesides Wister receipted bills, 1839–1864; Charles J. Wister and Charles J. Wister, Jr., transit instrument notations and astronomical observations, 1834–1889; Charles J. Wister, Jr., letterbook, 1857–1870, containing letters to family and friends together with science and music articles, poems and memoranda.

Among the related family papers are Miercken family receipt book, 1786–1890, carried on by several generations, primarily for St. Peters Church pew rent; Henry Miercken, Cape François merchant, family letters, 1791–1807; Sarah Miercken Whitesides tax and rent receipt book, 1821–1837, continued by Harriet Whitesides, 1838–1841.

There are additional scattered letters, receipted bills and other accounts, photographs, and other family keepsakes.
Gift of James W. Wister, 1931.

730
Wister, Sarah, 1761–1804.   Journal, 1777–1778.   (1 v.)

Journal written by Sarah Wister during the British occupation of Philadelphia, describes social life.
Gift of Owen Wister and Dr. James W. Wister, 1931.
Published in the *P.M.H.B.*, 9 (1885): 318–329, 463–473; 10 (1886): 51–60.

731
Wolf, George, 1777–1840.   Correspondence, 1826–1836.
(3 linear ft.)

The papers of George Wolf, Governor of Pennsylvania, relate to state administration and politics, including many letters from George M. Dallas, 1830–1835.

732
Wolsperger, Samuel.   Letters, 1738–1756.   (35 items.)

Letters of the Rev. Samuel Wolsperger, Ausburg, Germany, to the Rev. Fresenius, theologian at the Court of the Landgrave of Hesse, on publication of books, religious matters, social and charitable activities.

733
Women's Dental Association of the United States.   Record books, 1892–1921.   (2 v.)

Minutes, committee reports, and membership lists of the Women's Dental Association of the United States.
Gift of Dr. Eliza Yerkes.

734
Wood, Walter.   Papers, 1691–1910.   (ca. 100 items.)

Family papers, including deeds to Philadelphia properties, 1691–1910; correspondence of Peter Hahn, Philadelphia merchant, 1814–1831; certificates of stock in the Pennsylvania Academy of Fine Arts, New Theatre, German Society, 1814–1821; mercantile agreement on Chinese trade in Canton, 1824; powers of attorney, and other items.
Gift of the Walter Wood estate.

735
Wood, Walter.   Papers, 1889–1894.   (ca. 100 items.)

These papers include patents, agreements, and correspondence on gasometers, cranes, and other mechanical implements in which Walter Wood was financially interested and which he purchased from inventors in America and Europe.
Gift of R.D. Wood Company, 1936.

736
Woodhouse family.   Diaries, 1818–1867.   (5 v.)

The pocket diaries include Commander Samuel Woodhouse memoranda while in Brazil, [1818]. In addition, there are diaries of Dr. Samuel Washington Woodhouse, naturalist and surgeon: 1849, of U.S. topographical expedition, under Captain L. Sitgreaves and Lieutenant I.C. Woodruff, to survey boundary between the Creek and Cherokee Indian Nations; 1860, of trip from Philadelphia to England and Scotland and return; 1867, of trip from New York to France and England and return. The collection also contains an account of sale at vendue on the farm of the late Samuel Wood-house, Springton Forge, Chester County, with a list of articles, prices, and names of purchasers, 1853.

Gift of Samuel W. Woodhouse, Jr., 1935.

737
Woolman, John, 1720–1772.   Papers, 1669 (1752–1800) 1830. (29 items.)

John Woolman was a Mount Holly, N.J., Quaker minister who advocated the abolition of slavery.

These papers included John Woolman's spiritual autobiography, 1756–1770, which also contains his essay, "A Plea for the Poor." There are also John Woolman's daybook as a tailor, 1743–1746, continued as a ledger for his executorship of various estates, 1746–1765, and his dry-goods and other business ledgers, 1752–1798 (continued after Woolman's death). In addition, there are John Woolman letters, 1760–1772, to his wife and miscellaneous family legal papers, 1669–1830. The papers also contain Quaker preacher Elias Hicks letters, 1824–1827, to Woolman's grandchild Samuel Comfort, also a Quaker preacher, concerning the Society of Friends.

Gift of Major Samuel Comfort, 1912.

John Woolman's spiritual autobiography published in *The Works of John Woolman,* William A. Beardsley, ed.

738
World War, 1914–1918.   Collection, 1915–1922.   (25 items.)

Mementos, scrapbooks, poetry, pictures, and other items reflecting activities during the World War.

Gift of Mrs. E. Russell Jones.

739
Wroth, Peregrine.   Transcripts, 1879.   (1 v.)

Excerpts from "Discovery of the Site of New Yarmouth," "The Old Maryland Line," and "Retrospection," unpublished writings on local history by Peregrine Worth, scholar and physician of Chestertown, Md.

Copied by James H. Carr, 1879.

740
Yeates, Jasper, 1745–1817.   Papers, 1718–1876.   (ca. 7,500 items.)

Jasper Yeates papers, 1764–1816, reflect his activities as a leading lawyer in Lancaster County, and as judge of the Supreme Court of Pennsylvania;

they contain his notes on trials, evidence, arguments, depositions, and judicial opinions rendered in numerous legal cases. A large portion of the papers is his personal correspondence, 1780–1816, with noted men, such as Edward Burd, Thomas Hartley, Richard Peters, William Tilghman, and others, which deals with political events, public questions, congressional and administrative affairs; John Yeates papers, 1738–1865, relate chiefly to commerce, shipping between the Middle Atlantic colonies and Barbadoes, Antigua, and other islands in the West Indies; survey of Richard Hill's plantation in Philadelphia, by Jacob Taylor, 1718; Redmond Conyngham letters, essays, 1833; Peter Grubb estate papers, accounts, 1750–1759; Jasper Yeates Cunningham family papers, 1856–1876; chronology of the history of the world, from the creation to 1750; Yeates genealogical notes.

741
York County papers, 1738–1803.
(ca. 150 items.)

Miscellaneous material on local economic and political affairs: petitions, laws, deeds, and letters of prominent men. Purchased.

742
Young, William.   Family papers, 1745 (1800–1850).   (100 items.)

William Young was a Philadelphia bookseller and publisher who later established a paper mill at Rockland, New Castle, Del. The papers include Young's receipt book, 1819–1822, as treasurer of Philadelphia Society for the Promotion of National Industry. There are also miscellaneous deeds and other legal papers, 1745–1850, about his property, "Whitehall," on Spring Garden Street, and the Rockland estate. Other family papers are: receipt book, 1839–1846, of his son, William Wallace Young; newspaper extracts about his granddaughter Agnes Young McAllister and the 1819 Atlantic Ocean crossing of the steamship *Savannah;* memorabilia of a trip to Europe, 1841; family memoir, n.d.
Gift of Stan V. Henkels, 1911.

743
Zinzendorf, Nicholas Lewis von.   Papers, 1732–1741.   (7 items.)

Transferred to the Genealogical Society of Pennsylvania.

744
Milbourne, Thomas.   Testimonies, 1681.   (1 v.)

An Abstract of abbreviation of some few of the many (later and former) testimonies from the inhabitants of New Jersey and other eminent persons who have wrote particularly concerning that place : to contradict the disingenuous and false reports of some men who have made it their business to speak unjustly of New Jersey and our proceedings therein.—London: Thomas Milbourne, 1681.

Handwritten transcript by Mrs. John R. Bartlett, 1874.
Library of Mrs. John Carter Brown, Providence, R.I.
Gift of Brinton Coxe, 1883.

745
Peale, Titian Ramsay, 1799–1885.   Collection, 1794–1808.

Letters, records, and copies of correspondence gathered by Peale from the papers of his father, Charles Willson Peale relating to the founding, in 1794, of the Columbianum and its subsequent failure, as well as the founding and early years of the Pennsylvania Academy of Fine Arts. Included are copies of C.W. Peale's correspondence with Robert Fulton concerning an exhibition of Benjamin West's paintings, 1807; and a brief exchange of letters between C.W. Peale and West; 1808.

Some correspondence handwritten transcripts, 1877.
Gift of Titian Ramsay Peale, 1877.

746
Hopkinson, Francis, 1737–1791.   Papers, 1778–1780.   (1 v.)

Record of bills drawn on the Commissaries between France and the United Colonies by Francis Hopkinson while he was treasurer of the Continental Loan Office.

747
Irish Land Commission.   Reports, 1702–1705.   (1 v.)

Statutes affecting the restoration of forfeited estates in Ireland following the rebellion of 1641, with minutes of the Commission established for that purpose.

Contemporary transcript in several hands.
Purchased, Library Fund, 1896.

748
American Colonization Society.   Biographical catalogue of the portrait gallery, 1866.   (1 v.)

Biographical sketches of the 41 sitters for portraits collected by the Colonization Society, 1836–1866, including name of artist.

Gift of the Colonization Society, 1903.

749
Roberts, Samuel W., 1811–1882.   Notebook, 1830–1832.   (1 v.)

Account by Samuel W. Roberts, as engineer for the Allegheny Portage Railroad, of its construction, including notes on surveys, building specifications, lists of contractors, estimates of costs.
Gift of Joseph T. Richards, 1916.

750
Ludewig, Hermann E. (Hermann Ernst), 1809 or 10–1856.   Papers, 1853.   (1 v.)

"The Literature of American Local History. Second Supplement. Pennsylvania," an annotated bibliography, was prepared by Hermann Ludewig, a New York lawyer and bibliographer, to supplement his privately printed *The Literature of American Local History; a Bibliographical Essay.* (New York: The Author, 1848) and *The Literature of American Local History.* First Supplement; New York. (New York: R. Craighead, 1848).
Gift of Hermann E. Ludewig, 1853.

751
Vicary, John.   American Naval Signals, 1798–1800.   (1 v.)

An explanation of flag signals by Captain John Vicary.
Purchased, Dreer Fund, 1935.

752
Paxton Volunteers.   "Apology of the Paxton Volunteers," 1764.   (1 v.)

Draft of an unpublished pamphlet which blames Quakers in the Pennsylvania Assembly for attacks upon frontier settlements during the French and Indian War and for the massacre of Conestoga Indians in December, 1763. Continues with copies of depositions, 1764, detailing the losses of settlers.
Gift of N.W. Spear.

753
Appel, Charles D.   Diary, 1865.   (1 v.)

Charles D. Appel's diary, 1865, as conductor on the Philadelphia, Wilmington, and Baltimore Railroad and in charge of the special car which conveyed the remains of Abraham Lincoln from Washington to Springfield.
Gift of the Ellen I. Kenney estate, 1939.

754
Ashmead, John, 1738–1818. **Log and journal,** 1797–1798. (1 v.)

Log and journal, 1797–1798, of John Ashmead of the fourth voyage of the *India* from Philadelphia to Batavia and return with weather accounts and other nautical notations.

755
Ashmead, Lehman P. **Journals, 1841–1845.** (2 v.)

Journals of Lehman P. Ashmead, a midshipman with the United States Navy from 1841 to 1845, of a cruise on the U.S. Frigate *Constitution* commanded by Captain Philip F. Vorhees from Portsmouth, N.H., to the Mediterranean and from Brazil to Norfolk, Va.; lists of vessels of the United States Navy, notes on naval flag signals and storage and equipment of the *Congress,* and a selection of poetry and songs.
Gift of G.C. Callahan, 1913.

756
Association, club, and society records, 1764–1937. (110 v.)

Abolition Society of Delaware. Minutes, 1801–1819. (1 v.)
Academy of Medicine of Philadelphia. Minutes, 1798–1799. (1 v.)
Amateurs' Drawing Room Association (Philadelphia, Pa.) Record books, 1862–1865. (11 v.)
American Republican Society. High Street Ward (Philadelphia, Pa.) Minutes, 1809–1811.
American Society for Promoting Useful Knowledge. Rules and membership list, ca. 1790. (1 v.)
Amphion Amateur Musical Association. Minutes, 1849–1868. (1 v.)
Anti-Slavery Society of Pennsylvania. Minutes, constitution, papers, 1837, 1846–1856. (3 v.)
Artist Fund Society. Minutes and papers, 1835–1858. (3 v.)
Association of Aldermen (Philadelphia, Pa.) Constitution, by-laws, lists of members, 1865. (1 v.)
Association of Pennsylvania. Officers' minutes, 1764–1772. (1 v.)
Association of Survivors. Pennsylvania Volunteers. 95th Regiment Infantry. Minutes, 1875–1917. (1 v.)
Athenian Institute. Constitution, by-laws, minutes, 1837–1846. (1 v.)
Caballeros de la Luz. Record books, 1873–1919. (8 v.)
Central Phrenological Society of Philadelphia. Constitution and minutes, 1822–1827. (1 v.)
Citizens Temperance Union. Minute book, 1874–1875. (1 v.)

Clarkson Institute of Pennsylvania. Minutes, 1830–1838. (3 v.)
    Club Stable. Account book, 1831–1833. (1 v.)
Delta Kappa Psi. Alpha Chapter. Papers, 1849–1931. (1 v.)
Democratic Society of Pennsylvania. Minutes, 1793–1794. (1 v.)
Downingtown Lyceum. Minutes. 1841–1845. (1 v.)
First Female Beneficial Society of Philadelphia. Minutes, 1814–1840.
(1 v.)
    Franklin Literary Union. Minutes, 1859–1862. (1 v.)
Friends Historical Association. Papers, 1874–1878. (1 folder).
Gettysburg Battlefield Memorial Association. Minutes, 1872–1896.
(2 v.)
    Gloucester Fox Hunting Club (Gloucester, N.J.) Papers, ca. 1816. (1 v.)
Jockey Club. Register book and papers, 1766–1774, 1930. (3 v.)
Mercantile Club (Philadelphia, Pa.) Minutes, 1878–1895. (2 v.)
Neighbors' Club (Philadelphia, Pa.) Minutes, 1901–1912. (1 v.)
Ocean City Fishing Club (Ocean City, N.J.) Account book, 1916. (1 v.)
Patriotic Association. Record book, 1778. (1 v.)
Penn Relief Association. Record books, 1862–1865. (11 v.)
Pennsylvania Hall Association (Philadelphia, Pa.) Minutes, 1837–1864.
(2 v.)
    Pennsylvania History Club. Papers, 1905–1916. (ca. 250 items.)
Pennsylvania Literary Society. Papers, 1820–1826. (1 v.)
Pennsylvania Society for the Encouragement of Manufacturers and the
Useful Arts. Minutes, 1787–1789. (2 v.)
Pennsylvania Society for the Promotion of Public Economy. Papers,
1817–1854. (1 v.)
Philadelphia Child Welfare Association. Minutes, reports, resolutions,
1933–1937. (1 v.)
Philadelphia Anti-Slavery Society. Constitution, by-laws, names of
members, 1838. (1 v.)
Philadelphia Association of Young Men for Celebrating the 4th of July.
Record book, 1831–1833. (1 v.)
Philadelphia Medical Society and Institute. Minutes, 1817–1853. (2 v.)
Philadelphia Quoit Club. Minutes, 1839–1855. (2 v.)
Philadelphia Society for Alleviating the Miseries of Public Prisons. Min-
utes, 1787–1793. (1 v.)
Pike Beneficial Society of Philadelphia. Minutes, treasury accounts,
membership lists, 1814–1865. (19 v.)
Platonian Association. Constitution, by-laws, resolutions, 1823–1826.
(1 v.)
    Platonian Literary Association. Correspondence, 1827–1830. (1 v.)

Saturday Club (Philadelphia, Pa.) List of original members, ca. 1877–1878. (1 v.)

Schuylkill Fishing Company (Philadelphia, Pa.) Manuscripts, 1832. (1 v.)

Scott Legion of Soldiers of Mexican War. Roll of members, by-laws. constitution, 1868. (1 v.)

Société Française des Amis de la Liberté et de l'Egalité. Minutes, 1793–1794. (1 v.)

Society for the Commemoration of the Landing of William Penn. List of member and correspondence, 1825. (1 v.)

Society for Political Inquiry (Philadelphia, Pa.) Minutes, 1787–1789. (1 v.)

Society of Native Pennsylvanians. Minutes, 1812–1813. (1 v.)

Taylors' Company of Philadelphia. Minutes, 1771–1776. (1 v.)

Tinicum Fishing Company (Philadelphia, Pa.) Minutes, n.d. (2 v.)

Washington Benevolent Society. List of members, 1818–1828. (2 v.)

West Chester Debating Society. Minutes, 1821–1831. (1 v.)

757
Asylum Company.   Minutes, 1794 (1802–1804).   (1 v.)

The Asylum Company was founded by Robert Morris, John Nicholson, and others in 1794 to settle and improve tracts of land in Pennsylvania and to establish a colony for French refugees. After the bankruptcy of both Morris and Nicholson, the company was reorganized by a group of Philadelphia merchants in 1801.

Included here are two of the original articles of agreement, 1794, and the minutes and list of shareholders of the reorganized company.

Gift of Ferdinand J. Dreer, 1878.

758
Atlee, Samuel John, 1739–1786.   [Journal extract], 1776.   (1 v.)

This journal extract contains details of a battle between the British and Continentals.

759
Autograph Collection, 1813–1904. (27 v.)

Collection of autograph and sentiment books of: Sarah Coates, 1813–1814; J. Pattison, 1816–1818; Susanna Longstreth, 1823–1852; R.N. Paxson, 1824–1828; Frances McGregor, 1825; Mary Wells, 1825–1838; Susan L. Watson, 1831–1833; Ann Lippincott, 1835; Rhoda Ann Hampton, 1837–1852; Almira

Roberts, 1839–1842; Annie Wells Fisher, 1847–1853; Sally Bridges, 1849–1863; William E. Stokes, 1851–1860; Mary Anna Hughes, 1855; Henrietta N. Taylor, 1855; Helen N. Price, 1857–1880; Almira Galliard, 1859–1884; Josephine Griffith, 1862–1864; Harriet I. McCluen, 1862–1879, 1864–1892; Anna McCluen, 1879–1904; Alexander Mullen, 1880–1886. Also included are: autographs of members present at a dinner for Rear Admiral Charles E. Clark, U.S.N., 1904; autographs of prominent Philadelphians, 1705–1797; autographs of members of the Pennsylvania Legislature, 1874; Edward A. Groves collection of autographs and photographs of celebrated musical and traditional celebrities, 1859–1864; letters of medical men of Pennsylvania, 1747–1887; autographs of delegates to the Pennsylvania constitutional conventions, 1837–1838, 1872–1873; letters of French statesmen and soldiers associated with the American Revolution, 1778–1819.

760
Backhouse, Richard, 1793.   Account book, 1775.   (1 v.)

Accounts of Richard Backhouse, contractor of provisions for the Revolutionary army.
Gift of John Jordan, 1877.

761
Wilson, John.   Bahamas Islands report, 1783.   (1 v.)

Report of Lieutenant John Wilson, of the British army, on the military state and defenses of the Bahamas Islands; also data on the origin, number, customs, and occupations of the inhabitants and on their general economic condition.
Gift of William Gibbes, 1937.

762
Bank of Pennsylvania.   Minute book, 1793–1842.   (1 v.)

Minutes of stockholders of the Bank of Pennsylvania; names of officers and directors.
Gift of John D. Rogers, 1878.

763
Philadelphia and Reading Railroad.   Record book, 1884–1890. (1 v.)

Philadelphia and Reading Railroad Company's record of mortgage bonds and convertible script, Samuel W. Bell, trustee.

764

Stone, Frederick Dawson, 1841–1897.   Bibliography of the 4th of July, 1876.   (1 v.)

Annotated proof copy of the bibliography of the Fourth of July materials in the Historical Society of Pennsylvania.

765

Biddle, Clement, 1810–1879.   Papers, 1769–1896.   (600 items.)

Entry cancelled; see collection #1792A.

766

Billon, Frederick Louis, 1801–1895.   Research notes, ca. 1876–1887. (200 items.)

Research notes of Frederick L. Billon concerning: the number of slaves in each state in 1790; election returns in 1796; census returns for Philadelphia, 1800–1810, list of Philadelphia residents by street from city directories, 1795–1816; biographical material on several 18th and 19th century Philadelphians; city maps, 1885, 1887, and newspapers.

Purchased, 1902.

767

Great Britain. Board of Trade.   Papers, 1675–1782. (28 linear ft.)

Records of the Councils on Trade and Plantations created by Charles II, beginning in 1675, and continued by the Board of Trade, commissioned by William III in 1696. Prior to 1696 the records were assembled by a committee of the Privy Council but were then transferred to the first permanent secretary of the Board of Trade, William Popple, who served until 1709. Popple was followed by his son, William Popple, Jr., 1709–1722, and by his grandson, Alured Popple, 1722–1737. Thomas Hill, 1737–1758, John Pownall, 1753–1776, and Richard Cumberland, 1776–1782, served as secretaries until the board was dissolved in 1782. Generally the secretary was assisted by a chief clerk, several minor clerks, or writers, and a solicitor. The board met at least twice weekly during most of the 18th century

William III charged the board with "promoting trade of the kingdom and inspecting and improving the plantations in America and elsewhere." To this end, the board reviewed colonial legislation and the reports and correspondence of colonial governors and others.

These materials as well as their actions and replies are included. Each royal colony had its own file. Proprietary colonies such as Pennsylvania and company-charter colonies such as Rhode Island were grouped together under the heading of Plantation General. Some of these materials are included in the Historical Society of Pennsylvania's transcriptions.

Purchased, English Record Copying Fund, 1902.

Transcriptions prepared by B.F. Stevens in London, 1895–1905.

768
Boot and Shoe Manufacturers of the United States.
Banquet papers, 1880.   (100 items.)

Invitation responses and letters about the banquet of the Shoe and Leather Trades of Philadelphia for the Boot and Shoe Manufacturers of the United States, held on November 17, 1880, Alexander P. Brown, banquet committee chairman. The collection includes an invitation, menu, and a list of toasts.

Gift of Alexander P. Brown, 1903.

769
Symmes, John Cleves, 1742–1814.   [Land Agreement], 1788.
(1 v.)

Agreement in which John Cleves Symmes transfers two million acres of land between the Great Miami, the Little Miami, and the Ohio Rivers in Ohio to Elias Boudinot; with maps of the tract.

Handwritten transcript of agreement, ca. 1886.

Gift of the Howard Edwards estate.

In Boudinot Papers.

770
Braddock Expedition.   Papers, 1754–1755.   (1 v.)

Papers concerning Edward Braddock's expedition and defeat by French and Indian forces near Fort Duquesne including: lists of British army officers present, killed and wounded; diary of proceedings of Commodore Augustus Kepple detachment of seamen with account of Braddock's defeat; anonymous report sent to King George IV; Governor Horatio Sharpe letters, 1754–1755; and maps and plans.

Handwritten copies, ca. 1852.

Gift of Joseph R. Ingersoll, 1853.

List of officers published in the *P.M.H.B.*, 32 (1908): 499–501.

771
Hildeburn, Charles Swift Riché, 1855–1901.   Correspondence, 1893–1895.   (70 items.)

Correspondence of Charles R. Hildeburn, much with Robert Ludlow Fowler, on the reprinting of William Bradford's Laws of New York (1694). Gift of Charles R. Hildeburn, 1896.

772
Bright, A.L.   Notes, 1900.   (6 v.)

A.L. Bright's biographical notes on French officers connected with the American Revolution.

773
Brill Car Company.   History of war material production, 1919. (2 v.)

Gift of the Brill Company.

774
Jones, Charles.   Papers, 1671–1689.   (50 items.)

A small collection of accounts current, bills of exchange, powers of attorney, and some correspondence reflecting the trade of Charles Jones, merchant of Bristol, England with settlers in the Delaware Valley. Prominent in the papers are William Frampton, Jones's, agent in Philadelphia, and Thomas Taylor, master of Jones's ship.
Purchased, 1910.

775
Hildeburn, Charles Swift Riché, 1855–1901.   Collection, 1760–1777. (70 items.)

A miscellaneous collection of documents, copies, and abstracts collected by or made for Hildeburn and organized to reflect some of the activities of the British Army in North America.

Included are an account of liquor given Indians, 1765–1766; subsistence records for officers in New York, 1771; returns of prisoners taken by the Americans, 1775–1777; paroles issued to British officers, 1775–1777; as well as copies and abstracts made for the collector from British Army records. Included, too, are some early references to the fur trade in western Pennsylvania, 1767–1768.

776
Relief and Employment of the Poor.   Contributor's daybook, 1767–1768.   (1 v.)

Daybook of the contributors to the Relief and Employment of the Poor, recording receipts and disbursements for outdoor relief.
Gift of Mrs. Albert Henry Savery, 1967.

777
Bucks County (Pa.)   Register, 1682.   (1 v.)

Register of persons residing in Bucks County including freemen, children, servants, time of servants' freedom and wages, with date and ship by which freemen and servants arrived in America.

778
Hills, John.   Survey, 1799.   (1 v.)

Survey of Edward Burd's property, Ormiston Villa, on the bank of the Schuylkill River, showing land use and cultivation.

779
Burnside, James.   Correspondence, 1778–1779.   (1 v.)

James Burnside was Quartermaster at Morristown, N.J., during the Revolutionary War.
Correspondence of James Burnside with army officers, government officials, and others on the events of the Revolutionary War.
Gift of William Chauvenet, 1930.

780
Bush Hill Estate.   Survey, 1814 and plan, 1824.   (1 v.)

Robert Brook survey, 1814 and Joseph H. Siddel plan, 1824
Gift of William Brooke Rawle, 1912.

781
Camden and Gloucester Counties (N.J.)   Poll books, 1856. (2 v.)

Voter lists for Camden and Gloucester counties, N.J. Also a personal "poll book" kept by George M. Robeson, showing party affiliations of voters in Gloucester, N.J.
Gift of William John Potts, 1887.

782

Cammerhoff, John Christopher Frederick, 1721–1751.   Letters, 1747–1748.   (1 v.)

Excerpts from letters of John Christopher Frederick Cammerhoff, addressed to Nikolaus Ludwig Zinzendorf on early Moravian settlements in Pennsylvania; includes a biographical sketch of Cammerhoff and wash drawings of Gnadenthal, Bethlehem, 1784, Donegal Township, Gemeinhaus in Lebanon township, and Gemeinhaus in Oley, Bucks County, all presumably by John W. Jordan.

Gift of John W. Jordan, 1886.

783

Coleccion de canciones patrioticas . . . , 1814.   (1 v.)

Collection of anti-Napoleonic songs, published in Cadiz, sent to Robert Waln, Jr. of Philadelphia by Thomas R. Tunis in 1815. Included in Waln's translation of the first song, "Spaniards, Run to Arms . . . "

Gift of Emlen Wood, 1932.

784

South Carolina and Georgia Loan subscription list, 1781.   (1 v.)

List of Philadelphia subscribers for a loan to the citizens of South Carolina and Georgia, George Meade, treasurer.

Gift of George Meade, 1894.

785

Wayne, Anthony, 1745–1796.   Surveys, 1771, 1774.   (1 v.)

Anthony Wayne's survey of West Chester County lands belonging to West Jersey Society and the Thompson estate; also William Cleever land, Upper Merion, Montgomery County, 1771.

786

Chief justices of the Supreme Court of Pennsylvania collection, 1712–1910.   (50 items.)

Autograph letters of the chief justices of the Supreme Court of Pennsylvania with portraits by Albert Rosenthal.

Purchased, Gratz Fund, 1939.

787

Lewis, Thomas D.   Journal, 1807–1808.   (1 v.)

Journal kept by Thomas D. Lewis on board the *China Packet* on voyage from Philadelphia to Madras and Calcutta and return.

Purchased by the Dreer Fund, 1938.

788

Church Records, 1737–1847.   (8 v.)

First Presbyterian Church (Philadelphia, Pa.) Building Committee. Minute book, 1828–1829 and Church blotter, 1834–1846. Minute book, kept by E. Flint, secretary of the building committee for the First Presbyterian Church in Southwark, Philadelphia. Church blotter contains lists of pew rents. Gift of William John Potts, 1888.

First Independent Church (Philadelphia, Pa.) Youth's Missionary Society. Minute book, 1834–1839. Includes minutes for Youth's Female Missionary Society, 1835, which merged eventually with Male Missionary Society in 1836 to form the Youth's Missionary Society. Gift of Daniel W. Pannepacker, 1905.

Episcopal Church. Diocese of Maryland, General Conventions. Rough minutes, ca. 1840. Includes information on the condition and support of clergy for the Episcopal Diocese of Maryland with account of income and expenses for the Diocese. Gift of William John Potts, 1885.

Presbyterian Church (Beaver Meadow, Pa.) Papers, 1838–1839. Treasurer's accounts for the Building Committee with an account of money collected for building the meeting house; history of the church; and miscellaneous correspondence. Gift of Mary J. McNair, 1914.

Presbyterian Church in the U.S.A. Synod of Philadelphia. Minutes, 1737. Gift of William John Potts, 1885.

United Presbyterian Church (New York, N.Y.)   Register of members and their families, 1845–1848. Gift of William John Potts, 1893.

789

Almshouse (Philadelphia, Pa.)   Records, (1767–1768) 1837. (3 v.)

The City Almshouse and infirmary, established in 1732, provided "shelter, support, and employment for the poor and indigent, a hospital for the sick, and an asylum for the idiotic, the insane, and the orphan." Successor institutions that have carried on its services have been Blockley Almshouse, Philadelphia General Hospital, Philadelphia Hospital for Mental Diseases (Byberry), Home for Indigent (Holmesburg).

The record books are: ledger, 1767–1768; statistics, 1837, for the women's part of the Almshouse, listing name, age, birthplace, slave or free, marital status, probable cause of poverty, temperance habits, and employment, with comparative summaries for males and females.

Gift of the Genealogical Society of Pennsylvania, 1903.

790
United States. Army Commissariat.   Account book, 1861–1865. (1 v.)

Records of supplies and provisions furnished by the Commissary Department during the Civil War. Purchased, Dreer Fund, 1938.

791
Clement, John, 1818–1894.   Collection, 1616–1884.   (9 linear ft.)

Deeds, indentures, surveys, and other papers collected by John Clement, judge and antiquarian of Haddonfield, N.J. The manuscripts pertain largely to Gloucester County, N.J., but include some documents for Pennsylvania lands.

The New Jersey material consists of: deeds, 1677–1852; indentures, 1681–1884; warrants and surveys, 1616–1865; copies of maps and drafts; notes, maps, and memoranda on Newton Township; Newton Township town meeting minutebook, 1724–1822, with records of indentures and stray livestock; Camden City abstracts of titles with maps; copy of Pennsylvania Proprietary surveys in New Jersey. Also included are Pennsylvania deeds and indentures, 1681–1853.

Gift of John Clement Estate, 1899.

Finding aid available.

792
Coates, Samuel, 1711–1748.   Ciphering book, 1724.   (1 v.)

Copybook of Samuel Coates, Philadelphia merchant; continued as account book, 1733–1749, then invoice book, 1758.

Gift of John H. Lewis, 1920.

793
Pennsylvania.   Tax returns and accounts, 1832–1856.   (2 v.)

Miscellaneous returns and accounts for taxes largely in Crawford and Erie counties.

Purchased, Dreer Fund, 1934.

794
University of Pennsylvania.   Accounts, 1762–1788.   (2 v.)

Account of cash collected in England for the College of Philadelphia (University of Pennsylvania) and the College of New York (Columbia University) by William Smith and James Jay. Ledger, 1763, 1780–1788, of the College of Philadelphia (University of Pennsylvania) largely for mortgage, rent, and other investments, with some repair and tutorial accounts.

Gift of George Steinman, 1895.

795
Collin, Lewis.   Stagecoach book, 1795.   (1 v.)

Record of stagecoach house opposite City Tavern, containing names of passengers and destinations.

Gift of the City of Philadelphia.

796
Irwin, Matthew.   Accounts, 1777–1779.   (1 v.)

Accounts kept by Matthew Irwin at Morristown, N.J., as Commissary during the Revolution.

797
Pennsylvania. Committee of Assembly.   Receipt book, 1777–1780. (1 v.)

Receipts of money paid out by the Pennsylvania state treasurer on orders of the Committee of Assembly.

798
Tilton, Edward G., d. 1861.   Logbook, 1822–1824.   (1 v.)

Edward G. Tilton was a midshipman in the United States Navy.

The logbook is a record of voyages on the *Congress,* commanded by Captain James Biddle, from Norfolk, Va., to the West Indies, 1822 and from Wilmington, Del., to South America and return, 1823–1824; also voyage of *Grampus* commanded by John D. Sloat, from Hampton Roads, Va. to the African coast, 1824.

Gift of Charles Shivers, Jr.

799
Congressional Record.   Subscription list, 1788–1789.   (1 v.)

Gift of Mrs. R.I.G. Walker, 1906.

800

Connecticut claims papers, 1664 (1769–1806) 1837.   **(350 items.)**

Letters and legal papers of Pennsylvania officials and Wyoming Valley inhabitants, many concerning the boundary and land claims dispute with Connecticut.

801

United States. Continental Army.   **Returns, 1777–1778.**   **(1 v.)**

List of soldiers and contributing data on casualties in the Revolutionary War.

Gift of Francis J. Alison and Robert H. Alison, 1899.

802

United States. Continental Loan Office.   **Receipt book, 1786–1790.** **(1 v.)**

Receipt book of Thomas Smith, Continental Loan officer in Pennsylvania.

Purchased, 1899.

803

Caleb Cope & Company.   **Papers, 1716–1835.**   **(10 items.)**

Deeds and titles to premises occupied by Caleb Cope & Company at 429 Market Street and 7 and 9 North Fifth Street.

Gift of Porter F. Cope, 1924.

804

Pennsylvania. Provincial Council.   **Minutes, 1706–1707.**   **(1 v.)**

Extracts from minutes of the Pennsylvania Provincial Council on the controversy between the Council and the Assembly over the bill to establish courts and to impeach James Logan.

Full minutes published in *Colonial Records,* 2 (Harrisburg, 1852–1853).

805

Courts records, 1676–1825.   **(67 v.)**

Bucks County (Pa.). Dockets, 1774. (1 v.)
Chester County (Pa.). Docket, 1759–1771. (1 v.)
Germantown (Philadelphia, Pa.). Records of general court, 1691–1707) (2 v.)
Newcastle (Del.). Dockets, 1676–1699, 1760–1764. (5 v.)

Kent County (Del.). Records, 1683–1695. Records of wills, administrations, and marriages of Kent and Sussex counties.

Lancaster County (Pa.). Docket, 1775. (1 v.)

Montgomery County (Pa.). Docket, n.d. Kept by Michael Croll, justice of the peace. (1 v.)

Pastorius, Francis Daniel, 1651–1719. "Rules and regulations for settlers," 1689–1697. Also includes a copy of the patent of land in Germantown (Philadelphia) granted to Pastorius. (2 v.)

Pennsylvania. Supreme Court. Dockets, 1753–1799. (2 v.)

Philadelphia (Pa.). Records, 1681–1825 The records include: court dockets, 1686–1686, 1706–1776; index to wills and administrations, 1681–1825; miscellaneous legal papers, including grand jury lists, commitments, indictments, summonses, 1697–1821; petitions to quarter sessions at court, 1718–1775; account book of county tax office, 1770; minute book of commissioners and assessors, 1771–1774; quarter session docket, 1780–1785; jury lists, 1806–1818; docket of debt department of prison, 1832–1834. (44 v.)

Sussex County (Del.). Orphans Court docket, 1728–1743. (1 v.)

Upland (Pa.). Records, 1681–1688. (1 v.)

York County (Pa.). Docket, 1775–1774. (1 v.)

806

Coxe, Daniel, 1640–1730. [Agreement], 1688. (1 item.)

Agreement, February 2, 1688, made by Daniel Coxe on the behalf of the proprietors of West Jersey and Robert Barclay on the behalf of the proprietors of East Jersey, on the boundary lines between the two provinces.

807

Crawford County (Pa.) Daybook, 1816–1819. (1 v.)

Daybook kept by R. Alden, Treasurer of Crawford County.
Purchased, Dreer Fund, 1933.

808

United States. Board of the Treasury. Report on the financial condition of the United States, 1781–1783. (1 v.)

The committee of the Board of the Treasury, formed to report on the financial condition of the United States, included James Bunne, William Sharpe, and Oliver Wolcott.

809

Decatur, Stephen, 1779–1820. Letterbook, (1801–1805) 1820. (1 v.)

Entry cancelled; see collection #165.

810
Deed Collection, 1300–1901.   **(27 linear ft.)**

Arranged chronologically. Includes deeds for land in Bristol, England; Delaware; New Jersey; and Pennsylvania.

811
Defense of Philadelphia.   **Subscription list, 1813.**   (1 v.)

List of subscribers who contributed to a fund for the defense of Philadelphia during the War of 1812.
Gift of William Duane, 1851.

812
Martin, John Hill, 1823–1906.   **Delaware and Chester counties historical essays, 1874.**   (1 v.)

Handwritten copies some by John Hill Martin.
Gift of Mrs. Edward S. Sayres, 1923.

813
Porter, Andrew, 1743–1813.   **Memoranda book, 1793–1813.**
(1 v.)

Construction accounts, including payroll, and memoranda recorded by Andrew Porter, engineer for construction of the Delaware and Schuylkill Canal, 1793–1794; continued by Porter as a personal record of family lands and taxes paid in Western Pennsylvania, 1801–1813. Included, too, are a copy of the will of William Smith, ca. 1800, and a diagram of Count Rumford's Improved Chimney Fireplace, n.d.
Gift of W.W. Porter, 1923.

814
Smith, Benjamin H.   **Atlas, 1915.**   (1 v.)

Atlas of Delaware County and the Great Welsh tract in Pennsylvania.
Gift of Benjamin H. Smith, 1915.

815
Estaing, Jean Baptiste Charles Henri Hector, 1729–1794.
Reports, 1778–1779.   (1 v.)

Official narrative of the actions of the French fleet in North American and West Indian waters during the Revolution under the command of Comte Charles Hector d'Estaing.
Purchased, 1904.

816

Anonymous.   Travel diary, 1836.   (1 v.)

Diary of unknown travelers from Windham, Conn., to Philadelphia, August 22 to September 11, 1836.

817

Anonymous.   Diary, 1812–1813.   (1 v.)

Diary describing the military campaign in upper New York against Canadian-English forces, 1812–1813.
Handwritten copy.
Purchased, Publication Fund, 1891.

818

Dillworth, William.   Logbooks, 1711–1717.   (2 v.)

Log kept by William Dillworth, mate on the ships: *Jersey Galley, Mary, Young Mary Galley,* traveling to various ports in the West Indies.
Purchased, Dreer Fund, 1936.

819

Dougherty, Daniel.   Diaries, 1863–1864.   (2 v.)

Daniel Dougherty served with Company H, 63rd Regiment, Pennsylvania Volunteers.
These diaries describe Civil War campaigns in northern Virginia and Gettysburg.

820

Buck, Hammitt, Apple, and Company.   Accounts, 1846–1848.
(1 v.)

Accounts for the Doylestown and Philadelphia coach, 1846–1848.
Gift of Albert Cook Myers, 1904.

821

Fackenthal, Benjamin Franklin, Jr., 1851–1941.   Briefs of
title, 1936.   (1 v.)

Briefs of titles to real estate in Durham and adjoining townships in Pennsylvania and the partition and allotment of the Durham Iron Company among the partners as of December 24, 1773 and its subsequent owners. Also briefs in Springfield township and Nockamixon townships in Bucks county and in Williams and Lower Saucon townships, Northampton county Pennsylvania together with other historical data.

Gift of B.F. Fackenthal, 1936.

Typescript.

822

Sheeder, Frederick.   Historical sketch, 1846.   (1 v.)

Historical sketch of East Vincent Township, Chester County.

Gift of Frederick Sheeder, 1846.

823

Elmer, Ebenezer, 1752–1843.   Commonplace book, 1779–1781.   (1 v.)

Notes kept by Ebenezer Elmer while serving as surgeon of the 2d New Jersey Infantry include: a parody on the British crown and government; a "cursory history" of the Revolution to 1778; poems, many on love and marriage; medical notes; and some memoranda on military action.

Purchased, Morris Fund, 1934.

Complete diary published in *Proceedings of the New Jersey Historical Society*, 2:43–50.

824

English Heraldry, 1567, 1605, 1702.   (3 v.)

Transferred to the Genealogical Society of Pennsylvania.

825

Nicola, Lewis.   English Lines near Philadelphia, 1777.   (1 item.)

Manuscript map of the British forces around Philadelphia during the Revolutionary War.

Gift of Ebenezer Hazard, 1938.

826

Enterprise Telegraph Company.   Minutes, 1865.   (1 v.)

Enterprise Telegraph Company was a juvenile, amateur telegraph company which operated in Philadelphia, 1865.

Gift of Alexander E. Outerbridge, 1920.

827

British depredations, 1777–1778.   (1 v.)

Records of appraisals by various assessors in Philadelphia and adjacent territory of the damage done by the British during the Revolutionary War.

828
Ewing, Henry.   Accounts, 1844.   (1 v.)

Accounts, 1844, of Henry Ewing kept for the Philadelphia Stock Exchange.

Gift of the Charles G. Leland estate, 1905.

829
Anonymous.   History of cession of Louisiana to the Spaniards, 1765–1770.   (1 v.)

An anonymous account of events, 1765–1770, in Louisiana precipitated by the cession of that province by France to Spain, and particularly the Creole uprising against the Spanish governor, Antonio de Ulloa, 1768.

830
Mills, Charles K. (Charles Karsner), 1845–1931.
Collection, 1900–1928.   (8 v.)

Historical sketches of the community of East Falls, or Falls of the Schuylkill, and vicinity, ca. 1650–1928: "Pictorial history of the Falls of the Schuylkill and Environment," by Charles K. Mills, 1912; "The Falls of the Schuylkill—Military History," by Mills, 1912–1914; "Historical Memoranda relating to the Falls of the Schuylkill and Vicinity," by Mills, 1922; "A History of the Falls of Schuylkill," by Bernard Emmett Dowdall, a compilation of articles from *The Forecast,* a weekly newspaper, 1900–1901; and newspaper clippings from the *East Falls Herald* and the *Roxborough News,* gathered by A.C. Chadwick, Jr., 1925–1928.

Gift of Charles K. Mills estate, 1931.

831
Fayette County (Pa.).   Collection, 1764–1920.   (1 v.)

Manuscripts on inhabitants of Fayette County: New York City artist (sculptor) Rudolph O'Donovan letters, 1860–1920, to his sister and other relatives at Spring Mill Furnace; Civil War letters, 1861–1864, of James, Isaac, and William Abraham, and their cousin James Sturgis; Gaddis family papers, 1751–1879, with letters and documents, many of which concern life and land in Kansas and other frontiers; Mount Moriah Church of Christ minutes, 1784–1797; Nancy J. Kendall diary, 1847–1849; and miscellaneous letters, 1764, 1838–1867, largely to U.S. Senator Daniel Sturgeon, including 3 James Buchanan letters.

Typescript copies, ca. 1920.

832
Federal Reserve Bank of Philadelphia (Pa.)   Papers, 1914–1936.

Transferred to the Library of the Historical Society of Pennsylvania.

833
Feltman, William.   Papers, 1779–1782.   (2 v.)

Copy, 1779, of the final three chapters of von Steuben's *Regulations for the order and discipline of the troops of the United States,* first published in 1782, and a diary, 1781–1782 kept while Feltman served as lieutenant, 1st Pennsylvania Regiment, from its departure from York, to its arrival near Charleston, S.C., including the siege of Yorktown, Va.

Diary published in *Pennsylvania in the Revolution, Battalion and Line,* v. 2, p. 709–762.

834
Fernberger, Samuel Weiller, 1887–1956.   Collection, 1796–1819. (750 items.)

Miscellaneous legal documents, mainly of Portland, Maine; applications for the release of debtors, 1796–1805; writs of attachment, 1798–1816; bail bonds, 1797–1804; liberty bonds (for liberty of jail), 1798–1805; writs of executions of judgments, 1799–1819; other legal materials, 1801–1813; commitments, 1802–1805. The collection also includes Amos Partridge personal correspondence, 1799–1817; daybook, 1809.

Gift of Samuel Weiller Fernberger, 1938.

835
Fête Champêtre.   Proceedings, 1850.   (1 v.)

Minutes of the Board of Managers of the Fête Champêtre, Winthrop Sargent, secretary. Gift of Mrs. J. Madison Taylor, 1940.

836
Field, Mrs.   Cookery recipes, ca. 1880.   (1 v.)

Gift of Mrs. Field, 1904.

837
Fire Companies, ca. 1890.   (1 v.)

Transcripts of articles on the history of fire companies, published in the *Germantown Independent.*

Gift of Mary W. Shoemaker, 1936.

838
Fire companies of Philadelphia record books, 1742–1871. (14 v.)

Minutes, constitutions, expense accounts, and other records pertaining to the history of fire companies.

839
Fire Insurance Company of Philadelphia County (Pa.)
Record books, 1832–1841. (2 v.)

Ledger, 1832–1839, and cashbook, 1833–1841, kept by Jacob F. Holckley, treasurer.

840
Byers, William Vincent. **Collection, 1913–1914.** (1 v.)

Data on the first American movement west, 1750–1850, including the Ohio Company of Virginia, the Indiana Company, the Illinois Company, the Mississippi Company, the Grand Ohio Company and the Vandalia Company, Thomas Cresap, William Franklin, Christopher Gist, Solomon Henry, William Trent, Alexander Lowry, Joseph Simon, William Henry Harrison, George Morgan, and Edward Ward.
Typewritten transcripts.

841
Greenwich (Cumberland County, N.J.). **Vital Statistics, 1817–1886.** (4 items.)

Birth and death records of the township of Greenwich, compiled by Enoch Fithian.
Gift of Emlen Wood, 1938.

842
Fitzgerald, Thomas. **Plays, 1868.** (3 v.)

Manuscript copies of two plays by Fitzgerald: "Who Shall Win" and "Light at Last."

843
Hazard, Samuel, 1784–1870. **Forts of Pennsylvania, 1754–1783.** (1 v.)

An extra-illustrated edition of Samuel Hazard's "Notes of the Forts" published in *Pennsylvania Archives,* 1st series, v. 12, as an appendix. Contains

letters, notes, and maps on the history of Pennsylvania forts. Several forts are included that are not mentioned in the published edition.
Gift of Spenzer Hazard, 1940.

844
Eastern Penitentiary. Minute book, 1846–1858. (1 v.)

Records of and notes on prisoners in Eastern Penitentiary by William Parker Foulke.
Gift of E.A. Andrews, 1938.

845
Franklin (ship). **Logbook, 1817–1819.** (1 v.)

The *Franklin* was commanded by Henry N. Ballard, 1817–1818, and by John Gallagher, 1818–1819.

846
Herbst, John. Prayer for Franklin College, 1787. (1 v.)

Prayer delivered by John Herbst, minister of the United Brethren Congregation, at Lancaster on the day of dedication of Franklin College, June 6, 1787.
Gift of John W. Jordan, 1890.

847
Free Military School (Philadelphia, Pa.) Register, 1863–1864. (1 v.)

Record of admissions to the free military school of the "Philadelphia Supervisory Committee for recruiting colored regiments."
Gift of Abraham Barker, 1896.

848
Cappelis, de, Major. Account, 1781. (1 v.)

Account of supplies purchased from Breck and Green for the French squadron. Breck and Green were Boston merchants and agents for the French squadron in Newport, R.I.

849
Buck, William J., b. 1825. Letters, 1870–1873. (50 items.)

Letters written by William J. Buck to John Jordan containing biographical sketches of Friends in Pennsylvania and adjacent territories.

850

Fugger family.   Genealogy, 1700.   (1 v.)

Transferred to the Genealogical Society of Pennsylvania.

851

Committee of Defense.   Minutes, 1814–1815.   (3 v.)

Entry cancelled.

852

German heraldry books, ca. 1700.   (3 v.)

Transferred the Genealogical Society of Pennsylvania.

853

Anonymous.   Recipes, ca. 1750.   (1 v.)

Magical formulas for obtaining supernatural power and warding off evil spirits.

854

Germantown and Cresheim lots, 1824.   (2 v.)

General plan of the lands and lots of Germantown and Cresheim townships.

Copies; copied from Mathias Zimmerman's 1746 original and Christian Lehman's 1766 drafts.

855

**Germantown and Perkiomen Turnpike Company.
Papers, 1764–1808.   (26 items.)**

Correspondence, documents, and records of surveys relating to the construction of the Germantown and Perkiomen Pike, the Egypt or Norristown Road, and the Chestnut Hill and Spring House Turnpike Road.

Gift of John F. Lewis, 1920.

856

Germantown Home Guard.   Minutes, 1861–1863.   (1 v.)

Gift of Mary Quincy Butler, 1904.

857
Gibson, James.   Journals, 1786–1787.   (2 v.)

James Gibson journal, 1786, discusses college life at Princeton; his journal (by Leander), 1786–1787, describes social life in Philadelphia.
Gift of Edward Shippen, 1892.

858
Gilbert, George.   Wood engravings, ca. 1818–1839.   (1 v.)

Entry cancelled.

859
**Philadelphia (Pa.). Common Council.   Testimonial to E.B.
Gleason on his retirement.   (1 v.)**

Illuminated testimonial of the Common Council of Philadelphia to E.B. Gleason on his retirement.
Gift of Dr. H.M. Goddard, 1936.

860
**Gloucester County, (N.J.).   Docket books, 1754 (1782–1783).
(2 v.)**

General docket book, 1754, for Gloucester County, N.J., and a docket book for John Little, justice of the peace in Gloucester, N.J., 1782–1783.
Gift of Louis B. Runk, 1897 and W.K. Taylor, 1917.

861
Goshen (Chester County, Pa.)   Town book, 1718–1870.   (1 v.)

Chester County audits of overseers accounts; also a list of servants, 1736–1751, 1772, and officer list, 1844–1870.
Photostats.
Purchased, Wendell P. Brown Memorial Fund, 1935.

862
Pennsylvania Governors correspondence, 1778–1904.   (200 items.)

Correspondence to and from governors of Pennsylvania, 1778–1904 including: James Beaver, William Bigler, Andrew Gregg Curtin, John W. Geary, John F. Hartranft, Joseph Heister, Henry Martin Hoyt, William F. Johnston, Thomas Mifflin, William F. Packer, Robert E. Pattison, Samuel W. Pennypacker, James Pollock, David R. Porter, Joseph Ritner, John A. Schulze, Francis R. Shunk, Simon Snyder, William A. Stone, and George Wolf. Included are a small group of "crank" letters addressed to Beaver,

1888–1890, as well as several signed documents, addresses to the legislature, portraits, clippings, and obituaries.

863
Graham, Archibald Hunter, d. 1943.   Papers, 1927–1928.
(150 items.)

Archibald Hunter Graham was a Philadelphia physician and amateur sportsman.

The papers include a part of Graham's *History of Cricket in Philadelphia*, intended as a publication of the Historical Society of Pennsylvania, as well as copies of correspondence dealing with its compilation, editing, and the difficulties in securing money for publication.

864
Grafly, Daniel W.   Memior, 1897.   (1 v.)

Daniel W. Grafly served as an engineering officer in the Navy from 1862 to 1873 and later was a paint manufacturer in Philadelphia.

These memoirs, A years experience on the *Keystone State*, deal with his blockade duty off Charleston, S.C. in 1862.

Gift of Frederick Schober, 1898.

865
Great Central Fair of the United States Sanitary Commission (1864 : Philadelphia, Pa.) Newspaper committee.   Minutes, 1864.   (1 v.)

The Great Central Fair of the United States Sanitary Commission was held in Logan Square, from June 7 to June 28, 1864. During the fair Charles G. Leland edited a daily paper called *Our Daily Fair*.

Gift of Charles G. Leland, 1905.

866
Greene, Nathanael, 1742–1786.   Letters, 1780–1782.   (52 items.)

Nathanael Greene's letters to Henry Lee discuss the Continental Army and military operations during the Revolution.

Typescript copies.

Gift of Stan V. Henkels, 1909.

867
Greenewalt, Mary Elizabeth Hallock, 1871–1950.
Papers, 1897–1936.   (18 linear ft.)

Correspondence about Mary Hallock Greenewalt's invention of the color organ, which enabled changing colored lights to accompany the various moods of a piece of music; notes on, and plans and blueprints of, the color organ and related inventions; correspondence and notes on obtaining patents; patent certificates; copy of testimony of *Greenewalt v. Musical Arts Association,* 1935, in which she won the right to patent the color organ; notes on music and light; pamphlets on the theatre, light control, and other related subjects; personal correspondence largely about her family and career as a piano soloist; Hallock family biographical notes and photographs; and several rolls of film and gramophone records.

Gift of M.H. Greenewalt, 1936.

868
Conway, William Wright.   Collection, 1894–1895.   (2 v.)

Typescripts of articles appearing in Philadelphia and New York City newspapers, 1745–1749, prepared for William Wright Conway on the activities of a privateer captain, Richard Jeffries, particularly the engagement between the U.S. *Greyhound* commanded by Jeffries, and the French privateer *La Fleury.* Included, to, is *A Draught of and Engagement . . . between the Brig Greyhound . . . and La Fleury . . .* engraved by Henry Dawkins after a painting by J. Haviland, 1747, as well as acknowledgements from several historical societies for receipt of Gutekunst photograph of the Dawkins engraving.

Gift of Mrs. William Wright Conway, 1938.

869
Hamilton, James, 1710–1783.   Docket book, 1745.   (1 v.)

870
Hamilton family.   Letterbook, 1781–1790.   (1 v.)

The letters are chiefly in the handwriting of Jasper Yeates and relate to the estates of James Hamilton and William Hamilton in Lancaster.

871
Harper, B. Frank.   Abstracts of title, 1680–1872.   (1 v.)

Abstracts of title to three tracts of land in Northern Liberties, belonging to Robert Harper.
Typescript copy.
Gift of Miss E.E. Wright, 1921.

872
Society of Union Army.   Records, 1863–1865.   (3 v.)

General and special orders, 1863; provost marshall's records, kept by James W. Brady and others, detailing military service and physical descriptions of captured Confederate prisoners and actions taken against Union deserters; "Ration Book of Soldiers Rest," Harper's Ferry, 1864–1865.

Purchased, General Fund, 1935.

873
Hering, Constantine, 1800–1880.   Collection, 1840–1860.
(100 items.)

Collection of portraits and biographical notes on prominent men in Europe and America.

Gift of the family of Constantine Hering, 1918.

874
Hesselius, Andreas, 1677–1733.   Diary, 1711–1724.   (1 v.)

The diary of Andreas Hesselius, a Swedish Lutheran minister, reports on his journey to America, his ministry at Christiana, Del., and travels in other colonies.

Original located at the Royal Library at Stockholm.

English translations, 1889.

Gift of Charles J. Stillé, 1889.

875
Hessian, Waldeck, and British prisoners records, 1776–1779.   (1 v.)

List of prisoners of war received at Lancaster.

876
United States. Selective Service System. Philadelphia (Pa.)
History of Local Board No. 7, 1917–1919.   (1 v.)

The history of a local draft board, covering the ninth and tenth ward of Philadelphia with a list of registrants.

Gift of Edwin C. Atkinson, 1919.

877A
Wurts, Maurice, 1783–1855.   Land records.   (1 v.)

Copies of title papers and other records on the purchase of a half-interest in tracts of land in western Pennsylvania, once known as Holland Land Company lands, by the Wurts brothers, Philadelphia merchants, subsequently assigned to John B. Wallace, also of Philadelphia.

Purchased, Dreer Fund, 1934.

877B
Huidekoper, Alfred.   Lectures, 1872, 1876.   (1 v.)

Alfred Huidekoper's lectures on the Holland Land Company, 1876, and the Pennsylvania Population Company, 1872.
Typescripts.
Gift of Frederick W. Huidekoper, 1903.

878
Howell, Anna Hazen, d. 1936.   Collection, 1838 (1860–1910) 1930. (ca. 500 items.)

Estate papers of Elizabeth Hacker, Isaiah Hacker, Lloyd Mifflin Hacker, Mary B. Hacker, Rebecca H. Howell, and William H. Howell, 1891–1907; diaries of Isaiah Hacker, 1838–1866; diaries of Anna H. Howell of trips to Europe and western United States; diary of Edward I.H. Howell of trip to England, n.d.; cashbooks, 1898–1930, of Anna H. Howell; Edward I.H. Howell business correspondence and papers, 1879–1907; Hacker and Howell family papers, scrapbooks, photograph album, memorabilia, 1865–1909; Anna H. Howell minutes of the Botany Club of Germantown, 1884–1889; *John Howell and His Descendants* by Frank Willing Leach, 1912, *Instances of Slavery* by Rowland Green, 1859.
Gift of the Anna Hazen Howell estate, 1956.

879
Humphreys, A.A. (Andrew Atkinson), 1810–1883.
Biographical notes, 1865–1884.   (1 v.)

Collection of miscellaneous sketches and biographical notes on the life of General Andrew A. Humphreys who served during the Civil War.
Gift of H.H. Humphreys, 1917.

880
Illinois and Wabash Land Company.   Minutes, 1778–1812. (1 v.)

Lists of names of original purchasers and proprietors of lands in the Illinois country, minutes of company transactions, resolutions, and other data about lands purchased from Indians.
Purchased, Gratz Fund, 1938.

881

Immigrant lists, 1772–1775.   **(7 v.)**

Photostatic copies.
Originals in Pennsylvania State Library. Box 1026; Harrisburg, Pa.
17120.
Gift of John Frederick Lewis, 1933.

882

Jackson, David, 1747–1801.   Recipes, 1783–1800.   (1 v.)

David Jackson was a Philadelphia physician, apothecary, and member
of the Continental Congress.
Purchased, 1899.

883

Jackson, Joseph, 1867–1946.   Papers, ca. 1798–1916.   (50 items.)

Entry cancelled; see collection #314.

884

Jacobs family.   Account books, 1751–1818.   (5 v.)

Entry cancelled; see collection #316.

885

James, Thomas Potts, 1803–1882.   Letterbooks, 1851–1863.
(5 v.)

Thomas P. James was a Philadelphia druggist.
Gift of the Baker Library, 1937.

886

Japanese and Chinese War drawings, 1904–1905.   (1 v.)

Entry cancelled; transferred to Graphics Department.

887

Jenning, John, ca. 1738–1802.   Papers, 1757 (1766–1767).   (2 v.)

An account of John Jenning's trip from Fort Pitt to Fort Chartres and
New Orleans, 1766; account book of the sale of provisions and general
merchandize at Fort Chartres in the Illinois country.

888

Jones, John, 1796–1843/4.   Papers, 1814–1864.   (ca. 60 items.)

Personal and official papers of Colonel John Jones, brigadier inspector of the Pennsylvania militia; included are letters from George Bryan, auditor general, and a tax collector's book of Shamokin Township, Northumberland County, 1825.

Gift of Mrs. Charlotte E. Jones, 1939.

889

Jones, Lewis.   Papers, 1787–1876.   (ca. 140 items.)

Family and business papers of Lewis Jones of Gwynedd. Included are records of Clow and Company, 1787–1798; Franklin Foulke estate papers, 1839–1847; Charles Livezy letters, 1855–1876; Sarah Tyson estate papers, 1850–1859.

Gift of Harold E. Gillingham.

890

Jones, Paul.   Cartoons, 1778–1788, ca. 1830–1837.   (1 v.)

Cartoons of Jones Company, 1830–1837, and accounts of Paul Jones's naval exploits from the *Gazetteer and New Daily Advertisers* and the *London Chronicle*, 1778–1788.

Gift of Charles Morton Smith, 1930.

891

Coates, Joseph Saunders.   Letters, 1805–1806.   (1 v.)

Letters, mainly written to his father Samuel Coates, describing hardships while at sea including the loss of the brig *Kaderbox* off Java.

Handwritten copy made by Joseph Hartshorne (cousin of Joseph S. Coates).

Gift of Dr. Edward Hartshorne, 1880.

892

Allaire, Alexander.   Indenture, 1765.   (1 item.)

Printed indenture, July 26, 1765, for a public burying ground, granted by Alexander Allaire, and others to Emanuel Eyre and others in Kensington, Northern Liberties, Philadelphia.

Photostatic copy.

893
Kreitzer, John.   Journal, 1846–1848.   (1 v.)

John Kreitzer's account of the Mexican War as a private in Company
C of the Pennsylvania Volunteers.
Gift of W.R. Hutchinson, 1920.

894
**Marquis de Lafayette Reception Committee.   Papers, 1824.
(300 items.)**

Papers of the committee of arrangements for a Philadelphia reception
for Marquis de Lafayette; invitation lists; letters of Richard Peters, Joseph
Lewis, Rembrandt Peale, and Peter S. Du Ponceau.

895
*Laws of Pennsylvania, 1693-1700 : Under the administration of
Governors Fletcher and Markham.*   (1 v.)

Photostatic copy.
Original in American Philosophical Society. 105 South Fifth Street; Philadelphia, Pa. 19106. Original copy gift of J. Francis Fisher, 1835 to the American Philosophical Society.

896
Pemberton, Phineas, 1650–1702.   Laws, 1682.   (1 v.)

Phineas Pemberton's record of laws made at Chester, 1682.
Photostatic copy.

897
**Lehigh Valley Railroad.   Record books, 1858–1896.
(9 linear ft.)**

Purchased, Dreer Fund, 1939.

898
Levick, James J.   Collection, (1674–1782) 1888.   (40 items.)

An artificial collection of manuscripts of early Welsh Quakers in both
Wales and Pennsylvania, chiefly about the Jones, Lewis, Roberts, Thomas,
and Wynne families: deeds, surveys, letters, certificates of removal, as well
as several items on Quaker education.
Some letters in Welsh.
Gift of James Levick.

899
Anonymous.   Lewes (Del.) Collection, (1812–1813) (1926–1936).
(2 v.)

Notes, correspondence, newspaper clippings, and photographs, 1926-1936, on the history of Lewes, Del.; Sarah Marriner daybook of an inn at Lewes, 1812–1813.
Gift of Richard Paynter Lochner, 1938.

900
Lexington (ship).   **Accounts, 1828–1830.   (1 v.)**

Purchased, Dreer Fund, 1936.

901
Library Company of Philadelphia.   Papers, 1746–1747.   (2 v.)

Minutes of directors' meetings, 1746; agreement between the Library Company of Philadelphia and Robert Greenway, librarian, 1747.
Gift of Mrs. Rodman Wharton, 1914.

902
Pennsylvania. General Loan Office.   Register of indentures,
(1724–1730) 1785.   (2 v.)

Record of mortgages on property in various Pennsylvania counties held by the General Loan Office.
Gift of Charles Henry Hart, 1886.

903
Local Committee in Aid of the Belgians (Haverford, Pa.)
Papers, 1914–1921.   (100 items.)

The Local Committee in Aid of the Belgians was organized in October 1914, by Mary V. Lewis Sayers.
Minutes, correspondence, and clippings of the Local Committee in Aid of the Belgians.
Gift of Mrs. Edward S. Sayers, 1931.

904
Lochner, George W., 1841–1920.   Collection, 1812 (1860–1864) 1886.
(50 items.)

Family and personal correspondence collected by George W. Lochner, an immigrant from Bavaria who served as a corporal in the 72d Pennsylvania

Volunteers and had been imprisoned at Andersonville, 1864. Included are Lochner's naturalization papers, his Civil War letters to his mother, as well as correspondence from Frank M. Smythe and Harry Bell.

George W. Lochner's Civil War letters to his mother in german.

Gift of Richard P. Lochner, 1938.

905

Lodge records, 1731–1903.   (36 v.)

Armenia Rebekah Lodge. Cashbook, 1890–1901.

"Book of the Proceedings of the Mason's Lodge held at the Tun Tavern in Water Street, Philadelphia," 1749–1755.

Colfax Degree of Lodge No. 1. Index of order book, 1854–1888 and minutes, 1865–1878.

Grand Lodge. Receipt book, 1833–1865.

Harmony Encampment No. 65. Minutes, 1847–1877. (2 v.)

Herman Lodge No. 7. Semi-annual reports, 1870–1896.

Jefferson Lodge No. 48. Membership applications, 1873–1884.

Mount Olive Encampment No. 6. Minutes, 1839–1869.

Mount Olive Lodge No. 357. Minutes, 1849–1869 and treasurer's book, 1849–1854.

Minnehaha Lodge, I.O.S.M. Minute book, 1873–1878.

Northern Liberties No. 17. Minutes, 1859–1863.

Order of U.S. of A. Camp No. 2 (Camden, N.J.) Records, 1848–1854.

O.U.A.M. Nassau Council No. 103 (Princeton, N.J.) Minute book, 1873–1878.

St. John's Lodge. Account book, 1731–1737.

United Brothers Encampment No. 26. Membership applications, 1846–1881 and cashbook, 1877–1883.

Walhalla Lodge No. 7. Minutes, 1841–1849, 1883–1892.

906

Longstreth, Joshua.   Letterbooks, 1806–1833.   (2 v.)

Joshua Longstreth was a Philadelphia merchant.

Gift of Griffin C. Callahan, 1920.

907

Willits, Samuel C.   Papers, 1868–1885.   (2 v.)

Manuscript of Samuel C. Willits' history of Lower Dublin Academy and Holmesburg Library and biographical sketches of the trustees of these

institutions, 1882–1885; Holmesburg Mill Invoice Book, 1868–1870; map of Thomas Holme's grant from William Penn, drawn in 1884.
Gift of Mrs. I. Pearson Willits, 1934.

908
Loxley, Benjamin, 1720–1801.   Journal, 1776.   (1 v.)

Journal of Captain Benjamin Loxley of the first company of artillery of Philadelphia, containing account of the Amboy campaign, and muster roll for his company.

909
Lutz, William Filler.   Collection, 1762–1933.   (ca. 100 items.)

Miscellaneous papers of the Lutz family and the related Filler, Holliday, and Lowry families of Bedford County, chiefly consisting of personal and business correspondence; business papers, largely on real estate in Bedford County and the Lutz Woolen Mills, one of the first of its kind in the area, established about 1805 and operated by John and Michael Lutz; Jane M. Washington diary, 1833–1836, 1848; a corrected copy of a "list of deserters for Bedford County," 1864.
Gift of William Filler Lutz, 1939.

910
Land Association of Luzerne, Lycoming, Northampton, Northumberland and Wayne Counties.   Records, 1801–1806. (1 v.)

Names of members, memorials, rules, and regulations.

911
MacPherson, John, Jr., 1754–1775.   Notes on Law, 1771.   (1 v.)

Legal definitions, rules, and notes on the practice of law.
Gift of T.E. Marshall.

912
Mantua Academy (Philadelphia, Pa.)   Rollbook, 1868–1877. (1 v.)

Gift of Mrs. J.T. Allen, 1923.

913
Erskine, Robert.   Map of the Highlands (New York, N.Y.), 1779. (1 v.)

Entry cancelled; transferred to Graphics department.

914

Maps and plans of the Revolution, 1771–1851.   (ca. 35 items.)

Entry cancelled; transferred to Graphics department.

915

Martin, John Hill, 1823–1906.   Legal opinions, 1856.   (1 v.)

Opinions of legal authorities on marine insurance, 1856.
Gift of John Hill Martin, 1890.

916

**Market Street Bridge (Philadelphia, Pa.)   Photographs, 1886–1888.
(1 v.)**

Entry cancelled; transferred to Graphics department.

917

**Pemberton, Phineas, 1650–1702.   Marks and brands of cattle, 1684.
(1 v.)**

Sketches and descriptions by Phineas Pemberton of brands of cattle in
Pennsylvania.
Gift of the Court of Common Pleas, Bucks County, 1873.

918

Philadelphia (Pa.).   Marriage registers, 1835–1865.   (3 v.)

Registers of marriages performed by Lewis Swift, Bucks County justice,
1835–1839; by John Dennis, Philadelphia alderman, 1846–1852; and at the
mayor's office, Philadelphia, 1858–1865.

919

**Marshall House (Alexandria, Va.)   Register of guests, 1861.
(1 v.)**

Gift of John A. McAllister, 1880.

920

Martin, William, 1765–1796.   Medical notes, 1785–1786.   (6 v.)

William Martin's notes on lectures by Benjamin Rush, Joseph Black,
and Adam Kuhn while studying at the University of Pennsylvania.
Gift of J. Hill Martin, 1876.

921

United States. Army.   **List, 1863–1864.**   **(1 v.)**

List of passes issued at Martinsburg [West] Virginia, 1863–1864.
Purchased, General Fund.

922

McCall, Archibald, 1767–1843.   **Orders for marine insurance, 1809–1817.**   **(1 v.)**

Photostatic copies.
Gift of Harrold E. Gillingham, 1933.

923

McCrossin, Lawrence E.   **Scrapbook, 1901–1914.**   **(1 v.)**

Papers, letters, mementos, and newspaper clippings of Lawrence E.
McCrossin, relating to his activities as a Democratic party leader.
Gift of Lawrence E. McCrossin, 1918.

924

McReynolds, Benjamin F.   **Correspondence, 1862–1863.**   **(1 v.)**

Correspondence of Benjamin F. McReynolds, an army commissary,
relating to provisions.
Purchased, Dreer Fund, 1938.

925

McShea, Walter Ross.   **Genealogical records, ca. 1918–1929.**
(ca. 150 items.)

Genealogical notes on the families of Samuel Davis, Rozier Levering,
and Peter Wentz.

926

United States. Bureau of the Mint.   **Register of medals, 1841–1849.**
(1 v.)

Register was compiled by Franklin Peale, chief coiner of the United
States Mint.
Gift of Mrs. William H. Patterson, 1938.

927

Medical book collection, 1779–1896.   **(500 items.)**

Records of hospitals and dispensaries in Philadelphia; papers on the
history of Blockley General Hospital; Dr. James Stratton's record books,
1779–1816.

928
Philadelphia Gazette and Universal Daily Advertiser.   Subscription
list, 1797.   (1 v.)

This paper is a continuation of *Federal Gazette and Philadelphia Daily Advertiser.* The *Philadelphia Gazette and Universal Daily Advertiser* was published by Andrew Brown. As a result of a fire in his office, Andrew Brown died in 1797. The paper was succeeded by Andrew Brown, Jr., who formed a partnership with Samuel Relf under the name of Brown & Relf. In 1800 the title changed to *Philadelphia Gazette and Daily Advertiser.*

Each subscriber advanced five dollars to enable the conductor to buy and keep in repair a printing office for the use of the paper. In exchange, the subscribers were entitled to a reduced annual subscription rate of four dollars. In addition their advertisements were carried at half price.

Gift of John F. Lewis, 1920.

929
Merchants Coffee House (Philadelphia, Pa.)   Minutes, 1818–1853.
(1 v.)

Minutes of the subscribers to the Green Room at the Merchants Coffee House.

Gift of Henry C. Potter.

930
Merchants Exchange (Philadelphia, Pa.)   Minutes, 1841–1868.
(1 v.)

Minutes of meetings of a group of Philadelphia merchants at the Merchants Exchange giving information on local and national financial matters.

Gift of Henry C. Potter, 1900.

931
Merrill, Daniel S.   Notes, 1864–1868.   (250 items.)

Real estate notes giving location, size of lot, description, price, and page number as listed in *Folwell's Monthly Real Estate Register.*

Gift of Mrs. Daniel S. Merrill, 1916.

932
The Meschianza, 1778.   (1 v.)

The Meschianza was a large regatta and party given upon the acceptance of the resignation of William Howe by his officers. The grand entertainment opened with a regatta down the Delaware River and a mock tournament in which seven knights of the "Blended Rose" contended with seven knights of the "Burning Mountain" for 14 damsels in Turkish garb. This followed with dancing and full banquet, ending in a huge displays of fireworks.

Catalog of events that took place at the Meschianza.

933
Naylor, Charles, 1806–1872.   List of prisoners of the American army during the Mexican War, 1848.   (1 v.)

Charles Naylor served with the 22nd Pennsylvania Regiment.
Gift of William B. Mann, 1895.

934
Mifflin, Benjamin.   Journal, 1764.   (1 v.)

Benjamin Mifflin's journal from Philadelphia to Cedar Swamps and back.
Gift of Joseph A. Clay.

935
**Mifflin, Northumberland, and Bedford Counties (Pa.).
Conveyances, 1795.   (1 v.)**

Land transactions of members of the Gratz family, James Wilson, and others.

936
**Milestown School (Philadelphia, Pa.)   Records, 1818–1874.
(1 v.)**

Minutes, bylaws, names of officers, and subscribers for the Milestown School.

937
United States. Army.   Report, 1861.   (1 v.)

Report of the military reconnaissance of the Susquehanna River and of the country comprised within the river part of the Chesapeake shore and Delaware canal and a line drawn from Harrisburg to Philadelphia, 1861. Report made to General A.J. Pleasonton, Philadelphia. Brigadier General Pleasonton was in charge of organizing the defense of Philadelphia, 1861–1865.

938
Ministerial intrigues, 1716–1717.   (1 v.)

Private letters of Robert Walpole, Horace Walpole, Charles Townshend, James Stanhope, and Paul Methven. Transcript by Patrick Young, ca. 1717. Gift of Harrold E. Gillingham, 1937.

939
Mitchell, James T. (James Tyndale), 1834–1915.
Collection, 1659–1911.   (15 linear ft.)

Autograph letters and documents of distinguished jurist and other prominent persons, ca. 1659–1873; lists of grand jury indictments, 1701; Philadelphia court docket book, 1737; papers on land controversies in Maryland and New Jersey, 1753; contemporary copy of Penn's case relating to buying up of grants made to first settlers, 1769; letters reflecting events of the Revolutionary War and early national political questions, tariff, transportation, construction of turnpikes, bridges, etc, 1770–1860; Abraham van Vechten, correspondence from New York, 1780–1841; papers of Jacob Thornton's trial for conspiring to pass counterfeit banknotes, 1821; portraits of members of the bar.

James T. Mitchell's personal papers, records of his activities as a member of the bar and as chief justice of the Supreme Court of Pennsylvania; papers of D.B. Canfield, publisher of the *Law Register,* 1852–1888; James T. Mitchell portrait collection, 1888–1907; John Hill Martin's notes on members of the bar, 1882–1889; papers of *Commonwealth v. Alburger* about title of Franklin Square, 1836; Manayunk tax record, 1840; Erastus Corning correspondence, 1842–1864; and Peter A. Browne papers, ca. 1857.

Gift of the James T. Mitchell estate.

940
Montgomery, James A.   Collection, 1702–1903.   (ca. 500 items.)

Papers chiefly on prominent Maryland families: Colonel Thomas White, merchant, quitrent book, 1702, letterbook, 1751–1775; Thomas and Esther White estate papers, 1749–1803; Thomas R. White, Stafford Forge records, 1752; Bishop William White, correspondence and genealogical notes, 1769–1794; genealogies of families of Daniel Dulany, Daniel Charles Heath, Philip and Richard Key, 1710–1836; Edward Hall, merchant in West Indies, correspondence, 1796; Thomas H. Montgomery, correspondence, 1879–1903; indenture of sale of Baltimore Iron Works by Daniel Dulany and Robert Carter, 1770; view of Annapolis, 1787; letters to James Wilson, 1769–1794; and notes on Wilson genealogy.

Gift of James A. Montgomery, 1939.

941
Moore, Joseph Hampton, 1864–1950.   **Peace Jubilee Papers, 1898.**
(6 linear ft.)

The Peace Jubilee was originally intended as a local affair to celebrate the suspension of hostilities between Spain and the United States; it took on national significance. The festivities included military, naval, and civic parades.

Letters and photographs of the committee of arrangements for the Peace Jubilee celebration.

Gift of J. Hampton Moore, 1940.

942
Moore, Samuel.   **Receipt book and commonplace book,**
1765–1788.   **(1 v.)**

Samuel Moore was a landowner in Philadelphia and Chester County.
Gift of Alfred Prime, 1920.

943
Moore, William, 1699–1783.   **Papers, 1764–1777.**   **(2 v.)**

Papers and court docket of William Moore of Chester County.
Gift of John F. Lewis, 1937.

944
Martin, John Hill, 1823–1906.   *Moravian history at Bethlehem,* **1866.**
(1 v.)

This history was compiled by J. Hill Martin from notes of Rufus A. Grinder, 1866.
Gift of Mrs. Edward S. Sayers, 1923.

945
Shreve, Richard Cox, 1808–1896.   *History of Mount Holly,* **1882.**
(1 v.)

History of Mount Holly, N.J.
Gift of Isaac R. Pennypacker, 1910.

946
Rickey, Randal Hutchinson, 1799–1855.   **Moyamensing surveys,**
1833.   **(1 v.)**

Plans and drafts of Moyamensing.
Gift of Herbert DuPuy, 1910.

947
Martin, John Hill, 1823–1906. *Music at Bethlehem,* 1870. (1 v.)

This historical sketch of the music at Bethlehem for the period of 1742–1870 was compiled by J. Hill Martin from notes of Rufus A. Grider, 1870. Gift of John Hill Martin.

948
Collection of music books, 1800–1865. (6 v.)

949
Music manuscripts, ca. 1800. (2 v.)

Manuscripts of sacred music.
Purchased, Dreer Fund, 1935.

950
Muster rolls, 1776–1865. (26 v.)

Lancaster County, 1776; Captain David Greer's Company at York, 1776; Bucks County, 1776–1802; Philadelphia County, 1777–1789; Billingsport, 1778; Captain John Davis' company, North Pennsylvania regiment at West Point, N.Y., 1778–1780; French army in America, 1778–1783; 1st and 2nd battalions of Philadelphia Militia, 1778–1789; Captain Cox, 1781; 7th Company, 5th battalion, Philadelphia Militia, commanded by Lt. Col. John Shee, 1782; rolls of the six battalions of the city of Philadelphia, 1784; 1st battalion of Lancaster County, Captain John Wudhy, 1786; Pennsylvania troops commanded by Lt. Col. Josiah Harmar, headquarters at Vincennes, 1787; 69th regiment dragoons, Berks County, 1807; 7th Company, 84th regiment, Philadelphia militia, Capt. Francis Asbury Dickins commanding, 1824; 1st brigade District of Columbia Militia, 1828; Berks County, 1861–1865; and Company C 118th Regiment of Infantry, Pennsylvania Volunteers, 1862–1865.

Gift of Brinton Coxe, F.M. Etting, George Getz, Col. J.P. Nicholson, William S. Reed, Simon Stevens, and Isaac R. Walker.

951
Myers, A.   Diary, 1851.   (1 v.)

Diary of A. Meyers describes a trip to the Siskowit mine and other copper mines near Lake Superior.
Gift of Leonard G. Myers, 1919.

952
The Early history of the Human Freedom League . . . (1 v.)

This history contains *special reference to National Ensigns upon a white field : Being a collection of papers and publications relating to the H. F. League flags; their origin, early history, and presentation at peace conferences, patriotic assemblies, in public localities, upon national holidays* . . .
Originally owned by Henry Pettit; gift of Arabella Carter, 1931.

953
Rodney, George Brydges, Baron, 1719–1792.   Instruction to the captains of the British Navy, 1780–1781.   (1 v.)

Naval signals.

954
Hunter, William M.   Navigation treatise, 1808.   (1 v.)

General discourse on navigation by William M. Hunter, Hamilton Academy.
Purchased, Dreer Fund, 1936.

955
Patterson, Samuel D.   Navy agency records, 1845–1849.   (2 v.)

Samuel D. Patterson was the naval agent in Philadelphia.
Letterbook, 1845–1847, and ledger, 1845–1849.
Gift of Ethan Allan Weaver, 1929.

956
New Jersey Society for Promoting the Abolition of Slavery.   *Laws of New Jersey respecting Negroes and Mulatto slaves from 1682 to 1788, 1795.*   (1 v.)

These laws were compiled by Joseph Bloomfield for the New Jersey Society for Promoting the Abolition of Slavery, 1795.

957
New Hampshire Constitutional Convention.   Proceedings, 1791.   (1 v.)

These proceedings were attested to by John Calfe who served as secretary for the New Hampshire Constitutional Convention.

958
New York subscription book, 1790. (1 v.)

Autographs of subscribers to a literary publication, [possibly *The Miscellaneous Works of David Humphreys* (New York, 1790).]

959
Philadelphia. Committee of Observation. **Cargo manifests, 1774.**
(4 v.)

Manifests of imported merchandize conveyed to the Committee of observation of Philadelphia, Northern Liberties, and Southwark.

960
Non-Importation Resolution, 1765. (1 v.)

Declaration of non-importation made by the citizens of Philadelphia.
Gift of William Bradford, 1854.

961
Norris, George W. (George Washington), 1808–1875. **Collection,**
1695–1835. **(50 items.)**

Chiefly miscellaneous papers of Isaac Norris.
Gift of George W. Norris.

962
North, Frederick, Earl of Guilford, 1766–1827. **Arabic and**
Turkish tables of conjugation, 1825. (1 v.)

963
Land company records, 1792–1816. (1 v.)

Contains accounts, names of purchasers and shareholders, plans of association, and agreements for the North American Land Company, Pennsylvania Population Company, Asylum Company, and Pennsylvania Land Company.
Purchased, Dreer Fund, 1935.

964
Northern District of Kingsessing Meadows. **Ordinances,**
1761–1809. (1 v.)

Records of the local government including managers' minutes, laws, resolutions and regulations.

965

Northern Liberties. Board of Commissioners.   Ordinances, 1838–1854.   (1 v.)

Gift of A.S.W. Rosenbach, 1939.

966

Northumberland. Committee of Safety.   Minutes, 1776–1777. (1 v.)

Gift of J. Simon Stevens, 1846.

967

Norwich and Callowhill Markets (Philadelphia, Pa.)   Records, 1784–1845.   (1 v.)

Minutes of managers' meetings and miscellaneous records of Philadelphia markets.

968

Battle of Lexington report, 1775.   (1 v.)

Report of the battle, April 19, 1775, sent per Express from town to town, certified by the committees of correspondence at each stop.

969

***Directions for raising nurseries, planting orchards,* 1772.   (1 v.)**

Gift of Charles R. Hildeburn, 1892.

970

Obituary notices, 1909–1924.   (100 items.)

Collection of newspaper clippings, genealogical notes, and correspondence on prominent Philadelphians.
Gift of Charles Chauncey.

971

Duffield, Charles H.   "The Old Swedes Mill."   (1 v.)

Historical sketch of Old Swedes Mill, later known as Duffield's Mill, including its water rights and surrounding industries.
Gift of Charles H. Duffield, 1910.

972
Bertolet, Peter G.   **"Fragments of the past."**   (1 v.)

Historical sketches of Olney and vicinity.
Gift of Alfred S. Bertolet, 1884.

973
Order-books, 1775–1861.   (42 v.)

Collection of orderly books for: General William Smallwood, Small-wood's Brigade, 1778–1779; Colonel Daniel Morgan, 11th Virginia Regiment, 1777; Col. Christian Febiger, 2nd Virginia Regiment (kept by Francis Cowherd), 1778; Col. Christian Febiger, 1st Virginia Battalion of 1781; Col. William Thompson, Pennsylvania Rifle Battalion, 1775; Col. John Cadwalader, 3rd Battalion of Philadelphia Association (kept by Capt. Sharp Delancy), 1776; Lt. Col. Thomas Bull, 4th Battalion Chester County Associators (kept by William Armstrong), 1776; Col. John Bull and Col. Walter Stuart, Pennsylvania State Regiment, 1777; Col. Anthony Wayne, 4th Pennsylvania Battalion, 1776; Brig. Gen. Anthony Wayne (kept by Benjamin Fishbourne), 1778–1782, 1792–1794; Col. Henry Bicker, 2nd Pennsylvania Regiment, 1778; an unidentified Regiment at Whitemarsh, 1777; Col. Nicholas Haussegger, Lt. Col. George Stricker, and Col. Baron de Arent, Continental German Battalion, (kept by Capt. Charles Baltzel); 1776–1778, 1780; an unidentified Regiment at Valley Forge, 1778; Col. Moses Hazen, 2nd Canadian Regiment, 1778–1779; Col. Henry Bicker and Col. Walter Stuart, 2nd Pennsylvania Regiment, 1778–1779; Maj. Nicholas Dietrich Baron de Ottendorf (kept by Capt. Anthony Selin), 1777; Col. Daniel Brodhead, 8th Pennsylvania Regiment, 1778–1780; and Lt. Col. Calvin Smith, 6th Massachusetts Regiment, 1782.

Col. James Chambers, 1st Pennsylvania Regiment, 1778–1780; Gen. Alexander McDougal, 1780; an unidentified unit [Militia], 1780; an unidentified [North Carolina] Regiment, 1777; Col. Elias Dayton, 3rd New Jersey Regiment, 1780; John Ross, Brig. Gen. and Inspector of New Jersey Brigade, 1780; Elisha Williams, Adjutant to George Washington, 1776; 1st Regiment of Artillery, 1794–1809; Thomas Cadwalader and S. Anderson of Camp Dupont, 1814; 2nd Elite Corps, Virginia Militia, 1814; and Gen. Robert Patterson, 1861.

974
Great Britain. Army.   **Order-books, 1758 (1778–1780).**   (5 v.)

Sergeant Alexander Ross, at Camp Great Falls, Lake George, Fort Edward, and other points in New York, 1758; orderly books kept during occupation of Philadelphia, 1778; Captain R. Clayton, 17th regiment, headquarters at New York, 1777–1779; Lord Stirling's guards headquarters at Totoway, 1780.

**975
German Order-books, 1779–1780.   (2 v.)**

Lieutenant Colonel Hubley, commanding German regiment at Wyoming, 1779; Captain Charles Baltzel, commanding company of German infantry, headquarters at West Point, N. Y., 1780.
Gift of John Jordan and Jacob Weidman.

**976
Pannebecker, Henry.   Surveys of roads and townships.   (1 v.)**

Survey of roads and townships in Philadelphia, now Montgomery County, 1722–1742.
Photostatic copy, 1885.
Gift of S.W. Pennypacker, 1885.

**977
Penllyn (Wales).   Probate records, 1571–1700.   (1 v.)**

Copies made by Thomas Alan Glenn, 1914, for genealogical data on Welsh settlers in Pennsylvania.
Purchased, Library Fund, 1915.

**978
Delaware Indians.   Deed, 1682.   (1 leaf)**

Deed, July 15, 1682, to William Penn for land between the Delaware River and Neshaminy Creek.
Gift of Thomas Kimber, Jr., 1867.

**979
Penn Guarantee Association.   Minute book, 1878–1886.   (1 v.)**

The Penn Guarantee Association was formed for the purchase, sale, and improvement of real estate and the purchase, sale, and exchange of securities related to real estate.
Purchased, General Fund, 1939.

980

Penn family.   List, n.d.   (1 v.)

List of Penn relics at Penn's castle, Isle of Portland, near Weymouth Dorsetshire England belonging to J. Merrick Head, Esq.
Gift of William Brooke Rawle, 1911.

981

Penn Township (Philadelphia, Pa.)   Supervisors accounts, 1820–1870.   (1 v.)

Accounts kept for the collection of taxes and payments for highway improvements and other township needs.
Purchased, Dreer Fund, 1936.

982

Carter, Lucius.   Penn tracts of land in Northampton County, 1764–1776.   (1 v.)

List and draughts of Penn lands located in Northampton County as surveyed by James Scull.
Gift of Mrs. P.H. Ashbridge and Miss Benners, 1911.

983

Bank of the United States, (1791–1811).   Pennsylvania pension papers, 1790–1792.   (150 items.)

Chiefly powers of attorney of pensioners authorizing other persons to draw their pensions awarded for service during the Revolution.

984

Pennsylvania Assembly.   Minutes, 1724–1725.   (1 v.)

Minutes of representatives from Philadelphia, Bucks, and Chester counties. Gift of Jonathan Ingham, 1880.

985

Pennsylvania Assembly.   Records, 1682–1783.   (300 items.)

Miscellaneous papers reflecting activities of the assembly under the proprietary government: drafts of minutes and acts of assembly, 1701, 1706–1707, 1711–1712, 1715, 1717, 1720; attorney general's report on legislation, 1700, 1701; several items on Benjamin Franklin's anti-British activities.

986
Petitions against the slave trade, 1780.   (16 items.)

Petitions to the Pennsylvania Assembly from citizens of Philadelphia against the slave trade.

987
Porter, Andrew, 1743–1813.   Papers, 1785–1787.   (4 v.)

Journals and memoranda of Andrew Porter on his surveys of the Pennsylvania boundary line.
Gift of W.W. Porter, 1923.

988
Campbell, John H.   Pennsylvania Constitutional Convention minutes, 1872–1873.   (1 v.)

John H. Campbell's minutes of the committee on suffrage, elections, and representation of the Pennsylvania Constitutional Convention.
Gift of William J. Campbell, 1900.

989
Malin, William J.   *Sketch of the history of the Medical Library of the Pennsylvania Hospital,* n.d.   (1 v.)

History of the Medical Library of the Pennsylvania Hospital with a brief notice of the medical museum formerly belonging to that institution.
Gift of Mrs. G. Malin, 1902.

990
Pennsylvania. Militia.   Enlistments, 1781–1808.   (2 v.)

Records of enlistments in the Pennsylvania line, 1781, certified by Plunket Fleeson; artillery regiment muster rolls, 1781–1808.
Gift of William F. Corbitz.

991
Pennsylvania. Militia. Infantry Regiment, 98th.   Returns, 1827–1825.   (1 v.)

Return of absentees of the 4th Company, 2d Battalion, 98th Regiment, Pennsylvania Militia, commanded by John Early.
Gift of S.W. Brecht.

992
Richards, Joseph T., 1845–1915.   Memoranda relating to the Pennsylvania Railroad.   (2 v.)

Joseph T. Richards served as Assistant, Chief, and Consulting Engineer, 1893–1915 for the Pennsylvania Railroad.
Gift of the estate of Cephas G. Childs.

993
Pennsylvania Railroad.   Papers, 1889.   (1 v.)

General manager's report to the president and board of directors of the Pennsylvania Railroad, 1889, photographs and miscellaneous papers of the Johnstown flood.
Gift of Joseph T. Richards, 1921.

994
Pennsylvania Salt Works.   Waste book, 1776–1779.   (1 v.)

995
Pennsylvania. Treasury.   Accounts, 1795–1797.   (1 v.)

These accounts list income from land sales and taxes and payments for salaries, pensions, improvements, militia, and general expenses.

996
Pennsylvania. Valuation Commission.   Minutes, 1799.   (1 v.)

The Valuation Commission was established in 1799 in order to determine valuation for lands and dwellings and the enumeration of slaves.

997
Smith, Benjamin H.   Patent book, n.d.   (1 v.)

Patent book for lands in Delaware County.
Gift of the Frederick H. Shelton estate, 1925.

998
Anonymous.   Death records, 1812–1928.   (1 v.)

Record of deaths and interments of soldiers of the War of 1812 and the Pennsylvania Volunteers in the Civil War, 1861–1928.
Purchased, Dreer Fund, 1936.

999
Pennypacker, Samuel W. (Samuel Whitaker), 1843–1916.
Pennypacker's Mill in story and song, 1902.   (1 v.)

Historical sketches of the early settlement and development of the Perkiomen Creek region including the settlement, the French and Indian War, and the encampment of Washington's army, Sept. 26th, to October 8th 1777, before and after the Battle of Germantown.
Gift of S.W. Pennypacker, 1913.

1000
Perkins, Samuel C.   Naval general court martial docket, 1864.
(1 v.)

Samuel C. Perkins was a judge advocate.
Gift of S.C. Perkins estate, 1904.

1001
Permanent Bridge (Philadelphia, Pa.)   Account book, 1800–1809.
(1 v.)

Account of dividends received and signed for by stockholders in the company for erecting a permanent bridge over the Schuylkill River.
Gift of H. Griffiths, 1882.

1002
Philadelphia (Pa.).   Petitions, 1780–1831.   (200 items.)

Petitions to the Council of Philadelphia on the opening of new roads, paving and repairing of streets; included is an account of the estate of Benjamin Franklin.
Gift of Robert Bethell and George S. Bethell, 1871.

1003
Philadelphia and Lancaster Turnpike Road.   Papers, 1806.
(2 v.)

Surveys, sketches, notes, and photographs by Robert Brooke for the Philadelphia and Lancaster Turnpike Road.
Gift of William Brooke Rawle.

1004
Pennsylvania.   Philadelphia emergency campaign, 1868.   (1 v.)

The Philadelphia emergency campaign was the result of a plea from Governor Andrew G. Curtin to the banks and private corporations of Philadelphia to front $700,000 in payments to the Pennsylvania militia until such time that the state and national legislature could appropriate the needed funds.

These papers give an account of the money raised and the disbursement of funds to the militia.

Gift of Harry Rogers, 1914.

1005
Philadelphia to Bethlehem journal, 1773. (1 v.)

Description of a tour from Philadelphia through Bethlehem, Easton, Allentown, and Reading.

1006
Catalogue of books of the City of Philadelphia (Pa.) (1 v.)

List of books, letters, and miscellaneous communications housed in the various municipal departments of Philadelphia.

Gift of George S. Bethell, 1870.

1007
Philadelphia (Pa.). Catalogue of citizens, 1859. (1 v.)

List of citizens living within the city giving addresses only with no further information.

Gift of John B. Wood, 1910.

1008
Philadelphia (Pa.) Poor relief catalogue, 1766. (1 v.)

Catalogue of contributors, to the relief and employ of the poor of the City of Philadelphia, District of Southwark, Township of Moyamensing, Passyunk, and the Northern Liberties, 1766.

Gift of the Gilpin estate.

1009
Centre Square Water Works (Philadelphia, Pa.) List of subscribers, 1801–1806. (1 v.)

Gift of the Jenkintown Trust Company, 1936.

1010
Pennsylvania. Commission on Lots in Philadelphia.   Report, 1700.
(1 v.)

Report of commissioners containing the names of owners of properties, location, and acreage in Philadelphia.
Gift of John T. Morris, 1904.

1011
Philadelphia Committee of Public Safety (Pa.)   Minutes, 1861.
(1 v.)

The Philadelphia Committee of Public Safety was formed in order to protect the city during the Civil War. The committee called for ten regiments containing ten companies; each company composed of 80 men. The minutes give information on money raised, supplies purchased, and precautionary measures taken to protect the city.

1012
Philadelphia (Pa.) Common Council. Committee of Inspection and Observation.   Minutes, 1774.   (1 v.)

1013
Philadelphia County Board (Pa.)   Record book, 1835–1845.
(1 v.)

The County Board was composed of members of the Senate and House of Representatives of the state legislature for the city and county of Philadelphia and was responsible for miscellaneous public improvements through taxation.
Minutes and reports.
Gift of Samuel C. Perkins, 1940.

1014
Philadelphia County (Pa.)   Papers, 1671–1855.   (600 items.)

Miscellaneous papers, documents, correspondence, and surveys of land.

1015
Philadelphia Assembly.   Records, 1749–1916.   (100 items.)

The Philadelphia Assembly, sometimes know as the Philadelphia Dancing Assembly, was a social event in Philadelphia held among the most ancient and honored in Philadelphia. Being a subscriber to the dances was regarded as a mark of social distinction.

Treasurer's book, 1828–1831; subscriber and board lists; invitation cards; and miscellaneous items.

Gift of John William Wallace, 1883 and George L. Harrison, 1936.

1016
Pryor, Norton.   Memorandum book, 1791–1851.   (2 v.)

Entered by Norton Pryor, 1791–1815; Richard Loxely, 1815–1851; also Norton Pryor's weather records, 1786–1790.

Gift of Lewis C. Massey, 1886.

1017
The Philadelphia directory and annual register.   Subscription list, 1821.   (1 v.)

Autographs of subscribers to the proposal for publishing *The Philadelphia Directory and Annual Register.*

Purchased, Library Fund, 1904.

1018
Philadelphia dissected : or the metropolis of America.   Subscription list, 1800.   (1 v.)

Philadelphia Dissected, or the Metropolis of America was to consist of 25 to 30 prints principal buildings and views of Philadelphia.

Also included is a list of subscribers to William Birch's Views of Philadelphia, second edition.

1019
Philadelphia Insurance Company.   Records, 1814–1845.   (1 v.)

Philadelphia Insurance Company handled both marine and fire insurance.

Minutes, accounts, names of officers, and records of general transactions.

Gift of Mrs. Howard W. Page, 1934.

1020
Penn, Thomas, 1702–1755.   Memorandum, 1734. (1 v.)

List of names of the inhabitants in the county of Philadelphia with notations of land held by each compiled by Jonathan Hyatt by order of Thomas Penn.

Gift of Richard McCrain, 1846.

1021
Canby, Thomas.   Daybook, 1770–1788.   (1 v.)

Thomas Canby was a Philadelphia flour merchant.

1022
Philadelphia (Pa.)   Ordinances, 1722.   (1 v.)

Ordinances made and passed in Philadelphia by the mayor, recorder, alderman, and common council, October 15, 1722.
Gift of J.A. McAllister, 1882.

1023
Ffoulkes, Charles.   *Philadelphia pageant : sketches of military uniforms from contemporary sources,* 1912.   (1 v.)

Entry cancelled; transferred to the Graphics department.

1024
Philadelphia (Pa.).   Memorials, 1827.   (1 v.)

Memorials addressed to the Philadelphia select and common councils relating to the cutting of High (now Market) and Broad Streets through Penn's or Centre Square.

1025
**Philadelphia Sugar Refining Company (Pa.)   Records, 1816.
(1 v.)**

Articles of association, list of stockholders, constitution, bylaws, and other data on the Philadelphia Sugar Refining Company.
Gift of A.C. Kline, 1863.

1026
James, Abel.   Correspondence, 1773–1778.   (1 v.)

Correspondence of Abel James and Henry Drinker on severance of trade with Great Britain as a result of the tea party.
Typewritten copies made by Francis R. Taylor for an article, 1910.
Gift of Francis R. Taylor, 1921.

1027
Philadelphia tea shipment papers, 1769–1773.   (1 v.)

Papers relating to popular agitation in the colonies against the importation of tea and other commodities from England.
Gift of Mrs. F.M. Ives, 1923.

1028
Marine insurance records, 1804–1805.   (1 v.)

Philadelphia marine insurance records listing vessels insured, names of clients and captains.
Gift of Samuel Marshall, 1905.

1029
Warrington, Immanuel H.   Diaries, 1899–1902.   (2 v.)

Immanuel H. Warrington was a soldier in the United States infantry during the Philippine War.

1030
Philmore, J.   Account, ca. 1765.   (1 v.)

Entry cancelled.

1031
Pittsburgh (Pa.)   Minutes, 1794–1803.   (1 v.)

Minute book of the burgesses of Pittsburgh, containing rules and ordinances.
Purchased, Library Fund, 1912.

1032
Plans, ca.1685–1777.   (1 v.)

Entry cancelled; transferred to the Graphics department.

1033
Pomroy, Benjamin.   Journal, 1758–1763.   (1 v.)

Benjamin Pomroy was chaplain in one of the British regiments in upper New York state and Canada.

1034
Lightfoot, Benjamin, 1726–1777.   Survey notes, 1759.   (1 v.)

Benjamin Lightfoot was deputy surveyor of Berks County. These surveys notes covered the areas of Pottsville to Shamokin.
Gift of Jessie Lightfoot, 1850.

1035
Powell, Joseph.   **Account of philanthropy, 1755–1756.**   **(1 v.)**

Account of the benefactions received and his distribution thereof amongst the poor distressed back inhabitants who took their refuge to the United Brethren in their several settlements at Bethlehem, Nazareth, Friedensthal, Christian's Brun, and Gnadenthal and the Rose. This account was included in a letter of Joseph Spangenberg, 1757.

1036
Bradford, Thomas, 1745–1838.   **Records, 1778–1782.**   **(2 v.)**

Letters of Thomas Bradford, commissioner of prisoners, on the exchange and parole of prisoners of war; and records of provisions drawn for prisoners.

1037
Prophecy and dream, ca. 1757.   **(1 v.)**

Mystical religious sentiments.
Purchased, 1903.

1038
Pennsylvania.   **Act for regulating and establishing fees, 1711.**
(1 v.)

This act was passed in order to prevent extortion and undue exaction of fees of several officers and practitioners of law. Contains a list of permissible fees for specific legal tasks.
Gift of Harold E. Gilligham, 1936.

1039
Pennsylvania. Provincial Conference.   **Minutes, 1776.**   **(1 v.)**

Provincial conference of committees of the Province of Pennsylvania, 1776.

1040
Pennsylvania. Provincial Council.   **Papers, 1684 (1714–1823).**
(150 items.)

Miscellaneous letters and documents from early proprietary government officials largely on the sale of lands, and political and economic affairs.
Gift of the Numismatic and Antiquarian Society.

1041
Pennsylvania. Provincial Council.   Letters, 1754–1829.
(ca. 600 items.)

Letters of men who served as provincial delegates: Benjamin Franklin, written in London, 1762–1776; John Dickinson, 1754–1774; Anthony Wayne, 1776–1796; Thomas Fitzsimons, 1776–1783; James Irvine, 1760; John Cadwalader; Thomas McKean; Jacob Morgan; Robert Morris; Jacob Rush; Charles Thompson; Thomas Wharton; David Rittenhouse; Owen Biddle; P. Muhlenberg; Thomas Willing; Samuel Hunter; and others.

1042
Morhouse, Abraham.   Estate records, 1808–1832.   (1 v.)

Record of sale of the land from the estates of Abraham Morhouse and Andrew Y. Morhouse in Quachita, La.
Gift of Manuel E. Griffith, 1904.

1043
Pennsylvania.   Qualification book, 1720–1759.   (1 v.)

Oaths of allegiance to the British crown by persons taking office in departments of the government of the Province of Pennsylvania.

1044
Philadelphia (Pa.)   Qualification books, 1747–1765.   (2 v.)

Oaths of allegiance to the British crown by persons taking office in the city of Philadelphia.

1045
Anonymous.   Diary, 1863–1866.   (1 v.)

Diary of a British soldier, Queens redoubt, giving an accounts of the British military campaign in the Maori War in New Zealand.

1046
Radbill, Samuel X., 1894–1956.   Collection, 1855–1856, 1899–1900.
(300 items.)

Letters received by Lindsay and Blackiston, Philadelphia bookdealers and publishers, relating to the sale of books; cancelled checks of Jud I. McGuigan, 1899–1900.

1047
Read, George C., 1733–1798.   Naval Orders, 1836–1847.   (7 v.)

Journals and correspondence of Captain George C. Read, U.S. Navy, commander of the U.S. frigate *Columbia;* there are also colored drawings of flags and signals.
Gift of Joseph Henry Dubbs, 1876.

1048
Custom House (London, England). Redemptioners registry, 1774–1775.   (1 v.)

Gift of Cheesman A. Herrick, 1936.

1049
Redemptioners registry, 1785–1831.   (2 v.)

Register of German redemptioners indentured as servants in Philadelphia.

1050
Broom, Jacob.   Region of the Brandywine, 1777.   (1 item.)

Entry cancelled; transferred to the Graphics department.

1051
Port of Philadelphia (Pa.)   Registry, 1682–1686.   (1 v.)

Partial list of names of arrivals in Philadelphia.
Gift of J. Francis Fisher, 1852.

1052
Pennsylvania. Revenue board of commissioners.   Records, 1845.   (1 v.)

Accounts kept by Eli Kirk Price, commissioner of revenue, appointed to investigate the state of taxable property in various parts of Pennsylvania, and especially Philadelphia.
Purchased, Dreer Fund, 1934.

1053
McNachtane, John.   Logbook, 1769–1781.   (1 v.)

Logbook kept by Commander John McNachtane, on his various vessels *Sally, Neptune,* and the brigantines *Robert* and *Hannah* during his service in the Revolution.
Purchased, 1939.

1054
United States. Continental Army. Quartermaster.
List, 1776–1783.   (1 v.)

Names of artificers, prisoners, enlisted men, and officers killed in battle.

1055
Ridley Meadow Company.   **Cashbook, 1787–1793.**   (1 v.)

Treasurer's accounts, names of officers, record of taxes paid by the Ridley Meadow Company.

1056
Rittenhouse Bicentenary Celebration.   **Papers, 1932.**   (1 v.)

Photographs, newspaper clippings, articles, and astronomical calculations on the birth of David Rittenhouse.

1057
Ritter, Abraham, 1792–1860.   **"A Hundred years ago," n.d.**
(2 v.)

Traditional historical and reminiscent sketch of the villas of Bethlehem and Nazareth with portraits, sketches of characters. Copy by William H. Jordon from the original manuscripts.
Gift of John Jordan, Jr.

1058
Roach, Isaac, 1786–1848.   **Diary, 1812–1847.**   (1 v.)

Account of Isaac Roach's participation in the War of 1812 and the military campaign against Canada; also included is a brief genealogical introduction.
Gift of Walter T. Roach, 1934.

1059
Robbins, John F.   **Memoranda, 1862.**   (2 v.)

Notes and memorandum kept by John F. Robbins, March 12-April 25 and April 25-May 3, 1862.
Gift of Camille Reilly, 1934.

1060

Anonymous.   Diary, 1836.   (1 v.)

Diary kept by a young physician in Saint Louis, Mo., describing social conditions, illnesses, and mob violence against free Afro-Americans known to have committed crimes.

Gift of George P. Philes, 1889.

1061

Sandy Bank Cemetery (Media, Pa.)   List of persons buried, 1801–1855.   (1 v.)

Sandy Bank Cemetery consisted of approximately one acre of ground owned by the Society of Friends and had been used for burial since ca. 1750. Isaac Smedley, who owned and operated the farm at Sandy Bank, was responsible for burials in the cemetery. Escaped slaves and free blacks, as well as Friends were interred there.

Typescript by Edgar T. Miller, 1901.
Gift of Edgar T. Miller, 1905.

1062

Great Central Fair for the United States Sanitary Commission. Records, 1864.   (2 v.)

Minutes, memoranda, and correspondence of the Wholesale Dry Goods Department, Children's Department, and Ladies Central Committee for the Great Central Fair of the United States Sanitary Commission which was held in Philadelphia, 1864.

1063

Sargent, Winthrop, 1825–1870.   Commonplace book, 1845–1846. (1 v.)

Commonplace book of Winthrop Sargent containing extracts from various sources on the history of Pennsylvania and the Penn family.

1064

Scattergood, Mary R.   Genealogical records, 1872–1885. ([300 p.])

Genealogical records for the families of Arthur William Starr, William Cooper, and James S. Lippincott, of Pennsylvania.

1065

Schaffer, Charles.   Meteorological observations, 1854–1930.
(4 v.)

Gift of Mrs. Charles Schaffer.

1066

Schoolbook collection, 1667–1872.   (40 v.)

Miscellaneous school notebooks and texts, mainly mathematics, book-keeping, surveying, French lessons.

1067

***John* (ship).   Logbook, 1799.   ([12] p. and 2 loose leaves)**

Log of voyage from Philadelphia to Surinam.
Gift of Thomas A. Biddle Company, 1927.

1068

Schuylkill Arsenal (Philadelphia, Pa.)   Photographs, ca. 1890.
(1 v.)

Entry cancelled; transferred to the Graphics department.

1069

Schuylkill Bank (Philadelphia, Pa.)   Minutes, 1840–1843.   (1 v.)

Minutes relate chiefly to the liquidation of the financial affairs of Hosea J. Levis with the Schuylkill Bank by Eli Kirk Price, John R. Vogdes, and Charles Thomas Jones, assignees.
Gift of Dr. A.F. Twogood.

1070

Pennypacker, Isaac A., 1812–1856.   *The History of Schuylkill*
***Township*, n.d.   (1 v.)**

History of Schuylkill Township containing an account of the Indians, settlements, fisheries, and hunting of agriculture, horticulture, manufacturers, and mechanics of geology, mineralogy, and botany of wars, churches, school houses, and public improvements.
Gift of Isaac A. Pennypacker, 1845.

1071

Pennsylvania scrapbook, 1802–1890.   (1 v.)

Newspaper clippings on politics, commerce, shipping, and Indians in Pennsylvania.

1072
Sackville, George Germain, Viscount, 1716–1785.   **Secret orders, 1776.**   **(1 v.)**

Lord Germain's secret orders issued to Admiral Richard Howe and General William Howe.
>Handwritten copy by B.F. Stevens for Sydney G. Fisher, 1908.
>Originals in the British Records Office.
>Gift of Sydney G. Fisher, 1909.

1073
Seeley family.   **Genealogical records, 1934–1939.**   **(1 v.)**

1074
Hamilton, James, 1710–1783.   **Servants and apprentices records, 1745–1773.**   **(2 v.)**

Records of James Hamilton, mayor of Philadelphia, containing certification of indentures of servants and apprentices, 1745–1746; list of servants belonging to inhabitants of Pennsylvania, taken into British service without compensation to their masters, 1757; record of servants and apprentices bound and assigned before John Gibson, mayor of Philadelphia, December 5, 1772, to May 21, 1773.
>Purchased, Library Fund, 1909.

1075
Shearman, S.H., Mrs.   **Collection, 1678–1785.**   **(75 items.)**

>Quakeriana.
>Gift of Mrs. S.H. Shearman, 1915.

1076
Shelton, Frederick H.   **Papers, 1915–1922.**   **(5 v.)**

Correspondence and photographs on Frederick H. Shelton's *Milestones of the Philadelphia District in Pennsylvania.*
>Gift of the estate of Frederick H. Shelton, 1925.

1077
Shoemaker, Franklin.   **Diary, 1862–1867.**   **(2 v.)**

>Civil War diary of Franklin Shoemaker.
>Gift of Mary Shoemaker, 1938.

1078
Dussault, Chevalier.   Journal, 1780.   (1 v.)

Journal giving an account of the siege of Charleston.
In French.

1079
Siege of Quebec Journal, 1775.   (1 v.)

Copy, 1856.
George Chalmers purchased original in England.
Gift of Charles Hare Hutchinson, 1856.

1080
Skippack township (Montgomery County, Pa.)   Records of death,
1793–1844.   (1 v.)

1081
Mends, Robert, Sir, 1767–1823.   Report, 1822.   (1 v.)

Report of Sir Robert Mends of H.M.S. *Iphigenia,* at Sierra Leone, to
the British admiralty on slave trade on the western coast of Africa; also
genealogical list of the Mends family.
Gift of Captain Aubrey G.W. Mends, 1930.

1082
Smith, Charles Morton, d. 1914.   Collection, 1681–1848.
(400 items.)

Letters and legal documents of Charles Morton Smith on land in the
early frontier counties of Pennsylvania, 1720–1848. The correspondence includes letters of Hugh Roberts, prominent early Philadelphia Quaker,
George Roberts, and other members of the Roberts family.
Gift of Charles Morton Smith estate, 1927.

1083
Smith, Samuel, 1720–1776.   "The History of the Province of
Pennsylvania," 1760.   (1 v.)

1084
***George* (ship).   Logbook, 1805–1806.   (1 v.)**

The ship, *George,* was a trafficker of slaves and was confiscated by the
British at Kingston.

Diary and log of *George* on a voyage from Philadelphia to Cork, Iceland and to St. Thomas.

1085
Society for Improvement of Roads and Inland Navigation (Philadelphia, Pa.)   Journal, 1791–1793.   (1 v.)

The Society for Improvement of Roads and Inland Navigation was organized in Philadelphia with the intention of improving trade by building and extending roads westward and northward.

1086
Society for the Propagation of the Gospel in Foreign Parts. Letters, 1732–1779.   (1 v.)

Letters of missionaries and ministers of the Church of England relating to the activities of the society in Pennsylvania, especially the Radnor and Lancaster meetings.
      Copies.

1087
Jenkins, Francis.   Somerset County, Maryland land warrant book, 1670–1682.   (1 v.)

Francis Jenkins was deputy surveyor for Somerset County, Md.
      Gift of Hampton L. Carson, 1902.

1088
South Carolina photographs, ca. 1880.   (1 v.)

Entry cancelled; transferred to the Graphics department.

1089
Seymour, William.   Journal, 1780.   (1 v.)

Journal of William Seymour, sergeant major in the Delaware regiment, Maryland division, under the command of DeKalb on the march from Morristown, N.J. to Charleston, S.C.
      Gift of George Foote, 1855.

1090
Southern Whale Fishery.   Records, 1775–1790.   (1 v.)

Account of the whaling vessels from the port of London.

1091
Southwark (Philadelphia, Pa.)   Map, 1789.   (1 item.)

Entry cancelled; transferred to the Graphics department.

1092
Philadelphia (Pa.). Watering Committee of Spring Garden.
Register of water permits, 1844.   (1 v.)

1093
State Guards of 1814.   List of names, 1829.   (1 v.)

List of names of surviving Philadelphia members of the volunteer company of state guards who served in the campaign of 1814 at Camp Brandywine and Camp Dupont.
Gift of Miss Benners and Mrs. Ashbridge, 1911.

1094
Hawkins, John H.   Memoranda, 1780.   (1 v.)

Entries of state stores drawn for the non-commissioned officers and privates, Pennsylvanians in Col. Hazen's Regiment, 1780.

1095
Stauffer, David McNeely, 1845–1913.   Collection, ca. 1644–1884.
(20 linear ft.)

David McNeely Stauffer was an eminent civil engineer, author, and antiquarian. From 1893 to 1913 he devoted much of his time to the extra-illustration of "Westcott's History of Philadelphia, 1609–1829" as printed in the *Sunday Dispatch*.

The total collection amounted to 32 folio volumes and contained portraits of people mentioned in the text, signed letters, manuscripts relating to the city, maps, plans, prints and drawings. The volumes have since been disbound.

Letters of Queen Kristina of Sweden, 1644; John Printz, 1644; Peter Stuyvesant, 1653; Sir William Penn, 1655; William Penn to the Indians in Pennsylvania, 1681; James Harrison and William Turner to William Penn, 1686, 1690, 1697; William Markham and James Pemberton letters relating to lands and surveys, 1693, 1694; petitions for licenses for public houses, grand jury lists, mortgages, bonds, shipping bills, receipts, marriage and court records, 1709–1767; miscellaneous documents relating to extension of the frontier toward the Susquehanna River, whale boats on the Oswago,

Indian affairs, Fort Augusta, Fort Allen, Fort Pitt, treaty of Easton, French and Indian War, embargoes, smallpox epidemics, 1701–1763.

Letters of Jaspar Yeates, Sir William Johnson, Edward Penington, Sir William Keith, Jacob Arndt, John Bayard, William Parsons, Phineas Pemberton, Thomas Leach, Edmund Physick, Jacob Duché, Springett Penn, Nicholas Scull, Anne Caesar de la Luzerne, Isaac Norris, Thomas Bradford, George Washington, William Shippen, Dr. Caspar Wistar, Rembrandt Peale, Mary Masters Penn, Franklin Bache, Thomas McKean, Clement Biddle, and Joseph Watson; petitions of Mennonites and Quakers relating to the oath of allegiance, 1778; Revolutionary War items relating to confiscation of property, raising of troops, medical supplies, finance, distress on the frontiers, pensions to families of soldiers, armaments, enlistment, 1775–1783; portraits of eminent Americans and Europeans; views of colonial Philadelphia churches, inns, mills, bridges, and homes; miscellaneous maps, facsimiles, sketches, drawings, and broadsides.

Gift of David McNeely Stauffer.

1096
Cowper, James Hamilton. Account of the loss of the steam packet *Pulaski.* **(1 v.)**

Eyewitness account of shipwreck by James Hamilton Cowper of Hopeton, Ga.

1097
Anonymous. Survey, 1817. (1 v.)

Survey of land from Stoddartsville to Allentown.

1098
Sullivan, Thomas. Journal, 1775–1778. (1 v.)

Typescript.
Thomas Sullivan was a Sergeant of the British Army.
Purchased, Library Fund, 1905.

1099
Susquehanna Permanent Bridge Company. Account book, 1811. (1 v.)

The Susquehanna Permanent Bridge Company erected the bridge over the Susquehanna River at McCall's Ferry.
Purchased, Library Fund, 1903.

1100

Armstrong, John, 1717–1795.   **Susquehanna River and Schuylkill River Island Survey, 1759–1761.**   **(47 items.)**

Surveys of islands in the Susquehanna River and the Schuylkill River done by John Armstrong, Bartrem Galbraith, George Stevenson, and James Scull.

1101

Tax lists, 1693–1870.   **(19 v.)**

Philadelphia County taxables, 1693; Philadelphia, Chestnut, Lower Delaware and Walnut Wards, 1754–1767; Berks County taxables, 1758; Lower Delaware, High Street and North Wards, 1765; tax lists for city and county of Philadelphia, 1772; assessments, Northern Liberties, 1781–1792; North Ward, 1782–1783; overseer of poor cash account, 1780–1783; miscellaneous assessments, 1788; Germantown taxables, 1790; Philadelphia County taxables, 1800; Northern Liberties, 1815; Lower Delaware and South Mulberry Wards, 1829; assessments, Walnut Ward, 1841; Blockley poor tax, 1841–1845; and Camden, N.J., South Ward taxables, 1870.

1102

Begg, William.   **Journal,** 1812–1815.   **(1 v.)**

Journal kept by William Begg while on the *Tenedos* under the command of Captain Hyde Parker detailing sea voyages and naval accounts of the War of 1812.

Gift of W. Brotherhead.

1103

Kent, Sussex, and Newcastle (Del.)   **Papers, 1655–1805.** **(ca. 200 items.)**

Miscellaneous papers contributing material on the counties of Kent, Sussex and Newcastle in Delaware.

1104

Anonymous.   **Travel diary, 1871.**   **(1 v.)**

Travel diary entitled, "To my old armchair," 1871 of a trip from Philadelphia to California.

Gift of Mrs. J.W. Queen, 1907.

1105
Great Britain.   Treaty of Amity, Commerce and Navigation memorials, 1798.   (1 v.)

Memorials addressed to the commissioners charged with carrying out the sixth article of the Jay Treaty.

1106
Trent, William, 1715–1787?   (Journal, 1759–1763.   (1 v.)

Journal of William Trent's journey to Ohio to transact business with the western Indians as William Johnson's deputy.
Photostatic copy.
Original in the Cadwalader Collection, George Croghan section, Historical Society of Pennsylvania.
Published in the *P.M.H.B.,* 71 (1947): 305–444.

1107
Trent, William, 1715–1787?   (Journal, 1763.   (1 v.)

Journal kept by William Trent at Fort Pitt describing frontier conditions and Indian attacks on white settlements.

1108
Truxton, Thomas, 1755–1822.   Records, 1797–1801.   (4 v.)

Muster rolls, journal, and letterbooks on Thomas Truxton's command of the U.S.S. *Constellation,* particularly in West Indian waters.
Gift of Charles R. Hildeburn, 1877.

1109
Townsend, Joseph, 1756–1841.   *Historical Sketch of Turks Head Tavern,* 1800.   (1 v.)

Gift of William P. Townsend, 1876.

1110
Tyndale, Hector, 1821–1880.   Diary, 1842.   (1 v.)

Hector Tyndale was captain of the National Rangers of Southwark, later known as the Artillery Corps of Cadwalader Grays.
Gift of Mrs. E. Dallett Hemphill, 1920.

1111
Union Library Company of Hatborough (Philadelphia, Pa.)
Records, 1755–1827.   (2 v.)

Documents of the Union Library Company of Hatborough including names of subscribers and records of meetings of the director.
Purchased, Dreer Fund, 1934.

1112
United States. Army.   Records, 1861–1864.   (3 v.)

Company orders, 1861–1864; company morning reports, 1863–1864; company clothing, commissary department, 1863–1864.
Purchased, Dreer Fund, 1934.

1113
United States. Arsenal (Philadelphia, Pa.)   Receipts, 1839–1840.
(1 v.)

David S. Brown's receipts at the United States Arsenal for blankets delivered by him to military storekeepers for inspection.

1114
Coleman, C.C.   United States in the making, 1926.   (1 v.)

Historical notes on the states.
Gift of C.C. Coleman, 1926.

1115
***United States* (ship).   Log and journal, 1784–1785.   (1 v.)**

Log and journal of the ship *United States* on its voyage to India, China and Sumatra. Also included is Henry Kepple's arithmetic, 1761.
Gift of John Emory, 1889.

1116
United States.   Passport register, 1809–1825.   (1 v.)

Gift of John W. Brock, 1925.

1117
Anonymous.   Letters, 1887.   (1 v.)

Letters about William Usselinx, founder of the Dutch and Swedish West India companies.

Copies by Dr. J.F. Jameson.
In Swedish with some English translation.

1118
**United States. Continental Army.   Valley Forge court martial
records, 1778.   (1 v.)**

Records of the court-martial of Lieutenant McCalley and other prisoners, before Colonel Thomas Clark at Valley Forge.
Gift of William Lanier, 1909.

1119
**Valley Forge National Historical Park (Pa.)   Report to Governor
William C. Sproul, 1920.   (1 v.)**

Typescript.
Gift of John W. Jordan, 1920.

1120
Van Etten, John.   Journal, 1756–1757.   (1 v.)

Account by John Van Etten of military defense at Fort Hyndshaw.

1121
**Vigilant Committee of Philadelphia (Pa.)   Minute book,
1839–1844.   (1 v.)**

The Vigilant Committee was set up by blacks and whites to assist
runaway slaves in the years before the Civil War.
Minutes giving accounts of cases kept by Jacob C. White for the Vigilant Committee of Philadelphia.
Gift of Leon Gardiner, 1933.

1122
**Wallace, John William, 1815–1884.   Ancient Records of
Philadelphia, 1702–1770.   (60 items.)**

Miscellaneous records of the city of Philadelphia.
Gift of John William Wallace, 1847.

1123
Walmsley, William.   Warrant, 1749.   (1 item.)

Warrant signed by William Callender and Evan Morgan requiring William Walmsley, constable of Byberry, to make a census of his district.
Transferred to the Society Miscellaneous Collection.

1124

Anonymous. **"War in America : Observations for the King of France,"** 1780–1781. (1 v.)

Observations on the Revolutionary War made for the King of France.
Gift of Clarence B. Moore, 1893.

1125

Pennsylvania Railroad. Women's Division for War Relief. Papers, 1916–1919. (2 v.)

Letters, accounts and miscellaneous papers reflecting the activities of the Pennsylvania Railroad Women's Division of War Relief.
Gift of Mrs. Theo. L. Pomeroy, 1926.

1126

Patterson, William Houston. **History of the Artillery Corps of Washington Grays.** (4 v.)

The Washington Grays Artillery Corps was a volunteer militia unit from Philadelphia. It was organized in 1822 under the command of Cephas G. Childs.
Gift of William Houston Patterson, 1902.

1127

Anonymous. **Genealogical notes, ca.** 1914–1922. (1 v.)

Genealogical notes on the Welsh founders of Pennsylvania.
Gift of Mrs. Walter Ross McShea, 1938.

1128

West, Moses. **Treatise on marriage,** 1739. (1 v.)

Entry cancelled; transferred to the Library.

1129

West Bradford Township (Chester County, Pa.) **List of taxables,** 1802. (1 v.)

Names of taxables in West Bradford Township, showing amounts collected and paid to Evan Evans, treasurer for the poor.
Purchased, Library Fund, 1904.

1130
Pennsylvania. National Guard.   **West Chester National Guards**
Constitution, 1846–1851.   (1 v.)

Minutes, constitution, bylaws and list of members.

1131
Westcott, Thompson, 1820–1888.   *List of officers of Pennsylvania and*
Philadelphia, **1682–1888.**   (3 v.)

Also included is a manuscript index to Westcott's *History of Philadel-phia,* 1609–1829.

1132
United States. Army.   **Records, 1794.**   (2 v.)

Orders issued to Generals James Chambers and Thomas Procter at Bedford by General William Irvine during the Western Insurrection, journal kept by Major Edward Spear commanding the 1st battalion of Maryland militia, muster roll and accounts of Captain Machinheimer.

1133
Whales, Henry.   **Account book, 1830–1840.**   (1 v.)

Henry Whales was a dancing master.
Gift of Harrold E. Gillingham, 1932.

1134
Esling, Charles H.A., 1845–1907.   **Essay, 1885.**   (1 v.)

An essay read by Charles H.A. Esling before the Historical Society of Pennsylvania, May 4, 1885, entitled: "Governor Thomas Wharton : Escape at the British occupation of Philadelphia."
Gift of A.H. Wharton, 1922.

1135
University of Pennsylvania. Philomathean Society.
The Whetstone Essays, 1819.   (1 v.)

Miscellaneous essays and addresses written by University of Pennsylvania students.

1136
Wignell, William.   **Memoranda, 1771–1781.**   (1 v.)

Memoranda of William Wignell while managing the Philadelphia Theatre.
Gift of the Gilpin estate.

1137
Williamson, Peter.   Records, 1861–1874.   (2 v.)

Account book of the fund for the relief of families of Philadelphia volunteers, 1861–1886; record of names of orphans maintained and educated by the Philadelphia superintending committee of soldiers' orphans, 1864–1874.

1138
United States. Centennial Commission. Women's Centennial Executive Committee.   Minutes, 1874–1876.   (2 v.)

Mrs. Elizabeth Duane Gillespie served as president for the Women's Centennial Executive Committee which was formed to raise funds in support for the Centennial within the city.
Gift of Josephine Carr, 1890, and L.V. Carr, 1913.

1139
Young Men's Christian Associations (Philadelphia, Pa.)   Civil War casualty records, 1861–1865.   (3 v.)

Records of sick and wounded soldiers and hospital care and other aid rendered by the association.

1140
Young Republicans of Philadelphia (Pa.)   Minutes, 1903–1919. (1 v.)

Minutes, bylaws, resolutions and names of members.
Purchased, Library Fund, 1926.

1141
Young, Sgt.   Journal, 1776–1777.   (1 v.)

Sgt. Young served under Captain Thomas Fitzsimmons' Philadelphia infantry company.

1142
Ashmore, Edith Bancroft.   Collection, 1744–1821.   (105 items.)

Letters and documents about Dr. Edward Bancroft, including some of his correspondence, 1779–1789; letters to Bancroft, 1777–1819; information on *Two Books of Epigrams and Epitaphs* by Thomas Bancroft; and portraits, notes, letters and genealogical material relating to the Bancroft family.
Some of Dr. Edward Bancroft's correspondence is photostatic copies.
Gift of Edith Bancroft Ashmore, 1940.

1143
Birmingham Mills (Burlington, N.J.)   **Account book, 1860–1867.**
(1 v.)

Account book of Birmingham flour and feed mills.
Purchased, Historical Society.

1144
Betty **(ship).   Logbook, 1789.   (1 v.)**

Logbook of the *Betty,* commanded by Captain Edward Rice, from
Philadelphia to Port au Prince, and of the *Charleston,* S.C. from Newfound-
land to New York.
Purchased.

1145
Brodhead, Daniel, 1736–1809.   Letterbook, 1780–1785.   (1 v.)

Letterbook of Daniel Brodhead written while commander at Fort Pitt.
Material relates to the condition of the army and the forts depending on
Fort Pitt, the Indian troubles, events leading up to General Brodhead's court
martial, and a few business letters from Brodhead written in 1785.
Purchased.

1146
Brown, Mary Stockton.   Collection, 1764–1860.   (93 items.)

Letters to Samuel Cooper and others, 1819–1837, some relating to Cooper's Western expedition; papers from the estate of Mary Graham, Bordentown, N.J., 1817–1830, including the accounts of Newberry Smith, executor;
papers of John Harrison, including his will, 1826; marriage certificate of
Thomas Harrison and Sarah Richards, 1764; papers of M.G. Taylor & Co.,
1854–1860.
Gift of Mrs. Mary Stockton Brown.

1147
Business account books, 1845–1876.   (6 v.)

Journal of William Pollock, lumber merchant, 1851–1870; account book
of William Pollock, 1845–1853; ledger for a lumber and coal merchant, 1853–
1869; account book for a Pottsville coal merchant, 1872–1875; account book
for a coal merchant, 1872–1876; and account book, 1870–1872.
Gift of Mrs. Juliet C. Walker, 1941.

1148
Chambers, Gordon.   Collection, 1792–1823.   (44 items.)

Papers and correspondence of the Schuylkill and Susquehanna Navigation Company and the Union Canal Company. Records of payments, receipts, stock certificates; patent rights for swinging gates to increase the depth of water; contracts and laws governing lotteries; protests against abolition of lotteries; protests against the proposed union of the canal companies. Among the names mentioned are: Henry Drinker, James C. Fisher, Peter S. DuPonceau, William M. Meredith, Charles Ingersoll, William Milnor, Samuel Mifflin, Samuel Breck, Ebenezer Hazard, Thomas McKean, Simon Snyder, and others.

Gift of Gordon Chambers.

1149
Civil War papers, 1861–1865.   (533 items.)

Entry cancelled.

1150
Day, Alfred.   Letterbook, 1855.   (1 v.)

Alfred Day was a Philadelphia naval agent.
Purchased.

1151
Felton family.   Papers, 1839–1889, 1916–1920.   (ca. 500 items.)

The Felton papers consist of correspondence, memoranda, reports, of Samuel Morse Felton and his son Samuel Morse Felton, both civil engineers who became prominent railroad executives.

Samuel Morse Felton, Sr., was appointed president of the Philadelphia, Wilmington & Baltimore Railroad in 1851, and his letterpress book, 1857–1859, concerns his management of the railroad. The P.W. & B. was an important transportation route during the Civil War, and Felton's loose papers relate primarily to the foiling of an assassination plot against Lincoln in February, 1861, the transportation of Union troops and supplies (much of this material consists of cipher dispatches and telegrams), and the construction of the Hoosac Tunnel in Massachusetts, for which Felton served as commissioner, 1862–1865. After the War, Felton became president of Pennsylvania Steel, but his interest in railroading remained strong. A letterpress book, 1868–1874, contains his letters as president of the Delaware Railroad and other positions he continued to hold in the industry. Felton's correspondents include Craig Biddle, John B. Brooks, Simon Cameron, Samuel

F. du Pont, John M. Forbes, Alexander Holmes, Benjamin H. Latrobe, Jr., Benson J. Lossing, Allan Pinkerton, Fitz John Porter, Enoch Pratt, E.S. Sanford, Nathaniel Thayer, David Yulee, P.H. Hare, John Bingham, George McClellan, George Stearns, Thomas Blackwell, Robert Beale, and George E. Bent.

Samuel Morse Felton, Jr., also served as president and chairman of several railroad companies and industry associations. These papers relate in part to Felton's position as advisor to the U.S. Army Corps of Engineers in 1916 and illustrate preparations made by the Corps for war with Mexico. Most of the material is on Felton's activities as Director General of Military Railroads, 1917–1918. Correspondents include Wallace Atterbury, Maj. Gen. William Black, Col. W.C. Langrift, William G. McAdoo, and William B. Parsons. There is also a typescript of an official report compiled by Felton, History of Director General of Military Railways.

Gift of C.C. Felton, 1941, and Samuel Morse Felton, 1961–1963.

1152
Society of the Friendly Sons of Saint Patrick (Philadelphia, Pa.)
Papers, 1771–1982.   (75 items.)

The Society of the Friendly Sons of Saint Patrick was founded in 1771 as a social organization for men of Irish heritage. The original organization was dissolved by 1798. In 1792, the Hibernian Society for the Relief of Emigrants from Ireland was incorporated, with much of its membership overlapping with the Friendly Sons. In 1898 the Hibernian Society changed its name to the Society of the Friendly Sons of Saint Patrick for the Relief of Emigrants from Ireland.

Rules and minutebook, 1771–1797; minutebooks, 1813–1910, 1935–1956, 1960–1982; record of fees for membership, dinners and scholarship fund, 1954–1960; annual toasts, 1853–1880; portraits of early members; constitution and by-laws, 1941, 1945, 1951, 1971; membership lists, 1954, 1956, 1958, 1971; addresses presented to the society; dinner programs, 1939–1980; and other ephemera.

Gift of the Society of the Friendly Sons of Saint Patrick, 1941, 1979, 1980, 1982.

1153
Harvey, Isaac, Jr.   Papers, 1788–1856.   (15 v.)

Diary, 1820–1856, of Isaac Harvey, a Philadelphia merchant, recording events in Philadelphia, the weather; letterbook, 1788–1795 of Isaac Harvey, Sr., on the West Indian trade.

Purchased.

1154
Satterthwaite family.   **Papers, 1752–1845.**   **(10 items.)**

Papers on the Satterthwaite family including the will of Ann Satterthwaite, 1830; marriage certificates of Joshua Satterthwaite and Ann Middleton, 1785, Richard Satterthwaite and Elizabeth Wright, 1752, Richard Satterthwaite and Jemima K. Redman, 1831, Joseph Schofield and Lydia Satterthwaite, 1821; Lydia Satterthwaite's autograph book and book of poetry, 1817, and 1818; Richard Satterthwaite's book of poetry, 1852; four maps drawn at school by Lydia Satterthwaite.
Gift of Mrs. Logan Henshaw, 1940.

1155
Jackson, Joseph, 1867–1946.   **Collection, 1798–1941.**
(3 linear ft.)

Letters, correspondence and miscellaneous items including letters from Fanny Kemble; S. Weir Mitchell, 1912; Samuel W. Pennypacker, 1912; Agnes Repplier, 1916; Rudolph Blankenburg, 1912; and others. Cartoon "Congressional Pugilists," 1798; play bills; broadsides; material relating to Charles G. Leland, 1853–1893; list of subscribers to Philadelphia directory, 1820; W.W. Lamb's theatrical record, 1857; and miscellaneous material relating to Jackson's literary career.
Gift of Joseph Jackson.

1156
King and Wilson (Washington, D.C.)   **Letterbook, 1837–1838.**
(1 v.)

King and Wilson was a firm in Washington, D.C., interested in the buying and selling of public lands.

1157
Lawrence, Thomas, 1689–1754.   **Papers, 1684–1759.**   **(100 items.)**

Papers of Thomas Lawrence including correspondence, business letters, receipts, legal papers, accounts with Samuel Bronson, 1742–1748, and letterbook, 1746–1754.
Gift of Martha Morris Lawrence.

1158
Leisler Rebellion Papers, 1689–1691.   **(ca. 225 items.)**

When word reached to colonies that William had landed in England as a result of the Glorious Revolution, there was reaction throughout America. In New York the lieutenant-governor was deposed by a group led by Jacob Leisler. Leisler assumed the office of governor until further word from England. An ambiguous letter from King William authorized continuation of the Leisler government. In 1691 a new governor was appointed. Leisler hesitated to relinquish the office. As a result, he was charged with treason and hanged. In 1695 Parliament exonerated Leisler from all charges.

These papers are accounts of the events leading up to the conviction of Jacob Leisler and arguing for his exoneration.

Copies.

1159
Mary Anna Longstreth School. Alumnae Association (Philadelphia, Pa.)   Papers, 1829–1939.   (ca. 225 items.)

Business papers and correspondence of the Mary Anna Longstreth Alumnae Association, 1829–1939, including cancelled checks; bank statements, 1828–1835; list of members, 1925–1938; correspondence 1912–1939; bills, receipts, treasurer's reports, 1929–1936; newspaper clippings, pamphlets; school account books, 1829–1890; association account books, 1899–1901, 1901–1915, 1916–1931; officers' books, 1899–1907, 1907–1930; minute books; and memoirs.

Gift of Miss A.M. Archambault, 1941.

1160
Marchand, Lizzie.   Journal, 1864.   (1 v.)

Journal of Lizzie Marchand kept while attending Mrs. Cary's school in Philadelphia.

Gift of Charles Coleman Sellers, 1940.

1161
Young Men's Christian Associations. Philadelphia (Pa.)   *History of the Fifth Street Methodist Episcopal Church.*   (1 v.)

Manuscript apparently assembled for the fiftieth anniversary in 1882. Includes photographs and prints.

Purchased, Gratz Fund.

1162
Montgomery, William Woodrow, 1845–1921.   Papers, 1847–1922. (4 linear ft.)

Papers of W.W. Montgomery, attorney, including letters, legal papers, agreements, indentures, land warrants, drafts, deeds, articles of search, bonds, mortgages, judgements, tax bills, receipts, estate papers.

1163

Morgan, George, 1743–1810.   Letterbook, 1767–1768.   (1 v.)

Letterbook of George Morgan, Indian trader and speculator in western lands. The letterbook contains Morgan's correspondence addressed to Baynton and Wharton from Fort Charles and Kaskaskia giving many details of the Indian trade. There are also journals of the journey from Philadelphia to the Mengo town on the Ohio and a voyage down the Mississippi River from Kaskaskia to the Iberville River.

Gift of George Norris Morgan and Mrs. Henry W. Leiger, 1940.

1164

Johnston, Benjamin S.   Logbook, 1856–1860.   (1 v.)

Record of voyages in the ship, *Morning Light,* from Philadelphia to San Francisco; in the schooner, *Flying Duck,* from San Francisco to Honolulu; in the barque, *Francis Palmer,* from San Francisco to Honolulu; in the barque, *Godfrey,* from San Francisco to New York; in the barque, *Julia Castner,* from Philadelphia to San Francisco; and in the ship, *Old Colony,* from San Francisco to Callao and then to Leith.

Purchased.

1165

Neave, Samuel, d. 1774.   Accounts, 1737–1738.   (1 v.)

The accounts of Samuel Neave, Philadelphia furrier, kept in his copy of Bradford's almanac for 1738.

Purchased, Dreer Fund, 1941.

1166

Penn family. Lands records, 1683–1746.   (1 v.)

A record from the surveyor general's office showing Penn lands, warrants, surveys, returns of the manors and other tracts.

Purchased.

1167

Sergeant, Thomas, 1782–1860.   Papers, 1781–1853.   (115 items.)

Correspondence and legal papers for Thomas Sergeant, a Philadelphia jurist, including letters on the Philadelphia Post Office (1883); papers relating to the capital stock of the Albany Gas Light Company; reports on decisions of the Supreme Court of Pennsylvania; and similar matters. Correspondents include John Binns, William Davidson, William Findlay, John B. Trevor, George Wolf and John Wurtz.

Gift of William Pepper, 1941.

1168
Rittenhouse Boys Grammar School (Philadelphia, Pa.)
Examination results, 1866–1887.   (2 v.)

Gift of Wilbur S. Morris, 1941.

1169
Roberts, Thomas.   Account book, 1767–1810.   (1 v.)

The accounts of Thomas Roberts, III, of Bristol Township, including his farm accounts, 1767–1810; rents received from a house in Southwark, 1786–1796; and accounts as administrator of an estate in Germantown, 1768–1771, 1776–1782.

Gift of B. Frank Harper, 1941.

1170
Schulling, S.   Diary, 1824–1825.   (1 v.)

Diary of S. Schulling of summer trips through Pennsylvania, New York and New England.

Purchased.

1171
Scott, John Morin, 1789–1858.   Papers, 1782–1869.   (6 linear ft.)

Legal papers and correspondence of John M. Scott including: John M. Scott case book, 1822–1845, letterbooks, 1813–1860, correspondence, 1782–1869; Sarah Hopkinson estate account book, 1858–1869, receipt book, 1857–1865, account book, 1857–1864, memorandum books; and Meredith estate accounts.

1172
Shaler, William, 1778?-1833.   Papers, 1794–1832.   (ca. 700 items.)

Miscellaneous papers of William Shaler, U.S. Consul at Algiers: correspondence, 1799–1832; business papers, 1794–1829; notes on the Turkish language; and journal of the U.S. consulate at Algiers, 1827–1828.

Gift of Mrs. Walter Craig Hill.

1173
United Rifle Corps (Philadelphia, Pa.)   Papers, 1844–1861.
(3 linear ft.)

In 1844 the National Rifle Corps was formed as a volunteer corps. Its name was changed in 1846 to the United Rifle Corps.

Miscellaneous papers and minute book of the United Rifle Corps: notices, accounts, orderly sergeants' reports, receipts, 1849–1861; minutes, 1844–1849, 1850–1861; orders on the treasurer, 1858–1860; ledger, 1853–1857; account books of dues, 1844–1848.

1174
Walker, Juliet C.   Collection, 1788–1895.   (2 linear ft.)

Business papers, correspondence and legal papers of the Walker family of Pottsville, primarily the papers of Thomas H. Walker, lawyer, and Lewis S. Walker, physician. Papers on the Burd, Hubley, Shippen and Walker families, 1788–1895; Lewis Walker's medical lectures; and Lewis Walker's journal, 1848–1864.

Gift of Juliet C. Walker.

1175
Wicacoa and Moyamensing Meadows Company.
Papers, 1762–1900.   (2 v. and 1 item.)

Blueprint of land embraced within the charters, 1761–1765, 1828–1830; copy of assessments, 1899; return of names of landowners, 1762; and minute books, 1762–1824, 1825–1900.

1176
R. D. Wood and Company.   Papers, 1858–1905.   (15 linear ft.)

Business records of a foundry in Cumberland County, N.J., which made iron castings and pipe. These records include account books, 1871–1879, 1892–1895, 1896–1899; records of pipe made, 1860–1899; casting books, 1868–1898; and daybooks, 1873–1876, 1883–1886.

Gift of Spencer Hazard.

1177
Young, William, 1755–1829.   Correspondence, 1792–1827.
(ca. 1050 items.)

Correspondence of William Young, bookseller and printer of Philadelphia. Among the correspondents of Young were: Darton and Harvey, London; Dunlap and Claypoole; William Gilbert, Dublin; Joshua Gilpin; Richard Folwell; Benjamin F. Garrigues; Ross and Simpson; John Matthews; John Stockton and Son; William Warner and Company; and others.

Gift of Hiram E. Deats, 1941.

1178
Philadelphia (Pa.). General Hospital.   Papers.   (3 linear ft.)

Data on all the physicians who have been connected with Philadelphia General Hospital from its founding in 1731 as Blockley Alms House to 1939.
Purchased.

1179
Brisbane, John, 1730–1822.   Ledger, 1776–1779.   (1 v.)

Revolutionary War ledger of accounts of Capt. John Brisbane with other soldiers recording money paid and supplies purchased.

Gift of Susan Brisbane Lowrie, 1942.

1180
Carson, Hampton L. (Hampton Lawrence), 1852–1929.   Papers, 1874–1927.   (11 linear ft.)

Papers on the American Bar Association, of which Hampton L. Carson was president; testimonials to Mr. Carson; correspondence, 1875–1926; papers of the Commission on Revision of the Constitution of Pennsylvania, 1910–1920; Carson's speeches; docket books, 1874–1883, 1879–1890, 1890–1893.

Gift of Joseph Carson.

1181
Champion, Joseph.   Papers, 1774–1844.   (42 items.)

Forms of precepts for justices of the peace, 1797; and miscellaneous manuscripts.

Gift of Mrs. Margaret MacIntosh.

1182
Cope family.   Papers, 1692–1891.   (1 v.)

Letters, many to Caleb Cope, coats of arms, newspaper clippings and genealogical data relating to the Cope and allied families.

Gift of Porter F. Cope.

1183
Dreer Collection : Additional manuscripts, 1741–1812.
(ca. 170 items.)

Entry cancelled; see collection #175.

1184
DuBois, Henry C.   Papers, 1774–1890.   (31 items.)

Letters and papers on the DuBois, Ewing and Patterson families; letters of Robert Patterson, James Madison and Oliver Wolcott.
Gift of Henry C. DuBois.

1185
Fahnestock, Anna Maria, 1803–1890.   Diaries, 1863–1867,
1869–1873.   (7 v.)

Diaries of Anna Maria and George Wolff Fahnestock. In addition to the diaries there is a volume of clippings on the burning of the steamboat *United States,* December 4, 1868.
Gift of Bernard Bunting Fahnestock.

1186
Fair American (ship).   **Papers, 1793–1794.   (9 items.)**

Letters of Andrew Clow, Robert Cumming, and William Crammond, merchants on the voyages of the ship *Fair American.*
Purchased.

1187
United States. Army Commissariat.   Invoices, 1863.   (1 v.)

Invoice book of ordinance and stores of the Frankford Arsenal, sent of Captain Prince R. Stetson at Harrisburg, 1863.
Purchased.

1188
Franklin Reformatory Home for Inebriates (Philadelphia, Pa.)
Papers, 1872–1906.   (19 v.)

The Franklin Reformatory Home for Inebriates was incorporated in 1872 and located at 915 Locust Street. Its mission was to provide a home and support for individuals without economic means desirous of overcoming alcohol abuse. Samuel P. Godwin acted as the president. All present and previous patients of the home became members of the Godwin Association which contributed a large sum of money for operating costs each year.

Minute books, registers, constitution and bylaws, and a journal of daily events, 1880–1890.
Purchased.

1189
Gilmore's Auditorium (Philadelphia, Pa.)   Programs, 1895–1901. **(3 v.)**

Programs of entertainments given in Gilmore's Auditorium, Walnut Street above Eighth.
Purchased.

1190
Graff family.   Papers, 1727–1929.   (87 items and 6 v.)

Graff family Bible records, 1727–1908; letters of Frederick Graff, 1806–1829; letters of Charles Graff, 1819–1833; family correspondence, 1819–1833; autograph albums; diary, 1880; and a book of verse.
Gift of Mrs. Charles Graff.

1191
Greene, James M., d. 1871.   Letters, 1825–1835.   (24 items.)

Dr. James M. Greene was a medical officer in the United States Navy.

1192
Jackson, Joseph, 1867–1946.   Papers, 1926–1927.   (100 items.)

Joseph Jackson's correspondence with Dr. Robert B. Ludy on the book *Historic Hotels of the World,* and manuscript of this book.
Gift of Joseph Jackson.

1193
Jones, John, Jr.   Daybook, 1746–1765.   (1 v.)

John Jones, Jr. was a Philadelphia shoemaker.
Gift of Mrs. Harper Wilson.

1194
Jordan, Ewing, b. 1847.   Papers, 1846–1877.   (15 v.)

Diary, 1846–1877 of Francis Jordan; schoolbooks of Ewing Jordan, 1853–1861, used at Nazareth Hall; scrapbook kept by Ewing Jordan while at the University of Pennsylvania.
Gift of the estate of Ewing Jordan.

1195
Lippincott, Joseph W.   Papers.   (125 items.)

Papers on the early history of New Jersey; notes on the Lippincott and Roberts family.
Gift of Susan Wills Roberts.

1196
Mary Anna Longstreth School. Alumnae Association.
Papers, 1898–1942.   (80 items.)

Minute books and memoirs of the alumnae association.

1197
Lyons, Edward.   Diaries, 1830–1856.   (2 v.)

Edward Lyons' diaries discuss his membership in William Metcalfe's Philadelphia Bible-Christian Church, a fundamentalist sect believing in vegetarianism.
Gift of Albert J. Edmunds.

1198
Nelson, Thomas Forsythe.   Papers, [19—].   (4,000 items.)

Personal papers, bank drafts, and financial papers of Thomas Nelson.
Gift of Thomas Forsythe Nelson.

1199
Stoddard, J.K.   Collection, 1872–1926.   (3 linear ft.)

Primarily correspondence of the Newhall family.
Gift of Mrs. J.K. Stoddard.

1200
Paschall, Benjamin.   Record book, 1778–1784.   (1 v.)

Record book of Benjamin Paschall, Philadelphia Justice of the Peace. Includes recognizance, apprentice and service indentures, and Pennsylvania allegiance lists.
Gift of Clara Harrison Town.

1201
United States Custom House (Philadelphia, Pa.)
Records, 1803–1873.   (247 items.)

Ship manifests.
Purchased.

1202
Philadelphia (Pa.). Fire Department.   Records, 1884–1913.
(21 v.)

Gift of George A. MacManus.

1203
United States. Selective Service System. Philadelphia (Pa.)
Papers, 1917–1918.   (2,000 items.)

Papers of Clarence L. Harper, secretary for the Board, on the drafting of Philadelphians for World War II.
Gift of Mrs. Clarence L. Harper.

1204
Philadelphia (Pa.)   Tax books, 1803–1853.   (266 v.)

Entry cancelled; transferred to the Philadelphia Department of Records.

1205
Progressive Literary Association of Philadelphia (Pa.)   Minutes,
1860–1902.   (2 v.)

Entry cancelled; missing since 1954.

1206
Rawle family.   Papers, 1778–1921.

Correspondence and legal documents of the Rawle family of Philadelphia, lawyers. The papers include the court docket of William Rawle, 1807–1835; letterbook of William Rawle, 1848–1854; letters of William Rawle, Sr., 1778–1804; cash accounts, R. Rawle, 1821–1824; letterbook, R. Rawle, 1818–1819; contemporary copy of Penn's Frame of Government; book of surveys of Rawle properties; legal notebook, 1905–1916; maps; and engraved portraits.
Gift of Mrs. Charles Sanderson.

1207
Washington Righter's Sons (Columbia, Pa.)   Records, 1847–1881.
(36 v.)

Washington Righter's Sons, lumber merchants of Columbia, Lancaster County, and of Philadelphia, originally operated as Righter and Sutton.

Business records including receipt books, ledgers, journals, accounts and other papers.
Gift of Francis D. Brinton, 1941.

1208
Rodgers family.   Papers, 1791–1885.   (6 linear ft.)

Commodore John Rodgers entered the navy in 1798 as a lieutenant and in 1799 was promoted to captain. After the war he served briefly as the master of the *Nelly* sailing to Santo Domingo. He was arrested by the French, and his cargo was confiscated. He returned to active naval service in the Mediterranean Squadron. During the War of 1812 he was the thanking officer. In 1815 he was appointed president of the Board of Navy Commissioners.

In 1806 Rodgers married Minerva Denison, daughter of Gideon Denison, Jr., merchant of Sion Hill, near Havre de Grace, Md. Three of the Rodgers sons entered the Navy. Frederick, a midshipman, was drowned in 1828 at Norfolk. John, a surveyor and naval engineer, served in the Civil War and died as a rear admiral in 1882. Henry was lost off the California coast in 1854. Robert Smith Rodgers, the eldest, was a civil engineer; he operated the family farm at Sion Hill, and served in the Civil War as a colonel, and later was deputy collector of the port of Havre de Grace. He married Sarah Perry, daughter of Commodore Matthew C. Perry, in 1841, and two of their children, Frederick and John Augustus, also served in the navy.

Henry Denison, brother of Minerva Denison Rodgers, operated the family farm at Sion Hill before his nephew Robert and served as a U.S. Navy purser.

The bulk of the John Rodgers material relates to his various naval assignments: with the West Indies Squadron, 1799–1802, commanding the sloop of war *Maryland;* with the Mediterranean Squadron against the Barbary pirates, 1802–1806, commanding the sloop of war *John Adams,* the frigates *New York* and *Congress,* and at various times commander-in-chief of the entire squadron; commanding the New York Flotilla (of gunboats and bomb vessels) and Naval Station, 1807–1810, following the war scare occasioned by the *Chesapeake-Leopard* incident and, with the abandonment of the gunboat philosophy, directing his command of the brig *Argus,* the sloop of war *Wasp* and other vessels from the frigate *Constitution;* commanding "the northern division of ships for the protection of the American coast," 1810–1814, with the frigate *President* as his flagship; commanding the Delaware Flotilla and the frigate *Guerriere* under construction in Philadelphia, 1814; President of the Board of Navy Commissioners responsible for administering the navy material, 1815–1837, with two interludes—commanding the West Indies Squadron, 1823, aboard the schooner *Shark* in the relief expedition to Thompson's Island (Key West), and commanding the Mediterranean Squadron, 1825–1827, with the *North Carolina* as his flagship, and the *Constitution*, the frigate *Brandywine*, the sloops of war *Erie*, *Ontario*, and *Warren*, and the schooner *Porpoise* under his command.

The Commodore Rodgers materials include: Incoming correspondence, 1803–1835, mainly from fellow naval officers. Letterbooks (including incoming letters), official correspondence, 1799–1803, from the *Maryland*, *John Adams*, *New York*; 1802, from Baltimore, reporting to President Madison on Santo Domingo experience; 1814, from Philadelphia; 1823–1824, from the *Shark*; 1829–1830, from Navy Commissioner's Office; 1834, from Navy Board of Revision. Logs, 1812, of the *President*; 1824–1827, of the *North Carolina*. Court-martial proceedings, 1807–1808, for the bomb ketches *Vesuvius* and *Etna*; 1810–1812, for the *Wasp*, *Argus*, *Constitution*, sloop of war *Hornet*; 1826, for the *Constitution*. Stores books (receipts and expenditures), 1804–1805, for ship of the line *Constellation*, Mediterranean Squadron; 1809–1814, for the *Constitution*; 1819–1820, for ship of the line *Columbus*, built by Navy Commissioners Board; 1824–1827, for the *North Carolina*. Requisition books, 1814, for the *Guerriere*; 1825–1827 for the *North Carolina*, *Constitution*, *Brandywine*, *Erie*, *Ontario*, *Warren*, *Porpoise*. Survey order books, 1808–1812, for the New York Flotilla and for the Northern Division; 1825–1827, for the Mediterranean Squadron.

Account books, 1805–1806, for the *Constitution* and other Mediterranean vessels; 1807–1810, for the New York Flotilla, including specified gunboats, the *Constitution*, the schooner *Revenge*; 1810–1813, for the *President*; 1824–1827, for the *North Carolina* and the Mediterranean Squadron; some John Rodgers personal accounts, such as house expenses, 1815–1817, are interspersed in these volumes. General orders books, and quarter, station and other bills, 1802–1804, for the *John Adams*, *New York*, and *Congress*; 1807, for the New York Flotilla of Bombs and Gunboats; 1809, for the *Constitution*; ca. 1810, for the *President*; 1824–1826, for the Mediterranean Squadron. Record book of commercial vessels boarded, 1808–1809, by New York Flotilla gunboats and the *Constitution*. Muster roll, 1809–1811, for the *Constitution*. Meteorological diary, 1824–1827, for the *North Carolina*. Liberty books, 1826–1827, for the *North Carolina*. General orders and outfitting instructions for naval vessels, signal books, stores and requisition books, calculations for naval ship construction, ca. 1805, ca. 1815, 1825–1827, 1833–1834, n.d.

There is material for the sons and daughter of Commodore John and Minerva Rodgers. The material for Frederick Rodgers includes: astronomy copybook, ca. 1825; pocket station bill, 1825, for the *North Carolina*; black book or punishment book, 1825–1827, maintained by Frederick for the *North Carolina;* log, 1827, for the *North Carolina.*

For Henry Rodgers there are: logs, 1837–1840, aboard the sloop of war *Fairfield,* the brig, *Dolphin,* and ship of the line, *Independence,* 1842, aboard the brig, *Somers;* navigation work book, 1840–1842, aboard the sloop of war, *Levant;* at rear, arithmetic work book; personal logs and diaries, 1850, aboard the mail steamer *Georgia,* 1850–1851, aboard the mail steamer *Falcon,* 1852–1853, aboard unnamed steamer carrying mail, cargo, passengers; night order book, 1851, for the Falcon, continued as Robert S. Rodgers, survey notes, ca. 1850's, for the Hartford County, Md., properties.

For John Rodgers (Jr.) there are purser's accounts, 1840–1841, for the schooner *Wave.* Quarter, watch, and other bills, ca. 1841, for the schooner, *Boxer.*

For Robert Smith Rodgers there is incoming correspondence, 1835–1863, mainly family, and records for work as canal engineer, 1836–1838. Other volumes include prize agent's memorandum book, 1846–1847, for the steamer, *Mississippi;* diary and expense accounts, 1846–1857, at Sion Hill, with some ca. 1850's survey notes interspersed; custom house book, 1877–1885, weekly reports of collections at Havre de Grace. For Louise Rodgers there is an Arithmetic work book, 1826 and commonplace book, 1829–1836.

There are also papers for the grandsons of Commodore John and Minerva Rodgers. The material for Frederick Rodgers includes: diary, 1854, at Sion Hill; copybook, 1860, while at the Naval Academy, watch bills, (between 1855 and 1861) for the sloop *Marion,* 1862, for the frigate *Santee,* ca. 1864, for the screw steamer *Grand Gulf,* 1870, and for the sloop of war *St. Mary's;* letterbook, 1873–1876, official naval correspondence aboard the screw steamer *Despatch.*

The material for John Augustus Rodgers includes: diary, 1867, of summer cruise aboard the sloop of war *Macedonian* and Paris visit and notes on navigation, 1869, aboard the steam sloop *Pensacola.*

Papers for Minerva (Denison) Rodgers' father, brother, and brothers-in-law include: Gideon Denison letterbook, 1792–1794, business letters concerning trade matters; Ezra Denison letterbook, 1799, from Natchez, continued, Henry Denison, 1800–1801, from Natchez, New Orleans and Havre de Grace; Henry Denison letterbooks, 1808–1809, on settlement of father's estate; 1815–1821, official correspondence on his purser's accounts and assignments. Sion Hill account books, 1804–1807, estate accounts; 1816–1819, same, and at back, purser's accounts, 1816–1817, for the *Congress;* 1818–1819, personal house expenses. Incoming correspondence and accounts as purser, 1807–1821, including especially accounts while prisoner in England following August 1813 capture of the *Argus,* paying and supplying American naval prisoners at Chatham, Plymouth, Dartmoor. John D. Henley: Enlistment receipts, 1813, as recruiting officer at Baltimore for the schooner *Asp*. Correspondence, 1817–1818, official exchanges aboard the John Adams with General Louis de Aury on the surrender of Amelia Island to Rodgers. Log, 1819–1821, of the *Congress* on cruise to China from Norfolk and return, first American naval vessel to visit a Chinese port. Alexander S. Wadsworth: Log and regulations, 1829–1831, as captain of the *Constellation*.

The Commodore Matthew C. Perry materials include: correspondence, incoming and outgoing, 1825–1852; letterbooks, official correspondence, 1830–1832, as commander of the sloop of war *Concord* carrying John Randolph of Roanoke to Russia, continued 1833–1837, as second officer of the New York Navy Yard; 1842–1843, as commandant of the New York Navy Yard; 1846, from New York on the propriety of an increase of naval steamships, continued, 1847, aboard the *Mississippi*, commanding the Home Squadron at Vera Cruz, continued, 1848–1849, on special duty at New York superintending construction of ocean mail steamers; 1847, commanding the Home Squadron aboard the *Mississippi* at Vera Cruz, Tuxpan, Tabasco; 1848, commanding Home Squadron aboard the frigate *Cumberland;* log, 1832, of the *Concord;* record book, 1843–1844, containing minutes of conferences with native chiefs and of proceeding of councils of naval officers, as commander of the Africa Squadron; also notes of events at Cape Palmas involving difficulties between American settlers and native tribes; essay on the Society for the Colonization of Free People of Color and settlements established by the Society; letters, private, involving either colonization or aspects of the cruise.

A small collection of printed general orders, 1863–1865, Admiral John A. Dahlgren to the South Atlantic Blockading Squadron, is also included in this collection of Rodgers Family Papers.

Purchased.

1209
Order of United American Mechanics. Fredonia Council, No. 52 (Philadelphia, Pa.)   Records, 1850–1857.   (1 v.)

The Order of United American Mechanics was founded in 1845 for the protection and encouragement of workmen and the providing of relief funds.

Records of the Fredonia Council, located in West Philadelphia, of the Order of United American Mechanics.

Purchased.

1210

Stackhouse, William.   **Diaries, 1863–1865.**   **(3 v.)**

Diaries kept by William Stackhouse during his period of service with Company B, 119th Pennsylvania Volunteers, 1863–1865.

Gift of Mrs. Lilie Wilson and Charles S. Stackhouse.

1211

Thompson, Sarah, b. 1764.   **Commonplace book, 1782–1849. (1 v.)**

Commonplace book of Sarah Thompson, 1782–1785; notes by Rebecca Robinson; and miscellaneous genealogical notes on the Thompson, Robinson and Dunn families, 1784–1841.

Gift of John W. Cadbury.

1212

Union Burial Ground Society (Philadelphia, Pa.) Papers, 1827–1889.   **(3 v.)**

Records of owners of lots and of internments in the Union Burial Ground.

Gift of Mrs. A. Merrill Redding.

1213

United States. Marine Corps.   **Flight logbooks, 1919–1939. (10 v.)**

Purchased.

1214

United States. Marine Corps.   **Papers, 1811–1848.**   **(51 items.)**

Payrolls and size rolls of the Marine Corps.
Purchased.

1215

Vollmer, Charles.   **Ledger, 1860–1864.**   **(1 v.)**

Charles Vollmer was a Philadelphia cabinetmaker.
Business and personal accounts with description of a trip to Paris.
Gift of Mrs. F.E. Gramm.

1216
Wheeler, George.   Papers, 1900–1940.   (6 linear ft.)

Notes on Pine Grove and Schuylkill County, Pennsylvania canals and railroads, and Indian Wars.
Gift of Mrs. George Wheeler.

1217
Young Republican Club of the Twenty-Second Ward (Philadelphia, Pa.)   Minute book, 1892–1912.   (1 v.)

Minute book including correspondence, lists of members, bylaws, rules for Board of Governors, and miscellaneous accounts for the Young Republican Club of the Twenty-Second Ward located in Germantown.
Gift of Francis D. Brinton.

1218
Atlanta **(ship).   Invoice book, 1809.   (1 v.)**

The first part of this volume contains invoices of goods shipped on an unidentified schooner, records of sales. The second part lists the wares shipped on board the schooner Atlanta, with notes on the sale of the goods, and of purchases made in Puerto Rico. Both ships sailed from the Port of Philadelphia.

1219
**Atkinson, William B. (William Biddle), 1832–1909.
Notes on lectures, 1850.   (3 v.)**

Three small notebooks containing notes on British literature, religion and Italian.

1220
**Bailey, Gilbert Swartzlander, b. 1897.   Collection, 1897–1940.
(4 linear ft.)**

School notebooks, 1897–1940, of Gilbert S. Bailey while attending A.D. Bache School, Central High School, School of Pedagogy, Wharton School, Crozer Seminary and Temple University. Correspondence while in the Army, 1918, as well as minutes for the Junior Baptist Young Peoples Union (of Trinity Church), 1913, the Fifth Baptist Church, 1925, and the State Sabbath School Convention complete the collection. Also included is a series of baseball cards.
Gift of Mrs. Gilbert S. Bailey, 1943.

1221
Bedford, Isaac.   Papers, 1827–1846.   (ca. 300 items.)

Miscellaneous real estate papers, bills, and receipts, giving information on income from and improvements on properties owned by Isaac Bedford; some papers of Andrew McBride are also included documenting the building of a factory in Morrisville.

1221A
Bell, Richard, 1780–1866.   Diary, 1818–1827.   (1 v.)

Diary of Richard Bell kept on his voyage to America and during his residence in Delaware.
Typescript.
Gift of Malcolm A. MacQueen.

1222
Bentley, David.   Receipt book, 1822–1857.   (1 v.)

David Bentley was a Philadelphia coppersmith and regulator of weights and measures.

1223
St. Andrews Episcopal Church. Berean Society (Philadelphia, Pa.)
Minutes, 1823–1828.   (1 v.)

The Berean Society managed a Sunday School for boys under the direction of St. Andrews Episcopal Church.

1224
Decree of the Estate of Voisin of Argillieres, 1574.   (1 v.)

1225
Bogert, Judith.   Memoranda book, 1842–1847.   (1 v.)

Small notebook recording the expenses and income of Miss Bogert.

1226
Brayton, Annie Hare Powel.   Collection, 1681–1799.
(124 items.)

Deeds, 1681–1789, surveys and maps, 1683–1799, of the Philadelphia area.
Gift of Annie Hare Powel Brayton, 1943.

1227

Brissot de Warville, J.-P. (Jacques-Pierre), 1754–1793.   *Constitution de la republique de Pensylvanie, 1776.*   (1 v.)

History of the constitution of Pennsylvania adopted in 1776.

One section of the volume contains a translation of these essays into Italian.

These essays were published in Brissot de Warville' *Bibliotheque de Philosophie du Legislateur* (Berlin, 1782).

1228

Britannia (ship).   **Mustering book, 1773.**   (1 v.)

This record book was kept by Captain James Peters and contains a list of passengers brought by him on the *Britannia* from Rotterdam to Philadelphia. Accounts of the freight and head charges, and signatures of the passengers, most of whom were German, are included.

Gift of Deborah Fisher Wharton, 1876.

1229

Brown, Beulah.   **Book of verse, 1811.**   (1 v.)

1230

Brown family.   **Papers, 1742–1810.**   (15 v.)

Commonplace books of Elijah and Mary Brown containing articles and poems, chiefly from contemporary newspapers. A few letters and some material directly relate to Charles Brockden Brown are included.

Finding aid available.

1231

Brown, John.   **Memorandum book, 1762–1763.**   (1 v.)

Accounts of prize money paid, records of privateering enterprises, costs of shipping, of provisions.

Purchased, Fund, 1930.

1232

Browning Society of Philadelphia (Pa.)   **Records, 1903–1925.** (100 items.)

The Browning Society was formed in 1887 to promote the reading and study of the works of Robert Browning. It disbanded in 1922.

Minutes, cashbooks and clippings, 1903–1925.

Gift of the Browning Society through the kindness of Mrs. E.M. Ralston, 1943.

1233
Butler, Samuel Worcester.   Record book, 1849–1858.   (1 v.)

Medical records of births attended by Dr. Samuel Worcester Butler, a physician practicing in Burlington, N.J.

1234
Butler, Thomas, 1812–1870.   Memorandum book, 1844.   (1 v.)

Thomas Butler was a Philadelphia tinsmith.
Gift of Thomas Butler, 1941.

1235
Cadwalader, John, 1805–1879.   Account book, 1826–1840.   (1 v.)

Account book of John Cadwalader on legal matters.
Gift of S. Moyerman, 1941.

1236
Carr, Josephine.   Invitation and address book, 1888–1893.   (1 v.)

Notes on invitations received and a list of the names of prominent Philadelphia debutantes.
Gift of Miss Josephine Carr, 1914.

1237
Centennial Exhibition. Women's Centennial Committee.
Register of Visitors.   (1 v.)

Register of visitors to the Women's Pavilion of the Centennial Exhibition held in Philadelphia, 1876.
Gift of the Germantown Historical Society, 1931.

1238
Chambers, James.   Notebook, 1834–1841.   (1 v.)

Notebook containing essays, poems and puzzles of James Chambers of Philadelphia.

1239
Chandler, Mary Ann.   Notebooks, 1857–1858.   (3 v.)

School notes, poetry, essays and a list of pupils with their attendance recorded by Mary Ann Chandler.

1240

Chester County (Pa.)   Deed book, 1716–1730.   (1 v.)

1241

Cheyney, Thomas, b. 1731.   Docket book, 1779–1805.   (1 v.)

Docket of Thomas Cheyney, Chester County justice of the peace, includes records of cases brought before Thomas Cheyney and of the marriages performed by him.

1242

Chinese characters, 1825 and watercolors, 1891.   (2 v.)

Manuscript depicting the art of writing the Chinese language with the English equivalents, and a collection of watercolors illustrating Chinese system of justice and the customs of the country.

Gift of Richard J. Dunghier, 1873; and Mrs. R. J. C. Walker, 1904.

1243

United States Customs House (Philadelphia, Pa.)   Papers, 1882–1883.   (1 v.)

Records of arrival of passenger vessels in the Port of Philadelphia, lists of dutiable goods imported with amounts of duty paid.

1244

United States. Army. Commissariat.   Account book, 1863–1865.   (1 v.)

Commissary account book showing the purchase of provisions, clothing.

Purchased, Dreer Fund, 1938.

1245

Clark, Adele C.   Autograph book, 1888.   (1 v.)

Gift of Mrs. M. Van Gelder, 1941.

1246

United States Constitution Sesqui-Centennial Celebration. Papers, 1937.   (3 linear ft.)

Invitations; tickets; programs; text of radio address delivered by Mayors S. Davis Wilson and Fiorella H. La Guardia; essay on Pelatiah Webster by George W. Mingus; and similar items issued by the Pennsylvania Constitution Commemorative Committee.

1247
Cottrell, J.F.   **Receipt book, 1842–1848.**   **(1 v.)**

J.F. Cottrell was a Lancaster County ironmaster.

1248
Coxe, Robert D.   *Legal Philadelphia,* **1908.**   **(1 v.)**

Original manuscript of Robert D. Coxe's *Legal Philadelphia* (Philadelphia, 1908).
Gift of the publisher, William J. Campbell, 1920.

1249
Craft, James.   **Diary, 1796–1808.**   **(2 v.)**

Diary of James Craft of Burlington, N.J., chiefly recording weather conditions. There are some notes on current happenings.

1250
Curtin family.   **Clippings, 1894.**   **300 items.**

Largely clippings on the death of Andrew Gregg Curtin; miscellaneous clippings collected by Dr. Robert G. Curtin.
Gift of Miss Mary Curtin, 1935.

1251
Curtis, Cyrus Hermann Kotzschmar, 1850–1933.
Papers, 1912–1938.   **(667 items.)**

Personal letters to and from Cyrus H.K. Curtis, Philadelphia publisher. Many relate to the affairs of the Curtis Publishing Company and to the *Public Ledger*.

1252
Daix, Augustus F.   **Papers, 1889–1914.**   **(11 v.)**

Letterbooks, 1893, 1898–1914; order book, 1903; and real estate ledger, 1889–1896, pertaining to property in Philadelphia.

1253
Dallas, George Mifflin, 1792–1864.   **"Twelfth Night Ball," 1813.**
(1 v.)

Verse entitled "Twelfth Night Ball", dedicated to Mr. and Mrs. Thomas Willing.
Gift of Mrs. Thomas Willing.

1254
Darain, M.   Essay, 1762.   (1 v.)

Essay entitled "Idée générale de tous les gouvernemens de l'Europe."
Purchased, C. Percy de la Roche Fund, 1935.

1255
Daughters of the Founders and Patriots of America. Pennsylvania Chapter.   History, 1902–1939.   (1 v.)

History of the Pennsylvania Chapter of the Daughter of the Founders and Patriots of America.
Gift of Mrs. J. Wistar Evans.

1256
Davis, Charles H.   *Metallic money*, 1890.   (1 v.)

Treatise on the principles of banking and other monetary transactions.
Gift of Charles H. Davis, 1902.

1257
Cuesta, Josefa Espinosa de.   Correspondence, 1826–1842. (400 items.)

Letters addressed to Josefa Espinosa de Cuesta, a resident of Philadelphia, from relatives in Europe and South America.

1258
Philadelphia and Camden Bridge and Terminal Company (Pa.) Delaware River Bridge Survey, 1916.   (1 v.)

A preliminary report on the feasibility of bridging the Delaware River with drawings of proposed bridge and road map of the area.

1259
Dobler, Daniel, b. 1803.   Journal, 1819–1844.   (1 v.)

Daniel Dobler was an itinerant German Lutheran evangelist who travelled throughout Pennsylvania, New Jersey, Delaware and Maryland.
Journal kept while travelling mentioning anecdotes of the men met and manners of the Pennsylvania Dutch at the time.
In German.
Purchased, Elise Willing Balch Fund, 1940.

1260
Dobson, James.   **Collection, 1890–1920.**   **(2 v. and 70 items.)**

Letterpress copies of the letters of James Dobson, a Philadelphia carpet and plush manufacturer, and other correspondence on his business, investments, and personal affairs.
Gift of Mrs. Elizabeth Dobson Altemus Eastman, 1941.

1261
Drayton, William Henry, 1742–1779.   *The Confederation of the United States,* [1776].   (1 v.)

Manuscript copy.
Gift of Brinton Coxe, 1898.

1262
Ebeling, Christopher Daniel, 1741–1817.   **Histories, 1840, 1883.** **(2 v.)**

Manuscripts of *History of Delaware* 1799 and *History of Pennsylvania by Christopher Daniel Ebeling.*
Transcript made by John Eberle, ca. 1840, and Carl Ernst Bohen, 1883.
Gift of John A. McAllister, 1880; and Brinton Coxe, 1889.

1263
Ellis, Joseph.   **Notebook, 1837.**   (1 v.)

Notebook used for problems in arithmetic.

1264
Emerson, Daniel H.   **Journal, 1837–1868.**   (1 v.)

Journal of Daniel H. Emerson, includes lists of marriages, 1836–1853, of baptisms, 1837–1852, and of funerals, 1842–1852 while serving as a Congregational and Presbyterian minister in Northborough, Mass., 1836–1840; East Whiteland, Chester County, 1841–1845; York, 1846–1855; and St. George's, Del., 1855–1861.
Purchased, 1892.

1265
Esher family.   **Collection, 1794–1884.**   **(10 items.)**

Deeds of property belonging to the Esher family of Philadelphia and commissions to John Dunlap.
Gift of Mrs. M.H. Esher Kromer.

1266
Etting, Gratz.   Notes, 1818.   (1 v.)

Notes taken by Gratz Etting on Charles Smith's legal opinions on the land laws of Pennsylvania, citing numerous cases.
Gift of Harrold E. Gillingham, 1935.

1267
Evans, Lewis, 1700?-1756.   "A Brief account of Pennsylvania," 1753.
(1 v.)

Lewis Evans, in a letter to Richard Peters, gives an account of Pennsylvania in answer to some queries of a gentleman in Europe, 1753.
Photostatic copy also available.
Gift of Dr. George Fox.

1268
Everett, Edward, 1794–1865.   Speech, 1864.   (1 v.)

Patriotic speech to the Committee on Naval Affairs of the House of Representatives, March 12, 1864.
Given by him to Mrs. Julia K. MacAllister for the benefit of the Sanitary Fair. Gift of Miss Clementina R. Plumsted, 1864.

1269
Fahnestock family.   Papers, 1849–1873.   (11 v.)

Papers of the Fahnestock family comprise: George W. Fahnestock, diary, 1863–1867; Mrs. Anna M. Fahnestock diary, 1869–1873; newspaper clippings on the burning of the steamboat *United States,* 1868; executors' account of the estate of George W. Fahnestock, 1868; notes on the Fahnestock and the Wolff families.
Gift of C.H. Wolff, Mrs. Francis K. Wolff, and Bernard Bunting Wolff, 1939, 1941.

1270
Faris, John Thomson, 1871–1949.   Papers, n.d.   (2 v.)

Two unpublished books written by John Thomson Faris : *He Financed the War : a Life of Robert Morris* and *Steamboat Coming,* a history of the steamboat in the United States.
Gift of John T. Faris, 1943.

1271
Episcopal Female Tract Society of Philadelphia (Pa.)
Minutes, 1816–1834. (1 v.)

Minutes of an organization of Episcopal women dedicated to publishing and distributing religious tracts.
Gift of Mrs. DeRenne, 1886.

1272
Fitzsimons, Thomas, 1741–1811. **Papers, 1793–1800.** (2 v.)

Miscellaneous business papers and letters addressed to Thomas Fitzsimons. Roll of a militia company commanded by him and a book of receipts for money paid by Fitzsimons when he was commissioner for settling the claims of British subjects against the United States.

1273
Foulke, John. **Papers, 1769–1798.** (3 v.)

Receipt book of Judah and Mary Foulke, 1769–1798; receipt book, 1787–1796, of John Foulke, physician; manuscript of an oration on longevity delivered by John Foulke before the American Philosophical Society, n.d.

1274
United States. Bureau of the Mint. **George M. Fox Memorial volume, 1889.** (1 v.)

Memorial volume presented to George M. Fox on the occasion of his retirement from the Mint.
Gift of James E. Gibson, 1943.

1275
Franklin, Benjamin, 1706–1790. *Le Science du bonhomme Richard,* **1778** (1 v.)

Includes excerpts from Franklin's interrogations before the House of Commons, 1776; the constitution of Pennsylvania, 1776; and extracts from the treaty between France and the United States.
Translated and copied from the Morin edition (Paris, 1778).
Gift of Dr. Joseph J. Rosengarten, 1908.

1276
Franks, Rebecca. **Letter, 1781 Aug. 10.** (1 v.)

Letter of Rebecca Franks describing New York society.
Gift of Jacob Ritter, 1857.

1277
Free Society of Traders.   **Obligation to Nicholas More, 1685.**
(1 v.)

The Free Society of Traders was the first stock company to operate in Philadelphia. Although it was not a monopoly, the company was given extensive trade privileges in Pennsylvania. Nicholas More, a medical doctor of London, was one of the incorporators.

1278
Anonymous.   **Notes, 1688–1754.**   (2 v.)

Notes on the Friends' School consisting of extracts from Friends' records and biographical notes from Robert Proud's *History of Pennsylvania.*

1279
Du Roy l'Engagement (frigate).   **Journal, 1781–1782.**   (1 v.)

Journal of the frigate, *Du Roy l'Engagement,* which fought in the West Indies and Hudson Bay, 1781–1782, during the Revolutionary War.

1280
Gettysburg National Military Park (Pa.)   **Papers, 1893–1913.**
(1 v.)

Letters mainly addressed to Colonel John P. Nicholson on the attempt to force the Gettysburg Commission to change the name of United States Avenue to Hunt Avenue.
Gift of Colonel John P. Nicholson, 1913.
Some letters are photostatic copies.

1281
Gibbons family.   **Papers, 1760–1837.**   (27 items.)

Papers of a Chester County family: diary of James Gibbons, 1760 1769; school account books, 1781–1783; medical account book, 1836–1837.
Gift of Mrs. Isaac R. Davis, 1943.

1282
Gilpin, Thomas, 1776–1853.   **Papers, 1840.**   (3 v.)

Autobiographical account of Thomas Gilpin, 1728–1778, and *Memorial and reminiscences in private life* by Hannah Logan Smith with additions made by Thomas Gilpin in 1840.

1283
Gist, Thomas, b. 1744.   Journal, 1758–1759.   (1 v.)

Thomas Gist was taken prisoner in 1758 by the Wyandot tribe and escaped after a year of captivity.
The journal contains details of Indian life and treatment of captives.
Photostatic copy.

1284
Gorham family.   Genealogical records, 1550–1856.   (1 v.)

Genealogy of the descendants of James Gorham and Agnes Bernington Gorham.

1285
Gottschall, Jacob.   Medical notebook, 1825–1839.   (1 v.)

1286
Gould, Walter G., 1829–1893.   Autograph book, 1851–1852.
(1 v.)

Autographs of Officers of the Hungarian Army captured in Turkey, including Lajos Kossuth.
Signatures in Hungarian and English.

1287
Gregg, Lizzie R.   Notebook, 1883.   (1 v.)

English grammar and composition notebook of Lizzie R. Gregg, a schoolgirl from Cressona.
Gift of Francis D. Brinton, 1941.

1288
Verlenden family.   Collection, 1703–1863.

Papers on the Serrill, Pearson and Verlenden families.
Gift of Mrs. Samuel Blair Griffith and Edith Verlenden Paschall in memory of Mary Verlenden.

1289
Hamilton, Abigail Francis, 1744/5–1798.   Domestic receipts,
1784–1798.   (1 v.)

Abigail Francis Hamilton at this time was the widow of Andrew Hamilton.
Gift of H.C. Kuhn, 1943.

1290
Phillips, John.   Land book, 1784–1795.   (1 v.)

Land book of John Phillips and William Harrison giving information on sales, taxes, and improvements on lands in Pennsylvania and Virginia.
Gift of Harrold E. Gillingham, 1943.

1291
Hartshorne, Joseph, 1779–1850.   Malay-French dictionary, 1807.
(1 v.)

Gift of Dr. Edward Hartshorne, 1880.

1292
Herrick, Cheesman Abiah, 1866–1956.   Papers, 1933–1942.   (3 v.)

Program and letters about a dinner given in honor of Dr. Charles A. Herrick, 1933; address *William Penn High School for Girls, Some Early Beginnings,* and letters commenting thereon; and author's copy of *White Servitude in Pennsylvania,* and letters relating to the book.
Gift of Cheesman A. Herrick, 1942.

1293
Hight, William.   Letterbook, 1795–1796.   (1 v.)

William Hight was a Philadelphia merchant.
Gift of Mrs. Arnold Talbot, 1942.

1294
Crispin, M. Jackson, 1875–1953.   *Holme memorial,* 1624–1695.
(1 v.)

Commemorating the tercentenary, 1624–1924, of the birth of Captain Thomas Holme, collected and arranged by Thomas Butler at the request of M. Jackson Crispin.
Gift of M. Jackson Crispin, 1927.

1295
Kimber & Conrad and Johnson & Warner.
Subscription book, 1762.   (1 v.)

List of subscribers to the proposal of Kimber & Conrad and Johnson & Warner for publishing *A Large Map of Pennsylvania* by Reading Howell, 1762.

1296
Independence Hall (Philadelphia, Pa.)   Deposit book, 1873–1896.
(1 v.)

Deposit book stubs provide a list of donations, 1873–1896.

1297
Indian treaties and deeds, 1683–1756.   (2 v.)

Treaties and deeds for Pennsylvania.
Contemporary copies.

1298
Jennison, William, b. 1757.   Diary, 1776–1780.   (1 v.)

William Jennison was a lieutenant of the Marines, 1776, served with the Army later in the same year, and with the Navy, 1777–1780.
Diary kept while serving on board the ship *Boston,* giving brief description of his earlier service.

1299
Johnson, Jesse.   Diary, 1861–1864.   (1 v.)

Jesse Johnson's Civil War diary kept while serving with Company L, 2nd Regiment of the West Virginia Volunteer Cavalry. Johnson fought at Lewisburg, Sinking Creek, Wytheville, and Princeton, Va. Captured, but subsequently exchanged, he served in Washington, D.C. until mustered out.
Gift of Everlyn Abraham.

1300
Jones, Horatio Gates, 1822–1893.   *Early history of Roxborough and Manayunk,* 1855.   (1 v.)

Facts and traditions about the early settlement of Roxborough and Manayunk.

1301
Jones family.   Papers, 1681–1861.   (2 linear ft.)

Correspondence, accounts, business papers, legal papers and miscellaneous materials pertaining to the Jones family. In particular are papers for Owen Jones, Jr., merchant, 1768–1802; Jones and Foulke, merchants; Jonathan Jones, lawyer, 1780–1830; legal papers of Jonathan and Owen Jones, and Owen Jones, lawyer and member of congress, 1820's-1861.

1302
Justice, Jefferson, b. 1840.   Papers, 1862–1865.   (200 items.)

Papers of Jefferson Justice, regimental quartermaster, 100th Regiment Infantry, Pennsylvania Volunteers, on supplies issued to the regiment.
Gift of Eugene Klein, 1943.

1303
Almanacs, 1816–1820.   (2 v.)

Benjamin and Thomas Kite's *Town and Country Almanac* and a partial agricultural almanac published by Solomon W. Conrad of Philadelphia. Both almanacs contain miscellaneous notes and accounts.

1304
Keim, George May, 1805–1861.   Collection, 1814–1841.   (2 v.)

Copies of the *Star Spangled Banner* by Francis Scott Key and of *Home Sweet Home* by John Howard Payne, autographed by the authors.
Gift to George May Keim by authors; given to the Historical Society by Keim's heirs, 1876.

1305
Leach, Josiah Granville, 1842–1922.   Diaries, 1876–1920.   (39 v.)

Josiah Granville Leach was a Philadelphia lawyer, genealogist, and historian.
His diaries contain entries relating to his business affairs and to the social and political life of the period.

1306
Lee, William Atkinson, 1778–1848.   Account book, 1822–1848. (1 v.)

Accounts kept by William A. Lee of a select Philadelphia seminary for boys and girls which he ran under various names at various location within Philadelphia.
Gift of James E. Gibson, 1943.

1307
McCarter, William.   "My life in the army," 1862.   (11 v.)

Notes of William McCarter's experiences in the Civil War and accounts of the campaigns in which he participated.

1308

Martin, John Hill, 1823–1906.   **Papers, 1789–1872.**   (13 v.)

John Hill Martin practiced law in Philadelphia's Orphan Court and the Commonwealth's Admiralty Court from 1844 to 1881. He was the legal editor of the *Philadelphia Intelligencer* from 1857, a member of the Historical Society of Pennsylvania, and an inveterate compiler of lists.

Manuscript lists of names of *The Bench and Bar of Philadelphia, Chester and Delaware Counties, Pennsylvania, with other lists of Public Functionaries in the State and in the United States; The Miscellaneous Legal Literature of the Philadelphia Bar,* 1884; and the manuscript of the history of the town of Chester.

Gift of John Hill Martin, 1880, and Mrs. Edward S. Sayres, 1923.

1309

Miles, E.   **Abstracts, 1841.**   (1 v.)

Extracts from Mile's historical and statistical description of the Royal Naval Service of England and data on the building and extension of the United States Navy.

Gift of Rev. Joseph Henry Dubbs, 1876.

1310

Coxe, Brinton, 1833–1892.   **Collection, (1743–1876) 1880.**   (3 v.)

Histories on New Jersey including the manuscript of *The Note Maker Noted and the Observer Observed Upon . . . , A Pocket Commentary of the First Settlers of New Jersey . . . ,* and an account of the history of New Jersey, 1663–1775, written ca. 1880.

Gift of Brinton Coxe, 1884.

1311

Gibon, John H.   **Histories, n.d.**   (3 v.)

Histories of California, 1534–1850; Kansas, 1857; and of Mexico and Texas, 1845.

Gift of Colonel J.P. Nicholson, 1896.

1312

Parrish, Morris Longstreth, 1867–1944.   **Collection, 1833–1865.** (18 v.)

Scrapbooks containing clippings, engravings, business cards, and postcards; photograph albums; and letterbooks, 1833–1865 of Philadelphia merchant Richard Price about friends, family, local events and society.

Gift of Morris L. Parrish, 1943.

1313

Pennsylvania.   Papers, 1792–1907.   (3 v.)

Records of land warrants entered in 1792, bound in a volume, *Acts of the Assembly of Pennsylvania*; *A brief account of the Province of Pennsylvania lately granted . . . to William Penn*; parchment containing the printed constitution of Pennsylvania as adopted in Philadelphia in 1873, autographed by the delegates; and Samuel W. Pennypacker's manuscript of his *Desecration and profanation of the Pennsylvania capital*, ca. 1907.

A brief account of the Province of Pennsylvania lately granted . . . to William Penn hand copied, 1882.

Gift of Francis Rawle, 1913; E.C. Knight, 1874; and Samuel W. Pennypacker.

1314

Pennsylvania Hospital (Philadelphia, Pa.)   Papers, (1817–1818) 1895.

Visitor's book, Christ Healing the Sick, 1817–1818; account book of the monies received by the hospital; reports from the Board of Managers; letters to and from Benjamin West; papers on the publication of the history of Pennsylvania Hospital, 1895; and material on the controversy between Dr. William A. Armstrong and Dr. Thomas G. Morton.

Benjamin West letters copied.

Gift of Dr. William A. Armstrong, 1915, and Dr. Melvin M. Franklin, 1920.

1315

Pennsylvania. Militia. Philadelphia Associators.   Muster roll, ca. 1776.   (1 v.)

Muster roll of the Philadelphia Associators, organized mainly of merchants in order to protect Philadelphia and the city's commercial interests.

1316

Philadelphia (Pa.). Committee on Markets.   Minutes, 1829–1831. (1 v.)

1317

United States. Selective Service System (Philadelphia, Pa.)
Papers, 1918–1919.   (1 v.)

Papers of the United States Selective Service System during World War I.

Gift of John F. Lewis.

1318
Powers, Frederick Perry, d. 1927.   Papers, 1912.   (2 v.)

Manuscripts of *Old Pennsylvania on the Trail of Washington,* 1776–1794, and *Places of Worship,* both volumes contain photographs.
Gift of Mrs. Charles P. Turner, 1912.

1319
Scott, John M.   Court docket, 1819–1865.   (1 v.)

Court docket of John Morin Scott, lawyer and mayor of Philadelphia, with entries for Scott's son, Lewis Allaire Scott, who joined his father's law office in 1841.

1320
Sears, John V.   Essay, 1873.   (1 v.)

Essay entitled "Mound builders of the Missouri" on the terrain of the Missouri Valley, including a brief history of the Lewis and Clark expedition with biographical information on Meriwether Lewis, and a description of the various Indian tribes in the West. This essay was read before the Historical Society of Pennsylvania.
Gift of John V. Sears, 1902.

1321
Ships' register, 1741–1742.   (1 v.)

Register containing record of ships, where built, registered, names of owners and masters, manifests of cargoes; name of port not indicated.

1322
Solis-Cohen, Solomon, 1857–1948.   Papers, 1933–1943.
(2.5 linear ft.)

Solomon Solis-Cohen was a medical doctor, served as Chairman of the Board of Education for Philadelphia, and was active in the Zionist movement in the United States and many other philanthropic endeavors.

Correspondence, letters, petitions, invitations, broadsides, and programs relative to Solomon Solis-Cohen's activities. Much of the material deals with Philadelphia teachers' salaries, the Zionist movement in America, and World War II. The programs are generally for performances by the Philadelphia Orchestra.

1323
Anonymous.   South Street brief of title, 1671–1869.   (1 v.)

Brief of title to a piece of land on the south side of South Street in Philadelphia.
Gift of John H.L. Houston, 1917.

1324
Stewart, Walter, 1756–1796.   Orderly book, 1780.   (1 v.)

Orderly book of Walter Stewart for the Second Pennsylvania Regiment, headquartered at Morristown, N.J., notes, regimental orders, names of officers, and incidents of the Revolutionary War.

1325
Stratton, Joseph.   Collection, 1796–1915.   (89 items.)

Miscellaneous deeds to Philadelphia properties.
Gift of Joseph Stratton, 1943.

1326
Swift, John, 1720–1802.   Memoranda, 1742.   (1 v.)

Memoranda, accounts, and other notes made by John Swift, an early settler of Pennsylvania kept in his copy of Rider's *British Merlin* almanac for 1742.

1327
Talbot, Jeremiah.   Muster roll, 1776.   (1 v.)

Jeremiah Talbot's muster roll for his division under the command of William Irvine, First Pennsylvania Regiment.
Gift of the Vermont Historical Society, 1943.

1328
Union Canal Company.   Records, 1791–1922.   (6 linear ft.)

Correspondence, 1820–1922, for William Lehman and B.B. Lehman, both of whom served as general supervisors and engineers for the Union Canal Company; miscellaneous business records, 1822–1887; letterbooks, 1852–1891; letterbook of B.B. Lehman, 1849–1877; business books, 1822–1858; annual reports, 1791–1869; maps, charts, photographs, and diagrams.
Gift of George M. Lehman, 1943.

1329
United States. Army. Order book, 1838. (1 v.)

Order book for the 2d Brigade Army south of the Withlacoochie, Fla. Gift of Mrs. Arnold Talbot.

1330
United States. Marine Corps. Aviators' flight logbooks, 1919–1939. (10 v.)

Logbooks kept by members of the U.S. Marine Corps Air Force. Entries show number of hours flown, types of plane used.

1331
Essays on law, crime, and punishment. (1 v.)

Gift of Mrs. Juliet C. Walker, 1941.

1332
United States. Army. General orders, 1813–1815. (2 v.)

General orders from the adjutant general's office and from headquarters at Camp Marcus Hook, Philadelphia, and New York. Accounts of Army discipline, courts-martial.
Gift of Dr. W.A.N. Doland, 1923.

1333
Zschokke, Johann Heinrich Daniel, 1771–1848. *Settlement of Maryland*, 1850. (1 v.)

A romantic and fictional narrative by Johann Heinrich Daniel Zschokke written in the form of letters to Cecil Calvert, Lord Baltimore.
Gift of Edward S. Sayres, 1924.

1334
Adjuvant Horse Company. Records, 1838–1924. (2 v. and 28 items.)

The Adjuvant Horse Company was a Philadelphia company organized in 1838 to facilitate the recovery of stolen horses and the detection of thieves. It incorporated in 1865 and dissolved in 1924.
Minutes, 1838–1924; rolls, 1872–1924; and other records.
Gift of W. Austin Yerkes, 1944.

1335
Allen, Nathaniel.   **Ledgers, 1710–1752.**   **(2 v.)**

Nathaniel Allen was a Philadelphia merchant.
Gift of John William Potts, 1886.

1336
American Red Cross. Pennsylvania-Delaware Division.
Records, 1917–1919.   **(240 items.)**

Divisional reports, 1917–1918; letters; bulletins, 1917–1919, describing the activities of the Pennsylvania-Delaware Division of the American Red Cross during the First World War.

1337
Baltimore and Philadelphia Steamship Company.
Records, 1844–1936.

The Baltimore and Philadelphia Steamship Company was chartered in 1844 to provide steamboat service between Baltimore and Philadelphia via the Delaware and Chesapeake Canal. The Company ceased operation in 1935.
Minutes, 1844–1934; financial records; letters; reports and contracts, 1848–1936; reports to the Interstate Commerce Commission, 1930–1935; and reports to the Maryland-Philadelphia Service Commission, 1933–1935.
Gift of Miss Mary Helen Cadwalader and Miss Sophia Cadwalader, 1942.

1338
Barton, George Washington.   **Papers, 1841–1850.**   **(3 items)**

Manuscript of George Washington Barton include: journal of a voyage from New York, N.Y. to San Francisco, Cal. in the *Elsinore*, Captain Thomas S. Conden, 1850; address, *Ancestral Vanity*, delivered before the William Fisk Institute, 1841; and a manuscript entitled *The Age in Which We Live*.

1339
Biddle, Thomas, 1776–1857.   **Stock certificates, 1804–1866.**
(92 items.)

Stock certificates issued to Thomas Biddle. The businesses represented include canal, turnpike and bridge companies; railroads; banks; and insurance and mining companies.
Gift of Biddle-Whelen & Company.

1340
Brey, J.T.   Collection, 1697–1918.   (30 items.)

Deeds; marriage certificates of the Crossdale, Taylor, and Watson families; and charts of the Boker and Van Horn families.
Photostatic copies.
Gift of Mrs. J.T. Brey, 1942.

1341
Brown family.   Papers, 1693–1908.   (800 items.)

Letters on the education and career of Henry Armitt Brown; genealogical notes on the Armitt, Baker, Brown, Livezey, Robeson, and related families.
Gift of Mrs. Dorothy Burr Thompson, 1942.

1342
**Edmunds, Albert Joseph, 1857–1941.   Papers, 1850–1917.
(36 linear ft.)**

Albert Joseph Edmunds was a noted Biblical scholar and the cataloger of the Historical Society of Pennsylvania.
The collection includes: correspondence, 1867–1941, notebooks, diaries, 1874–1929, notes on religion, cults, ballads, writings, essays, poems, bills and receipts, and spiritual lectures.
The collection also includes correspondence to Benjamin Smith Lyman on vegetarianism while Lyman was in Japan.
Gift of Albert J. Edmunds.

1343
Fletcher, Thomas.   Letters, 1806–1855.   (275 items.)

Business letters to Thomas Fletcher, Philadelphia goldsmith and jeweler, some describing the affairs of the firms of Fletcher and Gardiner, 1810–1831, and of Fletcher and Bennett, 1839.

1344
Freas family.   Papers, 1754–1889.   (75 items.)

Papers of the Freas family of Whitemarsh Township, Montgomery County including: bonds, indentures, deeds, surveys, wills and papers of administration.
Gift of Alice B. Poopes, 1940.

1345
The Historical Society of Pennsylvania.   Correspondence, 1926.
(600 items.)

Correspondence on the luncheon given to the crown prince and princess of Sweden by the Council of the Historical Society of Pennsylvania and by the Swedish Colonial Society, June 2, 1926.
Gift of Miss M. Atherton Leach, 1931.

1346
Howell family.   Papers, 1688–1886.   (114 items.)

Letters and papers of the Gibbons, 1806–1834; Howell, 1811–1815; Richardson, 1834–1848; and related families. These include a letterbook of Rebecca Richardson, New York, 1688–1689.
Gift of Josephine R. Howell, 1942.

1347
Landon-Shattuck family.   Papers, 1849–1890.   (101 items.)

Family letters, most of them written to or by Mrs. Eliza Hinckly Landon and Mrs. M.M. Shattuck.
Purchased, 1942.

1348
Laux, James B.   Collection, 1757–1816.   (12 items.)

Materials on the French and Indian War including George Croghan's journal to Presque Isle, 1760; letter of Croghan and of Jacob Arndt, 1757; materials of the Revolutionary War period, including letters of Croghan, 1778, of Sol Jennings, 1778, petition of James Craig, 1775, and will of George Taylor, 1781; post Revolutionary period letters include Jacob Arndt, Jr., 1804, P. Doddridge, 1816, Thomas Jefferson, 1816, and Colonel Stephen Rochenfontaine, 1795–1796.
Gift of James B. Laux, 1920.
Photostatic copies.

1349A
Leach, Frank Willing, 1855–1917.   Papers, 1914–1915.
(1,000 items.)

Letters and notes compiled by Frank Willing Leach when writing "Pennsylvania in the United States Senate," a series of articles that appeared

in the Sunday *North American,* 1914; letters from descendants of the senators; genealogical notes of their families.
Gift of Miss M. Atherton Leach, 1944.

1349B
Leach, Frank Willing, 1855–1943.   Papers, 1914.   (300 items.)

Frank Willing Leach's notes, clippings, drafts, transcripts and some correspondence for research on his series of articles on duels, *Famous "Affairs of Honor" in America.*
Gift of Miss M. Atherton Leach, 1944.
Published in the *North American,* January 3 to April 25, 1915.

1350
Learned, Marion Dexter, 1857–1917.   Papers, 1524–1915.
(500 items.)

Papers and notes of Dr. Marion Dexter Learned, a professor at the University of Pennsylvania and a leader in societies interested in the study of German culture; diaries of members of the Learned family showing conditions in Europe in 1914.
Documents from German Archives are photographic copies.
Purchased, 1943.

1351
McCauley, Edward Yorke, 1827–1894.   Papers, 1840–1916.
(20 items.)

Certificates of appreciation presented to Daniel Smith McCauley, United States consul at Tripoli, 1841; commissions of Edward Yorke McCauley through the grades of midshipman to rear admiral; marriage certificate of Edward Yorke McCauley and Josephine Berkeley.
Gift of G.H. McCauley, 1943.

1352
McMichael, Clayton, 1844–1906.   Papers, 1861–1901.
(250 items.)

Clayton McMichael was the editor and proprietor of the *Philadelphia North American*; City Treasurer, 1898–1901; and Postmaster, 1902–1906.
These papers include: military correspondence, 1861–1865; papers relating to the take over of the City Treasurer's Office, 1897–1898; letters written to McMichael, 1872–1901; papers on the United States Mint in Philadelphia, 1872; papers on the office of postmaster, 1901; and clippings and speeches.
Gift of Mrs. Emory McMichael, 1944.

1353
Merion Cricket Club (Haverford, Pa.)   Papers, 1865–1923.
(10 v.)

Scrapbooks containing letters, announcements, photographs, and clippings on the activities of the Merion Cricket Club.
Gift of the estate of Edward S. Sayres, 1929.

1354
Mervine, William McKinley, 1874–1914.   Papers, 1688–1788.   (25 items.)

William McKinley Mervine was a Philadelphia genealogist and one of the Board of Managers of the Genealogical Society of Pennsylvania.
Records of Chesterfield Monthly Meeting, N.J., including minutes, 1685–1687; minutes of Women's meetings, 1688–1698, 1708–1712, 1756–1760; and certificates of renewal to Chesterfield Meeting, all relating to the Forman, Kelly, Van Horn, and Davies families.
Gift of Mrs. William Mervine, 1917.

1355
Pemberton family.   Correspondence, 1740–1787.   (3 v.)

Correspondence of Israel, James, John, and Mary Pemberton.
Copies; originals of many of these letters are in the Pemberton Papers. See collection #484.
Gift of the Friends Historical Association, 1941.

1356
Pennsylvania. National Guard. Infantry Regiment, 1st.
Records of Company D, 1861–1923.   (6 v.)

Letters, notices of musters, clippings, and other records on the Philadelphia militia regiment that took part in suppressing the labor troubles at Hazelton in 1875 and at Pittsburgh in 1877, and which saw service as the 109th Regiment during World War I.
Gift of the estate of Edward S. Sayres, 1931.

1357
Philadelphia Bicycle Club (Philadelphia, Pa.)   Papers, 1882–1902.
(347 items and 10 v.)

Papers of the Philadelphia Bicycle Club including: minutes, 1895–1902; treasurer's accounts, dues books, 1890–1902; charter, bylaws and amend-

ments, 1885–1895; papers on the construction and repair of the clubhouse
and on the running expenses of the Club, 1886–1902.

Gift of Henry W. Wills, 1942.

1358
Philadelphia Bourse (Philadelphia, Pa.)   **Papers, 1891–1900.**   **(161**
items.)

The Philadelphia Bourse was a corporation formed in 1891 to protect
and further the business and commercial interests of the city. The Bourse
Building, was built to house exchanges, the Board of Trade, and similar
groups.

These papers relate to the organization of the Bourse Corporation and
to the erection of the Bourse Building. They are chiefly letters of John
Frederick Lewis, attorney for the corporation.

1359
Philadelphia Child Welfare Association.   **Papers, 1893–1933.**
(5 v.)

Minutes of the Philadelphia Juvenile Court and Probation Association,
1903–1917; minutes of the Philadelphia Child Welfare Association, 1917–1933;
constitution of the Philadelphia Juvenile Court and Probation Association;
bylaws of the Philadelphia Child Welfare Association; history of the House
of Detention, 1898–1923; Judge Staake remarks on the administration of the
Juvenile Court, 1908; correspondence regarding cooperation of the police
and the schools with the Court, 1906.

Gift, 1937.

1360
Philadelphia public building papers, 1860–1881.   **(19 items.)**

Ordinances and papers on the location of City Hall; reports of committees; and manuscript and corrected proofs of a history of City Hall.

1361
Pennsylvania. Philadelphia County Board of Assistance.
Papers, 1941.   **(2 linear ft.)**

Testimony before the Reviewing Board of the Philadelphia County
Board of Assistance on the appeals of 50 employees discharged for alleged
communist affiliation, 1941.

Typewritten transcripts.

Gift of James E. Gibson, 1943.

1362
United States. Selective Service System (Philadelphia, Pa.)
Records, 1917.   (50 items.)

Lists of men registered in the 51 local draft boards of Philadelphia, July, 1917.

1363
Philadelphia lawyers collection, 1847–1939.   (300 items.)

Miscellaneous collection of letters, most of them addressed to members of the law firm of [John F.] Lewis, [Francis] Adler and [Francis] Laws; letters addressed to the Poor Richard Club on conventions held in Philadelphia, 1926; and a folder of letters to L.C. Siner, Philadelphia gunsmith and sporting goods dealer.

1364
Philadelphia legal papers, 1702–1744.   (75 items.)

Pleas before the Court of Common Pleas of Philadelphia County; and decisions of the Court and of the Supreme Court of the Province of Pennsylvania.

1365
Philadelphia War History Committee.   Papers, 1917–1919.
(1 v.)

The Philadelphia War History Committee was appointed by the Mayor of Philadelphia to gather facts about the city in World War I.

These papers include: notes on Base Hospital No. 20; a history of the 19th Grand Division Transportation Corps; list of personnel, 108th Field Artillery; brief history of the 79th Division, by Major General Joseph E. Kuhn; history of the 103rd Trench Mortar Battery, by James J.D. Spillan; personnel, Tank Corps, by Harold N. Hill; notes on Philadelphia casualties, recruiting, draft boards.

This material was gathered preparatory to the publication of *Philadelphia in the World War,* 1914–1918 (New York, 1922).

1366
Pile family.   Papers, 1793–1836.   (129 items.)

Letters to Captain Samuel Pile of Philadelphia and to other members of the Pile family, include personal news and considerable information on Philadelphia, New York, and New Orleans.

Gift of Annie Pile, 1944.

1367
Powers, Frederick Perry, d. 1927.   Papers.   (600 items.)

Lectures by Frederick Perry Powers on *Songs of the Revolution* and *War Songs*, and the notes on which these lectures were based.
Typescripts.
Gift of Mrs. Frederick Perry Powers, 1931.

1368
Robins, Edward, 1862–1943.   Papers, 1939–1942.   (43 items.)

Manuscripts and clippings of articles and addresses by Edward Robins dealing with literary and historical matters, and personal letters to Robins.
Gift of Mrs. Edward Robins, 1943.

1369
Sayres, Edward Stalker, 1850–1923.   Papers, 1866–1923.
(650 items.)

Papers of Edward S. Sayres on his activity in the Civil Service Reform Association and in the First World War; clippings, letters and notes relating to the Society of the War of 1812, the Military Order of Foreign Wars of the United States; the Colonial Society of Pennsylvania, and the Society of Colonial Wars in the Commonwealth of Pennsylvania, in all of which Mr. Sayres held office.
Gift of Mrs. Edward S. Sayres.

1370A
Lewis, Henry Carvill, 1853–1888.   Papers, 1874–1929.
(200 items.)

Henry Carvill Lewis was a geologist with undergraduate and graduate degrees from the University of Pennsylvania in 1873 and 1876.
Papers of Henry Carvill Lewis consist primarily of correspondence of proposed members with Henry Carvill Lewis, secretary of the Science and Art Club of Germantown, 1874–1884; letters, articles and clippings showing some of the scientific ideas current, 1874–1879; and printed reports of the Club, 1884–1929.
Gift of Mrs. Edward S. Sayres, 1931.

1370B
Lewis, Henry Carvill, 1853–1888.   Papers, 1861–1890.   (350 items.)

Letters, notes, programs, clippings, obituaries, and some photographs of his schooling, lectures, travels, and the clubs and organizations with which he was involved.

1371
Scioto Land Company.   **Papers, 1789–1792.**   **(76 items.)**

The Scioto Land Company, organized in 1787, had options on approximately 5,000,000 acres of land in Ohio. The French land company failed in 1792.

The collection contains letters and papers of the Scioto Land Company.

1372
Sheafer, Peter Wenrick, b. 1819.   **Papers, 1873–1875.**
(150 items.)

Peter W. Sheafer, a geologist and mining engineer, compiled the *Historical Map of Pennsylvania* (Philadelphia, 1875).

Letters on and corrected proofs of the Map.

1373
Shower family.   **Collection, n.d.**   **(1 v.)**

Entry cancelled; transferred to the Genealogical Society of Pennsylvania.

1374
Shunk family.   **Collection, 1760–1923.**   **(400 items and 6 v.)**

Drafts of letters, mainly personal, written by Francis Rawn Shunk; and letters of the Shunk family.

1375
Smith family.   **Papers, 1728–1846.**   **(600 items.)**

Family papers containing letters, bills, receipts of Lamar, Hill, Bisset and Company, wine merchants of Madeira, 1762–1802; business papers of Joseph Wharton, 1728–1771, pertaining chiefly to land in Philadelphia County; letters of John Ely, Controller of New York, to Miers and Samuel Fisher, regarding lands in Otsego and Montgomery Counties, N.Y., 1800–1829; letters to Charles Wharton from Calcutta, Lisbon, and Leghorn, 1783–1809; business letters to James Moffat from Europe, 1794–1813; miscellaneous deeds, letters, and broadsides.

Gift of Mrs. Edward Wanton Smith, 1942.

1376
Smith, Franklin R.   **Papers, 1848–1858.**   **(217 items.)**

Letters to Franklin R. Smith, physician living in Bellefonte, primarily from his brothers, Pemberton Smith and Charles Smith, on business conditions in Pennsylvania. There are also accounts of Dr. Smith with Pemberton Smith.

1377
Smith, Persifor Frazer, 1798–1858. Papers, 1770–1873.
(300 items.)

Persifor Frazer Smith, an officer in the U.S. Army, served in the Seminole War, 1836–1838, in the Mexican War, 1846–1848, and commanded the Pacific Division, the Department of Texas, 1850–1856, the Western Department, 1856–1858, and the Department of Utah, 1858.

The Smith papers include letters and a letter book relating to the war with Mexico, 1847–1848; military letters to General Smith, 1838, 1850–1858; miscellaneous legal papers, 1770–1873; daybook, Springton Forge, 1803–1804, 1833–1842; accounts of Matthew Stanley, 1815–1841; and legal notes.

Gift of Mrs. Talbot, 1939.

1378A
Smith, Uselma Clarke, 1841–1902. Collection, 1688–1899.
(1,000 items.)

Uselma Clarke Smith was a Philadelphia lawyer and collector of deeds, wills, commissions, estate papers, family letters, genealogies, and other materials. Smith was particularly interested in his great-uncle William Jones, an army and naval officer during the Revolution, about whom Smith planned to write a biography.

William Jones, was both an army and a navy officer during the Revolution and great-uncle of Uselma Clarke Smith. In 1795 Jones returned from South Carolina to Philadelphia. He served in Congress, as a Democrat, 1801–1803, and was appointed secretary of the Navy from 1813 to February 1814. He returned to private business in order to save himself from bankruptcy and was elected first president of the Second Bank of the United States in 1816. After two and a half years he resigned under charges of incompetence and fraud. He joined Joshua and Samuel Humphreys in a company to build steamships and served as collector for the Port of Philadelphia.

These papers reflect Jones's activities, his descendants, and other related families.

Gift of John H. Dilkes, Jr., 1942.

1378B
Smith, Uselma Clarke, 1841–1902. Collection, 1691
(1768–1828) 1899. (185 items.)

Jones family letters, 1784–1828; Lloyd Jones letters and documents, 1813–1815, on his assignment as commander of the U.S.S. *Neptune* during its mission as transport for the United States peace negotiators to St. Petersburg, Fla. and Ghent; and deeds, commissions, and estate papers of the Jones, Loxley, and Lownes families.

Gift of William J. Smith, 1945.

1378C
Smith, Uselma Clarke, 1841–1902.   Collection, 1740–1900.
(200 items.)

Benjamin Loxley memorandum book, 1767–1771, 1787, with notes and accounts of the Carpenters' Company, particularly for the construction of Carpenters' Hall; William Jones miscellaneous including an examination of difficulties and solutions to winter navigation on the Delaware River; estate papers of William Jones involving protracted French spoliation claims, 1886–1900; estate papers of Jane Loxley Clarke; and estate papers of Elizabeth Loxley Jones.

Gift of John H. Dilkes, 1958.

1378D
Smith, Uselma Clarke, 1841–1902.   Collection, 1791–1888.
(600 items.)

This collection includes additional William Jones material, incoming correspondence, 1791–1827, mainly addressed to Jones in his capacities as secretary of the navy, acting secretary of the treasury, and Second Bank of the United States president. It includes a small group of letters, 1813, mostly from Judge Joseph H. Nicholson of Baltimore, concerning Joshua Barney's duel with Lemuel Taylor. There are a few letters from family or merchants including Joshua and Samuel Humphreys.

Among other William Jones papers are: a logbook, 1805–1806, kept by Jones as master of the ship *Ploughboy*; copies of U.S. Navy estimates for dimensions and equipment of ships of war; estate papers; newspaper clippings; and Smith's biographical notes.

The collection includes other miscellaneous letters and genealogies of Smith's family. Clarke, Jones, Loxley and related lines are represented. There is a logbook kept by Lloyd Jones, 1797–1798, of two voyages made by the brig *Benjamin Franklin* between Philadelphia and Bordeaux.

Uselma Clarke Smith's own papers are few: Pennsylvania Supreme Court Chief Justice George Sharswood letters, 1864–1871, concerning property settlement; letters and documents, 1868–1888, relative to the schooling of his son Robert M. Smith at Bordentown Military Institute; estate papers, 1863–1899, of Jane Loxley Clarke, Charlotte Jones Smith Goodrich, Catherine Loxley Jones, Mary P. Loxley, and others; law school notes; and miscellany.

Gift of Mrs. John H. Dilkes, 1964.

1379
Spofford, Ernest.   Papers, 1929.   (1 v.)

Corrected proofs of Ernest Spofford's book, *Armorial Families of America*.

Gift of Ernest Spofford.

1380
Strayer, Francis M.   Collection, 1781–1822.   (100 items.)

Papers on tax collections in Chester County, 1781–1822, including a few tax lists.

Gift of Francis M. Strayer, 1938.

1381
Suydam, Mary Francis Ludwig.   Collection, 1475–1904. (100 items.)

Letters from minor German princes, 1475–1811; and letters, signatures, and autographs of prominent Americans including Henry Ward Beecher, William Cullen Bryant, Millard Fillmore, John Hay, and William Dean Howells.

Gift of Mary Ludwig Suydam, 1919.

1382
Trigg, Ernest T., 1877–1957.   Papers, 1910–1917.   (1 v.)

Ernest T. Trigg was a Philadelphia paint manufacturer and president of the Philadelphia Chamber of Commerce.

The papers include a scrapbook of clippings, letters, and invitations relating to Ernest T. Trigg's activity in the Chamber of Commerce; Trigg's report as regional advisor to War Industrial Board, 1918; letters, forms, on the work done to organize Philadelphia for war.

Purchased, 1943.

1383
Union League of Philadelphia (Pa.)   Papers, 1896–1909. (300 items.)

Notices, lists of candidates for membership, appeals for support, and form letters showing the League's activities.

Gift of Henry Paul Busch, 1941.

1384

Union Library Catalog of the Philadelphia Metropolitan Area. Inauguration reception papers, 1935. (217 items.)

Acceptances and regrets from Philadelphians invited to a reception to inaugurate the newly organized *Union Catalog*.

Gift, 1935.

1385

Warren, M.I. **Collection, 1786–1919.** (100 items.)

Holograph sermons by Erza Stiles, 1794, and by Cyrus Gildersleeve, 1797; notes from Mr. Webster's lectures on the English language, 1786; manuscript of Professor Pearson of Harvard on prosody, ca. 1893; and notes on the history of English literature, based on material in the British Museum and the Bibliothèque Nationale.

1386

Woodhouse, Samuel Washington, b. 1875. **Collection, 1743–1858.** (3 linear ft.)

Bills, receipts, canceled bank checks, and other business papers of the Meredith family, 1743–1858; shipping papers, 1776–1803; and accounts of the Commissioners of Naval Stores for outfitting ships of the Continental Navy, 1776.

Purchased, 1943.

1387

Worrall family. **Papers, 1724–1892.** (8 v. and 108 items.)

Papers of the Worrall family of Philadelphia and Delaware County. They include: deeds, wills, marriage certificates, and other legal papers of the Crosby, Paul, and Worrall families; contracts for materials for the Delaware Bay Breakwater, 1831, and for the Baltimore and Ohio Railroad, 1872; justice of the peace docket book, 1835–1862, 1886; account books of Israel Thomas, 1813–1828, and of William and Edward Lane, 1745–1813; other Philadelphia merchants' business papers and miscellaneous family papers.

Gift of Mrs. John S. Mershon, 1944.

1388

Ziegler, John Williamson, 1868–1938. **Papers, 1911–1917.** (4 linear ft.)

John Williamson Ziegler took active interest in the General Alumni Association of the University of Pennsylvania and the bulk of his papers are on this Association. There is material on independent political action in Delaware County, on Sabbath Schools, and on the attempts to secure local option in Pennsylvania.

Gift of the estate of John Williamson Ziegler, 1942.

1389
Pennsylvania. Court of Admiralty.   Records, 1770–1804.
(3 linear ft.)

Records of the Admiralty Court, 1770–1797; papers of Blair Mc-Clenachan, merchant, banker, and financial supporter of the American forces, in account with Matthew Clarkson, 1777–1801; log of ship *Imperial,* 1803–1804; and miscellaneous papers on other ships.

Part the gift of the Common Pleas Court of Berks County, part purchased, 1945.

1390A
Bank of the United States of Pennsylvania.   Papers, 1840–1855.
(6 linear ft.)

Papers of John Bacon, Alexander Symington, and Thomas Robins, trustees, on the liquidation of the Bank of the United States of Pennsylvania after its suspension in 1841. Deed of trust, June 7, 1841; records of sales of property in various parts of the United States, 1840–1855; stock transactions, 1844–1853; bills and receipts, 1843–1854; and reports of bank agencies, 1840–1841.

Deposited by the Fidelity-Philadelphia Trust Company, 1945.

1390B
Bank of the United States of Pennsylvania.   Trusteeship papers,
1828–1865.   (275 items.)

A small collection documenting efforts of bank trustees to conclude the affairs of the second Bank of the United States, by paying the debts of the corporation and compensate its stockholders. Also included are: agency accounts for Erie, 1841–1842; Cincinnati, Ohio, 1844; inventories of real estate and other assets; correspondence to James Dundas, Edwin M. Lewis, and Charles S. Folwell, all bank trustees.

Purchased from Freeman's with the Mifflin Fund, 1972.

1390C
Bank of the United States of Pennsylvania.   Papers, 1814 (1841–
1853) 1866.   (8 linear ft.)

These records concern the overall transactions of the trusteeship for the second Bank of the United States (of Pennsylvania) and of specific agencies. Much of the material relates to the liquidation of real estate assets. The general series contains trustees minutebook, 1841–1855; Pittsburgh, Washington and other agency letters; trustees accounts filed with the court; records for Buffalo, Cincinnati, Erie, Mobile, Pittsburgh, and Washington consist of accounts of varying detail and series of letters from Cincinnati, 1845, Erie, 1843–1845, and Mobile, 1841–1853. There are also some early records of the United States Bank: ledger, 1814–1816, and checkbook stubs, 1818–1822.

Gift of Howard W. Lewis, 1938.

1391
Boggs, Benjamin Randolph.   **Papers, n.d.**   **(2 linear ft.)**

Clippings, photographs, and typescripts of articles on old Philadelphia and the inns and taverns of the city.

Gift of the Benjamin Randolph Boggs estate, 1944.

1392
Lobdell Car Wheel Company.   **Papers, 1817–1929.**
(30 linear ft.)

Papers of Lobdell Car Wheel Company of Wilmington, Del., firm that specialized in railroad equipment. Most of the papers are letters received by the company from their agents and customers and include interesting material on the development of the railroads.

1393
Clover Club (Philadelphia, Pa.)   **Papers, 1918–1921.**   **(186 items.)**

The Clover Club was a dancing club founded in 1881. It was famous for its distinguished guests and for its lack of seriousness in entertaining them.

The papers of the Clover Club are those kept by James McCartney, secretary of the Club.

1394
Doran family.   **Papers, 1797–1880.**   **(20 v.)**

Michael Doran's journal of domestic accounts, 1797–1823; receipt book, 1815–1825; ledger, 1797–1816; receipt book,1828–1834 for money received for shipments made by Doran; day book, 1829–1832; expense book, 1848–1859; Michael Keppele's docket, 1806–1807; bills of lading, Port of Philadelphia, 1820–1826; Lydia C. Warner's music book; Joshua Longstreth's letter book,

1822–1827; J. Warner Irwin's diary, 1854, and sketch book; Mrs. Joseph M. Doran's diary and memo book, 1871; and H.C. Borden's diary, 1880.

Gift of S. Hamill Horne, 1945.

1395
Davis, E.M., Mrs.   Elfreth's Alley papers.   (3 v. and 55 items.)

Typed history, scrapbook, and genealogical notes on the people and the houses of Elfreth's Alley.

Gift of Mrs. E.M. Davis.

1396
Emlen family.   Papers, 1715–1885.   (115 items.)

Letters and correspondence of various members of the Emlen family and related families including: commonplace book of Ann Emlen Mifflin and her religious meditations, 1775–1800; notebooks of Ann Emlen Mifflin and of Samuel E. Mifflin, 1779.

Gift of John T. Emlen, 1945.

1397
Fothergill, Samuel.   Journal, 1806–1808.   (1 v.)

Journal by Samuel Fothergill of a trip from Philadelphia to the settlements in Luzerne County, 1806; and another briefer journal of a similar trip in 1808. Recorded are descriptions of events, places, opinions of people, conditions of roads, and inns.

Gift of Miss Edith Newbold, 1945.

1398
Hazard family.   Papers, 1770–1818.   (190 items.)

Journals of Ebenezer Hazard, 1770–1771, 1772–1773, 1777–1778; journals of Samuel Hazard, 1806–1813; medical recipe book of Samuel Hazard, 1818; correspondence of Samuel Hazard, including letters of Benjamin Franklin and George Washington; and the history of the Philadelphia Hose Company.

Gift of Spencer Hazard, 1945.

1399
Hubbard, C. Evans.   Collection, 1780–1801.   (300 items.)

Bills and receipts for goods, mostly rum, shipped from the West Indies to Philadelphia; accounts of Walter Stewart, surveyor of the Port of Philadelphia, 1794–1795.

Gift of C. Evans Hubbard, 1945.

1400
Indigent Widows and Single Women's Society of Philadelphia.
Papers, 1823–1862.   (400 items.)

The Indigent Widows and Single Women's Society of Philadelphia was founded in 1817 by Sarah Ralston, a Quaker. She organized this charitable organization for women of good "Christian" character. The name was eventually changed to the Ralston House when the organization admitted men.

Correspondence, 1824–1862, account books, and other business papers.

1401
Isabella Furnace (Chester County, Pa.)   Papers, 1880–1921.
(33 linear ft.)

Correspondence and business papers of Isabella Furnace, one of the last charcoal burning furnaces in the United States.

Gift of William Wikoff Smith, 1944.

1402
Jenkins, Charles Francis, 1865–1951.   Collection, 1762–1807.
(500 items.)

Autograph letters of members of Old Congress.
Gift of Charles F. Jenkins, 1945.

1403
Jones, Andrew M.   Papers, 1833–1883.   (1,600 items.)

Andrew M. Jones was a Philadelphia merchant.
The papers of Andrew M. Jones contain correspondence, and bills and receipts on stocks, bonds, dividends, and real estate owned by Jones.
Gift of Mrs. Charles Willing, 1945.

1404
Miller, Joseph, d. 1798.   Docket book, 1794–1815.   (1 v.)

Continuance docket of the Supreme Court of Kent County, Del., kept by Joseph Miller, one of the lawyers admitted to practice before the Court. It is continued by John Fisher, another lawyer, as political and personal memoranda, 1802–1815.
Gift of Joseph M. Ritter, 1945.

1405
King, Duncan.   **Papers, 1820.**   (1 v.)

Manuscript by Duncan King of a proposed botanical and agricultural monthly.
Purchased, 1944.

1406
Masters family.   **Estate papers, 1746–1850.**   (3 linear ft.)

Business papers on the estates of William Masters and Mary Masters Ricketts, and genealogical notes on the Penn-Masters families including: bills and receipts, 1830–1856; real estate papers, 1808–1853; trustee account books, 1832–1856; check books, 1834–1848; and legal documents, 1840–1859.
Gift of Francis D. Brinton, 1945.

1407
Meade, George Gordon, 1815–1872.   **Papers, 1863–1869.**   (33 v.)

Letters and telegrams sent and received by General George Gordon Meade, 1863–1865; proceedings of board for recommending brevet promotions, 1866; testimony of Meade and Butler on battle before Petersburg, 1864; records, 3d Military District of the South, 1868–1869.
Gift of George Gordon Meade, 1945.

1408
Moore, James Clark.   **Papers, 1683–1830.**   (88 items.)

Papers for James Clark Moore and William Colmer Moore include early surveys of Pennsylvania lands including the first draft of a survey for Germantown, and cashbook for Richard Peters, 1755–1758.

1409
Newhall, Walter Symonds, 1841–1863.   **Letters, 1862–1863.**
(2 v.)

Letters of Walter Symonds Newhall while serving in the Third Pennsylvania Cavalry.
Gift of Daniel A. Newhall, 1945.

1410

Newton family.   Papers, 1799–1903.   (450 items.)

Letters, journals of trips abroad, manuscript sermons, and notes on church activities of the Reverend Richard Newton and the Reverend R. Heber Newton.

Gift of Richard Newton, Jr. and F. Maurice Newton, 1945.

1411

Philadelphia (Pa.). City Council.   Minute book, 1789–1793. (1 v.)

Minute book of the City Council of Philadelphia containing the "Act of Incorporation," May 12, 1789, and meeting minutes, 1789–1793.

Contemporary copy.

Purchased, 1945.

1412

Rush, Richard, 1780–1859.   Papers, 1812–1847.   (1 v.)

Papers of Richard Rush include: letters to James Madison, 1812–1831, many written during Madison's presidency offering suggestions about appointments to office and later ones discussing politics and contemporary events; letters to Mrs. Madison, 1820–1847; and letters of Mrs. Rush.

1413

Science and Art Club of Germantown (Philadelphia, Pa.)
Papers, 1880–1944.   (4 v.)

Lists of members; correspondence, 1880–1943; and minutes, 1911–1944.

Gift of Donald Ruhel, 1945.

1414

Shoemaker, Rebecca.   Papers, 1780–1786.   (1 v.)

Letters and diaries of Rebecca Shoemaker and of her daughters Anna Rawle and Margaret Rawle, loyalists during the American Revolution.

Typescript.

Gift of Henry F. Pommer, 1945.

1415

Society for the Relief of Poor and Distressed Masters of Ships, Their Widows and Children.   **Records, 1765–1923.**   **(7 linear ft.)**

The papers of the Society for the Relief of Poor and Distressed Masters of Ships, Their Widows and Children include minute books, 1765–1922; dues books, 1768–1922; and other similar records.

Deposited by the Fidelity-Philadelphia Trust Company, 1945.

1416

Universalist Church of Philadelphia.   **Records, 1820–1920.** **(7 v.)**

Minute book, First Universalist Church, 1875–1879; minute books, Second Universalist Church, 1820–1893, 1906–1920; secretary's book, Sunday School Association, Second Universalist Church, 1844–1867; minute book, Universalist Church of the Restoration, 1893–1906.

Gift of Thomas Butler.

1417

Barr, Samuel Victor, 1863–1946.   **Collection.**   **(300 items.)**

Family notes, photographs, correspondence, on Samuel Price, his services in the Navy during the Civil War, and his later life as a marine engineer.

Gift of Samuel Victor Barr, 1946.

1418

Building and Loan Association (Philadelphia, Pa.) **Records, 1871–1909.**   **(3 linear ft.)**

Jenkintown Building and Loan Association minute book, 1878–1909; Logan Square Building and Loan Association account books, minute books, ledgers, and journals, 1871–1886; and Humboldt Building and Loan minute book, 1876–1880.

Purchased, 1946–1947.

1419

Butler, Thomas, d. 1945.   **Papers, n.d.**   **(12 items.)**

Teacher's certificates and diplomas granted to Rev. Thomas Butler.

Gift of Rev. Thomas Butler, 1945.

1420
Camac, William Masters, 1802–1842.   Estate papers, 1799–1860.
(4 v.)

William Masters Camac will, 1841–1842; brief of title to real estate in the county of Philadelphia belonging to the Camac's estate; and papers, 1852–1860, on the estate of Camac and Mary Ricketts, 1799–1859.
Gift of Dr. Charles N.B. Camac, 1936.

1421
Citizens' Permanent Relief Committee (Philadelphia, Pa.)   Papers,
1885–1899.   (21 linear ft.)

The Citizen's Permanent Relief Committee was a local philanthropic group which aided the sufferers in many disasters between 1878 and 1900, notably the Charleston Earthquake, 1885, the Johnstown Flood, 1889, the Russian famine, 1892–1893, and the Armenian massacres in 1896. During the Spanish-American War the Committee under the name National Relief Commission, helped soldiers, sailors, and their families.
Correspondence, business papers, magazines, clippings, applications for relief, treasurer's reports, minutes, investigations and field reports related to each disaster for which the committee provided relief.
Gift of Justice Williams, 1947.

1422
Cresson, John Elliott.   Diary, 1795–1796.   (3 v.)

Diary, 1795–1796, of John Elliott Cresson, relates the daily happenings in the life of a Philadelphia Quaker.
Gift of John E. Cresson, 1946.

1423
Curtis, John.   History of Grand Opera in Philadelphia, 1922.
(7 v.)

Gift of John Curtis, 1942.
Typescript.

1424
Dorland, W.A. Newman (William Alexander Newman), 1864–1956.
History of the Second Troop, Philadelphia City Cavalry, 1775–1917.
(2 linear ft.)

The Second Troop, Philadelphia City Cavalry was organized in 1775, disbanded in 1850, and reorganized in 1896.

Gift of Dr. W.A. Newman Dorland, 1947.
Published in *P.M.H.B.*, 46–79 (1922–1954).

1425
Flagg, Josiah Foster, 1828–1903.   Papers, 1821–1859.   (87 items.)

Diary, 1849, and letters, 1849–1855, of Josiah Foster Flagg on a trip to California and residence there during gold-rush days. There are letters, 1821–1824, of Adin G. Croft and a diary of John Foster Brewster Flagg, 1859, kept during a trip to Europe.
Gift of Mr. and Mrs. Henry V. Gummere, 1946.

1426
Girard College.   Letters, 1884–1946.   (ca. 300 items.)

Letters to Dr. John S. Boyd, 1884–1894, superintendent of admissions and indentures at Girard College, include: letters recommending admittance of certain boys to the college; letters from businessmen reporting favorably or unfavorably upon boys employed; and letters from former students telling of their life after leaving the college, 1942–1946.
Purchased, 1947.

1427
Hamilton & Hood.   Records, 1803–1863.   (12 linear ft.)

Hamilton & Hood were Philadelphia wholesale grocers and wine merchants. This firm was preceded by two firms: Lentz & Hood, 1803–1806, and Hamilton & Drew, 1805–1810.
The records include: correspondence, and financial records, 1808–1838. The account books for Hamilton & Hood are: wastebooks, 1814–1825; daybooks, 1813–1833; ledgers, 1816–1832; receipt books, 1816–1833; letterbook, 1824–1837; and miscellaneous accounts, 1816–1837.
Also included are: business and personal correspondence and accounts of the two partners, John Hamilton, 1809–1833, and John M. Hood, 1819–1848; account books for Lentz & Hood, 1803–1807; accounts, 1805–1807, of Hamilton & Drew. ' Papers of John Hamilton include: daybooks, 1804–1819; ledgers, 1808–1828; receipt books, 1804–1833; letterbook, 1809–1813; and Robert Harris' account as guardian of the children of John Hamilton. Papers of John M. Hood include: daybooks, 1819–1847; ledger, 1831–1840; receipt books, 1806–1848; and Eliza Hood's receipt book for the Estate of John M. Hood.
An artificial collection assembled from Gratz Fund purchases, the Harold E. Gillingham gift, and Dreer Fund purchases.

1428
Jones, Andrew M.   Papers, 1833–1883.   (600 items.)

Personal correspondence, bills, and receipts of Andrew M. Jones, Philadelphia merchant.
Gift of Mrs. Charles Willing, 1945.

1429
Konkle, Burton Alva, 1861–1944.   Papers, n.d.   (2 linear ft.)

Burton Alva Konkle was a prominent Pennsylvania historian and biographer.
This collection includes manuscript notes on his work, particularly on the lives of George Bryan and John Motley Moorhead.
Gift, 1947.

1430
McMaster, John Bach, 1852–1932.   Collection, 1889.
(100 items.)

John Bach McMaster, a prominent historian, was employed to write the history of the Johnstown Flood Relief Commission.
This collection contains the maps, proclamations, letters and printed histories gathered to further the work.
Gift of Dr. Philip D. McMaster, 1932.

1431
Martin, John, 1789–1854.   Notes on British painters, engravers, and architects.   (2 v.)

Short notes by John Martin on the artists of Great Britain who died in the period between 1816 and 1835.
Gift of Norbert Considine, 1942.

1432
North American Land Company.   Records, (1793–1810) 1898.
(200 items.)

The North American Land Company had interests in Pennsylvania, the District of Columbia, Georgia, Kentucky, North Carolina, South Carolina, and Virginia. Some of those associated with the company include: James Greenleaf, Robert James, Tobias Lear, Robert Morris, John Nicholson, Benjamin Tilghman, and James Wilson.

North American Land Company minutes, 1795–1805; correspondence, 1765–1874; land records including descriptions, maps, deeds, 1793–1898; financial records including daybooks, ledgers, receipt books, 1795–1876.

Purchased by the Gratz Fund, 1950.

1433
Paschall family.   Papers, 1734–1875.   (50 items.)

Wills, deeds, and other papers on the estates of Paschall and related families as well as notebooks and poetry of Ann Sellers, George Sellers, and Mary Frances Paschall.

Gift of Miss Ann Paschall, 1930.

1434
Pearce, Harry B.   Collection, 1689–1836.   (44 items.)

Miscellaneous legal and business papers including letters addressed to William Till, a Philadelphia merchant, 1735–1742, and legal and business papers for Andrew and William Hamilton of Philadelphia, 1736–1803.

Gift of Harry B. Pearce, 1938.

1435
Penington family.   Papers, 1764–1882.   (9 linear ft.)

Papers of the Penington family include: account books, 1769–1826, of the sugarhouse of Edward Penington and son Edward Penington; observations on the making of sugar; correspondence and business papers, 1840–1862, of John Penington, rare book dealer; and diary, 1827–1841, of Henry I. Baird.

Purchased, Mifflin Fund, 1946.

1436
Pennsylvania Civil Service Reform League.   Papers, 1881–1935.
(6 linear ft.)

The Pennsylvania Civil Service Reform League was a voluntary organization whose purpose is to strengthen civil service laws particularly in Philadelphia and Pennsylvania.

Correspondence and reports of the Pennsylvania Civil Service Reform League, 1881–1935.

Gift of Albert S. Faught, 1946.

1437
Naval Order of the United States. Pennsylvania Commandery.
Papers, 1895–1925.   (1.5 linear ft.)

Minute books, accounts, and lists of members of a local branch of a patriotic organization, the Naval Order of the United States.

1438
Philadelphia Board of Trade.   Papers, 1880–1941.   (15 linear ft.)

Entry cancelled; see collection #1791.

1439
Philadelphia Cricket Club (Philadelphia, Pa.)   Papers, 1854–1921.
(1.5 linear ft.)

The Philadelphia Cricket Club was founded in 1854.
Minutes, 1854–1879; annual reports, 1883–1921; year books, 1883– 1911; material on international cricket matches, 1868, 1872; and reports, 1878–1880, of the Chestnut Hill Cricket Club.
Gift of Percy H. Clark, 1952.

1440
Philadelphia Vacant Lots Cultivation Association (Philadelphia, Pa.)
Papers, 1895–1928.   (5 v.)

Scrapbooks and minutebooks of the Philadelphia Vacant Lots Cultivation Association, an organization that helped the poor secure and cultivate gardens on the vacant lots of the city.
Purchased, 1947.

1441
Scott, Hannah L.   Papers, 1903–1909.   (ca. 200 items.)

Personal and household receipted bills of Hannah Scott, a member of a prominent Philadelphia family.
Gift, 1946.

1442
Kuesel, Mary H. Stillwell.   Correspondence, 1893–1933.
(82 items.)

Correspondence of Dr. Mary H. Stillwell Kuesel, pioneer woman dentist, on the Association of American Women Dentists.

Gift of Dr. George C. Kuesel in the name of Dr. Mary H. Stillwell Kuesel, 1941.

1443
Stoddard, J.K.   Collection, 1870–1930.   (3 linear ft.)

Personal and business letters written to various members of the Newhall family of Philadelphia.
Gift of Mrs. J.K. Stoddard, 1941.

1444
Willard family.   Papers, 1730–1880.   (100 items.)

Legal and land papers on the Willard family of Hartford County, Conn. Included is a journal of the Newington School, 1828, giving information on students, daily assignments, and credits earned.
Gift of Dr. DeForest Willard, 1946.

1445
Wilson, William Hasell, 1811–1902.   Papers, 1779–1900.   (ca. 250 items.)

Entry cancelled; see collection #725A.

1446
Hamilton, James, 1710–1783.   Papers, 1733–1783.   (ca. 60 items.)

Official papers of James Hamilton, mayor of Philadelphia and lieutenant governor of Pennsylvania, include: his commissions as prothonotary of the Court of Common Pleas of Philadelphia County, and bond for the same; personal account book, 1768–1782; cashbook, 1739–1757; letterbook, 1749–1783; daybook, 1759–1783; instructions from the proprietaries; miscellaneous papers on Pennsylvania and the Penns; and some surveys.
Deposited by the trustees of the estate of Henry Beckett, 1908.

1447
Butler family.   Papers, 1771–1900.   (8 linear ft.)

Pierce Butler resigned his commission in Her Majesty's 29th Regiment in 1773 and devoted his life to planting and politics. From 1778 to 1782 and from 1784 to 1789, he was a representative in the South Carolina state legislature. He disregarded the planter-merchant group in politics, championing the democrats of the back country. He pushed for reform of representation, removal of the state capital, and revaluation of property. As a delegate to the Federal Convention, he proposed a strong central government with property as part of the basis for representation. He was the author of the fugitive slave clause. Though strong in the back country, his support waned in the tide waters. He resigned from politics in 1806 and retired to his plantations in South Carolina.

These papers concern Major Pierce Butler, his estate, and his heirs. The family members represented include: Sir Thomas Butler, Sir Richard Butler, Sarah Middleton Guerard, Benjamin Guerard, Mary Izard Brewton, Miles Brewton, Mary Brandford Bull, Elizabeth Izard Blake, Mary Middleton Butler, Thomas Butler, Pierce [Mease] Butler, Sarah Butler Wister, Owen J. Wister, Frances Butler Leigh, and James W. Leigh.

The papers include South Carolina legislature papers, 1775–1805; U.S. Congressional papers, 1789–1800; Bank of the United States papers, 1801–1819; Georgia plantation managers' correspondence, including George Hooper, 1786–1803, Roswell King, 1802–1830, Roswell King, Jr., 1815–1854, Alexander Blue, 1847–1859, and James M. Couper, 1879–1885; plantation crop and livestock reports, 1800–1884; shipping agents' correspondence and accounts, including Harrison & Latham, 1807–1834, Simon Magwood, 1814–1829, John McNish, 1815–1826, Chisholm & Taylor, 1825–1835, and William Lawton, 1847–1857; slave lists, 1775–1815; birth and death lists, 1800–1834; transactions, 1780–1804; wills and estate papers for above-mentioned family members, 1771–1860; deeds and leases, 1782–1786, 1801–1812, 1833–1840, 1865–1886; Pennsylvania property correspondence and receipts, including Armstrong County, 1818–1838, Bedford and Cumberland Counties, 1804–1821, Huntington County, 1766–1819, Indiana County, 1815–1821, Jefferson County, 1824–1836, Lycoming County, 1797–1818, and Northumberland County, 1802–1809; Georgia property correspondence, including St. Simon's Island, 1891, Hampton, 1894, and General's Island, 1895–1900; and lawsuits involving Major Pierce Butler, 1780–1830, 1864–1881.

Gift of Owen J. Wister, 1947.

1448
Adelman, Seymour.　Collection, 1787–1884.　(12 items.)

Miscellaneous papers collected by Seymour Adelman include: letters, 1797–1800, from Rufus King to Major Lennox on assistance to American sailors stranded in England; list of articles required to be sent to Algiers as tribute, 1799; journal of Benjamin Eakins, 1883–1884; short letters by General W.H. Taylor, 1836, Robert E. Lee, 1864, Millard Fillmore, 1836, James Anderson, 1849. The collection also contains prints by Felix O.C. Darley, n.d.

Gift of Seymour Adelman, 1947.

1449A
Apprentices Library (Philadelphia, Pa.)   Records, 1813–1945.
(6 linear ft.)

Apprentices Library was the first free circulating library in America, founded in 1820.

The records include: minute books of the Board of Managers, 1834–1937; minutes of the Committee on Attendance, 1830; minutes of the Committee for a Girls Library, 1842–1847; minutes of the Library Committee, 1858–1945; record book, 1820–1821; cash ledgers, 1925–1935; correspondence on the library; bookplates; and miscellaneous papers on the library.

Gift of the Apprentices Library, 1947.

1449B
Apprentices Library (Philadelphia, Pa.)   Records, 1923–1946.
(200 items.)

Reports of Librarian, Book Committee, and Board of Managers, with some additional miscellaneous records.

Gift of Mrs. E.N. Cooper, 1971.

1450
Ashhurst family.   Papers, 1704–1874.   (50 items and 7 v.)

Papers of the Ashhurst and Hazlehurst families of Philadelphia and Burlington County, N.J., include mostly personal letters, diplomas, certificates, but include 2 letters from Alexander Hamilton, 1793, and a letter from Henry Clay, 1816. The books comprise account and memorandum book, 1850–1873, of the Clover Hill estate at Mount Holly purchased by Lewis K. Ashhurst in 1850; receipt book of Samuel Hazlehurst, 1830–1849; notes on sermons heard by L.K. Ashhurst, 1831–1835; and private account book of Lewis K. Ashhurst, 1847–1874.

Gift of Richard Ashhurst, 1947.

1451A
Biddle and Craig family.   Papers, 1779–1837.   (800 items.)

Correspondence primarily about Mrs. John Craig, mother of Jane Craig Biddle, containing material about the Biddle and Craig families.

Gift of Mrs. Harold Paumgarten in memory of Jane Craig Biddle and Meta Craig Biddle, 1947.

1451B
Biddle and Craig family.   **Papers, 1748–1866.**   **(100 items.)**

Papers of Margaret M. Craig correspondence, 1776–1814, including letters to and from her daughter, Jane Craig Biddle, and her son-in-law, Nicholas Biddle; Jane Craig Biddle, incoming correspondence, 1818–1840; miscellaneous correspondence, including letters by George Whitefield, clergyman, 1748–1757, Charles Biddle, 1799–1819, and James S. Biddle, 1833, 1851; and miscellanea.
Gift of Mrs. John Tyson, 1976.

1452
Bonnaffon family.   **Papers, 1897–1912.**   **(2 v.)**

Logbook of Edmund W. Bonnaffon, Paymaster, United States Navy, 1896–1897, describing life in Alaska, 1897; register of allotments aboard the U.S.S. *Massachusetts*, 1903; invitations, clippings, and souvenirs of E.W. Bonnaffon, as well as two letters to Captain Sylvester Bonnaffon, 3rd, Paymaster, United States Army, 1912.
Purchased, 1947.

1453
The Pennsylvania Four Minute Men.   **Records, 1917–1919.**
(ca. 200 items.)

The Pennsylvania Four Minute Men was organized to provide men for theaters and other rallies to make short speeches on various designated topics concerning the war. They also participated in the Liberty Loan campaigns.
The records include: correspondence, 1918–1919; schedules, 1918–1919; and notes on speeches and many printed releases dealing with local war activities.
Gift of Clarence C. Brinton, 1947.

1454
Cadwalader family.   **Papers, 1630–1900.**   **(300 linear ft.)**

The principal divisions are the papers of General John Cadwalader, Phineas Bond, General Thomas Cadwalader, Judge John Cadwalader, General George Cadwalader, Dr. Charles E. Cadwalader, and the Honorable John Cadwalader, Jr.
The papers of General John Cadwalader include: material on the Trenton-Princeton campaign; letters of George Washington, 1776–1778; Cadwalader's memorandum book, 1776–1777; letters of Thomas Wharton; documents relating to the Cadwalader-Reed controversy; James McHenry

letters, 1781; an Alexander Hamilton letter, 1783; revolutionary matters; family papers; papers of Cadwalader Evans, 1735, and Joseph Rose, 1737; and an account book.

The correspondence of General Thomas Cadwalader is broad in scope and embraces letters of many prominent persons. It is rich in family letters and contains material on the Port Folio, the Assembly, clubs. Included are letter books, 1812–1840. His military papers relate mainly to the War of 1812, covering the services of Philadelphia troops, Aug.-Dec. 1814. In 1817 he took over the management of the Penn family affairs in America. Material collected by earlier agents was placed in his hands. This included many of William Penn's own files on the lower counties, as well as manuscripts collected later to substantiate Penn's claims. Many of the Penn family's original deeds relating to their interests in Pennsylvania are included here, as well as agreements for the Mason-Dixon surveys. The coverage of the Penn agency is very broad. Included in it is voluminous correspondence of the Penns starting with Thomas Penn. Many drafts, surveys, and maps are in the collection.

Another large category of General Thomas Cadwalader's papers reflects his career as a lawyer. Richest of all the material preserved here are the George Croghan papers, 1744–1782. These papers deal with Croghan's life as Indian trader, Indian agent, and land speculator. They include a number of his journals, and letters from Sir William Johnson, the Franklins, Gates, Gage, Monckton, Trent, the Whartons, Lord Dunmore and many soldiers and traders of the frontier. Many other cases dealing with the affairs of prominent persons and concerns of General Cadwalader's times are included, notably those concerning the American Iron Company and the West Jersey Society.

Judge John Cadwalader's papers relate principally to the law cases he handled prior to his elevation to the bench. In addition, there is material of interest relating to President Buchanan. Present also are Judge Cadwalder's letter books, 1830–1859.

Phineas Bond, the British consul, is represented by papers, much of biographical interest, Revolutionary material primarily relating to the affairs of Judge William Moore of Moore Hall, as well as many law cases. Bond represented English concerns having interests in this country. Many of these cases he passed on to his nephew, General Thomas Cadwalader.

General George Cadwalader's papers furnish information on military subjects, 1834–1865, are rich in militia affairs, include information on the "Awful Riots of 1844," day-by-day coverage of the Mexican War, and much excellent Civil War material. His interests as a sportsman in yachting and duck shooting are well represented, as are his extensive farming and cattle-raising activities in Maryland. Business interests include papers relating to the Baltimore and Philadelphia Steamboat Company, 1840–1878; estate papers, many inherited from his father, General Thomas Cadwalader; and railroad and mining interests.

Dr. Charles E. Cadwalader's papers consist principally of extensive historical and genealogical notes on the Cadwalader and allied families, as well as photographs of family portraits, relatives, and family houses.

Among certain miscellaneous items not included in the above items are account books of John Moore, 1710–1717; John Kearsley, 1711–1720; John Cadwalader, 1711–1724; Patient Usher, 1737–1741; Dr. Phineas Bond, 1758–1759, 1762–1769; and Dr. Thomas Cadwalader, 1767–1768.

Also included is the correspondence of Richard Peters. The correspondence includes incoming letters and drafts of Peter's outgoing letters, concerning the editorial projects, legal and political affairs. The major correspondent is Joseph Story, Associate Justice of the Supreme Court, but there is correspondence with many other judicial and public figures, including Henry Clay, John Marshall, Charles Sumner, and Roger Brooke Taney.

Gift of the Cadwalader family at various times, the bulk in 1947.

1455
Chew family. **Papers, 1739–1768.** **(ca. 250 items.)**

Entry cancelled; see collection #2050.

1456
Civil War papers. **(ca. 500 items.)**

Entry cancelled; see collection #1546.

1457
Clark, Ephraim. **Papers, 1779–1886.** **(2 linear ft.)**

Correspondence, legal papers, and account books of Ephraim Clark, a Philadelphia real estate agent. A few early items relate to Bedford County. Gift of Miss Bertha Clark, 1948.

1458
Coles family. **Papers, 1762–1887.** **(ca. 600 items.)**

Letters, documents, and business papers of Edward Coles, abolitionist and second governor of Illinois. Also included are: correspondence, 1810–1868, consisting of letters primarily from his family and contain information on: the War of 1812; Washington, D.C. during James Madison's administration; Coles's business activities, 1833–1868; and slavery. Also included are: autobiographical sketch; speeches on slavery; essays on the emancipation of his slaves, 1827; Russian trade documents; and account books. There is a small group of correspondence for his son, Edward Coles, Jr.

Gift of Oliver W. Robbins, 1948.

1459
Croghan, George, d. 1782.   Papers, 1754–1808.   (200 items.)

Letters and documents on George Croghan's work with the Indians. Photostatic copies.
Gift of the University of Pennsylvania Library, 1947.

1460A
Dallas, George Mifflin, 1792–1864.   Papers, 1791–1880.
(ca. 1,400 items.)

Correspondence of Alexander James Dallas and George Mifflin Dallas. Included among George Mifflin Dallas' papers are letters to his wife Sophia Chew Nicklin Dallas, 1831–1857; letters from his wife and their children; the manuscript of the life he wrote of his father, Alexander James Dallas; and letters received by George Mifflin Dallas, 1813–1864.
Purchased, 1947.

1460B
Dallas, George Mifflin, 1792–1864.   Letters, (1819–1831) 1852.
(82 items.)

Letters to Samuel D. Ingham, many of which were written during the first two years of the Andrew Jackson administration, 1829–1831, while Dallas was U.S. District Attorney at Philadelphia and Ingham was Secretary of the Treasury. They concern financial difficulties, political patronage recommendations, and running commentary, at times in code, on political affairs and personalities in Pennsylvania and the nation. Principle issues discussed are the tariff, nullification, the Bank of the United States, and the Margaret (Peggy O'Neale) Eaton affair which led to the resignation of Ingham. There is a long letter, September 17, 1829, which Ingham, in slightly revised form, used as the administration reply to Nicholas Biddle in an argument about the Bank of the United States.
Purchased, 1963.

1461
Edmonds, Franklin Spencer, 1874–1945.   Papers, n.d.
(ca. 60 items.)

Papers of Franklin Spencer Edmonds, lawyer, educator, and author, including: an essay entitled "Progressive Education in the Nineteenth Century;" and correspondence and notes about his papers on Albert H. Smyth, George Davidson, John G. Johnson, and Ulysses S. Grant.

Gift of Mrs. Franklin Spencer Edmonds, 1947.

1462
Fisher, Sidney George, 1809–1871.   Diaries, 1834–1871.
(9 linear ft.)

The diaries of Sidney George Fisher, Philadelphia lawyer and gentleman, whose interests included local history, agronomy and national politics. The diaries give a portrait of the social, political and economic life of Philadelphia and its people. Nicholas Biddle, Pierce Butler, George Cadwalader, and the Fisher and Ingersoll families are among the prominent Philadelphians scrutinized.

Included are the Mount Harmon diaries, recording his enthusiastic although not altogether successful efforts to operate his Maryland farms.

Gift of R. Sturgis Ingersoll, 1948.

Published in *A Philadelphia Perspective : The Diary of Sidney George Fisher Covering the Years,* 1834–1871. / N.B. Wainwright, ed. (Philadelphia: Historical Society of Pennsylvania), 1967.

Portions also published in *P.M.H.B.,* 74–89 (1952–1965).

1463
Fort Necessity (Pa.)   Papers, 1932–1943.   (ca. 200 items.)

Notes, pamphlets, letters and plans on the efforts to make Fort Necessity a national monument.

Gift of Mrs. Evelyn Benson and Miss Perie Abraham, 1946.

1464A
Harrison, George L., b. 1874.   Papers, 1946.   (7 v.)

George L. Harrison was a man of leisure who concerned himself with civic affairs and hunting.

This papers consist of manuscripts entitled "Memories of Sixty Years" and "Extracts from the Journal of Edward Waln," written by George L. Harrison, civic leader and sportsman. The first mentioned work is autobiographical in nature and mainly deals with hunting and shooting in western America, Canada, Mexico, Africa, and Scotland. The journal of Edward Waln presents a lively picture of the life of a well-to-do man who was interested in politics and country life, 1861–1887.

Gift of George L. Harrison, 1946.

Edward Waln journal transcript made by George L. Harrison, 1946.

1464B
Harrison, George L., b. 1874. "Philadelphia as I remember it, 1875–1950." (3 v.)

These volumes present a picture of Philadelphia social life from the perspective of this prominent Philadelphian.
Gift of George L. Harrison, 1951.

1465
Hobbs, Henry J.P. Papers, 1937–1946. (ca. 300 items.)

Pamphlets, letters, and notes, relating to the activities of Henry J.P. Hobbs, a civilian in England during World War II and the years immediately before and after.
Gift of Henry J.P. Hobbs, 1947.

1466
Jackson, Joseph, 1867–1946. Papers, 1926–1939. (2 linear ft.)

Manuscripts of articles and books, and correspondence related to articles and books, by Joseph Jackson, a prominent Philadelphia historian. Topics include George Cruikshank and George Lippard.
Gift of Mrs. Joseph Jackson, 1947.

1467
Laurence, Thomas. Papers, 1684–1759. (100 items.)

Correspondence and business papers primarily of Thomas Laurence, prominent merchant and mayor of Philadelphia.
Gift of Martha Morris Laurence.

1468
Lumberman's Exchange (Philadelphia, Pa.) Papers, 1886–1905. (5 v.)

Papers of the Lumberman's Exchange, a Philadelphia business association, including: a scrapbook of social events, 1886–1905; and minute books, 1887–1891, 1893–1894. Also, the minute book, 1893–1894, of the Retail Lumber Merchants' Protective Association, an organization formed to combat price cutting in the lumber trade.
Purchased, Library Fund, 1947.

1469
Lycoming Mining Company.   Records, 1891–1938.
(21 linear ft.)

Minute books, 1891–1938; ledgers, 1892–1938; letter books, 1893- 1938, of Lycoming Mining Company in Lycoming County.
Gift of William W. Smith, 1947.

1470
Martin, John Hill, 1823–1906.   Correspondence, 1859–1886.   (ca. 200 items.)

Correspondence relating to John Hill Martin's history of Chester and to his historical sketches of Bethlehem.

1471
Midland Mining Company.   Records, 1880–1939.   (19 v.)

Midland Mining Company was a coal mining company located in Clinton and Centre Counties.
Letterpress books, 1880–1939; geological reports, 1880–1895; and stock ledger and daybook, 1892–1931, of Midland Mining Company.
Gift of William W. Smith, 1947.

1472
Noyes, Stephen H., 1881–1932.   Papers, 1913–1925.
(ca. 300 items.)

Captain Stephen H. Noyes served as an aviator in World War I. He was awarded the Croix de Guerre and the Distinguished Service Cross.
Letters, orders, maps, photographs, and instruction books.
Gift of Stephen B. Leece, 1947.

1473
Pennsylvania. National Guard. Regiment, 20th.   Records, 1877.
(2 v.)

Orders, letters, and muster rolls of the 20th Regiment, Pennsylvania National Guard, Colonel S. Bonnaffon, Jr., commanding, on strike duty at Wilkes-Barre, July 29-September 19, 1877.
Purchased, Library Fund, 1947.

1474
Pennsylvania. Board of Wardens for the Port of Philadelphia.
Papers, 1881–1908. (ca. 400 items.)

Letters and reports of the administrative body responsible for the Port of Philadelphia. Includes anchorage regulations and anchorages, harbor lines, harbor defenses, depth of water in harbor, docks and wharves, and obstructions in the river.
Gift, 1947.

1475
United States. Federal Civil Works Administration.
Historical records survey reports, 1934–1940. (1.5 linear ft.)

Preliminary reports on the holdings of the American Philosophical Society, the Historical Society of Berks County, the Northampton County Historical and Genealogical Society, and the Historical Society of Frankford, by the workers of the Federal Civil Works Administration; reports on the records of some older Philadelphia business houses and on the municipal records of Norristown, Pottstown, and Conshohocken; workers' manuals, 1940's, of the Works Progress Administration; lists of records found in preliminary surveys of Philadelphia by the Federal Civil Works Administration, 1934; and list of city and county records of Philadelphia prepared by the Works Progress Administration, 1938.
Deposited, 1947.

1476
Garden Club of Philadelphia (Pa.)   **Records, 1904–1962.**
(6 linear ft.)

The Garden Club of Philadelphia was organized in 1904 for the purpose of "promoting an interest in gardens, their design, and management."
Charter, 1907; minute books, 1904–1937, 1944–1962; "yearbooks," 1904–1953, which are scrapbooks of miscellaneous correspondence, some minutes and committee reports, transcripts of lectures and poems read at meetings, photographs, clippings; additional lectures delivered at meetings, 1905–1936; and annual meeting reports, 1904–1936. One small group of papers deals with the Club's participation in the Women's Land Army of America, 1917–1918, and agricultural reconstruction in France in 1918.
Deposited by the Garden Club of Philadelphia, 1925, 1965.

1477
Ringgold Brass Band.   Musical scores, ca. 1870–1880.
(ca. 150 items.)

Musical scores used by a local band.
Purchased, Dreer Fund, 1941.

1478
St. David's Church (Radnor, Pa.)   Records, 1705–1961.
(6 linear ft.)

St. David's Church is an historic Episcopal church located in Radnor.
Parish records, 1705–1805; record book, 1820–1894; rector's record, 1833–1900; minute book, 1894–1921; correspondence, 1734–1905; and drawings for the construction of the Parish House.
Deposited by St. David's Church, 1947, 1961.

1479
World War II Collection, 1938–1949.   (20 linear ft.)

Organized in three series. The first section consists of correspondence, pamphlets, press releases, photographs, and posters presented by volunteer and community organizations. Included are: America First Committee, Philadelphia chapter, releases, pamphlets, correspondence, and ephemera, 1939–1941; Committee to Defend America by Aiding the Allies, Conyers Read, Philadelphia chairman, correspondence, 1939–1941; Fight for Freedom Committee, Philadelphia chapter, correspondence, 1939–1941; and a number of smaller groups of materials representing, for example, the Anti-defamation League, the American Palestine Committee, Fellowship House of Philadelphia, the American Friends Service Committee, the Friends of the Spanish Republic, and several Afro-American, German-American, and Italian-American organizations.

The second section consists of press releases and speeches prepared or distributed by the Office of War Information, 1942–1944. Much concerns agreements achieved by the Office of Price Administration and is arranged by product groups.

The third section contains the records of the United Service Organization of Philadelphia, an organization offering recreation and assistance to members of the armed forces and their families. The Philadelphia United Service Organization was the result of a 1941 cooperative agreement among the Jewish Welfare Board, the Y.M.C.A., the Y.W.C.A., the Salvation Army, Travelers' Aid, and the National Catholic Commission Services. The section includes: administrative and financial records of the United Service Organization Council, 1941–1947; Stagedoor Canteen, administrative and operational records, statistical records, programs, and photographs, 1942–1947; Jewish Welfare Board, minutes, correspondence, and financial records, 1941–1948; Labor Plaza, minutes and committee reports for this facility providing outdoor entertainment for servicemen and women, 1943–1946; subsidiary organizations operated by the United Service Organization, reports and receipts, 1942–1947; and letters written in answer to those sent by a letter-writing group at St. Mark's Church in Philadelphia, 1943–1945.

In late 1942 the Historical Society of Pennsylvania solicited materials to form an artificial collection which would document the war effort of a number of community and social service agencies. The result is a miscellaneous and uneven group of papers presented over a number of years by the organizations and their officers.

Finding aid available.

1480
Swift family.　　Papers, 1716–1857.　　(ca. 400 items.)

Family and business papers of the Swift family from Philadelphia and Bucks County. Most of the letters are personal, but some show business conditions in the West Indies, 1820–1850.

1481
Herndon, John G. (John Goodwin), b. 1888.　　Papers, 1945–1946. (ca. 100 items.)

Dr. John G. Herndon's papers on the efforts to have Philadelphia made the headquarters of the United Nations.

Gift of Dr. John G. Herndon, 1947.

1482
United States Centennial Commission.　　Papers, 1872.　　(1 v.)

Letters of the Executive Commission; copies of letters written by W.P. Blake primarily on the proposed sale of stock in the Exhibition of 1876.

1483
Wheatley Dramatic Association (Philadelphia, Pa.)
Papers, 1860–1921.　　(4 v.)

The Wheatley Dramatic Association was a Philadelphia amateur theater group, organized in 1860. It disbanded in 1880.

Programs and clippings and some subsequent material which shows the continuing interest of E.S. Hulfish in the theater.

Gift of Arthur H. Hulfish, 1941.

1484
L.H. Alden and Company (Aldenville, Pa.)   Records, 1829
(1848–1883).   (9 linear ft.)

L.H. Alden and Company was a leather-tanning company and the single industry of Aldenville, Wayne County.

The collection includes store records, wage contracts and payments, factory accounts, and grist mill accounts. There are a few records, 1829, of the library at Windham, N.Y.

Purchased, 1949.

1485
Baldwin Locomotive Works.   Records, 1834–1868.
(39 linear ft.)

The Baldwin Locomotive Company was founded by Matthias W. Baldwin in 1831. In 1926 the Company moved from Philadelphia to Eddystone.

Included in these papers are letter books, 1842–1866; letter book of Matthias W. Baldwin, 1837–1839; of the New York office, 1865–1867; of Gilead A. Smith, New York office, 1861–1865; and of Matthias W. Baldwin, 1834–1841; day books, 1835–1866; journals, 1839–1867; ledgers, 1839–1867; cash books, 1839–1867; receipt book, 1849–1854; loans ledger, 1866–1868; apprentices books, 1854–1868; charge books, 1846–1849, 1853–1867; charge book for shop work, 1858–1859; orders book, 1853–1858; goods received book, 1855; extra orders book, 1854–1869; specifications books, 1836–1843; John Gulliver's American Systematic Beneficial Society, 1856–1858. The books cover every activity of the firm for the first 35 years of its existence.

Gift of the Baldwin Locomotive Works, 1946.

1486A
Cope family.   Papers, ca. 1800–1925.   (475 v.)

Thomas Pym Cope was already an established Philadelphia merchant in 1821 when he began the first regular packet line between Philadelphia and Liverpool. The business continued throughout most of the nineteenth century, with the company name changing as successive generations assumed responsibility. The shipping company section here is primarily a record of the business conducted out of Liverpool where the packets unloaded cotton, flour, wheat, turpentine, resin, and bark, and took on salt, pig iron, tin, and ash. The line also developed a sizable passenger business.

Business records of Thomas P. Cope and Sons, Cope Brothers, Philadelphia Steam Tow Boat Company, and associated business firms; shipping business predominates. There are many letter books and a few miscellaneous items, including memorandum books, estate and family accounts.

Gift of E.W. Evans, 1949.

1486B
Cope family.   Papers, 1787–1908.   (12 linear ft.)

Organized in three series: business papers, Cope family papers, and related family papers. Business papers arranged by name of ship and number of voyage.

Business papers include captains' letters, cargo books, bills of lading, disbursement vouchers, passenger lists and tickets, bills for ship maintenance, seamen's articles of agreement, orders for wages, and various other papers. Additional series in this section consist of "domestic letters," 1844–1884, requesting steerage tickets, together with some instructions for shipping materials. "Foreign letters," 1854–1863, are mostly from Tapscott, Smith & Co., Cope's passenger agents in Liverpool. Brown, Shipley & Co. acted as assignee and agent in Liverpool, and there is a group of Brown, Shipley & Co. letters, 1829, 1836–1874, reporting on unloading, sales, and loading of goods, and market conditions. There are further miscellaneous financial papers, cancelled checks, passenger certificates and lists.

The Cope family section contains random correspondence and other papers of several members: Thomas P. Cope correspondence concerning the charter and location of Haverford School, 1831, the commission to enquire into the best means of conveying merchandise from the wharves to the Broad Street rail road, 1835, and the Irish Relief Committee, 1847; Thomas P. Cope receipt books, 1789–1792, 1806–1810; Francis Reeve Cope incoming letters from James S. Cox concerning the state of Lehigh Coal and Navigation Company affairs, 1867, and from others concerning later personal and philanthropic business, 1902–1903; Francis R. Cope personal receipt book, 1847–1892, Penn Normal and Agricultural School, S.C., contribution records, 1901–1908, and receipted bills, 1906; sundry family estate papers with letters and documents concerning property in Dauphin, Centre, and Susquehanna Counties; Pleasant family estate account books, 1838–1862; letters from Rebecca Drinker, Samuel Reeves and his heirs regarding payments from estate monies. The Reeves letters have further interest because of the story they tell of Samuel C. Reeves, from the witnessing of his father's death, through a troubled adolescence, to his adult struggles with drinking and finding occupation.

The bulk of the section of papers from related families appears as a result of Francis R. Cope's marriage to Anna S. Brown, daughter of Jeremiah. Jeremiah and Moses Brown were commission merchants in textiles and other "domestic goods" coming to them primarily from Boston, Providence and New England mills, but also from Wilmington and Baltimore. The incoming correspondence, 1814–1819, and invoices, receipted bills, and accounts, 1815–1819, are from manufacturers among whom are: Almy, Brown & Slater, Providence; Lyman, Tiffany & Co., Boston; David Our & Co., Wilmington; and Sterling Manufacturing Co., Providence. Occasional letters from purchasers and a small group of letters from Moses to Jeremiah concern the sale of merchandise to western Pennsylvania, Ohio, Kentucky and other markets of the interior. Later Brown family papers consist of Susan S. Brown diary, 1893–1909, recording her medicinal treatments, and cancelled checks, 1885–1896. Henry Sandwith Drinker correspondence, 1787–1810, with his father Henry Drinker and his father-in-law James Smith reveals continuing disputes between the families, seemingly inspired by young Drinker's financial incompetence.

Gift of Edward Evans, 1967, and George W. Emlen, Jr., 1964.

1487
Rosengarten and Denis (Philadelphia, Pa.)   Records, 1818–1853.
(36 linear ft.)

Business papers of the firm, Rosengarten and Denis, Philadelphia chemists; contains some correspondence with family and friends.
Gift of G.D. Rosengarten, 1948.
Some family correspondence in German.

1488
Grubb family.   Papers, 1834–1869.   (6 linear ft.)

Contains papers on the St. Charles Furnace, 1854–1861; Henry Clay Furnace, 1852–1853; Manada Furnace, 1837–1862; and Chestnut Hill ore bank, 1851–1865; Union Canal boat permits, 1849–1850, and the correspondence of Clement B. and Edward B. Grubb, 1834–1869.
Gift of Mrs. William S. Morris, 1949.

1489
Hahn, Peter.   Papers, 1802–1834.   (75 items.)

Legal and business papers, 1802–1834, of Peter Hahn, Philadelphia merchant. Included are letters from New York and Liverpool, England, telling of business conditions in 1829, and a few plans of properties.
Gift of the College of Physicians, 1948.

1490
Murray family.   Collection, 1837–1853.   (ca. 150 items.)

This collection contains correspondence, 1837–1853, addressed to Joseph D. Murray, postmaster at New Hope, and to his son Thomas, on business affairs, particularly the lumber trade; bills of lading of the Lehigh Coal and Navigation Company, White Haven, 1838.

1491
Great Britain. Board of Commissioners for Trade and Plantations.
Lists, 1771–1772.   (10 items.)

Lists of the quantities of different commodities shipped by and into various American ports.
Photostatic copies.

1492
Charles D. Barney and Company.   Letters, 1933–1934.
(100 items.)

Form letters sent out by Charles D. Barney and Company, a New York stock brokerage firm, advising investors and commenting on political and market trends.

1493
Lardner, Alexander.   Account books, 1830–1847.   (9 v.)

Alexander Lardner was a Philadelphia stock broker.

1494
Yeates family.   Papers, 1733–1894.   (3 linear ft.)

Business and social correspondence, financial accounts, and miscellaneous papers of the Yeates, Burd, and allied families.
Gift of Mrs. T. Duncan Whelen.

1495
Point No Point (Philadelphia, Pa.)   Land title papers, 1726–1873.
(50 items.)

Deeds and briefs of title to land situated at Point No Point on the Delaware River in Philadelphia.

1496
Queens County (N.Y.). Loan Office.   Record book, 1770–1778.
(1 v.)

Records of loans on real estate.

1497
Briefs of title, 1820–1900.   (9 linear ft.)

A collection of papers tracing the titles of various pieces of real estate in Philadelphia.
Gift of Cornelius Stevenson, 1921.

1498
Fairman family.   Papers, 1671–1828.   (75 items.)

Deeds, orders for surveys, originating in the Fairman family of Philadelphia. Many of the orders for surveys are signed by Thomas Holme.
Gift of John Howell and John S. Harmstead, 1948.

1499
Cheyney, Waldron J., 1831–1906.   Papers, 1853–1906.
(56 items.)

Waldron J. Cheyney, who served as secretary of the Board of Awards, Centennial Exposition, was also interested in lands in New Jersey and in mining ventures in Georgia and California.
These papers deal chiefly with California mines.
Purchased, 1948.

1500
Wharton family.   Legal papers, 1825–1875.   (4 linear ft.)

Legal papers, memorandum books, documents, and correspondence of Thomas I. Wharton and Henry Wharton, Philadelphia lawyers.
Gift of the Wharton family, 1946.

1501
Alexander, Lucien Hugh, 1866–1926.   Papers, 1899–1911.
(300 items.)

The papers of a controversy between Lucien H. Alexander, Philadelphia lawyer and member of the James Wilson Memorial Committee, and Burton Alva Konkle, historian and secretary of the committee that originated the idea of bringing the remains of James Wilson from North Carolina to

Philadelphia in 1906. There is also material on an attempt by Alexander to publish a commemorative volume.

Gift of Dr. John Alexander and Miss Helen Alexander through the Clements Library, 1937.

1502
Fox, Isaac, d. 1865.   Papers, 1863–1869.   (50 items and 3 v.)

This collection contains the diaries, 1863–1864, of Sergeant Isaac Fox, Company F, 114th Pennsylvania Volunteers. Also included are his letters to his family, 1862–1865; the discharges of his brothers Charles and William; a poem upon his death; and Civil War song sheets and copy of a Southern song.

1503
Irwin, John.   Diaries, 1863–1865.   (3 v.)

The diaries of Lieutenant Colonel John Irwin of the 149th Pennsylvania Volunteers tell of his experiences in most of the battles of the Army of the Potomac from Chancellorsville to Petersburg, Va.

Gift of Mrs. J.P. Orlady, 1948.

1504
Dotterer, Henry Sassaman, 1841–1903.   Papers, ca. 1900.   (ca. 20 items.)

Notes and a few manuscripts of papers written by Henry S. Dotterer on Pennsylvania Germans, the Reformed Church, and Montgomery County.

Gift of Mrs. Henry S. Dotterer, 1947.

1505
Binney, Horace, 1780–1875.   Papers, 1836–1858.   (11 v.)

Horace Binney served as the director of the first U.S. Bank, 1808 and was active in Pennsylvania and Philadelphia politics. He was admitted to the Philadelphia bar in 1800 and was recognized as a leader of the Philadelphia bar after he earned his reputation winning two important cases. In *Lyle v. Richards,* he argued for the application of common law to property. In the Girard Trust Case, Binney defended Philadelphia's right to hold a trust. This Supreme Court appearance was Binney's last case. He retired in 1850 but continued to be a prolific writer throughout his life.

Journals kept by Horace Binney, American lawyer and legal writer, on a trip to Europe, 1836–1837; commonplace book written by Binney for his daughter Susan, 1858; and the *Autobiography of Horace Binney,* 1780–1868, together with essays by Binney and some notes on the Binney family.

Gift of Horace Binney Montgomery, 1949.

1506

Pommer family.   Papers, 1800–1900.   (100 items.)

Business papers, legal records, and memoranda relating to the Pommer family.

1507

Pleasants family.   Papers, 1689–1843.   (100 items.)

This collection is composed primarily of deeds and agreements to sell lands in western Pennsylvania to Samuel Pleasants, Charles Pleasants, and Charles E. Pleasants. Included are a few letters to Charles E. Pleasants on a law suit with Colonel Love of Tennessee.

1508

Pleasants, Henry, b. 1884.   Collection, 1693–1825.   (125 items.)

Papers collected by Henry Pleasants include: Captain Thomas Mason's account of a voyage to Europe to secure arms for the colonies, 1775–1776, and papers on his disputes, 1776–1784, with Robert Morris and Jacob Winey, his partners, over the proceeds of the voyage; letters, 1775–1783, written by Thomas Shirley of London give the viewpoint of a moderate Englishman on the American Revolution; commonplace books, 1789–1816, of Israel Pleasants, containing notes on insurance and other mercantile enterprises; and miscellaneous manuscripts of Thomas and John Mason, 1693–1825.

Gift of Dr. and Mrs. Henry Pleasants, Jr., Henry Pleasants, 3rd, William Wilkins Pleasants, Howard Spencer Pleasants, Richard Rundle Pleasants, Mrs. Nathaniel Bowditch, Dallas Franklin Pleasants, and Ann Franklin Pleasants, 1948.

1509

Meredith family.   Papers, 1756 (1793–1866) 1888.   (65 linear ft.)

These papers document the personal and professional lives of four generations of the Meredith family of Philadelphia, beginning with Jonathan Meredith, who emigrated from Leominster, Herefordshire, England, to Pennsylvania in the 1750's, where he established a successful tanning business. Other family members and associates present include: Jonathan's sons, David Meredith, who inherited and lost most of his father's fortune as an unsuccessful merchant in France, and William Meredith, lawyer and president of the Schuylkill Bank; Gertrude Gouverneur Ogden Meredith, William's wife and litterateur; their sons, William Morris Meredith, lawyer and Whig politician, and Sullivan Amory Meredith, forty-niner in California and Union general in the Civil War; David B. Ogden, Gertrude's brother and New York lawyer; and Joseph Dennie, editor of the Port Folio and close friend of Gertrude and William Meredith. Jonathan's youngest son, Jonathan Meredith, Jr., and his sister Mary's husband, Thomas Hawthorne, merchant, are also present.

The correspondence, 1756–1888, bulks between 1793 and 1866. Subjects addressed include: banking, including the recharter of the Second Bank of the United States; churches and charities, particularly Christ Church in Philadelphia, for which both William and William M. Meredith were wardens and vestrymen; Federalist, Whig, and Republican politics at the local, state, and national levels; education; prison reform; and arts and letters. Principal correspondents include: Alexander Dallas Bache, James C. Biddle, Horace Binney, Samuel Breck, Mathew Carey, Henry C. Carey, Charles and Henry Gilpin, Robert Hare, Charles Jared Ingersoll, Reverend Johnson, Abbott Lawrence, David Parish, John Hare Powel, and Eli Kirk Price. Also present are: William Rawle, Richard Rush, John Sergeant, Robert Walsh, and Thurlow Weed.

There are also family accounts, bills, and receipts, 1778–1884; and drafts, pamphlets, statutes and legal papers. The subject categories are: banks, 1807–1866, including material relating to the legislative charters of several Pennsylvania banks; canals, 1822–1865, including the Delaware and Hudson and Union canals; charities, 1821–1873, including material on the Philadelphia Almshouse and the Greek Relief Fund; education, 1809–1859, concerning both the University of Pennsylvania and its Free School, of which William M. Meredith was president of the Board of Trustees; Meredith family lands in Pennsylvania and elsewhere, 1785–1860; miscellaneous leases and other legal papers, 1760's–1860's; railroads, 1834–1865, including material on the Northern Liberties and Penn Township Railroad, the Pennsylvania Railroad, and others; ships, 1763–1852, with maritime insurance policies, claims; verse, mostly written by William M. Meredith, 1814–1857; and the Port Folio, 1801–1807, concerning its publication and circulation.

Business records of Jonathan Meredith include: letter books, 1786–1811⊥rsonal memoranda, 1780–1794; blotters, 1784–1797; waste book, 1795; day books, 1786–1794; ledgers, 1772–1788; cash books, 1795–1804; receipt books, 1779–1799; real estate tax receipts, 1788–1801; bills payable, 1793–1803; accommodation notes, 1795; memorandum book of interest payable; list of expenses for repairing the estate opposite Samuel Powel, Esq., 1790–1792; and bank books for the Bank of North America, 1787–1799, the Bank of Pennsylvania, 1793–1818, and the Bank of the United States, 1791–1794.

Personal, professional, and business papers of Jonathan's son, William Meredith, include: letter books and letterpress books, 1802–1838; cash book, 1799–1803; receipt books, 1795–1838; rent books, 1827–1837; appearance dockets for the Supreme Court, 1797–1826, for the Court of Common Pleas, 1797–1818, for the Philadelphia District Court, 1811–1826, and for the Court of Quarter Sessions, 1814–1819; legal memoranda, 1797–1838; report of the City Solicitor on titles to city property, 1810–1839; accounts for the Committee for the Necessitous Poor, 1823–1824; and bank books for the Commercial Bank, 1813–1815, the Bank of Pennsylvania, 1811, and the Schuylkill Bank, 1814–1829.

Also present are: David Meredith, bank books with the Bank of Pennsylvania, 1808–1818, letter book, 1806–1816, and day book, 1787–1790; and some business and professional papers of William M. Meredith, including diaries, 1814–1825, legal and personal memoranda, 1818, notes on practice, n.d., appearance docket for Philadelphia District Court, 1819–1834, letter books, 1849–1850, while Secretary of the Treasury, and letter book, 1865. There are trial dockets for Philadelphia Aldermen's Court, 1830, Quarter Sessions, 1831–1832, and the Court of Oyer and Terminer, Philadelphia, 1829–1830. Each includes a jury list.

Miscellaneous accounts of Meredith legal clients as well as other members of the family include: Joseph Anthony, bank books, 1794–1799, ledger, 1760–1782, and receipt book, 1773–1787; John Du Barry, receipt book, 1806–1815; William Baker, receipts, 1812–1815; Baltimore Mail Coach, passenger and cargo book, 1823–1824; Hawthorne & Kerr, waste books, 1795–1801, journal, 1793–1795, ledger, 1793–1795, receipt book, 1795–1800, and invoice book, 1805–1807; James Hawthorne, waste book, 1793–1797; Thomas Hawthorne, invoice book, 1805–1807; Lain I. Johnson, merchant of Richmond, Va., record of collections in northern Virginia, 1789; Richard Littlewood, ledger, 1786–1793; J. Lupton, ledger, 1784–1797; Thomas Lupton, accounts for the estate of J. Lupton, 1799–1812; Hugh Maxwell, memorandum of book sales, 1806; Daniel McCarney and James Sterrit, whiskey dealers, sales book, 1818–1820; Daniel McKaraher, receipt book, 1804–1813; and record prepared by William M. Meredith for the Vestry of Christ Church, 1832, of bequests and gifts to the Church from Dr. John Kearsley and Joseph Dobbins.

Miscellaneous legal papers include materials on the estates of the Anthony, Bond, Carey, Morris, Ogden, Robinson, Stockton, Westcott, and Wurts families; business papers on lands in Pennsylvania, Virginia, Jew Jersey, and New York; materials on maritime shipping and insurance; and wills, leases, briefs, abstracts, and other legal papers.

Gift of Samuel W. Woodhouse, 1940.

1511
Trimble, James, 1755–1836.   Papers, 1791–1833.   (33 items.)

James Trimble was the first Deputy Secretary of the Commonwealth of Pennsylvania, 1777–1836.

These papers include his commissions as deputy secretary, 1791–1833; a few personal papers and family letters; and a plan of the town of Shenango, 1808.

1512
Broomall, John Martin, 1816–1894.   Correspondence, 1867–1868. (300 items.)

John Martin Broomall was a Representative in Congress from Delaware County, 1863–1869.

Correspondence dealing with the routine work of a congressman, and some letters on conditions in the southern states during Reconstruction are included.

Purchased, 1948.

1513
Hoopes, Alban Williamson, b. 1904.   Collection, 1808–1948. (2 linear ft.)

Family papers collected by Alban W. Hoopes, teacher and author of articles on the history of the American Indians, include: typescripts of articles and book reviews; family and business letters, 1939–1948; business and personal papers, 1860–1905, of Azariah Hoopes, Philadelphia businessman, are in the collection.

Gift of Alban W. Hoopes, 1948.

1514
Gratz, Louisa.   Estate papers, 1825–1891.   (50 items.)

Estate papers of the Gratz sisters relate to their real estate and personal property and contain some correspondence on Judaism and the Mikveh Israel Synagogue.

1515
Smith, Abraham Lewis, 1831–1914.   Correspondence, 1846–1913. (115 items.)

Correspondence of Abraham Lewis Smith, prominent lawyer, covers his activities as the first president of the Delaware County Historical Society and as a member of the Alumni Society of the University of Pennsylvania. There are also a few personal letters.

1516
Cresson family.   Papers, 1828–1920.   (9 linear ft.)

Business and social correspondence of Caleb Cresson, William Penn Cresson, Francis Macomb Cresson, George Vaux Cresson, and other members of the Cresson family of Philadelphia; accounts and other papers on St. Philip's Church and the Church of the Epiphany, Philadelphia; St. Paul's Church, Oaks; and churches at Claymont and in Brandywine Hundred, Del., are included. The collection also contains miscellaneous family photographs, mementos.
Purchased, 1948.

1517A
St. Andrew's Church (Philadelphia, Pa.)   Papers, 1800–1905.
(3 linear ft.)

St. Andrew's Church is a West Philadelphia Episcopal Church.
Correspondence and bills, 1831–1902; miscellaneous legal papers, including many deeds of the Church; scrapbook and journal of the Rev. E.D. Saunders, with some records of his military school, 1852–1870, in West Philadelphia.

1517B
St. Andrew's Church (Philadelphia, Pa.)   Records, 1823–1896.
(450 items.)

Records of St. Andrew's Church including Gregory Townsend Bedell's letters to the Vestry, 1823–1834; correspondence of the Vestry, 1834–1882, concerning finances and other Church affairs; records of pew rents, 1823–1896; and miscellaneous financial records, 1823–1876, including investment and operating records.

1518
Reformed Church in America (Philadelphia, Pa.)
Records, 1837–1895.

Records of the First Reformed Dutch Church include: minutes of the organization of officers and teachers in the Sunday School for the Sabbath School Association, 1859–1885, and minutes containing records of the numbers attending and other notes on the services for the Sunday School, 1845–1856, 1861–1863; Sunday School receiving books, 1844–1862, containing names and addresses of the pupils, and frequently noting the name and occupation of the father; Young Peoples Missionary Society minutes, 1883–1885; list of girl pupils, n.d.; superintendent's attendance records and Sunday School minute book, 1872–1873; miscellaneous orders, bills, and receipts, 1877–1895, for the upkeep of the church; Crown Street Sabbath School Missionary Society minutes, 1838–1842; accounts, 1837–1849.

Purchased, 1948.

1519
Burrell, Stephanie L.   Collection, 1928–1943.   (100 items.)

Letters, notes, and pamphlets gathered in preparation for an address on the history of the American flag. Material on the flags and seals of the original thirteen states is included.

Gift of Stephanie L. Burrell.

1520
McCormick, Robert Laird, 1847–1911.   Diaries, 1859–1866.
(5 v.)

These diaries were begun by R. Laird McCormick in 1859, when he was twelve years old. Entries for the period 1859–1862 are fragmentary, but the life of a boy in Clinton County, is well depicted. The years 1865–1866 describe the activities of Saunders Institute, a boys' school in Philadelphia, and of other schools in the state.

Gift of W.L. McCormick, 1948.

1521
Nazareth Hall School for Boys.   Account books, 1786–1850.
(9 linear ft.)

Account books for the Nazareth Hall School for Boys, a well-known school for boys, founded in 1755 and conducted by the Moravians, included are general account books, 1786–1846; cash books, 1788–1845; journals, 1799–1820; waste book, 1788–1796; pay book, 1823–1850; rosters of pupils, 1814–1819; private lessons, 1832–1842; annuities, pensions, and salaries, 1799–1853; quarterly disbursements, 1793–1810; inspectresses' house store books, 1839–1844; bills and drafts, 1822–1829. The collection also contains linen-mending book, 1839–1848; pocket money for students, 1827–1841; clothing repairs, 1840–1850; clothing and washing, wash-house book, 1841–1848.

Purchased, Dreer Fund, 1948.

1522

Friends Library Association of West Chester (West Chester, Pa.)
Papers, 1880–1896.   **(150 items.)**

Bills and receipts for books purchased and services rendered.
Purchased, 1946.

1523

Indian Rights Association.   **Papers, 1830 (1884–1967) 1969.**
(246 linear ft.)

The Indian Rights Association was founded in Philadelphia in 1882 to "bring about the complete civilization of the Indians and their admission to citizenship." In 1884 the Indian Rights Association opened a Washington office to act as a legislative lobby and liaison with the Board of Indian Commissioners and the Board of Indian Affairs. The Philadelphia and Washington offices maintained almost daily correspondence until the latter office closed in 1939. Much of this correspondence is included in the collection. The Indian Rights Association also maintained close contacts with Indian agents and with Indians themselves through correspondence and almost annual field trips to reservations and settlements. The papers include many reports and letters reflecting these contacts.

The responsibility for the Indian Rights Association's programs fell, largely, to five men, all of whom had lengthy careers with the Indian Rights Association: Herbert Welsh, Matthew Sniffen, and Lawrence E. Lindley, active in Philadelphia; and Charles C. Painter and Samuel M. Brosius, Washington agents.

The collection contains correspondence, 1864–1967, and letterpress books, 1886–1943; organizational records, 1882–1973; printed matter, including early Indian pamphlets, Indian Rights Association Annual Reports and draft legislation, 1830–1969; Herbert Welsh papers, 1877–1934; photographs, mainly from Western field trips, ca. 1910–1930; Council on Indian Affairs materials, 1943–1968; manuscripts dealing with traditional Pueblo Indian dances, 1912–1915, and the legal rights of Oklahoma Indians under that state's probate laws, 1912–1916.

Gift of Indian Rights Association, 1942–1978.

Microfilm available from the Microfilming Corporation of America. 21 Harristown Road; Glen Rock, NJ 07452.

1524

Lotus Club (Philadelphia, Pa.)   **Minute book, 1873–1879.**   **(1 v.)**

The Lotus Club was a social and political club of Philadelphia.
Purchased, 1948.

1525
Malta Boat Club (Philadelphia, Pa.)   Papers, 1870–1912.
(4 linear ft.)

The Malta Boat Club, a Philadelphia athletic and social club, was founded in 1860.

Financial accounts, correspondence, miscellaneous papers, and lectures on banking.

Purchased, 1948.

1526
Ocean City Fishing Club (Ocean City, N.J.)   Minute books,
1913–1928.   (4 v.)

The Ocean City Fishing Club, established in 1913, was devoted to saltwater fishing.

Gift of Dr. W.M. Miller, 1946.

1527
Franks, Isaac, 1759–1822.   Account book, 1819–1824.   (1 v.)

Isaac Franks served as prothonotary of the Supreme Court of Pennsylvania, 1819–1822.

This account book lists the sums owed him by various lawyers for services rendered in his official capacity, some of which were paid after his death.

1528
Long, George V.Z.   Papers, 1918–1919.   (3 items.)

Diary telling of the experiences of George V. Z. Long as Y.M.C.A. secretary with the 89th Division, American Expeditionary Forces in France, 1918, and letters praising his efforts.

Gift of George V.Z. Long, 1936.

1529
Welsh, John, 1805–1886.   Papers, 1837–1878.   (1,500 items.)

Correspondence of John Welsh, Philadelphia philanthropist, covering his service as ambassador to England, 1877–1879, and as president of the Centennial Exposition in 1876. There is some correspondence of John Welsh, Jr.

Gift of Edward Lowber Stokes, 1946.

1530
Paschall family.   Papers, 1705–1770.   (6 v.)

Commonplace book of John Paschall consisting primarily of notes from the alchemic and philosophical writings of Thomas Vaughan; iron account book of Stephen Paschall, 1735–1756; and malt and barley book of Thomas Paschall, 1705–1711, 1713–1728.

Gift of Elliston J. Morris, 1944.

1531
Willing family.   Papers, 1761–1866.   (6 linear ft.)

The papers of the Willing family include: papers of Thomas Willing, Philadelphia lawyer, merchant, and partner of Robert Morris, some of which relate to the Revolutionary War, especially Willing's statement of his part in transmitting General Howe's peace offer to Congress in 1778; correspondence and personal papers of Richard Willing, Dr. Charles Willing, and other members of the Willing family; some correspondence of the Crammond family, 1816–1839, and of the Rev. Nicholas Power Tillinghast, 1837–1866.

Gift of Horace Hare, 1947.

1532
Dudley, Thomas Haines, 1819–1893.   Papers, 1854–1911.
(6 linear ft.)

Correspondence and legal papers of Thomas Haines Dudley, Edward Dudley, and Israel Roberts, Camden, N.J., attorneys.

Purchased, Mifflin Fund, 1948.

1533
Oxford Horse Company.   Minute book, 1854–1916.   (1 v.)

The Oxford Horse Company was organized to apprehend horse thieves.

Gift of Francis R. Taylor, 1948.

1534
World War II collection, 1938–1949.

Entry cancelled; see collection #1479.

1535
Archambault, Anna Margaretta.   Collection, 1876–1945.
(1,000 items.)

Entry cancelled; see collection # 11.

1536
Winner, Septimus, 1827–1902.   Collection, 1845–1902.   (41 v.)

Diaries, letters, and music notebooks of Septimus Winner, American composer. Original manuscript of "Listen to the Mocking Bird;" catalog of music for piano and organ, 1874; music for violin; Hannah Winner's illustrated volume of songs with music by Winner under the pseudonym of Alice Hawthorne.
Gift of Charles Eugene and Donald Claghorn, 1946.

1537
Wharton, Anne Hollingsworth, 1845–1928.   Papers, 1852–1926.
(7 linear ft.)

These papers include many writings and historical notes of Anne Hollingsworth Wharton, American author, widely known for her books on colonial customs and society. They contain biographical material, reproductions of portraits, and newspaper articles on persons and places of the colonial period.
Gift of Anne Hollingsworth Wharton.

1538
Konkle, Burton Alva, 1861–1944.   "A Life of Nicholas Biddle,"
1928.   (1 v.)

Unpublished biography.

1539
Bunting, William M.   *Sowing and Reaping : a novel.*   (1 v.)

Manuscript of *Sowing and Reaping,* a novel set in Philadelphia about 1880.

1540
Business, professional, and personal accounts, 1734–1936.   (107 v.)

Armstrong, William A. Receipt book, 1867–1875. William A. Armstrong was a Philadelphia stone contractor. (1 v.)
Atkins & Hughes. Letterbook, 1865–1867. Atkins & Hughes were Philadelphia commission merchants. (1 v.)
Baker, Pennell and Blanchard & Marsh. Account book, 1844–1858. (1 v.)
Bertolet, Amos. Account book, 1839–1861. Bertolet was a Norristown liquor merchant. (1 v.)
Black, Samuel A. Accounts, 1856–1920. Black was a Philadelphia building contractor. (2 v.)

Bonsall, John. Daybook, 1815–1831. Bonsall was a Philadelphia real estate conveyancer. (1 v.)

Booksellers daybook, 1869–1870. (1 v.)

Thomas Borbridge & Company. Receipt book, 1822–1829. (1 v.)

Burr, H. Daybook, 1835–1839. Burr operated a Vincentown, N.J. general store. (2 v.)

Chevalier, John. Daybook, 1760–1766. John and Peter Chevalier were Philadelphia and China merchants of rugs, blankets, dry goods, and general merchandise. (1 v.)

Clarkson, William. Ledger, 1767–1791. Clarkson was a Philadelphia general merchant.. (1 v.)

Coates, Mary. Personal receipt book, 1760–1770. (1 v.)

Columbia Transportation Line. Daybook of shipments, 1823–1824. (1 v.)

Commercial Banker's Accounts, 1859–18861. (1 v.)

Connelly, Lemuel S. Cashbook, 1851–1858. Connelly was a Philadelphia ship captain. (1 v.)

Coxe, Daniel W. Records, 1815–1849. (5 v.)

Cummings, Albert F. Account books, 1891–1931. (5 v.)

Daix, Augustus F. Letterpress book, 1907–1909. (1 v.)

Dobbins Soap Manufacturing Company (Camden, N.J.) Records, 1892–1936. (2 v.)

Emlen, George—Estate. Personal account book, 1784–1811.

Evans, William. Receipt book, 1836–1857. Evans was a Philadelphia publisher. (1 v.)

Evans, William. Records, 1818–1868. Evans was a Philadelphia druggist. (3 v.)

Everett, Hicks, & Caldwell. Receipt book, 1858–1861. Philadelphia merchants. (1 v.)

Farmers and Mechanics Bank (Philadelphia, Pa.) Bankbook of deposits, 1841–1846. (1 v.)

Fitzwater, John and Jacob. Records, 1813–1860. John and Jacob Fitzwater were Fitzwatertown lime-makers and general store operators. (1 v.)

Footman, Richard T. Letterbook, 1791–1793. Footman was a Savannah, Ga., general merchant. (1 v.)

Fraizer, F.W. Account book, 1842–1850. Fraizer was a Philadelphia real estate dealer. (1 v.)

Frazier, Nalbro. Cashbook, 1805–1811. Frazier was a Philadelphia insurance agent. (1 v.)

General merchant records, 1821–1885. (9 v.)

Green, Henry. Records, 1859–1887. (1 v.)

Haines, Joshua. Account book, 1796. Haines was a Philadelphia importer. (1 v.)

Hill, John and Samuel. Records, 1835–1908. John and Samuel Hill were Philadelphia rental agents. (1 v.)

Charles Hillman & Company. Records, 1853–1896. (2 v.)

Holbrook and Hughes. Letterbook, 1863–1867. Holbrook and Hughes were commission merchants. (1 v.)

Howell, Arthur. Account book, 1791–1799. Howell was a Philadelphia courier. (1 v.)

Hudson, Arnold. Account book, 1765–1780.

Robert Jenks and Son. Windsor Forge records, 1830–1839. (2 v.)

Melchior and John Larer. Receipt book, 1815–1820. The Larers were Philadelphia brewers. (1 v.)

Linvill, S.D. Receipt book, 1885–1886. Linvill was a Chester County farmer. (1 v.)

Mason, Richard. Daybook, 1784–1788. (1 v.)

McCalla, Alexander. Daybook, 1814. McCalla was a Philadelphia innkeeper. (1 v.)

McCally, John. Account books, 1805–1825. McCally was a Philadelphia merchant. (1 v.)

Abraham Mitchell and Company. Daybook, 1844–1858. Abraham Mitchell and Company were New York liquor merchants. (1 v.)

Morris, Luke W. Receipt book, 1799. Morris was a Philadelphia brewer. Receipts for goods and services furnished the Orphan's Home. (1 v.)

O'Neil, Henry. Account book, 1846–1848. (1 v.)

Philadelphia National Bank (Philadelphia, Pa.) Signature book, 1856–1868. (1 v.)

Pryor, Joseph. Journal, 1796–1805. Pryor was a Philadelphia grocer. (1 v.)

Rex, S.S. Account book, 1834–1835. Accounts for the Scheafferstown general store. (1 v.)

Richardson, Joseph. Records, 1796–1801. Richardson was a gold and silversmith. (3 v.)

Root, R.M. Account books, 1880–1899. (1 v.)

Scott, Lewis A. Account books, 1840–1847. Scott was a Philadelphia lawyer. (1 v.)

Sharswood, William. Journal, 1811–1812. Sharswood was a Philadelphia brewer. (1 v.)

Simpson, Thomas C. Personal cashbook, 1865–1867. (1 v.)

Swift Sure Line Mail Stage. Account book, 1811–1814. (1 v.)

Steel and Smith. Ledger, 1818–1823. Steel and Smith were Chester County millers. (1 v.)

Stock, John. Receipt books, 1784–1841. Stock was a Philadelphia painter. (2 v.)

Super, John. Account book, 1828–1831. Super was a Philadelphia blacksmith. (1 v.)

Thompson, William P. Ledger, 1831–1835. (1 v.)

Trumbauer, William T. Daybooks, 1857–1863. Trumbauer was a Schuylkill County merchant. (3 v.)

Vaughan and Lyman. Records, 1853–1896. Vaughan and Lyman were Philadelphia shipbuilders. (1 v.)

Vollmer, Gottlieb. Records, 1863–1869. Vollmer was a Philadelphia housefurnishing merchant. (1 v.)

Wescoat, William. Ledger, 1827–1829. Wescoat was a general merchant. (2 v.)

Western Transportation Line. Shipments between Philadelphia and Baltimore, Md., 1827–1838. (1 v.)

Whitaker and Stickel. Journal 1863–1881. Whitaker and Stickel was Philadelphia publishers. (1 v.)

Isaac S. Williams and Company. Receipt book, 1883–1890. Williams and Company were Philadelphia housefurnishing merchants. (1 v.)

1541

Moore, Joseph Hampton, 1864–1950.   **Papers, 1884–1949.**
(33 linear ft.)

The personal papers of J. Hampton Moore, one of the civic and political leaders of 20th century Philadelphia, fall into five sections, each covering a phase of Moore's career.

The earliest papers, 1884–ca. 1900, pertain to his early life and his start in politics. Many clippings and letters reveal his activities as a reporter and editorial writer, 1884–1894. Some material on the Johnstown flood, 1889, is also included. For the period 1894–1906, there is considerable information on local politics.

The second group of papers, pertains to the period when Moore was a U.S. congressman, 1906–1920, is voluminous and reveals the activities of a hard-working and influential big city representative and disclose the pressures exerted by various economic, social, religious, cultural and national groups about proposed legislation. There is much on World War I, 1914–1918.

The third group pertains to Moore's career in local politics and includes: correspondence, reports, and clippings on his two terms as Mayor, 1920–1924, and 1932–1936; some correspondence and clippings, 1920–1949, on other political and local affairs.

The fourth section pertains to Moore's activities in social and political clubs. The Five O'Clock Club, a well-known dining club organized in 1883, is represented by correspondence, notes, and invitations, 1890–1930. Correspondence, 1900–1912, of the National League of Republican Clubs is also contained in this group.

The last major group of papers is that of the Atlantic Deeper Waterways Association. Moore was president of this group from its organization in 1907 to 1948. Correspondence, clippings, and pamphlets on the efforts to construct a deep-channel, protected waterway from Boston to Miami.

Correspondents include: W.J. Bryan, John J. Pershing, Al Smith, Charles Warren Fairbanks, Boies Penrose, Zane Grey, Grover Cleveland, W.G. Harding, Cyrus Curtis, Theodore Roosevelt, George Dewey, Mark Hanna, Elihu Root, A. Graham Bell, Calvin Coolidge, William McKinley, Joseph Grundy, Edward Bok, Georges Clemenceau, John Burroughs, Henry Ford, and others.

Gift of J. Hampton Moore, 1944–1949.

1542
McKesson, Irvin H., Mrs.   Collection, 1750 (1760–1870) 1917. (44 v.)

Papers of Samuel Jones and three generations of his descendants. Samuel Jones, a minister of Pennypack Baptist Church, Philadelphia, 1763–1814, is represented by incoming correspondence, sermons, personal and church records, and some miscellaneous legal items. There are papers, 1748–1812, of Alexander Edwards, Philadelphia storekeeper and active member of Jones' church, including incoming family correspondence, financial records, and miscellaneous legal papers.

Jones's daughter, Sarah, married Robert Henderson, and then Theophilus Harris. Harris was a minister and justice of the peace for Philadelphia County, and some personal incoming correspondence, 1810–1845, court dockets, 1819–1833, daybook, 1822–1841, and miscellaneous legal items are found here. There is family correspondence, 1815–1861, of Samuel Jones Henderson, son of Sarah and Robert Henderson. Of special interest are Civil War letters between Laura Henderson Dade and her husband Frank Dade while he was serving as a Union Army physician stationed at Beaufort, S.C.

Gift of Mrs. Irving H. McKesson.

1543
Bank of North America.   Records, 1780–1923.   (150 linear ft.)

The Bank of North America was the first chartered bank in the United States, chartered by the Second Continental Congress in 1781. It was established primarily to aid Congress in providing supplies and money for the prosecution of the Revolutionary War. In 1916 the bank bought the assets of the National Bank of the Northern Liberties; in 1923 it merged with the Commercial Trust Company to form the Bank of North America and Trust Company; six years later the merged institution was itself absorbed by the Pennsylvania Company.

Minute books and letterbooks, 1780–1923. The minute books, are complete from the very beginning of the bank until its merger with the Commercial Trust Company, with brief records of meetings of the Board of Directors and some of meetings of stockholders.

The documents include formal bank communications, memoranda, announcements, copies of letters, financial statements, and the like. The most interesting of the documents is a long report from the Joint Committee of the Philadelphia banks, April 13, 1816, recommending that specie payments be resumed as soon as the Bank of the United States commenced giving discounts, that each bank pay out its own notes only (except those for less than $10), and that the banks refrain from an immediate reduction of discounts. There are photographs and engravings of bank people. There are also a few caricatures and silhouettes. In addition there are numerous prints and engravings of Robert Morris and the first seven presidents of the bank: Thomas Willing, John Nixon, John Morton, Henry Nixon, John Richardson, James Dixon, and Thomas Smith.

Miscellaneous items include: deeds of sundry lands contracted for in 1793 and 1794 by Robert Morris, John Nicholson, and James Greenleaf, totaling over 3.5 million acres in Georgia, South Carolina, Virginia, and Kentucky, at an average price of over a shilling an acre; letter book of John Nixon, Philadelphia merchant; checkbooks and bank books; scrapbook, 1904–1920, of antiquarian interest; unclassified books and pamphlets on finance; and an extra-illustrated, three-volume folio edition of Lawrence Lewis' History of the Bank of North America.

Deposited by the Pennsylvania Company, 1939.

Finding aid available.

McClurkin, A.J. "The Bank of North America and the Financial History of Philadelphia," *P.M.H.B.,* 64 (1940).

1544
Centennial Exhibition.   Records, 1876–1879.   (12 linear ft.)

Soon after the Civil War, many individuals in various parts of the country began to consider how the United States' centennial year should be spent. In 1871 Congress provided that "the first century of our national existence shall be commemorated by an exhibition of the natural resources of the country and their development, and of its progress in those arts which benefit mankind, in comparison with those of older nations."

The collection covers many aspects of the Exhibition. Most important in the collection is the Documentary Record of the Centennial. This is a group of scrapbooks that primarily focuses upon the United States Centennial Commission. The Commission was responsible for soliciting support through its Board of Finance, organizing the centennial celebration and exhibits, and building the extensive exhibition grounds.

There are reports, pamphlets, form letters, lists of regulations, and news releases. Information on the various Bureaus of Administration (Agriculture, Horticulture, Transportation, Machinery) and foreign and state exhibits is present.

Most correspondence consists of form letters to legislators, supporters, and exhibitors.

There are architectural plans submitted in the Centennial building competition with descriptions by the architects. Ephemera (trade cards, visitors' cards, invitations, programs, and newspaper clippings) fills out the collection.

There are many photographs and stereoscopic views of the exhibition grounds, buildings, and exhibits.

Finding aid available.

1545A
City National Bank (Philadelphia, Pa.)   Records, 1857–1900.
(2 v.)

Records of the City National Bank, including a signature book, 1870–1900, and a stock transfer book, 1857–1900.

Gift of the Free Library of Philadelphia, 1947.

1545B
City National Bank (Philadelphia, Pa.)   Records, 1892–1894.
(1 v.)

George Albert Lewis, cashier, letterpress book with incoming and outgoing correspondence, reports, and memoranda.

1546
Civil War papers, 1861–1878.   (6 linear ft.)

These papers contain primarily Union Army muster rolls, consolidated reports, returns, enlistment certificates, with some Civil War correspondence, official and personal, reminiscences, miscellaneous manuscripts and memorabilia.

Major groups of regimental papers are: Eastern Shore Maryland Volunteers, 2nd Regiment, enlistment certificates for Company G, 1862, orders, 1862, and muster rolls, October 1864; New York Volunteers, 67th Regiment (Long Island Volunteers, 1st Regiment) Company K, muster rolls, 1862–1864, return notices, 1863–1864, and morning reports, July-November 1862; Pennsylvania Volunteers, 96th and 98th Regiments, scattered muster rolls; Pennsylvania Reserve Volunteer Corp, 7th Regiment, Company G, record books, 1861–1864, of clothing, personnel descriptive list, orders, and morning reports; Matthew Hasting Independent Keystone Battery record books, 1862–1864, morning reports, post guard reports, and clothing.

Enlistment related papers consist of Marine Corps enlistment certificates at Philadelphia, November, 1862 to January, 1863; Citizens Bounty Fund Committee, Philadelphia, muster rolls of reserve units, September, 1862; Philadelphia Sixth Ward enlistment certificates, 1864–1865, and some financial papers; Camden City Middle Ward enrollment list, August, 1862. There are also Office for the Relief of the Families of Philadelphia Volunteers payment orders, 1861–1865.

Additionally there are copies of correspondence, 1861–1862, between Major General Robert Patterson and General Winfield Scott on military operations of the first Bull Run Campaign; William H. Manley, private with Pennsylvania Volunteers, 72nd Regiment (Baxter's Fire Zouaves), letters, 1861–1862; David D. Jones, officer with Pennsylvania Volunteers, 88th Regiment, letters, 1862–1863; and [John F.] Reynolds Monument Committee, minutes and papers, 1864–1878.

A small section of Confederate miscellany includes some letters, 1861–1862.

1547
Sesqui-Centennial papers, 1926.   (100 **items.**)

A small collection of booklets, advertising matter, invitations, printed plans, and views of the celebration of the 150th anniversary of American Independence.

1548
Foulkrod, John C.   Collection, 1853–1915.   (2 v.)

Papers collected by John C. Foulkrod include: invitations, notices, programs, insignia, rules and bylaws of the volunteer fire companies of Philadelphia, 1853–1873. Also included is material on the election of the chief engineer of the fire department, 1867–1868, and a history of the volunteer department which appeared in the *Philadelphia Sunday Dispatch*. A few letters and invitations of the Firemen's Active Association of Philadelphia,

1910–1915, together with photographs and clippings relating to the activities of the local volunteers, 1873–1910, complete the collection.

Gift of Mrs. F. Foulkrod, 1927.

1549

Magee, Horace, 1846–1912.   Collection, 1861–1862.   (1 v.)

A small volume containing 6 numbers of *The Union*, an amateur paper published by four youthful Philadelphians: Horace Magee, Walter Lippincott, Francis H. Williams, and Thomas H. Lyman. Also included are some patriotic appeals and a few business cards.

Gift of Miss M. Atherton Leach, 1931.

1550

Bancker family.   Papers, 1735–1869.   (1,000 items.)

Entry cancelled; returned to family.

1551

Pennsylvania. Council of National Defense.   Papers, 1917–1918. (2 v.)

The Council was established in March, 1917, as a civilian organization to provide safety for the Commonwealth of Pennsylvania and later became a cooperative agency of the Federal Council of National Defense. This group advised Governor Brumbaugh, promoted civilian affairs, and assisted businessmen in the war effort. George Wharton Pepper served as chairman.

Minutes of the Advisory Committee; correspondence file of George Wharton Pepper; publicity information on Pepper's efforts; treasurer's reports, 1917–1918.

Gift of George Wharton Pepper, 1948, 1955.

1552

Insurance papers, 1726–1900.   (1,500 items.)

A collection of insurance policies that includes marine insurance, 1726–1843, and fire insurance, 1796–1900. Most of the policies are placed on Philadelphia properties. The collection contains Levi Hollingsworth's insurance subscription book, 1784–1788.

1553

Greeting card collection, 1770–1940.   (3 linear ft.)

A collection of greeting cards, invitations, admission tickets, funeral notices, Christmas cards, birthdays cards, and valentines.

1554

Brinton, John Hill, 1772–1827.   **Papers,** 1790–1890.

Entry cancelled; returned to family.

1555

Pricipio Iron Works.   **Papers,** 1724–1903.   (31 v.)

Entry cancelled; returned to family.

1556

J.G. Brill Company (Philadelphia, Pa.)   **Records,** 1876–1940.
(ca. 10,000 photoprints.)

These records contain shop records and photographs of the J.G. Brill Company, manufacturers of street cars and buses. They include: cabinet shop work order books, 1876–1884; shop work order books, 1887–1940; photographs of street cars and buses and of their construction and parts.

Gift of A.C. Brill, 1946.

1557

Mask and Wig Club.   **Papers,** 1889–1937.   (5,000 items.)

Papers of the Mask and Wig Club, the dramatic organization of the University of Pennsylvania, including: historical data, yearbooks, membership lists, minute books, orchestrations, librettos and lyrics, prompt books, publicity releases.

Deposited by the Mask and Wig Club, 1941.

1558

Citizen's Bounty Fund Committee (Philadelphia, Pa.)   **Papers,**
1862–1866.   **(6 linear ft.)**

The Citizen's Bounty Fund Committee was formed to encourage enlistments through payments of bounties during the Civil War.

The papers include: subscriptions to the fund, 1862–1863; correspondence, 1862–1863, on enlistments and donations of tents and other equipment; certificates of volunteer enlistments; financial records, 1862–1866; and minutes, 1862–1863.

Gift of the Lorin Bloget estate, 1911.

1559

Confederate States of America.   **Currency,** 1861–1864.
(1,000 items.)

This collection contains examples of the paper money issued by the Confederate government, 1861–1864, with notes on the printing and rarity of each issue. There is also material on the money issued by the various southern states, 1861–1864, and examples of nontaxable certificates, state bonds, subscriptions blanks, surety's oaths, bonds, currency, local and national receipts.

1560
Philadelphia (Pa.)   Records, 1810–1858.   (21 v.)

Financial records of the city and county, 1810–1858. The collection includes auditors' minutes, 1810–1854; auditors' journals, 1841–1843, 1846–1848; auditors' bill books, 1849–1854; treasurer's accounts, 1854–1857; treasurer's daybook, 1851–1853; expense accounts of public works, 1839–1853; building and material agreements, 1834–1848; work and labor agreements, 1836–1853; city election office pay roll, 1851–1854; inventory of city property, 1852–1855; tobacco warehouse ledgers, 1845–1858; District of Richmond Board of Commissioners minute book, 1847–1852.

1561
Historical Society of Pennsylvania. War Service Committee. Papers, 1918–1919.   (5,000 items.)

Invitations, programs, bills, receipts, and vouchers showing how the Historical Society assisted in entertaining servicemen, 1918–1919. There is some correspondence relating to the work and to the publicity given it.

1562
Bank records, 1789–1849.   (36 items.)

Collection of protested notes at Philadelphia banks. Among the banks represented are Girard, Mechanics', Bank of North America, Bank of the Northern Liberties, Bank of Pennsylvania, Bank of Philadelphia, and the Schuylkill Bank.

1563
Janney, Samuel McPherson, 1801–1880.   *History of the Religious Society of Friends,* 1859.   (1 v.)

The original manuscript of the last part of Samuel M. Janney's *History of the Religious Society of Friends* (Philadelphia, 1859) dealing with the Hicksite schism in America.

1564
Parke, James P.   Marriage and death records, 1751–1850.   (1 v.)

Daily entries of marriages and deaths with occasional entries reporting weather and local events.

1565
Stone, Frank S.   Collection, 1764–1859.   (30 items.)

A collection of Philadelphia deeds, 1764–1859, and a few miscellaneous legal papers, judgement searches, 1823–1855.
Gift of Frank S. Stone.

1566
Hutchinson, J.B.   Collection, 1889–1930.   (500 items.)

This collection contains passes on various railroads, steamship lines, and other forms of transportation issued to J.B. Hutchinson, an official of the Pennsylvania Railroad.

1567
Liberty Bell petitions, 1912.   (3 v.)

Signed petitions presented to Philadelphia City Council against permitting the removal of the Liberty Bell from Independence Hall for any reason.
Gift of the Philadelphia Chapter of the Daughters of the American Revolution, 1948.

1568
Historical Survey of Philadelphia : record survey, 1934.   (10 items.)

Entry cancelled; see collection #1474.

1569
Book-plate collection.   (1,500 items.)

1570
Pennsylvania Court papers, 1773–1845.   (15 linear ft.)

A collection of legal papers of cases tried before various Pennsylvania courts. A few dockets are included.
Gift of the Eli Kirk Price estate, 1933.

1571
Gratz, Simon.   Correspondence, 1858–1923.   (9 linear ft.)

Correspondence of Simon Gratz, Philadelphia lawyer, autograph collector, and member of the Philadelphia Board of Education, including letters from most of the politically prominent Philadelphians of the period. There is considerable material on the public schools of Philadelphia.

1572
Philadelphia (Pa.). Department of City Transit.   Collection, n.d.
(100 items and 26 v.)

Entry cancelled; transferred to the Graphics department.

1573
United States. Army.   Muster rolls, 1809–1812.   (100 items.)

Purchased, 1900.

1574
Courtland Saunders Post No. 21 (Philadelphia, Pa.)
History, 1890–1923.   (3 v.)

Sketches of the war experiences of the various members of the post and notices of their deaths, 1890–1923. A list of those taking the oath of allegiance to the United States, 1863–1864, at Bridgeport, Ala., is included, as well as a report of the operations of the 2nd Division, 12th Army Corps, U.S. Army, from April 27 to July 26, 1863.

Gift of Courtland Saunders Post No. 21.

Cover title: Personal War Sketches Presented to Courtland Saunders Post No. 21 Department of Pennsylvania / by Frank F. Bell et al.

1575
O'Donovan, William Rudolph, 1844–1920.   Letters, 1861–1920.

(150 items.)

Letters of William Rudolph O'Donovan, noted American sculptor, to his family in Fayette County. Most of the letters were written between 1871 and 1887 from New York and tell of the sculptor's experiences there. There are letters telling of O'Donovan's sympathy with the South and his services in the Confederate Army.

Gift of Mrs. Evelyn Benson and Miss Pierie Abraham.

1576
Edmunds, Albert Joseph, 1857–1941.   Papers, 1861–1941.
(21 linear ft.)

Papers of Albert J. Edmunds, noted biblical scholar and long-time cataloger of the Historical Society of Pennsylvania, includes his personal correspondence, 1861–1941, notes on his published works, and manuscripts. The papers also includes some correspondence, 1874–1904, of Benjamin Smith Lyman, and a typescript of his book, *Vegetarian Diet and Dishes*.

1577
Penrose, Boies, 1860–1921.   Collection, n.d.   (5,000 items.)

Entry cancelled; removed to Graphics Department.

1578
Kimball family.   Scrapbook, 1861–1902.   (1 v.)

This volume contains photographs of members of the Kimball family, their residences, and the placed they visited. A few letters and manuscripts are included. There is a short poem signed A. Conon Doyle, 1890, mentioning Kimball and Lippincott in Philadelphia.
Gift of Arthur J. Sussel, 1935.

1579
**Historical Society of Pennsylvania.   Records survey, 1934–1940.
(50 items.)**

Entry cancelled; see collection #1475.

1580
Fales, Samuel B.   Collection, 1861–1880.   (9 linear ft.)

Bills, receipts, correspondence, and newspaper clippings present a comprehensive view of the activities of the Union Volunteer Refreshment Saloon, 1861–1865. This organization cared for thousands of Union soldiers as they passed through Philadelphia, and the papers and books name many of those so helped. The hospital books, 1861–1865, in particular, give the name, regiment, and home of each man treated. Another book gives names and addresses of Southerners separated from their families. Other books give donations and subscriptions.
Gift of Samuel B. Fales.

1581
Birch, William Russell, 1775–1834.   Autobiography.   (2 v.)

Autobiographical notes written by William Russell Birch, American painter and engraver, telling of his life in England and his removal to and early life in this country. Included is a note on enamel painting by Birch and a list of paintings by him.
Gift of Albert Rosenthal, 1927.
Typescript.

Powel family.   **Papers, 1700–1925.**   **(51 linear ft.)**

The papers of several related families, long prominent in Philadelphia, Newport, R.I., and Jamaica, B.W.I., are represented in this collection.

The first part contains business letters and records, 1700–1748, of Samuel Powel, the original settler, and of his son Samuel. They were general merchants trading with Europe and the West Indies. The next Samuel Powel was mayor of Philadelphia in 1775 and again in 1789. He married Elizabeth Willing who became well known as a social leader. Present are Samuel Powel's exercises at the University of Pennsylvania, 1759; his business papers, 1767–1771; and a list of his property, 1779. The papers of Elizabeth Powel comprise a group of pocket almanacs, 1793–1822, with diary entries; receipt books, 1793–1801; personal account books, 1794–1800; and correspondence, 1772–1823, including copies of her own letters. Among the correspondents are George Washington, Bishop William White, William Bingham, Rev. Jacob Duché, and others of equal prominence.

The remainder of the Powel papers are those of Elizabeth's nephew and adopted son, and his descendants. John Hare Powel, who changed his name from John Powel Hare in 1807, was active in public affairs and was much interested in improving breeds of cattle in America. His correspondence, 1806–1839, contains much on these matters as well as on early railroads, the location of tracks in the city of Philadelphia, and on canals. A group of papers, 1830–1850, on coal lands in Pennsylvania describes their possibilities. Personal papers include: a diary, 1806, of a trip to Calcutta; letter books, 1827–1830 and 1849–1853; a commonplace book; and an abridgement of Robertson's *History of Charles V* complete his personal papers. His business papers showing the activities of a well-to-do landowner cover the years 1820–1856.

Samuel Powel, son of John Hare Powel, lived in Philadelphia and Newport. His papers largely supplement those of his father and deal with similar subjects. They include business papers and accounts, 1843–1885, with many bills and receipts, 1856–1857, on the construction of the Newport house; a diary kept while in Europe, 1841, and personal correspondence, 1843–1884, containing many letters to members of his family and a number, 1843–1869, from Dorothea Dix.

Among the remaining Powel papers are those of Mary Edith Powel, including her garden notebooks, 1894–1919; journal, 1898–1907, 1923–1926; correspondence, almost entirely personal, 1883–1925; genealogical notes; and several scrapbooks and notebooks.

Samuel Powel married Mary Johnston who was born in Jamaica, B.W.I. Through her came a large group of papers of the Johnston, Taylor, and Cole families of Jamaica. They deal largely with the operation of plantations on that island. Dr. Alexander Johnston, a physician, is represented by daybooks, 1782–1783; ledgers, 1764–1769, 1773–1775; journal, 1760–1772; diaries, 1773–1775 and 1787; and commonplace book, 1764, containing medical discourses delivered at Aberdeen, Scotland. Of James Johnston there is correspondence, 1807–1836; accounts, 1821–1830; and a few military papers, 1793–1833, showing the life of a Jamaica planter.

The bulk of the Johnston papers are those of Robert Johnston, who spent most of his life in England, moving to Newport, R.I., about 1832–1834. The Robert Johnston papers include the original journals of his travels in northern Europe and Russia, 1814, in Scotland, 1810 and 1813, and in Ireland, 1812. Also included are journals of a voyage from London to Jamaica, 1813, and one of his residence at Newport, 1835–1839; correspondence, 1802–1839, dealing with business, literary, and personal affairs; and business papers, 1817–1836, concerning his Jamaica plantation and a projected railroad from London to Southampton, a plan he originated.

Business papers, 1783–1813, of John Taylor and of Jacob Thomas Cole, Jamaica planters, are also in this collection.

Gift of the Powel family, 1949.

1583
Bingham, William, 1752–1804.   Papers, 1777–1917.
(69 linear ft.)

This collection pertains primarily to the administration of the estate left by William Bingham, financier and United States senator from Pennsylvania. Some letters, 1783–1784, from William Bingham in Europe to Thomas Willing, deal with business matters. Some of the early papers, 1777–1779, pertain to the business interests of Bingham during the Revolutionary War.

The estate was invested primarily in undeveloped lands in Pennsylvania, New York, and Maine.

The papers on the Maine lands include most of the important papers connected with the Knox-Duer purchase of Maine lands in 1791; descriptions of the country, surveyors' field books, and similar accounts of Maine in the 1790's; papers on the attempt to plant a French colony in Maine under Madame Leval; documents on the transfer of this purchase to William Bingham in 1792–1793; a series of letters, 1793–1795, from William Jackson while he was in Europe attempting to sell Maine lands to British capitalists and the French government; correspondence with Generals Henry Knox, Henry Jackson, and David Cobb, all concerned in one way or another in the development of the purchase; material on the sale of one half of the

Penobscot Tract in 1796 to Alexander Baring, acting for the house of Baring and Hope; letters from Harrison Gray Otis, Thomas Russell, John and Stephen Codman, John Richards, and other prominent Massachusetts citizens, 1791–1830; papers explanatory of the suit of *Cabot et al v. Bingham,* arising from Bingham's actions while agent for the Continental Congress in Martinique, 1779–1804; reports on Maine developments from General David Cobb, John Black, and other agents, 1795–1850; reports of the trustees of the Bingham estate on the Maine property, together with their correspondence with various agents, 1804–1850; and numerous accounts, vouchers, deeds, contracts and court papers illuminating almost every phase of this venture.

The papers on the Pennsylvania and New York lands are similar in content. They contain many letters and reports from the agent at Wellsboro, 1855–1917, to the trustees of the estate. A few letters, 1879–1911 mention oil leases.

Deposited by R. Sturgis Ingersoll, 1949.

1584
Drayton family.   Papers, 1796–1896.   (28 linear ft.)

Papers of the Drayton family, a prominent South Carolina and Philadelphia family. The largest part of the collection consists of the legal papers, 1851–1893, of William Heyward Drayton. Among these are a small number of papers of Frances Butler, 1828–1886, and of Pierce Butler, 1800–1822.

The letters of various members of the Drayton family reflect their opinions on nullification, the Mexican War, the Civil War, and other subjects. Of special interest are the letters of General Thomas Drayton, U.S. Army, and the correspondence of Captain Percival Drayton, U.S. Navy, 1840–1866. The latter has much on naval matters. The letters, 1817–1846, received by Colonel William Drayton illustrate the feeling of the times. The collection contains considerable printed material on nullification, states rights, slavery, and the tariff, 1796–1840.

Deposited by the Estate of Henry F. Drayton, 1939.

1585
**Bureau of Unemployment Relief.   Papers, 1930–1932.
(2,000 items.)**

Check stubs, banknotes, warrants, bills, reports, contributions, food orders, and other business papers of the Bureau of Unemployment Relief, formed to relieve the distress of the unemployed, 1930–1932. Included are papers on the Clearing House for Homeless Men, 1931; Temporary Shelter for Homeless Men, 1931–1932; Emergency Aid, 1932; and the United Campaign, 1932.

Gift of Horatio Gates Lloyd, 1947.

1586
Brown, David S. & Co.   **Records, 1828–1910.**   **(204 linear ft.)**

David S. Brown entered into his brothers' Philadelphia firm, J. and M. Brown, in 1817. In 1821 he became a member of the firm of Hacker, Brown and Co., which existed until 1830 when its name was changed to David S. Brown & Co., Philadelphia commission merchants dealing in dry goods.

Brown served as Director of Girard Bank, 1840–1843. In 1844 he built and was president and manager of the Washington Manufacturing Company in Gloucester, N.J., which manufactured cotton. Washington Mills, owned by the Washington Manufacturing Company, contained both mills and boarding houses for single workers. Following this he established the Gloucester Manufacturing Company for the production of printed calicoes. In 1859 Brown built the Gloucester Gingham Mills, incorporated in 1872. In 1864 he established and was president of the Gloucester Iron Works, which was incorporated in 1871.

Other companies David S. Brown established include the Gloucester Print Works and the Gloucester Land Company. He founded the Ancona Printing Company in 1871, which introduced new methods of applying colors which had been successful in Europe but previously untried in the United States.

The collection includes records of David S. Brown & Co.: correspondence, letter books, cashbooks, ledgers, receipt books, sales books, invoice books, sample books, stock books, purchase books, daybooks, sketch books, account sale books, journals, merchandise blotters, cash blotters, order books, checks, miscellaneous books, and other titles.

Other Brown companies are represented by assorted records: Washington Manufacturing Company, 1844–1895, minutes of the stockholders, ledgers, payroll books, superintendent's cashbook, and rent roll; Gloucester Manufacturing Company, 1868–1879, ledgers and stock book of prints; Gloucester Gingham Mills, 1871–1908, correspondence, ledgers, supply book, legal papers relating to a suit between Gloucester Gingham Mills and Gloucester Cotton Mill Company, office letter book, letter books, cashbooks, daybook, receipt book, purchase books, stock book, sales books, monthly reports, and invoice books; Gloucester Iron Works, 1873–1910, correspondence, letter books, cashbooks, sales books, time book, ledger, and check stubs; and the Ancona Printing Company, 1877–1880, letter books, account sales books, cashbooks, stock book, stock print books, receipt book, and invoice book containing fabric samples.

Other records include Gloucester Library and Library Company minutes, 1850, and accounts, 1851–1854.

Gift of David S.B. Chew.

1587

Parker, Daniel, 1782–1846.   Papers, 1761–1838.   (12 linear ft.)

The Parker papers consists almost entirely of correspondence and business records of the Collins and Marshall families. Zaccheus Collins, a Philadelphia merchant, was the father-in-law of General Parker, who administered his estate. The papers consist of correspondence, 1798–1831, much of it with members of his family, but including letters, 1820–1829, from Constantine Samuel Rafinesque on business and botanical matters, and letters from Charles Lee, Edmund J. Lee, R.B. Lee, R.H. Lee, and William Lee, 1790–1829. The business records include a letterbook, 1801–1804; ledgers, 1787–1791 and 1794–1805; receipt book, 1794–1831; receipts, 1800–1831; papers relating to lands taken up in Pennsylvania, 1793–1795, 1812; and some correspondence relating to trade with India, 1801–1809. A book of letters and legal opinions, 1831, by William Rawle in regard to the Zaccheus Collins estate and General Daniel Parker's accounts of the estate complete the Zaccheus Collins portion.

For Stephen Collins, father of Zaccheus, the collection contains old bonds and deeds, 1761–1795; bankbook, 1791; letter book, 1783–1792; and letters from Colonel Robert Hampden Pye, 1778–1779.

Christopher Marshall, Jr., the father-in-law of Zaccheus Collins, is represented by a diary, 1806, and a waste book, 1797–1798. In addition there is a ledger, 1775–1797, of the firm of Christopher and Charles Marshall, Philadelphia drug and paint manufacturers, and an account book, 1811, of Christopher's estate.

The collection also contains Elizabeth Marshall's ciphering book, 1782; inventory of the estate of Thomas Paschall, 1796, Christopher Marshall executor; an account of the estate of Anne Collins, 1807–1815; and General Parker's letters relating to his venture in the horse-breeding business with General Irvine, 1818–1838, and book entitled War and Peace Register and Regulations, 1814–1838, which contains copies of orders and regulations issued by the War Department.

1588

Wilson, William Bauchop, 1862–1934.   Papers, 1913–1921.
(54 linear ft.)

Papers from the private files of William B. Wilson, who served as the first U.S. Secretary of Labor, 1913–1921, mention labor conditions, strikes, efforts to secure employment under the government, patronage, and other routine work of a cabinet officer. A section of political letters shows activities in the national campaigns, 1914–1920.

Deposited by Paul W. Pritchard, 1942.

Finding aid available.

1589

Wood and Bacon.   Account books, 1787–1824.   (3 linear ft.)

The books of Wood and Bacon, general merchandise firm in Greenwich, N.J., include: are daybooks, 1787–1820; ledgers, 1791–1824; invoice books, 1796–1803; and arithmetic book of David Wood, 1794.

Deposited by Richard D. Wood, 1937.

1590

Markham, William, 1635–1704.   Papers, 1681–1698.   (4 items.)

Entry cancelled; transferred to the Society collection.

1591

Strubing family.   Papers, 1786–1864.   (23 items.)

This is a group of Strubing family papers including primarily those of Philip Strubing, a Swiss who served as an officer in the Continental Army during the Revolutionary War. Included are his commissions as a lieutenant and as a captain; letters testifying his services signed by Baron Von Steuben and George Washington; a certificate of membership in the Society of the Cincinnati, 1784; family letters, 1785–1822; and some personal papers, bills, accounts, and passports, 1785–1831. The collection also contains the naturalization petition of Patrick Devitt, 1808; marriage certificates of John K. Strubing and Julianna Kelley, 1841, and of Philip H. Strubing and Mary Devitt, 1864; a deposition about James Strubing, 1842; and John K. Strubing's discharge from the Army, 1863.

Deposited by John K. Strubing, Jr., 1939.

1592

St. James Church (Perkiomen, Philadelphia, Pa.)
Vestry book, 1740–1866.   (1 v.)

Vestry book of St. James Church contains early entries that are fragmentary. There is also an envelope containing some papers on repairs to the parsonage, and to renting the rectory.

Deposited by the Vestry of the Church, 1929.

1593
Dealy, Dennis F., d. 1887.   Papers, 1853–1887.   (50 items and 3 v.)

A collection of diaries, 1853–1857, 1858–1860, and 1887, of Dennis F. Dealy, Philadelphia publisher. There are also clippings, letters of condolence on Dealy's death in 1887, and a letter from George W. Childs, 1880.

Deposited by C. Victor Dealy, 1939.

1594
Bond, George.   Papers, 1775–1792.   (5 items.)

Entry cancelled; transferred to the Society collection.

1595
Bayard, Mabel.   Collection, 1777–1831.   (3 items.)

Entry cancelled; transferred to the Society collection.

1596
Revolutionary soldiers and pensioners papers, n.d.   (500 items.)

Transferred to the Genealogical Society of Pennsylvania.

1597
Smith family.   Real estate papers, 1890–1934.   (300 items.)

Deeds, mortgages, and insurance on properties at 1019–1021 Reed Street, 1327 South Warnock Street, and 4220 and 4224 Westminster Avenue, all in Philadelphia, owned by the Smith family. There are also bills and receipts, 1901–1934, on the upkeep of the properties.

Gift of John Gibbs Smith, 1946.

1598
Philadelphia legal records, 1776–1915.   (3 v.)

Appearance book, 1776; docket, 1870–1915, of Cornelius Stevenson, a Philadelphia lawyer; docket, 1813–1817, of James B. Harris.

1599
Montgomery County (Pa.)   Dockets, 1821–1835.   (3 v.)

Dockets for a justice of the peace of Limerick Township, Montgomery County.

1600

Futhey, J. Smith.   **Papers, 1776–1880.**   **(500 items.)**

A collection consisting mainly of newspaper clippings gathered for use in writing *The History of Chester County* by J.S. Futhey and Gilbert Cope, published in Philadelphia, 1881. There are letters, 1870–1800, relating to the history and containing information, and notes used in compiling the history.

1601

Welsh Society (Philadelphia, Pa.)   **Minutes, 1798–1911.**   **(3 v.)**

The Welsh Society was founded in Philadelphia in 1798 "for the relief of such emigrants as may arrive in this country from Wales."

General minutes, 1798–1911, and Acting Committee minutes, 1858–1869.

Deposited by the Welsh Society.

1602

Borie family.   **Papers, 1799–1886.**   **(6 linear ft.)**

This collection includes business and personal letters of John Joseph Borie, of his wife Sophie, and of his sons and daughters and relatives in France. A large portion of the papers and documents relates to Santo Domingo, with letters from Toussaint Louverture and others residing on the island at the beginning of the 19th century who were connected with J.J. Borie, as well as miscellaneous papers, accounts, and bills. Also included is material on the *Rogé v. Borie* case, and letter books and account books belonging to the shipping firms of J.J. Borie, J.J. Borie & Son, and Borie and Laguerenne.

Gift of Beauveau Borie, 1948.

1603

Banknotes, 1787–1863.   **(1,000 items.)**

Banknotes issued by various banks, railroads, turnpikes, and other companies, 1787–1863, by state and political subdivisions. The collection also includes specimens of fractional currency issued primarily in 1815, 1837, and 1863; counterfeit notes; notes issued by the Confederate States of America and its political divisions; local notes issued in the South during the Civil War; private currency issued by individuals; few notes from Haiti, Russia, and Mexico.

1604
Colonial and Continental paper money, 1723–1786. (1,000 items.)

A collection of the various types and denominations of paper money issued by the colonies and states, 1723–1786, and by the Continental Congress, 1775–1779.

1605
Civil War envelope collection, 1861. (25 items.)

A collection of the envelopes used at the outbreak of the Civil War, most of which display a patriotic slogan and cartoon at the left side of the face of the envelope.

1606
Collis, Charles H.T. (Charles Henry Tucky), 1838–1902.
Letterpress books, 1863–1868. (3 v.)

Letters of General Charles Henry Tucky Collis telling mainly of his Civil War experiences.
Gift of Joseph F.A. Jackson, 1911.

1607
McGown, James Milton, 1844–1863. **Diary, 1863.** (1 v.)

The diary, of James Milton McGown, who enlisted in Company A, 76th Regiment of Infantry, Pennsylvania Volunteers, on October 1, 1861, was wounded and captured July 11, 1863, at Fort Wagner, S.C., and died in Libby Prison, Richmond, Va., on November 27, 1863.
Gift of Ralph C. McGown, Jr., 1949.

1608
Benners, Henry B. **Diaries, 1857–1879.** (2 v.)

Henry B. Benners was a Philadelphia glass manufacturer.
Diaries which contain notes and comments on daily events.
Gift of Mrs. P.H. Ashbridge and Miss Benners, 1911.

1609
Lynch, John Wheaton. **Letters, 1860–1866.** (150 items.)

This is a group of letters written by Captain John Wheaton Lynch of the 106th Regiment, Pennsylvania Volunteers to his fiancée, Miss Bessie Mustin of Philadelphia. Most of the letters are personal, but those written during his army service, May 1861-September 1863, contain details of camp life and army gossip.

Purchased, 1949.

1610

Cassel, Abraham H., 1820–1908.   Collection, 1680–1821.   (41 v.)

This group of manuscripts includes items on the Ephrata Cloister: hymnbooks; letter book, 1755, of Conrad Beissel; collection of songs composed and arranged by Johannes Kelpius; death register of the Cloister, 1728–1821. The remainder of the collection is comprised of religious tracts, hymnbooks, and school books, recipe book, n.d., of Christopher Sauer, and an extra-illustrated rare book by Friedrich Adolph Lampe, *Short Instructions in the Foundations of Reformed Christianity* (Philadelphia, 1762) with manuscript notations which include Bible quotations commenting on the text, and personal remarks at the beginning and end of the volume.

Purchased from Abraham H. Cassel, 1882.

Many of the hymnbooks are beautifully illustrated. Some of the personal remarks entered in the Lampe volume are crossed out but are still legible.

1611

Extra-illustrated books.   (9 v.)

These volumes include two sets of *The Diary of Christopher Marshall* (Albany, 1877) edited by William Duane, Jr., and one set of Henry Simpson's *Lives of Eminent Philadelphians* (Philadelphia, 1859) which have been expanded by the addition of manuscripts, prints, and maps relating to the subjects covered.

1612

Hamilton, James.   Papers, 1750–1899.   (21 linear ft.)

Organized in the following series: James Hamilton (d. 1819); James Hamilton (d. 1873); Robert Magaw; Samuel Postlethwaite and John Davis; Joseph Murray; and Collector of the Port of Philadelphia and miscellaneous volumes.

Hamilton was born and educated in Ireland. He settled in Carlisle in 1780, where he became a member of Robert Magaw's law office. Upon Magaw's death, in 1788, Hamilton took over the practice. Hamilton, a Constitutionalist and Jeffersonian Republican, served as U.S. Attorney for Western Pennsylvania, and as President Judge of Pennsylvania's 9th Judicial District.

Chiefly papers from the law offices of James Hamilton but includes files from the offices of James Wilson and Robert Magaw. Revolutionary material and western Pennsylvania is represented in the papers of Magaw, Samuel Postlethwaite, Edward Hand and John Davis. The collection contains letters of or pertaining to: George Washington, Benjamin Rush, Anthony Wayne, Rev. Richard Peters, John Witherspoon, Robert Whitehall, George Croghan, John Fraser, Andrew Gregg, Samuel Miles, George Ross, Arthur St. Clair, Thomas McKean, William Thompson, General Samuel Smith, William Crawford, Tench Coxe, Joseph Reed, Robert Morris, George Clymer, A.J. Dallas, John Harris, and Thomas Mifflin.

Other materials relate to: the Carlisle-Presbyterian Church, Carlisle Associators, and the Collector of the Port of Philadelphia.

Purchased, 1950.

Finding aid available.

1613
Blankenburg, Rudolph, 1843–1918.   Papers, 1881–1913.
(150 items.)

Philadelphia reform leader and mayor, 1911–1915.

Correspondence concerning Philadelphia politics, including statements concerning graft in the City Treasurer's Office, 1881, as well as material on high speed transit and the Philadelphia Rapid Transit Company, the sending of the Liberty Bell to San Diego,1915, and other items showing interest in good government for the city. Correspondents include: Wayne MacVeagh, Edward T. Stotesbury, and Morris L. Cooke. Some miscellaneous pamphlets and clippings.

1614
No entry.

1615
Rodenhausen's Excelsior Wagon Works.   Records, 1859–1900.
(40 v.)

Journals, ledgers, wage books, and other account records of Rodenhausen's Excelsior Wagon Works, Philadelphia wheelwright and wagon maker.

Purchased, 1950.

1616
MacVeagh family.   Papers, 1850–1950.   (15 linear ft.)

Wayne MacVeagh was a lawyer, a Civil War Captain, and both an active Republican and Democrat. (MacVeagh switched to the Democratic Party in

1892.) He also served as minister to Turkey, 1870–1871, as Attorney General of the United States under Garfield, 1881, and held other state and national offices.

Correspondence, 1850–1917, covering MacVeagh's personal affairs and public life. Correspondents include: MacVeagh's father-in-law, Simon Cameron, Joseph J. Lewis, Franklin MacVeagh, and John J. Pinkerton. Also letters from: Andrew G. Curtin, Charles Francis Adams, Brooks Adams, Henry Brooks Adams, and Andrew D. White. Major national political figures wrote MacVeagh including: William Jennings Bryan, Rutherford B. Hayes, Theodore Roosevelt, William Howard Taft, and Woodrow Wilson. There is a series of letters to Mrs. Cameron during MacVeagh's service in Turkey. There are personal letterpress books, 1876–1891, mostly concerned with MacVeagh's private financial dealings, including the Cameron estate; legal letterpress books, 1874, 1876; and fee books, 1856–1894; also typescript narrative on the history of the Panama Canal, 1904; and typescript "William Cromwell, Diplomat and Revolutionist" by Earl Harding, 1910. There are miscellaneous papers of other MacVeagh family members including: Margaret (Mrs. Simon) Cameron letters, 1870–1871, to her daughter Virginia C. MacVeagh; Mrs. Benjamin Warder letters, 1912, while living in Buenos Aires; and Mrs. Warder letters, 1913, 1916.

Gift of Edwin C. MacVeagh, 1951.

1617
Brown Family.   **Papers, 1788–1915.**   **(6 linear ft.)**

In 1815 Moses Brown, Dover, N.H., Quaker, came to Philadelphia and became engaged in domestic textile trade with his brother Jeremiah. He married Mary Waln Wister.

Early correspondence, 1810–1840, consist of letters to Moses Brown from his brothers, Jeremiah and David Sands Brown, and from other relatives on family matters, together with some letters on business. Later correspondence, 1840–1915, contains miscellaneous letters of T. Wistar Brown, as well as letters to his daughter, Agnes from her father and from her future husband, Henry Goddard Leach. There are also various family commonplace books, financial memoranda, clippings, and photographs. The small section of Wistar family papers include: Elizabeth Waln Wistar incoming family letters, 1846–1880; miscellaneous Caspar Wistar and Thomas Wistar papers.

Gift of Henry Goddard Leach, 1951.

Genealogical materials in the Library of the Historical Society of Pennsylvania.

1618
Lloyd, Malcom, Jr.   **Collection, 1749–1822.**   **(75 items.)**

A collection of letters, documents, and genealogical data pertaining to the related family of Carpenter, Howell, Ladd, Lewis, Lloyd, and Malcom. The collection also contains: Isaac Lloyd miscellaneous Civil War papers while serving as lieutenant in the Pennsylvania Volunteers, 92nd Regiment, 9th Calvary; Camden, N.J., lawyer Richard Washington Howell legal case books, 1854–1859, each continued, 1865–1874, by his son J.L. Howell, also a Camden lawyer.

Gift of Malcom Lloyd, Jr., 1949.

1619
Brinton, Jasper Yeates, b. 1878.   **Collection, 1762–1916.**
(18 linear ft.)

The collection is arranged in following three series: Steinmetz, Smith, and Brinton sections.

The John Steinmetz section, 1762–1792, concerns primarily the Philadelphia wholesale merchant and import business which Steinmetz operated with his brother-in-law Henry Keppele. Steinmetz was an active supporter of the Revolution, but the bulk of the correspondence is for the pre-Revolutionary period and some material for the 1790's, with little for the intervening period. Major correspondents are: James Arbuckel (Chester County), William Bell (Lancaster), Nathaniel Blencowe (Kingwood, W.Va.), Benjamin and John Bower (Manchester, England), Alexander McCauley (Chester County), and Parr, Bulkeley and Company (Libson, Portugal). Receipted bills, invoices, manifests, and other financial papers are more evenly distributed although there is still a dearth of material on the war years. There are also letters, 1790–1798, concerned with son [John] Henry Steinmetz's divorce.

The rest of the collection deals mostly with real estate transactions of William Smith and his son Charles Smith, and other family landholdings, 1763–1835. Although William Smith was provost of the University of Pennsylvania, an organizer of the Protestant Episcopal Church, and an active Loyalist during the Revolution, there is little material for these activities. Correspondence, legal papers, surveys and field books pertain to lands in Pennsylvania, New York (among which appear some Tench Coxe letters on political questions), Maryland, Maine, and Nova Scotia, along with similar papers of Charles Smith as executor of his father's estate.

Additional Charles Smith papers, 1791–1835, relate to his own interests in landholdings. Smith sat as president judge of the Pennsylvania District Court at Lancaster, 1820–1824, reflected by a few letters of Andrew Gregg and Smith's trial notes. There are also letters, 1836–1843, concerning a dispute over Charles Smith's estate revealing domestic difficulties between Smith's daughter and son-in-law Thomas B. McElwee.

A small section of miscellaneous Brinton family papers includes Lt. Ward Brinton letters, July–October, 1916, to his mother while on duty in the Medical Reserves Corps during Mexican border actions.

Gift of Jasper Yeates Brinton, 1951.

1620
Congdon, James A.   Letters, 1862–1865.   (100 items.)

Letters of Lieutenant Colonel James A. Congdon, 12th Cavalry, 113th Pennsylvania Volunteers, to his father-in-law, William T. Bishop, concerning Congdon's efforts to gain promotion. Also represented are Congdon's repeated efforts to force the removal of his commanding officers, Colonel Lewis B. Pierce and Lt. Darius Titus. When not detailing Congdon's pursuit of advancement, the correspondence centers on the regiment's competent officers, lack of discipline, and low morale.

Gift of Clement H. Cogdon, 1943.

1621
Biddle, James Stokes.   Papers, 1833–1859.   (150 items.)

Papers of James Stokes Biddle consist largely of orders and other official incoming correspondence he received while serving in the United States Navy, with some unofficial letters from Commodore Christopher Raymond Perry Rodgers. Biddle's Vera Cruz letterbook, 1845, reports on the state of affairs in Mexico. There is also a Commodore James Biddle naval commonplace book, ca. 1840's.

1622
No entry.

1623
Barton, Benjamin Smith, 1766–1815.   Lecture notes, 1813–1815.
(6 linear ft.)

Benjamin Smith Barton was a Philadelphia physician and a naturalist. He taught at the University of Pennsylvania.

Lecture notes used in the "practice of medicine" course at the University of Pennsylvania.

1624
Gorman, Frederick J., b. 1885.   Collection, 1928–1949.
(500 items.)

Notes and copies of deeds, grants, surveys, and court records primarily concerned with land in Passayunk Township and Kingsessing Township in Philadelphia County. There is also information on Limerick and Moyamensing Townships as well as information on Bucks, Chester, Delaware, and Montgomery counties. The emphasis is on roads and highways. There is a small amount of personal correspondence and a copy of persons who worked on the dikes in the Swedish settlement.

Gift of Frederick J. Gorman, 1949.

1625A
Wister family.   Papers, 1747–1902.   (22 v.)

Records of the Wistar family begin with those of John Wister who, having purchased property on Market Street between 3rd and 4th Streets, started his wine merchant business. Successive generations of Wisters, their partners, and one clerk carried on as dry good merchants at this same location. They include: John Wister; his sons Daniel and William; Daniel's sons John Jr., and Charles Jones; Daniel's son-in-law John Morgan Price; Charles Jones's son Charles Jones, Jr. (who was not a merchant); William's partner George Aston; one-time clerk turned merchant in his own right, Adam Konigmacher, his partner Yardley, and John Cameron, a Lancaster merchant of unknown connection.

Ledger kept by John Wister, 1747–1766; Daniel Wister, 1762–1770; John Cameron, 1767–1770; William Wister, 1792–1796; Wister and Aston, 1788–1791; John M. Price and Co., 1795–1814 and letterbook, 1794–1796; Adam Konigmacher, 1806–1836, with letterbook, 1806–1816; Konigmacher, Yardley and Co., 1819–1822, 1838; Yardley and Co., 1821–1834; Charles J. Wister, Jr. meteorological journals, 1845–1858, 1876–1902; Sarah Whitesides Wister household account, 1861–1874.

John Wister ledger, 1747–1766 mostly in German.

Finding aid available.

1625B
Wister family.   Papers, 1792–1840.   (15 v.)

Records of: William Wister, 1796–1801, with letterbook, 1792–1801, 1827; William Wister estate, 1801–1837; Wister, Price and Wister, 1797–1801, 1834; William and John Wister, Jr., 1797, 1800–1806, 1833; John and Charles J. Wister, 1802–1818, 1840; Wister, Price and Wister, 1815–1822, 1827; with letterbook, 1815–1823.

Gift of the Germantown Historical Society, 1937.
Finding aid available.

1626
United States. Army. Pennsylvania Infantry Regiment, 52nd (1861–1865).   Papers, 1861–1864.   (300 items.)

Consolidated morning reports; several muster rolls; general orders; letters; and other miscellaneous papers.

1627
Dorsey, Greensbury, d. 1807.   Family papers, 1734–1861. (300 items.)

Mainly papers of Greensbury Dorsey, ironmaster of Barree Forge, Huntingdon County. and his son-in-law Samuel Miles Green, who eventually became manager of the forge. Greensbury Dorsey incoming correspondence, bills, and receipts, 1780–1847, concern personal financial affairs. Letters, 1824–1866, to Samuel Miles Green also relate to finances. There are additional Dorsey and non-Dorsey family papers including: Edward B. Dorsey incoming family correspondence, 1800–1829, and memorandum books, 1815–1829, of business transactions in western Pennsylvania; Richard Peters land and draught book, 1744–1757, 1776, mostly for Lancaster County, and materials on his own properties; miscellaneous papers on Pennsylvania lands of William Meredith and Benjamin Wilson.
Finding aid available.

1628
Smith and Waln family.   Papers, 1774–1891.   (9 linear ft.)

James Somers Smith was a Philadelphia lawyer. His son, Richard Rundle Smith was also a lawyer who served as a delegate to the Pennsylvania House of Representatives.
James Somers Smith's correspondence, 1804–1841, deals with his financial agency for Talbot Hamilton, Philadelphia; Sarah Bunner, New York City; Francis Gurney and his estate coming from John Fine, Ogdensburgh, N.Y.; and Thomas Burnside, Lewistown. Also James S. Smith receipt books, 1803–1840, for business and taxes; Francis Gurney estate receipt book, 1815–1820.
Richard Rundle Smith's correspondence, 1841–1879, is primarily on law office business, but also includes letters, 1848–1849, reporting on his activi-

ties as a delegate to the Pennsylvania House of Representatives. In addition there are letters, 1850–1878, of Gideon J. Ball to Smith on the subject of railroad expansion, especially the Sunbury and Erie Railroad and the Philadelphia and Erie Railroad. R. Rundle Smith receipt books, 1839–1891, concern legal services and rents.

Robert Waln was at one time a prosperous Philadelphia merchant with interests in a cotton mill and iron works. However, in 1819, Waln was forced to make an assignment of his property to Benjamin Rawle Morgan and John C. Smith.

Many of the papers, 1819–1836, relate to Waln's financial affairs following the assignment, including correspondence with Morgan as well as Morgan's own correspondence. There is also Waln's correspondence with Gideon H. Wells, his brother-in-law and partner in the Eagle Factory at Trenton, N.J., on the cotton mill. Robert Waln's active support of protectionism is evident in correspondence, 1832, with Charles J. Ingersoll and Benjamin B. Howell on new tariff laws being considered in Congress.

There are Robert Waln account books; receipt books, 1785–1800, 1810–1819, for taxes and personal expenses, and assignee's accounts, 1819–1830.

Lewis Waln, Robert Waln's son, was also affected by his father's financial reverses. Much of the Lewis Waln material, 1819–1863, refers to efforts to collect accounts due to the merchant firm Large and Waln which dissolved in 1819. The major correspondent is D.E. Wilson, Waln's agent in Lexington, Ky. Other agents are Benjamin Gratz (Lexington, Ky.), Robert Hall (Sunbury), Joseph Taylor (Cynthia, Ky.), and more. There are also letters to Lewis Waln from John King, Ceres, and William Bache, Wellsborough, concerning family lands in Potter and Tioga counties, and from William Rawle [Jr.] on family estate questions. Lewis Waln's letterbook, 1820–1849, contains letters mostly to Gideon H. and Charles M. Wells concerning the cotton mill operation in which Lewis also had an interest; some later letters concern mercantile matters and Potter County lands. Lewis Waln account books include: account books, 1837–1858; D.E. Wilson (for Large and Waln) pocket ledgers, 1817–1821.

There is a large group of bonds, bills, accounts, and legal papers relating to the Waln's business, estate, and personal transactions. Third party account books are here presumably because of family or estate connections: Samuel Richards receipt book, 1783–1793, for personal expenses; merchant Benjamin Fuller receipt book, 1786–1794, cash and expense book, 1787–1789, both containing business with some personal transactions; Thomas Longhead receipt book, 1824, continued by Samuel Broom & Co., 1825–1828, for confectionery business.

Gift of James Somers Smith, 1950.

1629

Clement, Samuel M.   Collection, 1770–1909.   (22 items.)

This autograph collection contains: single letters of prominent early American figures including United States presidents; autograph book, 1862–1907; and an extra-illustrated *The Life of Abraham Lincoln* by Ida M. Tarbell, 1909, with autograph letters and documents of Lincoln's cabinet members, generals, and other prominent contemporaries.

Gift of Mrs. Samuel M. Clement, Jr., 1930.

1630

Bedford Street Mission.   Records, 1870–1929.   (4 v.)

The Bedford Street Mission was established in 1852 to "promote physical, moral, and religious well being," and provided food, clothing, shelter, and education for children and adults.

The records are Board of Managers minute books, 1870–1882, 1908–1929; record book, 1894–1901, with accounts, statistics, reports, clippings, and other information.

Gift of Mrs. Erza Evans, 1951.

1631

Philadelphia Record.   **Assignment books, 1930–1941.   (8 v.)**

Newspaper assignment books for reporters by the City desk; includes 1936 notes relating to news items and assignments.

Gift of the *Evening Bulletin,* 1951.

1632

No entry.

1633

McHenry, Margaret.   Notebooks, 1929–1949.   (19 v.)

Margaret McHenry received her doctorate in education from the University of Pennsylvania in 1931 and went to teach at Roxborough High School (Philadelphia, Pa.)

These notebooks, most of which are in diary form, contain McHenry's memoranda on education, religious faith, art, as well as comments on her own professional and personal activities. McHenry mentions suffering from newzathemia and was evidently prone to nervous disorder.

Gift of the University of Pennsylvania, 1951.

1634
No entry.

1635
McCall, George Archibald, 1802–1868.   Papers, 1818–1864.
(150 items.)

George A. McCall was an 1822 West Point graduate and a career soldier.

The papers provide a fragmentary record of McCall's rise through the ranks from 2nd Lieutenant to Brigadier General of the Pennsylvania Reserve Corps (a.k.a McCall's Division) in the Civil War. Most of the correspondence is routine; but there are some references to McCall's service in the Seminole War, 1835–1842, and Mexican War. The Civil War correspondence consists primarily of letters about rumors of McCall's removal from command. There are also descriptions of the battles at New Market Crossroad, June, 1862, and Drainsville, December, 1861. Major correspondents include General Edmund P. Gaines and Governor Andrew Gregg Curtin.

1636
DuBois, Abraham.   Papers, 1792–1809.   (150 items.)

Abraham DuBois was a Philadelphia merchant trading with the West Indies.

The papers include correspondence from agents, bills of lading, and other miscellaneous material.

A few items in French.

1637
William and Levi Garrett (Philadelphia, Pa.)   Account books,
1795–1807.   (3 v.)

William and Levi Garrett were Philadelphia tobacco merchants.

[William and Levi Garrett] ledger, 1795–1800; Levi Garrett daybook, 1804–1807; Unidentified super phosphate and tobacco grower book of sales, 1874–1881.

Gift of Mrs. W.W. Pagon, 1951, 1952.

1638
Stokes, William E., b. ca.1875.   Collection, 1836–1948, 1836, 1897–1948.   (5 linear ft.)

William E. Stokes was born West Philadelphia and lived there until 1936 when his position as a lawyer with the Norfolk and Western Railroad necessitated his move to Roanoke, Va.

His scrapbook, entitled, "Personal Narrative," 1920–1943, is an annual record in scrapbook form of his various professional, social, and Presbyterian Church (Walnut Street Presbyterian Church in particular) activities. There are clippings, programs, invitations, letters, memoranda, and photographs. The early volumes contain family history and reminiscences of growing up. In addition, there are further personal scrapbooks, 1896–1947, and notes and memorabilia on West Philadelphia compiled by Stokes. Unaccountably, some miscellaneous records of John Meredith Read, Philadelphia lawyer, are also included: account book, 1836–1838, legal commonplace book, n.d., and miscellaneous bankbooks, 1841–1889.

Gift of William E. Stokes, 1950, 1956.

1639
Harris family.   Papers, 1750 (1820–1839) 1844.   (525 items.)

Letters to Stephen Harris, Chester County, physician, and to his mother, Mary Harris, are primarily from family members and concerns family business and personal matters. Major correspondents are: James B. Harris, Genesceo, N.Y., farmer; John Harris, Captain Thomas Harris, Philadelphia doctor. There are some additional miscellaneous Harris family documents.

Gift of George B. Harris, 1949.

1640
James, Dorothy Biddle.   Collection, 1787–1871.   (18 items.)

Correspondence, 1788–1789, from Ann Biddle Wilkinson to her father, John Biddle; some letters of Sally Biddle, James Wilkinson, and others; and various deeds of John Dunlap and Thomas Savery. Genealogical notes for the Wilkinson and Penrose families.

Gift of Mrs. J. Robert James, 1949.

1641
Navy League of the United States Philadelphia Branch.
Records, 1917–1922.   (9 linear ft.)

The Navy League of the United States, Philadelphia Section, was formed June, 1917, by consolidation of several other local Navy League organizations. However, the membership consisted largely of the Women's Section of Navy League and remained composed almost entirely of women.

The records are mostly correspondence which covers the League's many activities in support and service to the U.S. Navy: producing, collecting, and distributing knitted garments as well as other clothing and supplies, raising funds for the Liberty Loan Campaigns, giving aid to the Seamen's Church Institute, and operating cafeterias for seamen. There are also some account books and other miscellany.

Gift of Richard W. Lloyd, 1949.

1642
Clay, Cecil, fl. 1861–1890.   Papers, 1862–1890.   (150 items.)

Special and general orders to the 58th Regiment, Pennsylvania Volunteers, and miscellaneous correspondence including several letters to Cecil Clay recollecting actions at Fort Harrison in September, 1864.

Gift of Curtis L. Clay, 1949.

1643
Browning, Mrs. Edward.   Collection, 1891–1916.   (75 items.)

A collection of posters, photographs, schedules, menus, and other miscellaneous material, 1891–1916, of several coaching clubs, and organizations concerned with the running and driving of coaches in Philadelphia.

Gift of Mrs Edward Browning, 1949.

1644
**Mary Ann Furnace and Forge.   Account books, 1827–1838.
(27 v.)**

Account books of Mary Ann Furnace and Forge, iron furnace on Trough Creek in Huntington County, owned by John Savage: daybooks, ledgers, receipt books, settlement books, account books, record book, blast book, pig iron book, cordwood book, and provision book, 1833–1838; also memo book of other furnaces, 1827–1834.

Gift of George Thompson for the Executors of John Savage, 1950.

1645
Levy family.   Papers, ca.1790–1885.   (100 items.)

The Levy family papers include correspondence, marriage certificates, wills, land surveys, and deeds. There is also a Hebrew Pentateuch with manuscript notations in both Hebrew and English. The documents give a very sketchy picture of the Levy family with only a few items to represent each generation. The bulk of the material concerns Aaron Levy, the founder of Aaronsburgh, and his nephew Aaron Levy, Jr., a Philadelphia merchant. Civil War letters of Aaron Levy, Jr.'s grandsons, Myer and Elias Levy, are included in the collection.

Hebrew Pentateuch with Hebrew and English notations.

Gift of Louise M. and Miriam E. Levy, 1946.

1646
Physick family.   Papers, 1680–1899.   (300 items.)

This very miscellaneous collection letters and documents relates primarily to Henry White Physick and his estate, with some other immediate and not so immediate family papers also present. The major correspondent is George Haynes, Physick's father-in-law.

Gift of W.H. Noble, 1950.

1647
Brown, Peter Arrell.   Papers, 1806–1864.   (150 items.)

Commissions, deeds, miscellaneous legal papers, and correspondence of Philadelphia lawyer Peter Arrell Brown.

1648
Walton family.   Papers, 1809–1868.   (100 items.)

Cashbooks, journals, receipt books, and miscellaneous financial records of David and Silas Walton's grain business in Morrestown, N.J.

1649
Bank of Pennsylvania (Philadelphia, Pa.)   Records, 1720 (1790–1831) 1861.   (150 items.)

Primarily grants of the power of attorney to transfer shares of stock in the Bank of Pennsylvania; some correspondence; wills, deeds; and miscellaneous legal papers; two manuscripts, 1798, concerning Patrick Lyons who was accused of having robbed the bank.

Gift of Mrs. Nancy Patterson Bright, 1950.

1650
**Sartain family.   Collection, 1771 (1830–1897) 1929.
(15 linear ft.)**

John Sartain was born in London and came to the United States in 1830. He was a Philadelphia engraver and publisher. Sartain produced engravings at home and abroad for books, magazines, and framing; he edited *Campbell's Foreign Semi-Monthly Magazine* from 1843 until his 1848 purchase of an interest in a New York publication, which became *Sartain's Union Magazine of Literature and Art*. He was a Director of the Academy of Fine Arts for 23 years. Sartain served as chief of the art departments for both the 1876 Centennial Exhibition at Philadelphia and the 1887 American Exhibitions in London. A member of many art societies, he was prominent in local associations.

The John Sartain papers include: letterpress books, 1869–1871, 1875–1876, concerning his Philadelphia and London exhibitions work and other business; outgoing letters, 1850–1897, mostly during trips to Europe on business and pleasure; letters from his son Samuel, an engraver, while in London on business for John, 1850; letters from another son William, a painter, 1862–1888, many written while living in Paris from 1872 to 1875; random portions of his professional and personal correspondence, 1845–1897. Additional papers are: manuscript and expense book for *Sartain's Union Magazine*, 1849–1852; the manuscript Sartain's autobiography, *Reminiscences of a Very Old Man;* Artist Fund Society papers, 1838–1846; Graphic Association of Philadelphia minutes, 1849–1855; Philadelphia Union of Associationists minutes, 1847–1854; National Art Association record book, 1858–1859; artist Rembrandt Peale's unpublished *Notes of the Painting Room*.

Also represented are John Swaine, Sartain's father-in-law and the English engraver with whom Sartain apprenticed with in London, John Barak Swaine, English artist, and three of Sartain's children: Emily Sartain, noted woman artist, Samuel Sartain, engraver, and William Sartain, painter. These papers include: Samuel Sartain's outgoing family correspondence, engravings, and other papers; personal letters to and by Emily Sartain; William Sartain's outgoing family correspondence and sketchbook, genealogical data, and miscellaneous materials. The Swaine family papers include drawings by John Swaine and John Barak Swaine, a letterpress book of John Barak Swaine's letters to his father, 1834–1837, and genealogical data on the Swaine and allied families.

The collection also includes 122 drawings by Thomas Birch and seven steel plates, a set of engraving tools, and oil paintings by Swaine.

Gift of Harriet Sartain, 1950.

Birch drawings removed to the Print Department.

Swaine oil paintings transferred to the Museum Department.

Finding aid available for graphic items.

1651

Waln, Richard, 1737–1808.   Papers, 1759–1888.   (900 items.)

Richard Waln was a Philadelphia Quaker merchant engaged in the colonial trade. In 1774 he moved to Crosswicks (Monmouth County, N.J.), where he built "Walnford" and established a flour mill. Following the Revolution, Waln became involved again in Philadelphia commerce.

His papers relate almost entirely to business. The larger portion concerns his early mercantile activities from 1759, when he served as a factor in Barbados, until 1774. The collection includes: letterbooks, 1759, 1762, 1762–1773, 1799; incoming letters and accounts from David and John Barclay, Harford and Powell, Neate and Pigou, all of London, Robert Wilson, Barbados, Anthony Golley, master of several Waln ships, and others at home and abroad; brother Nicholas Waln letters, 1764, report on colonial politics in England; day books and other miscellaneous accounts, 1759, journals, 1761–1775; ledgers, 1761, 1761–1777, 1800. There is also an Upper Delaware Ward tax assessment, 1767, Richard Waln assessor.

The smaller portion concerns a grist mill and other business associated with Walnford: incoming letters and accounts from Henry Lisle, Downing & Thomas, both of Philadelphia, and Robert Bowne, William Remsen & Co., Jacob Seamen, all of New York; son Joseph Waln letters, 1787–1799, reporting on market conditions in Philadelphia; correspondence with son Richard Waln, Jr., 1792–1808, also on commercial affairs. Nicholas Waln, another son of Richard, managed the Walnford mill after his father's return to Philadelphia. His correspondence and accounts, 1788–1838, from Smith & Nevins, New York City, Thomas Ridgeway, Philadelphia, and others concern flour sales. Several miscellaneous Walnford account and record books, 1774–1888, span several generations of ownership.

Gift of Mrs. Benjamin Rush, 1951.

Finding aid available.

1652

Baldwin and Spooner.   **Records, 1819–1833.**   **(200 items.)**

Letters and ship invoices from Philadelphia clients of [Simeon] Baldwin and [Francis J.] Spooner and successor firms Baldwin and Forbes and Baldwin and Co., New York commission merchants.

1653

Parrish family.   **Papers, 1614–1874.**   **(350 items.)**

This collection consists of letters, memoranda, and notes of members of the Society of Friends, chiefly from the Pemberton and Parrish families of Philadelphia. Letters are of personal and religious matters. Among correspondents are John and Ann Ball, Robert Barclay, Abraham Scott, and Richard Vaux. Papers of the Society of Friends include epistles, testimonies, memorials; extracts from earliest records of the Friends meetings in America at Salem and Plainfield, N.J.; and extracts from Friends writings. Among the other manuscripts are: minutes, 1756–1759 of the Friendly Association for Regaining and Promoting Peace with the Indians; James Carter account of sufferings of his family as slaves, 1807; Ann Parrish case book recording her "Visitations of the Sick," 1841; transcripts of Joseph Parrish articles on capital punishments, Friends doctrines, the popular worm, and the death of John Randolph; Robert Proud "extracts of letters and memorandums relative to Pennsylvania in former times," 1785–1806.

Gift of Anna H. Denniston, 1936.

James Carter Account published in *P.M.H.B.*, 105 (1981):335–339.

1654
Knight, Daniel.   Mathematics notebooks, 1831–1834.   (4 v.)

Notebooks used at the Byberry School (Philadelphia, Pa.) by Daniel Knight, a 10–13 year old boy.

Purchased, Mifflin Fund, 1950.

1656
Adelman, Seymour.   Collection, 1708–1884.   (300 items.)

This highly miscellaneous collection of deeds, surveys, and correspondence relates in part to Chester and Delaware County and includes: plans for the new Free Quaker Meeting House in Philadelphia, 1783; receipt book, 1799–1817 of Caleb Cresson; anonymous hardware store journal, 1800–1802; "Book of Truth," 1842–1843, containing revelations made to an anonymous Philadelphian; minute book, 1845–1846 of the Granite Arch Club (a "society for social, moral, and intellectual improvements"); journal, 1883–1884, of Benjamin Eakins, Philadelphia ornamental writing master, of personal and business accounts, kept by his son, Thomas Eakins.

Gift of Seymour Adelman, 1947–1965.

1657
Price, Joseph.   Papers, 1783–1828.   (50 v.)

Daily memoranda of Joseph Price, Lower Merion Township Montgomery, County, recording weather, farm work for both himself and his neighbors, coffin-making and other carpentry business. There are some miscellaneous accounts, "harvest book," 1816–1823, and Blockley Township, Philadelphia, return of taxables, 1783.

1658
Clark, William Bell.   Collection, 1917–1918.   (5 items.)

Lists of Pennsylvania killed, wounded, or captured while serving with the United States Navy or Merchant Marine, 1917–1918, compiled by Clark when he was Assistant Secretary of the Pennsylvania War History Commission.

Gift of William Bell Clark, 1949.

1659
Society of Arts and Letters of Philadelphia.   Papers, 1908–1921. (450 items.)

The Society of Arts and Letters of Philadelphia encouraged original work in music, literature, and allied arts.

The papers include: programs, 1908; letterbooks, 1908–1911; incoming correspondence, 1910–1921.

Gift of Jessie Roger Greaves, 1949.

1660
Robertson family.   Papers, 1787–1889.   (60 items.)

Family and personal correspondence and miscellaneous papers of the following: James Robertson, president of the Bank of the United States during the 1840's, 1798–1854, with household account book, 1800–1827; his daughter, Helen Robertson, his son-in-law, the Rev. Robert B. Croes, and his granddaughter, Helen Croes, 1824–1889. Also, Bishop John Croes, First Protestant Episcopal bishop of New Jersey, and father of Robert B. Croes, 1801–1832; and Robert Smith, Philadelphia merchant, brother-in-law of Alexander Robertson, uncle of James, 1787–1816, all incoming correspondence. There is also an unidentified household account book, 1866–1868.

1661
Bank of Germantown (Philadelphia, Pa.)   Ledgers, 1822–1855. (8 v.)

The Bank of Germantown opened in 1814 and was rechartered with John Fanning Watson as cashier, 1814–1847.

Included are: general ledger, 1822–1831, and depositors' ledgers, 1827–1855.

1662
Pennsylvania Company for Insurances on Lives and Granting Annuities.   Journals, 1849–1879.   (9 v.)

The Pennsylvania Company was chartered in 1812. In 1836 the company was authorized to enter into the business of executing trusts, which thereafter became its chief activity.

The journals include trust and account daybooks.
Purchased, 1953.

1663
Brinley family.   Papers, 1744–1880.   (300 items.)

Manuscript and typescript correspondence of Brinley family members on family and social matters. Elizabeth Parker letters, 1798–1808, are particularly illustrative of life in that period. Other correspondents include: Edward Brinley, 1783–1801, from Shelburne, Nova Scotia; Francis Brinley, 1744–1765; G.A. Gilpin, 1820–1841; and E.P. Halsey, 1861–1880.
Gift of B. Borie, 1949.

1664
Association of the Foundation of the First Naval Battalion of Pennsylvania.   Records, 1925–1945.   (3 v.)

Minutes and notes with some photographs of annual meetings first held in 1925.
Gift of the Association of the Foundation of the First Naval Battalion of Pennsylvania, 1950.

1665
Infant School Society of Philadelphia.   Records, 1827–1947. (18 items.)

The Infant School Society of Philadelphia was a charitable organization providing pre-primary instruction for both black and white children from 1827–1940.
Included are: Coloured School Committee letterbook, 1828–1936; Board of Managers letterbook, 1827–1830; Board of Managers minutes, 1827–1899, 1906–1940; account book, 1827–1891; and miscellaneous business papers, 1827–1947.
Gift of Burton Chance in the name of Elizabeth Chance, 1950, and Walter Biddle Saul, 1960.

1666
Stokes, James.   Business Papers, 1783–1828.   (4 v.)

James Stokes was a Philadelphia merchant who dealt in dry goods and hardware.
Business records are letterbooks, 1791–1800, 1804–1817, and ledgers, 1783–1828.
Gift of Mrs. Harold Paumgarton, 1951.

1667
Lewis, John F.   Papers, 1942–1948.   (300 items.)

Correspondence, minutes, newsletters, from the file of John F. Lewis, Jr., founder and president of the Philadelphia branch of the United Seamen's Service, formed during World War II for the benefit of the merchant marine.
Gift of John F. Lewis, Jr., 1949.

1668
Read, John Meredith, 1797–1874.   Papers, 1797–1917.
(12 linear ft.)

These papers deal generally with the legal career of John Meredith Read, prominent Pennsylvania lawyer and jurist. Letters primarily concerned with court cases, estates, and business interests, and touche only occasionally on Read's political interests as a state Republican leader. There is some correspondence, 1825–1831, between Read and his first wife Priscilla. Many of the letters from 1840 to 1874 are from other family members, chiefly his father John Read who wrote from Trenton of financial matters, and his son John Meredith Read, Jr., who wrote from school and later from his law office in Albany, N.Y. A series of letters from Col. Charles H.T. Collis, 1862–1864, covers Collis' court martial case and his observations on the progress of the Civil War. A letterbook, 1842–1846, also relates to Read's general legal and financial matters, and another letterbook, 1846, cover his tenure as attorney general of Pennsylvania. Read's several judicial appointments are documented: court docket books, 1818–1841, which cover first the period of private practice and later his cases as U.S. district attorney for eastern Pennsylvania, and personal court docket books, 1859–1860, 1867–1870, 1873, kept during his tenure as Pennsylvania Supreme Court justice. Read was an active member of the Masons, and a number of manuscripts relate to the Grand Lodge of Pennsylvania, including a record and account book, 1825–1834.

There are small account books of John Meredith Read and John Read as well as Philadelphia lawyer Thomas Kittera's receipt book, 1827–1839.
Purchased, 1952; Gift of Richard S. Rodney, 1953.

1669
Painter, Uriah Hunt, 1837–1900.   Papers, 1855–1936.
(21 linear ft.)

Uriah Hunt Painter was a newspaper correspondent, lobbyist, and businessman of West Chester County, and of Washington, D.C.

The main body of the collection consists of incoming and outgoing correspondence, 1855–1900. During the Civil War, Painter was a Washington correspondent of the *Philadelphia Inquirer* and there is some routine correspondence from this period. The bulk of the correspondence is for the years 1875–1900 and deals with Painter's numerous business interests. This material is also largely routine, but it represents a variety of industrial enterprises. Among the companies are: The Edison Speaking Phonograph Co., American Graphophone Co., Western Union Telegraph Co., New York, Pennsylvania, and Norfolk Railroad Co., Pennsylvania Railroad, Denver and Rio Grande Railroad Co., Union Pacific Railroad Co., Edison Electric Light Co., Edison General Electric Co., Western Electric Co., General Incandescent Arc Light Co., and Interior Conduit and Insulation Co.. The correspondents include: Thomas A. Edison, Thomas T. Eckerts, President of Western Union Telegraph Co., and Grenville M. Dodge, President of the Colorado and Texas Railway Construction Co.. The correspondence includes letterbooks dealing with the New York, Pennsylvania, and Norfolk Railroad Co.; Edward H. Johnson letterbooks of the Edison Company for Isolated Lighting; and business letterbooks of William Painter, Uriah Painter's brother.

The collection also contains the business records of two Painter enterprises: Edison Speaking Phonograph Co., 1878–1880, including letterbooks, account books, and other material, with letters to and from Thomas Edison; and Danville Furnace, Danville, 1879–1884, including correspondence, receipted bills, other accounts, and records.

1670

Musical Fund Society.   Records, 1820–1939.   (35 v. and 300 items.)

The Musical Fund Society was established in 1820 to provide relief to "decayed musicians and their families."

Among the scattered records here are: minutebooks, 1867–1926, of the Committee on Relief, and of other committees; account books; engagement books, 1847–1870; scrapbooks; and some correspondence, membership lists, legal papers.

Gift of the Musical Fund Society, 1953.

1671

Burton, Alexander, b. 1780.   Collection, 1684–1856.   (75 items.)

Letters, 1822–1856, addressed to Alexander Burton, U.S. Consul at Oporto, Portugal, and Cadiz, Spain, with single items from: Lewis Cass, A.C. Dodge, Alexander Hamilton, Washington Irving, and Martin Van Buren; 2 letters from John Quincy Adams; and 3 letters from William H.

Prescott. Some genealogical material on the Burton, Hickling, and Prescott families.

Gift of the Genealogical Society of Pennsylvania, 1953.

1672
Warren, William J.   Business Papers, 1855–1866.
(ca. 400 items.)

Mostly bills and receipts, some correspondence and miscellany for William J. Warren's furniture business in Philadelphia.

Finding aid available.

1673
Fallon, Christopher.   Papers, 1824 (1850–1863).   (100 items.)

Christopher Fallon served as legal counsel and president of the Sunbury and Erie Railroad, later the Philadelphia and Erie Railroad.

Primarily business correspondence dealing with his work for the railroad; includes some letters in Spanish pertaining to Fallon's representations of Spanish interests in the United States, and other miscellaneous letters on his various business interests.

Some letters in Spanish.

Exchanged with Chester County Historical Society, 1953.

1674
Nathan Trotter and Company.   Correspondence, 1825–1859.
(100 items.)

Nathan Trotter was a Philadelphia copper and tin plate merchant.

These papers are the incoming correspondence for the merchant company.

Exchanged with Chester County Historical Society.

1675
Clark, John Y.   Papers, 1839–1866.   (250 items.)

Papers of John Y. Clark include, primarily, letters from John Y. Clark and Charlemagne Tower dealing with the purchase of the Northampton and Luzerne Coal Company.

Exchanged with Chester County Historical Society, 1953.

1676
Bradford Family.   Papers, 1747–1847.   (350 items.)

Thomas Bradford and his father, William, were Philadelphia printers and booksellers.

Miscellaneous papers of Thomas and William Bradford reflecting their business, political, and family affairs. The bulk of chronologically arranged correspondence is addressed to Thomas: from William Bradford; Rachel Budd Bradford, his mother; Rachel and Tace Bradford, his sisters; as well as cousins, and business associates. Included in this group are: James Adams, the Wilmington printer; Elias Boudinot; William Cobbett; Benjamin Fuller; Lewis Hallam; Ebenezer Hazard; Thomas Leaming, Jr.; Timothy Pickering; and Abraham Skinner. Also in the series are letters addressed to Thomas Bradford's son Thomas, a Philadelphia lawyer, reflecting his political ambitions. Correspondents in this group include: Nicholas Biddle, James Buchanan, Richard Peters, Jr., John Tyler, and Abel Upshur.

A group of miscellaneous volumes includes: partnership accounts of William and Cornelius Bradford, 1761–1769; journal and ledger, 1766–1768, of William Bradford for his share in the schooner Rachel; six subscription books for the *Pennsylvania Journal,* 1766–1782; a memorandum book of Thomas Bradford, 1766; a list of members and expenses of an unidentified Philadelphia club of which William Bradford was a member, 1772; an anonymous diary of imprisonment by the British, 1781; and several other volumes.

1677

Stambaugh, Samuel C.   Papers, 1807–1859.   (100 items.)

Samuel C. Stambaugh served as a U.S. Indian agent in Green Bay, Mich. During his service, he became involved with the proposed organization of the Territory of Huron.

Miscellaneous accounts, reports, and correspondence with Lewis Cass and others while acting as U.S. Indian agent, 1830–1840, particularly his negotiations with the Green Bay Menominee tribe, 1831, and the Cherokee and Creek tribes, 1833. Some of the correspondence also relates to Democratic party politics in Pennsylvania.

Gift of George A. Landell, 1953.

1678

**Cordorus Forge (York County, Pa.)   Papers, 1738–1861.
(45 items.)**

Chiefly deeds and land drafts for Cordorus Forge property, Hellam Township, York County.

Gift of Mrs. W.S. Morris, 1953.

1679
Lorimer, George Horace, 1867–1937.   **Papers, 1900–1947.**
(3 linear ft.)

George Lorimer was editor of the *Saturday Evening Post* from 1898 to 1936.

The main body of the collection consists of incoming and outgoing professional and personal papers; and a 1932 scrapbook of Lorimer's editorials for the *Post.* There are letters from many prominent individuals, including: Albert J. Beveridge, Josephus Daniels, Theodore Dreiser, Herbert Hoover, Huey Long, Will Rogers, Franklin D. Roosevelt, Billy Sunday, Woodrow Wilson, and P.G. Wodehouse.

The collection also includes papers of Adelaide W. Neall, an associate editor for the *Saturday Evening Post* for most of the time she worked for the journal, 1909–1942. The major part of this group consists of papers collected by Neall for a projected biography of Lorimer. Also included is an album of photographs of *Post* authors and editors. A scrapbook of letters written to Neall by prominent contributors to the *Post* includes: Pearl S. Buck, Calvin Coolidge, William Durant, F. Scott Fitzgerald, Ring Lardner, Sinclair Lewis, and Will Rogers.

Gift of Mr. and Mrs. Graeme Lorimer, 1960.

1680
Lewis, William David, 1792–1881.   **Papers, 1800–1918.**
(33 linear ft.)

William David Lewis arrived in Europe in 1814 at the conclusion of the Napoleonic Wars and the War of 1812. Having obtained passage from New York as a secretary to the United States peace commission, Lewis soon resigned his office to join the employ of his brother John Delaware Lewis, a commission merchant in St. Petersburg, Russia. William spent the following ten years there. In 1820, William Lewis was sued for slander by the consul at St. Petersburg, Leavitt Harris, and the seven year litigation involved eminent officials in the United States and in Russia, including John Quincy Adams and James Monroe. Lewis began his own import commission business in Philadelphia in 1825, helped finance several early railroads, and was cashier of Girard Bank, 1832–1842. He served as collector of customs for the Port of Philadelphia, 1849–1853, despite the strenuous efforts against confirmation by his fellow Whigs from Pennsylvania. Lewis then retired to his estate near Florence, N.J., where he continued to take an active interest in business affairs. He was an ardent supporter of the Union during the Civil War.

The incoming letters relate mainly to Lewis's financial interests, but touch on all phases of life. Especially rich are the manuscripts generated by Lewis himself: letterbooks and letterpress copybooks, diaries and diary extracts, 1839, 1843–1881, and autobiography to 1841, reflecting 19th century economic, political, and social life. The autobiography is particularly interesting for Lewis's accounts of life and travels in Russia and Europe, his duel with John L. Harris (nephew of Leavitt Harris and also a consul at St. Petersburg), his early interests in the railroad industry, and his involvement with the bank crisis of the 1830's. In addition, there are: letters, depositions, evidence, and other materials relating to *Harris v. Lewis;* Girard Bank accounts, correspondence, and reports during Lewis's tenure as cashier; literary pieces, mostly poetry by Lewis; John D. Lewis letters, 1810, 1814–1830, 1841, mostly on Russian business; arrivals and clearances of vessels at Philadelphia, 1826–1827; William D. Lewis, Jr., diary of a trip to Europe, 1853; Thomas Neilson (son-in-law of Lewis) diaries, 1856–1857; and scrapbooks, 1840–1918 including Civil War and World War I clippings.

Gift of Mrs. Lewis Neilson, 1952.

1681
Benedick Club.   Records, 1898–1939, 1947.   (36 v.)

Minutes, 1925–1939, 1947, and lists, 1898–1939, of the persons invited to the annual ball given by the Benedicks, a social club of 21 prominent Philadelphians.

Gift of the Benedick Club, 1953.

1682
William Mann Company.   Account books, 1854–1902.   (12 v.)

The William Mann Company did business as stationers, blank book manufacturers, lithographers, and printers both in Philadelphia and in New York.

The account books are: record book, almost entirely personal, containing annual financial statements, 1854–1880, ledger accounts, 1856–1871, and real estate records, 1856–1879; journals, 1854–1856, financial statements, 1880–1885, including New York store statements; banks and bankers order book, October-December, 1872.

Gift of William Mann Company, 1934.

1683
Philadelphia Musical Association.   Records, 1864–1918.   (4 v.)

The Philadelphia Musical Association was incorporated in 1865 as a protective, regulatory, and beneficial organization for professional musicians. Its charitable activities continued after its other responsibilities were assumed by a national union.

The records are: charter, constitution, bylaws, and amendments, 1865–1869; minute book, 1864–1878, with some material on the early history of the Philadelphia Orchestra; and executive committee minute books, 1895–1918.

1684
Athletic Club of the Schuylkill Navy of Philadelphia. Records, 1876–1923. (100 items.)

The Athletic Club of the Schuylkill Navy of Philadelphia was an organization of wealthy men interested in amateur athletics.

The charter, reports, programs, and other miscellaneous material of the Athletic Club of the Schuylkill Navy of Philadelphia.

Gift of Frank Weiner, 1953.

Almost no manuscript material is included, but there is some information on amateur athletics, 1887–1894.

1685
Wainwright, Nicholas Biddle.   Invitations, 1933–1942. (700 items.)

Nicholas Biddle Wainwright served as Assistant Librarian and later as Director of the Historical Society of Pennsylvania in Philadelphia.

Personal invitations received by Nicholas Biddle Wainwright.

Gift of Nicholas Biddle Wainwright, 1949.

1686
Darlington, William, 1782–1863.   Papers, 1829–1861. (150 items.)

Papers of William Darlington, lawyer of West Chester and chairman of the Anti-Masonic Committee of Correspondence of Chester County, consist mainly of letters on politics, legal, and family matters; included is a small group of letters to his wife, Catharine. There are miscellaneous accounts, bills, and receipts.

1687
Northern Dispensary of Philadelphia for the Medical Relief of the Poor.   Records, 1816–1904.   (17 v.)

The Northern Dispensary was chartered in 1817 for the purpose of furnishing gratuitous medical assistance to those who, though not destitute, could not afford medical care. The corporation, governed by a board of managers, was supported by membership, donations, legacies, and investment and rental incomes. It served the Spring Garden, Northern Liberties, and Kensington districts.

The records consist of board of managers minutes, 1816–1876; Medical Board minutes, 1841–1872; register of patients, 1816–1862; in-door register of patients, 1873–1874, 1877–1880; occulists' register of patients, 1886–1888; and register of female patients, 1891–1896, 1901–1904. All of the patient registers record: name, admission date, age, residence, occupation, disease or diagnosis, and results. The earlier registers may record color and birthplace as well, while later registers are more detailed as to diagnosis and prescribed treatments.

Purchased, 1939.

1688
MacPherson family.   **Correspondence, 1766 (1766–1813) 1855.** (250 items.)

John MacPherson, Jr., served as Richard Montgomery's aide-de-camp during the Revolutionary War. He died in the attack on Quebec. His brother, William MacPherson, was an army officer whose several commands included: a Pennsylvania militia battalion (MacPherson's Blues) in the 1794 Whiskey Insurrection; a legion formed during the 1798 conflict with France; and troops sent to enforce revenue laws in Northampton County during the 1798 Fries Rebellion.

Correspondence of the MacPherson family of Philadelphia includes: personal letters, 1766–1773, of John MacPherson, Jr., to William Patterson of N.J., and a letter, 1775, written a few hours before his death. The bulk of the collection consists of letters to William MacPherson on his military service, as well as land transactions and other business affairs. There are also a few letters, 1804–1807, written to William from Jamaica by his brother John Montgomery MacPherson about family affairs and business trade in Jamaica.

Gift of Mrs. William Horner, 1951.

1689
Hollis, Louis H.   **Collection, 1817–1902.**   (100 items.)

The collection was assembled to write the *History of the Improved Order of Red Men* by Morris H. Gorham, with additions by William G. Hollis (Philadelphia, 1884). Records of the Order which were evidently gathered in preparation for the book include: Great Council of Maryland minutes, 1842–1849; Osceola Wigwam No. 2, New York, minutes, 1848–1851; Oneactah Wigwam No. 4, New York, minutes, 1848–1851; Tecumseh tribe No. 1, Pennsylvania, constitution, bylaws, membership, n.d., and membership lists, 1817–1837. A scrapbook contains clippings and some Great Council of Redmen U.S. correspondence, 1850's. There are letters in response to research inquiries and publication, sales accounts, manuscript chapters for the book, together with notes for Gorham's lectures on the Improved Order of Red Men. There is a small group of Hollis family notes.

Gift of Louis H. Hollis, 1951.

1690
Steinmetz, Mary Owen.   Collection, 1770–1948.   (150 items.)

Mary Owen Steinmetz was a genealogist from Reading.

The collection of research letters and lecture notes of Mary Owen Steinmetz contains information on the history of clocks and clockmakers of Reading, 1770–1810, and newspapers of Bucks County, 1790–1810. There is also material on: soldiers (primarily genealogical), 1775–1864; slavery, 1780–1825; market houses, 1850–1870; and copies of Berks County muster rolls for the Whiskey Insurrection, 1794 and 1814.

Gift of the Genealogical Society of Pennsylvania, 1952.

1691
Rulon, John W.   Papers, (1807–1845) 1861.   (6 linear ft.)

John W. Rulon was a general merchant in Philadelphia engaged in the import-export trade with India and China.

Loose correspondence, 1815–1845, and letterbook, 1844, reflect business affairs including the shipping of wild animals to America, 1833–1838, by Rulon and his associates. Financial records include various accounts, inventories, shipping lists, of domestic and foreign trade. Also included is a letterbook, 1833–1835, of Canton China, commission merchant Nathan Dunn & Company.

Gift of William Coles, Jr., 1951.

1692
Henderson, Robert, d. 1805.   Papers, 1779 (1781–1805) 1823. (6 linear ft.)

Robert Henderson was a merchant of Philadelphia and American partner of the firm of [William] Gardner & Henderson of Glasgow, Scotland, trading as Robert Henderson & Company in Philadelphia. Henderson imported soft goods, acted as commission merchant in indigo, rice, and tobacco and as a factor for Pennsylvania and New Jersey grains.

Correspondence, 1785–1797, including letters from a many Scots and Americans of Scottish descent, reflects extensive trade with England, Scotland, the West Indies, the American South, and the Mississippi territory. The correspondence reveals a particularly close network of merchants of Scottish descent who were interdependent in their dealings in commodities, land speculation in North Carolina and the Illinois country, stock in the First Bank of the United States, and speculation in ship bottoms and cargoes. Bills and receipts, 1783–1801, confirm the picture.

Also included are: letterbooks, 1784–1798; daybooks, 1781–1794; journals, 1781–1823; ledgers, 1779–1794; cashbook, 1785–1795; receipt books, 1781–1823; invoice book, 1784–1793; Henderson's laundry list, begun in London and continued in Philadelphia, 1784–1800; Gardner & Henderson's inventory of goods, n.d.; and a stockholder list of an unidentified Philadelphia company, 1809.

Represented in the collection are: Buchanan & Dunlap, Petersburg, Va.; Alexander Addison, Washington, D.C.; William Galt, Richmond, Va.; Alexander Glen, Glasgow, Scotland; David Lamb, Glasgow, Scotland; William Liddell, Glasgow, Scotland; William Nimmo, Richmond, Va.; Mair & Gordon, Charleston, S.C.; and Andrew van Tuyl, New York, N.Y.

Gift of Mary H. McKesson, 1935.

1693
Central Congregational Church (Philadelphia, Pa.)   Records, 1864–1923.   (600 items.)

Records of Central Congregational Church includes: correspondence, letters, and certificates of recommendations and dismissal, reports, financial records, and miscellaneous items; minute books, 1864–1898 of the Central Congregational Society of Philadelphia; annual meeting minutes and reports, 1872–1903, of the Congregational Association of New Jersey.

Purchased, Mifflin Fund, 1952; and gift of Mrs. P. Donald Folwell, 1957.

1694
Brolasky family.   Papers, 1842–1914.   (6 linear ft.)

Simon Brolasky was a dry-goods merchant who acquired substantial rental properties. Simon's son, Henry Connelly Brolasky, who was also engaged in the dry-goods business, eventually established a real estate office and looked after his father's property. Howell de Coursey Brolasky, Henry's son, was a fabric salesman/representative for Lee Brothers and Company (Philadelphia) then for Brigg, Enty, and Company (New York, N.Y.), as its Philadelphia agent.

Professional and personal account books, financial memoranda, and other papers of three generations of the Brolasky family of Philadelphia make up the bulk of this collection.

Simon Brolasky's records consist of receipt books, 1869–1880, for property and personal payments, and a personal expense book, October, 1880 to January, 1881.

The account books for Henry Connelly Brolasky as a dry-goods merchant are: journals, 1859–1862; ledger, 1859; bills payable and receivable, 1859–1866. There are rental records, 1866–1873, kept as continuations of two account books. As executor of the Simon Brolasky estate there are: cash accounts, 1881, 1887–1894; receipt book, 1881–1910; receipted bills, 1881–1904, which include the Mary Ann Howell estate. There is additional miscellaneous business and personal correspondence, receipted bills, legal documents, and financial memorandum books.

There are sundry memorandum books for Howell de Coursey Brolasky on orders, expenses, and his letterbook, 1885–1887, while with the New York firm. There is also: some correspondence; a European diary, 1875; notebooks as a Captain in the Pennsylvania National Guard; and financial papers.

Among the few items apparently not of the Brolasky family are: Gurney & Co., N.Y., silk manufacturer, account book, 1845–1846, with Benjamin P. Gurney's record of business in Philadelphia, and sales journal, 1857–1858. Henry S. Leech, New York, N.Y., stock ledger, 1871–1873; George J. Scott, Philadelphia glue manufacturer, business and estate receipt book, 1851–1871; mimeograph copies of *Pathology. Prof. James Tyson. General Pathological Anatomy,* and *Theory & Practice of Medicine. Prof. [Alfred] Stille. Nervous Diseases,* n.d

Gift of George C.C. Stout, 1954.

1695
Larned family.   Papers, 1777–1822.   (7 v.)

Simon Larned, later a Pittsfield, Mass., merchant and banker, served in the Revolution as captain, 4th Massachusetts regiment, Colonel William Sheppard commanding. Larned's brother, Thaddeus, was a Thompson, Conn., farmer, magistrate, and land speculator. Noadiah Larned, son of Thaddeus, also farmed in Thompson, Conn.

Simon Larned's papers include regimental orderly books, April 21 to October 26, 1777, and May 17 to July 25, 1778, containing, as well, results of courts martial; a contemporary copy of [John Armstrong's] Newburgh Addresses with Washington's replies, March, 1783; and a memorial to the General Court of Massachusetts concerning officers' pensions, continued with an anonymous New Year's satire [1783].

There is also: a diary, 1791–1817, for Thaddeus Larned including farm rental accounts maintained as agent for Thomas Dawes of Boston, 1791–

1803; and a diary for Noadiah Larned, 1821–1822, in Simon Larned's 1778 orderly book.

Gift of Hope B. Tyler Montgomery, 1951.

1696
Clymer family.   Papers, 1807–1899.   (325 items.)

Maria O'Brien Clymer was the wife of George Clymer, Jr., daughter-in-law of George Clymer, the signer of the Declaration of Independence. Her son Meredith Clymer studied medicine in Europe, practiced in Philadelphia and New York, specializing in nervous disorders, became president of Pridedale Iron Company, New York City, returned to medicine as assistant surgeon general during the Civil War, and thereafter continued his practice in New York and Albany with some apparent difficulty.

A portion of these papers consist of Maria Clymer's personal incoming correspondence, 1807–1848.

For Meredith Clymer there is a diary fragment, June-July, 1840, of his visit in Germany. His correspondence and military papers, 1841, 1853–1870, 1899, concern his Civil War service and other professional activities as well as personal affairs, particularly his estrangement from his wife Eliza L. Snelling in 1866. There are also some genealogical notes.

Formerly part of 138.

1697
No entry.

1698
No entry.

1699
Sinclair, Robert Lincoln.   Papers, 1858–1931.   (150 items.)

Robert Lincoln Sinclair was a Philadelphia bookkeeper who immigrated from Ireland and became a United States citizen in 1858.

Sinclair's letters mention politics and religion. Some of the correspondents include: George Potter Darrow, Gifford Pinchot, and John Wanamaker. There are also some letters from relatives in Ireland.

1700
William H. Horstmann and Sons.   Records, 1836–1888.   (7 v.)

William H. Horstmann and Sons (later Horstmann Brothers and Company), established in 1815, were Philadelphia importers and manufacturers of military uniforms, insignias, and flags.

The records include: cashbook, 1858–1860; machine book, 1845–1875; register of employees, 1876–1875; ribbon sample books, 1850–1876; book of labels used on silks and ribbons; scrapbook of newspaper clippings, 1867–1888.

1701
Burrough, Marmaduke.   Papers, 1814–1843.   (38 items.)

Marmaduke Burrough was a Philadelphia physician and United States consul in Vera Cruz, ca. 1820–1840.

Burrough's papers consist primarily of correspondence on his interests in wild animal trade, especially from India. Some printed material includes a proposal for a coffee growing settlement in Florida.

Gift of H. Genet Taylor, 1952.

1702
No entry.

1703
Biddle, Alexander.

Entry cancelled; see collection #1792B.

1704
Union Canal Company of Pennsylvania.   Records, 1792–1833.
(10 v.)

The Schuylkill and Susquehanna Navigation Company, founded in 1791, and the Delaware and Schuylkill Navigation Company, founded in 1792, merged in 1811 to form the Union Canal Company for the purpose of building an east-west canal through Pennsylvania.

These records include Schuylkill and Susquehanna Navigation Company stock transfer book and minute book, 1792–1797, 1800–1811; Delaware and Schuylkill Navigation Company subscription book, 1792, and minute book, 1798–1811; and Union Canal Company minute books, 1811–1827, 1830–1833.

1705
No entry.

1706
Shippen, Edward, 1826–1911.   Papers, 1849–1875.   (250 items.)

Edward Shippen was a United States Naval Surgeon.

Papers of Edward Shippen include personal correspondence, mainly letters to and from his wife, Mary Katherine Paul Shippen, and some incoming U.S. Naval correspondence. There is almost no material on Shippen's practice of medicine.

Purchased, 1952.

1707
No entry.

1708
Snow, Edward Taylor, 1844–1913.   Papers, 1890–1913.
(200 items.)

Edward Taylor Snow was a Philadelphia artist.

Mostly incoming correspondence on exhibitions, sales, and other activities of the Art Club of Philadelphia.

Purchased, 1952.

Print material removed to print collections.

1709
Pennsylvania Society for the Prevention of Cruelty to Animals.
Records, 1867–1921.   (300 items.)

The Pennsylvania Society for the Prevention of Cruelty to Animals was incorporated in 1868.

The records include: letterpress book, 1872–1876; membership records, 1871–1885, n.d.; case books, 1867–1873, 1884–1893, recording offenses on which the S.P.C.A. acted; reports of disabled animals, 1878–1883, 1907–1921; arrival of livestock, 1917–1921; income and payment book, 1877–1883; receipt book, 1878–1887; miscellaneous papers including correspondence, reports, and lists of fines collected.

Purchased, 1952.

1710
Philadelphia General Hospital. Woman's Advisory Council.
Records, 1915–1957.   (12 linear ft.)

The Woman's Advisory Council of the Philadelphia General Hospital was a hospital auxiliary originally organized to advise the Philadelphia director of Health on conditions at the hospital.

Records include correspondence, minutes, hospital shop reports, journals, bills, and receipts. There are some papers of the Social Service Auxiliary, Philadelphia General Hospital, 1945–1950.

Gift of Mrs. Harry Snellingburg, 1958.

1711
Colton, Richard Francis, 1843–1880.   Notebooks, 1856–1874.
(11 v.)

Richard Francis Colton was a Philadelphia theological teacher and Episcopal clergyman.

His notebooks cover topics ranging from theology to political economy and are written in several languages, including English, Greek, and German.

1712
No entry.

1713
Benjamin Franklin Parkway.   Papers, 1907–1917.   (300 items.)

Correspondence and papers primarily on the acquisition of real estate along the proposed Benjamin Franklin Parkway in Philadelphia. Many of the letters are addressed to Mayors John Edgar Reyburn, 1907–1911, and Rudolph Blankenburg, 1912–1913. There is also outgoing correspondence from the Mayor's Office on the project.

Gift of J. Hampton Moore, 1946.

1714
Pennsylvania Court.   Records, 1797–1835.   (50 items.)

The miscellaneous records of both civil and criminal proceedings in Pennsylvania courts in Philadelphia county. Includes: argument lists, case books, case lists, and jury lists.

1715
Genealogical Society of Pennsylvania.   Collection, 1642–1806.
(14 linear ft.)

Entry cancelled; transferred to the Pennsylvania Historical and Museum Commission, 1985.

1716
DuPonceau, Peter Stephen, 1760–1844.
Correspondence, 1777–1844.   (2 v.)

Peter S. DuPonceau was a Philadelphia lawyer, author, and linguist.

These copies were made by Job R. Tyson. One volume consists mainly of incoming letters, 1777–1785, 1808–1839, on political and legal matters from John Adams, John Quincy Adams, Washington Irving, Marquis de Lafayette, Edward Livingston, James Madison, James Monroe, and others. There are some copies of outgoing correspondence.

The other volume is DuPonceau's reminiscences of his life to 1783 in the form of letters, 1836–1844, mainly written first to Robert Walsh and then to DuPonceau's granddaughter, Anne L. Garesch. The memoirs concern his formal and informal education in France and his service as an aid to von Steuben and Greene during the American Revolution.

Both volumes contain a table of contents. There are also a few miscellaneous letters and notes.

Gift of Edward T. Stuart.

"The Autobiography of Peter S. DuPonceau" / edited by James L. Whitehead. *The Pennsylvania Magazine of History and Biography,* 1939–1940.

1717
Hubbell, Helena.   Collection, 1679 (1800–1895).   (300 items.)

Autograph collection of cut signatures, letters, and signed photographs, mainly of prominent American men in the 19th century. Included are two scrapbooks of Civil War miscellany.

Gift of Helena Hubbell, 1944.

1718
No entry.

1719
Robinson, Jonathan John.   Papers, 1815–1860.   (60 items.)

Jonathan John Robinson was a Philadelphia dry goods and commissions merchant.

Account books and financial records of Jonathan John Robinson including: letterbook, 1815–1829; journal, 1816–1824; ledger, 1816–1822; bankbook, 1816- 1821; miscellaneous accounts and other financial records, 1832–1860; personal account book, 1844–1853, with some notes of his activities at his farm in Abington; and some estate and inventory records, 1825–1869.

1720
Weirs family.   Records, 1830–1860.   (7 v.)

Robert and Uriah Weirs were blacksmiths of Christiana, Del.

Included are Robert Weirs's ledgers, 1830–1841, 1848–1849, and Uriah Weirs's daybooks, 1839–1860.

Purchased, Dreer Fund, 1935.

1721
Clark and Raser.   **Records, 1817–1849.**   **(14 v.)**

The firm was founded by John C. Clark and Matthias Raser, both Philadelphia printers, in 1817. The partnership continued until 1831, after which it became John C. Clark & Company. Clark was joined by his son in 1857. The firm did job printing for several major Philadelphia publishers including Blanchard, Desilver, and the American Sunday School Union.

Included in the collection are: journals, 1817–1824, 1832–1837; compositor's bill books, 1821–1825, 1845; cash sales book, 1831–1832; invoice book, 1831; ledger, 1831; cashbooks, 1831, 1832, 1837–1840, 1845, 1849; letterbook, 1832; expense book, 1832, printing order book, 1833–1838; and orders for binding, 1836–1841.

Purchased, Library Fund, 1947.

1722
Besson family.   **Papers, 1718 (1806–1884).**   **(75 items.)**

The Bessons were a retail merchant family in Philadelphia, descended from French immigrants, Anthony and Marie Louise Vernier Besson.

Naturalization papers, passports, certificates, a few letters, and miscellaneous items.

There are a few French documents, 1718–1806, that predate Anthony Besson's naturalization.

Gift of Howard B. Knight, 1954.

1723
Jellett, Edwin Costley.   **Papers, 1848–1849, 1860–1921.**
(3 linear ft.)

Edwin C. Jellett, and his father, Morgan W. Jellett, resided in Germantown.

Diaries recording Jellett's walks, visits, and other daily activities. The diaries for the 1860's give fragmented reminiscences. There are also 2 small financial memorandum books, 1848–1849, of Morgan Jellett.

1725
Smyth family.   **Papers, 1785–1897.**   **(1,000 items.)**

Correspondence and legal papers on the estate of Jacob Baker, his son-in-law John William Baker, who lived in Cuba, and son-in-law Cornelius Comegys. The responsibility for the estates all eventually devolved to Isaac S. Smyth, Comegys' son-in-law. (John W. Baker's estate was particularly confused by the claims of illegitimate children. There is some family and other personal correspondence, including letters, 1816–1855 of John W. Baker to his sister Catherine Comegys, and business papers of Cornelius Comegys.

Purchased, 1955.

1726
Hazlett and Moss.   **Records, (1904–1928) 1938.**   **(26 v.)**

Hazlett and Moss was a Philadelphia real estate, mortgage, insurance, and trust estate agency that managed financing for the construction of residential developments in the city and its suburbs. The business was operated chiefly by Frank Hazlett Moss from 1902 to 1927, when the firm name was changed to Frank H. Moss & Company.

The records are: operations books, 1904–1938, with accounts of mortgages, loans, and schedules of construction costs; plan books, 1906–1935, with architectural drawings; building specification books, ca. 1911.

1727
MacDade, Albert Dutton, 1871–1954.   **Memoirs, 1950–1954.**
(ca. 400 items.)

Albert Dutton MacDade was born and raised in Delaware County, where he was admitted to the bar in 1894, served as district attorney, 1905–1912, served in the Pennsylvania State Senate, 1920–1928, then was elected judge of Delaware County Court of Common Pleas, 1928–1948, and became president judge in 1943.

His reminiscences deal at length with his legal career; political intrigues of judicial election; cases in which he was involved; and are filled with his outspoken views on a multitude of subjects including: the legal system, judicial behavior, juvenile delinquency, divorce, and prejudice against men over forty. Many judges of the Pennsylvania courts are frequent targets of his praise and criticism. Governor William C. Sproul was a childhood and close personal friend of MacDade and figures prominently in the memoirs. There is also an account of a trip to Europe in 1950. The memoirs are composed of a 1,200-page typescript narrative, copies of letters and articles for newspapers and speeches. There are also clippings of MacDade's newspaper contributions.

Gift of Albert Dutton MacDade, 1954.

1728
No entry.

1729
Redwood, William, 1726–1815.   **Account books, 1749–1811.**
(10 v.)

William Redwood was a merchant of Newport, 1749–1762, 1778–1782, Philadelphia, 1762–1778, 1787–1815, and Antigua, 1782–1787. While in Antigua, he also operated the family plantations.

Included in the collection are: Redwood's journal and ledger, 1749–1760 of his Newport partnership with Elias Bland; wastebook, 1775–1778, 1788–1791; ledger 1775–1778, 1788–1807, showing extensive importation of wine and teas; daybook, journal, ledger, 1787–1790; and a daybook, 1797–1811, showing some activity in the China trade.

1730
No entry.

1731
Blackwell, Robert, 1748–1831.   **Estate papers, 1791–1853.**
(100 items.)

Robert Blackwell was the minister of Saint Peters Church (Episcopal), Philadelphia.

Legal and other papers relating to the estate of Robert Blackwell. There is some correspondence, 1833–1853, from the U.S. Treasurer's Office to James S. Smith and Henry Hollingsworth, trustees of Blackwell's estate. Miscellaneous legal papers include land patents and deeds, 1791–1853, and Blackwell's bank book, 1817–1831, gathered by the trustees.

1732
Calvin, Samuel, 1811–1890.   **Papers, 1837 (1848–1865) 1870.**
(300 items.)

Samuel Calvin practiced law in Hollidaysburgh, and was the U.S. Congressman (Whig) from Blair, Hunington, Juniata, and Centre Counties from 1849 to 1851.

Papers include incoming correspondence and miscellaneous bills and receipts. The letters pertain to his law practice, Republican politics, and family matters. Among correspondents are Andrew Gregg Curtin and William F. Johnston.

1733

Society of the Sons of Saint George.   Records, 1772–1949.
(25 v. and ca. 400 items.)

The Society of the Sons of Saint George was organized in Philadelphia in 1772 for the purpose of "giving advice and assistance" to Englishmen in distress.

Included here are: minute books, 1772–1949; stewards' records, 1861–1938; treasurers' account book, 1875–1923; members dues book, 1897–1909; Saint George's Hall Association (stockholders in the Society's building at 13th and Arch streets) minute books, 1875–1898; some miscellaneous loose records, among which is the original charter.

Gift of the Society of the Sons of Saint George, 1955, and Paul Lester, 1960.

1734

Hockley family.   Papers, 1731–1883.   (450 items.)

The papers of the Hockley and related families of Philadelphia include: incoming business letters, 1784–1804, of George Wescott, Philadelphia copper merchant, and his letter and order book, 1790–1802; receipt book with sections for Thomas Hockley, 1772–1796, George Wescott, 1800, and Mrs. [Thomas] Hockley, 1813–1827; letterbook and accounts, 1819–1824, of Thomas Hockley as supercargo for Philadelphia merchants Nixon & Walker, Joseph Sims, Stephen Russel and others, on voyages to West Indies, Brazil, Madeira, Gibraltar, Malay, and other ports; receipt book on behalf of Ann P. Anderson, 1876–1883, of Thomas Hockley ; receipt books, 1817–1826 of Cornelius Stevenson; loose papers of various family members, deeds, certificates, accounts, and other miscellany.

1735

Beale, Leonard T.   Collection, 1746–1892.
(1,000 items and 16 v.)

The main body of the collection relates to the business activities, beginning in 1780, of the Lewis family. The early correspondence and financial papers of Mordecai Lewis and his sons Mordecai and Samuel N. Lewis, Philadelphia merchants, pertain to trade with the West Indies, Europe, and Asia, and contains some ship records. Samuel N. Lewis ledger, 1800–1840, and Mordecai and Samuel N. Lewis journal, 1817–1849, cover the period of their bankruptcy in 1817 and eventual recovery by 1842 as lead manufacturers. The later incoming correspondence and financial records relate to the Lewis' industrial enterprises including the Philadelphia Lead Works. There are account books of the trustees of Rebecca C. Lewis, 1820–1849. The collection also holds marine insurance ledgers, 1755–1757, 1759; account books of Philadelphia merchants Thomas Wharton, 1747–1783, and James C. Fisher, 1783–1789; and Henry Steele letters, 1760–1761, from London to his sister.

Gift of Leonard T. Beale, 1955.

1736
Lewis, Eleanor Parke Custis, 1779–1852.   Letters, 1794–1852. (2 v. and 49 leaves.)

Eleanor Parke Custis Lewis was the daughter of Martha Parke Custis Washington and George Washington's adopted daughter.

These are typescripts of letters to her friend Elizabeth Bordley Gibson of Philadelphia. The early letters relate to family life with her grandparents at Mount Vernon. Later letters are written from the Lewis plantation in Woodlawn, Va., and from her trips in the United States and England. Also included is a transcript of an address, 1924, by Roland S. Morris to the Historical Society of Pennsylvania about the letters.

Gift of Roland S. Morris, 1950.
Typescripts.
Originals owned by Mount Vernon Ladies Association.

1737
Frankenfield, Samuel P.   Account books, 1852–1901.   (14 v.)

Journals, ledgers, cashbooks, carriage books of Samuel P. Frankenfield, Philadelphia undertaker, 1871–1901. There is also a daybook, 1852–1860, of Goucher and Frankenfield, an unidentified business.

Gift of H. Guy Boohar, 1955.

1738
Cushman and Wetherill families.   Papers, 1803–1907. (80 items.)

The papers of the Cushman and Wetherill families of Philadelphia consist largely of letters between George H. Cushman and Susan Wetherill during their courtship; also Susan's letter to her siblings, George's letters from their children, and letters to their daughter, Ida Cushman. There is a Rebecca Wetherill diary, 1907, with brief daily memoranda.

Gift of Mr. and Mrs. W. Chatlin Wetherill, 1956.

1739
Lancaster and Schuylkill Bridge Company.   Records, 1811–1842.
(ca. 400 items.)

The Lancaster and Schuylkill Bridge Company was incorporated in 1811 to construct a bridge across the Schuylkill River at Upper Ferry in Philadelphia. Completed in 1813, "Wernwag's Bridge" was regarded as an engineering phenomenon because of its single-arched span.

Included in the records are: charter and acts of incorporation, 1811–1812 and minutes, 1811–1837. Also included are: incoming correspondence, 1811–1841, dealing with construction and financial details; treasurer's reports, 1811–2827; miscellaneous accounts, 1814–1832; bankbooks, 1811–1820; ledger, 1812–1813; cancelled checks, 1812–1841; bills, 1811–1839; lists of stockholders, 1812–1826; and miscellaneous material relating to shareholders, 1811–1842.

1740
Holdem, Erza, 1803–1846.   Biographical notes.   (ca. 150 items.)

Erza Holden was the editor of the *Philadelphia Saturday Courier,* 1836–1846.

Notes and partial typescript of Mr. and Mrs. George Glen Gould for a projected biography of Erza Holden. Most of the source material comes from newspapers of the period, particularly Holden's.

Gift of Mr. and Mrs. George Glen Gould, 1955.

1741
West family.   Business records, 1769–1804.   (10 v.)

William West was a Philadelphia dry-goods merchant. He was followed in the business by his sons Francis and John in Philadelphia and James in Baltimore, Md.

These records of the West family business interests include: journals, 1769–1796; ledger, 1770–1777; letterbooks, 1783–1788; William West estate journal, 1783–1790; James Fuller, Philadelphia merchant, volume of letter drafts, accounts, and other memoranda, relating in part to the West estate; and James West daybook, 1799–1804.

Gift of Mrs. Henry C. Bailey, 1954.

1742
Aero Club of Pennsylvania.   Papers, 1908–1953.   (350 items.)

The Aero Club of Pennsylvania was founded in 1909 in Philadelphia for the "encouragement and development of interest and activity in aeronautics and aviation."

Minutebook, 1909–1953; record of daily activities, 1930–1932; correspondence, 1929–1950; drafts for a club history, 1932–1939; membership lists, 1945–1949; miscellaneous pamphlets, 1910–1931; and scrapbooks, 1908–1910, 1915, 1929–1932.

Gift of Norman J. Greene, 1953.

1743A
Irvine family.   Papers, 1777–1869.   (750 items.)

William Irvine served as Colonel with the 6th Pennsylvania Regiment during the Revolution. His son, William Neill Irvine began a career as a lawyer and served as a Colonel in the War of 1812 when he raised the 42nd Regiment of Infantry.

The papers of the Irvine family begin with a series of William Irvine letters, 1777–1778, to David Grier on military supplies and recruitment. William Neill Irvine's military papers include: correspondence, returns, accounts, recruitment reports, and court martial proceedings for William Hull and others. Following the war, there are papers on legal matters and incoming correspondence to William N. Irvine and his son Galbraith A. Irvine on state and national politics, with letters from James Buchanan, John Galbraith, and other Pennsylvania politicians.

Other papers of Galbraith A. Irvine a Warren physician with business interests include material on the Warren Bridge Company, of which Irvine was treasurer, and a dispute with William A. Irvine over lands inherited from their grandfather William Irvine.

Purchased, 1956.

1743B
Irvine family.   Papers, 1778–1843.   (220 items.)

Correspondence and other papers of General William Irvine and his son Callander Irvine. General Irvine's papers, 1778–1804, concern his command of Fort Pitt, his services as commissioner of accounts, 1793, and as superintendent of military stores, 1801–1804. The papers also relate to national and state politics, particularly in letters from William Findley and Andrew Gregg.

Over half of the letters, 1803–1843, to Callander Irvine, U.S. Army commissary general, are from John Armstrong who writes as secretary of war, 1813–1814, and later as a retired gentleman farmer.

Purchased, 1963 (through the kindness of Mrs. Caryl Roberts).

1744
Maitland family.   Papers, 1729 (1779–1896).   (300 items.)

There is one section of papers, 1729, 1806–1896, for John Maitland, merchant, and Thomas Maitland, grocer, and their descendants, a Philadelphia Irish-American family. It includes incoming correspondence, personal, family, and business records, deeds, and John J. Maitland account of his Civil War experiences as a Confederate officer in Virginia.

The other section consists of papers, 1779–1811, of Thomas Fitzsimons, Philadelphia merchant, political figure, signer of the Constitution, and Maitland family in-law. His papers deal mainly with business matters and include incoming correspondence, miscellaneous business and legal records, and material on the construction of the frigate *Philadelphia*. His correspondence includes a few letters from Robert Morris.

Purchased, 1956.

1745
Anderson family.   Papers, 1797–1913.   (ca. 2400 items.)

The Anderson family lived in Lower Merion Township, Montgomery County. James Anderson was a physician, civic leader, and 1816–1817 member of the Pennsylvania House of Representatives. His son, Joseph W. Anderson, was also a physician.

The papers of the Anderson family are chiefly those of James Anderson. His correspondence, 1805–1858, letter and memorandum book, 1817–1828, and letterbooks, 1831–1852, 1855–1858, relate to personal, business, and political matters. Material on Anderson's medical career include: ledgers, 1808–1858; casebook, 1804–1806, of patients treated at a Philadelphia almshouse; and notes on Benjamin Rush lectures, 1797–1798.

Among other family papers are: reminiscences, 1835, Isaac Anderson, father of James, about Charlestown Township, Chester County; James' father-in-law Joseph Wilson's contested estate papers, 1816–1845; miscellaneous correspondence, 1846–1903, receipt book, 1865–1890, and medical notes, n.d. of Joseph W. Anderson; Corona Anderson, James's daughter, incoming correspondence, 1859–1913, from friends living and traveling abroad; and anonymous recipe books, notes and clippings, ca. 1750–1900.

Gift of Joseph W. Anderson, 1956.

1746
Chew, Samuel, 1795–1841.   Papers, 1826–1850.   (250 items.)

Samuel Chew, Philadelphia lawyer, acted as agent for the corvette *Kensington (Tepeyac)*, built for the Mexican government, and for which Mexico eventually defaulted payment.

These papers include bills and accounts for the construction and letters from Mexican and American officials on payment from Mexico. The correspondence occasionally reflects the political turmoil of Mexico's First Federalist Régime.

Purchased, 1956.

1747
Blockley Baptist Church (Philadelphia, Pa.)   Records, 1804–1891.
(5 v.)

The Blockley Baptist Church, a West Philadelphia church, was founded in 1804.

Includes constitution and minutes of the Bible Society of Blockley; pew book; church dues book; treasurer's accounts; Sabbath School treasurer's accounts; and a few miscellaneous papers.

Purchased, 1956.

1748
Wickham, Benjamin C.   Collection, 1823–1898.   (150 items.)

Benjamin C. Wickham served as president of Tioga County Bank.

The collection includes: incoming business and personal correspondence, miscellaneous business papers dealing with the sale of land and banking matters, and miscellaneous records of the Tioga County Bank. Also included are deeds, miscellaneous correspondence, and business papers of other Tioga County businessmen.

Purchased, 1956.

1749
Cornett, Jane, d. 1903.   Papers, 1834–1904.   (115 items.)

Papers of Jane Cornett of Phoenixville. Mainly incoming family correspondence. Includes forty Civil War letters, 1861–1865, of J.A. and Joseph P. Cornett, brothers of Jane Cornett. The letters were written from Union Army camps in Beaufort, S.C., and eastern Virginia, including Appomattox Court House, and contain personal accounts of the course of war in those areas. Also included are a few miscellaneous financial records, 1835–1888, of Samuel Cornett.

Acquired in 1955.

1750
Fox, Samuel M.   Correspondence, 1838–1841.   (50 items.)

Samuel M. Fox was a Philadelphia brickmaker.
Incoming business and family papers.

1751
Naval and Military Order of the Spanish-American War.
Pennsylvania Commandery.   Records, 1908–1951.   (200 items.)

The Commandery was an association of veteran officers of the War with Spain, together with their lineal descendants.

The records include: outgoing and incoming correspondence, 1912–1951, constitution and by-laws, and membership lists.

Gift of Charles H. Speckman.

1752
Penfield, Frederick Courtland, 1855–1922.
Collection, 1909 (1913–1917) 1921. (140 items.)

Frederick Courtland Penfield served as Ambassador to Austria-Hungary, 1913–1917.

Over one-half of the collection is made up of photographs, mainly of the Austrian royal family. There are copies of some diplomatic correspondence, printed documents, and reports prepared for the State Department, including *Austria-Hungary after Two Years of War.*

1754
Turvey, Caroline Schetky, 1866–1954. **The Log of a Long Voyage.**
(300 items.)

The Log of a Long Voyage, a two-part typescript biography of Charles Alexander Schetky from the notes he dictated to his daughter, Caroline Schetky Turvey, during the last years of his life. The first part relates stories of his childhood and tales of his younger years at sea. The second part begins with his entrance into the United States Navy in 1863, his service during the Civil War and thereafter, until his retirement from the Navy in 1889. Other biographical information is included about Schetsky's retirement in Haddonfield, N.J., 1889–1901. Some correspondence, 1949–1954, between Turvey and her godson, Ralph W. Wescott, on the biography; and some clippings about Schetky.

1755
Biddle-Rush papers.

Entry cancelled; see collection #1792H.

1756
Borman family. **Papers, 1837–1898.** (ca. 50 items.)

Johann Karl Edward Borman, in 1837, migrated from Dresden, Germany, to Philadelphia, where he first worked as a tool and dye maker and then as a merchant of glass and mirrors.

Included are Borman's school diploma from Dresden, 1837; his passport, 1838; and the diary of his trip to Philadelphia, 1839. There are also letters to and from family and friends in Germany, 1849–1872, especially the letters from Johann Eckardt, 1861–1872, all in German. The collection also includes a miscellany of bill-heads, business cards, stage coach tickets in France, and 2 letters on Borman's descendants, A.G. Brook's appointment to the Navy, 1898.

1757
Law, Samuel Andrew, 1771–1845.   **Correspondence, 1817–1849.**
(80 items.)

Letters to Samuel Andrew Law, land agent from New York, primarily on appraisal and sales of land, especially of the Henry Drinker estate. Correspondents include James C. Fisher and Thomas Stewardson, both from Philadelphia. The last few letters are directed to Law's relatives and also deal with land concerns.

1758
Starr, Floyd T.   **Collection, 1750 (1828–1869) 1876.**
(ca. 150 items.)

A miscellaneous collection of papers including the letters, 1827–1829, of Dr. John White of Lewes, Del., while a member of the Delaware House of Representatives for Sussex County to his sons John P. White and Joseph H. White, both in Philadelphia. Dr. White, a Whig, comments on Jacksonian politics in lower Delaware as well as upon family affairs.

Included, too, are some papers of three naval officers whose careers brought them to Philadelphia: James Madison Frailey, personal copies of orders and circular letters reflecting his commands on the blockading squadron during the Civil War, 1861–1866, and his commissions, 1851–1870; James R.M. Mullany commissions, 1861–1870; Charles Stewart, 1 letter, 1864. A small group of Philadelphia deeds, 1750–1867, completes the collection. Gift of Floyd T. Starr, 1953.

1759
Walker, George.   **Records, 1775 (1829–1873).**   **(75 items.)**

George Walker was a Susquehanna County, surveyor and prothonotary.

The bulk of the collection is made up of the survey notes, 1829–1873, of Walker, Orrin S. Beale, Robert B. Beath, and unidentified volumes. The survey notes are mainly for lands in Susquehanna County, with some notes for Tioga, Bradford, Wayne, and Luzerne Counties. Also included are miscellaneous land records, land patents, deeds, and survey maps.

1760

Drinker, Elizabeth Sandwith, 1734–1807.   **Diaries, 1758–1807.**
(33 v.)

Elizabeth Sandwith Drinker of Philadelphia was the daughter of William Sandwith, merchant and shipowner; in 1761 she married Henry Drinker, also a merchant.

Elizabeth Sandwith Drinker composed memorandum books for her own personal recollections, which constitute a day-by-day account of the life of a well-to-do Quaker woman. Elizabeth Drinker's interests were diverse but she was little concerned with political or economic questions, except insofar as they directly touched upon her family. The bulk of the entries deal with strictly private or family matters, particularly the health of her family. She gives particular consideration to the Yellow Fever outbreaks in Philadelphia after 1793, especially the epidemics of 1793 and 1798. Elizabeth Drinker and her family were conscientious Quakers and there is material on the Society of Friends in Philadelphia.

Of special note is the material on the American Revolution which includes detailed descriptions of the treatment of Quaker non-combatants, and of the British occupation of Philadelphia, principally during 1777.

Gift of Mr. Henry S. Drinker, 1955.

Typescript in 7 v., diary for 1801 lacking.

The volumes for 1787–1788 were destroyed. No diary entries exist for May, 1786, to July, 1789.

Henry Biddle, ed., *Extracts from the Journal of Elizabeth Drinker, 1759–1807*, Philadelphia: J.B. Lippincott Company, 1889.

1761

Foering, John Oppell, b. 1843.   **Papers, 1861–1908.**   **(35 items.)**

John Oppell Foering was a soldier and officer with the Pennsylvania Volunteers, 28th Regiment of Infantry, which saw action at Cedar Mountain, Antietam, Chancellorsville, Gettysburg, Missionary Ridge, Ringgold, Pine Knob, Peach Tree Creek, and in the Atlantic, Savannah, and Carolinas campaigns.

With these papers is Foering's account, which apparently relies on a diary, of the Regiment's service. There are also drafts and notes for speeches and a history of the 20th Army Corps, miscellaneous papers and photographs.

Gift of H.M. Lippincott, 1958.

1762
Lewis family.   Papers, 1774–1940.   (3 linear ft.)

Papers of the Lewis family reflect their business and cultural activities. A major portion of these papers are receipted bills and other accounts, 1774–1859, for the management of the Philadelphia properties of the George Blight estate. There is a Phoenix Mutual Insurance Company minute book, 1852–1876, and dividend book, 1856–1877. Two Philadelphia amateur music clubs are represented: Melody Club, history and by-laws, 1893–1907, and Wednesday Music Club, by-laws and programs, 1893–1918. Lewis family material includes wedding invitation responses for the marriage of Eleanor Lewis to C. Whalen Vaughn, 1907, and Eleanor Lewis to W. Furness Thompson, 1940, and miscellaneous bills and letters, 1937–1940, to Clifford Lewis III.
Gift of Clifford Lewis, III.

1763
Entry cancelled.

1764
Entry cancelled.

1765
Entry cancelled.

1766
Yuengling family.   Papers, 1815–1953.   (9 linear ft.)

Papers of the Yuengling family, owners of the Yuengling Brewery, Pottsville, collected or retained by David Gaul Yuengling.

There are letters addressed to Dr. George Douglas, Yuengling's great-great grandfather from Orwigsburg, Schuylkill County, from sister Mary, sons Andrew and John, conveyancer,land agents Andrew D. Cash and Thomas Spotswood of Philadelphia, and others on personal and business matters, 1815–1857. There are also letters written by Yuengling's mother, Augusta Roseberry, while a student at Springside School, Philadelphia, 1896–1900. Roseberry's uncle, Charles H. Moore, is represented by miscellaneous papers on his career as a civil engineer with various railroads, 1895–1937.

The bulk of the collection consists of files of correspondence maintained by Yuengling, 1931–1953, with friends from: Pottstown, the Georgetown School of Foreign Service, Trinidad (where he was employed on the construction of the U.S. Naval Air Station during World War II), teaching positions, and with friends made during his many travels. His most frequent correspondents are his mother, Bertram Anderson, Raymond J. Greene, Elizabeth G. Koenig, and Peter Milivojevic, a Yugoslav priest.

Gift of David Gaul Yuengling, 1956.

1767
Drinker, Henry, 1734–1809.   **Papers, 1747–1867.**   **(1,100 items.)**

Henry Drinker was a merchant, land developer, and ironmaster of Philadelphia. He was a member of the Society of Friends.

The bulk of the collection consists of Drinker's business correspondence, including some of the firm of James & Drinker, which Drinker had formed with Abel James. In 1773, the East India Company consigned a shipment of tea to the firm; there is a good deal of material concerning the resulting controversy and non-importation. Of particular interest are the letters from Pigou and Booth, London merchants, showing the British point of view. There are several letters on the war-time disruption of trade.

The collection also includes typescripts of correspondence, 1777–1778, between Drinker and his wife, Elizabeth Sandwith Drinker, written while Drinker was exiled to Winchester, Va., by the new Pennsylvania government.

Drinker's correspondence after the war, 1783–1809, is largely concerned with land development and speculation in northern and western Pennsylvania. His correspondents include: Benjamin Rush, Benjamin West, James Wilson, and Aaron Burr.

Also included in the collection are other items created or collected by Drinker's descendants: a late 19th century transcription of Henry Drinker's *Journal of a Voyage to England,* 1759–1760; business letters, 1808–1867, of Henry Drinker's nephew Henry Drinker, Jr.; correspondence and two journals of Drinker's grandson, Sandwith Drinker, including the journal of his voyage to India, 1838, and to Zanzibar, 1840, and correspondence addressed to Nathan Kite, Philadelphia merchant and one of the administrators of the estate of Henry Drinker; annual trial balances, 1833–1838, of John Wheeler Leavitt, maternal great-grandfather of Henry S. Drinker; a diary, 1842–1854 of Leavitt's youngest daughter, Emily Austin Leavitt; and the manuscript for a story, 1887, by Thomas A. Janvier, husband of Sandwith Drinker's daughter Kate.

Gift of Mr. and Mrs. Henry S. Drinker, 1956.

Originals of typescript Henry Drinker letters, 1777–1778, are located at the Haverford College Library.

1768

Collins, Zaccheus, d. 1831.   Papers, 1760–1847.   (450 items.)

Papers of Zaccheus Collins, Philadelphia merchant, include: correspondence on land speculation in Susquehana County, and elsewhere, and miscellaneous accounts, 1793–1831; Pennsylvania land surveys, 1786–1809, in Armstrong, Bedford, Cambria, Luzerne, Northampton, and Somerset Counties; miscellaneous land patents, 1795; papers of Collins's estate, 1832–1847, administered by his son-in-law Daniel Parker. There are miscellaneous certificates, 1760–1786, of Collins's father, Stephen Collins, also a Philadelphia merchant.

Gift of Vincent Young, 1956.

1769
No entry.

1770
Citizens' Municipal Associations.   Records, 1893–1907.
(300 items.)

The Citizens' Municipal Association was organized in 1886 in order to promote better local government in Philadelphia.

Small amount of incoming correspondence, 1893–1907, concerning cases, meetings, and salaries. Some correspondence and membership lists, 1895–1896, of the Eighth Ward Association of the Municipal League. Cases, 1888–1903, on municipal problems and scandals. Financial records, including contribution lists, 1898–1907, and Citizens' Municipal Association's bills and receipts, 1893–1907. Miscellaneous printed material of the Citizens' Municipal Association, 1893–1896.

Gift of Albert Smith Faught, 1956.

1771
Sherborne family.   Papers, 1798–1899.   (40 items.)

Miscellaneous papers of several unrelated Philadelphia businessmen includes: farm account book, Queen Charlton Parish, Somerset England, 1798–1803 of William Sherborne; receipt book, 1808–1837, with entries for William Sherborne who became a Philadelphia baker, William V. Sherborne, and Thomas P. Sherborne for the estate of William V. Sherborne; a few business papers, 1839–1899 of Thomas P. Sherborne, cabinet maker, Thomas H. Sherborne, merchant, and Hiram Miller; John Craig estate papers, 1809–1829; immigration papers and 23 letters, 1831–1854, in German to Christian Gessler, jeweler.

Christian Gessler letters in German.

1772
Cozens, William Barr Nash.   **Papers, 1864–1871.**   **(150 items.)**

William Barr Nash Cozens was a Philadelphia merchant accused of defrauding the United States government in a contract to supply tents during the Civil War.

The papers, which include affidavits in support of Cozens' case, deal with his arrest in 1864, trial, conviction, and fight for vindication. Correspondence from Cozens' lawyer, Jeremiah Sullivan Black, a copy of a letter, 1867, from Andrew Johnson disapproving the findings of the court's conviction, some of Cozens' account sheet, and a memorandum book, 1864–1871, complete the collection.

Gift of Clifford Lewis, III, 1956.

1773
Weems, James N., d. 1822   **Records, 1810–1831.**   **(8 v.)**

Business and estate records of James N. Weems, Philadelphia merchant in tea and soft goods trading to Delaware and the South alone and in partnership with Richard Benson and Benjamin Rawlings. Included are: letter book, 1810–1814; scrapbook of bills, 1811–1812; cash books, 1810–1814; day book, 1810–1814; letter book of Weems & Benson, continued by Weems & Rawlings, 1815–1823; Weems & Rawlings day book, 1818–1822; Eli Kirk Price's administrator's accounts of the estate of James N. Weems, including an inventory of household goods, 1822–1831.

Purchased, Dreer Fund, 1934.

1774
Hagstoz, Thomas.   **Collection, 1865–1914.**   **(150 items.)**

Thomas Hagstoz was a Philadelphia manufacturer of watch cases.

Clippings, photographs, trade cards, and trade announcements on the making of watches and cases.

Gift of George S. Hagstoz, 1956.

1775
Buckley, D. Penrose, d. 1862.   **Papers, 1861–1866.**   **(110 items.)**

Primarily correspondence of D. Penrose Buckley to his family while serving with the 3rd New Jersey Volunteers during the Civil War. The letters describe the training period in New Jersey, encampment outside of Washington, D.C., and events of the Peninsular Campaign. Captain Buckley died from wounds received in the Battle of Gaines Mill, June, 1862. Additional letters document the efforts of Buckley's family to confirm his death, to retrieve his possessions, and to have Buckley reinterred.

Gift of Mrs. Albert Nalle, 1957.

1776
Fels, Samuel Simeon, 1860–1950.   Papers, 1889–1973.
(18 linear ft.)

Seven series of papers including: correspondence, publications, Fels and Company, financial records, legal papers, biography, and miscellaneous.

Samuel Simeon Fels, youngest son of Lazarus and Susanna Fels, was born in Yanceyville, N.C., on February 16, 1860. His family moved north to settle in Philadelphia, where in 1876 Samuel joined the soap manufacturing business established that year by his older brother. The firm, Fels & Co., was incorporated in 1914, and Samuel became its first president, holding the office until his death in 1950. (The company was sold to Purex Corporation in 1964.) While remaining active in the affairs of Fels & Co., he also became one of Philadelphia's most prominent philanthropists. He took an active interest in, and gave generous support to civic, scientific, cultural, and educational causes. In 1936 Fels established the Samuel S. Fels Fund to continue financial support in these areas.

The correspondence series, 1889–1957, is comprised primarily of Fels' personal letters and business correspondence. The letters reflect Fels' philanthropic services as well as his interests in civic affairs and government reform. Financial concerns as well as Fels' interest in the medical field, in scientific research, and in music and musicians are also documented in this series. There is also a section in this series for the Samuel S. Fels Fund.

There is Fels & Co. Executive Committee and Board of Directors correspondence, 1952–1965; Board of Directors minutes, 1914–1965; and annual reports 1951–1964.

The publication series contains notes, drafts, correspondence, and comments concerning Fels' book *This Changing World* (Boston, 1933), his pamphlet, "A Layman's Program for Peace" (reprint from the New York Times Magazine, 1943), and some miscellaneous writings, mostly about education, and war, and plans for peace.

Financial records, 1904–1954, consist of Fels' personal tax returns and related papers; his personal and business bank books; bills and receipts; miscellaneous stock and insurance certificates; and estate papers.

A small group of legal papers, 1916–1952, contain miscellaneous deeds, agreements, and estate papers.

The biography series, 1950–1973, includes groups of letters on the death of Fels, as well as correspondence and some working papers concerning publication of a Fels biography written by Dale Phalen in 1969.

The miscellaneous series contains clippings, photographs, blueprints, printed material, records, and scrapbooks concerning various projects and interests of Fels.

Gift of Samuel S. Fels Fund, 1971.

Finding aid available.

1777
No entry.

1778
Haines, John S.   Records, 1849–1890.   (1,400 items.)

John S. Haines was the botanist of Wyck, Germantown.

Financial records including bills, receipts, and account books of personal and household expenses and account books, 1853–1886, of his farm receipts and expenditures.

Gift of Mrs. Samuel Emlen, 1957.

1779
Mulford family.   Papers, 1757–1867.   (150 items.)

Deeds, agreements, leases, and other legal papers on land of the Mulford family in Cumberland County, N.J. Several accounts and miscellaneous receipts, 1862–1865.

1781
West Philadelphia Maennerchor.   Records, 1890–1906.   (13 v.)

Records of West Philadelphia Maennerchor, German singing society, include: minute book, 1890–1906, and manuscript song books Tenor I, Tenor II, Bass I, and Bass II.

Song-books in German.

1782
Wallgren, Abian A.   Collection, 1917–1947.

Wallgren drew cartoons for *The Stars and Stripes,* the official newspaper of the American troops in France during World War I, for the American Legion magazine, and for several syndicated comic strips.

The bulk of the collection is made up of scrapbooks of cartoons and comic strips. There are also clippings about his activities, and letters to him from prominent persons including Walt Disney, Herbert Hoover, and John J. Pershing.

Gift of Mrs. Abian A. Wallgren, 1958.

1783
Ludwick Institute (Philadelphia, Pa.)   Records, 1801–1950.
(300 items and 6 v.)

The Ludwick Institute, organized in 1799 as the Philadelphia Society for the Free Instruction of Indigent Boys, chartered in 1801 as the Philadelphia Society for the Establishment and Support of Charity Schools, was the first free educational plan in Philadelphia. Girls were admitted in 1811. In 1872 its name was changed to Ludwick Institute after its chief benefactor Christopher Ludwick. With the establishment of the tax-supported Public School system, the Ludwick Institute stopped holding classes around 1890, but continued to sponsor a course of free lectures at the Academy of Natural Sciences.

The records include: enrollment books, 1801–1858; minutes and extracts of minutes of the board of managers and of the contributors, 1832–1951; minutes of the Committee on Instruction and Lectures, 1904–1940; miscellaneous correspondence, 1899–1950; miscellaneous financial records including check stubs, 1859–1898, 1912–1916, and treasurers' reports, 1886–1918; and two typescript biographies of Christopher Ludwick, one by Edward W. Hocker and one anonymous.

Gift of the Ludwick Institute through John M. Fogg, 1958.

Finding aid available.

1784
Union Benevolent Association (Philadelphia, Pa.)
Records, 1831–1967.   (12 linear ft.)

The Union Benevolent Association was a private relief agency founded in Philadelphia in 1831 by a group of philanthropists opposed to the existing almshouse system of relief.

The association's records contain material on many periods of economic depression, including the Great Depression, 1929–1939. They also reveal the gradual evolution of theories and practice of social welfare.

The records include: minutes, 1831–1967; minutes of the Ladies Branch, 1832–1845; reports, 1937–1941; miscellaneous items; and incoming with some outgoing correspondence, 1908, 1921–1950. Among the correspondents are the Welfare Federation of Philadelphia, Pennsylvania Department of Welfare, Social Security Board, and the American Red Cross. The financial accounts include: cash journals, 1876–1892, 1894–1920, 1933–1949; receipt book, 1876–1891; ledger, 1933–1940; budgets, 1923–1935; and miscellaneous accounts, including records of legacies and trusts.

There are also some records of Southwark Soup Society, Philadelphia, organized in 1805: constitution and by-laws; minutes, 1855–1949; ledger, 1887–1949; and a few miscellaneous papers.

Gift of the Union Benevolent Association, 1958 and 1970.

1785
Roussel, Euguene. **Papers, 1835–1888.** **(8 v.)**

Eugene Roussel, Philadelphia manufacturer of mineral water, ledger, 1850–1876, weather journals, 1855, 1857, *Notes et regettes de Liquers de Tables;* Peter Perlet, Philadelphia watchmaker, ledgers, 1861–1867, 1875–1881; unidentified travel notes in North America and Europe, 1872–1873; unidentified medical lectures and case notes, 1883–1888.

Gift of M.D. Weihrnmeyer and members of the Roussel family, 1958.

1786
McCall family. **Papers, 1764–1891.** **(750 items.)**

Correspondence, 1798–1889, and other records of the McCall family of Philadelphia, include: business letters, 1798–1839, to Archibald McCall, a general merchant, many from his brother Samuel McCall, on trade, especially with South America; some of their accounts and inventories, 1802–1817, including ledger, 1810–1817, bills payable/receivable, 1804–1813, and insurance book, 1809–1817. Also included are: letters, 1825–1862, of Archibald McCall's son, Major-General George Archibald McCall, original commander of the Pennsylvania Reserve Corps, to his sisters, mostly about his European travels; and his almost daily correspondence, 1852, 1861–1862, with his wife Elizabeth McCurtie McCall, which reflect his service in various Indian wars, the Mexican-American War, and the Civil War; and her letters, 1861–1863, to him. There is an unidentified commonplace book, ca. 1787, some miscellaneous papers, 1764–1758, and clippings, 1864–1891, mostly about Major-General George A. McCall.

Gift of Frances M. Bradford, 1958.

1787
Plumsted family. **Papers, 1726–1890.** **(250 items.)**

The miscellaneous papers of the Plumsted family include personal and business correspondence, financial records, land papers for family property in Pennsylvania and Virginia. The major portion of the papers relate to William Plumsted, Pennsylvania merchant. There are a few items of Clement Plumsted and his son William, both of whom served as mayors of colonial Philadelphia, and cookbook, 1776, of Mary McCall (Mrs. William) Plumsted. There is some correspondence, 1825–1838, of William Plumsted, U.S. Navy Surgeon, to his sister Clementina Ross Plumsted. Also copies of the by-laws, muster rolls, and papers, 1774–1815, extracted from the archives of the 1st Troop Philadelphia Cavalry.

Gift of Frances Bradford, 1958.

Cookbook, 1776, of Mary Plumsted reported to NUCMC as cashbook.

1788
Hay, Malcom, 1842–1885.   **Papers, 1815 (1854–1885).**
(250 items.)

Malcom Hay of Pittsburgh was a lawyer and prominent figure in the Democratic Party.

Incoming personal and political correspondence, 1854–1885, including a few letters, 1885, while he was assistant postmaster general; newspaper clippings and a few printed documents, 1872–1873, on the Pennsylvania Constitutional Convention.

Gift of Roger Butterfield, 1958.

1789
Lovering family.   **Papers, (1817–1868) 1903.**   **(150 items.)**

There is some material on three generations, but best represented are Mary (Shallcross) Lovering and her son Joseph S. Lovering, a sugar refiner in Philadelphia. Included are typescripts and some originals of family correspondence, 1817–1903; letter press book, 1839–1863, of Joseph Lovering; accountbook, 1860–1868, for Hope Farm, the Lovering home near Wilmington, Del.; and receipt book, 1824–1849, of Mary and Sarah Lovering.

Gift of Henry R. Pemberton, 1958.

1790
Edward A. Green and Company.   **Correspondence, 1878–1893.**
(68 v.)

The Philadelphia firm of Edward A. Greene & Co., commission wool merchants, with a branch office in Boston, opened in 1881. Members of the firm included Eugene van Loan, joined 1882, William Coffin, joined in 1883, and Francis Hathaway and John Dickey, joined in 1892. The firm apparently dissolved in 1893 with Greene's death. The firm had extensive trading contacts with growers in the South and West as well as with mills in New Jersey, Pennsylvania, and New England.

Incoming correspondence, 1878–1893, and a letterpress book, 1878.
Purchased, 1952.

1791
Philadelphia Board of Trade.   **Records, 1801–1942.**
(21 linear ft.)

The Philadelphia Board of Trade was the precursor of the Philadelphia Chamber of Commerce. A group of Philadelphia merchants organized the Board of Trade in 1833 because of the restrictive nature of the old Chamber of Commerce which had been founded in 1801, primarily to foster the shipping interests of the city. The Board of Trade united with the old Chamber of Commerce in 1845, and it came to represent most of the commercial and industrial interests of the city. In 1891, a new Chamber of Commerce was organized and there was no unified commercial organization in the city until 1942, when the Board of Trade combined with the Chamber of Commerce.

The records of the Board of Trade are organized chronologically by month. The records for each month are arranged by subject in the order they were presented at the monthly meetings. Included are incoming and some outgoing correspondence, reports, and miscellaneous items, 1889, 1891, 1897–1900, 1904–1916, 1919, 1921–1925, 1930–1933, 1939–1942. Many of the records, including reports, are recorded in the Minutes, 1833–1940. There are also annual reports, 1904–1922, 1929–1941; correspondence and reports, 1880–1909, on deepening the harbor, Port of Philadelphia. There are three volumes of records of the old Philadelphia Chamber of Commerce: an Award Book, 1801–1808, which contains the proceedings of the Committee of the Chamber of Commerce that acted as arbiter in commercial disputes; a letterbook, 1801–1826, of which many of the letters were written by Thomas Fitzsimons, president of the Chamber of Commerce, 1801–1811, Philadelphia merchant, political figure, and signer of the Constitution; and minute book, 1837–1846.

Also included in the collection are minutes, 1868–1900, of the Executive Council of the National Board of Trade; Port of Philadelphia statistics, 1924–1934; Minutes and miscellaneous records of the Pennsylvania Tax Conference, 1892–1994, a conference of various economic interests to consider a revision of the assessing and taxing laws of the state; Minutes and a few miscellaneous items, 1895–1898, of the Sound Money League of Pennsylvania, an organization formed to maintain the gold standard; and letter press correspondence, 1863-1879, of Henry Preaut, merchant and Russian Vice Consul in Philadelphia.

Gift of Free Library of Philadelphia, 1958 & 1960.

1792
Biddle, Thomas, 1776–1857.   Family papers, 1769–1954.
(3 linear ft.)

Thomas Biddle married Christine Williams, the daughter of Jonathan and Marianne Alexander Williams. Christine Williams Biddle's brother, Henry Jonathan Williams married Julia Rush, the daughter of Benjamin and Julia Stockton Rush.

The manuscripts consist of correspondence and other papers of Thomas and Christine Biddle and their descendants, as well as aunts Berthia, Christine and Jane Alexander and Isabelle Alexander Hankey, all of whom report on politics and family affairs in Scotland, England, and France. Another major correspondent is Apolline Agatha Alexander, a member of the Kentucky branch of the family who was orphaned and subsequently raised by Mrs. Biddle, with letters from London following her marriage to Thomson Hankey, Jr.

The individual units of the collection were once likely a single body of family papers which were divided among various relatives. Although emphasis may differ with each entry, material found in one may also be found to some degree in others.

1792A
Biddle, Thomas, 1776–1857.　　Family papers, 1769–1898.
(450 items.)

Thomas Biddle incoming letters, 1806–1871, consists primarily of letters from his father-in-law, Jonathan Williams, on his finances and from Isaac Abrahams (Peru, Ill.), Henry Lardner (Niles, Mich.), Charles Loeser (Pottsville), Volney L. Maxwell (Wilkesbarre), and other agents for Biddle's land transactions.

Small groups of other family papers include: George Washington Biddle letters and documents, 1804–1809, on Stephen Girard's suit against Biddle over a tea shipment from Canton; Anne and Alexander W. Biddle incoming family and social notes, 1893–1898.

Gift of Clement Biddle estate.

1792B
Biddle, Thomas, 1776–1857.　　Family papers, 1768–1899.
(600 items.)

Thomas Biddle's incoming letters, 1807–1844, is concerned primarily with his brokerage business. There are also letters of Christine Williams to Biddle before their marriage. Christine Williams Biddle's incoming correspondence, 1807–1848, includes letters from her "daughter" Apolline Alexander Hankey, her Scottish aunts, and her son Henry J. Biddle. Other miscellaneous Biddle family materials include Alexander Biddle's stockbook/ledger, 1884–1899.

Henry J. Williams' incoming correspondence, 1812–1871, includes miscellaneous financial and personal letters, and letters from the Alexander sisters. There are also letters from Mariamne to Jonathan Williams, 1785–1789, while the latter was in the United States, discussing Jonathan Williams' financial affairs and reporting her own activities.

There is also a small group of personal and political correspondence, 1768–1809, of Benjamin Rush, and a Rush family genealogy.

Gift of Alexander Biddle, 1952.

1792C

Biddle, Thomas, 1776–1857. **Family papers, 1828–1917.** **(900 items.)**

These are the papers of three generations of proprietors of Lanoraie, a farm established by Henry J. Williams in Springfield Township, Montgomery County. The major portion of this section contains correspondence and accounts of Louis Alexander Biddle and Lynford Biddle, grandsons of Thomas and lawyers, concerning horse and dog breeding at Lanoraie, shooting, European travel, cricket and social club activities, and stocks.

There is a small group of legal papers, 1828–1877, of Williams dealing with family estates and including his personal receipted bills.

Another small group contains family and social notes of Alexander and Julia Williams Rush Biddle, 1874–1896.

There is also some Yarrow & Van Pelt correspondence, 1916–1937, on Philadelphia real estate brokerage.

Purchased, 1958.

1792D

Biddle Thomas, 1776–1857. **Family papers, 1773–1862.** **(3 linear ft.)**

The letters and miscellaneous papers of Alexander, Biddle, Rush, and Williams families in this section relate mostly to family and personal affairs, with some business papers included. Of particular significance are the letters from the Scottish branch of the Alexanders reporting from Scotland, England, and France on politics, society, and family affairs.

The Jonathan Williams, Jr., correspondence, 1773–1815, includes family letters.

Mariamne Alexander Williams' correspondence, 1778–1816, includes letters from her sisters Bethia, Christine, and Jane Alexander and Isabelle Alexander Hankey, as well as from Henry Jonathan Williams, Margaret M. Craig, and Jonathan Williams, Jr.

The Thomas Biddle papers, 1800–1846, consist primarily of business letters and related documents involving his brokerage firm. There are also some family letters from various Alexanders abroad and in Kentucky, his son Henry Jonathan Biddle, his brother John G. Biddle, and his wife Christine Williams Biddle.

Christine Biddle's correspondence, 1794–1856 includes letters from the four Alexander aunts, Margaret Green, her "daughter" Apolline Agatha Alexander Hankey, and her "granddaughter" Apolline Alexander Blair of the Kentucky branch of the Alexanders, her five sons, particularly Henry Jonathan Biddle, as well as Thomas Biddle and Thomas Hankey, Jr.

The Henry Jonathan Williams correspondence, 1812–1862, includes letters from his four Alexander aunts, Thomas Hankey, Jr., on remittances, his parents, and from various others on legal, personal, and military matters. There is also a scrapbook of "Family Memorials," begun by Williams and continued after his death, which includes genealogical and biographical materials on the Alexander, Biddle, Rush, and Williams families.

Julia Rush Williams correspondence, 1823–1866, includes letters to her mother, Julia Stockton Rush, and letters from various relatives.

Other family members are represented by small groups of miscellaneous papers: Clement Biddle, 1776, 1813, mostly as deputy quarter master for the Pennsylvania and New Jersey militia; Benjamin Rush, 1768–1810, with letters from Alexander Leslie (Lord Balgonie) and others; and Julia Stockton Rush, 1813–1840, on social and family matters.

Gift of Mrs. John Penn Brock, 1959.

1792E
Biddle, Thomas, 1776–1857.   **Family papers, 1790–1916.**
(400 items.)

Henry J. Williams' legal papers and receipted bills, 1827–1877; Alexander and Julia Williams Rush Biddle's family and social correspondence, 1860–1896; Louis and Lynford Biddle's incoming correspondence on Lanoraie operations, cricket and club activities, 1890–1916.

Gift of Samuel Moyerman, 1960.

1792F
Biddle, Thomas, 1776–1857.   **Family papers, 1778–1954.**
(375 items.)

Of particular interest in this section are the diaries: Julia Williams Rush, 1852; Horace Brock, 1877–1878; Anne McKennan Biddle, 1885, concerning a European trip; Alexander Biddle, 1889, 1897 of European trips; Pauline Biddle, 1892–1894, 1924, covering the years before and after her marriage to John Penn Brock in 1905, including two European tours; and Christine Biddle, 1917–1918, describing her activities with the American Red Cross at Toul, France.

Also included are some Jonathan Williams family papers, 1779–1828; Alexander Biddle's letters to his wife written while he toured Europe, 1878, and other family correspondence.

Gift of Pauline Biddle Brock, 1968.

1792G
Biddle, Thomas, 1776–1857.   Family papers, 1779–1957.
(100 items.)

Letters, wills, and other miscellaneous papers of the Alexander, Bent, Biddle, Brock, Coleman, and Williams families. Among the correspondents are Christine Alexander, 1833–1838, and Jonathan Williams, 1779–1815.
Gift of Horace Brock, 1972.
Finding aid available.

1792H
Biddle, Thomas, 1776–1857.   Family papers, 1776–1876.
(176 items.)

This miscellaneous group of letters is written mainly by members of the Biddle and Rush families. The largest group of letters in this section are those of Richard Rush, 1812–1857, covering his career as Comptroller of the Treasury, acting Secretary of State, Minister to Great Britain, Secretary of the Treasury, Minister to France, and private citizen. Some of the Rush letters deal with domestic politics and foreign policy, but the greater part is either routine official business or personal in nature.
Clement Biddle's letters, 1781–1813, relate mostly to business affairs. There are also two smaller groups: Nicholas Biddle's papers, 1824–1842, concern banking and the Second Bank of the United States; and Episcopal Bishop of Alabama Richard H. Wilmer's letters, 1812–1857, discuss church matters.

1793
Lee, Franklin.   Papers, 1807–1861.   (400 items.)

Franklin Lee was a masonry contractor of the Northern Liberties.
Ledger, 1813–1852, contracts, receipts, and miscellaneous financial records of Franklin Lee & Son, bricklayers and corders; papers and financial records on various estates of which Lee was executor or trustee.
Purchased, Gratz Fund, 1959.

1794A
Townsend family.   Collection, 1761–1858.   (262 items.)

Washington Townsend of West Chester, served as a United States congressman from 1869 to 1877.
These papers include letters: 1812–1832 on military and political matters to Isaac Dutton Barnard, a Chester County lawyer who served as an officer during the War of 1812, held several elective local and state offices, including senator (Federalist), 1827–1831; 1826–1858 to Anthony Bolmar on the West

Chester boys schools he operated; 1761–1858 to the Townsend family of West Chester, principally to Washington Townsend; 1838–1854 to General Persifer F. Smith, mainly on the Mexican War; 1852 to and from Henry S. Evans regarding legal efforts of the Pennsylvania legislature to free Rachel Parker from slavery; and a few letters addressed to others.

Gift of Mrs. Frederick J. LeMaistre, 1959.

1794B
Townsend family.   Collection, 1784–1893.   (700 items.)

David Townsend was cashier of the Bank of Chester County from 1817 to 1849 and was involved in civic affairs. His son, William, was also associated with the Bank of Chester County, was a lawyer, and served as U.S. congressman, 1868–1876.

David Townsend's incoming letters, 1812–1854, from William Dillingham, solicitor for the Bank of Chester County, and from others concerns the recharter of the bank and some political issues. Townsend's incoming letters, 1833–1893, concerns mostly family matters.

Isaac Dutton Barnard incoming correspondence, 1820–1832, is mostly from his father-in-law Isaac Darlington. Barnard, a lawyer and officer in the War of 1812, became a U.S. senator and served in various Chester County political and business offices. Darlington was serving as president judge of the Chester and Delaware Counties judicial district, and the letters report on Court cases, politics, and appointments.

1795
Chapman, Herman H.   *Biography of Herman Haupt*, 1817–1905.
(1 v.)

Herman Haupt, civil engineer, author, and inventor, was born in Philadelphia in 1817 and was graduated from West Point in 1835. Soon thereafter he resigned his commission to become a railroad surveyor. Later Haupt became an authority on bridge construction and served as chief engineer or superintendent of several large railroads including the Pennsylvania Railroad, the Northern Pacific Railroad, and the Hoosac Tunnel in Massachusetts. He was chief of United States military railroads in Virginia, 1862–1863.

The biography treats the Civil War experiences in detail, quoting extensively from the war *Reminiscences of General Herman Haupt,* published privately in 1901. Also included is a typescript, written in 1859, of the *Memoirs of Herman Haupt* up to the age of 21.

Gift of Martin H. Verner, 1959.

1796
Norris family.   Papers, 1822–1917.   (50 items.)

Miscellaneous papers, letters, and documents of members of the Norris family, including William Norris and Septimus Norris.
Finding aid available.
Gift of H. Norris Harrison, 1959.

1797
Minford, William Alexander McAllister, b. 1881.
Papers, 1884–1946.   (300 items.)

William Alexander McAllister Minford, born in Ireland, immigrated to the United States from Buenos Aires, Argentina, was employed as an accountant, and eventually settled in Philadelphia.
Correspondence, memoranda, and financial papers relate to Curwin's Accountancy Corporation, North Bend, Ind., where Minford was manager of the Services Department, and to a piece of property in Wilkes Barre, owned by his cousin Sarah Patterson. Some of the material concerns financial hardships brought on by the Depression. There are several unidentified photographs.
Gift of Edward Pinkowski, 1959.

1798
Hart, Francis F.   Collection, 1681–1925.   (70 items.)

A small collection of letters and documents gathered by Francis Fisher Hart primarily from the Fisher and Harrison families. Most individuals are represented by a single item; included in the collection are: Robert Barclay, Nicholas Biddle, Joseph Bonaparte, George Fox, Sir Philip Frances, Joseph Hopkinson, James Logan, Thomas Sully, William White, and others.
Gift of Dr. Francis F. Hart, 1959.

1799
Wheeler, Mabel Brice.   Collection, 1914–1945.   (800 items.)

Mabel Brice, before her marriage to Walter Wheeler, was an officer of the Belgian Relief Committee of the Emergency Aid of Pennsylvania, a volunteer agency for the relief of victims of World War I.
Contained in the collection are incoming letters addressed to Miss Brice, as well as flyers, pamphlets, and photographs dealing with the work of the Belgian Relief Committee. Also included are anonymous notes and reminiscences on a wide variety of topics: Spanish colonies, volunteer fire

departments of Philadelphia, packet ships serving Philadelphia, coal lands, and the settlement of Pennsylvania.

Gift of Mrs. Walter Wheeler, 1959.

1800
Infants' Clothing Association.   Records, 1813–1963.   (200 items.)

The Infants' Clothing Association of Philadelphia, a charitable organization of 18–20 women, was founded in 1814 by members of the Society of Friends. Originally called "The Utilian," it became known as "The Antediluvian" after 1900. In the early days the members collected and remade used clothes for direct distribution; after 1920 they began to contribute clothes and money to organized charities, especially to the Visiting Nurse Society of Philadelphia.

The records include minutes, 1836–1963; annual reports, 1901–1941; account books, 1814–1942; miscellaneous financial records; membership lists; histories of the association, 1910 and 1957; and a few miscellaneous letters.

Gift of the Infants' Clothing Association, 1964.

1801
Magee family.   Papers, 1833–1910.   (250 items.)

In 1824, James Magee and George Taber purchased the southern branch of the saddlery firm of Peter Dickson and Company and thereafter, until Magee's retirement in 1847, maintained a profitable trade through the port of New Orleans. James Magee, after retiring from Magee, Tabor, and Company, became an incorporator and director of the Pennsylvania Railroad.

Through most of his life, Horace Magee's principal energies were devoted to the organization and management of coal, iron, and urban transportation systems. Magee was also the founder of Jeanette, a company town near Pittsburgh.

The Magee papers include correspondence, bills and receipts, invoices of James Magee and his son Horace, both Philadelphia businessmen. Most of the James Magee papers, 1833–1886, relate to his first enterprise, although there is some correspondence with Thomas A. Scott pertaining to their purchase of the Rock Furnace Company of western Pennsylvania. Correspondents include Henry Horn, Henry Muhlenberg, and Scott.

Horace Magee's papers consist mostly of business correspondence, and reflect his interests in numerous ventures. Among those represented here are the Buffalo Railroad Company, Rochester Street Railway Company, Citizens Street Railroad Company, of Indianapolis, Chambers and Magee Glass Company, and the Bethlehem Steel Company. There are several letters from Bishop Courtland Whitehead concerning the erection of a new church building in Jeanette. Approximately thirty letters from the Bowley's Quarter Ducking Club reflect Magee's sporting interests. Correspondents include: H.M. Watson, H.H. Littel, Nathaniel E. Janney, and H. Sellers McKee.

1802
Parker family.   Papers, 1787–1904.   (6 linear ft.)

The papers of the Parker and related families of Philadelphia include miscellaneous correspondence, and financial and estate records. Most of the correspondence is on routine family matters and local gossip, some is on politics, current events, and family conflicts over courtship and marriage. The collection includes: wastebook, 1798–1799, 1804–1806 of Christopher Marshall, Jr.; miscellaneous papers, 1807–1832, of Zaccheus Collins, merchant, mostly records on the estate of Marshall, Collins' father-in-law; receipt book, 1787–1835, of George Aston including financial memoranda and estate papers (Z. Collins and D. Parker, successive executors); papers, 1816–1846, of Daniel Parker most of which is correspondence, with Zaccheus Collins, Anne Collins Parker, and others on the secret marriage of Anne and Daniel, child raising, the 1824 election, and the Zaccheus Collins estate; letters, 1841–1848 to Charles Collins Parker from his father Daniel, classmates, and "guardians" Edward and Eliza Bull giving advice, reporting on friends and current events.

Also included are letters, ca. 1838, from Caroline Willing to Dr. Edward Peace protesting his forbidden courtship; notes, ca. 1840, to Anna Coleman (who would marry first C.C. Parker and second Dr. Peace), mostly from Ellen S. Rand urging Anna to turn from her wicked ways; financial memoranda, 1845–1857, account, books and letterpress book, 1845–1857, of Edward Peace on his estate, 1879–1887, James Rawle and John W. Watts executors; personal letters, 1830, to Joseph Peace, and ledger, 1843–1848, of Washington Peace; diary, 1869–1870, of Rawle & Company Shingle Mill; letterpress book, 1885–1887, of James Rawle on legal and personal business; and miscellaneous Rawle family papers on real estate interests.

Gift of James Rawle, 1960.

1803
Zeller, Edwin Adrian, Jr.   Papers, 1886–1946.   (600 items.)

Edwin Adrian Zeller, of Germantown, managed the Franklin Sugar Refining Company of Philadelphia.

There are business papers as well as reports and circular letters from the City Party and the City Club which reflect Zeller's involvement with local reform politics. There is also some correspondence from the Presbyterian Sunday School Superintendents Association, of which Zeller was a member.

Purchased, 1959.

1804
Faires family.   Papers, 1811 (1837–1918).   (100 items.)

Miscellaneous papers, 1891–1918, on the education of James D. Faires, a civil engineer of Philadelphia. Also includes a few personal letters, 1837–1897, to various members of the Faires family; and other miscellaneous items.

Gift of James D. Faires, 1960.

1805
No entry.

1806
Harvey, Samuel.   Papers, 1771–1848.   (400 items.)

The business papers, 1797–1848, of Samuel Harvey, importer, hardware merchant, and banker of Philadelphia, includes: incoming business correspondence, 1798–1830; miscellaneous business records, 1797–1848; and receipt books, 1797–1824. The bulk of the correspondence and a few of the records are on Harvey's management of the business affairs of Elizabeth (Freeman) Kershaw, heir to the estate of Mark Freeman, Philadelphia merchant. A few miscellaneous items, 1771–1786, relate solely to the Freeman estate.

Purchased, 1959.

1807
Lossing, Benson John.   Papers, 1712–1892.   (150 items.)

Miscellaneous collection, 1712–1851, of Pennsylvania land, legal, and military documents and letters, 1852–1892, to Benson John Lossing on his *Pictorial Field Book of the Revolution,* (1850–1852) and *Pictorial Field Book of the War of* 1812, (1868), and other historical writings, as well as personal correspondence.

Purchased, 1959.

1808
United States. Army. Pennsylvania Infantry Regiment, 29th (1861–1865).   Papers, 1861–1912.   (250 items.)

Miscellaneous papers, 1861–1912, of the 29th Regiment, Pennsylvania Volunteers, popularly called the Jackson Infantry, include: minutes and notes on the organization of the regiment in Philadelphia, 1861; minutes, 1888–1900, of the Survivors Association; and the manuscript of David Mouat's reminiscences entitled *Three Years in the Twenty-Ninth Pennsylvania Volunteers,* 1861–1864. Mouat, a private in Company G, gave accounts of the organization of the regiment, his capture in 1862, and his participation in several battles, including Front Royal, Va.; Chancellorsville; Gettysburg; Lookout Mountain, Tenn.; and Resaca, Ga.

Purchased, 1960.

1809
Heckman, Charles Adam, 1822–1896.   Papers, 1861–1863.   (5 v.)

Record books of Union troops commanded by Charles Adam Heckman in eastern North Carolina during the Civil War, including the 1st Brigade, Naglee's Division, and the 3rd Brigade, Eighteenth Army Corps: letterbook, 1863, of correspondence written and received; General Orders, 1863; Special Orders, 1862–1863; and a descriptive roll, 1861, of the members of Company D, 1st Regiment, Pennsylvania Volunteers.

Gift of the Free Library of Philadelphia, 1960.

1810
Knowles, Gustavus W.   Records, 1875–1895.   (9 v.)

Records of Gustavus W. Knowles, Philadelphia merchant dealing in railroad ties and cotton and wool waste products and trading as Hagy & Knowles, 1875–1877, and his own name 1877–1895.

Includes: letterpress book, 1891–1895, on railroad ties; receipt books, 1875–1893; cashbooks, 1875–1893; daybooks, 1876–1893; journal, 1875–1892; ledger, 1877–1888; of storm damages to the barge "L.B. Mayhew" and its cargo of railroad ties.

Gift of Robert C. Alexander, 1959.

1811
Bining, Arthur C., b. 1893.   Collection, 1787–1908, 1957.
(850 items.)

Letters and miscellaneous items collected by Arthur C. Bining, Philadelphia historian. About one-third of the collection consists of letters, 1804–1844, which originally formed part of the correspondence of the United States Customs House of Philadelphia, on routine customs matters and addressed to the collector of Philadelphia. Major Customs House correspondents are: Joseph Anderson, William H. Crawford, Alexander James Dallas, George Mifflin Dallas, Henry D. Gilpin, Charles J. Ingersoll, Jared

Ingersoll, Joseph R. Ingersoll, William Morris Meredith, John Meredith Read, Jonathan Roberts, Richard Rush, and Henry Miller Watts.

About one-fourth of the collection consists of papers, 1787–1812, in French, of Joseph R.E. Bunel, paymaster general of the French colony of Santo Domingo, Haiti, and Marie F.M. Bunel, businesswoman in Santo Domingo. In 1804, following the successful Haitian revolution, the Bunels moved to Philadelphia. Included are their incoming personal and business correspondence and a few miscellaneous financial records.

The remainder of the collection contains letters of: James Barker, 1814–1815, army officer and agent for fortification, Philadelphia; William Shaler, 1807–1832, United States consul-general to Algiers and Cuba, and commissioner in the negotiation of the United States-Algiers treaty of 1815; Henry Stanton, 1843–1848, army officer; Abbot H. Thayer, 1876–1897, painter and naturalist; Edward Thursby, 1803–1819, merchant of Philadelphia; and James Trimble, 1809–1835, Pennsylvania political figure. There are also a few miscellaneous papers, 1853–1896, of August F.W. Partz, a German immigrant and inventor; papers, 1877–1878, on efforts by producers and carriers of anthracite coal in Pennsylvania to limit production and control prices; miscellaneous letters, business papers, deeds, military discharge papers of various persons and firms.

1812
**Ingersoll, Charles Jared, 1782–1862.   Papers, 1803–1862.
(675 items.)**

There are letters to Ingersoll from many public men of the period, 1812–1847, on a wide range of national and foreign policy topics. Of these, some 300 are from Richard Rush, a close friend of Ingersoll. Almost one-half of the Rush letters were written while he was comptroller of the United States Treasury, 1812–1814, and relate especially to the War of 1812. The remainder were written while Rush was minister to Great Britain, 1817–1825, secretary of the Treasury, 1825–1829, private citizen, 1829–1847, minister to France, 1848, and discuss domestic and international affairs, especially Anglo-American relations. Ingersoll correspondence also contains: letters, 1814–1837 from John Forsyth, a member of Congress, minister to Spain, governor of Georgia, and secretary of state; letters, 1846–1848, from British author Sarah Mytton Maury on personal and political matters in the United States and England; and letters, 1814–1830, by James Monroe, principally on financial loans to Monroe.

Several public figures are represented by letters: John Quincy Adams, 1821, 1831–1832; John Binns, 1813, publisher of the *Democratic Press,* on the War of 1812 and the publication of political matters in newspapers; James

Buchanan, 1838, 1839, 1843; James Burn, army officer, 1813, on military and naval action against the British forces; John C. Calhoun, 1816–1845; Thomas Abthorpe Cooper, actor, 1828–1833, on financial matters; William H. Crawford, while secretary of the Treasury and private citizen, 1816–1831, on politics, American Indians, revenue, tariff, manufacturing, and banks; Peter Stephen Du Ponceau, 1813–1814, authority on international law and practice, on legal questions; Bolling Hall, congressman from Georgia, 1815–1830, on political matters; Edward Livingston, principally while he was secretary of state, 1831–1833; James Kirke Paulding, naval officer and secretary of the Navy, 1832–1841, on personal and naval matters; Joel R. Poinsett, Representative from South Carolina, Minister to Mexico, and secretary of war, 1818–1840; and J.M.P. Serurier, French minister to the United States, 1815–1834, on a wide range of personal and political topics. Other public figures, including five presidents, are represented.

There are letters, 1803–1846, of Ingersoll on politics, diplomacy, and economic and legal matters; Ingersoll's diary, February 1823; and manuscript notes by Ingersoll for projected work on *Slavery, The Origins of the War with Mexico,* 1846–1848, and a *History of the Territories of the United States.*

Also included are letters, 1814–1842, 1855, from Ingersoll's brother, Joseph Reed Ingersoll, Philadelphia lawyer and congressman, mostly to Henry Dillworth Gilpin, United States attorney general, on legal and political matters.

Letters from J.M.P. Serurier written in French.

Gift of R. Sturgis Ingersoll, 1959, 1961, 1966.

1813

Civic Club of Philadelphia.   Records, 1893–1957.   (51 v.)

The Civic Club of Philadelphia, organized in 1894, consisted of prominent Philadelphia women who sought to promote "by education and active cooperation a higher public spirit and better public order." Initially the club was organized into four departments, Municipal Government, Education, Social Service, and Art, each of which operated somewhat autonomously and created its own committees or task forces. The Education Department had committees on public schools, free libraries, and free kindergartens and the Municipal Government Department included committees on sanitation, civil service reform, and police patrons. Despite its interest in social and political reform, the club refused on several occasions to take part as "disfranchised citizens" in meetings of the Anti-Spoils League and the National Civil Service Reform Convention. By the 1920's, after the passage on the suffrage amendment, the club structure changed, the Departments were abandoned, and the committees reduced in number and given new, more limited charges. In 1959, the membership voted the Club out of existence and transferred its assets to other civic organizations.

Included in the records are: director's minutes, 1899–1959; minutes of the general meetings, 1893–1948, 1959, primarily recording addresses to the membership; and minutes of the Art Department, 1894–1903, reflecting interest in free art exhibitions at Philadelphia museums, summer and community concerts, as well as parks and playgrounds. There are also published annual reports, 1894–1935, including the constitution, by-laws, lists of officers and members, and financial summaries. Published bulletins and calendars, 1907–1959, give summaries, often monthly, of club activities. Also included are pamphlets and publications, 1894–1948; clippings, 1894–1903; a fiftieth anniversary volume, including lists of officers, 1944; and a volume containing four memorial addresses for distinguished members: Alice Lippincott, Anna Hallowell, Mary Channing Wister (Mrs. Owen Wister), and Sarah Yorke Stevenson (Mrs. Cornelius Stevenson).

Gift of the Civic Club, 1959; purchased, 1972.

1814
Pennsylvania Academy of the Fine Arts. Minutes, 1817–1831. (2 v.)

Fragmentary minutes of the Academy, primarily in the hand of Francis Hopkinson.

Gift of Charles R. Hildburn, 1877.

Formerly part of 745.

Appear to be partial transcriptions of originals still in the possession of the Pennsylvania Academy of the Fine Arts.

1815
Smith, Mary Bainerd. Diaries, 1894–1957. (64 v.)

Philadelphia diaries of Mary Bainerd Smith on the domestic concerns of the Smith family and their friends. There is little commentary or mention of public affairs.

Gift of Edith Smith Gaskill, 1960.

1816
Philadelphia Gazette Publishing Company. Records, 1891–1954. (1,050 items and 369 v.)

This Philadelphia publishing firm was known first as The German Daily Gazette Publishing Company, 1891–1918, and then as The Philadelphia Gazette Publishing Company, 1918–1954. The firm published the principle

German language newspapers of Philadelphia: *Philadelphia Gazette-Demokrat; Philadelphia Sonntags-Gazette; Philadelphia Tageblatt,* 1933–1944; and the *Philadelphia Sonntagsblatt;* also, it did a large scale printing business, including the printing for publishers of other Philadelphia area newspapers.

Financial records make up the main body of the collection, and may be divided into general accounts, advertising accounts, branch accounts, carrier's accounts, subscriber's accounts, special accounts, and miscellaneous accounts. Included are journals; ledgers: general ledgers, advertiser's ledgers, branch ledgers, carrier's ledgers, commission ledgers, subscriber's ledgers, miscellaneous ledgers; cashbooks: general cashbooks, advertiser's cashbooks, carrier's cashbooks, subscriber's cashbooks; subscriber's receipt books; indexes to the record books; special accounts: advertising contract records, payroll records, trial balances, voucher registers; and miscellaneous financial accounts.

The collection also contains minutes, 1891, concerning the organization of the company; miscellaneous non-financial records; correspondence, financial records, and miscellany, 1923–1954, of the publishing company, and also, of the Mayer family, proprietors of the company. Members of the Mayer family represented include Gustav Mayer, Theodore Mayer, and Louis Mayer.

Purchased, 1959.

1817
Snyder, Henry F.   Business records, (1816–1861) 1913.
(200 items.)

Receipted bills and incoming business correspondence of Henry F. and John L. Snyder, proprietors of a general store in Somerset. After 1820, when John Snyder continues with the business alone, there is a smattering of papers on his office as treasurer of Somerset and his land interest.

Purchased, 1960.

1818
Cohen, Charles Joseph, b. 1847.   Papers, 1922–1927.
(3 linear ft.)

Mostly incoming correspondence acknowledging receipt of *Rittenhouse Square, Past and Present* by C.J. Cohen, 1922, and replying to Cohen's request for reminiscences and photographs in preparation of *Memoir of Rev. John Wiley Faires,* (1926), with biographical sketches of pupils of the Classical Institute, Philadelphia; typescripts, manuscript notes, correspondence, photographs, clippings, and other memorabilia, all primarily biographical material, intended to be published as "Part II" of *Rittenhouse Square;* two scrapbooks of photographs and typescripts on Chestnut Street; one scrapbook of miscellaneous research, also including typescripts and photographs of people and places.

Gift of Mrs. Albert M. Cohen, 1956, 1958.

1819
No entry.

1820
Penn Athletic Club.   Papers, 1922–1934.   (300 items.)

Correspondence to and from several members of the membership committee of the Penn Athletic Club of Philadelphia, organized in 1922, showing their effort to create a large membership and to maintain that membership during the 1930's. Bills and other financial records of the club's house committee are also present.

Gift of Samuel Moyerman, 1960.

1821
No entry.

1822
Philadelphia. Mayor's Committee for the 1948 Republican Convention. Auxiliary Housing Division.   Records, 1948. (700 items.)

Correspondence of the committee, chaired by Frank C.P. McGlinn, responsible for housing arrangements for the 1948 Republican Presidential Convention in Philadelphia, and other papers of the committee, including rental application forms and assignment notifications.

Gift of the Free Library of Philadelphia.

1823
Quitman, Frederick Henry, d. 1884.   Papers, 1841–1858. (97 items.)

The bulk of the collection consists of letters, 1841–1858, addressed to young F. Henry Quitman, in Natchez, Miss., and a while at college at Princeton from his father, John Anthony Quitman. The elder Quitman served as a brigadier-general of militia during the Mexican War, governor of Mississippi, 1850–1851, and as a member of Congress, 1855–1858. His letters concern Cuban independence, with which he was sympathetic, states rights, secession, and other Southern political issues, as well as family affairs. Also included are several letters of other family members.

Gift of Mrs. Alexander Leon, 1960.

1824
No entry.

1825
Grand Army of the Republic. Department of Pennsylvania. Schuyler Post, No.51.   Records, 1877–1928.   (41 v. and 600 items.)

The Philadelphia post of the Grand Army of the Republic, a fraternal, charitable, and patriotic organization of Union veterans of the Civil War, and its auxiliary organizations was founded in 1874.

The Post records include: constitution and by-laws, with members' register, 1877; minutes, 1874–1919; journals of members' accounts, 1881–1917; dues ledgers, 1903–1912; "black books," 1875–1886; minutes of the Guard, 1898–1908; miscellaneous loose material of correspondence, bills, receipts, committee reports, and applications for the Citizens Corps.

Records of the Sons of Veterans, P.R. Schuyler Camp No. 2, Philadelphia, include: minutes, 1889–1922; and dues ledgers, 1899–1928.

Ladies Aid Society, No. 4, Captain Schuyler Camp No. 2, Sons of Veterans Inc. (later changed to Auxiliary No. 4) records include: minutes, 1892–1903, 1917–1924; dues ledgers, 1893–1928; receipt books, 1893–1928; and account book, 1906–1928. Also one unidentified dues ledger, 1890–1914.

Gift of Philip R. Schuyler Post No. 51, GAR through Maxwell Whiteman, 1961.

1826
Norris, George William, 1875–1965.   Papers, 1898–1962.   (10 v.)

George William Norris was a Philadelphia physician and president of the board of trustees of the Mutual Assurance Company of Philadelphia. Norris was also a very talented amateur photographer who exhibited in the Photographic Society of Philadelphia's 1893 exhibition and at both the first and second Philadelphia Photographic Salon exhibitions.

Personal narratives, memorabilia, and a family history, all with accompanying photographs, of Dr. George William Norris. Included in the collection are: European travel diary, 1898; transcription of a diary kept by Norris during his service with the U.S. Army Medical Reserve Corps in England and France, May, 1917-December, 1918; *Medical Memories* of his years as a medical student at the University of Pennsylvania, 1895–1899 (ca. 1960); a social and biographical memoir of the Mutual Assurance Company;

History of the Norris Family compiled by George Washington Norris, William Fisher Norris, and George William Norris, n.d.; and a family scrapbook, n.d. There are three Norris photograph albums, ca. 1890–1950, of portraits, scenery, and the buildings, grounds, and personalities of "Woodburne," the family residence in Susquehana County.

Gift of Norris, 1960 and the Norris estate, 1966.

1827
Morris, Samuel Wells, 1786–1847.   Correspondence, 1799–1852.
(400 items.)

Incoming correspondence of Samuel Wells Morris and his wife Anna Ellis Morris of Wellsboro. The early letters, 1799–1839 are mostly from family members to Anna Morris on domestic matters and include letters from Samuel on family business and his political activities while serving as a state legislator, 1832–1836, and as a democratic congressman, 1837–1841. The correspondence, 1840–1847, to Samuel reflects his interests in politics, northern Pennsylvania coal lands, and the Tioga Navigation Company. Correspondents are John Laporte, Frederick A. Muhlenberg, A.G. Ralston, various politicians, and members of the Morris and Ellis family.

Purchased, 1962.

1828
Philadelphia Independence Homecoming Committee.
Records, 1951.   (1,050 items.)

The Philadelphia Independence Homecoming Committee was organized "to recognize the 175th Anniversary of the signing of the Declaration of Independence; to rededicate the American people to the ideals of democracy."

The papers include correspondence, speeches, publicity announcements, and miscellaneous publications and photographs. Much of the correspondence is of their chairman of the board, Edwin O. Lewis, and of the Committee president, Clement Vincent Conole.

Gift of Thomas V. Labrum, 1960.

1829
John Cummins and Company.   Correspondence, 1800, 1812.
(90 items.)

Incoming business correspondence, 1800, 1812, of John Cummins and Company, merchant firm in Duck Creek and Smyrna, Del., dealing in grains, flour, lumber, and dry goods. A few of the letters, April, 1800, are to George Kenard of Duck Creek, also a merchant.

Gift of James P. Faires, 1961.

1830
Norris, Thomas G.   **Collection, 1786–1911.**   **(78 items.)**

This collection of papers on the iron industry of Cumberland County, includes: Pine Grove Furnace day book, 1789–1790; Cumberland Furnace miscellaneous record book, 1795–1808; cordwood book, 1878, charcoal book, 1878, and analysis book (of various iron ores), 1880–1901, apparently of the South Mountain Mining and Coal Company; Pennsylvania Geological Survey Maps of the South Mountain, 1880–1889; land records, 1887–1892, primarily on Cumberland County; and a few miscellaneous records, 1864–1911, of the South Mountain Mining and Coal Company.

Gift of Thomas G. Norris, 1961.

1831
Clothier, Clarkson, 1846–1917.   **Collection, 1895–1909.**
(41 items.)

A small collection of letters addressed to Clarkson Clothier, president of Strawbridge and Clothier, Philadelphia department store, and his wife Agnes Evans Clothier. Included among the correspondents are prominent actors, writers, educators, and politicians such as William McKinley and Dwight L. Moody.

Gift of Marion Clothier, 1961.

1832
Wanamaker, John, 1838–1922.   **Collection, 1779–1892.**
(300 items.)

John Wanamaker was founder of a Philadelphia department store.

Small autograph collection assembled by John Wanamaker, consisting of autograph letters, clipped signatures, documents, and illustrative engravings and lithographs, representing mostly early 19th century American political, military, and literary figures. Included are such figures as Matthew Carey, Charles Carroll of Carrollton, Millard Fillmore, Timothy Pickering, Joel Roberts Poinsett, Gideon Welles, and John Greenleaf Whittier.

Gift of Wanamaker's Department Store of Philadelphia, 1959.

1833
Freeman and Frost families.   **Papers, 1809–1929.**   **(800 items.)**

Incoming correspondence, business records, estate records, diaries, and miscellaneous family papers of the Freeman and Frost families of Philadelphia. Tristram William L. Freeman, auctioneer, is represented by business correspondence and a few miscellaneous business records, 1835–1848; his brother, Henry G. Freeman, lawyer, by a few business letters, 1847–1848;

and Henry Freeman's son, Charles D. Freeman, lawyer, by correspondence, business records, and papers, 1842–1891, on his tenure as a New Jersey land commissioner.

The papers of Isabel Freeman Frost, Charles Freeman's daughter, make up the largest part of the collection. They include family and personal correspondence, 1873–1928; papers of the Whist Club of Philadelphia, 1879–1905; a memo book, 1897 apparently by Isabel Frost; diary, 1914; and personal account book, 1880–1819. Her correspondence contains letters from Sarah Augusta Cushing Freeman, her mother; Canfield Darwin Freeman, her brother; Augusta Frost Eisenbrey, her daughter; Emily Louise Phillips Frost, her sister-in-law; and ethnologist, Matilda Coke Evans Stevenson.

Her husband, Charles W. Frost, advertising agent, is represented by personal and business correspondence, 1881–1927; records of the Frost Block Company, 1901–1903, a firm organized to manufacture building blocks, toy, and novelties; and some correspondence and miscellaneous financial items, 1896–1897, of *City and State,* a Philadelphia reform newspaper with which Frost was associated.

There is also a diary, 1837, perhaps of Elizabeth Raney Frost; and a diary, 1870–1871 of Mary Ann Dorr Frost, daughter of Elizabeth Frost, about travel in western Europe.

Gift of J.F.K. Eisenbrey through Mr. Schwartz, 1961.

1834
Spring Garden Soup Society (Philadelphia, Pa.)
Records, 1852–1929.   (300 items.)

The Spring Garden Soup Society was a private relief agency, organized in 1852 in the Spring Garden district of Philadelphia.

Minute book, 1852–1854; register of society members, 1853–1898; register of applicants for assistance, 1853–1929; a receipt book of donations, 1898–1916; and coal orders, 1891–1905. There is also a register of applicants for assistance from the Ladies Spring Garden Beneficial Society, 1861. Loose items, 1852–1914, include: the original list of subscribers, by-laws, bills, receipts, treasurer's reports, a few minutes, incoming correspondence, and miscellanea.

Gift of the Spring Garden Soup Society.

1835
Philadelphia Drug Exchange.   Records, 1861–1957.   (10 v.)

The Philadelphia Drug Exchange was founded in 1861 to promote the interests of the local drug and allied industries.

These records include: minutes, 1861–1955, of the board of directors and of annual meetings; roll of officers and members, 1861–1912; circulars, 1873–1877; and annual reports, 1875–1957.

Gift of Philadelphia Drug Exchange.

1836
Tucker, William Robinson, 1845–1930.   Correspondence, 1882–1898.   (1,500 items.)

Tucker was manager for the counting house of John R. Penrose which operated a line of sailing vessels between Liverpool and Philadelphia and was primarily involved in the salt trade. At the same time, Tucker was secretary of the Philadelphia Board of Trade and served in various capacities with the Board of Port Wardens, Joint Executive Committee for the Improvement of the Harbor, the National Board of Trade, and the Philadelphia Bourse.

Major business correspondents are C.A. McDowell and W.S. McDowell of Nicholas Ashton and Sons, Liverpool, salt proprietors; William A. Hazard of Francis D. Moulton and Company, New York, salt merchants; and Samuel Thompson's Nephew and Company, New York, importers of burlaps, bagging, yarns. The correspondence is also reflective of his involvement in the development of Philadelphia's harbor and commerce. Many letters to Tucker, an avid sportsman, concern various club activities, particularly the League of American Wheelmen and other bicycling associations. There is scattered material from family of routine nature including many notes from his sister Irene H. Clark.

Gift of the Free Library of Philadelphia, 1960.

1837
Davis, William Watts Hart, 1820–1910.   Papers, 1809–1908. (3 linear ft.)

William Watts Hart Davis was graduated from military school in Norwich, Vt., in 1842, was professor at Portsmouth (Va.) Military Academy, studied law, was an officer in the Mexican War, returned home to Doylestown and practiced law, was appointed to various government offices for the territory of New Mexico, 1853–1857, returned home where he purchased the Doylestown "Democrat," recruited the 104th Regiment, Pennsylvania Volunteers, and served through the Civil War, returned home to spend the rest of his life managing and editing the *Democrat,* and speaking and writing on historical subjects.

Davis arranged his papers into several volumes. His incoming correspondence, 1832–1846, 1857–1860, 1880–1882, from family and friends touches on all his activities, with many passing references to politics, although the content is primarily of personal affairs. One volume of the correspondence has been designated "autographs" and includes letters of political and military men, together with clipped signatures.

Davis also compiled two volumes of *Literary Remains* containing school essays, articles, addresses, reminiscences, diary entries, queries, acknowledgements, invitations, and clippings. There are additional manuscripts of consolidated reports, returns, special and general orders of his command which included regiments of 11th Maine, 56th New York State, 52nd Pennsylvania, and 104th Pennsylvania; *History of One Hundred and Fourth Regiment, Pennsylvania Volunteers;* other works on the Mexican War and Bucks County; more scrapbook material, invitations, cards, notes, and newspaper clippings. The Doylestown Guards minute book, 1849–1860, is also found in these papers.

Purchased, in part, 1961.

1838
No entry.

1839
Pennsylvania State Sabbath School Association.
Records, 1862–1922.   (11 v.)

The Pennsylvania State Sabbath School Association was organized to promote Sunday School attendance and to encourage participation in church activities in Pennsylvania.

Minutes, 1873–1921, of the executive committee and the board of directors, with index; Convention records, 1862–1922, which include general news and summaries of the proceedings of the annual convention, as well as clippings, and a significant amount of material (in the 1922 volume) on John Wanamaker, president of the association, 1895–1906, and then honorary president and chairman of the board until his death in 1922; county records, arranged alphabetically by county including clippings and a brief history of the Sunday schools and the association within each county.

Gift of C.R. Blackwell, 1923.

1840
Morrow, John Harcourt Hague.   Papers, 1932–1939.
(300 items.)

Papers on the political activities of John H.H. Morrow, Philadelphia lawyer. Most of the collection is made up of the papers of the Young Republicans of Philadelphia, in which Morrow held several offices and includes: by-laws and rules, 1932; minutes, 1932–1934; correspondence,

1934–1939; papers on the Philadelphia mayoralty campaign, 1935; and miscellaneous items. Morrow was president of the Young Republican National Federation, 1938, and the correspondence, 1937–1939, includes material on the National Federation.

There are also papers on the proposed division of the 46th ward, West Philadelphia, south of Market Street, in 1936.

Gift of Ethel Morrow, 1961, 1967.

1841
No entry.

1842
No entry.

1843
No entry.

1844
Chadwick, Alexander C., Jr.   **Papers, 1909, 1927, 1931.**   **(12 v.)**

Alexander C. Chadwick was editor of first the *Roxborough Times* and then the *Suburban Press* newspapers which served Philadelphia's northwest communities.

Chadwick's interest in the past, present, and future of the Falls of Schuylkill neighborhood and the Wissahickon Valley are reflected in the 200 letters to him and in scrapbooks of newspaper clippings and photographs. Titles of the scrapbooks are: "Falls of Schuylkill"; "Falls of Schuylkill, Educators and Schools"; "Wissahickon"; "Wissahickon Valley (concerning construction of Henry Avenue Bridge); "Fairmount Park at Our Back Door"; "Philadelphia."

Purchased, 1962.

1845
Brown, Henry Paul.   **Invitations, 1914–1954.**   **(200 items.)**

Engraved invitations received by Dr. and Mrs. Henry Paul Brown.
Gift of Mrs. Francis James Dallet, 1961.

1846
No entry.

1847
Franklin Inn Club.   **Archives, 1902–1974.**   **(3 linear ft.)**

The Franklin Inn Club is a private club for authors, illustrators, editors, and publishers organized in 1902 at Philadelphia.

Correspondence; biographical data on the members, and manuscripts or other examples of their work; minutes, 1902–1955; account books, 1923–1950, invoices, 1927–1937, financial reports, bills, and receipts, and miscellaneous financial records; entertainment records, including texts of speeches, papers, and plays given before the club; and miscellany of other materials. The collection also contains three book length manuscripts: George Gibbs, *The Secret Witness*, (1917); John Bach McMasters, *Life and Times of Stephen Girard*, (1918); and Felix Emanuel Schelling, *A History of English Drama*, (1914).

Deposited by the Franklin Inn Club.

1848
Read family.   Papers, 1810–1852, 1879.   (175 items.)

Papers of John Read and of his son John Meredith Read, Philadelphia lawyers. The John Read items, 1810–1833, consist almost entirely of letters, primarily from Henry Clymer, and legal documents on estate of George Clymer.

The John Meredith Read items, 1832–1852, 1879, include correspondence on legal matters, a few family letters, and some miscellaneous financial items. None of the papers touch upon Read's public career.

Purchased, 1961.

1849
Ernst, Johann Friedrich, 1748–1805.   Papers, 1776–1819.   (4 v.)

Letters, mostly in German, detail Johann Friedrich Ernst's personal and professional life in Northumberland County and Easton, 1776–1783; his letterbook, 1780–1786, contains copies of letters to such fellow pastors as Frederick Muhlenberg, Wilhelm Lehman, Immanuel Snozl as well as to Philadelphia printer, Charles Cist; a small personal diary, n.d.; and a religious and personal diary in the *Americanisher Stadt und Land Calender*, (1791), continued in another hand [Rev. Frederick Hauser] in English in an unidentified 1819 German almanac.

1850A
Fisher, Sidney George, 1809–1871.   Papers, 1823–1887.
(3 linear ft.)

Personal correspondence of Sidney George Fisher, Philadelphia author and diarist, and his wife Elizabeth Ingersoll mostly on family matters: letters, 1851–1853, from Fisher to John W. Burton, giving instructions on the management of Mount Harmon, Fisher's Maryland farm; letters, 1852–1859, from Fisher to Elizabeth; and letters, 1864–1866, from Elizabeth to George. Also Edward Ingersoll's correspondence and memoranda, 1850, on the finances of John Ingersoll of Vicksburg, particularly John's mortgaged slaves.

Gift of R. Sturgis Ingersoll, 1961.

1850B
Fisher, Sidney George, 1809–1871.   Papers, 1832–1895.
(700 items.)

Letters, 1850–1869 of Sidney George Fisher to and from his wife Elizabeth Ingersoll, mainly while Fisher was in Richfield Springs, N.Y., taking the cure; letters, 1833–1855, to Elizabeth from her father Charles Jared Ingersoll; and letters, 1832–1859, to Elizabeth from various family members. The correspondence is mostly on routine social and family news. Also included in the papers are: Ann Eliza George Fisher (mother of Sidney George Fisher) account book, 1809–1820; Sidney George Fisher docket books, 1835–1850, account book, 1840–1841, and scrapbooks, 1833–1870, of his articles; Elizabeth Ingersoll Fisher diaries, 1855–1863; Sydney George Fisher (son of Sidney George Fisher and Elizabeth Ingersoll Fisher) miscellaneous papers, 1875–1895.

Gift of Anna Warren Ingersoll, 1970.

1851
Kane, John Kintzing, 1795–1858.   Papers, 1826–1860.
(ca. 1200 items.)

John Kintzing Kane was appointed attorney general of Pennsylvania in 1845, a position he resigned in 1846 to serve until his death as a U.S. District Court judge for eastern Pennsylvania.

These papers are mostly petitions and letters directed to Kane in 1845 recommending candidates for deputy attorney offices. There is some personal and family correspondence and letters of condolence to his family written after Kane's death in 1858.

Miscellaneous papers, 1853–1860, of Elisha Kent Kane, naval surgeon, explorer, and son of John Kintzing Kane, includes correspondence on the Second Grinnell Expedition to the Arctic in 1853 under Kane's command, condolence letters upon his death in 1857, and a small amount of correspondence on the establishment of Kane Lodge and an effort to finance a small monument to Kane.

Purchased, 1961.

1852
No entry.

1853
No entry.

1854
No entry.

1855
Miscellaneous Government Records, 1664–1950.   (72 v.)

An artificial, miscellaneous collection of official records or retained copies created by or for individual officer holders, governmental or quasi governmental bodies. Grouped with these entries are transcriptions of legislative hearings or court trials retained by parties to the proceedings. The assessment records described include taxes on real and personal property and list the taxable's name, the property taxed, and the assessed valuation. Duplicates are the records of taxes collected retained by the several collectors.

Arch Street Prison (Philadelphia, Pa.) Building Committee. Minutes, 1807–1813, 1820–1823. Arch Street Prison, first called "New Prison," was intended as a Pennsylvania state penitentiary. These minutes include construction accounts. Deposited by F. Theodore Walton, 1873. (1 v.)

Bethel Township (Lebanon County, Pa.) Auditor's records, 1822–1863, of settled and audited accounts. Also includes clerk's notices, 1845–1869, of strayed animals. Purchased, 1956. (1 v.)

Camden (N.J.) South Ward state, county, city, ward, school, poll, and dog tax assessment, 1870. With tabular totals, and amounts raised for each tax. Gift of William John Potts, 1889. (1 v.)

Chester Borough (Pa.) Town Council minutes, 1826–1849, with ordinances and resolutions, some tax and financial records. Gift of Mrs. Frank E. Seletz, 1976. (1 v.)

Chester County (Pa.) West Chester Township school tax assessment duplicate, 1835. Ezra Haines, collector. (1 v.)

Delaware County (Pa.) Registry of voters for Marple Township. Lists names and occupations including number of housekeepers per household when given. (1 v.)

Delaware County (Pa.) Ridley Township school assessment duplicates, 1855, 1881, 1882. Tinnicum school tax assessment duplicates, 1859, 1862, and road tax assessment duplicate, 1861. Gift of Lillian Hutchinson Mousley, 1959. (5 v.)

Eastern Penitentiary (Philadelphia, Pa.) Discharges, 1885–1889, containing almost no information. In part used as a scrapbook, 1890, for clippings about Richard Vaux. Gift of Eastern Penitentiary, 1950. (1 v.)

Great Britain. Board of Trade. Hearing proceedings, [May 15, 1759], on Benjamin Franklin's petition to the King in Council in behalf of Tedyuskung and the Delaware Indians who accused the Pennsylvania proprietors with land fraud, with arguments and supporting documents; report, January 6, 1758 of Committee of the Provincial Council appointed to enquire into complaints of the Delaware Indians at the Treaty of Easton. Contemporary copies. (2 v.) 1758 Report published in *Colonial Records, First Series*, 8: 246–261.

Massachusetts. House of Representatives. General Court. Journal, 1803–1804. Copy. (1 v.)

Montgomery, Morton Luther. Reading (Berks County, Pa.) lawyer and local historian. Berks County taxables, 1758. Compiled by Morton Luther Montgomery from provincial and county records at the Historical Society of Berks County. Purchased, 1911. (1 v.)

Creigh, John. Tyrone Township (Perry County, Pa.) Justice of the Peace. Docket book, 1812–1813. Gift of the Chicago Historical Society, 1948. (1 v.)

New York. General Assembly. Journal extracts, 1766–1767. Copy by Henry Dilworth Gilpin. (1 v.)

New York. Records, 1664–1682. Relating to Delaware, New Castle, and the Whore=Kill. Copied, 1740. (1 v.)

New York. Police patrol. Roll, 1848–1851, of the first and second platoon, 8th Patrol District; continued as Edward Riehl and Ann Sickles, Philadelphia accounts and memoranda, 1890, for construction of two houses. (1 v.)

Northampton County (Pa.) Property tax assessments, 1818, by township. Purchased, 1958. (1 v.)

Pennsylvania. Laws. Laws of Pennsylvania, 1693–1700. Photostatic copies; originals in the collections of the American Philosophical Society. (1 v.)

Pennsylvania. Laws. *The Statutes at Large of Pennsylvania from 1682–1801, compiled under the authority of the Act of May 19, 1887*, by James T. Mitchell and Henry Flaunders, commissioners. Volume 1 (incomplete) containing laws, 1682–1699, with additional material. Typescript. (1 v.)

Pennsylvania. General Assembly. Proceedings of the General Assembly, 1779–1788, and Supreme Executive Council, 1785, regarding the Commonwealth's settlement with the Penn estate, Also: Great Britain. Parliament. *An act for settlement of an annuity to the heirs of William Penn*, 1790. Proceedings are a contemporary copy, 1788. Gift of Lindsay Harkness, 1948. (1 v.)

Pennsylvania. Constitution. Autograph album, 1837, signed by delegates, secretaries, stenographers, doorkeepers, and other personnel connected with the Pennsylvania Convention to Revise the Constitution. Continued with additional autographs and poems, 1840–1842. (3 v.)

Pennsylvania. Council of Censors. Minutes, 1783–1784, of proceedings to consider whether the 1776 Constitution had been preserved inviolate and to recommend amendments. Gift of the Lutheran Theological Seminary, 1965. (1 v.)

Pennsylvania. Provincial Council. Drafts of minutes, 1757–1758. Richard Peters, Secretary. The proceedings during this period were primarily concerned with negotiations with the Delaware Indians. Published in *Colonial Records,* 7:652–783, 8:1–123. (1 v.)

Pennsylvania. Province. Register General. Marriage register, 1682–1689, kept by Christopher Taylor, James Claypool, and others. Gift of Joshua Francis Fisher, 1845. (1 v.)

Pennsylvania. Supreme Court. Scrapbook, 1731–1882, of autograph letters and documents of approximately 50 Chief Justices and Associate Justices of the Pennsylvania Supreme Court. Gift of Mrs. Oscar H. Rogers, 1934. (1 v.)

Pennsylvania Canal. Records, (1859) 1864, with measurements and notes on structures of Eastern, Lower Juanita, and Upper Juanita divisions, with some 1864 notes for the Wisconesco division. (1 v.)

Philadelphia (Pa.). City Charter Commission. Public hearing transcripts, 1949–1950, preparatory to proposal of 1951 City Charter. Gift of Frederick D. Gorman, 1950. (1 v.)

Philadelphia (Pa.). City Council. Lighting Committee. Proceedings, 1931, of public meetings held on "matters pertaining to the wholesale price of gas and gasoline lamps, cost of maintenance and other subjects in connection with the alleged overcharge for service to the City of Philadelphia." Typescript. Gift of Joel Harris Mustin, 1973. (1 v.)

Philadelphia (Pa.). Alderman. Marriage register, 1846–1852, kept by John Dennis, alderman. Gift of Mrs. Joseph Y. Jeanes, 1933. (1 v.)

Philadelphia (Pa.). Court of Common Pleas. and Court of Quarter Sessions. Proceedings, 1694–1695; also record of deeds acknowledged in open court, 1695–1696. Gift of Mrs. Benjamin Rush, 1951. (1 v.)

Philadelphia (Pa.). Court of Common Pleas. Attachments for debt and other case reports, 1710–1713. (1 v.)

Philadelphia (Pa.). Courts. Grand Jury. Minutes, 1844. This jury considered many of the cases arising from the anti-Catholic riots of 1844 in Kensington and Southwark. (1 v.)

Philadelphia (Pa.). Justice of the Peace. Marriage register, 1814–1839, kept by Edward D. Cornfield, justice of the peace. Gift of Samuel Castner, Jr., 1916. (1 v.)

Philadelphia (Pa.). City Surveyors. Lot surveys and notes, 1780–1842, of street and alleys from Market Street to Pine Street and Front Street to 6th Street. James Pearson and others surveyors. Often gives lot owners names. (1 v.)

Philadelphia (Pa.). Committee on Public Safety. Minutes, 1861–1862. Gift of the American Negro Historical Society. (1 v.)

Philadelphia (Pa.). Department of City Transit. Photographic Division. *Historical Buildings in Philadelphia,* compiled under the direction of Joseph Jackson, 1934. Typescript. (1 v.)

Philadelphia (Pa.). Department of Police. Receipts for warrants on the City Treasurer, 1855. Listing names of payee and receipted by ward lieutenants. (1 v.)

Philadelphia (Pa.). Mayors Court. Docket book, 1767–1771. Includes indictments, appointments for constables and overseers of the poor, recommendations for public housekeepers and liquor licenses. Purchased, 1962. (1 v.)

Philadelphia (Pa.). Mayor's Office. Notes and Statistics from the Mayor's Office marriage register, 1858–1865, Alexander Henry, Mayor. Gift of Mrs. Bayard Henry, 1938. (1 v.)

Philadelphia (Pa.). Municipal Court. Civil Division. Court transcript, 1935, of the case of *Snepp v. Del Goleto.* Petition of Mary Orth Seth for revocation of adoption of Delores Del Goleto by Ernest Del Goleto. Gift of Joel Harris Mustin, 1973. (1 v.)

Philadelphia (Pa.). Overseers of the Poor. Chestnut, Lower Delaware, and Walnut poor tax duplicate, 1769. William Savery, collector. (1 v.)

Philadelphia (Pa.). Overseers of the Poor. Account books, 1780–1784. Contains both professional and personal accounts. Includes North Ward poor tax duplicates, 1782. Gift of the heirs of Eliza F.E. Fraser, 1926. (2 v.)

Philadelphia (Pa.). Overseers of the Poor. Blockley Township poor and dog taxes duplicate, 1844. Lists name, occupation, property or personal assessment. Gift of Jacob H. Stadelman, 1918. (1 v.)

Philadelphia (Pa.). Receiver of Taxes. Tax list, 1693. One penny tax assessment, copy of John Claypoole, collector. This was the first tax list for Philadelphia County. Published in *P.M.H.B.,* 8 (1884): 83–105. (1 v.)

Philadelphia (Pa.). Receiver of Taxes. Chestnut, South, and Middle Ward tax duplicate, 1754. Copy of William Savery, collector. Names published in *P.M.H.B.,* 14 (1890): 414–420. (1 v.)

Philadelphia (Pa.). Receiver of Taxes. City Wards tax assessment, 1756. Recorded by wards with names, occupations, and assessment. (1 v.)

Philadelphia (Pa.). Receiver of Taxes. Lower Delaware, High Street, and North Wards watch and lamp, highway and water/sewage tax duplicate, 1765. Joseph Ogden, collector. Purchased, 1926. (2 v.)

Philadelphia (Pa.). Receiver of Taxes. Tax receipts, 1770. With summary statements, by ward and township, of total receipts due and amounts received from collectors, allocations made, and fees paid. Gift of Thomas Archer, 1902. (1 v.)

Philadelphia (Pa.). Receiver of Taxes. Tax list, 1772. Fifteenth eighteen penny provincial tax assessment. Transcript. Gift of Sarah H. Lockrey, 1902. (1 v.)

Philadelphia (Pa.). Receiver of Taxes. State of the Accounts of the County Treasurer, 1798–1799, and of the County Commissioners, 1798–1800. Continued as Philadelphia County in account with public landings and hay scales, 1798–1800. Last page missing. Gift of J. Welles Henderson. (1 v.)

Philadelphia (Pa.). Receiver of Taxes. Northern Liberties tax duplicate, 1781. Valentine Ulrick, collector. (1 v.)

Philadelphia (Pa.). Receiver of Taxes. Southwark public landings tax duplicate, 1788. Include occupations, James Jordon, collector. Purchased, 1906. (2 v.)

Philadelphia (Pa.). Receiver of Taxes. Germantown Township penal tax duplicate, 1790. The tax was collected for the purpose of "building cells for the convicts." Mathias Roop, collector. Purchased, 1889. (1 v.)

Philadelphia (Pa.). Receiver of Taxes. Northern Liberties and Blockley Township poor, county, and road tax accounts, 1790–1793. James Swain, collector, 1790–1800. (1 v.)

Philadelphia (Pa.). Receiver of Taxes. Roxborough Township tax duplicate, 1790. William Rittenhouse, collector. Gift of Mable Kirkbaugh, 1960. (1 v.)

Philadelphia (Pa.). Receiver of Taxes. Tax list, 1800. Enumeration of taxables and slaves by township, listing taxables and their occupations, slaves and their ages and owners. Gift of G.B. Keen, 1887. (1 v.)

Philadelphia (Pa.). Receiver of Taxes. Blockley Township personal and poor tax assessment, 1815. Gift of Bart Anderson, 1947. (1 v.)

Philadelphia (Pa.). Receiver of Taxes. Northern Liberties tax assessment, 1815. Frederick Sigmund Hoeckley, assessors. Continued with unidentified account, 1819–1820, in German. (1 v.)

Philadelphia (Pa.). Receiver of Taxes. Lower Delaware and South Mulberry Wards tax duplicate, 1829. Charles W. Schreiner, collector. Includes recapitulations for each ward. Purchased, 1903. (1 v.)

Philadelphia (Pa.) Receiver of Taxes. Walnut Ward tax assessment, [1842]. William B. Chambers, assessor. Gift of Amos G. and William B. Chambers, 1929. (1 v.)

Philadelphia (Pa.). Receiver of Taxes. Letterbook, 1841–1846, kept by Penrose Ash, county treasurer. Purchased, 1944. (1 v.)

Philadelphia (Pa.). Receiver of Taxes. 22nd Ward tax duplicate, 1859–1860. George Widdis, collector. Gift of Marjorie Mayrott, 1973. (1 v.)

Philadelphia County (Pa.). Register of Wills. Receipt book, 1800–1808, kept by Charles Swift, Registrar. (1 v.)

Port of Philadelphia. Captain's Reports, 1797–1802, of vessels entering the Port of Philadelphia. Lists date of entry, commander, owner or consignee, port of origin or destination, pilot and draught. Purchased, 1976. (1 v.)

1856
Darlington, Nina Kelton, b. 1866.   **Papers, 1892–1929.**
(40 items.)

Nina Kelton Darlington was an author and educator in kindergarten music in Philadelphia and Boston, Mass.

These papers included the manuscript of *Heart Songs of Degrees. Lessons in Verse for the Uni-verse,* c. 1903, Darlington's applications for copyrights, and other miscellaneous papers.

Gift of Mrs. Theopolis W. Shields, 1961.

1857
No entry.

1858
Fisher, Joshua Francis, 1807–1873.   **Papers, 1755–1865.**
(500 items.)

Miscellaneous papers of the Joshua Francis Fisher family of Philadelphia family include: letters, 1767–1768, of Tench Francis to his wife, on business activities in England; Fisher family letters, 1775–1777, on revolutionary activities in America; George Harrison papers, 1792–1842, including some business papers and accounts, correspondence with William Tilghman on the Tench and Ann Francis estate and with Horace Binney on William Waln property; and Joshua Francis Fisher papers, 1819–1865, on family matters and a dispute with William Logan Fisher over the estate.

Gift of Mrs. James B. Drinker, 1961.

1859
White, Charlotte.   **Collection, 1801 (1827–1886).**   **(4 v.)**

Commonplace books of Philadelphians: Elizabeth Webb, n.d., copied 1801, with testimony by Thomas Chalkley; Thomas Shipley, hardware merchant, 1827–1834; Samuel Richards Shipley, salesman, ca. 1846–1859; and Earl Shinn, art critic and writer, 1872–1886.

Gift of Charlotte White, 1961.

1860A

Unger, Claude.   Collection, 1706–1937.   (ca. 7000 items.)

Letters and documents representing some 2,000 individuals relate to a wide variety of subjects. Large groups of papers concern Philadelphia merchants of the late 18th and early 19th centuries and include correspondence, accounts, bills of lading, ships papers. Firms represented are: Richard Ashhurst and Sons, which traded in dry goods primarily with Alabama, Louisiana, and Mississippi; Thomas Astley, trading with England, whose papers mostly pertain to land investments in western Pennsylvania; Andrew Clow and Company, with offices in Philadelphia and London, traded with England and Europe, here mostly with Rathbone and Benson, Liverpool; Dutilh and Wachsmuth and affiliate companies, trading mostly with the West Indies but also with Europe.

There are account books representing a variety of businesses of Pennsylvania Germans, and also some court dockets and school exercise books. The bulk of this material consists of the records, 1840–1890, of Jonas Robinhold's dry good store, Port Clinton; blotters, journals, and ledgers; also Jonas Robinhold justice of the peace docket books, 1845–1863; and Port Clinton tax collection records, 1872, Hiram Robinhold, collector.

Additional records include: Heidelberg Township accounts of supervisors, 1775–1836; Peter Hoffman ledger, 1817–1831 (labor); Aaron Keffer, ledger, 1845-1853; David Rinewald, linen merchant, daybook, 1797–1815; John Romich, lumber merchant, ledger, 1844–1888; William Weiler, dry goods merchant, ledger, 1851–1859; and others.

Dutilh and Wachsmuth—1,000 items in French.

Aaron Keffler ledger in German.

Purchased, 1959.

1860B

Unger, Claude.   Collection, 1760–1900.   (ca. 4500 items.)

A miscellaneous section contains single items and small groups of papers of approximately 700 individuals. There are large groups of papers of Philadelphia merchants including: Richard Ashhurst and Sons, particularly in regard to its business in Tennessee; and Dutilh and Wachsmuth.

Additional groups of papers are: Manuel Eyre, also an early 19th century Philadelphia shipping merchant, correspondence and accounts on property development of Delaware City and other Delaware land interests, farming, and several voyages of the *Charleston Packet* to France and the West Indies; George Louis de Stockar, merchant of Nantes, France, incoming letters, 1760- 1796; Philadelphia surveyors papers used to make assessments for paving streets and for the Watering Department in the 1830's and 1840's, giving block by block measurements of street frontage in the Northern Liberties; and miscellaneous legal papers including some Berks County court records and John M. Read legal notes.

George Louis de Stockar incoming correspondence in French and German.

Gift of Franklin and Marshall College, 1967.

1861
Wharton, Katherine Johnston Brinley, 1834–1925.
Papers, 1723–1923.   (11 v. and 130 items.)

Diaries, 1856–1922, of Katherine Johnston Brinley Wharton of Philadelphia and Newport, R.I., reporting on personal activities and public events. The loose papers include some letters to Mrs. Wharton as well as letters and papers of Godfrey Malbone, Jr., John Malbone, and other ancestors of Mrs. Wharton.

Gift of Mrs. James Drinker, 1961.

1862
No entry.

1863
Bradford family.   Papers, 1774–1923.   (700 items.)

Papers of the Bradford family and related families. The papers, 1800–1814, of Samuel Fisher Bradford, bookseller, stationer of Philadelphia, consists of bills, receipts, and some business correspondence.

There is a Charles S. Bradford, Jr., journal of a trip to Paris, 1860, and a volume of James Hewson Bradford's household accounts, 1853–1858.

The papers of James Sydney Bradford, engineer and military officer of Philadelphia, includes: a scrapbook, 1900–1913, of Company "B" Engineers Battalion, National Guard of Pennsylvania, which Bradford joined, 1909; and incoming and outgoing family correspondence written while he served on the Mexican border, 1916, in Camp Meade, Md. and Hancock, Ga., 1917–1918, and with the American Expeditionary Forces in France, 1918–1919.

The remainder of the collection consists primarily of Bradford, Hewson, and Caldwell miscellaneous family letters, 1774–1923.

Gift of Frances Margaret Bradford, 1961.

1864
Smith, Sarah A.G.   Collection, 1716–1816.   (550 items.)

The Sarah A. G. Smith collection consists primarily of the business correspondence and records of several 18th-century Philadelphia merchants.

About half of the collection is made up of the papers of Charles Wharton, his father, Joseph Wharton, both merchants, and other related members of the Wharton family, and includes: Charles Wharton business correspondence; business records; letter books, 1779–1785, 1800–1828; account book with the Bank of Pennsylvania, 1794–1809; an index to shipping adventures and merchants who did business with Charles Wharton; and an unidentified letter book, 1766–1769, 1771.

One-third of the collection consists of the business papers, 1756–1798, of [Thomas] Lamar, [Henry] Hill, [Robert] Bisset Company, a partnership of three brothers-in-law who traded between Philadelphia, London, England, and Madeira, Portugal, and consist mainly of the correspondence between the partners and a few miscellaneous records. There are letters by Mary Lamar, the widow of Thomas Lamar, about her estate.

The remainder of the collection includes: correspondence, 1768–1774, of Anthony Clarkson, merchant of Philadelphia, from John and Arthur Burrows of St. Vincent and Jamaica; Joshua Fisher and Sons, merchants of Philadelphia, business records, 1745–1775; and miscellaneous items.

Gift of Sarah A.G. Smith, 1962, 1966.

1865
Eberlein, Harold Donaldson.   **Papers, 1923–1962.**
(ca. 4000 items.)

Harold Donaldson Eberlein was a Philadelphia antiquarian and author of books and articles on American history, historic houses, architecture, interior design, and decorative arts. He also wrote on wine, gardens, and Italian architecture. Many of his books are written with Cortland Van Dyke Hubbard.

Typescripts, research notes, and correspondence. The material also includes several unpublished projects: *The Making of Long Island,* written with Hubbard and Elled D. Wagner, *Social Life in the Federal Period,* and a biography of Benvenuto Cellini. There are seventeen small volumes of Eberlein's personal expenses, 1940–1960.

Gift of Harold Donaldson Eberlein.

Houses of the Hudson Valley / by Harold Donaldson Eberlein and Cortland Van Dyke Hubbard. New York: 1942.

Manor Houses and Historic Homes of Long Island and Staten Island / by Harold Donald Eberlein. Philadelphia: 1928.

Portrait of a Colonial City, Philadelphia, 1670–1838 / by Harold Donaldson Eberlein and Cortland Van Dyke Hubbard. Philadelphia: 1939.

The Practical Book of Chinaware / by Harold Donaldson Eberlein and Roger Wearne Ramsdell. Philadelphia: 1925.

The Rabelelasian Princess, Madame Royale of France / by Harold Donaldson Eberlein. New York : 1931.

Diary of Independence Hall / by Harold Donaldson Eberlein and Cortland Van Dyke Hubbard. Philadelphia: 1948.

American Georgian Architecture / by Harold Donaldson Eberlein and Cortland Van Dyke Hubbard. Bloomington, 1952.

Historic Houses of George-Town and Washington City / by Harold Donaldson Eberlein and Cortland Van Dyke Hubbard. Richmond: 1958.

The Practical Book of Garden Structures and Design / by Harold Donaldson Eberlein and Cortland Van Dyke Hubbard. Philadelphia: 1937.

1866
E.W. Clark and Company.   Papers, 1837–1948.   (425 items.)

Papers collected for writing a history of E.W. Clark and Company, an investment banking and brokerage house founded in Philadelphia in 1837 by Enoch W. Clark and Edward Dodge. Significant activities of the firm included financial backing for the Mexican War and for the development of American railroads. The papers include some original correspondence, 1837–1937, miscellaneous legal and business records, news clippings, pamphlet, photographs, and typescript histories. There is also some material on Clark, Dodge, and Company, a New York banking house affiliated with the Clark Company, 1845–1857.

Gift of Sydney P. Clark, 1962.

1867
Moore, Clara Jessup, 1824–1899.   Correspondence, 1890–1896.
(82 items.)

Clara Jessup Moore was a Philadelphia author and philanthropist residing in London, best known as the principal supporter, 1881–1896, of John W. Keely's fraud, the Keely motor.

Most of the letters are to Cornelia Frothingham of Readville, Mass., and Philadelphia, several of them on the Keely motor. There are also a few from Keely and others.

Gift of Katherine Brinley Estate through John B. Meir, 1962.

1868
Boyd, John C., d. 1849.   Correspondence, 1819–1849.
(53 items.)

A small collection of the correspondence of John C. Boyd of Danville, including family and business letters. Many of the latter deal with Boyd's frequently less-than-successful business speculations.

Purchased, 1962.

1869
Yeomans, John William, 1800–1863.   Correspondence, 1841–1849.
(150 items.)

The incoming correspondence of John Williams Yeomans, Presbyterian clergyman and educator, pertains to his term as president of Lafayette College, 1841–1843, and as the minister of the Presbyterian Church of Danville, 1846–1849.
Purchased, 1962.

1870
Harrisburg Bridge Company.   Papers, 1812–1850.   (125 items.)

The Harrisburg Bridge Company was incorporated in 1809 to erect and operate a bridge over the Susquehanna River at Harrisburg.
Incoming correspondence and material on stock sales, original financing, repairs, tolls, complaints on service, and applications for work.
Purchased, 1962.

1871
Smith, Thomas W.   Letters, 1862–1864.   (100 items.)

Thomas W. Smith was a sergeant in Company 1, 70th Regiment, Pennsylvania Volunteers (6th Pennsylvania Calvary).
The letters report on the Peninsular Campaign of 1862, the Battle of Antietam in 1862, the Gettysburg Campaign of 1863, and the beginning of Grant's offensive in 1864.
Purchased, 1962.

1872
Buchanan, Alexander, d.1913.   Papers, 1855–1913.   (236 items.)

Correspondence and miscellaneous papers of Alexander Buchanan, Philadelphia police officer on his police work, with receipts and other miscellaneous personal papers.
Gift of David B. Shaw, 1963.

1873
Watson, Joseph, 1784–1814.   Correspondence, 1824–1828.
(400 items.)

Incoming correspondence of Joseph Watson, mayor of Philadelphia, 1824–1828, on patronage positions, counterfeiting of currency, clemency for prisoners, and the sale of Philadelphia blacks, especially children, into slavery. There are also a few copies of Watson's outgoing correspondence.

Purchased, 1962.

1874
Willing and Francis.　　Records, 1794–1822.　　(150 items.)

Records of the merchant firm of Thomas Willing, Thomas Mayne Willing, and Thomas Willing Francis of Philadelphia. A majority of the papers pertain to the China trade, 1805–1822, and to William Read, a merchant of Philadelphia, who represented the firms of Willing and Francis and Willing and Cuwen, some outgoing correspondence of Willings and Francis, invoices of goods shipped, and other financial records, documenting trade in opium and tea, including probably the first recorded arrival of an American opium ship in China in 1805, the *Bingham,* owned by Willing and Francis, and a dispute involving the efforts of the Chinese merchant, Consequa, to recover a debt owed by Willing and Francis. There are also a few letters and other records, 1796–1800, on the ship *Mount Vernon* and a claim against Willing and Francis by William Mayne Ducanson, a few land papers, 1794–1811, of Thomas Willing, and Willing family land deeds.

Gift of Leonard T. Beale, 1963.

1875
No entry.

1876
Hey, Emanuel, 1821–1892.　　Papers, 1866–1896.　　(75 items.)

Legal papers primarily about Emanuel Hey, Philadelphia yarn manufacturer, his real estate interests, the estate of his father, Moses Hey, and Emanuel Hey's own estate.

Gift of Mrs. L.M.C. Smith, 1973.

1877
Hey, Moses, 1792–1866.　　Papers, 1817–1868.　　(78 items.)

Correspondence to and from Moses Hey, Springfield Township, Delaware County, with some of Hey's speech drafts. Early correspondence concerns his yarn manufacturing business and personal interests. Half of the letters are written by Hey to local newspapers expressing his strong Republican views during the Civil War.

Gift, 1962, Donor unknown.

1878
Sword family.   Papers, 1819–1850.   (ca. 1,000 items.)

The Sword family was a merchant family of Philadelphia and New Castle, Del., prominent in the China trade. John D. Sword was a supercargo to the West Indies, South America, and China. Mary Sword accompanied him to South America, 1837–1838, and to China, 1841–1845, where she lived at Macao while he did business at Canton.

Principally family correspondence, with a few diaries and business papers; includes original and a typescript copy of most items. The first two generations of Swords in America are represented by a small number of family letters, 1751–1790, of William Sword, a sea captain, of his wife, Penelope Haley Sword, and of their son, John Ewer Sword, also a sea captain.

More than half of the collection is made up of the papers of John Dorsey Sword, the son of John Ewer Sword, and his wife Mary Parry Sword.

The larger part of the papers of John D. and Mary Sword are for the years 1836–1850 and pertain to the China trade. Their numerous and detailed family letters contain material on almost every aspect of the China trade, including descriptions of the voyage to Canton, the Opium War, and the social life of westerners at Macao. John D. Sword's papers include family correspondence, 1819–1850; business correspondence, 1825–1842, including a number of letters from his business partner John B. Trott; and a business letterbook, 1825–1826. Mary Sword's letters contain numerous references to Americans at Macao. There are also extracts of her letters making reference to the Delano family, the grandparents of Franklin Delano Roosevelt. Also included are outgoing family letters from Rio de Janeiro and Valparaiso, 1837–1838, and from Macao, 1842–1845; letters to John D. Sword at Canton, 1842–1845; incoming social letters, 1837–1845; South American diary, 1837–1838; China diary, 1841–1842; diary, 1841–1844, from her brother Thomas Parry on life in Philadelphia.

The papers of William Sword Ash, at Canton with his uncle, James D. Sword during 1847–1848, also relate mainly to the China trade and include family correspondence, 1841–1848; a letter press copy of business letters, 1847–1848; and a diary, 1846–1847, of the journey from New York to Canton.

The remainder of the collection is made up of the family and personal correspondence of James D. Sword's sister, Sarah Dunn Sword, 1819–1849; of his brother, James Brade Sword, supercargo and businessman, 1818–1839; and a diary, 1863, of his son, John Sword.

Gift of the estate of Mary Parry Farr, 1962.

1879
Meredith, Joseph D.   Papers, 1845–1857.   (300 items.)

Correspondence and title papers of Joseph D. Meredith, a land agent of Pottsville, on the ownership and development of lands in the Schuylkill and Luzerne counties. The papers reflect the development of Middlesport, the Summit Branch Railroad Company, and early coal companies. Correspondents include: Horatio N. Burroughs, Joseph Casey, John C. DaCosta, Eli Kirk Price, and A.G. Waterman.

Purchased, 1963.

1880
Miscellaneous monographs, 1740–1973, n.d.   (37 v.)

Brand, Robert. A Study of General Howe's Influence on the Defeat of Saratoga, 1966. (Ph.D.) Dissertation—University of Pennsylvania. Gift of Robert Brand, 1966. (1 v.)

Brecher, Ruth E. Study, [1965]. Two chapters of a study: William Smith of Pennsylvania; The Early Years . . . in Scotland and England; and Tutor in the Colony of New York. Typescript. Gift of Ruth E. Brecher, 1965. (2 v.)

Brenner, Walter C. "Notes on Rising Sun, Fair Hill and Vicinity, 1680–1900," n.d. Brenner was a Philadelphia clerk and local historian. This was meant as a continuation of "Old Rising Sun Village." Typescript, 1932. Gift of James Rawle, 1962. (1 v.)

Brenner, Walter C. "A List of Philadelphia Inns and Taverns, 1680–1900," 1928. Typescript. Gift of Walter C. Brenner, 1929. (2 v.)

Burkhardt, John, 1893–1969. "A History of the Academy of Stomatology," [1964] / John Burkhardt and Ray Hand. An account of a Philadelphia dental society founded in 1894. Gift of John Burkhardt, 1965. (1 v.)

Butler, Thomas. "Studies in Education," 1921–1922. Term paper—University of Pennsylvania. Gift of Thomas Butler, 1945. (1 v.)

Butler, Thomas. "Universalism in Pennsylvania," 1934. Butler was a Universalist Convention Minister and Philadelphia teacher. This work is a scrapbook compiled as Historian for the Pennsylvania Universalist Convention. Gift of Thomas Butler, 1935. (1 v.)

"Continuation of Lectures on the Steam Engine," [1850]. (1 v.)

Edmunds, Albert Joseph, 1857–1941. Essay, 1916. Edmunds was a Philadelphia and Cheltenham librarian. This essay is a textual comparison between his report and the "mangled articles" in the *Evening Bulletin* and *Friends Intelligencer* concerning the 1916 Orthodox and Hicksite Friends reunion in Germantown (Philadelphia, Pa.) Gift of Albert J. Edmunds, 1917. (1 v.)

Findlay, William, 1768–1846. History of Pennsylvania, [1811–1812]. Abstract prepared for William Plumer, Governor of New Hampshire, then collecting materials for a History of America. Copy. (1 v.)

[Fryeburg, Gertrude.] Notebook, n.d. Notebook describing arrangement and contents of Philadelphia County Road Records on file in Quarter Session. (1 v.)

G., H. "Observations respectfully submitted to the consideration of Matthew Carey, Esqr. Aug. 1834," n.d. A Federalist/Whig review of past administrations and recommendations for future constitutional amendments and economic policies. (1 v.)

Gorman, Frederick J., b.1885. Research, [1937]. Data gathered for Gorman's article "Penn's Manors," published in the *P.M.H.B.*, 67 (1943). Gift of Frederick J. Gorman, 1942. (1 v.)

Gutleben, Dan. "A Record of the Behavior of the Men and Machines in the Pennsylvania Sugar Refinery, 1868–1960". Gutleben was a engineer for the Pennsylvania Sugar Company (Philadelphia, Pa.) Letters, abstracts from records, interviews, notes, clippings, photographs, and diagrams compiled for a history of the people, the plant and the processes of the Pennsylvania Sugar Company. Gutleben began his compilation in 1935. Gift of Dan Gutleben, 1967. (1 v.)

Hall, John Elihu, 1783–1829. Critical essay, n.d. This essay was prepared for the *Port Folio* on Charles Sedley's translation of the *Memoirs of Anacreon* and Thomas Moore's translation of the *Odes of Anacreon*. Gift of Gregory Keen, 1920. (1 v.)

Hartwell, Henry. "An account of ye present State and Government of Virginia," [1696] / Henry Hartwell, James Blair, and Edward Chilton. Published as *The Present State of Virginia, and the College* (London, 1727). Purchased, 1938. (1 v.)

Historical notes, [1740–1743]. These notes regard major events and countries of the world. Primarily on old german; continued as a ciphering book in old german, [1752]. Gift of Rev. Amnon Stapleton, 1900. (2 v.)

History of the Brethern Church, 1834 Feb. 6. This history begins with the Ancient Church and continues to the Modern or Renewed Church. Much in german. (1 v.)

History of Mount Joy Borough (Lancaster County, Pa.), 1709–1886. With pen and ink drawings. Purchased, 1958. (1 v.)

Irwin, Samuel Dale. Scrapbook, 1873–1874. Irwin was a Tionesta (Forest County, Pa.) attorney. His scrapbook contains clippings of newspaper articles written by Irwin including "History of Forest County" and "Petrography by Indians." Gift of Samuel D. Irwin, 1875. (1 v.)

1880

Jones, Charles S. History of Darby, Pa., 1946. Includes photographs. Typescript. Gift of Edith Jones, 1954. (1 v.)

Lamb, Andrew, b. 1684. "New Rules for finding Longitude," 1754. Prepared for the Lords of the Admiralty. (1 v.)

McCusker, John James, b. 1939. "The Pennsylvania Shipping Industry in the Eighteenth Century," 1973. Typescript. Gift of John J. McCusker, 1974. (1 v.)

Macfarlan, Douglas, 1887–1966. "Mills along the Wissahickon Creek," 1947–1950. Macfarlan was a Philadelphia physician, professor, and local historian. Contains maps, sketches, clippings, and notes from the notebooks of James F. Magee, Jr. Originals at the Free Library of Philadelphia. Gift of Douglas Macfarland, 1965. (1 v.)

MacMaster, John Bach, 1852–1932. "A Partial Account of the Pennsylvania Floods of 1889," n.d. Begun and discontinued under the direction of the Flood Relief Commission. Purchased, 1973. (1 v.)

Petshek, Kirk R., d. 1973. "Policy Making in a Major City : Urban Development in Philadelphia," [1972]. Published as *The Challenge of Urban Reform : Policies and Programs in Philadelphia* (Philadelphia, 1973). Gift of Kirk R. Petshek, 1972. (1 v.)

Plan for the General Government of America : under which America is governed by Great Britain, 1780. Gift of Samuel N. Lewis, 1907. (1 v.)

Reichel, William Cornelius, 1824–1876. *A Red Rose from the Olden Time; or, A Ramble through the Annals of the Rose Inn and the Barony of Nazareth, in the Days of the Province,* 1752–1772 / by William C. Reichel, John W. Jordan, ed., 1883. From *Transactions of the Moravian Historical Society.* Extra-illustrated by John W. Jordan, 1886. (1 v.)

Roberts, Thomas. "A History and Analysis of Labor-Management Relations in the Philadelphia Transit Industry," 1959. Ph.D. dissertation—University of Pennsylvania. Typescript. [Gift of Thomas Roberts.] (1 v.)

Shaw, Joshua, ca. 1777–1860. Palette, [1820]. Shaw was a Philadelphia and Bordentown, N.J., artist and inventor. This palette contains an explanation of colors and how to mix them. (1 v.)

S. Kind & Sons. Corporate history, 1872–1938 / compiled by Joseph W. Halberstadt for S. Kind & Sons. S. Kind & Sons were Philadelphia jewelers. Gift of Oscar Kind, 1964. (3 v.)

Smith, Harry A. "The Distribution and Organization of the British Army in America from 1763 to 1774," 1930. (M.A.) thesis—Miami University. (1 v.)

Union Canal Company of Pennsylvania. "General Description," [1847]. Gift of Wilson Lundy, 1947. (1 v.)

Zschokke, Johann Heinrich Daniel, 1771–1848. "The Dead Guest."
Translated by A.A.H. (1 v.)

1881
Biddle, James Cornell, 1835–1898.   Civil War letters, 1861–1865.
(317 items.)

Letters of James C. Biddle to his wife report on Civil War military
operations and strategy of the capture of Fort Hatteras, the occupation of
New Orleans, and with George Gordon Meade's staff at the battles of Chancellorsville, Gettysburg, and Appomattox. There are many sketches of the
position of the troops and frequent references to Union and Confederate
leaders, especially Ulysses S. Grant, Joseph Hooker, Stonewall Jackson, Robert E. Lee, and George Gordon Meade.
      Purchased, 1963.

1882
No entry.

1883
Colt, Roswell L. (Roswell Lyman), 1779–1856.   Papers, 1808–1854.
(ca. 1200 items.)

These papers consist primarily of business, political, and social correspondence of Roswell L. Colt of Paterson, N.J. The material reflects Colt's
penchant for speculation in lands in Oneida, N.Y., Pennsylvania, Maryland,
and western property, as well as coal, iron, canals, and railroads. His debts
to the Bank of the U.S. and the estate of his father-in-law are also treated.
There is evidence of Colt's position as financial advisor to his brother, John
M. Colt, textile manufacturer, his cousin Samuel Colt, arms manufacturer,
Nicholas Biddle, and Daniel Webster. American politics are frequent topics
in the letters. Much of the later correspondence concerns his agricultural
and horticultural interests, from Nicholas Biddle, Richard M. Blatchford,
John W. Bloomfield, William A. Bradley, John M. Colt, Samuel Colt, Herman P. Cope, John Devereux, R.M. Gibbes, D.M. Perine, Daniel Webster,
and various members of the Hone Club of New York. There are also some
bills, receipts, and other miscellaneous papers.
      Gift of Mrs. E. Perot Walker and Mrs. A. Reid Johnson, 1963.
      Finding aid available.

1884
Miscellaneous Military records and Orderly books,
1675–1864.   (24 v.)

Great Britain. Office of the Royal Ordnance. Treasurer's and paymaster's account book, 1675–1676. Kept by George Wharton, showing sums paid for allowances, wages, annuities, services, and supplies. Gift of Mr. and Mrs. Eugene Newbold, 1961. (2 v.)

Pennsylvania. Militia. Records, 1815–1821. Records of vouchers kept by Harman Vansant, Brigade Inspector of the Pennsylvania Militia, for exonerations for Militia and Exempt for 33rd, 42nd, and 59th Regiments. Includes Vansant's account with the State of Pennsylvania, 1821. (1 v.)

United States. Continental Army. Records, 1776–1782. The records include:

Order-book, 1776. For 4th Pennsylvania Battalion, commanded by Colonel Anthony Wayne, Feb. 27-June 20, 1776, headquarters at Marcus Hook, New York, Camp Cadwell (Long Island, N.Y.), Albany, and the Isle of Noix. Gift of Francis Etting. Published in *P.M.H.B.,* 29 (1905): 470–478; 30 (1906): 91–103, 206–219. (1 v.)

Order-book, 1776. For Colonel Paul Dudley Sargent's Brigade (composed of various Massachusetts and Connecticut Regiments), headquarters at Beekman's Seat between New York and Harlem, Feb. 7-June 25, 1776. Gift of Hyde Appleton, 1921. Portions published as "Elisha Williams' Diary of 1776," Pennsylvania Magazine of History and Biography; v. 49, p. 44–60. (1 v.)

Order-book, 1777. Kept, Feb. 7-June 25, 1777, for and unidentified North Carolina Regiment, headquarters at Haddrills Point, Wilmington, Halifax, Roanoke, and Middle Brook. Gift of the Lanier bequest. (1 v.)

Order-book, 1777. Kept, April 14-Oct. 9, by Colonel Daniel Morgan for the 11th Virginia Regiment, headquarters at Princeton, Bridgewater, Bound Brook, Morristown, Cross Roads, Wimington, Birmingham, and Pottsgrove. Gift of William S. Febiger, 1963. (1 v.)

Order-book, 1777–1778. Kept by Colonel Anthony Morris and Colonel Richard Butler for the 9th Pennsylvania Regiment, headquarters at Morristown, Middle Brook, and Valley Forge. With some Quartermaster accounts. Purchased, 1955. (1 v.)

Order-book, 1778. Kept, Jan. 28-Feb. 20, for General Enoch Poor's Brigade (composed of the 1st, 2nd, 3rd New Hampshire and 2nd, 4th New York Regiments). Purchased, 1947. General Orders published in *Valley Forge Orderly Book of General George Weedon,* (1902). (1 v.)

Order-book, 1778. Kept, Jan. 8-March 11, by Colonel Christian Febiger for the 2nd Virginia Regiment, headquarters at Valley Forge. Gift of William

S. Febiger, 1963. Brigade orders published in *Valley Forge Orderly Book of General George Weedon*, (1902). (1 v.)

Records, 1779–1782. Kept by Thomas Grosvenor, Lieutenant Colonel of the 3rd Connecticut Regiment and Sub-Inspector reporting to Major General William Heath, commander of troops east of the Hudson River. Contains General Order extracts, return abstracts, and copies of documents concerning payment for service with the Connecticut Line. Copy. Gift of John H. Hall, 1951. (1 v.)

Order-book, 1780. Kept, Aug. 18–28, by Lieutenant Colonel George Smith for the 1st Pennsylvania Battalion, headquarters at Trenton. Purchased, 1955. (1 v.)

Order-book, 1781–1782. Kept by Colonel Christian Febiger and Lieutenant Colonel Thomas Posey for the 1st Virginia Battalion, headquarters near Yorktown and at Cumberland Old Court House. Gift of William S. Febiger, 1963. (1 v.)

Order-book, 1782. Kept, May 23-Aug. 19, by Colonel John Durkee and Lieutenant Colonel Thomas Grosvenor for the 1st Connecticut Regiment, headquarters at Highlands, Newburgh. Copy. Gift of John H. Hall, 1951. (1 v.)

Order-book, 1782 July. Kept, July 28-Dec.27, by Lieutenant Colonel Henry Dearborn for the 1st New Hampshire Regiment, headquarters at Saratoga. Indexed. Deposited by Thomas Seymour Scott, 1900. (1 v.)

United States. Army. Records, 1798–1863. The records include:

Order-book, 1798–1801. For U.S. Infantry, 2nd Regiment, Lieutenant Colonel Commandant David Strong, headquarters at Wilkinson Ville, Ill., 1798–1801. (1 v.)

Records, 1794. Kept, Oct. 11-Nov. 31, by William Irvine, Major General of the Pennsylvania Line during the Whiskey Insurrection, including orders, miscellaneous accounts, and letters. (1 v.)

United States. Army. Paymaster. Department of Pennsylvania. Accounts, 1863–1864. Kept by Samuel Bell, Jr., Paymaster. Purchased, 1946. (1 v.)

United States. Board of War. *Description of the Susquehanna River and the country which borders it, from Harpers Ferry to the mouth . . . made by order of the Board of War, in May* 1778. Typescript of Library of Congress transcript of French original in Cornwallis Papers, P.R.O., with translation. Gift of the Historical Society of York County. (1 v.)

United States Navy Yard (Philadelphia, Pa.) Officer of the day log, 1837–1844. Report of ship work assignments, Sailing Master Day report, yard laborer and ordinary work assignments. Gift of Seymour Adelman, 1956. (4 v.)

United States Naval Yard (Philadelphia, Pa.) Purser's letterbook, 1843. Kept, Mar. 24-Oct.4, by Abraham Levy as Assistant to the Purser, David H. Bowen. Gift of the Genealogical Society of Pennsylvania, 1967. (1 v.)

1885
No entry.

1886
Perot family.   Papers, 1819–1956.   (109 v. and 800 items.)

Francis Perot began a Philadelphia brewing and malting business in 1818. About 1825 he absorbed the brewery which had been founded in 1687 by Anthony Morris, Jr., and which was then owned by Perot's father-in-law, Thomas Morris, 2d. The Perot Malting Company gave up brewing in 1850, eventually closed its manufactories in Philadelphia and Oswego, N.Y. (acquired in 1882), and used only their malting plant in Buffalo, N.Y., which had been built in 1907. The company was acknowledged as the oldest American business firm until it was sold in 1963.

The smattering of records here, consisting of 88 volumes and 200 loose papers, are all that survive housecleaning. They include ledgers and cashbooks, 1818–1953; salesbooks, 1873–1879, 1885–1953; minutes, receipt books, barley and malt accounts, rents and interests, contracts for the Buffalo plant construction.

Perot family papers include: Francis Perot account books, 1823–1843, 1863–1885; William S. Perot, lawyer and estate executor for Sansom Perot, account books, 1836–1846; Elizabeth Marshall estate papers, 1862–1883; Mary Ann Marshall estate papers, 1881–1913; Elliston Joseph Perot diaries of academic, social, and church related activities, 1877–1901; and transcriptions of responses from the beyond to questions of T. Morris Perot, ca. 1890.

Among the T. Morris Perot, Jr., papers, 1893–1945, is correspondence with Sarah Tyson Hallowell and her niece Harriet Hallowell, both living in Moretsur-Loing outside of Paris, on financial affairs and family news.

In addition, the letters of Sarah Hallowell give glimpses of the coming of World War I, the Hallowells' hospital war work (financially supported by Perot), and post-war France. Harriet, who died in 1943, gives some commentary on the events of World War II, but the restrictions which the war placed on communications with France limits this information.

There are also correspondence and annual reports of the Santo Domingo Silver Mining Company, with mines in Chihuahua, Mexico, of which Perot was a major stockholder, and correspondence on the Association of Centenary Firms.

Gift of the Perot Malting Company, 1963.

1887
Breck, Samuel, 1771–1862.   Notebooks, 1800–1862.   (21 v.)

Samuel Breck was a member of a prominent Philadelphia merchant family, a founder of the Pennsylvania Institution for the Blind, an amateur historian, and an officer of the Historical Society of Pennsylvania.

He kept what he called diaries, 1800–1862, which might more accurately be described as diaries-cum-commonplace books, frequently illustrated with woodcuts, engravings, and Breck's watercolors. The "diaries" comment fully on most public figures, issues, and events in both the United States and Europe. They contain a full measure of travel memoirs, personal and social gossip, as well as comments on manners and society. In 1830, Breck began to organize and condense the diaries into a volume of autobiographical "Recollections," that he carried to 1797 and in which he tells of his childhood in Boston, his education in France, and the family's move to Philadelphia in 1792. Included in the collection are special journals which Breck maintained while serving in the Pennsylvania Senate, 1819–1820, as a member of Congress, 1823–1824, and during trips to Boston, Mass., 1822, and to Quebec, 1838. There are also manuscripts of his speeches and published and unpublished articles a wide range of topics including George Whitefield to the Marquis de Lafayette, as well as four other miscellaneous volumes.

The collection has been assembled from the gifts of several donors: Mrs. C.P. Beauchamp Jeffreys, Mrs. Henry Shaw, Mrs. A.G. Grove, and the Philadelphia Art Museum, 1963.

Much of the "Recollections" and selections from other diaries published in *Recollections of Samuel Breck.* H. E. Scudder, ed. (Philadelphia: Porter and Coates), 1877.

1888
Clayton, John.   Papers, 1832–1881.   (700 items.)

Family and business papers of John Clayton, Philadelphia lawyer, including: letters, 1832–1848, of his mother Sarah Medford Clayton; letters, 1842–1851, of his wife Anna Colton Clayton, many of them mentioning her father Matthias W. Baldwin, founder of the Baldwin Locomotive Works; record book of legal fees charged, 1841–1881; and incoming business letters and papers, 1877–1879.

Gift of Mrs. Stanley Bright, 1963.

1889
Betts, Charles Malone, 1838–1905.   Papers, 1862–1865.
(225 items.)

Charles Malone Betts was an army officer with the 106th Regiment Pennsylvania Volunteers, 15th Pennsylvania Cavalry (known as the Anderson

Cavalry) which served in the East Tennessee Campaign until the final months of the Civil War when it engaged in a campaign that carried it into Virginia, North and South Carolina, Georgia, and Alabama.

The papers contain Betts's incoming letters, orders, and other military papers, 1862–1865; and material prepared by members of the 15th Pennsylvania Cavalry for a proposed history of the cavalry, including a memo from the diary of Betts, an account of the 15th Pennsylvania Cavalry by Betts, and an account of the First East Tennessee Campaign by Charles Lamborn.

Purchased.

The manuscript by Charles B. Lamborn, "First East Tennessee Campaign," is published in the *History of the Fifteenth Pennsylvania Volunteer Cavalry* (Philadelphia: 1906): 331–339.

1890
Irvine-Newbold families. **Papers, 1776–1956.** **(13 linear ft.)**

Papers covering five generations of a family of Philadelphia and Brokenstraw, Warren County. Business records make up the bulk of the collection, but there are also family letters, miscellaneous records and photographs. The first generation is represented by the papers, of William Irvine, physician and revolutionary military officer, including correspondence, 1783–1804, on family matters and land speculation; land papers; account book, 1776–1781, of his military expenses; record book, 1781–1782, of clothing disbursed by Irvine at Fort Pitt; miscellaneous account books, 1793–1796, 1802–1808; orderly book, 1778–1779, and roll book, 1776–1777, of a British unit, the 1st Battalion of Guards.

General Irvine's son, Callender Irvine, served as the U.S. army commissary general from 1812 to 1841, and the papers on his military career include an account book, 1812–1829, and loose and letterpress correspondence. Although he lived in Philadelphia, Callender Irvine annually visited and took great interest in the Warren County lands inherited from his father, and there are incoming correspondence, account books, and other records which relate to land speculation, Brokenstraw farm, horse breeding, lumbering operations, and a general store. Callender Irvine's brother, Dr. John W. Irvine shared in the management of the store, along with Robinson R. Moore, until 1820, after which he practiced medicine in Brokenstraw, and his medical accounts and private business receipts are also included, 1821–1829.

The major portion of the papers belong to William A. Irvine, M.D., son of Callender, who settled in Brokenstraw in 1825, and who spent his life attempting to turn the Irvine property to profitable commercial ventures. Among his many enterprises were a lumbering business, the general store started by his father, a wool factory, an iron foundry, and further speculation. Correspondence, bills, receipts, legal records, memoranda, journals, and other account and record books cover the full range of Irvine's business interests, as well as his farm, internal improvements, and the post office where he served as postmaster. Additional account books relate specifically to the woolen factory, 1845–1856, the foundry, 1845–1854, the blacksmith shop, 1849–1854, and the Irvine post office. In the mid-1850's, Irvine was forced to give up most of his business, retaining the farm, the lumbering concern, and land on which he later developed oil. Irvine Tract papers, 1836–1881, include incoming letters, financial, and legal records.

William A. Irvine's personal papers include student medical notes, and incoming letters, 1849–1884. The papers of his wife Sarah Duncan Irvine include an account book, 1835–1838, scrapbooks, and an Irvine Sunday School minute book, 1838.

The fourth and fifth generations of the Irvine family are represented by the papers, 1865–1956, of William and Sarah Irvine's daughter Sarah Irvine Newbold and her five daughters: Elizabeth I. Newbold, Mary M. Newbold, Margaret E.I. Newbold, Emily D. Newbold, and Esther L. Newbold. The papers of the Newbold women include incoming letters, financial, legal and estate papers, and miscellaneous items.

There is also correspondence, 1910–1952, of August Gross, caretaker of Brokenstraw.

Gift of Mrs. Caryl Roberts and John L. Welsh, Jr.

The Irvine Story / by Nicholas B. Wainwright. Philadelphia: Historical Society of Pennsylvania, 1964.

1891
Kneass family.   Correspondence, 1835–1878.   (ca. 600 items.)

The Kneass family members include: Samuel Honeyman Kneass, a Pennsylvania engineer involved with the railroads; his son William Harris Kneass, a civil engineer; William's wife, Amelia Stryker Kneass (also known as Pettie), who died in Vevey, Switzerland; their son Samuel Stryker Kneass, a Philadelphia physician who graduated from the University of Pennsylvania; and William's uncle, Strickland Kneass, chief engineer and surveyor for the city of Philadelphia.

The first section includes: Samuel H. Kneass' business correspondence on his work on the Delaware-Schuylkill Canal, 1835–1839, and his appointment as principal city surveyor, 1849–1853; Miscellaneous correspondence on financial matters resulting from his career as an engineer, 1836–1857; annual reports to the North Western Railroad and the Delaware-Schuylkill Canal Company, 1839–1856; essays, speeches, his will, and various legal documents; as well as a miscellany of printed specifications, an architectural drawing, and stock shares, 1837–1860.

The second section of the collection consists of the private correspondence of William Harris Kneass and his immediate family including: letters from William to his son Samuel, after Amelia separated from him, telling Samuel to remember his father fondly, 1871–1876; letters from William to Amelia before they were married, 1862–1863, and after they were estranged, 1873–1876. There are also other family papers including: several letters, 1876–1877, from Samuel to his mother, while he was in school in Europe, and some of his school compositions; letters from Strickland Kneass to his niece-by-marriage Amelia, 1868–1876, revealing efforts to reconcile Amelia and William; bill from Strickland for a sewer survey, 1870, while he was chief engineer and surveyor for Philadelphia. Several volumes complete the collection: essays by William, 1856–1857, Amelia's book of poetry and her domestic accounts, 1873–1878, miscellaneous bills and receipts, stock shares, and advertisements.

There is also a seemingly unrelated collection of papers of the Steele family consisting of a brief family genealogy, financial records, and a letter dated 1825 from Eugene describing the railroads in England.

Gift of Mrs. Dudley Kneass, 1979.

Finding aid available.

1892
Faught, Albert Smith, 1883–1965.   Papers, (1907–1916) (1934–1961). (275 items.)

The papers of Albert Smith Faught, Philadelphia lawyer, on Pennsylvania politics include: letters, 1907, reflecting the efforts to organize support for presidential candidate William Howard Taft and John O. Sheatz for state treasurer; correspondence, 1910, on the Pennsylvania gubernatorial election; papers, 1912–1913, of the Pennsylvania Electoral College of 1912, and on the formation of an Electoral College Association comprised of its members; papers, 1916, on the attempt of the members of the Pennsylvania Electoral College of 1912 to organize in support of Charles Evans Hughes as the Progressive candidate for president; records and correspondence, 1934–1944, of the Philadelphia Committee on Public Affairs; miscellaneous records and correspondence, 1943–1961, on city policy, and the Philadelphia mayoral election of 1943.

Gift of Albert Smith Faught, 1963.

1893
Belfield, Percy C.   Papers, 1917–1947.   (1,800 items.)

Papers of Percy C. Belfield include: bills, receipts, and correspondence on the operation of his farm in Swarthmore, including items on house repairs, alterations, and care for the grounds. There are also some personal financial records of Belfield, a Philadelphia teacher.

Gift, 1964.

1894
No entry.

1895
West End Free Library.　　Records, 1912–1937.　　(300 items.)

The West End Free Library of Chester, chartered in 1907, later became a branch of the J. Lewis Crozier Library.

Librarians' records of the West End Free Library include: correspondence; annual reports, 1914, 1930–1937; bills and receipts; book orders; and bibliographies.

Gift, 1964.

1896
Willits, Edith W. Bullock.　　Papers, 1812–1863.　　(150 items.)

Incoming letters on personal and family matters and some correspondence and papers of other family members.

Gift of Mrs. James Emack, 1963.

1897
Cruice, Robert Blake, d. 1899.　　Papers, 1853–1899.　　(300 items.)

Robert Blake Cruice was a surgeon, secretary of the Board of Managers, and president of St. Joseph's Hospital.

Most of the papers relate to estates for which Cruice was appointed executor and under whose care the testators died. Several of the wills, which often included bequests to the hospital, were contested. There is also correspondence, 1888–1899, with his attorney, Theodore Finley Jenkins, an account book, 1887–1897, and correspondence on family property in Glenamaddy, County Ballinasloe, Ireland.

Gift of Dr. W.B. McDaniel, 1964.

1898
Jessup family.　　Records, 1814–1896.　　(175 v.)

Records of the Jessup family include primarily: journals, ledgers, and memoranda books on the legal practice of William Jessup and his son William Hunting Jessup of Montrose. In addition to the Jessup firm records, there are account books of several of the clients including: Drinker estate,

James C. Biddle and Henry Drinker, executors, 1834–1865; Charles Fraser, M.D., 1825–1838; Arthur King Harroun, D.D.S., 1884–1888; George C. Pride, general merchant of Haverford, 1848–1857; Joseph Richards, lawyer, 1835–1854; and Robert H. Rose estate, 1836–1858. As agriculturists and trustees of large tracts of land in Susquehanna County, several of their records concern lumbering and farming, including William H. Jessup's diary of farm work, 1871–1896.

Finding aid available.

Purchased, 1961.

1899

Lippincott family.   Papers, 1814–1950.   (ca. 2000 items.)

Primarily the personal papers of several related Philadelphia families, including correspondence, financial records, estate records, diaries, photographs, and much miscellanea. The earliest papers, 1814–1858, are by members of the Shaw, Craige, and Lippincott families, and include: correspondence; miscellaneous receipts; Sarah Lippincott's receipt book, 1826–1858; and the diary, 1839–1840 of Josephine Craige who in 1845 married J.B. Lippincott, the founder of the publishing house.

The Sigmund H. Horstmann papers include a few personal letters, 1869–1870; and miscellaneous business records, 1851–1864, of Horstmann Brothers and Company, importers and manufacturers of military uniforms, insignias, and flags. His wife, Elizabeth West Horstmann, is represented by account books of household expenses, 1864; servant's wages, 1856–1896; travel expenses in Europe, 1869–1870; and two miscellaneous volumes. Also included are the European diaries, 1869–1870, 1873, of her daughters Sarah and Elizabeth Horstmann.

The bulk of the collection is made up of the personal papers, 1860–1927, of Walter Lippincott, son of J.B. Lippincott and husband of Elizabeth Horstman. It contains: incoming correspondence; accounts; bills and receipts; contracts; real estate records; tax records; household accounts; inventories; instructions to servants; photo albums; Lippincott's diary, 1892–1919, with brief notations on routine activities; transcript of Lippincott's interview with Admiral George Dewey on the problems of the German fleet at the battle of Manila Bay; school records and reports; and other miscellanea.

Elizabeth Horstmann is represented by incoming letters, account book, 1884–1919, scrapbooks, school papers, and miscellanea.

The papers, 1906–1950, of Bertha Horstman Lippincott Coles, the only child of Walter and Elizabeth Lippincott, include a few letters, some regarding her published writings; financial records on the large estate inherited from her parents and other properties; a diary, 1906–1907; papers on her work with the U.S. Service Club; and the manuscript of her book, *Wound Stripes,* (1921.)

Gift of Mrs. Coles Langhorne, 1964.

1900A
Vauclain, Samuel Matthews, 1856–1940.   **Papers, 1905–1931.**
(6 linear ft.)

Vauclain was the president of the Baldwin Locomotive Works.

The material reports on production and sales and is inconsistent in subject and chronology: advertising department memoranda, 1920; cabinet meeting minutes, 1923–1924; comptroller's reports, 1920–1921, 1924, 1928; domestic sales department reports, 1919–1920, 1924; drawing room reports and memoranda, 1920–1921, 1923–1924; foreign sales department coded telegrams from Europe, 1923; personnel records, 1919–1920; general superintendent reports, 1923–1926; and vice-president in charge of manufacture memoranda, 1919. There is also correspondence, 1905, on locomotives for the Atchinson, Topeka, and Santa Fe Railway; scrapbook with miscellaneous correspondence and newspaper clippings on Baldwin Locomotive's war work; photographs of the Baldwin Locomotive Works and of Vauclain as chairman of the Philadelphia Gas Works Commission; letters, 1909, from Vauclain's family while they travelled in Europe; and family photographs.

Purchased, 1965.

Finding aid available.

1900B
Vauclain, Samuel Matthews, 1856–1940.   **Papers, 1915–1930.**
(3 linear ft.)

Papers of Samuel Matthews Vauclain as a member of the Delaware River Bridge Joint Commission on the planning, construction, and operation of the bridge, now named the Benjamin Franklin Bridge. They include: correspondence, much of which is with Ralph Modjeski, chief engineer; minutes of the Joint Commission Executive Committee; financial reports; blueprints and maps; photographs; scrapbooks. There are also 6 blueprints of the Remington Arms Company plant built by The Baldwin Locomotive Works in 1915 under Vauclain's direction.

Gift of Samuel Matthews Vauclain, III, 1964.

1901
McCarty and Davis.   Account books, 1816–1851.   (37 v.)

Account books, 1816–1844, of McCarty and Davis, Philadelphia booksellers and printers, covering the period of the partnership: daybooks, ledgers, receipt books, bank books, and notes receivable. Also small notebooks of Thomas Davis's family expenses, 1839–1851.

Purchased, 1964.

1902

Lee, George F., d. 1893.   Papers, 1820–1893.   (ca. 3,000 items.)

George F. Lee worked for his father's bricklaying business in Philadelphia and then started his own business as contractor and engineer for the construction of gas works. After Lee lost interest in this business, he concerned himself principally with real estate investments.

There are Franklin Lee and Sons account books, 1820–1844. The majority of the papers, 1844–1853, include business correspondence and accounts and personal receipted bills. They relate to the building of plants in Albany, Troy, and Utica, N.Y., St. Louis, Mo., and Chicago, Ill. The remainder of the correspondence concerns the management of mortgages he held and his own properties, particularly in Chicago, where his interests were much affected by the fire of 1871, and in Troy. Correspondents include James K. Burtis, superintendent of the St. Louis and Chicago gas works and also Lee's personal agent in Chicago, Burtis' successor Junius Mulvey, and Lee's agent in Troy S.S. Dauchy.

Gift of Harry E. Sprogell, 1964.

1903

Jayne, Horace H.F.   Collection, 1849–1897.   (275 items.)

Letters, 1849–1882, of Kate Rodgers of Philadelphia mainly to members of her family in regard to personal and family matters; letters, 1862–1863 from her husband Horace Rodgers, an agent for the United States Sanitary Commission, a few of which were written from the scene of Civil War battles in Maryland and Virginia; and a few papers, 1884–1897, of the Henry Seybert Commission appointed by the University of Pennsylvania to investigate spiritualism, including correspondence, financial records, and news clippings, some of which pertain to the Preliminary Report of the Seybert Commission for Investigating Modern Spiritualism, 1887.

Gift of Horace H.F. Jayne, 1963.

1904

Vetterlein, Theodore H.   Papers, 1868–1886.
(200 items and 9 v.)

Papers of two Philadelphia cigar manufacturers and dealers in tobacco: Theodore H. Vetterlein incoming business and family correspondence,

1868–1886; Julius Vetterlein and Company letterpress books, 1869–1885; and Henry E. Klein and Company letterpress book, [1876–1877].
Purchased.

1905
Coates, Elmer Ruan, 1831–1889.   Papers, 1854–1889. (2.5 linear ft.)

Elmer Ruan Coates was a Philadelphia Quaker "literary journalist" and temperance advocate.

Manuscripts of poems, plays, lectures. A small amount of correspondence from newspaper and magazine editors, printers, and fellow-scribblers concerns personal and professional matters. Gift of Mrs. T.C. Kundy, 1964.

1906
Frankford Mutual Fire Insurance Company.   Records, 1843–1885. (ca. 1,100 items.)

Records of the Frankford Mutual Insurance Company, located in the Frankford district of Philadelphia. The majority of the records are property surveys of the company, 1843–1885, containing detailed descriptions of each building surveyed. Most of the buildings described are in the Frankford, Bridesburg, and Kensington sections of Philadelphia County. The remainder of the records include miscellaneous legal and financial records, and a cashbook, 1863–1877.

Purchased, 1962.

1907
Autocar Company.   Records, 1899–1954.   (11 v.)

The Autocar Company was located in Ardmore. Founded in 1899 by Louis S. Clarke and his brother John S. Clarke, the Autocar Company became a pioneer of the automotive industry, producing passenger cars and commercial motor vehicles. After 1910 the company produced commercial motor vehicles exclusively. The company became a division of White Motor Company in 1954.

The records include: minutes, 1899–1953, 1953–1954; annual reports, 1929–1952; ledgers, 1909–1952, contain year-end figures; list of officers and directors, 1899–1925; and miscellaneous items. Much of the material, 1942–1945, is on Autocar Company war production of heavy duty military vehicles.

Gift of C.R.C. Custer, 1964.

1908

Clearing House Association of Philadelphia.   **Records, 1858–1958.**
(ca. 2400 items.)

The Clearing House Association of Philadelphia was organized in 1858 to provide a common place where representatives of the associated banks could exchange checks and settle balances.

The records include: correspondence, 1858–1958, primarily with the member Philadelphia banks; financial reports, 1885–1909, on gold certificates, U.S. legal tender certificates, collateral securities, and gold coin held by the Clearing House for member banks; semi-annual statements, 1858–1939, of expenditures and expenses; journals, 1887–1957; cashbooks, 1858–1940; ledger, 1890–1895; account books, 1949–1958; records on other clearing houses in the United States, 1914, 1929–1957, including correspondence, reports, and miscellaneous items; Keystone National Bank liquidation records, including journals, 1890–1891, correspondence and miscellaneous financial records, 1891–1930; Union Bank and Trust Company liquidation records, 1929–1934; examiner's report on the Kensington Security Bank and Trust Company, 1931; claims of members against other banks, 1931; and settlement sheets, 1930–1931.

There are also a few records on bank mergers in Philadelphia; the clearing of ration checks, 1943–1946; miscellaneous scrapbooks; National Currency Association of Philadelphia minutes, 1908–1914; and other records.

Gift of Charles R. Whittlesey, 1964.

1909

Burd-Shippen-Hubley papers.

Entry cancelled; see collection #595B

1910

Acton, Edward A., 1829–1862.   **Letters, 1861–1862.**   **(41 items.)**

Letters of Edward A. Acton, officer with the 4th Regiment, New Jersey Volunteers, and the 5th Regiment, New Jersey Volunteers, primarily to his wife Mary Woodnut Acton. The letters, 1861–1862, include detailed accounts of Acton's participation in the Peninsular campaign to capture Richmond, Va., 1862. There are four letters regarding Acton's death at the 2nd Battle of Bull Run, August 29, 1862.

Gift of Mary Acton Hammond, 1965.

1911
Speckman, Charles H.   Papers, 1898–1899.   (30 items.)

Charles H. Speckman served as Captain of Company A, Second Regiment, Pennsylvania Volunteers which guarded to Dupont powder works at Carney's Point, N.J., during the Spanish-American War.

His papers include: daily memoranda book, muster rolls, payrolls, clothing and material issues, and inventories.

1912
Ashhurst family.   Account books, 1796–1890.   (6 v.)

Personal and business account books collected by the Ashhurst family of Philadelphia include: Manuel Eyre, shipping merchant, ledgers, 1796–1798, 1801–1845; Richard Ashhurst, merchant, ledger, 1813–1817; Richard Ashhurst & Sons, merchants, journal, 1839–1848; John Ashhurst investment ledger, 1864–1867, and general ledger, 1864, 1880–1890, 1892.

Gift of John Ashhurst Richards, 1965.

1913
Orphan Society of Philadelphia.   Records, 1815–1963.
(6 linear ft.)

Records of the Orphan Society of Philadelphia, a privately supported orphanage established in 1815 by a group of Philadelphia women, include: incoming correspondence, 1815, 1900–1920, 1949; minutes, 1814–1938, 1938–1956 unbound; reports of the visiting committees on living conditions at the orphanage, 1819–1924; registers of children admitted, 1815–1955; records of children indentured by the society, including registers, 1815–1867; account books, 1878, 1920–1963; and miscellaneous items and volumes.

Gift of Orphan Society of Philadelphia, 1965.

1914
Wistar, Caleb Cresson, 1846–1916.   Papers, 1861–1916.
(31 v. and 200 items.)

Personal papers of Caleb Cresson Wistar, wholesale oil dealer of Philadelphia, include: outgoing family correspondence and incoming family and personal correspondence, 1861–1874; diaries, 1861–1864, kept while a student at Haverford College, Haverford; student notebook, 1864; notebooks of songs, 1862–1863; personal memoranda and account books, 1864–1875; personal cashbooks, 1886–1916; notebook on the wool and insurance industries, 1867–1869; commonplace book, 1870; address book; photographs; student notebooks of his children, Elizabeth Vaux Wistar and Frederick Vaux Wistar; and a personal account book of Frederick Vaux Wistar, 1907–1910.

There is also a receipt book for the estate of Benjamin Hooton, 1792–1799; a Joseph Cresson personal receipt book, 1801–1852; and two Charles Caleb Cresson letterbooks, 1898–1902.

Purchased, 1956, 1966.

1915
Pennsylvania Seamen's Friend Society (Philadelphia, Pa.)
Papers, 1844–1903.   (450 items.)

The Pennsylvania Seamen's Friend Society was incorporated 1846 to promote "social and moral improvement" of sailors. The society has been affiliated with the Seamen's Church Institute since 1920. The Society maintained the Sailors' Home until 1930 where seamen could receive lodging, financial aid, and spiritual guidance. Much of the reform efforts centered on temperance.

These papers concern primarily the Sailors' Home. Included here are the superintendent's reports on activities at the home, receipted bills and financial statements, correspondence relating to fund raising activities in churches throughout the state, and scrapbooks.

Purchased, 1965.

1916
Port of Philadelphia.   Bills of lading, 1866–1869.   (1,050 items.)

A collection of bills of lading and manifest prepared for the collection, Port of Philadelphia, listing importers, goods, vessel, and point of origin.

Gift of Dunn and Bradsheet, 1965.

1917
Grahame, Israel J.   Records, 1848–1897.   (19 v.)

Journals, ledgers, cashbooks, receipt book, stock book, and prescription memoranda, all in varying broken series, of Israel J. Grahame, Philadelphia druggist. Although Grahame apparently did not open his Philadelphia store until 1868, there are some early accounts that include a dry goods business ledger, 1857–1866, and an unidentified cashbook, 1848–1861.

Gift of Mr. and Mrs. E. Perot Walker, 1965.

1918
Brown, Coleman Peace, 1882–1964.   **Papers, 1885–1957.**
(9 linear ft.)

Coleman Peace Brown was headmaster, 1909–1915, of the Delancey School, Philadelphia. The boys preparatory school was founded in 1877 by Brown's father. It merged with the Blight School in 1911 and was absorbed into the Episcopal Academy in 1915.

Included are: Delancey School registers of teachers and students, 1893–1905; teachers record books, ca. 1899–1914; *The Delancey Weekly,* 1901–1907, the school's newspaper; school catalogues, 1887–1914; correspondence, 1911–1957, mainly from alumni to Brown concerning the Episcopal Academy merger and a 1956 alumni dinner; and miscellanea. There are many photographs of the school.

A small portion of the collection is made up of miscellaneous personal papers of Coleman P. Brown, including incoming correspondence, 1923–1957; photographs; and genealogical data on the Brown and related families.

Gift of Mrs. Coleman Peace Brown, 1965.

1919
Allen, William Frederick, 1846–1915.   **Papers, 1860–1865.**
(62 items.)

Correspondence received during the Civil War by William Frederick Allen of Bordentown, N.J., who later became a civil engineer instrumental in the adoption of standard times for railways in the United States. Allen was 14 years old when the Civil War began and the correspondence is mainly from young friends who had grown up with him, and mainly on the Virginia campaign of the war, 1861–1865, by Amos H. Evans, 9th Regiment, New Jersey Volunteers, and John W. Mitchell, 12 Regiment, New Jersey Volunteers. There are also four early letters, 1861, from Richard Watson Gilder, editor and poet.

Purchased, 1965.

1920
Philadelphia Time Telegraph Company.   **Records, 1877–1884.**
(350 items.)

The Philadelphia Time Telegraph Company furnished electric clocks for offices that registered standard time as telegraphed from Washington, D.C.

The records include: letterpress book, 1877–1879; bills and receipts, 1885–1889; account books, 1887–1892, and stock certificates, 1886; and miscellaneous records.

Gift of David Wallace, 1965.

1921
Kelley, William D. (William Darrah), 1814–1890.
Correspondence, 1837–1903.   (600 items.)

William Darrah Kelley was an influential Republican congressman from the 4th district (Philadelphia) of Pennsylvania. He was a leading congressional advocate of high tariffs, especially for iron and steel.

Incoming political correspondence, 1852, 1862–1889, includes letters from many of the major and minor political and business figures of the period. Many of the letters relate to the tariff question. Most of the correspondents are represented by only 1 letter each, but James M. Swank and Joseph Wharton of the American Iron and Steel Association are represented by 25 letters, 1882–1883, on tariff duties.

Family correspondence, 1837–1903, includes letters from William D. Kelley to his wife, Caroline Bonsall Kelley, and to his children; letters from Caroline Bonsall Kelley to William Darrah Kelley; and a few letters from Albert Bartram Kelley to his mother Caroline Bonsall Kelley.

Purchased, 1966.

1922
Faires family.   Papers, 1849–1901.   (100 items.)

A few papers of the Faires family of Philadelphia, including miscellaneous school papers and records of William John Faires, Bessie Dobbin Faires, and James Dobbin Faires; and 21 letters, 1849–1850, of Thomas Smith, a trader on the Mississippi River and great grandfather of James Dobbin Faires, to his wife, Elizabeth McLaughlin Smith.

Gift of James Dobbin Faires, 1966.

1923
Fisher, Sarah Logan, 1751–1796.   Diaries, 1776–1795.   (25 v.)

The diaries of Sarah Logan Fisher, wife of Thomas Fisher, Philadelphia Quaker merchant, detail domestic and family concerns of a well-educated Quakeress. There is some account of the Fisher family's passive resistance to the Revolutionary government, and a single volume of religious meditations.

Deposited by Benjamin R. Cadwalader, 1965.
Extracts published in *P.M.H.B.*, 82 (1958).

1924
Day, Anna Blanchard Blakiston, 1868–1952.   Papers, 1905–1961.
(6 linear ft.)

Anna Blanchard Blakiston Day, a supporter of reform politics, served as an officer in several Philadelphia women's organizations involved in local and national civic affairs.

Represented in Day's papers are: Women's Committee of the City Party, executive committee minutes, 1905–1907; its successor organization, the Women's League for Good Government scrapbook, 1913–1914, executive committee minutes, 1915–1918, and correspondence, 1920–1921; Franklin Party, George W. Porter for mayor scrapbook, 1915; Monday Conference membership lists, with some correspondence, particularly the correspondence of Martha Thomas, chairperson of the program committee for the 1928 Conference in Philadelphia and other material, 1917–1929; Committee on the Cause and Cure of War correspondence, clippings, and pamphlets, 1928–1938.

The majority of the papers, correspondence, bills and receipts, deeds, and mortgages concern the finances, particularly for property of Mrs. Day, her estate, and the estates of other Blakiston family members. There are Anna Blanchard, Harriet Blanchard, Maria Blanchard and unidentified diaries, 1861–1899, of travel in Europe and southern and western United States. There are also invitations, 1905–1909 addressed to Mrs. Day and her husband Frank Miles Day.

Gift of Mrs. James Hays, 1966.

1925
Hale, John Mulhallan.   Papers, 1837–1864.   (ca. 1,400 items.)

John Mulhallan Hale was a merchant, supplier, druggist, and insurance executive of Centre County and later Philadelphia. During the Civil War Hale served as Union captain in the Quartermaster Corp at Nashville.

Business papers, 1837–1860, make up one-third of the collection and relate to Hale's wide-ranging business interests and speculations in central Pennsylvania, including incoming correspondence, bills, receipts, and miscellaneous financial records.

The papers of the Nashville department of the Quartermaster Corp, 1861–1864, make up the rest of the collection, including incoming correspondence, invoices, receipts, reports, requisitions, vouchers, and financial reports.

Gift of John F. Steinman, 1966.

1926

Rayes, Mrs. Mario.   Collection, 1857–1920.   (60 items.)

A few miscellaneous items of the Calvert, Baltzell, Elliott, Miller,and Nevins families of Baltimore, Md., and Philadelphia and a few poems and other items by Harvey Maitland Watts, journalist, poet, and lecturer.

Gift of Mrs. Mario Rayes, 1939.

1927

Roset family.   Papers, (1794–1857) 1897.   (80 items.)

Papers of the Roset family of Germantown, including correspondence and miscellanea of Jacob Roset, Jr., dry goods merchant, and his wife, Cecilia Luff Roset.

Gift of John H. Ferguson, 1964.

1928

Hand family.   Papers, 1823–1866.   (78 items.)

Papers of the Hand family of Cape May, N.J., and Philadelphia, including letters, 1823–1824, written between Captain Noah Hand and his wife, Cornelia Foster Hand of Cape May; and incoming and outgoing family correspondence, 1833–1866, of Jacob Foster Hand, hardware merchant of Philadelphia. The Jacob Foster Hand correspondence contains letters, 1862–1863, from his nephew Israel K. Barnes, a few of which relate to his service with the Army of the Potomac.

Gift of Helen Hand, 1966.

1929

Corson, Edward F., 1833–1864.   Papers, 1859–1864.   (100 items.)

Edward F. Corson, commissioned as assistant surgeon in the Navy, served on the U.S.S. *Hartford* in the East India Squadron, 1859–1861. The *Hartford* cruised in and out of Hong Kong, Shanghai, Manilla, and other Far East ports. Corson was promoted to surgeon in 1862 and assigned to the U.S.S. *Mohican* which had a roving commission to capture confederate privateers. Although the *Mohican* did not see much action, Corson had ample opportunity to visit Brazilian ports, including Porto Grande, Bahia, and Rio de Janeiro.

These papers consist almost entirely of Corson's letters to his family describing the people, places, and events, on and off shore, during these two tours of duty.

Gift of Edward F. Corson, 1965.

1930
Fahnestock family.   Papers, 1726–1879.   (300 items.)

Papers of the Fahnestock family include: 6 letters in German with translations, 1726–1765, by Johan Dietrich Fahnestuck of Ephrata, to relatives in Germany describing conditions in America; copies of letters, 1860–1861, by Benjamin A. Fahnestock and his wife, Anna Maria Wolff Fahnestock of Philadelphia, written while on a European trip; and miscellaneous correspondence and other papers including acknowledgements to George W. Fahnestock for his book *Wolff Memorial*, 1863, and depositions concerning the 1868 Ohio River steamship collision which killed George W. Fahnestock and his daughter.

Six letters in German.

Gift of Roy W. Wolff, 1966.

1931
Allen, Samuel.   Papers, 1798–1841.   (100 items.)

In 1825, Samuel Allen went to Chester County, to settle his father's estate leaving his family in Slippery Rock for five years to fend for themselves and to cope with the debts left behind.

Correspondence with his wife Margaret and children. There are also deeds, depositions, wills, and a small group of broadsides.

Purchased, 1966.

1932
Harley, Herbert.   Scrapbooks, 195-   (25 items.)

The scrapbooks, 1950's, of Herbert Harley were compiled on Philadelphia and other topics of personal interests. His subjects include: Chalkley House, Lubin Film Studios, Peter Becker and the Church of the Brethern, and General Herbert Harley ("Hap") Arnold, World War II Chief of Army Air Force. The scrapbooks contain clippings and extracts from primary and secondary sources, and Harley's own compositions.

Gift of Herbert Harley, 1966.

1933
Wells, Samuel Calvin, 1849–1932.   Correspondence, 1869 (1890–1924).   (200 items.)

Samuel Calvin Wells worked for the *Philadelphia Press* from 1881 until its demise in 1920 and was editor-in-chief from 1908 to 1918.

His correspondence consists of some letters from fellow editors and journalists, Princeton 1873 classmates and family, but primarily of letters from individuals commenting on, or submitting background material for *Press* editorials. There are letters, 1891–1902, from Michael Arnold, president judge of the Court of Common Pleas, Philadelphia, on court issues, and Nicholas Murray Butler letters, 1912–1922, to Wells as member of the Advisory Board of the School of Journalism at Columbia, involving the Pulitzer Prize awards.

Purchased, 1965.

1934A
Drinker family.   Papers, 1722–1889.   (600 items.)

Papers of several generations of a Philadelphia Quaker merchant family including: family correspondence, primarily between Henry and Elizabeth Sandwith Drinker, diarist; letters, deeds, and surveys concerning Drinker family lands; William Drinker's accounts and papers on the estate of Mary Sandwith, his aunt and sister of Elizabeth; wills, marriage certificates, and other family material.

Papers relating to the business and domestic affairs of the Drinkers from 1722 to 1850, with strength in the pre-Revolutionary period. Included is the original copy of the memorial of the Virginia Exiles, dated December 2, 1777, to the President and Council of Pennsylvania, signed by all the Exiles including Thomas Affleck. There is also a 1790 letter of George Washington.

Some of the manuscripts were removed from the volumes (presumably by the family) before coming to the Historical Society, most notably about 50 letters of Henry Drinker to Elizabeth Drinker during the Quaker exile.

Gift of the Drinker family through Ernesta Drinker Ballard, 1968.

1934B
Drinker family.   Papers, 1777–1965.   (3 linear ft.)

Henry Sturgis Drinker graduated from Lehigh University in 1871 as a mining engineer, but soon turned to law. He was an attorney, general solicitor, and assistant to the president for the Lehigh Valley Railroad until his 1905 election to president of Lehigh University where he served until 1920. Drinker was a founder of the American Institute of Mining and Metallurgical Engineers, an organizer and promoter of the Military Training Camps before, through, and after World War I, a conservationist, and an appointee to various state advisory boards.

Dr. Drinker's son, Henry Sandwith Drinker, was a Philadelphia lawyer, becoming a senior partner of Drinker, Biddle & Reath in 1932. Drinker was an avid amateur musician; he hosted monthly choral music parties, translated classical music texts, and established the Drinker Library of Choral Music.

The papers of Henry Sturgis Drinker are mostly scrapbooks containing clippings and letters from political, military, and educational figures. Much of the material centers on the Lehigh University appointment and retirement, but his other interests are also represented. Of special note are some small groups of correspondence with Theodore Roosevelt on military preparedness, 1915–1917, and with William Howard Taft on fortification and administration of the Panama Canal, 1910–1912.

For Henry Sandwith Drinker there is a First Troop Philadelphia City Cavalry diary, 1909–1910, and a diary, 1930, of a trip with his son to British Columbia on a bird-watching and hunting expedition. He was a frequent author of articles on law and other subjects of personal interest, and among the papers are typescripts of articles on Anthony Trollope and a history of his law firm. Drinker's musical interests and activities are represented by some miscellaneous articles, speeches, clippings, and other materials.

Sophie Lewis Hutchinson, wife of Henry Sandwith Drinker, wrote a history of her and her husband's lives. In it she relied on Henry's own records to describe his private and professional life. In recounting her own activities she told of her family life, her increasing involvement in public affairs and literary pursuits, and her growing interest in feminism.

A preliminary typescript for *History of the Drinker Family* is supplemented by additional family material used in its preparation: typescripts of Henry Drinker and Elizabeth Sandwith Drinker correspondence, 1777, during the Quaker exile; contemporary copies of Sandwith Drinker letters, 1838–1840, while on his voyage to Canton; an anonymous diary, 1856–1857, of an American in China and Manilla; and family photographs.

Gift of Catherine Drinker Bowen, 1971.

1934C
Drinker family.   Papers, 1759–1956.   (30 items.)

This miscellaneous group of papers includes: Henry Sturgis Drinker clippings and tributes; Henry Sandwith Drinker notes from research on music and attendance record, 1932–1956, for his choral music parties; family genealogical notes.

Gift of Sophie H. Drinker.

1935
Markoe family.   Papers, 1773–1940.   (700 items.)

Abraham Markoe of St. Croix was a wealthy planter and merchant who moved to Philadelphia ca. 1770. He left his son, Abraham Markoe, Jr., behind to manage the sugar plantations. Abraham Markoe's papers contain letters, 1773–1803 from Abraham Markoe, Jr., on the operation of the plantations; a few letters from his son Peter Markoe, poet and dramatist; and a few letters, 1805–1809, of Abraham Markoe, Jr., to his brother John Markoe.

Other items of special note include a letterbook, 1810–1812, of Daniel Holsman of New York, supercargo and half-owner of the ship *Maria,* on the French confiscation of the ship and its cargo and on efforts to recover the vessel; Civil War papers, 1861–1863, 1895, of John Markoe, an officer with the 71st California Regiment, Pennsylvania Volunteers, containing outgoing family correspondence and incoming official correspondence and documents on his service in Virginia, his imprisonment at Richmond, 1861–1862, and his role at the battle of Fredricksburg, and a report, 1902, by Gerald Holsman, son of Mary Markoe Holsman, civil engineer and vice-president of the Investment Company of Philadelphia, on the building of the Guayaquil and Quito Railway in Ecuador.

The remainder of the papers include: James Markoe diary, ca. 1825, on travel in Italy; estate papers of several members of the Markoe and Holsman families; miscellaneous property papers; photographs; and other miscellanea.

Gift of Mary Dewitt Pettit, 1966.

1936
Whitcomb, Louis F.   Sesquicentennial papers, 1904 (1926–1927).
(200 items.)

Departmental orders, final reports, concessions contracts, ticket and pass samples; general orders, accounting systems memorandum, reports from previous expositions; and printed material, chiefly advertisements and promotions of products and places.

Gift of Mrs. L.M. Whitcomb, 1967.

1937
Belmont Driving Club.   Dissolution records, 1925–1926.
(200 items.)

Records of D. Yeakel Miller, auditor, on the dissolution of the Belmont Driving Club, Montgomery County, includes files of correspondence, with stockholders and court transcripts of claims made against the club.

Purchased, 1967.

1938
Gulager family.   Papers, (1813–1889) 1949.   (300 items.)

Papers of the Gulager family, including miscellaneous correspondence, 1821–1889, financial and legal records, and miscellanea. Among the financial records are a personal receipt book, 1813–1835, of Mary Malyar Gulager of Philadelphia, wife of Christian Gulager, artist; account books, 1831–1863 of Christian Gulager, Jr., sea Captain of Philadelphia, mainly on shipping; and personal receipt book, 1855–1882, of William Gulager. There are also personal and business accounts of John Christopher, a lumber merchant of Philadelphia and of his wife, Martha Christopher: receipt books, 1826–1833, 1848–1866; account book, 1840–1854.

Gift of Jan Kyle, 1966.

1939
Chambers family.   Papers, 1694–1963.   (24 v.and 300 items.)

The Chambers family of this collection first appeared as farmers of White Clay Creek, New Castle County, Del. In the latter half of the 19th-century, the locus moved to West Grove, Chester County, where four brothers engaged in the coal and lumber business.

These papers include: family letters, 1768, 1869–1927, 1957, with correspondents John J. Chambers, Rebecca Ballard Chambers, Samuel Kimble Chambers, and a multitude of family members all writing to each other and particularly to Mary J. Chambers; diaries, 1826–1857, of various members, most notably those of Mary Ballard Chambers while she was a student at Smith College, 1900–1904, and while being courted by her future husband, Philip Donald Folwell; financial papers, among which are Richard Chambers account books, 1796–1808, anonymous daybook, 1811–1824, and daybook, 1826–1854, of John Chambers; and estate papers of several members of the Chambers family.

Gift of Nathan Folwell and members of the Chambers family, 1967.

1940
League of Women Voters of Philadelphia.   Records, 1920–1961.
(ca. 3,000 items.)

In addition to educating the public during election campaigns, the League took stands on local issues concerning child care, city management, housing, public education, public health; national issues of the legal status of women and taxation of oleo margarine; and foreign policy questions including the United Nations and the Marshall Plan. The Philadelphia chapter communicated with the national and state League organizations, politicians, civic leaders, and organizations.

Correspondence, board minutes, budget and other committee reports, memoranda, circulars of League of Women Voters of Philadelphia. Most of the material is for the years 1941–1959, but the files are neither complete nor consistent.

Gift of the League of Women Voters of Philadelphia, per Mrs. Herbert Catheart, 1966.

1941

Dixon, Samuel Gibson, 1851–1918.   Papers, 1884 (1905–1918), 1953. (4.5 linear ft.)

Samuel Gibson Dixon was a physician, a scientist, and served as first commissioner of health for the state of Pennsylvania.

The bulk of the collection is made up of typescripts and printed copies of lectures, articles, and pamphlets on all the subjects that concerned Dixon from 1905 to 1918 including: public health, diseases, preventative medicine, hygiene, and sanitation. A small part of the collection is made up of incoming and some outgoing correspondence on public health issues such as sanitary and safety conditions of rural schools in Pennsylvania.

The remainder of the collection includes medical school notes, 1884; material on Dixon's pioneer research on immunity in tuberculosis; photographs; newspaper clippings; and miscellanea.

Gift of Mrs. John S. Sharpe, 1967.

1942

Philadelphia National Bank.   Records, 1804–1956. (30 linear ft.)

The Philadelphia Bank, organized in 1803, merged with several financial institutions to create the Philadelphia National Bank.

Minute books of the several banks represented make up the bulk of the collection and include board of directors' minutes, stockholder's minutes, executive committee minutes, Investment and credit committee minutes, loan and trust committee minutes, and other minutes.

Institutions represented by minute books are: Allegheny Realty Company, 1920–1955; Bristol Trust Company, 1907–1956; Cambridge Trust Company/Chester-Cambridge Bank and Trust Company, 1901–1954; Chester National Bank, 1883–1930; Commercial National Bank, 1857–1900; Fairhill State Bank/Fairhill Trust Company, 1921–1929; Farmers and Mechanics National Bank, 1807–1939; First National Bank of Conshohocken, 1872–1929; Fourth Street National Bank, 1886–1926; Franklin Fourth Street National Bank, 1926–1928; Franklin National Bank, 1900–1928; Franklin Securities Corporation, 1919–1924; Girard National Bank, 1864–1927; Independence National Bank, 1883–1901; Mechanics National Bank, 1810–1900; The Ninth Bank and Trust Company, 1923–1951; The Ninth National Bank, 1885–1923; The Ninth Title and Trust Company, 1920–1923; Northern National Bank, 1928–1929; Philadelphia National Bank, 1803–1868; Philadelphia-Girard National Bank, 1926–1928; and The Philadelphia National Company, 1929–1934.

Other record books include: Cambridge Trust Company/Chester-Cambridge Bank and Trust Company recommendations, reports, and financial statements, 1903–1954; Mechanics National Bank letterbook, 1824–1846; and Ninth Bank and Trust Company signature books, ca. 1885–1915.

Gift of the Philadelphia National Bank, 1966, 1967, and 1978.

1943
Philobiblon Club.   Archives, 1893- op2(ca. 1000 items.)

The Philobiblon Club, Philadelphia, was founded and incorporated in 1893 as a men's association of bibliophiles; it began admitting women in 1974.

The records relate to the arrangement of meetings, membership, and production and distribution of the club's publications. Included are: correspondence, bank statements, membership lists, program announcements, and other records.

Deposited by the Philobiblon Club, 1967.

1944
Philadelphia Bible-Christian Church.   Records, 1817–1929. (ca. 300 items.)

The Philadelphia Bible-Christian Church was a fundamentalist protestant church organized in Philadelphia ca. 1817 by emigrants from England, where they had been members of the Sanford Bible-Christian Church. The sect required its members to be strictly vegetarian and to abstain from alcoholic beverages.

Philadelphia Bible-Christian Church records include: record books, 1828–1919, containing minutes, financial records, addresses, correspondence, and reports; minutes, 1828–1929; registers, 1817–1929, recording the baptism of children, church attendance, deacon's meetings, membership, and interments; account books, 1865–1916; miscellaneous legal records, including marriage records and deeds for cemetery lots; and printed addresses, books, and pamphlets.

Many of the Bible-Christian Church associated themselves with the American Vegetarian Society, organized in 1850, and the church's records include some material on that organization.

Gift of Frances M. Schiebner, 1968.

1945
Lawyers' Club of Philadelphia.   Records, 1892–1960.   (6 v.)

The Lawyers' Club of Philadelphia, which was primarily a social club, was founded in 1892.

The minutes of the Board of Governors, 1892–1915, 1920–1957, and Club minutes, 1893–1911, concern receptions, smokers, and membership. There are also: treasurer's letterpress book, 1899–1906; notices of meetings, 1941–1960; and the club charter. Gift of Francis Shunk Brown, 1968.

1946
Pennsylvania Prison Society.   Records, 1787–1966.   (4 linear ft.)

The Philadelphia Society for Alleviating the Miseries of Public Prisons was organized in 1787 to promote penal reform. Its early members included: William White, Benjamin Rush, Roberts Vaux, Dorthea Lynde Dix, and Rose Steadman. In 1886 the Society's name was changed to its current name, the Pennsylvania Prison Society.

Minutes of the society, 1787–1832, 1852–1919, include its original constitution and discussion of news and legislation on the condition of prisons and prisoners. Topics include: prison administration; solitary confinement to hard labor (the Pennsylvania System); the establishment of the Western Penitentiary in Pittsburgh, authorized in 1818, the Eastern Penitentiary in Philadelphia, authorized in 1821, the House of Refuge, in 1828, a House of Correction, opened in 1874, an "industrial home," opened in 1889, and an asylum for insane criminals, opened in 1905; separation of men and women prisoners, of juveniles, and of the insane; and the parole system.

Minutes of the acting committee of the society, 1798–1966, contain reports of prison visits by members and by case workers; news of associated correctional facilities; the establishment of a half way house, and of a Narcotics Anonymous; gifts to the society; and other matters of concern and topics discussed at the general meetings.

Minutes, 1854–1885, of the Committee on the Eastern Penitentiary contain reports on the conditions of prisoners, including criminals, delinquents, and the insane; news from the library, which was maintained by the Society; and summaries from case-workers concerning discharged prisoners.

Copies of miscellaneous letters, 1816–1819, from Caleb Cresson, Jr., as secretary of the Society, and printed report, 1887, of the Society's 100th anniversary.

Gift of the Pennsylvania Prison Society, 1968.

1947
Brown, Abraham.   Papers, 1798–1848.   (200 items.)

Professional papers of Abraham Brown, a Mount Holly, N.J., lawyer and Burlington County surrogate, include: wills, deeds, leases, estate accounts, probate and other court records.

Gift of Mrs. William West Frazier, 1968.

1948
Bunting, Samuel J., 1889–1959.   Papers, 1719–1959.   (17 items.)

Miscellaneous papers of Samuel J. Bunting, Jr., Philadelphian active in the Society of Friends: *The Life of Jesus,* 1916, by Bunting is an analysis of Christ as depicted in the New Testament; Bunting's articles and diary entries, 1917, concern the Philadelphia Friends' response to World War I; 1920 journal of a trip to the London Conference of Friends records the voyage and travel through Great Britain; notes and drafts for a proposed *Life of William Penn* for young people. Also some family manuscripts: *Philadelphia Yearly Meeting Book of Discipline,* 1719; Samuel Bunting copybook, 1727; and Martha J. Gibson copybook of poems, 1839.
Gift of Mrs. J.G.M. Bunting, 1967.

1949
Predmore family.   Collection, 1699–1919.   (35 items.)

Deeds, 1701–1733, to land in Shrewsbury, N.J., and autographs of governors of New Jersey.
Gift of Fidelity Philadelphia Trust Company, n.d.

1950
Morris family.   Letters, 1862–1923.   (800 items.)

The three members of the Morris family represented in this correspondence are Thomas Burnside Morris, his wife, Sarah Arndt Sletor Morris, and their son Roland Sletor Morris. The letters of Thomas B. Morris include: 1861–1862, to his family from Panama, where Morris worked loading and unloading ships cargo; 1868–1869, to his family reporting on his work as an engineer with the Union Pacific Railroad from Green River to Promontory, Utah; 1870–1873, to his family and fiancee while an engineer in Ohio and with the Northern Pacific Railroad in Minn.; 1875–1885, to his mother and brother on family matters, from San Rafael, Cal., where he settled and became president of the Renton Coal Company.

Roland S. Morris maintained a faithful correspondence with his mother and his letters, 1884, 1890–1906, 1920, recount particularly activities as a student at Lawrenceville School, N.J., and as a freshman at Princeton University. After 1899 the correspondence is strictly of a family nature, with a few 1920 letters mentioning Morris's role as ambassador to Japan.

The remainder of the correspondence, 1909–1915, 1923, is from Sarah S. Morris to her son on family matters with some commentary on Roland's growing involvement in Democratic politics and the effects of war in Germany where Mrs. Morris lived from 1912 to 1915.
Gift of Mrs. William F. Machold, 1967.

1951
David H. Bowen and Son.   Records, 1839–1939.   (6 linear ft.)

David H. Bowen was a Philadelphia cabinetmaker until 1848. He then became an undertaker; his company was carried on by Clement R. and Charles H. Bowen.

Daybooks, 1839–1888, 1929–1939; funeral record books, 1888–1902; memorandum books, 1888–1923, giving vital statistics as well as funeral arrangement information; and auto wagon expense book, 1913–1922. A portion of one daybook, 1856, contains an unidentified "Ladies Lodge" dues ledger, 1846–1857; another daybook 1850–1852, includes some letterbook entries, 1843, of Abraham Levy as assistant to the purser, United States Navy Yard, Philadelphia. Also among the records is [William] Welsh and [Charles W.] Naulty, undertakers, daybook, 1878–1884.

Gift of David H. Bowen Company, Kindness of the Genealogical Society of Pennsylvania, 1968.

Daybooks and funeral records, 1845–1901, memorandum books, 1889–1899, and Ladies Lodge ledger available either on copyflow or transcription.

1952
Beelen family.   Papers, 1690–1959.   (ca. 60 items.)

Frederic Eugéne François Bertholff was the first Austrian representative in the United States. His descendants shortened the family name to Beelan.

The papers include correspondence, 1784–1885, some of which is in French; a Nuremburg, Germany almanac, 1690, with many contemporary annotations in German script; naturalization certificate and sketch book of Anthony Beelen, begun in 1794 in Pittsburgh, as well as several other miscellaneous notebooks in German, French, and Latin; a typescript biography of Milnora de Beelen Roberts of Seatle, Wash., as well as other family notes.

Some correspondence in French.

Almanac in German.

Gift of the Milnor Roberts Estate, 1959.

1953
Fels, Joseph, 1884–1914.   Papers, 1865 (1901–1930), 1956.
(ca. 1200 items.)

Joseph Fels, Philadelphia-London soap manufacturer, was a leader in the Single Tax movement. After his death in 1914, the Single Tax was carried on by the Joseph Fels Fund Commission.

Correspondence discussing economic and political reform in the United States, Europe, South American, and China, includes letters of Antonio Albenden, Earl Barnes, Gilbert Keith Chesterton, James Ludwig Hardie, Peter Kropotkin, William Hesketh Lever, Meyer Lissner, Wilhelm Ludwig Schrameier, and Samuel Fels, his brother and partner in Fels and Company, manufacturers of Fels-Naptha Soap. Copies of letters, 1899, 1906–1909, on the Fairhope Single Tax Colony in Alabama. Correspondence, 1906–1914, with Israel Zangwill, and others, on the establishment of Jewish Agricultural Settlements by the Jewish Territorial Organization (I.T.O.). Miscellaneous speeches and articles by and about Joseph Fels. There is also correspondence, 1915–1918, of Daniel Kiefer, the Chairman of the Joseph Fels Fund Commission.

Papers, 1907–1952, of Fels's wife, Mary Fels include: discussions of women's politics, Zionism, business, financial, and personal matters. Correspondents include: Rifka Aaronsohn, Newton Diehl Baker, Anna Barnes, Walter Coates, "Gypsy Bill" Cortez, and Frank Smith. Letters, reviews, and clippings about her writings including a typescript with notes of *The Life of Joseph Fels*. Scrapbooks with clippings about Joseph Fels, on his death, including *In Memorium*.

Guest book, 1906–1908, of Fels' home in Bickley, Kent.

Correspondence, 1953–1956, and notes, clippings, and printed material of Arthur Power Dudden, relating to his research for Joseph Fels and the single tax movement, 1971.

In Memorium in Danish and Swedish with English translations.

Gift of Arthur Power Dudden, 1968.

1954
Taylor, Fred Walter, 1848–1919.   Papers, 1888 (1905–1914), 1919. (200 items.)

Fred Walter Taylor was a steamship agent and broker of Philadelphia.

Incoming and outgoing correspondence and miscellanea on the improvement of the Delaware River ship channel, the development of Philadelphia port facilities, and the Delaware River Front Strike, 1913; and account books, 1889–1899, mainly on the shipping of coal.

Gift of Florence E. Taylor, 1967.

1955
Fisher, Samuel W.   Papers, 1762 (1783–1813), 1868.   (100 items.)

Samuel W. Fisher was a Pennsylvania state legislator and president of the Philadelphia Insurance Company.

Papers of the Fisher and Rhoads families of Philadelphia include: personal and family correspondence, 1783–1813, of Samuel W. Fisher mainly to

Benjamin Morgan, Jr., and from his wife Elizabeth and his mother-in-law Sarah Pemberton Rhoads; documents, 1800, on the investigation of the fracas between Fisher and George Logan on the floor of the Pennsylvania House of Representatives; Sarah P. Rhoads daybooks, 1796–1798, 1802–1803, commonplace books, and a reminiscence of her daughter Elizabeth Rhoads Fisher.

Gift of W.B. Shubrick Clymer, 1969.

1956
Ingersoll, Edward, 1817–1893.   Accounts, (1839–1860) 1890. (1,200 items.)

Personal and household bills and receipts, 1839–1860, of Edward Ingersoll, Philadelphia lawyer and legal writer, and his wife Anne Warren Ingersoll; and receipt book, 1862–1890, of the executors of the estate of Charles Jared Ingersoll, Edward's father.

Gift of Anna W. Ingersoll, 1970.

1957
Morris, Robert, 1734–1806.   Papers, 1756–1782.   (273 items.)

Robert Morris papers include incoming correspondence, 1776–1782 on Morris's private commercial connections, with some material on his public career as member of the Pennsylvania Council of Safety, Continental Congress, and Pennsylvania Assembly. Also included are miscellaneous business accounts.

Collected by Russel T. Levis; gift of Mrs. Russel T. Levis, 1968.

1958
Clark, Joseph Sill, 1901–1990.   Papers, 1947 (1956–1968.) (44 linear ft.)

Joseph Sill Clark was a Democratic reform politician from Philadelphia. Early in his career he served as campaign manager for Richardson Dilworth's mayoral campaign, 1947, and as Philadelphia city controller, 1950–1951. He served as mayor of Philadelphia, 1951–1956, and from 1957 to 1968 he was a United States senator from Pennsylvania.

This is a partial record of the career of Joseph Sill Clark. It consists primarily of material gathered by staff, reports, memoranda, clippings, news releases, articles, with some correspondence, all on issues and events with which Clark was involved.

A small portion of the papers are concerned with Clark's early activities as campaign manager for Richardson Dilworth's mayoral campaign, 1947, and as Philadelphia city controller, 1950–1951, for which there are campaign and office files. Clark's records as mayor of Philadelphia, 1951–1956, include campaign papers, some general office files, and transcripts of speeches.

The bulk of material covers Clark's years as United States senator from Pennsylvania, 1957–1968. There are papers for his three senatorial campaigns, 1956, 1962, and especially 1968. His Washington office general file reflects his interest in disarmament, the United Nations, Vietnam, and other matters before and after his appointment to the Senate Foreign Relations Committee in 1965. Although correspondence is scattered throughout the papers, there is a correspondence series, 1966–1968, and form letters used to answer constituents. Additional congressional files include press releases, speeches, newspaper clippings; bills sponsored and co-sponsored by Clark; Clark's voting record; television scripts and tapes, 1959–1967, principally of a program done with Pennsylvania Senator Hugh Scott; clippings from the *Congressional Record* referring to Clark.

Extra-senatorial activities for which there is material are the 1964 primary campaign of Genevieve Blatt (D.) for Senate, whom Clark supported, and the Pennsylvania State Planning Board, 1967–1968, of which Clark was a member.

Gift of Joseph S. Clark, 1968.

1959
**Greenfield, Albert M., 1887–1967.   Papers, 1921–1966.
(400 linear ft.)**

Albert M. Greenfield was a real estate broker, banker, and philanthropist of Philadelphia. He had many business interests among which were: Albert M. Greenfield & Co. (real estate), Bankers Securities Corporation, City Stores Co. (a chain of department stores), Bankers Bond & Mortgage Co., the Philadelphia Transportation Co., and its predecessor, the Philadelphia Rapid Transit Company.

Politically, Greenfield provided financial and other support to candidates for public office, including Edwin S. Vare of Philadelphia, Republican candidate for the United States Senate, 1926, and Lyndon B. Johnson, Democratic candidate for the presidency, 1960 and 1964; he was a delegate to the Republican National Convention, 1928; a delegate-at-large to the Democratic National Conventions, 1948–1964; and a presidential elector, 1960.

The large array of organizations in which Greenfield held prominent positions includes: Sesqui-Centennial Exposition of 1926; the Pennsylvania Constitutional Commemoration Commission, 1938; Pennsylvania Commission of Celebration of the 150th Anniversary of the Declaration of Independence; World Affairs Council; Philadelphia Chamber of Commerce; Pennsylvania Water Resources Committee, 1951; Philadelphia National Shrines Park Commission, 1946–1956; and Fairmount Park Commission.

He contributed to many institutions and organizations, including cultural and educational institutions such as Philadelphia Orchestra, Philadelphia Museum of Art, Lasalle College, and Lincoln University. In addition he founded the Albert M. Greenfield Foundation, a philanthropic institution created during his later years.

Greenfield also supported a variety of Jewish institutions and organizations such as Federation of Jewish Charities, National Conference of Christians and Jews, Development Fund for American Judaism, American Jewish Tercentenary, 1954–1955, and Israel Philharmonic Orchestra.

These papers constitute the selected office files of Albert M. Greenfield. Incoming and outgoing correspondence make up the bulk of the collection, but there is also a great quantity of other material, including appointment books, photographs, newspaper clippings, pamphlets, periodicals, and reports. The papers for 1921–1966 cover several categories: personal, business, political, civic, philanthropic, Jewish affairs, and miscellaneous.

The personal papers include mainly family, social, and private correspondence. They are interspersed throughout and constitute a small but important part of the collection.

The collection contains, in addition, papers of Greenfield's two confidential secretaries, Donald Jenks, 1951–1954, and John O'Shea, 1954–1964, including correspondence, drafts of speeches, appointment books, and miscellaneous materials; and a few personal papers, 1922–1930, of Greenfield's first wife Edna Kraus Greenfield, including personal and social correspondence, financial records, and record book of the Ladies Auxiliary of the Jewish Hospital-Emergency Fund, Philadelphia, 1922.

Gift of Alfred M. Greenfield, 1968.

Permission to use the papers must be secured from the Albert M. Greenfield Foundation. 1315 Walnut Street; Philadelphia, PA 19107.

1960
No entry.

1961
Philadelphia Society for Organizing Charity.   Records, 1878–1928.
(27 linear ft.)

The Philadelphia Society for Organizing Charitable Relief and Repressing Mendicancy (now the Family Service of Philadelphia), a private relief agency was organized in 1879 by a group of men connected with the Soup Houses and other charitable agencies.

The correspondence files constitute the largest group of material and include: letterpress books of general correspondence, 1878–1911; incoming general correspondence, 1899–1908; incoming correspondence, 1900–1909, of general secretary Mary Richmond, a central figure in the emergence of professional social work in the United States; incoming and outgoing correspondence of the supervisor of districts, 1915; miscellaneous correspondence.

Minute books, 1878–1928, include minutes of the Commission on Organizing Charities, 1878–1879; minutes of the Board of Directors; minutes of the Ward Associations; minutes of various committees. Some of the minute books also contain case records. Other records include application books, 1902–1909; case records, 1890–1923; annual reports of the Board of Directors, 1879–1900; annual reports of the Ward Associations, 1879–1902; scrapbooks, 1878–1879, 1895–1900; photographs; printed material such as "The Charity Organization Bulletin," and "The Monthly Register," 1879–1900, the first journal of social work to have a national circulation.

The records do not include many financial accounts of the society, but there are a few miscellaneous financial records, among which are an account book, 1916–1921; minutes of the Committee on Finance, 1884–1894, 1904–1916; and a volume of papers, 1879–1882, primarily on financial matters.

The collection contains, in addition, records of the Philadelphia Social Workers Club: incoming and outgoing correspondence, 1907–1922; minutes, 1905-1920; account book, 1916–1921; and scrapbook of programs, 1917–1922.

Gift of Family Service of Philadelphia, 1969.

1962
Wister family.   Papers, 1730–1940.   (20 linear ft.)

Frances Ann Kemble, a well-known English actress, and Pierce Butler, a Philadelphia gentleman, were married in 1834. They had two children. Fanny Kemble and her daughters are the central individuals in this collection.

Fanny and Pierce Bulter were separated and finally divorced in 1848. Fanny Kemble lived alternately in the United States, 1848–1862, 1867–1877, and England, 1845–1848, 1862–1867, 1877–1894, during which time she returned to the stage, performing dramatic readings of Shakespeare, publishing her diary and memoirs, writing some dramatic criticism. Most of the Fanny Kemble items consists of social and family correspondence. Fanny Kemble's letters comment on current events and prominent public leaders various cultural interests. They also reveal her more private concerns: her relationship with her children and the increasing frustrations of old age.

The letters of Frances Butler Leigh, the younger daughter of Fanny and Pierce, deal most significantly with the post-bellum South, where she and her sister maintained the Butler plantation after their father died until 1877.

The early portion of the Sarah Butler Wister papers focus on the Civil War years. In addition to Mrs. Wister's own opinions and activities, reflected in her letters and in her diary, there is correspondence from Jeannie L. Field, daughter of David Dudley Field. Jeannie Field regularly relayed to her friend pieces of the military and political information which her father, a prominent New York Republican, had received through his political connections. Also a series of letters from County Scull, Union commissary officer stationed on Hilton Head Island, provide information about the various military units which passed through Hilton Head post, and general views about Union military activities in the South.

Mrs. Wister and Agnes Irwin edited an 1877 volume of biographical sketches of American women, *Worthy Women of Our First Century*. There are fifty letters from individuals such as Anne Fiske, Faith Hubbard, Mary Eliot Parkinson, Catherine Pennington, Sarah Randolph, and Helen Stryker, which are filled with discussions about the qualities which a woman ought to possess to merit inclusion in the book.

The later portion of the Frances Wister correspondence deals with racial attitudes and relationships in both the North and the South during the years at the turn of the century. There are many letters from English feminist, Frances Power Cobbe, 1873–1898.

The material for Fanny Kemble, Frances Butler Leigh, and Sarah Wister offer a researcher material on politics, culture, family history, and the history of women.

Sarah Butler Wister's husband, Dr. Owen Wister, served as an assistant surgeon on the *Plymouth* with the U.S. Navy from 1848 to 1850. The few letters and a portion of a diary kept from this period are filled with descriptions of: wardroom quarrels, general ship life, dirty ports, Malayan natives, the American diplomatic mission to China, Chinese customs and traits, and retired white missionaries living in Hawaii. The remainder of his correspondence concerns the local news of Germantown and its citizens.

The collection offers only background sources for Owen and Sarah Wister's son, Owen Wister, author of *The Virginian*.

There is a section of business correspondence which relates to the management, financing, and eventual division and sale of the Butler plantation estate and the Germantown estate lands.

Also included is a miscellaneous section of family members. The genealogical connections are obscure, but all old Philadelphia families are related to each other somewhere along the line.

In this section there are miscellaneous manuscripts of Samuel Bradford, including papers relative to the disagreement with his father, Thomas Bradford, over the family printing business. There are letters of Dr. Edward Florens Rivinus to his brother-in-law Dr. James H. Bradford, son of Samuel Bradford. Dr. Bradford's father-in-law David Caldwell, is represented by a small group of miscellaneous items.

Finally there are miscellaneous manuscripts of Sarah Yorke Stevenson (Mrs. Cornelius Stevenson), archeologist, columnist, and civic leader. Most of these documents are notes and drafts for lectures and articles in connection with the Pennsylvania Museum and School of Industrial Art, for which she served as curator.

1963
Krumbhaar family.   Papers, 1732–1951.   (200 items.)

Miscellaneous family papers, genealogical notes, and letters gathered mainly by Edward Bell Krumbhaar in his roots pursuits. Among small groups of papers are: Christian Ludwig Lewis Krumbhaar letterbook, 1816–1820, on his Philadelphia mercantile business conducted from Hamburg, where Krumbhaar lived for the duration of the War of 1812, and from Philadelphia to which he returned in 1816, and on family business including lands in Kentucky and New York; William W. Stone letters, 1855–1861 on his business problems and Maryland's resistance to the passage of Northern troops through to Washington, D.C., at the start of the Civil War; Charles Hermann Krumbhaar scrapbooks, 1876–1893, on his political activities as city councilman, county commissioner, sheriff, and Pennsylvania superintendent of banking. Related families represented in the papers are Ramsay, Turnbull, and Bell.

Christian Ludwig Lewis Krumbhaar letterbook in German.
Gift of Peter D. Krumbhaar, 1969.

1964
Pennsylvania. Militia. National Guard.   Record books, (1861–1917) 1951.   (13 v. and 150 items.)

Company "D," Gray Reserves, was organized in Philadelphia, April 25, 1861, for the special defense of the city. Following a brief hiatus as a social organization, 1864–1866, Company "D" was reorganized within the Pennsylvania militia system and became part of the Pennsylvania National Guard in 1875.

The Company "D" books consist of: minute books, 1861–1914; Roll book, 1861–1876; constitution and by-laws with membership lists, 1861–1906; standing resolutions, 1861–1906; enlistment and descriptive book, 1878–1894; camp pay book, 1907–1915; company register, 1914–1917; and roll book for annual dinners and meeting, 1922–1942. A folder of miscellaneous materials, receipted bills and correspondence, 1875–1951, contains a "Muster-In-Roll," 1899, and a 1951 membership roll.

Gift of Earle Hepburn, 1969.

1965
Philadelphia Public Schools. 16th District. Records, 1835–1914. (15 v.)

Records of a local Philadelphia school board include: board of director's minute books, 1854–1906; Jefferson Grammar School for girls registers, 1835–1899; Jefferson Grammar School for boys (formed 1843) applications, 1847–1870, withdrawals, 1847–1887, and registers, 1870–1899; Jefferson Combined School (boys, girls, grammar, and primary) registers, 1899–1914; and George Wolfe Primary, No. 2 (organized 1849) registers, 1881–1906. The registers provide the pupils' names, ages, grade assignments, parents' occupations, dates and causes for leaving.

Gift of Miss Adelaide Conrad, 1971.

1966
Forsyth, Joseph W. Papers, 1835–1877. (200 items.)

Miscellaneous papers of Joseph W. Forsyth, Philadelphia plumber include: incoming correspondence pertaining mainly to promissory notes held by Forsyth and personal household bills, 1871–1877.

Gift of Helen H. and Elizabeth A. Livingston, 1971.

1967A
Grubb family. Papers, 1730–1950. (12 linear ft.)

These papers cover several generations of the Grubb family of Lancaster, and the iron manufacturing interests over which they presided. The founder of the family business was Peter Grubb [I] and he is represented here by only a Peter Grubb and Curtis Grubb ledger, 1745–1750.

A small portion of the papers consist of correspondence and financial papers, 1767–1793, relating to Peter Grubb's [II] military career as a Revolutionary War colonel in the 8th Battalion of Lancaster County, to his business career as owner of the several Pennsylvania iron forges, and to his estate.

The bulk of the collection centers around Colonel Grubb's grandson, Clement B. Grubb. This material, 1823–1871, gives a partial account of his management of the family iron furnaces, a responsibility which he shared with his brother Edward B. Grubb until 1851. A record book, 1841–1862, contains furnace memorandum and accounts and Lebanon and Manheim Plank Road accounts and minutes. There is correspondence between Grubb and his siblings, particularly Edward B. Grubb, A. Bates Grubb, and Mary Grubb Parker, on the interconnected aspects of the E. & C. B. Grubb partnership and the estate of their father Henry Bates Grubb, as well as family news.

Harriet B. Grubb's letters home to Clement and Mary Anne Brooke Grubb, 1852–1864, reveal the reactions of a daughter attending boarding school in Philadelphia.

There are personal receipted bills of Clement Grubb. The emotional difficulties of Henry Carson Grubb, a half-brother, also emerges from family letters to him and a few of his own notes, 1821–1873. Miscellaneous papers, deeds, land surveys, wills, and newspaper clippings complete the Grubb family material.

Apparently unrelated to the Grubb family is Mrs. Mary Ella Johnson Stuart incoming family and social correspondence, 1858–1868, much of which is from Anne and Theodore Mead in Boston.

Gift of Mrs. Charles S.W. Bissell, Mrs. James Rawle, and Mrs. Herbert S. Morris.

Finding aid available.

1967B
Grubb family.   Papers, 1707–1856.   (40 items.)

Additional business and family letters, surveys, and other documents of various Grubb family members.

1968
No entry.

1969
Rosenblum, Allen M.   Papers, 1957–1968.   (150 items.)

Notes and court transcripts, many being Master's reports on divorce cases, from the law office of Allen M. Rosenblum.

Gift of Edward Pinkowski.

1970

Lighthouse.   **Records, 1893–1965.**   **(ca. 155 v.)**

The Lighthouse, a settlement house, was founded as a social center for the mill workers of the Kensington section of Philadelphia. It shortly expanded to include a Boys' Club, Men's Club, Girls' Club, Women's Club, Baldwin Day Nursery, and a several other activities, with the boys' sports program as its most viable activity.

The records contain, in varying series, minutes, accounts, other operational records, scrapbooks and photograph albums of the Lighthouse, its' clubs and programs.

General: Executive Committee minutes, 1911–1918; cash receipts, disbursements, ledgers, and other account books, 1909–1963; front desk book diaries, 1908–1965, with messages, appointments, and activities.

Boys' Club: Council minutes, 1931–1951; "Reports" on finances and other proceedings, 1940–1949; scrapbooks of clippings, programs, photographs and photograph albums, 1895–1951?, of activities, especially sports, camps, and Websterians.

Old Timers' Association minutes, 1941–1943.

Men's Club minutes, 1934–1941.

Women's and Girls' Club minutes, 1907–1912.   Girls' Club: minutes, 1912–1934; daybooks, 1946–1964; group leader reports, 1957–1964; camp applications, 1950s; reports, 1930–1958; membership records of "dropouts," 1940–1959; scrapbooks, 1911–1930. Women's club minutes, 1919–1954.

Baldwin Day Nursery: minutes, 1898–1923; and application book, 1922–1925.

Lighthouse Beneficial Society minutes, 1917–1945.

There are assorted dues books, address books, and rollbooks of the clubs.

Gift of the Lighthouse, 1967.

1971

Loudoun.   **Papers, 1696 (1760–1895), 1939.**   **(40 linear ft.)**

A collection of papers accumulated by several generations of residents of Loudoun, a mansion in Germantown, built in 1801 by Thomas Armat, Philadelphia merchant. Included are papers of five related Philadelphia area families: Armat, Skerrett, Logan, Norris, and Dickinson.

The bulk of the Armat family section consists of the business papers of Thomas Armat. The most significant part of his papers is for the years, 1784–1804, when Armat was a prominent merchant trading in goods, especially with Great Britain. The papers for the merchant years contain the business records of Thomas Armat, his son Thomas Wright Armat, and two Armat partnerships: Thomas Armat & Son, 1795–1797, and [Thomas] Armat & [James C.] Copper, 1799–1806. After 1800 Thomas Armat turned increasingly to other business enterprises, especially dry-goods merchandizing and real estate, and from about 1820 he was known simply as Thomas Armat, gentleman.

The Thomas Armat business papers include incoming correspondence and loose financial records, 1779, 1784–1820, 1831; letterbooks, 1781–1798; journals, 1782–1800, 1818; ledgers, 1781–1805, 1818; receipt books, 1779–1829; miscellaneous account books, including four volumes on his property holdings; pocket diaries, 1790–1818; household journal, 1817–1829; and estate papers. Among the Armat & Copper records are a letterbook, 1801–1806, journals, 1799–1804, and an inventory book, 1801; Thomas Armat & Son records are limited to journals, 1795–1797; Thomas W. Armat business records consist of a letterbook, 1798–1801, journals, 1798–1799, receipt books, 1796–1807, and a journal of Thomas W. Armat's estate, 1806–1808.

Additional Armat family papers include: papers, 1780–1851 of Ann Smart Armat, Thomas Armat's fifth wife, Elizabeth Smart Rooker, Ann's sister, and James Rooker, Elizabeth's husband and pastor of the Presbyterian Church of Germantown, including incoming correspondence, loose financial records, and account books; James Rooker diary, 1811–1827, pertaining to church activities; Presbyterian Church of Germantown record book, 1818–1827; Thomas Armat, treasurer of St. Luke's Episcopal Church of Germantown, correspondence and financial records, 1817–1826; St. Luke's pew rent books, 1821–1825; Protestant Episcopal Association of Germantown subscription book, 1815–1816; St. Luke's Contingent Fund, 1922; business correspondence and financial records, 1800–1803, of Asbury Dickins, Philadelphia bookseller.

The Skerrett family section, 1805–1877, includes: family and personal correspondence, 1821–1849, of Jane Caroline Armat Skerrett, daughter of Thomas W. Armat and wife of James J. Skerrett, gentleman; her expense book while in Europe, 1836–1837; account book of Jane and James Skerrett on their real estate holdings, 1830–1860; Jane Skerrett estate papers, including financial records for rents collected from houses occupied by black tenants, 1856–1868. The larger portion of this section consists of James J. Skerrett financial records, 1805–1877, and estate papers.

The Logan family section, 1768–1939, contains four generations of Logan family papers, beginning with Deborah Norris Logan, collector of historical records. Her papers include outgoing family correspondence, 1768–1836; loose financial items; 1822 memoir of her husband George Logan, physician and legislator; commonplace books; and estate records.

Other Logan family papers include: James Logan medical receipt book, n.d.; loose financial records, 1808–1848, and account book of Sommerville Farm, 1818, of Albanus Charles Logan, physician; personal correspondence, 1792–1844 of Maria Dickinson Logan; Charles F. Logan ledger, 1823–1825; incoming correspondence, 1830–1871, loose financial records, miscellaneous account books, and ledger, 1861–1863, of Gustavus George Logan, gentleman; incoming correspondence and loose financial records, 1858–1895, of Anna Armat Logan; her receipt book, 1870–1895, miscellaneous account books, address book, desk book diaries, 1874–1894, fragments of a diary, ca. 1864–1867, on her separation from Gustavus George Logan, and estate papers; loose financial records and account books, 1852–1854, on building Restlerigg Hall on Stenton farm; incoming correspondence, loose financial items, account books and desk book diaries, 1874–1929, of Albanus Charles Logan, gentleman; his Stenton Stock Farm records, 1876–1886, containing horse and boarding records; incoming correspondence and loose financial records, 1880–1939, account books account book of wages paid Loudoun servants, 1884–1895, Loudoun cash book, ca. 1899, and commonplace book of Maria Dickinson Logan.

The Norris family section, 1706–1855, includes a few papers, ca. 1761–1766, of Isaac Norris [II] relating to his property holdings; correspondence, 1759- 1766, financial records, 1804–1809, and estate papers of Charles Norris, brother of Deborah Norris Logan; and miscellaneous Norris family papers.

The Dickinson family section, 1760–1856, includes: John Dickinson, lawyer and statesman, incoming official and personal correspondence, outgoing family correspondence, especially to his wife Mary Norris Dickinson, and loose financial records, 1760, 1780–1804; Mary Norris Dickinson, incoming and outgoing family correspondence, 1794; their daughter, Sarah Norris Dickinson's financial papers containing correspondence, deeds, and bonds relating to her property holdings, 1794, 1810–1834, 1856.

Other Loudoun records include: broadsides; deeds; photographs; account book, 1760–1765, of William Hicks of Staten Island.

Of special note are a few papers of Jonathan Dickinson, an importing merchant and landowner of Philadelphia and Jamaica, including incoming correspondence, 1698–1713, primarily on his mercantile pursuits. Eighteen of the letters are from John Askew, his factor, friend, and business associate in London. Also included is an incomplete manuscript of the "Jonathan Dickinson Journal," 1696: "A Journey of the Travels of Several Persons and their Sufferings being cast-away in the Gulph among the Cannibals of Florida," a narrative describing a shipwreck experienced by Dickinson, his family, and ten of his slaves on a journey from Jamaica to Philadelphia.

Deposited by the Commissioners of Fairmount Park, 1968.

Finding aid available.

1972A

Ashhurst family.   **Papers, 1797–1907.**   **(3 linear ft.)**

This collection contains random gatherings of the papers of the Ashhurst and related families of Philadelphia. The most complete series consists of John Ashhurst personal receipted bills, 1837–1883, and caretaker of Samuel H. Hibbard's accounts, 1863–1877, of the Grange, Ashhurst's summer estate in Havertown. Also John Ashhurst correspondence, 1834–1892, which includes some family letters, often referring to estate and financial matters, and some personal business letters and papers.

Other family members represented are: [I.I.] Wheeler & [Richard] Ashhurst, merchants, petit cashbook, 1808–1811; Richard Ashhurst, dry goods merchant, letterbook, 1822–1827; Richard Ashhurst & Son, dry goods merchants, receipt book, 1833–1839, and loose financial correspondence, 1821–1857, 1878; Richard L. Ashhurst letters (typescript), September, 1862—June, 1863, as Adjutant of the 150th Regiment, Pennsylvania Volunteers; Manuel Eyre estate papers, and assorted Stokes family correspondence, most notably Caleb P. Wayne's off again, on again courtship of Mary Stokes, 1802–1803.

1972B

Ashhurst family.   **Papers, 1796–1890.**   **(4.5 linear ft.)**

Additional miscellaneous Ashhurst family papers include: Richard Ashhurst & Sons, merchants, incoming correspondence, 1804–1890 primarily from the South; receipted bills and accounts, both business and personal, of Richard Ashhurst, John Ashhurst, and their families; Manuel Eyre incoming correspondence, 1796–1845, mostly on farm properties, and personal receipted bills; Manuel Eyre estate accounts, receipts, and legal papers; and John Connelly estate papers, 1827–1855.

Gift, 1967; Donor unknown.

1973

West family.   **Papers, 1764 (1828–1871), 1893.**   **(150 items.)**

Miscellaneous personal papers of the Nixon, West, and Hemsley families, three related Philadelphia families, including correspondence, legal records, photographs and miscellanea. Among the individuals represented are Francis West, merchant, and his wife, Mary Nixon West; Francis West [II], physician; Emily Cox Hemsley, whose incoming family correspondence includes letters, 1861, from her husband, Alexander Hemsley, inventor and manufacturer of photographic supplies, written while he served with the First Troop Philadelphia City Cavalry.

Purchased, 1968.

Finding aid available.

1974

Lerner, Albert.   Papers, 1918 (1942–1945).   (100 items.)

Albert Lerner, Philadelphia pharmacist, correspondence and miscellany on the two World Wars. There are five letters by Lerner while serving in the World War I medical corps of the 314th Regiment infantry in France; censored letters, 1942–1945, of Lt. Joseph Lerner, Albert's brother, from North Africa and Europe; and other World War II correspondence to Albert and his wife.

1975

Western North Carolina Land Company.   Records, 1873 (1874–1896), 1945.   (400 items.)

The Western North Carolina Land Company, incorporated in 1874, was organized by J. Grier Ralston, John K. Ralston, and other Philadelphia area entrepreneurs for the purpose of speculating in land in western North Carolina.

Almost half of the collection is made up of correspondence, 1877, 1890–1896, of John K. Ralston, secretary and treasurer of the company, and other officers. Among the other items are: miscellaneous financial records; title records; reports, including survey reports; photographs of western North Carolina; and miscellany.

Gift of Mrs. Conrad Wilson, 1968.

1976

Atherton, Humphrey, 1784–1845.   Papers, 1788 (1809–1845). (9 v. and 1,800 items.)

Humphrey Atherton, Philadelphia lawyer, correspondence, notes, accounts, and other legal papers on his cases, along with his docket book, 1811–1824, receipt books, 1809–1824, and financial memorandum books, 1809–1822. Also European travel diaries, 1833–1835, n.d., and copybooks of his daughter Emily Atherton.

Finding aid available.

1977

Purdon, James, Jr.   Correspondence, 1839–1841.   (95 items.)

Correspondence of James Purdon, Philadelphia lawyer, with family and friends, reporting on life in Easton, Wilkesbarre, and Bremen, Germany.

Gift of Mrs. Charles Murray Rudolph, 1968.

1978
Hopkinson family.   Papers, 1735–1863.   (19 v.)

The Hopkinson family was a prominent political family of Philadelphia and Bordentown, N.J. Thomas Hopkinson, 1709–1751, was a merchant, a lawyer, and judge of the vice-admiralty for the province of Pennsylvania. His son, Francis Hopkinson, 1737–1791, was a jurist, author, musician, and signer of the Declaration of Independence. Joseph Hopkinson, 1770–1842, son of Francis, was a Federal congressman from Pennsylvania, 1815–1819, federal judge, 1828–1842, and author of *Hail Columbia*. His son, Oliver Hopkinson, 1812–1905, served during the Civil War with the 1st Regiment, Delaware Volunteers and with the 51st Regiment Infantry, Pennsylvania Militia.

The Hopkinson papers cover four generation. The collection consists principally of incoming correspondence, but there is also some outgoing correspondence, documents, manuscript notes, and miscellany. The first generation is represented by the incoming correspondence, 1735–1747, of Thomas Hopkinson, and pertain mainly to his activities as an importing merchant. There are a few incoming letters, 1754–1766, to his wife Mary Johnson Hopkinson, and 3 letters from Benjamin Franklin.

The papers of Francis Hopkinson, includes incoming and outgoing correspondence, 1765–1789, and a few manuscript notes. Among his correspondents are: Benjamin Franklin, Thomas Jefferson, Robert Morris, and George Washington.

The bulk of the collection is Joseph Hopkinson's correspondence, 1815–1842. Joseph Bonaparte's letters to Hopkinson and his wife are mostly personal, but there is some mention of Bonaparte's financial interests while living in the United States. Other correspondents are eminent politicians and other nineteenth century figures among whom are: John Quincy Adams; Louisa Catherine Johnson Adams; Henry Baldwin, jurist; Samuel Rossiter Betts, jurist; Horace Binney, lawyer and congressman; John C. Calhoun; Henry Clay; Peter S. DuPonceau, authority on international law and practice; Edward Everett; William Gaston, jurist; Henry Dilworth Gilpin, lawyer and U.S. attorney general; Marquis de Lafayette; Louis McLane, U.S. senator, secretary of treasury, minister to Britain; John Marshall; Richard Peters, lawyer; Joel Roberts Poinsett, diplomat and secretary of war; Richard Rush, politician and diplomat; John Sergeant, lawyer and congressman; Jared Sparks, editor and historian; Richard Stockton, lawyer and congressman; Joseph D. Story, jurist; Robert Walsh, author and editor; Bushrod Washington, jurist; and Daniel Webster.

There are additional Joseph Hopkinson family and personal letters, notes, typescripts of essays, and materials relating to *Hail Columbia*. Hopkinson, an admirer of Alexander Hamilton, presumably collected the few Hamilton papers, 1794–1802, which include letters on military and political matters and a proposal for a military academy. There is also personal and family correspondence of Emily Mifflin Hopkinson, Joseph's wife.

The papers, 1853–1878, of Oliver Hopkinson consist primarily of Civil War correspondence on his service with the 1st Regiment, Delaware Volunteers, and then the 51st Regiment Infantry, Pennsylvania Militia.

Gift of Edward Hopkinson, Jr., 1946–1948.

Finding aid available.

1979
Richards, Howard, 1840–1911.   Papers, 1808–1912.   (3 linear ft.)

The papers of Howard Richards, lawyer of Philadelphia and Elizabeth, N.J., consist of legal correspondence and records, mostly from his New Jersey office, together with some family estate and personal papers. The legal material includes: Howard Richards letterpress book, 1865–1866, of legal and Pearson Petroleum Company business; Richards law office diary, 1876–1878, kept by an unidentified associate; papers on Civil War soldiers' claims, and other case papers. There are Richards' pocket diaries with memoranda of professional and personal activities, 1864–1883; his miscellaneous financial records; and State Charities Aid Association of New Jersey financial records, 1887–1892. Additional papers include: Augustus Richards' letters, 1848–1851, to his family reporting on his employment difficulties in California; Benjamin Wood Richards estate income, 1865–1905, from John G. Hewes, agent for family properties in Pottsville; Sarah Ann Richards estate papers; Mayo family correspondence, among which are letters, 1842–1844, of Winfield Scott; Mayo family estate papers; and "Journal of the Labrador Exploring Expedition of 1886," author unknown, mainly on travel in Quebec.

1980
Westcott and Thompson.   Records, 1856–1924.   (3 linear ft.)

Westcott and Thompson, compositors, job-printers, and stereotypers, specialized in book work for publishers such as Harper & Brothers, J.B. Lippincott, Lea & Febiger, and Saunders.

These volumes comprise a partial record of the company, including: wastebooks, 1856–1862; journals, 1858–1862, 1880–1902; trial-balance ledgers, 1900–1916; receipt book, 1864–1870; cashbooks, 1880–1920; sales books, 1890–1905; wage book, 1907–1918; composing room work orders, 1910–1924; record of children under 16 employed, 1895–1914; and Job printing billing book, 1900–1916.

Part gift of Mrs. Charles W. Singer, 1972; part purchased, 1972.

1981
Contemporary Club (Philadelphia, Pa.)   Papers, 1886–1951.
(3 linear ft.)

The Contemporary Club, was organized in 1886 to hold discussions on outstanding questions of the day and to present scholarly papers by public figures. Membership was open to men and women, most of whom were distinguished in the academic, artistic, and literary worlds of Philadelphia.

Correspondence, 1886–1951, makes up the bulk of the papers, including: outgoing correspondence of club presidents; incoming correspondence of individuals invited to speak; miscellaneous correspondence to Thornton Oakley and other club officers. Among the other papers are executive committee minutes, 1894–1919; photographs; year books; and miscellanea.

These papers were collected by Thornton Oakley, a Philadelphia artist, muralist, and officer of the club, 1933–1941.

Gift of Mrs. Lansdale Oakley Humphreys, 1972.

1982
Ewing, James Hunter, 1842–1922.   Accounts, 1859–1884.   (10 v.)

James Hunter Ewing was an investment banker and gentleman farmer of Philadelphia and Villanova.

These accounts document Ewing's efforts to improve the farm at Woodstock and the family estate at Villanova. Included are: account books and farm diary, 1859–1860, of Ewing's attempt at chicken farming; account book, 1861–1862, 1867; journal, 1874–1876; ledgers, 1863–1884; diaries, 1861–1879, recording farm work done at Woodstock and Ewing's social life; and a scrap book. Additionally, there is a Caldwell & Ewing account book, 1869–1872, the "suspended accounts" of a short-lived partnership with Robert S. Caldwell in the wholesale fish trade.

Gift of Lansdale Oakley Humphreys, 1972.

1983
No entry.

1984
Dallas, Constance H., 1902-   Papers, 1951–1956.
(13.5 linear ft.)

Constance H. Dallas was the first woman to be elected to the Philadelphia City Council where she represented the 8th district (21st and 22nd Wards) composed of Germantown, West Oak Lane and Chestnut Hill.

The papers include incoming and outgoing correspondence, reports, and other printed matter, published materials, clippings, and miscellanea and consist of six series: general files, having to do with council activities as well as papers on the Menniger Foundation, the Pennsylvania Federation of Democratic Women, and the World Affairs Council; committees of Council, largest of the series, consisting of material prepared for or used by the councilmanic committees, especially the committees of Public Welfare and of Public Health on which Dallas serves, together with papers on the Public Health Code of 1955 drafted by the Public Health Committee; administration, relating to various government departments including: City Planning, Police, Public Welfare, and Streets; political papers, files generated during Dallas's first successful campaign for City Council and its aftermath, 1951–1952, the election files for 1953, and for the Pennsylvania gubernatorial election of 1954; constituency affairs, includes material relating to the 8th district.; reports of various city departments.

Gift of Constance H. Dallas, 1972.

1985
Foster, Frank B.   Records, 1897–1923.   (8 v.)

These are the personal account books of Frank B. Foster, Philadelphia industrialist. The records include journals: 1904–1907, 1907–1914, and 1915–1920; ledgers covering the periods 1904–1914, 1904–1917, and 1914–1923; as well as farm accounts from the years 1916–1917. Another volume contains the stock lists of sheathing at Mount Airy, 1897–1900.

Gift of John H. Foster, 1980.

1986
**Roberts and Smith family.   Papers, 1702 (1801–1898).
(3.5 linear ft.)**

Estate papers of George Roberts, ironmonger of Philadelphia, and his heirs: Hugh Roberts, George Roberts [II], Elizabeth F. Roberts, Charles F. Roberts, Mary Roberts Smith and her husband John Jay Smith, Mary Roberts Smith, George Roberts Smith, Thomas Newbold Smith, Harry M. Smith, Charles Morton Smith, Sarah Emlen Roberts Ingersoll, and other grandchildren, great grandchildren, and their spouses. Much of the estate was derived from property in Philadelphia and various pieces of land in Centre, Clearfield, and Elk Counties, and much of the financial and legal papers are concerned with the management of this property.

The small groups of correspondence also refer mostly to family estate business, but there are Bainbridge, Ansley & Co. business letters, 1805–1810, to James Smith, Jr., Philadelphia merchant.

Also Harry M. Smith letters, 1846–1855, describe his expatriate life in Paris, viewed with disfavor by his brother.

1987
School books and lectures, 1755–1904.　　(30 v.)

Anderson, John. Music book, ca. 1793. This music book includes lessons given by John Anderson, a Bally Bay (Ireland) vocal teacher to Samuel Harkness. (1 v.)

Arithmetic work book, 1762-[1779]. Gift of Albert Fogg, 1913. (1 v.)

Arithmetic work book, [1800]. Gift of Anne Mott Rosengarten, 1961. (1 v.)

Baird, F. Music book, 1755. Music book for James Hunter as taught by F. Baird. (1 v.)

Bowne, Thomas. Arithmetic work books, 1786–1787. Gift of the Philadelphia Museum of Art, 1948. (3 v.)

Buzby, John Burrows. Report cards, 1863–1865. These report cards show Buzby's grades while a student at Central High School. (1 v.)

Carvill, Emma H. Music work book, [1850]. Gift of Mrs. Edward S. Sayres, 1931. (1 v.)

Dickson, William. Student notebook, 1850–1851. Notebook for a course in bookkeeping, includes "Daybook and Journal A, 1850" and Index to Ledger A, Ledger B and Sales Book B." Gift of Independence National Historic Park, 1967. (2 v. in 1 v.)

Fish, Asa Israel, 1820–1879. Student notebook, 1840–1842. Asa Israel Fish was a Philadelphia lawyer. This is a notebook of college themes submitted while a student at Harvard College. (1 v.)

[Fisher, Johannes]. Notes in Latin and Greek, n.d. (1 v.)

Haupt, Lewis Muhlenberg. Work book, 1866–1867. Lewis Muhlenberg Haupt attended the United States Military Academy, Class of 1867. This work book contains civil engineering notes, poetry, and miscellaneous personal notes and sketches. Purchased. (2 v.)

Kindergarten teaching programs, 1898 (1903–1904). Notebook of a Philadelphia kindergarten teacher. Gift of Ezra Evans, 1915. (1 v.)

Mahan, Abel. Bookkeeping work book, [1859]. Gift of Harrold E. Gillingham, 1933. (1 v.)

Mahan, William. Bookkeeping work book, [1828]. Work book of William Mahan apparently while a student in Joseph Flowers' and Absalom Michner's schools. Gift of Harold E. Gillingham, 1933. (1 v.)

McKean, William Wister, 1800–1865. Music notebook, [1822]. Music notebook of William Wister McKean consisting mainly of waltzes. Gift of Mabel Bayard Kane, 1936. (1 v.)

Milliman, Francis A. Arithmetic and bookkeeping work books, 1833–1834. Gift of Mary E.W. Milliman, 1933. (2 v.)

Music work books, [1850]. Gift of Mrs. Edward S. Sayres, 1931. (2 v.)

Panseron, A. *The A B C of Music : with additions by F. Dorigo,* 1846. Interleaved with manuscript notes. Gift of Mrs. Edwards S. Sayres, 1931. (1 v.)

Penrose, Martha T. Arithmetic work book, 1832. (1 v.)

Rowland, Mary Potts. Writing exercise book, 1851. Writing exercise book of Mary Potts Penores while attending the Diamond Rock School near Valley Forge. (1 v.)

Rush, Benjamin, 1745–1813. Manuscript Lectures of the Theory and Practice of Physick, 1790–1791. Gift of Dr. Solomon Solis-Cohen estate, 1948. (1 v.)

Sergent, Winthrop, 1825–1870. Notebook, 1845–1847. Notebook of Winthrop Sergent, author, mainly regarding historical figures. Gift of Winthrop Sergent. (1 v.)

Shaum, Eliza. Music work book, n.d. Purchased, 1895. (1 v.)

Walton, Lydia, 1821–1857. Arithmetic work books, 1827–1831. Arithmetic work books used by Lydia, Ann and Macre Walton, students from Moreland, Montgomery County. Gift of Miranda S. Roberts, 1924. (2 v.)

Wooddeson, Richard, 1745–1823. Lecture notes, 1777, on British Governmental law. Wooddeson was an English jurist, Magdalan College professor, and author. (1 v.)

Zerr, Paul G. Arithmetic work book, 1840. Work book used by Paul G. Zerr, a Berks County student, while attending Trapp Boarding School, Montgomery County. (1 v.)

1988A
Wurts family.   **Papers, 1796 (1824–1884).**   **(3 linear ft.)**

More than half of these papers of the Wurts and related Philadelphia families consist of the business papers, 1824–1859, of four Wurts brothers: Charles Stewart, John, Maurice, and William. These papers consist of incoming correspondence, correspondence between the brothers, and a few receipts and other loose accounts on their involvement in the Delaware and Hudson Canal Company, the dry goods firm of Wurts, Musgrove, & Wurts, and land speculation and related activities, especially speculation in anthracites coal lands in northern Pennsylvania.

Other Wurts family papers include: correspondence and loose accounts, 1838–1884, on family lands in Missouri; Dr. Charles Stewart Wurts [II] receipted personal and household bills, 1869–1900; miscellaneous deeds; genealogical notes; and miscellanea.

Related family papers include: Charles J. Wister poems, personal and business correspondence, 1796–1837; John Wister III, President and Treasurer of Duncannon Iron Company, outgoing family letters, 1846–1900; miscellaneous Wister family papers, including recipe books; and Ravenel family of Virginia correspondence, 1851–1857.

Gift of John Wister Wurts, 1969.

Finding aid available.

1988B
Wurts family.   Papers, 1817 (1845–1907).   (6 linear ft.)

These papers contain additional material of the four Wurts brothers. Maurice Wurts papers include: incoming business correspondence, 1849–1854, as manager of the Delaware and Hudson Canal Company; Delaware and Hudson Canal Company account book, 1847–1851; miscellaneous account book, 1848–1852; and miscellaneous loose accounts.

Charles Stewart Wurts [I] papers include: outgoing family and business correspondence, 1817, 1820–1854; account book, 1845–1846, on the Delaware and Hudson Canal Company and to land purchases; loose accounts, 1847–1861; and estate papers.

Mary Vanuxem Wurts (Charles' wife) papers include: personal correspondence, 1847–1851; account books, 1869–1877, on her property assets; and a record book, 1860–1867, on Illinois lands.

John Wurts is represented by correspondence and accounts, ca. 1845–1857.

The bulk of the papers is comprised of Charles Stewart Wurts [II] financial records, including receipted personal and household bills, 1889–1907; cashbooks, 1875–1885, 1895–1906; and miscellaneous account books. There are additionally a few items on other members of the Wurts family.

Gift of Mrs. John Wister Wurts, 1976.

1989
Pennsylvania. Magistrates Court. (Philadelphia Judicial District). Records, 1875–1903.   (8 v.)

Miscellaneous record books of Philadelphia magistrates include: landlord and tenant cases heard before John F. Poole, Court No. 10, 1875–1881, Thaddeus Stearne, Court No. 21, 1877–1879, and William A. Thorpe, Court No. 9, 1879–1885; charge books, 1875–1877, 1880–1883 (Blue Law violations), 1903; judgement book, 1889–1890; and marriages performed by Ebenezer Cobb, Court No. 10, 1885–1897.

Anonymous Gift, 1972.

1990
Lloyd, Malcolm, 1837–1911.   Papers, 1855–1911.   (50 items.)

Malcolm Lloyd owned the Gibson Point Refinery which was located on the Schuylkill River, Philadelphia. Lloyd, a pioneer in the oil refining field, was appointed Vice President of the Atlantic Refining Company following its purchase of the Gibson Point Refinery in 1888.

Contracts, patents, and patent assignments on Lloyd's oil refining business at Gibson Point on the Schuylkill River. Also membership certificates, leases, and obituaries.

Gift of Mrs. Nathan Hayward, 1970.

1991
Horn, Henry, 1786–1862.   Papers, 1816 (1826–1845), 1872.
(49 items.)

Henry Horn, a Philadelphia lawyer, served as a U.S. congressman, 1831–1833, and customs collector, 1845–1846.

These papers are mostly letters to Horn concerning state politics and congressional issues, with some family correspondence.

Gift of Mrs. Edna T. Stewart, 1970.

1992
Ashhurst family.   Papers, 1834–1890.   (122 items.)

Lewis Ashhurst was a Philadelphia merchant, bank director, and active in the Protestant Episcopal Church.

Ashhurst's diaries, 1834–1874, contain brief memoranda of his daily personal and professional activities. Mary Hazlehurst Ashhurst, wife of Lewis, diaries, 1834–1890, reflect her constant spiritual evaluation of herself and her family, and her religious activities. There are letters, 1865–1866, of Lewis R. and Mary Ashhurst and their children to others and also of their children while on a family tour through Europe.

Purchased, 1971.

1993
Coombe family.   Papers, 1751–1805.   (150 items.)

Thomas Coombe, Jr., studied for the Anglican ministry, 1768–1771. He returned to America as assistant minister to Christ Church and Saint Peter's Church in Philadelphia, but because of Loyalist sympathies, he removed to England in 1778.

Family correspondence, accounts, estate papers, and other legal papers of Thomas Coombe, collector of the Port of Philadelphia, and his children,

Sarah Coombe Shields and Thomas Coombe, Jr. The bulk of the correspondence are letters of Coombe, Jr., from England. Coombe writes home about family affairs, religion, and politics, with frequent mention of Benjamin Franklin whom he visited. The letters written from 1778 to 1803 relate mostly to family matters.

1994
No entry.

1995
Diaries and letterbooks, [1658]-1939, n.d.   (80 v.)

Alexander, John B. Memorandum book, 1812–1814. John B. Alexander was captain of a Company of Pennsylvania Volunteer Riflemen. This memorandum book contains notes of a march to join the Northwest Army, accounts, and muster roll. (1 v.)

Askew, Mary Brown, 1796-ca. 1887. Diaries, 1857–1869, 1873–1887. Diaries of family and social life in Burlington, N.J., with some account of Mrs. Askew's Brown relatives of Philadelphia. Gift of Thomas R. Adams and the University of Pennsylvania Library, 1951. (1 v.)

Bagnell, Edward. Letterbook, 1815–1816. Edward Bagnell owned St. Margaret's Hill plantation in Trinidad. This letterbook, kept while in New England and New York, covers Bagnell's efforts to stave off creditors; interspersed are food and health recipes, and expense accounts. (1 v.)

Baker, Anna Keyser. Diary, 1874–1876. Diary of Anna Keyser Baker, a Philadelphia Swedenborgian reporting on religious and social activities, with frequent mention of brother William Spohn Baker's family, and nature's wonders. Gift of Mrs. William Baker Whelen, 1951. (1 v.)

Barnitz, Euginia Landenberger, b. 1882. *Reflections of a Mid-Victorian* / edited by Rebecca Lycett Halsey, 1963. Personal memoirs of childhood, growing up, courtship, marriage, motherhood, divorce, earning a livelihood, ancestors, family, friends. (1 v.)

Barr, John P., b. 1839. Pocket diaries, 1862–1865. Diaries kept by John P. Barr, Brevet Major with the Pennsylvania Volunteers, 64th Regiment, reporting on guard, scout and picket duty, brigade headquarters assignments, occasional skirmishes and battle news, while with the Army of the Potomac in the Peninsular, Antietam, Fredericksburg, Chancellorsville, Gettysburg, Bristoe and other campaigns. Purchased, 1966. (8 v.)

Barrickman, John. Journal, 1812–1813. Kept while under the service of brigadier general Richard Crooks and Major General W.H. Harrison, recording travel of a marching detachment through Pittsburgh and Ohio. (1 v.)

Barton, Hetty Anne. Diary, 1803. Diary, May, 1803, of a family trip from Lancaster to visit Richard Peters Barton of Winchester, Va. The family returned through Washington, D.C., for dinner with President Jefferson. (1 v.)

Barton, Thomas, 1730–1780. Diary, 1758. Barton was an Episcopal missionary and clergyman. Diary kept as chaplain accompanying Brigadier General John Forbes's expedition against Fort Duquesne. Gift of the Dietrich Foundation, 1970. (1 v.)

Boyts, Franklin, 1840–1911. Diaries, 1862–1865. Boyts was a Somerset County, Union soldier, serving as a Sergeant with the Pennsylvania Volunteers, 142nd Regiment. His diaries, with letters inserted, describe action in campaigns of Fredericksburg, Chancellorsville, Gettysburg, and Wilderness, where he was wounded, duty in Commissary Department of Columbian College Hospital (Washington, D.C.) and defense of the capitol. Gift of Beatrice Edgerly, Boyt's granddaughter, 1967. (1 v.)

Brinley family. Papers, 1738–1800. Copies of letters and other documents concerning family news and business, with some references to the effects of the Revolutionary War on loyalist sympathizers. Gift of Beauveau Borie, 1949. (1 v.)

Calfe, John. Pocket devotional book, 1690. Contains direction for preparation and administration of Holy Communion according to the Church of England. With table of contents. Gift of J.C. Lightfoot, Jr., 1938. (1 v.)

Cavada, Adolph Fernandez, 1834-ca. 1871. Diary, 1861–1863. Kept while serving as Captain with Pennsylvania Volunteers, 23rd Regiment and as Inspector General and Special Aide de Campe to General Andrew Atlinson. Cavada reports on guard and picket duty and skirmishes during the Peninsular campaign, and on the Fredericksburg, Chancellorsville, Gettysburg, Bristoe, and Mine Run campaigns, with a detailed personal account of the Battle of Gettysburg. Copyflo. Gift of Mrs. Joseph Carson, 1973. (1 v.)

Clark, William J., 1839–1889. Scrapbook, 1861–1889. Clark was a Philadelphia journalist. Scrapbooks contains Civil War letters, commissions, and orders while serving on the South Atlantic blockading squadron. Also included are letters of condolence and obituaries of his death. Gift of Elizabeth E. Clark, 1951. (1 v.)

Clinton, Dewitt, 1769–1828. Diary extracts, 1826–1828. Contains brief memoranda of personal social and public activities, including a New England tour. Copy. (1 v.)

Clunn, John Hugg, 1770–1798. Diary, 1794. John Hugg Clunn was quarter master in New Jersey detached Militia, Artillery Battalion to brigadier general Joseph Bloomfield's Infantry Brigade, describing march from Trenton to Pittsburgh and back to quell the Whiskey Rebellion; continued as anonymous recipes, prose, and poetry. Diary portion published in *P.M.H.B.*, 71 (1947): 44–67. (1 v.)

Clymer, George, 1767–1830. Estate letterbook, 1815–1830. Contains letters of Clymer's son Henry and grandson William Bingham Clymer, mostly concerning management of Pennsylvania lands. Purchased, 1895. (1 v.)

Clymer, Meredith, 1817–1902. Diary, 1839–1840. Travel diary of Meredith Clymer, physician, professor, and author. Gift of George F. Howland, 1965. (1 v.)

Colt, Judah, 1761–1832. Diary, 1797–1811. Diary as an agent for the Pennsylvania Population Company, giving account of settlement of the Erie Triangle, disputes between the land company title holders and earlier settlers, and Colt's own farming activities. Typescript from microfilm at the Pennsylvania Historical and Museum Commission. Gift, 1963. (1 v.)

Colton, William Francis, 1841-ca. 1918. Diaries, 1862–1918. Recording Civil War service with the Pennsylvania Volunteers, 160th Regiment. Colton performed scouting duties in the Army of the Cumberland; his travels as an engineer for William Jackson Palmer's agent in Mexico, 1873–1874; with additional entries and memoranda on his other personal and professional activities. Gift of Hood Worthington, 1966. (1 v.)

Dickson, Robert. Diary, 1864. Dickson was Lawrence County Presbyterian minister. This diary was kept as chaplain with the Pennsylvania Volunteers, 100th Regiment, reporting on activity during the Wilderness, Spotsylvania, Petersburg campaigns, and North Anna River and Cold Harbor battles. Purchased, 1954. (1 v.)

Dillon, Romaine, b. ca. 1800. Letters, 1807 (1838–1862), 1881. Romaine Dillon was a New York city lawyer and diplomat. Letters to family matters, trips to Europe, diplomatic appointments, and other matters. Typescripts. Source unknown, 1965. (1 v.)

Drinker, Henry, 1734–1809. Diary, 1759. Describes voyage to England, with family reminiscences by Albert Gardner Clark appended. Gift of Mrs. John McDuffie, 1961. Copy. (1 v.)

Embree, George. Report, 1795. George Embree, John Murry, Jr., and Thomas Eddy, New York Quakers report on a journey undertaken to various Indian tribes on the New York western frontier by direction of the Meeting for Suffering and the Committee on Indian Affairs of the Yearly Meeting of New York. Gift of Friends Historical Association, 1954. (1 v.)

Emlen family. letters, 1772–1816. Mainly letters between Samuel Emlen and his wife, Sarah Mott Emlen while Samuel was on religious mission in Great Britain. There is some other family correspondence as well. Collected and arranged by Philip Syng Physick Conner. Gift of Mrs. W.H. Noble, Jr., 1950. (1 v.)

Fisher, Sarah Logan, 1751–1796. Diaries, 1776–1795. Sarah Logan Fisher's diaries are a record of domestic and family affairs, social and religious gatherings, and spiritual contemplations. Mrs. Logan reports, from the royalist perspective, on events of her husband, Thomas' exile to Virginia. Deposited by Benjamin R. Cadwalader. Diaries, Nov. 30, 1776-June 18, 1778 June 18 published in *P.M.H.B.*, 82 (1958). (24 v.)

Graff, Charles. Diaries, 1800–1823. Graff, a Philadelphia merchant, records voyages to Batavia, Macao, Wampao, New York State, and Western Pennsylvania. Purchased, 1955. (4 v.)

Gray, Isaac, b. 1747. Memorandum book, [1763]-1777. Gray's memorandum book includes recipes, weather observations, and Gray family genealogical notes. (1 v.)

Green, John, b. 1736. Records, 1784–1785. John Green was a sailing master and Revolutionary War naval Captain. These records provide log, diary, accounts and manifests at Canton for the *Empress of China,* the first ship to travel from America to China. Photostat. Original owned by Carrow Thibault, Jr. Purchased, 1956. (1 v.)

Grier, Helen S., 1842–1917. Diary, 1862–1863. Reports on her work for the United States Christian Association with the Army of the Potomac in Virginia. (1 v.)

Guest, Rebecca. Diary, 1800–1810. Diary of her life in England and in Philadelphia and vicinity, giving an account of her voyage to America. (1 v.)

Gummere, John. Diary, 1863. Gummere was a captain of the Lindis Battery, 1st Philadelphia Artillery. (1 v.)

Harris, G.W. Diary, 1841–1842. This diary was kept by a Washington County farmer. Purchased, 1975. (1 v.)

Harris, George M. "Journal of a Cruise in the U.S. Gunboat *Fort Henry,*" 1862. Harris writes of blockade duty off the coast of Georgia during this cruise. (1 v.)

Harrison, Joseph, 1810–1874. Letterpress books, 1844–1865. Joseph Harrison was a Philadelphia civil engineer. These letterpress books cover Harrison's family life, and his activities as a manufacturer of equipment for the St. Petersburg to Moscow Railroad, 1844–1862, developer and manufacturer of the Harrison Steam Boiler, real estate and stock investor, traveller, and art collector. The letters are written from St. Petersburg, Europe, and Philadelphia to family and business associates, including Annie Harrison Barry, Lewellyn F. Barry, Sarah Poulterer Harrison, William Henry Harrison, Thomas L. Luders, Stephen Poulterer, Anna McNeill Whistler, George Williams Whistler, Thomas DeKay Winans, William L. Winans. Purchased, 1962. (10 v.)

Harvey, Samuel. Letterbook, 1818–1823. Gift of George L. Harrison, 1952. (1 v.)

Hawley, Warren A. "The Trip of the Sloop Yacht *Restless* August 6–10, 1888." With pen-and-ink sketches. Gift of Everett M. Hawley, 1957. (1 v.)

Hazlehurst, Isaac, 1808–1891. Memorial volumes, n.d. Contain photographs. Gift of Craig D. Ritchie, 1901. (2 v.)

Hoopes, Penrose R. Weather diaries, 1863–1881. Penrose R. Hoopes was a Philadelphia merchant. Gift of Florence S. Hoopes, 1975. (2 v.)

Ivins, James. Diary, 1844. Largely meteorological and agricultural accounts for Bristol. Purchased, 1979. (1 v.)

Jessup, William. Diary, 1788–1789. Jessup was a Methodist preacher. This diary outlines his ministry in Nova Scotia, Maryland, and Delaware. Purchased, 1954. (1 v.)

Jones, Isaac Cooper. Collection, 1688–1880. Primarily marriage certificates of Cooper, Carpenter, Firth, and Jones family of Pennsylvania and New Jersey with several wills and estate inventories. Gift of Anna Woodruff Jones Bennett, 1940. (21 items.)

Jones, Lloyd, 1768–1820. Papers, 1796–1814. Jones was a Philadelphia shipmaster. Log for voyages between Philadelphia and Bordeaux; letterbook, 1813–1815, containing reports as Commander of the U.S.S. *Neptune* while waiting in various European ports for instructions for the transportation of U.S. delegates to the peace negotiations with Great Britain; incoming letters, 1806, 1813–1814, from Albert Gallatin, William Jones, George M. Dallas, and others relating mostly to the command of the *Neptune,* together with some accounts and lists of stores, 1811–1814. Gift of Robert M. Smith, 1952. (3 v.)

Jones, William Thomas. Letters, 1861–1864. Letters while serving as a private with the Pennsylvania Volunteers, 23rd Regiment, and as clerk for Army of the Potomac. Jones reported on Army life and action, including the Battles of Fair Oaks and Gettysburg. Typescript by Kenneth Trotter from the originals owned by Ann Elizabeth Savage and Sydney Jones Trotter. Gift of Kenneth Trotter, 1970. (1 v.)

Judd, Frank S. Diary, 1865. Judd was a Cheshire and West Meriden, Conn. Union soldier and button business man. His diary describes service as an engine room "oiler" aboard the U.S.S. *Grand Gulf* on the West Gulf Blockade; with some notes, 1864–1866, on civilian activities. (1 v.)

Keyser, Edmund, b. 1823. Record book, 1846–1865. Keyser was a Philadelphia saloon keeper and Democratic ward leader. This record book lists horse races and other competition for which Keyser seemingly look bets; continued as a diary, 1867–1876, recording weather, political maneuvering and other activities. Purchased, 1958. (1 v.)

Laughlin, Mrs. Tucker C., b. 1859. Pocket diary, 1888–1890. Mrs. Laughlin was a Chestnut Hill seamstress and housewife. In her pocket diary she reports on the household, sewing, family, and social activities. Gift of Joseph and Ruth Pascarell, 1976. (1 v.)

Lea, Thomas Gibson, 1785–1844. Diary, 1822. Cincinnati naturalist, Thomas Gibson Lea writes of his family's move from Pittsburgh to Cincinnati by flat boat. Gift of Mrs. James Febiger Lea, 1959. (1 v.)

Lear, Tobias. Diary, 1799–1801. Lear served as Secretary to George Washington. This diary gives an account of the last illness, death, and funeral of George Washington. There is also an account of consular appointment and voyage to Santo Domingo. Bequest of John Gribbel estate, 1947. (1 v.)

Leslie, Charles M.S. Narrative, 1873. Charles M.S. Leslie was a Philadelphia conveyancer. Narrative of the events leading to the failure of his real estate ventures written from Rio de Janeiro. Purchased, 1979. (1 v.)

Lewis, William David, 1792–1881. Letterbook, 1821–1822. Letters of William David Lewis, Philadelphia merchant to brother, John Delaware Lewis, commission merchant in Russia, regarding mercantile matters and Levett Harris' lawsuit against William. Also some letters to Samuel Williams concerning finances. (1 v.)

Longstreth, Charles. Diary, 1816. This diary is an account of a trip to England made by Longstreth, a Philadelphia merchant; with letters of introduction. Purchased, 1955. (1 v.)

Man, Daniel. Log, 1799–1800. Man was a Philadelphia sea captain and merchant. This is a log of two voyages between Philadelphia and Puerto Cabello, Venezuela, on board the schooner *Seaflower*. (1 v.)

Manigault, Harriet, 1793–1835. Diary, 1813–1816. The diary of this Philadelphia belle depicts family life and society in Philadelphia and at Clifton near Bristol. *The Diary of Harriet Manigault, 1813–1816* / Virginia and James S. Armerntrout, Jr., editors. (Philadelphia : Colonial Dames of America, Chapter II), 1976. Gift of Anna W. Ingersoll, 1960. (1 v.)

Matlack, Robert C. Statement, 1884. This statement, July 10, of Robert C. Matlack, Philadelphia Protestant Episcopal clergyman, concerns connections and business transactions with the Page family of Philadelphia. Purchased, 1948. (1 v.)

McAteer, Simon. Diary, 1864. Simon McAteer served as a Corporal with the Pennsylvania Volunteers, 113th Regiment. His diary reports on guard, scout, and picket duty, occasional skirmishes, and news of Shenandoah Valley campaign battles. Gift of Jack Burgess, 1943. (1 v.)

McCahan, Thomas S. Diary, 1862–1864. Kept while serving as Captain with the Pennsylvania Volunteers, 92nd Regiment describing skirmishes, battles and other activities with the Army of the Cumberland in Kentucky, Tennessee, Alabama, and Georgia. Copy, with additions to 1865. (1 v.)

McKnight, Charles. Diary, 1864–1865. McKnight was a Sergeant with the Pennsylvania Veterans Volunteers, 88th Regiment. This diary describes action in the campaigns of wilderness, Spotsylvania, Cold Harbor, Petersburg, and Appomatox. Gift of Wallace Weaver, 1954. (1 v.)

McManus, Susan Ritter Trautwine, 1841–1881. Diary, 1857–1881. Susan Ritter Trautwine McManus was a Philadelphia Moravian evangelical. In this diary she is reporting on religious work as well as domestic, social, and health matters; also biographical notes, 1863–1864, of Union soldiers at Turners Lane and other hospitals. Gift of Rosalie M. Mongel, 1960. (1 v.)

Mease, Thomas C. Diary, 1788. Mease was a farmer; the diary includes sporadic entries on garden planting and weather. (1 v.)

Mercer, John, 1704–1768. Diary, 1740–1768. Mercer, a Stafford County, Va., lawyer makes one line entries of his engagements. (1 v.)

Mercer, Joseph, 1837–1922. Notebook, 1859–1862. Joseph Mercer, Philadelphia conveyancer, realtor, and surveyor, kept miscellaneous notes in this book including a partial "Account of the taking of New Orleans & running Forts St. Phillip & Jackson," while aboard the U.S.S. *Pensacola*. (1 v.)

Merklee, Amanda L. Diary and record book, 1860–1866. In her diary, Amanda L. Merklee, Philadelphia trimmer, gives an account of her spiritual and temporal participation in the Tenth Baptist Church, other personal activities, dying and death, and Civil War news; record book, 1859–1870 for Ladies Christian Union Association and Ladies Hospital Aid Association, both of which Merklee served as an officer, with membership, subscriptions, donations. Gift of Helen G. Snyder, 1967. (2 v.)

Mervine, Charles R., b. 1847. Diary, 1862–1864. Kept while aboard the U.S.S. *Pohatan* on blockade and convoy duty in Atlantic and West India waters. Purchased, 1946. (1 v.)

Mervine, Isaac. Memorandum book, 1850–1863. Isaac Mervine was a Philadelphia police officer. This memorandum book consists primarily of a record of past and current unusual weather, conflagrations, and calamities; Mervine's sympathy with the American Party is evident in his reports and opinions on Philadelphia mayoralty elections. Purchased, 1946. (1 v.)

Mickley, Joseph J., 1799–1878. Diary, 1852. Daily entries made by Mickley, his wife, and four children. Joseph J. reports on his piano manufacturing and repairing business and coin collecting; Josephine C.A. notes comings and goings; the children tell of going to school; the entire family remarks on music lessons, performing or attending concerts, and other shared family activities. Gift of Paul Jones, 1958. (1 v.)

Miller, Morris Booth. Diary, 1917–1919. Diary while serving aboard the U.S.S. *Harrisburg* and the U.S.S. *President Grant*. Typescript copy. Gift, 1970. (1 v.)

Miskey, William F., 1816-ca. 1892. Autobiography, 1816–1892. Miskey, a Philadelphia clerk and merchant, recollects life in Philadelphia where he grew up and worked as a *United States Gazette* country collector and bookkeeper, and eventually became a partner of a gas fixtures manufacturing firm. Copy. (1 v.)

Mitchell, S. Weir (Silas Weir), 1829–1914. Autobiography, n.d. Typescript. (1 v.)

Moore, William Reed. Reminiscences, 1913. William Reed Moore was a Union soldier from Mercer County. In his reminiscences he recounts his service with the Pennsylvania Volunteers, 139th Regiment, which was held in reserve at the Battle of Fredericksburg. He also served with the 211th Regiment which participated in skirmishes and battles of the Petersburg campaign. Typescript. Gift of Maire Pinney, 1967. (1 v.)

Morgan, Samuel Rodman. Letterbook, 1861–1890. Morgan was a Philadelphia real estate and stock investor. His letterbook concerns personal and family investments in Philadelphia and Massachusetts property and stock, particularly in the Duncannon Iron Company, together with miscellaneous papers. (1 v.)

Morton, James, b. 1792. Writings, 1852–1853. Eastern State Penitentiary prisoners. These writings were undertaken to relieve the monotony of Morton's sixth and seventh years of solitary confinement. Included are a treatise on the decay of the Christian Church, especially the threat of popery, and an indictment of the penal system, police, courts, solitary confinement and the Pennsylvania Prison Society, naming officials particularly responsible for his treatment. Gift of Richard W. Foster, 1958. (1 v.)

Myer, Philip. Memorandum book, 1810–1811. Philip Myer was a Berks County land speculator. His memorandum book lists land transactions in Northumberland County, and other minor transactions. (1 v.)

Nicholson, James B., b. 1845. Diary, 1862–1865. Kept while serving as a Philadelphia Union sailor while at sea and port with U.S. Sloop of War *Jamestown,* sailing from Philadelphia to China, Japan and East India Stations, returning to San Francisco; with summary of important events. Scrapbook of clippings, 1863–1865, published from Nicholson's letters. Gift of Charles G. Simpson, 1957. (1 v.)

Nimocks, Franklin B. Papers, 1845–1849. Franklin B. Nimocks was a Carthage, N.Y., Mexican War officer. His papers consist mostly of military correspondence and orders as Acting Assistant Adjutant General, Department of Tampico Headquarters. (1 v.)

Nixon, John, 1733–1808. Estate letterbook, 1809–1810. John Nixon was a Philadelphia Revolutionary patriot. This estate letterbook, primarily in regard to Pennsylvania lands, was kept by Henry Nixon and Thomas Mayne Willing, executors. Gift of George L. Harrison, 1952. (1 v.)

Norcross, Aaron. Diary, 1775–1776. Norcross was a Northampton County Revolutionary War soldier. In his diary Norcross is reporting on service outside of Boston with Colonel William Thompson's Battalion of Rifleman (later the First Regiment of the Continental Army) and in the

Battle of Long Island with the First Regiment of the Pennsylvania Line in the Continental Service. (1 v.)

Norris, Septimus Henry. Memoir, [1894]. For Philadelphia lawyer relating family and social activities at the family "county seat' (20th and Norris Streets), details of his father William Norris' locomotive building business, a year residence in Austria, and other recollections of life in Philadelphia. Gift of Mrs. H. Norris Harrison, 1967. (1 v.)

Oldden, James, 1781–1832. Diary, 1800–1801, 1806, 1824. James Oldden was a Philadelphia merchant. His diary gives details of a trip to the British Isles and Europe; with biographical entries, 1806, 1824, describing his business career and his recovery from alcoholism. Purchased, 1969. (1 v.)

Partridge, William, 1669–1693. Notes, 1692. Partridge was a Wethersfield, Conn., Congregational minister. These are his notes on religious doctrine. (1 v.)

Patterson, Hamilton. Journal, 1852–1855, 1865. Journal of the Perry Expedition. Transcribed by George E. Chambers, 1855, continued as a scrapbook by Chambers, 1855–1865. (1 v.)

Patton, George Washington, 1817–1882. Diary, 1845–1869. Patton was a Blair County merchant. This diary reports on his business, family, social, and civic activities, local and national events. Typed extracts with notes by Patton's son, John Howard Patton. Purchased, 1957. (1 v.)

Paul, Mickle Cooper, b. 1837. Diary, 1864–1865. Cooper was a Philadelphia Union soldier and shoe merchant. Paul kept this diary while serving with the Signal Corps, Army of the Cumberland, and describing the Cumberland's participation in the Atlanta campaign, and his own subsequent duty in charge of Signal Corps mail at Atlanta and Chatanooga; with observations on army life in general. Gift of Paul Maloney, 1965. (1 v.)

Payne, Sarah Panill Miller, 1820–1910. Letters, 1865–1872. These letters describe the doings and whereabouts of various family members, farm life, social and economic adjustments during Reconstruction, with thoughts on the Civil War, secession and slavery; epilogue, 1910. Gift of Addison B. Freeman, 1958. (1 v.)

Pennington, Mary Proud Springett, ca. 1625–1643/4. *A Brief Account of Some of My Exercises,* [1658–1681]. Mary Pennington was an English Quaker married to William Pennington. In this account she gives a spiritual autobiography; biographical sketch, 1680, of her first husband, William Springett, a Parliamentary officer who died at the 1643/4 siege of Arundel Castle; continues with additional Christian narrative of others, 1743–1793. Published as *Experiences in the Life of Mary Pennington* / Norman Penney, ed. (1911) Purchased, 1941. (1 v.)

Pennypacker, James W. Diary, 1877–1878. Pennypacker describes in part his five months at Greytown (San Juan del Norte), Nicaragua, with a dredge construction project; and family and social life in Phoenixville. Purchased, 1956. (1 v.)

Philadelphia (Pa.). Commissioners for the Erection of Public Buildings. Letterbooks, 1875–1901. Kept by Samuel Perkins, president, mostly on finances and contracts for construction of Philadelphia City Hall; also Resolutions, June 26, 1901, in appreciation of Perkins's services as President. Bequest of Samuel C. Perkins, 1904. (3 v.)

Pitt, Benjamin, 1781–1864. Diary, 1834–1851. Pitt was schoolmaster of Colchester England and then of Covesville, Monroe County. Gift of Martin Winar, 1967. (1 v.)

Plummer, Charles Henry, b. 1822. Diaries, 1837–1847. Plummer was a Philadelphia Evangelist preacher, temperance lecturer, boot and shoe manufacturer. These diaries begin at age 16, recording debates, literary and temperance association activities, conversion to and preaching for the Christian Church, a variety of business ventures, courtship and marriage, and travel to New England to canvass for subscriptions to *The Christian*. Purchased, 1955. (6 v.)

Porter, Frederick W. Diary, 1829–1830. Porter served as Corresponding Secretary of the American Sunday School Union. This diary and memorandum book concerns personal and business matters. Gift of Henry F. Pommer, 1951. (1 v.)

Post, Christian Frederick, 1710?-1785. Diary, 1760. Post was a Moravian lay missionary to the Indians. This diary records a thwarted mission as a representative of the Governor and Council of Pennsylvania to the Ohio Valley Indians where he was particularly interested in gaining the release of prisoners. Accompanied by Tedyskung, Post turned back under the threat of attack by Mingoes. Copy. Gift of Friends Historical Association, 1949. (1 v.)

Preston, Samuel, 1756–1834. Diary, 1787. Preston was a Buckingham Township conveyancer and surveyor. He records trips to Delaware, Maryland, and through Pennsylvania as a business agent for Philadelphia merchants John Field, John Thompson, Henry Drinker, Mordecai Lewis, and others; also as a land agent for Drinker. The diaries record business activity, much of it consisting of debt collection, and observations on people and places. (1 v.)

Reed, William W. Diary, 1862. Reed was a Harrisburg Union soldier. This diary was kept while in Harrisburg at an undetermined occupation, and letter camp life and picket duty with the Pennsylvania Volunteers, 127th Regiment. (1 v.)

Richards, William 1738–1823. Memorandum book, 1781–1784. Richards was a New Jersey iron manufacturer. This book was kept by Richards while manager and owner of Batsto Iron Works, Batsto, N.J. Gift of Mr. and Mrs. H.L. Richards, 1940. (1 v.)

Richardson, Rebecca, 1821–1896. Diaries, 1853–1893. Rebecca Richardson was a Byberry Quaker gentlewoman. Her diaries consist of one line daily weather reports and occasional entries on comings and goings at Chestnut Glen, Byberry. Gift of Frances Richardson, 1957. (4 v.)

Roberts, Solomon White, 1811–1882. Diary, 1860–1861. Roberts was a Philadelphia civil engineer, canal and railroad expert. His diary was kept while general superintendent of the North Pennsylvania Railroad, commenting on business and social contacts, family and domestic affairs; with personal expense accounts. Gift of George Mayer, 1964. (1 v.)

Ruston, Thomas, 1742–1811. Diary, 1785. Thomas Ruston was an American physician at Exter, England, and Philadelphia. This diary records a visit to Paris and of conversations with Franklin, Jefferson, and other prominent people. Copy. (1 v.)

Sandel, Andreas, d. 1744. Diary, 1701–1719, 1721–1743. Andreas Sandel was a Swedish Lutheran Minister at Wicaco (Gloria Dei) Church. In this diary Sandel gives an account of his voyage to America, his life and ministry in the colonies, and return voyage to Sweden; continued with diary extracts, 1721–1743, on Sandel's American connections. Copy of translation by B. Elfoing. 1701–1719 published in the *P.M.H.B.*, 30 (1906): 287–299, 445–452. (1 v.)

Sayres, Edward Smith, 1797–1877. Memorandum book, 1828–1876. Sayres was a Philadelphia merchant and vice consul. His memorandum book includes some accounts, on his various occupations: supercargo on his brig *Clio* trading with Brazil, 1823–33; merchant of general goods, oil, and wine; vice consul for Brazil, Denmark, Norway, Portugal, and Sweden; farm owner. Family and household memos run throughout. Gift of the Free Library of Philadelphia, 1960. (1 v.)

Schaeffer, Ernestine Hochesang, 1829–1920. Memoirs, 1829–1892. Schaeffer reminisces of his childhood in Germany, 1848 emigration to America, marriage and raising a family in Philadelphia. Translation from Germany by Alice Rodman Ecroyd. Typescript. Gift of Henry Ecroyd, 1971. (1 v.)

Sherman, S.W. Pocket diaries, 1871–1892. S.W. Sherman was a Tioga County farmer. These diaries record day to day farm operations and activities, with some account of community activities and events. Purchased, 1977. (1 v.)

Shoemaker, Rebecca Warner Rawle, 1730–1819. Diary, 1813. Rebecca Shoemaker was a Philadelphia Quaker. Her diary records a summer at Woodford with her daughter Margaret Wharton and family, giving comings and goings of the Rawle, Shoemaker, Wharton, and Clifford families. Typewritten copy. Gift of Henry R. Pemberton, 1959. (1 v.)

Shrigley, James, b. 1814. Papers, 1863–1865. Shrigley was a Universalist Minister and librarian of the Historical Society of Pennsylvania. These papers are his official correspondence, orders, reports as chaplain at McClellan U.S.A. General Hospital, Philadelphia. Copy. Gift of James Shrigley, 1887. (1 v.)

Simpson, Robert. Letterbook, 1788–1796, 1800–1807. Simpson was a Scottish emigrant to Philadelphia. These letters home concern passage to America, life as apprentice printer, publishing business venture, and his decision to return to Scotland; continued with notes, 1800–1807, on sermons and brushes with death. Also in typescript. Purchased, 1958. (1 v.)

Smith, Persifor Fraser, 1798–1858. Letterbook, 1851–1854. Contains official correspondence and orders while Brevet Major General Commanding the 8th Military Department (the Department of Texas). Gift of Mrs. Arnold Talbot, 1942. (1 v.)

Stokes, Sallie, McG. Pocket notebook, 1859–1864. Sallie Stokes lived in Germantown. This notebook contains diary entries, copies of letters from her brother Wyndham, and other memoranda relating to social activities and Civil War. (1 v.)

Thackara, William Wood, 1791–1839. Diary, 1738–1816. William Wood Thackara was a Philadelphia conveyancer. His diary begins with notes on family history, continuing as diary entries which become more expanded, reporting on personal, family, public events, and service with Pennsylvania Volunteers, 1st Regiment, 1814, at Camp DuPont, with poems. Purchased, 1952. (1 v.)

Tozier, Frederic A. Pocket notebook, 1872–1878. Tozier was an Elk and Lycoming County lumber foreman. This notebook contains personal and lumber accounts; also notes, 1876, on trip to the Centennial Exposition. Gift of Gladys Tozier. (2 v.)

Troth, Henry, 1793–1842. Diary, 1813–1815. Henry Troth was a Philadelphia druggist, civic and business leader. His diary relates largely to his literary interests, books read, and meetings of the Philadelphia Literary Association, with some explanatory notes by his son Samuel Troth. Gift of Emma Troth, 1939. (1 v.)

Tucker, Joseph B., 1831–1867. Diary, 1852–1856. Tucker was a Cumberland County, N.J., glass works employee. In this diary he reports on family, social, Methodist Church, and civic activities, with some mention of glassworks employment. Typescript edited, with explanatory notes, by William McClure Dougherty. Indexed. Gift of William McClure Dougherty, 1967. (1 v.)

Vaux, Roberts, 1786–1836. Chemistry notes, 1807, and diary, 1808. Vaux was a Philadelphia philanthropist. His diary describes a horseback journey from Philadelphia to Clarks Valley, Schuylkill County. (1 v.)

Vining, Donald, b. 1917. Diary, 1926–1927, 1931–1939. Donald Vining was a New York City writer, editor, and publisher. This diary was kept while growing up in Pennsylvania, primarily as a student at West Chester State Teachers College, and reporting on his employment, his theater activities, and homosexuality. Typescript by Vining condensed from original in Yale University Library. Portions published in *A Gay Diary*, 1933–1967 (New York, 1979–1981). Gift of Donald Vining, 1963. (1 v.)

Wagner, Charles Mackinett, d. 1883. Notes, 1850–1875. Wagner was a Philadelphia attorney. These notes were received from Philadelphia lawyers regarding legal matters. Purchased, 1955. (1 v.)

Walker, James H. Diary, 1861–1864. Walker was a Union soldier. He kept this diary describing service in the Pennsylvania Volunteers, 81st Regiment, and its action with the Army of the Potomac, during the Peninsular, Chancellorsville, Gettysburg campaigns and later battles of Mine Run, Spotsylvania, North Anna River, Totopomoy Creek and Cold Harbor. Walker's account is most often concerned with daily army life, but there is some reporting on the battlefields. Donor unknown, 1966. (1 v.)

Watson, John Fanning, 1779–1860. *Bible Thoughts*, 1823–1859. Watson was a Philadelphia antiquarian, publisher, and financier. An examination of Christian doctrine, practice and belief by an "original enquirer after the truth." Purchased, 1970. (1 v.)

Wayne, Isaac, 1772–1852. Diary, 1821–1822. Isaac Wayne was Chester County Congressman and lawyer. In this diary Wayne describes farming and other activities at Waynesborough. Purchased, 1949. (1 v.)

Wayne, William H., 1809-ca. 1891. Meteorological diary, 1831–1835. Wayne was a Philadelphia clerk. His diary contains notes on odd and natural phenomena and some mention of current events; continued with miscellaneous items, 1841–1844, relating to Bucks County property. (1 v.)

Wehner, Jacob H. Medical notes on illness and treatment, n.d. Purchased, 1944. (1 v.)

Wenrick, James, 1829–1864. Diary, 1864. Wenrick was a Philadelphia Union soldier. This diary described his capture at Cypress Swamp, Tenn., and his imprisonment at Macon, Savannah, Charleston, and Columbia, where he died. Contemporary copy. Purchased, 1945. (1 v.)

Wharton, Anne Hollingsworth, 1845–1928. Dairy, 1903–1909. Anne Hollingsworth Wharton was a Philadelphia writer. Her diary gives an account of travels at home and abroad, social and literary gatherings, Society of Colonial Dames meetings, and her writing of *Italian Days and Ways*, (1906) *An English Honeymoon*, (1908) and other pieces. Gift of Genealogical Society of Pennsylvania, 1951. (1 v.)

Wharton, George Mifflin, 1806–1870. Legal records, 1826–1866. George Mifflin Wharton was a Philadelphia attorney and counselor and district attorney. These legal records include dockets, accounts, case book, letter-book, with some personal and miscellaneous accounts. (5 v.)

Wilcocks, Charlotte Manigault, d. 1875. Diary, 1842. Wilcocks was a Philadelphia belle. This the diary of the orphaned niece of Joseph Reed Ingersoll, depicting Washington and Philadelphia social life and gossip. With typescript. Gift of Anna Warren Ingersoll, 1963. (1 v.)

Williams, Richard Norris. A Survivor's Account of 1913 Sinking of the Titanic, 1933. With photographs. Richard Norris Williams was the director of the Historical Society of Pennsylvania. Gift of Richard Norris Williams. (1 v.)

Wilson, James Alexander Lesley. Diary, 1856–1859. Wilson was a Philadelphia clerk. This diary is mainly a record of social and church activities with young friends, courtship, and marriage. Gift of Mrs. W.A. White, 1958. (1 v.)

Windrim, James H., 1840–1919. Letterpress book, 1889–1891. Windrim was a Philadelphia architect. This letterpress book was kept by Windrim as Supervising Architect of U.S. Treasury Department. (1 v.)

Wood, George Bacon, 1797–1879. Diary, 1817–1829. Wood was a Philadelphia physician. His diary contains sporadic entries relating to his study of medicine, early career, and family trips to New York (State) and New England. Typescript, with introduction by grand nephew George Bacon Wood. Gift of DeForest Willard, 1946. (1 v.)

Yeates, Jasper, 1745–1817. Letterbook, 1769–1771. Yeates was a Lancaster attorney and jurist. His letterbook contains personal and business correspondence. Purchased, 1949. (1 v.)

Yeates, Jasper, 1745–1817. Pocket diary and memorandum book, 1764–1769. Notes and accounts relate to family, personal, and professional activities. Purchased, 1952. (1 v.)

Ziegler, Samuel William. Diary, 1857. Ziegler was a Philadelphia and Lewisburg Baptist Minister. His diary reports on work as colporteur and assistant at West Philadelphia Baptist Church, and on other Philadelphia Baptist ministers. Gift of College of Physicians, 1944. (1 v.)

1996
Longstreth, Thatcher.   Mayoralty campaign papers, 1971.
(300 items.)

Copies of letters and press releases of Thatcher Longstreth, 1971 Republican candidate for mayor against Frank Rizzo. The papers touch on the bicentennial, city finances, housing, education, and other campaign issues. The letters, in which Longstreth gives his positions, are addressed to Philadelphia's political, civic, and media leaders.

Gift of Thatcher Longstreth, 1972.

1997
Chamber of Commerce of Greater Philadelphia.
Records, 1891–1968.   (30 v. and 3,200 items.)

The Chamber of Commerce of Greater Philadelphia was formed by the 1915 merger of the Trades League of Philadelphia and the Merchants and Manufacturers Association, and followed by the 1942 merger with the Philadelphia Board of Trade. The Chamber of Commerce is an independent organization for the promotion and improvement of local commerce, business, and manufacturing interest.

The earliest records here are Trade League of Philadelphia minute books, 1891–1898. Minute books continue for the Chamber of Commerce Board of Directors, 1913–1968, some of which include full committee reports, and for the Executive Council, 1942–1958. There are also scattered minutes of various standing and special committees: Bridge, 1895; Reorganization, 1914–1915; Fire and Insurance, 1921–1944; Aviation, 1927–1946; Foreign Trade, 1933–1947; Transportation, 1934–1946; and Safety, 1958–1959. There are volumes of highly miscellaneous financial and organizational material.

The Chamber of Commerce loose files, 1949–1966, contain irregular records of correspondence, memoranda, and background material for committees and projects. Among the file labels are: Commerce and Industry Council, Manpower Resources Committee, Philadelphia Industrial Development Corporation, National Aeronautics and Space Administration, 1963–1964, and 30th Street Stadium, 1964.

Gift of the Chamber of Commerce, 1969.
Finding aid available.

1998
Barringer, Brandon, b. 1899.   Papers, 1956–1960.   (400 items.)

Brandon Barringer, treasurer of Curtis Publishing Company in Philadelphia, was active as a member of Hospital Council of Philadelphia, "a non-profit organization devoted to the improvement and coordination of hospital services." He held the offices of the secretary and acting chairman of secretary and acting chairman of the Blue Cross Relations Committee.

These papers for Brandon Barringer relate to his activities with the Hospital Council of Philadelphia. Types of papers include: incoming and outgoing correspondence, memoranda, minute, reports, and other materials.

Gift of Brandon Barringer, 1972.

1999
Public Baths Association of Philadelphia. Papers, 1890–1950. (50 items.)

The Public Baths Association of Philadelphia was a private charitable organization in 1895 to provide inexpensive bathing and laundry facilities to "the self-respecting poor" in working-class neighborhoods of Philadelphia. The Association, distinct from the City Baths which were swimming pools open only during the summer months, opened its first bath house in 1898, its fifth in 1928. The association functioned until 1946.

The papers consist of: trustee minutes, 1902–1950; scrap books, 1898–1944, of newspapers clippings, fund-raising letters, and other records on the association's real property, 1890–1944.

Gift Stephen R. Newman, 1972.

2000A
Morris family. Papers, 1723–1930. (20 linear ft.)

These papers contain correspondence, accounts, bills and receipts, deeds, surveys, and memoranda of the Morrises, a prominent Philadelphia family. This material is primarily concerned with family estates and lands in Philadelphia, western Pennsylvania, and New Jersey, with some business papers included.

Luke Wistar Morris Section, 1770–1881: accounts, 1811–1826, of his firm Morris and [John D.] Smith, lumber merchants. There are loose papers and account books, 1817–1828, relating to Morris' guardianship of the children of William Penrose. His estate papers refer to western Pennsylvania real estate and consist of correspondence to his son Samuel Buckley Morris and his grandson Elliston Perot Morris and business papers.

Samuel Buckley Morris Section, 1808–1912: business correspondence and accounts, 1808–1818, as a member of the shipping firm of [Jacob S.] Waln and Morris, as well as miscellaneous family estate material.

Elliston Perot Morris Section, 1725–1922: these papers are concerned with personal and family property management of the affairs and estates of John Perot Downing, Perot Lardner, Charles Perot, Edward Perot, John Perot, Beulah Sansom Morris Rhoads, Esther F. Wistar, and Mifflin Wistar. They include letterpress books, 1836–1914, correspondence, bills, receipts, account books, deeds, surveys, and other real estate papers.

Marriott Canby Morris Section, 1881–1930: letterpress books, 1914–1930, relate to personal and family property in Philadelphia, Pocono Lake, and Sea Girt, N.J., and various community projects of Germantown where Morris lived. Also personal accounts, 1881–1897.

Gift of Elliston P. Morris and Ann Morris courtesy of the Quaker Collection, Haverford College, 1972.

Finding aid available.

2000B
Morris family.   Papers, 1766–1959.   (9 linear ft.)

Additional Morris family accounts, receipted bills, family and social correspondence.

Wistar Section, 1733–1816: Caspar Wistar letterbooks, 1733–1737, and incoming correspondence, 1732–1754, many from George Frederick Holtzer concerning family, business, and politics; Sarah Wistar miscellaneous financial and estate papers, 1762–1816.

Luke Wistar Morris Section, 1787–1830: domestic receipted bills, 1810–1830; bills, accounts, legal papers, with some correspondence, 1816–1829, concerning Morris' guardianship of the children of William Penrose, Abigail, Ann, Hannah, Norwood, Samuel, and Thomas; and some of Morris' business papers.

Israel Wistar Morris Section, 1856–1903: personal and private business receipted bills, 1871–1886; Morris and [Henry W.] Murray, coal merchants, receipted bills, accounts, bills of lading, correspondence, 1856–1859; Morris' papers as land agent for Lehigh Valley Coal Company, 1864–1903, including correspondence, accounts, deeds, and other land papers.

Effingham Buckley Morris Section, 1865–1879: class notes, speeches, while a student at the University of Pennsylvania, together with letters from his fiancee Ellen Burroughs.

James Cheston Morris Section, 1837–1923: letters from family and friends, 1837–1922; physician's visiting record books, 1856, 1863; farm and household bills and receipts, 1904–1923; accounts of West Philadelphia properties, 1905–1912.

Lawrence Johnson Morris Section, 1881–1889, 1942: family letters and miscellaneous papers.

Mary Windor Morris Section, 1927–1959: social and family letters, newsletters and other mailings from various conservative organizations, and meditative diaries, 1953, 1954.

Letters from George Frederick Holtzer (Wistar Section) in german.

2000C
Morris family.   Papers, 1794–1913.   (9 linear ft.)

Business account books, letterbooks, and correspondence complimenting other Morris family papers.

Luke Wistar Morris Section: Luke W. Morris & Co. [Isaac W. Morris], brewers, letterbook and account book, 1794–1800; Morris and [Joseph] Maxfield, lumber merchants, account books, 1810–1814, 1816; Morris & [John D.] Smith, lumber merchants, account books, 1814–1819; Sarah Wistar estate account books, 1816–1827.

Perot Section: James and Sansom Perot, merchants, letterbook, 1817–1819; Charles and Joseph Perot, merchants, daybook, 1820–1821.

Israel Wistar Morris Section: Morris and [Henry W.] Murray, coal merchants, letterpress books, incoming correspondence, and account books, 1856–1859; Israel W. Morris letterpress books, 1856–1897, concerning Morris' continuing employment in the anthracite coal industry and his family and personal real estate and financial interests; incoming correspondence, 1868–1870, as president of Coal Ridge Coal Company; personal account books, 1852–1905; personal business papers after his death continued as Annie Morris Buckley papers, 1898–1914, consisting mostly of receipted bills with some incoming correspondence concerning finances.

There is also Church Home for Children, St. Andrews Church, record of contributors, 1866–1896; school notes of Effingham Buckley Morris and other family members.

Received, 1958.

Finding aid available.

2001
Miscellaneous Professional and Personal Business Papers, 1732–1945. (253 v.)

Adams, Zephaniah and Thomas Grover. Ledger, 1822–1830. Adams and Grover were Philadelphia Wharf Builders. Gift of H.W. Dyson, 1963. (1 v.)

Aldred, Thomas J., 1803–1880. Papers, 1821–1864. Thomas J. Aldred was a Chester County farmer. The papers include a commonplace book of recipes and remedies, n.d.; ledger, 1821–1862; journal, 1827–1860; journal of farm sales, 1855–1864; and auction account, 1853. (5 v.)

Anderson, Samuel V. Letterbook, 1835–1837. Samuel V. Anderson Son & Co. were Philadelphia wholesale grocers. Purchased, 1956. (1 v.)

Anderson Manufacturing Company (Lancaster, Pa.) Time book and journal, 1860–1867. Purchased, 1957. (1 v.)

Arch Street Theatre (Philadelphia, Pa.) Subscription book, 1828–1859. Subscription book contains building proposal and cash accounts kept by Peter Hertzog, Secretary; continued by Ann Hertzog, widow of Peter, with household accounts and notes, 1855–1859. Gift of Ogden D. Wilkinson Estate, 1940. (1 v.)

Ashton Brothers. Memorandum book, 1851–1857. Ashton Brothers was a Philadelphia real estate agent and conveyancer. The memorandum book contains management and settlement of properties. Purchased, 1959. (1 v.)

Baker, George A. Ledger, 1792–1803. Baker was a Philadelphia scrivener. Gift of John F. Lewis, 1895. (1 v.)

— Baynton, Wharton and Morgan. Journal, 1765–1767. Baynton, Wharton, and Morgan were Philadelphia merchants. This journal is a record of transactions at Fort Pitt Trading Post. Photostat. Original at the Historical Society of Western Pennsylvania. Indexed. Gift of the Pittsburgh Chapter of the Daughters of the American Revolution, 1948. (1 v.)

Beidler, Susanna. Receipt book, 1831–1847. Receipts for the estate of Christian Beidler. (1 v.)

Bentley, David. Daybooks, 1822–1824, 1842–1870. Purchased, 1946. (3 v.)

Bethany & Dingman's Choice Turnpike Road Company. Stock transfer book, 1813–1864. Purchased, 1961. (1 v.)

Bickham, Martin. Sales accounts, 1818–1824, and letterbook, 1829–1832. Bickham was a Port Louis (Isle de France) ships' factor. (2 v.)

Biddle, William. Receipt book, 1841–1871. Biddle was the Secretary for Mine Hill and Schuylkill Haven Railroad. Gift of Mrs. Robert James, 1949. (1 v.)

Billmeyer, John and Jacob. Letterbooks, 1809–1818. John and Jacob were Philadelphia flour merchants. Purchased. (2 v.)

Binny and Ronaldson. Specimen book, 1804–1816, 1830–1831. Archibald Binny and James Ronaldson formed a partnership in 1796 and founded America's first type founding plant. Specimen book, 1804–1816, with prices; continued as newspaper clippings, 1830–1831, on economics and politics. (1 v.)

Bolton, Mary and Emma. Ledger, 1846–1857. The ledger is for domestic expenses. Gift of the Free Library of Philadelphia, 1950. (1 v.)

Boys, Abraham and Thomas Sinnickson. Daybook, 1810–1814. Boys and Sinnickson were Philadelphia merchants. Purchased, 1959. (1 v.)

Bricklayers Company of Philadelphia. Records, 1792–1917. These records consist of the constitution, by-laws, and minutes. Deposited by the Bricklayers Company of Philadelphia, 1957. (3 v.)

Buchanan and McGill. Daybook, 1859–1861. William Buchanan and John McGill were South Hermitage, Lancaster County, grocers. Continued by John McGill with plans for Hugh W. Black and Joseph Clough's Dye House. Gift of John McGill Cooper, 1958. (1 v.)

Burd family. Accounts current, 1841–1846. These accounts are with the Farmers' and Mechanics' Bank of Philadelphia. Purchased, 1935. (1 v.)

Burr, Joseph. Daybook, 1759–1773. Burr was a New Jersey merchant. Gift of Mrs. Robert Link, 1979. (1 v.)

Cadbury, Richard, 1825–1897. Receipt book, 1850–1892. Cadbury was a Philadelphia dry goods merchant. Personal receipt book with entries for mortgage payments and other receipts. Gift of Richard Cadbury, 1949. (1 v.)

Campbell, Thomas. Receipt book, 1807–1812, 1828–1832. Thomas Campbell was an inhabitant of Albany, N.Y.; his wife Mary moved to Philadelphia after his death. Receipt book, 1807–1812, in part as partner of Macauly and Campbell; continued by Mary Campbell of Philadelphia, 1828–32. Also contains medicinal recipes. (1 v.)

Carpenter, John M. Daybook, 1857–1858. John M. Carpenter was a Salem, N.J., grocer. Daybook with entries for coffee, sugar. Purchased, 1959. (1 v.)

Chandler, James B. Memoranda, 1838–1839. James Chandler was an employee of Philadelphia merchants Moore, Heyl and Company. Memoranda book, 1838–1839, contains duties on dry goods and other notes. Purchased, 1959. (1 v.)

Chapman, Nathaniel, 1780–1853. Receipt book, 1820–1834. Nathaniel Chapman was a Philadelphia physician. Receipt book, 1820–1834, containing entries for mostly personal expenses. (1 v.)

Chase, George Clinton. Receipt book, 1837–1855. George Clinton Chase was a Philadelphia carpenter. Receipt book, 1837–1855, with entries for work done. Original privately owned. Photocopy gift of Historical Society of Wisconsin. (1 v.)

City National Bank of Philadelphia. Director's Minutes, 1896–1901. City National Bank was a Philadelphia bank, founded in 1855. Minutes for twice weekly meetings of the Board of Directors. (1 v.)

John W. Clark's Sons. Daybook, 1837–1847. John W. Clark was a Philadelphia bookbinder. Daybook, 1837–1847, with some description of services rendered. (1 v.)

Clark, Thomas. Account books, 1812–1820. Thomas Clark was a Philadelphia bookbinder and bookseller. Daybook, 1812, and ledger, 1812–1820, with entries for books and writing materials sold. (1 v.)

Clark, Thomas. Ledger, 1840–1881. Thomas Clark was a Philadelphia bookbinder and bookseller. Ledger 1840–1881, including list of books for Presbyterian Board of Publications. (1 v.)

Clement, Mark, b. 1790. Account books, 1815–1857. Mark Clement was a Deptford, N.J., brick and lumber yard owner. Daybook, 1815–1857, and ledger, 1815–1851 with entries for transport of wood an well as for sales. Purchased, 1956. (2 v.)

Clifford School District (Susquehanna County, Pa.) School Accounts, 1872–1891. The Clifford School District, in Clifford, is near Carbondale in Susquehanna County. Accounts list wages paid to employees of the school district with notations for state school appropriations. (1 v.)

Clifton, Anna Maria, d. 1811. Receipt book, 1795–1811. Anna Clifton was a resident of Philadelphia. Receipt book with entries for personal expenses. Purchased, 1959. (1 v.)

Coates, Samuel, 1711–1748. Personal receipt book, 1732–1740. Purchased, 1958. (1 v.)

Coates, Samuel. Journal (bookkeeping), 1760–1776. Coates was a Philadelphia merchant. Photostat. Original privately owned. (1 v.)

Coates, Samuel. Bills of Lading, 1791–1812. Coates was a Philadelphia merchant. Photostats. Originals privately owned. (1 v.)

Coleman, Philip E. Daybooks, 1850–1883. Coleman was a Philadelphia conveyancer and secretary. These daybooks cover bonds, mortgages, deeds, and other legal documents; personal business account book, 1861–1894, of mortgage, rent, investment income; continued from Washington Sparkassen Verein daybook, 1848–1851, of a Philadelphia savings association; John Naglee estate account book, 1852–1854, including inventory of Union Mill. Purchased, 1959. (1 v.)

Colfelt, Charles, b. 1815. Ledger and miscellaneous accounts, 1844–1857. Charles Colfelt was a Mifflin County farmer. Ledger and miscellaneous farm accounts. (1 v.)

Concord School House of Upper Germantown (Philadelphia, Pa.) Records, 1775–1945. The Concord School House was built by the residents of the upper end of Germantown in a portion of the upper Burying Ground. Funds were raised by subscription. Board of Trustees minutes, consisting largely of elections and treasurer reports. Treasurer accounts also. Permanent deposit by Concord School House of Germantown and the Upper Germantown Burying Ground Board of Trustees. (1 v.)

Concord School House of Upper Germantown (Philadelphia, Pa.) Treasurer's Accounts, 1851–1953. The Concord School House was built by the residents of the Upper end of Germantown on a portion of the Upper Burying Ground. Funds were raised by subscription. Treasurer's accounts for fuel and other expenses. Gift of Doris Ritzinger, 1972. (1 v.)

Connolly, Arthur J. Ledger, 1880, 1885. Arthur J. Connolly was a Philadelphia tinsmith. Purchased, 1959. (1 v.)

Cowperthaite and Co. Daybook and journal, 1891–1892. Cowperthaite and Co. were Philadelphia school book publishers. (1 v.)

Cramond, William. Receipt book, 1814–1815. Cramond was a Philadelphia merchant. (1 v.)

George Dabbs & Co. Daybooks, 1858–1860. George Dabbs & Co. was a Philadelphia photographic supply merchant. Originally partner in Dabbs & Birmingham with James Birmingham. Daybooks with entries for sales all along the east coast. Gift of Henry S. Cole, through Chester County Historical Society, 1967. (3 v.)

Elijah Davis & Co. Daybook, 1843–1847. Elijah Davis was a Philadelphia white lead manufacturer. Daybook, 1843–1847, with shipping entries. Gift of Sarah A.G. Smith. (1 v.)

DeLancey, William Heathcote, 1797–1865. Record book, 1831–1840. William DeLancey was an Episcopal clergyman. He was assistant minister of the United Church of Christ, St. Peter's and St. James in Philadelphia, the rector of St. Peter's and the bishop of the Diocese of Western New York. Record book, 1831–1840, includes lists of marriages, confirmations and baptisms at the United Church of Christ, St. Peter's and St. James in Philadelphia. Also an alphabetical list of St. Peter's Church communicants, 1833–1839. Gift of Museum of the City of New York, 1954. (1 v.)

Delaware and Schuylkill Canal Co. Minutes, 1835–1842. The Delaware and Schuylkill Canal Company was established for opening a canal and lock navigation between the Delaware and Schuylkill rivers through the southern section of Philadelphia County. Board minutes with stockholders annual meeting minutes. Gift of Mrs. Henry Wharton, 1950. (1 v.)

Diamond, William J., fl. 1833–1869. Receipt book, 1842–1869. William J. and Thomas M. Diamond were potters who ran an earthenware manufactory in Salem, N.J., which opened in 1833. Receipt book contains entries primarily for rent. Purchased, 1959. (1 v.)

Downing, Charles H., b. 1843. Docket book, 1861–1874. Charles Downing worked in a Philadelphia alderman's office. Docket book with an alderman's cases. (1 v.)

Doyle, Dennis, d. 1803. Receipt books, 1802–1834. Dennis Doyle was a Philadelphia resident. After his death his wife Ann married John Maypother, a resident of Lower Dublin. Receipts relating to a Philadelphia shopkeeper, Lower Dublin farm, taxes, tuition, medical treatment, burials and other expenses. Purchased, 1959. (2 v.)

Dreer, Frederick, 1782–1864. Cashbook, 1835–1838. Frederick Dreer was the proprietor of the American Museum, at 5th and Chestnut Streets. Cashbook, 1835–1838, with receipts and expenses for exhibitions at the American Museum. Purchased, 1954. (1 v.)

Dubarry, Jean. Documents and depositions, 1793, 1825–1826. Jean Dubarry was a Santo Domingo merchant. These documents and depositions refer to compensation claims against the French government for losses sustained in 1793. Purchased, 1874. (1 v.)

Edwards, William L., b.1815. Daybook and Cashbook, 1856–1875. William Edwards was a Philadelphia wool merchant. Daybook, 1856–1874, and cashbook, 1859–1875, with business accounts to 1863 and personal investment accounts thereafter. Gift of Chester County Historical Society, 1967. (2 v.)

E. Headley Bailey & Co. Protest ledger, 1893–1920. This was a Philadelphia Custom House Brokerage firm. Gift of Lena Scheindlinger, 1966. (1 v.)

Evans, Peter. Account book, 1767–1828. Peter Evans was a Montgomery County grain merchant. Account book, 1767–1788, mostly for grain sales; continued as Baptist Church of Christ subscription list, 1815; continued as receipt book, 1823–1828, for David Evans as executor for Peter Evans estate. (2 v.)

Eyre, John, d. 1781. Receipt book, 1776–1795. John and Lydia Eyre were Philadelphia residents. Household receipt book, 1776–1795, with receipts paid for taxes in the Northern Liberties. (2 v.)

Eyre, Manuel, 1774–1845. Account books, 1798–1838. Manuel Eyre was a Philadelphia merchant. Invoice book, 1798–1801; continued as bills payable and receivable, 1801–1802; Kensington farm day book, 1831–1835; lead factory cash book, 1831–1838. (3 v.)

Fegley, George. Journal, 1841–1845. George and Nathan Fegley were Mauch Chunk merchants. Mauch Chunk is now Jim Thorpe. Journal, 1841–1845. Purchased, 1967. (1 v.)

Joshua Fisher & Sons. Journal, 1776–1796. Joshua Fisher and Sons were Philadelphia merchants. Journal, 1776–1779, 1784–1796, with accounts of the closing of Fisher's store by the Committee of Safety, 1776. Gift of William J. McCouch, 1950. (1 v.)

Thomas, Samuel & Miers Fisher. Journal, 1784–1788, and ledger, 1792–1796. Gift of Henry Austin Wood, 1792. (2 v.)

Fitler, Elvina, fl. 1865–1874. Daybook, 1865–1874. Elvina Fitler was a West Chester milliner. Daybook, 1865–1874, with listings of hats made for each patron. Purchased, 1959. (1 v.)

Fitzsimons, Thomas, 1741–1811. Journal, 1781–1785. Fitzsimons was a Philadelphia congressman. Gift of Willis Blayney, 1973. (1 v.)

Foulke, Eleanor Parker, d. 1859. Account book, 1835 (1843–1847). Eleanor Foulke was a Philadelphia resident. Account book, 1835 (1843–1847), with real estate and domestic expenses. Gift of John W. Cadbury, 1944. (1 v.)

Foust and Weaver. Journal, 1854–1861. William H. Foust and David P. Weaver were Philadelphia stonecutters. (1 v.)

Frankford Academy. Minute book, 1798–1809. The Frankford Academy, a subscription school, was built in 1798 and sold in 1806. Contains subscription list, cash book and trustees minutes, 1798–1806, 1809. Purchased, 1958. (1 v.)

Frazier, Nalbro, 1759–1811. Account books, 1805–1851. Nalbro Frazier, father and son, were Philadelphia merchants. Cashbook, 1805–1811, and journal, 1842–1852. Gift of Mrs. Edmund Purvis, 1940. (1 v.)

Fuller & Sinnickson. Ledger, 1763–1782. (Benjamin) Fuller and Sinnickson were Philadelphia vendue masters. Ledger, 1763–1782. Purchased, 1975. (1 v.)

Gap Mining Company of Lancaster County. Minutes, 1851–1867. The Gap Mining Company operated copper mines and, later, nickel mines in Bart Township. Minutes of Board of Director's meetings, with treasurer's reports. Gift of Mrs. Henry Wharton, 1950. (1 v.)

John Gay's Sons. Journal, 1876–1916. John Gay's manufactured carpets at the Park Carpet Mills, Philadelphia. John Gay in partnership with sons James H. and Thomas S. Gay. Daily notebook of operations, 1876–1916, with notations on strike activities of weavers in Kensington, and elsewhere. Purchased, 1956. (1 v.)

Germantown Petroleum Company (Philadelphia, Pa.) Minutes, 1865–1868. (1 v.)

Girard Trust Corn Exchange Bank (Philadelphia, Pa.) Record book, 1902–1922. Girard Trust Company incorporated in 1836 as the Girard Life Insurance Annuity and Trust Company and merged in 1951 with Corn Exchange National Bank. Record book, 1902–1922, of real estate sales in central Philadelphia; includes block maps and street index. Gift of Chester County Historical Society, 1967. (1 v.)

Greenhill estate. Title Papers, 1694–1866. The Greenhill estate included land in Lower Merion Township, Montgomery County and Blockley Township in Philadelphia. Title papers including deeds. Gift of Mrs. W. Logan MacCoy, 1964. (1 v.)

Griffith, Samuel, b. 1810. Ledgers, (1829–1849) 1881. Samuel Griffiths was a Robeson Township, Berks County blacksmith. Accounts receivable ledgers, (1829–1849) 1881. Purchased, 1959. (4 v.)

Haines, Reuben, 1727–1793. Journal, 1779–1785. Haines was a Philadelphia brewer. This journal (bookkeeping) contains business and house accounts; continued as John Thompson, Centre county Justice of the Peace, docket book, 1823–1831; continued as H.F. Hess, Boalsburg, Centre County miscellaneous notes and accounts, 1894–1896. Gift of the Institute of Early American History and Culture (Williamsburg, Pa.), 1953. (1 v.)

Hall, John. Estate account books, 1811–1818. John Hall was a resident of New Castle, Del. Estate journal and ledger, 1811–1818. Purchased, 1935. (1 v.)

Harrison, George, 1762–1845. Ledger, 1805–1807. George Harrison was a Philadelphia merchant. Ledger, 1805–1807, with accounts for shipping ventures. Gift of Mrs. James Drinker, 1961. (1 v.)

Hayes, Richard, fl. 1708–1740. Ledger, 1708–1740. Richard Hayes was a Philadelphia miller. Ledger, 1708–1740, contains entries for grain and for mercantile shipping voyages. Gift of B. Hayes and S. Anderson, 1907. (1 v.)

Hewes, Aaron, 1742/3–1789. Estate account books, 1789–1791. Hewes was a Gloucester County, N.J. leather merchant. Josiah Hewes, administrator. Purchased, 1959. (1 v.)

Higbee, Lucy Ann, d.1853. Diary, 1837. Lucy Ann Higbee lived in Richmond Hill near Trenton, N.J. Travel diary describing a trip through Pennsylvania, Ohio, and New York starting and ending in Richmond Hill, N.J. Describes coach, train, river and canal transportation as well as interesting anecdotes about towns and cities visited. Gift of Peter S.H. Moore, 1987. (1 v.)

Hilliard, Samuel. Estate vendue book, 1837–1838. Hilliard was a Salem, N.J., farmer. George M. Ward, administrator. Purchased, 1959. (1 v.)

Hopkins, Albert Cole, 1837–1911. Land records, 1872–1915. Albert Hopkins, a resident of Lock Haven, was a wholesale lumber merchant selling pine, hemlock and hardwood. He was also a Congressman, 1891–1895, and State Forestry Commissioner, 1899–1904. Surveys and land records of timber and coal lands in western Pennsylvania. Gift of Eastern Washington State Historical Society. (1 v.)

Hough, Oliver, 1763–1804. Ledger, 1796–1798. Hough was a Bucks County ironmonger. Gift of the Oliver Hough estate, 1915. (1 v.)

Hubley, James B. Legal case book, 1808–1812. Hubley was a Reading attorney. This legal case book contains information on Berks, Northampton, and Schuylkill County suits. Gift of Juliet C. Walker, 1941. (1 v.)

Huggins, Benjamin. Journal and Memorandum book, 1807–1824. Huggins was a supercargo on several voyages trading to Europe and West Indies. (1 v.)

Hughes, John. Journal, 1767–1773. Hughes was a Philadelphia merchant. Gift of Mrs. W. Logan MacCoy, 1964. (3 v.)

Humes and Rogers. Daybook, 1811–1815. Hughes and Rogers were Philadelphia hardware merchants. (1 v.)

Humphreys, Samuel. Journal, 1818–1845. Samuel Humphreys was a U.S. Naval constructor. This journal concerns shipbuilding at the Philadelphia Navy Yard. Includes ships surveys and reports on repairs, with copies of letters from commanders concerning performance of their ships. Gift of C.R. Humphreys, 1973. (1 v.)

Hunter, George. Daybook, 1788–1791. Hunter was a Philadelphia coachmaker. Also includes clippings of poetry. Purchased, 1959. (1 v.)

Hunter, William. Daybook, 1801–1810. Hunter was a Philadelphia coachmaker. Purchased, 1959. (1 v.)

Hutchinson, John P. Account books, 1808–1837. Hutchinson was a Philadelphia merchant. These accounts include invoices, accounts current, sales, letters, poems, remedies, recipes, and estate papers. (1 v.)

Hytest Board Company. Prospectus, 1931. Hytest Board Company manufactured kraft or sulphate pulp fibre board in Oregon with sales and distribution located in Philadelphia. (1 v.)

Insurance Company of the State of Pennsylvania (Philadelphia, Pa.) Letterbook, 1794–1804. The Insurance Company of the State of Pennsylvania was a marine insurance company. Purchased, 1959. (1 v.)

Insurance Company of the State of Pennsylvania (Philadelphia, Pa.) Letterbook, 1804–1807. Purchased, 1954. (1 v.)

Irwin, James. Accounts, 1848–1856. Irwin was a Philadelphia broker. These accounts record bills and notes payable and receivable. Gift of Caroline B. Taylor, 1958. (1 v.)

Janney, Aquila. Daybook and Ledger, 1791–1792. Janney was a Philadelphia merchant. Continued as a commonplace book, n.d. Gift of the Ohio Historical Society, 1962. (1 v.)

Jewitt, John. Ledger, 1805–1830. Jewitt was a Dutchess County, N.Y., farmer. This ledger contains mostly farm accounts but also includes records on cider sales, land surveys, and legal work. Purchased, 1959. (1 v.)

Jones, Clarke, & Cresson. Receipt books, 1783–1797. Jones, Clarke, & Cresson were Philadelphia lumber merchants. Gift of the Chester County Historical Society. (1 v.)

Josephine (ship). Adjustor's statement, 1882–1883. This adjustor's statement, kept by O.C. Cranmer, ship master, after the *Josephine* struck on the Delaware Breaker icebreaker, April 20, 1882, on voyage from Jacksonville, Fla. to Philadelphia. Statement includes log of the voyage and the salvage operations, the marine surveyor's report, and the costs of salvage and repairs. Gift of the Free Library of Philadelphia, 1960. (1 v.)

Keefer & Keller. Daybook, 1829–1830. Keefer & Keller were Harrisburg carpenters and joiners. Gift of Mrs. Dean A. Fales, 1976. (1 v.)

Kuntz, M. Account book, 1870–1872. Michael G. Kuntz was treasurer of Washington Borough, Washington County. Purchased, 1954. (1 v.)

Lancaster & Jenkins. Records, 1815–1830. Lancaster & Jenkins were Philadelphia dry goods merchants. The records include daybooks, 1820–1830, ledger, 1815–1823, and Charles Jenkins' daybook, 1829. Gift of the Historical Society of Montgomery County, 1965. (7 v.)

John and Melchior Larer. Receipt book, 1815–1820. John and Melchior Larer were Philadelphia brewers. (1 v.)

Le Blanc, Joseph. Receipt book, 1785–1792. Joseph Le Blanc was a Philadelphia women's goods merchant. This book contains both personal and business receipts; continued by William H. Henry for letter drafts and memoranda, [1828]. Gift of Hamilton H. Gilkyson, 1968 (1 v.)

Levis, Hosea J. Records, 1836–1843. Levis was the cashier for the Schuylkill Bank, Philadelphia. The records include lists of bills for stocks purchased and sold, 1836–1839; stock accounts and letters to Levis concerning transactions, 1836–1839; minutes/letterbook, 1840–1843, kept by John R. Vodges, Eli K. Price, and Charles Thomson Jones, assignees appointed to resolve debts Levi incurred while mismanaging Schuylkill Bank funds. (3 v.)

Levy, Joseph. Receipt book, 1860–1891. Personal receipts. Gift of Miriam Levy, 1957. (1 v.)

Lewis, William David, 1792–1881. Employee Records, 1849–1853. Lewis was Philadelphia Collector of Customs. Purchased, 1941 (1 v.)

Linn, William. Receipt book, 1830–1832. Linn was a Philadelphia textile manufacturer. Contains personal and business receipts. Purchased, 1959. (1 v.)

Lippincott, Joshua Ballinger, 1813–1886. Ledger, 1853–1862. Lippincott was a Philadelphia publisher. Contains accounts for real estate and stocks. (1 v.)

Lipps, John. Receipt book, 1789–1790. Lipps was a Philadelphia tailor. Contains personal receipts; continued by Mary Lipps Keyser Maze, 1790–1821. Gift of Benjamin Moskowitz, 1976. (1 v.)

Little, Theodore. Case book, 1848–1870. Little was a Morristown, N.J., attorney. Contains information on Morris County, N.J., suits, primarily in the Circuit Court. (1 v.)

Livezey, Samuel, 1760–1840. Letterbook, 1824–1828. Livezey was a Plymouth Meeting merchant and a Quaker minister. (1 v.)

Logan, James, 1644–1751. Ledger, 1712–1714. Contains personal and proprietary accounts. Gift of J. Welles Henderson. (1 v.)

Long, William. Receipted bills, 1866–1873. Bills kept by William and Ida Long. (1 v.)

Lorain, John. Receipt book, 1809–1811. Lorain was a Philadelphia merchant. (1 v.)

Lower Marsh Creek Presbyterian Church (Adams County, Pa.) Receipt book, 1769–1778, 1786–1789, 1793–1849. For salaries paid to John Slemons, John McKnight, and William Paxton, ministers. Purchased, 1950. (1 v.)

Loxley, Benjamin, 1720–1801. Daybook, 1771–1785. Contains both personal and financial memoranda, including accounts as artillery store keeper for the Province of Pennsylvania and for canons, wagons, and other Revolutionary militia supplies. Gift of Library Company of Philadelphia, 1967. (1 v.)

McCall, Samuel, 1710–1761. Journal, 1743–1749. McCall was a Philadelphia merchant. Purchased, 1959. (1 v.)

Marsh, Ann. Accounts, 1774–1783. Ann Marsh was a Philadelphia educator. Accounts while teaching at the Dame School. Bequest of John Marshall Phillips, 1954. (1 v.)

Mathew, Joseph. Ledger, 1820–1841. Joseph Mathew was a New Britain Township physician. Ledger contains patient accounts. Purchased, 1944. (1 v.)

May, Thomas. Receipt book, 1764–1793. Contains personal receipts. Gift of William M. Beck, 1954. (1 v.)

Samuel and Joseph Mechlin. Journal (bookkeeping), 1794–1796 and ledger, 1794–1796. Samuel and Joseph Mechlin were Philadelphia grocers specializing in linseed oil. Purchased, 1959. (1 v.)

Meeker, Samuel, d. 1832. Ledger, 1807–1810. Meeker was a Philadelphia merchant. Ledger contains accounts of trade with New Orleans, Ohio, and Kentucky; also as agent for William Meeker, London merchant. (1 v.)

Mendelhall & Cope. Record book, 1789–1837. Mendelhall & Cope were Philadelphia merchants. Contains accounts of cash, 1789; sales, 1790; journal entries, 1790–1792, 1795; continued as Thomas P. Cope journal, 1836–1837. Gift of Mrs. Alfred Cope Garrett, 1949. (1 v.)

Meredith, Jonathan, 1740–1811. Order book, 1787–1798. Meredith was a Philadelphia tanner and currier. Purchased, 1959. (1 v.)

Mildred & Roberts. Accounts, 1777–1778. Mildred & Roberts were London merchants. These accounts are for their trading with Philadelphia merchants. (1 v.)

Miller, Henry. Estate accounts, 1807–1843. Miller was a Huntington Borough storekeeper. Jacob Miller, administrator; continued as Jacob Miller personal and business cashbook, 1850–1862. Gift of Charles A. Miller, 1962. (1 v.)

Monks, John. Ledger, 1795 (1812–1847). Monks was a Philadelphia County weaver. Ledger of accounts receivable. Purchased, 1959. (1 v.)

Moore, John. Daybook, 1816–1826. Moore was a Salem, N.J., farmer. Purchased, 1959. (1 v.)

Moore & Illig. Waste book, 1857–1868. Moore and Illig operated a Philadelphia livery stable. Purchased, 1954. (1 v.)

Morton, Robert. "List of mortgages, ground-rents, stocks, etc.," [183-] (1 v.)

Needles, Joseph A. Blotter, 1818. Joseph and John Needles were Philadelphia wire workers. Contains accounts and correspondence for Joseph A. and John Needles. Purchased, 1966. (1 v.)

Needles, Joseph A. Daybook, 1817–1824. Purchased, 1966. (1 v.)

New York Insurance Company. Receipt book, 1797–1799. Contains records for payments of shipping losses. Copy. Purchased, 1959. (1 v.)

North, Edwin. Account book, 1874–1883. Private account. Gift of Mrs. Herbert Foster. (1 v.)

Ogden, Joseph, d. 1787? Invoice book, 1749–1755. Ogden was a Philadelphia general merchant. Gift of Edward Jenkins, 1975. (1 v.)

Ogden, Joseph, d. 1787? Ledger, 1749–1755. Ogden was a Philadelphia general merchant. Purchased, 1959. (1 v.)

Ogden, Joseph. Account books, 1769–1771, 1795–1799. Ogden was a Philadelphia innkeeper and operator of Middle Ferry. Purchased, 1959. (2 v.)

Oliver, John. List of purchased from Susannah Thompson, 1798. (1 v.)

O'Neil, Henry. Account book, 1845–1849. O'Neil was an agricultural laborer and handyman. Contains personal accounts. (1 v.)

Otto, Jacob. Account of sales, 1851–1863. Gift of Chester County Historical Society, 1967. (1 v.)

Pennebacker, Abraham. Account book, 1862–1868. Pennebacker was a Berks County farmer. Purchased, 1959. (1 v.)

Peters, Richard, 1744–1828. Estate cash account, 1828–1848. Account for Belmont and undivided part of Mantua properties; Richard Peters, Jr., trustee. Purchased, 1972. (1 v.)

Peterson, Derrick. Ledger, (1790–1797) 1822. Peterson was a Philadelphia lumber merchant. Ledger contains business and personal accounts and includes real estate transactions. Gift of Mrs. A. Stanley Peterson through the Chester County Historical Society, 1967. (1 v.)

Philadelphia. City Treasurer. Receipt book, 1825–1826. John Bacon was a Philadelphia City Treasurer. Copies of receipts given by Treasurer John Bacon for monies received, listing date, amount, person from whom received, his signature, Treasurer's signature, and frequently the reason for payment. (1 v.)

Philadelphia and Trenton Railroad. Surveyor's notes, 1833. Notes cover the territory from Poqueston Creek to Kensington. (1 v.)

Pilling, Ralph, d. 1851. Estate receipt book, 1851–1852. Pilling was a Philadelphia print mill operator. William Overington and James Horricks, executors. Gift of Theodore Ashmead Longstroth, 1965. (1 v.)

Piper, Frederick A. Daybook, 1812–1814. Piper was a physician. Daybook contains fragment of lectures on heat and evaporation. Purchased, 1959. (1 v.)

The Portland Stage Company (Portland, Me.) Stage book, 1830–1831. Daily passenger and express bookings to Berwick, Kennebunk, Alfred, and Portland. (1 v.)

Potts, John, 1710–1768. Estate ledger, 1768–1782. Purchased, 1953. (1 v.)

Potts, Jonathan, 1745–1781. Invoice book of expenses, 1772–1774. Potts was a Reading physician. Purchased, 1953. (1 v.)

Powel, John Hare, 1786–1856. Account with William Hughs, 1830–1835. John Hare Powel was a Philadelphia soldier, statesman, agriculturist, and author. Hughes was superintendent of Powel's Powelton and Woodlands estate. This account concerns mainly cattle at Powel's estates. Purchased, 1941. (1 v.)

Pricket Mill Company (Medford, N.J.) Record book, 1765–1834. The Pricket Mill Company was a lumber mill and was primarily owned by the Haines family. Purchased, 1959. (1 v.)

Rambo, Abel. Receipt book, 1862–1871. Kept as guardian of A. Reiner Rambo. Gift of Bart Anderson, 1947. (1 v.)

Reeves, John. Account book, 1759–1760. Kept as executor of the James Johnson estate. Purchased, 1959. (1 v.)

Reynell, John. Journal, 1764–1778. Reynell was a Philadelphia merchant. Photostat. Original privately owned. (1 v.)

Richardson, Francis, d. 1688. Letterbook, 1681–1688. Includes letters of his wife, Rebeckah Hayward Richardson. Purchased, 1959. (1 v.)

Riché, Thomas. Receipt book, 1760–1769. Riché was a Philadelphia merchant. Purchased, 1958. (1 v.)

Ridge Turnpike Company (Philadelphia, Pa.) Journal (bookkeeping), 1811–1822 and receipt book, 1811–1815. Gift of Mrs. G. Lloyd Wilson, 1958. (1 v.)

Rittenhouse, Peter, 1797–1870. Ledger, 1846–1850. Rittenhouse was a Philadelphia merchant. Gift of Martin P. Snyder, 1969. (1 v.)

Sack, John, Mrs. Account with J.W. Pommer & Bro., 1878–1879. John William Pommer and Edward Pommer were Philadelphia grocers. Gift of Mrs. Samuel Eisenhofer, 1960. (1 v.)

Sager, John. Daybook, 1805–1817. Sager was a Philadelphia cabinetmaker. Purchased, 1956. (1 v.)

Sands, Isaac R. Records, 1865–1876. Sands was a Berks County blacksmith. The records include daybooks, 1865–1867, 1873–1876 and a ledger, 1862–1867. Purchased, 1959. (4 v.)

Santo Donimgo Silver Mining Company (Chihauhua, Mexico). Letterpress book, 1891–1892. Letters of E.L. Stillson, Superintendent to John P. Logan, President (Philadelphia), reporting on operations, finances, legal affairs, and politics. Purchased, 1953. (1 v.)

Santo Donimgo Silver Mining Company (Chihauhua, Mexico). Account book, 1897–1898. Giving reports on ore and silver production and payroll. Purchased, 1959. (1 v.)

Savery, Elizabeth. Receipt book, 1833–1855. Receipts for rents of properties owned by Elizabeth and Rebecca Savery. Gift of the Chester County Historical Society, 1967. (1 v.)

Schurmann, Edmund J., d. 1875. Daybook, 1861–1866. Schurmann repaired watches and did part sales for William G. Billin. (1 v.)

Schurmann, Edward W. Account book with M. Sickels, 1877–1880. Schurmann was a Philadelphia watchmaker. (1 v.)

Segner & Maxwell. Account of stock, 1866–1867. Segner & Maxwell were Harrisburg jewelers and clockmakers. Continued as a ledger, 1866–1871, and the as clocks account, 1871–1873. Gift of Mrs. Dean Fales, 1976. (1 v.)

Sharples, Joshua. Memorandum books, 1812–1859. Sharples was a Philadelphia carpenter and a Chester County farmer. These memorandum books record hardware sales, rents, bonds, mortgages, and farm animals. Gift of Bart Anderson, 1947. (2 v.)

Sharples, Joshua. Ledger, 1803–1809. Gift of Chester County Historical Society, 1967. (1 v.)

Sharples, Joshua. Receipt book and miscellaneous notes, 1813–1849. Gift of Chester County Historical Society, 1967. (1 v.)

Shepperd, George. Receipt books, 1766–1801. Personal receipts. Gift of Isaac Sutton, 1950. (2 v.)

Shinn, Earl. Receipt book, 1818–1846. Shinn was a Philadelphia bricklayer. Gift of Richard Cadbury, 1949. (1 v.)

Shippen, Edward, 1729–1806. Cashbook, 1781–1806. Shippen was a Philadelphia jurist. Cashbook of income from real estate sales, rents, farm production, and from professional duties; together with records and accounts, 1746–1806, of rents and ground rents on his own property of Edward Shippen estate. Purchased, 1953. (1 v.)

Shippen, Evans Wallace. Ledger, 1891–1910. Shippen was a Meadville oil producer. This ledger contains oil well, dam, real estate, and other personal investment accounts. Gift of Chester County Historical Society, 1967. (1 v.)

Shirk, David O. Ciphering book, 1850–1851. Gift of Mrs. Dean A. Fales, Jr., 1976. (1 v.)

Shoemaker, Shoemaker, and Berrett. Marine insurance records, 1796–1797. Shoemaker, Shoemaker, and Berrett were Philadelphia insurance brokers. Gift of the Chester County Historical Society, 1967. (1 v.)

Singleton, Stephen C. Waste book, 1869–1877. Singleton was a Philadelphia paperhanger. Gift of Mrs. Edwin Morris Singleton, 1953. (1 v.)

Sinnickson, Andrew. Ledger, 1803–1821. Sinnickson was a Salem, N.J., general store proprietor. Purchased, 1959. (1 v.)

Sinnickson, John. Receipt book, 1797–1815. Personal receipts. Purchased, 1959. (1 v.)

Slough, Matthias. "To the Stockholders of the Philadelphia and Lancaster Turnpike Road," 1793. Slough was the manager of the Philadelphia and Lancaster Turnpike Road. Transcript by the Historical Society of Pennsylvania, 1896. (1 v.)

Smith family. Papers, 1863–1892. Papers include Ladies' Soldiers' Aid Society minute and letterbooks, 1863–1877, Mary P. Wilson Smith, Secretary, recording efforts to aid sick and wounded soldiers, soldiers' widows and orphans, and freedmen; Xanthus Russell Smith diary, 1883, 1891–1892, commenting on his professional activities as a marine, landscape, portrait, and historical painter in Glenside and Philadelphia, on his family life, his experiments in photography, and his father Russell Smith's work as a Painter. Purchased, 1939. (4 v.)

Smith, Howell, & Barr. Duplicate letters and receipt book, 1844–1846. Smith, Howell, & Barr were Philadelphia dry goods merchants. Gift of Mr. and Mrs. James Kotlar, 1969. (1 v.)

Smith, Joseph. Ledger, 1813–1814. Smith was a Philadelphia iron merchant. The ledger was filled with iron and investment accounts. Gift of Mary V. Baldwin through the Chester County Historical Society, 1967. (1 v.)

Smith, Daniel B. Records, 1826–1829, 1851. Daniel B. and Benjamin R. Smith were Philadelphia druggists and chemists. These records are accounts and other memoranda; later used for children's crayon drawings. Gift of Sarah A.G. Smith. (1 v.)

Smith, Moses B. Estate receipt book, 1855–1887. Receipts for coal rents of East Sugar Loaf. Purchased, 1959. (1 v.)

Souder, Thomas M. Bank book, 1814–1822. Souder was a Philadelphia bricklayer and merchant. Gift of Curtis Allen, 1961. (1 v.)

Spear, Joseph. Daybook, 1816–1817, and ledger, 1817–1818. Spear was a carpenter and furniture maker. Purchased, 1959. (1 v.)

Spear, Joseph & Company. Ledger, 1764–1765. Joseph Spear & Company were Fort Pitt Indian traders. This ledger contains records of sales of provisions, primarily liquors, to Crown agents, officers, settlers, and others. Gift of Elliston J. Morris, 1944. (1 v.)

Spear, Thomas G. Receipt book, 1835–1841. Thomas G. Spear was a Philadelphia dry goods merchant. Purchased, 1959. (1 v.)

Spear, Thomas G. Cashbook, 1846–1849. Thomas G. Spear was a Philadelphia printer. Purchased, 1959. (1 v.)

Steel, Alexander. Ledger, 1797–1819. Steel was a Southwark surveyor. Gift of Joseph Hewlett. (1 v.)

Steele, Elizabeth. Accounts, 1821–1839. Also includes estate accounts with Lydia R. Bailey. Purchased, 1959. (1 v.)

Stevenson, Cornelius, 1779–1860. Receipt book, 1830–1842. Stevenson was Philadelphia city treasurer. Personal receipts. Purchased, 1955. (1 v.)

Stewardson, Thomas, 1762–1841. Ledger, 1788–1841. Includes estate, real estate, and financial transactions. Purchased, 1959. (1 v.)

Stewart, H.B. Letterbook, 1809–1811. Stewart was a Philadelphia supercargo on the schooner *Dolphin.* Contains some accounts. Gift of Ashurst family, 1911. (1 v.)

Stockton, William T. Account book, 1823. Stockton was a Philadelphia proprietor of stage coaches. Purchased, 1959. (1 v.)

Swedish Church, *Archivum Americanum,* 1891. Transcriptions and translations of documents relating to the Swedish Churches on the Delaware at the Consistory of Upsal, Sweden, done for C.J. Stille under the supervision of Col. Elfving and Dr. Wuselgrin. Purchased, 1895. (2 v.)

Tatnall, Robert. Wastebook, 1736–1745. Tatnall was a Chester County yeoman and member of the Provincial Assembly. His wastebook contains records of sales of lumber and farm items, loans. (1 v.)

Todhunter, William. Ledger, 1837–1840. Todhunter was a Philadelphia merchant. This ledger was kept for the Committee of Creditors of Mackinley. Gift of Drexel University, 1966. (1 v.)

Towanda Bank (Towanda, Pa.) Daybook, 1841–1842. Purchased, 1938. (1 v.)

Trenton, Thomas. Weaving draft notes, 1813–1815. Purchased, 1946. (1 v.)

Tuft & Hancock. Daybook, 1795–1796. Tuft & Hancock were Philadelphia merchants. Continued as Tuft & Yorke, 1796–1798, and Yorke & Paullin, 1802–1805, with inventories of stocks. Gift of Friends Hospital, 1971. (1 v.)

United States Insurance Company (Philadelphia, Pa.) Records, 1809–1843. The United States Insurance Company was chartered in 1810 and dealt in marine insurance. The records include: stockholders receipt book, 1809–1835; general receipt book, 1836–1843; stockholder meeting minutes, 1826–1843. Purchased, 1953. (3 v.)

Unrod, Ann. Receipt book, 1826–1846. Receipt book, primarily for taxes paid by Ann and Elizabeth Unrod. (1 v.)

Upper Germantown Burying Ground (Philadelphia, Pa.) Record book, 1724–1908. Mostly burials and accounts. Portions published in *P.M.H.B.,* 8 (1884): 414–426. Permanent deposit of Concord School House of Germantown and Upper Germantown Burying Ground Board of Trustees. (1 v.)

Walker, John V.L., d. 1816. Estate account book, 1816–1823. Beulah Walker, administrator. (1 v.)

Walnut Street Land Company (Philadelphia, Pa.) Minute book, 1854–1870. Minutes kept for corporation of stockholders investing in West Philadelphia real estate. Purchased, 1947. (1 v.)

Warren, E. Burgess. Receipt books, 1868–1871. Warren was a Philadelphia roofer and builder. Personal and business receipts for Warren, Kirk, & Co. Gift of the Free Library of Philadelphia. (1 v.)

Wells, Gideon H. Letterbook, 1802. (1 v.)

Wemyss, Francis Courtney, 1797–1859. Prompt book, [1830]. Francis Courtney Wemyss was a an actor and theatre manager. This prompt book was for the production of *Isabelle; of Woman's Life* by John B. Buckstone, performed at the Walnut Street Theatre. Purchased, 1911. (1 v.)

Wescoat, William. Ledgers, 1827–1829. Wescoat was a merchant. (2 v.)

West, Benjamin, 1730–1813. Subscription account book, 1811. The subscription was for James Heath's engraving of *Death of Lord Nelson* after West; another volume contains a list of English names and addresses. Gift of Samuel P. Avery, 1899. (2 v.)

West, Francis. Letterbook, 1788–1798. Letterbook for Francis and John West, Philadelphia merchants. Purchased, 1975. (1 v.)

West, Sarah. Receipt book, (1804–1828) 1831. Sarah West was a Philadelphia shopkeeper. Receipts for business and personal expenses. (1 v.)

Wetherill, John. Estate inventory for Chalkley House, Frankford, 1851. Gift of Walter C. Baker, 1944. (1 v.)

Wharton, Charles, 1744–1838. Receipt book, 1799–1803. Gift of Sarah A.G. Smith, 1968. (1 v.)

Wharton, Thomas, 1730–1782. Ledger, 1752–1756. Gift of Leonard T. Beale, 1956. (1 v.)

Wharton, William, 1740-ca. 1805. Receipt book, 1765–1791. Gift of Sarah A.G. Smith, 1963. (1 v.)

Wharton & Lewis. Records, 1787–1801. Isaac Wharton and David Lewis were Philadelphia merchants and insurance brokers. The records include receipt book, 1787–1792, and account of policies underwritten, 1795–1801. Gift of Chester County Historical Society, 1967. (2 v.)

Williams, Henry Jonathan, 1791–1879. Records, 1833–1874. Williams was a Philadelphia attorney. The records include: ledger, 1833–1839 of business and personal accounts; letterpress book, 1847–1849, concerning business matters including the Alexander family estate; and memoranda of personal bills and receipts, 1867–1874. Purchased, 1949, and Gift of Edwin Wolf, 1967. (3 v.)

Williams, Howard. Receipt book, 1813–1822. Personal receipts. (1 v.)

Williams, Jonathan, 1750–1815. Receipt book, 1792–1799. Personal receipts mostly for labor on his Mount Pleasant property. Purchased, 1959. (1 v.)

Williams, Thomas. Receipt books, 1812–1832. (2 v.)

Willing, Charles, 1806–1887. Papers, 1858–1887. Charles Willing was a Germantown, Philadelphia gentleman. The papers include letterbooks, 1858–1887; journal, 1860–1877; and ledger, 1859–1875. Gift of Rosenbach Co., 1972. (4 v.)

Wister, John, 1708–1789. Receipt book, 1749. Deposited by Alice Strickland, 1977. (1 v.)

Wood, George, d. [1817]. Estate accounts, 1827–1828. Accounts kept by Coleman Sellers, executor of the estate of George and Ann Wood. (1 v.)

Wood, Richard, 1755–1822. Estate receipt book, 1822–1827. Richard Wood was a Greenwich, N.J., merchant. George Bacon Wood and Charles Wood, executors. Purchased, 1959. (1 v.)

Yarnell, Ellis, 1757–1848. Receipt book, 1794–1810. Yarnell was a Philadelphia merchant. Receipts of both a business and personal nature. (1 v.)

Yeates, Jasper, 1745–1817. Account book, 1802–1814. Yeates was a Lancaster lawyer and jurist. Accounts with Edward Hand estate. (1 v.)

Young, Stephen. Cash disbursements, 1809–1811. Record of cash disbursements for the sloop *Cape May* carrying freight primarily between Philadelphia and Richmond, Va. (1 v.)

Zarfoss, Samuel. Journal (bookkeeping), 1844–1858. Zarfoss was a Lancaster County cabinetmaker. Purchased, 1956. (1 v.)

Zartman, George. Wastebook, 1819–1826. In German. Purchased, 1956. (1 v.)

2002
City History Society of Philadelphia.   Papers, 1887 (1900–1978), 1980.   (ca. 1600 items.)

The City History Society of Philadelphia was founded by C. Henry Keim in 1900 as the City History Club of Philadelphia and changed in 1906 to the City History Society of Philadelphia. The purpose was to interest the teachers of the city in local history, so that they in turn, would stimulate their students to understand the importance of Philadelphia. The society's activities included publication of lectures and more detailed histories of Philadelphia, as well as excursions. The Society dissolved in 1980.

The papers consist of: correspondence, 1910–1963; correspondence 1978–1980, mainly on the dissolution of the society; membership records, 1932–1978; minutes of meetings; legal documents; charters and by-laws; financial records, including treasurer's accounts, 1940–1966; copies of papers read before the Society; *Sunday Republic* series, "Rich Men of Philadelphia forty years ago," 1887–1888; printed pamphlets; scrapbooks, 1900–1915, 1951–1959, of correspondence, clippings, invitations, and photographs compiled by the society's photographic committee, 1900–1920; and photographs reproduced in the Society's publications. Photographs, mounted in scrapbooks and identified, comprise a large part of the collection and include historic, commercial, public, and residential buildings, bridges, streets, and other city scenes.

Gift of the Society, 1972–1980.

2003

Pennsylvania Society of New York.   Papers 1899–1922.   (66 v.)

The Pennsylvania Society of New York was organized in 1899 "to cultivate social intercourse among its members and . . . to collect historical material relating to the state of Pennsylvania" by a group of former Pennsylvanians living in New York.

The papers consist of scrapbooks of newspaper clippings, correspondence, invitations, programs, and other memorabilia having to do with the activities of the Society. Several of the scrapbooks are devoted to specific topics including Society biography and obituary and visits to the United States by Cardinal Desire Joseph Mercier of Belgium, 1919, French marshall Ferdinand Foch, 1921, and French marshall Joseph Joffre, 1922.

2004

**Newton, Joseph Fort, 1876–1950.   Papers, 1919 (1930–1950).
(300 items.)**

Joseph Fort Newton was a Protestant clergyman and author. He was associated with Saint James Church and the Church of Saint Luke and the Epiphany, both of Philadelphia.

The bulk of the material consists of typescripts of Newton's sermons, addresses, articles, and two books: *What Have the Saints to Teach Us,* and a volume of 100 sermons. Incoming correspondence, 1919, 1939–1950 includes letters from readers of his writings and letters on his ministry, masonry, and the efforts of Ebed Van der Vlugt, a Dutch Barrister, to avoid deportation from the United States in 1941. There are also four small commonplace books.

Gift of Sarah Hollis, 1970.

2005

Kirk family.   Papers, 1688 (1840–1863), 1897.   (400 items.)

Edward Needles Kirk, Sterlin, Ill., lawyer, was killed in the Civil War while serving as an officer with the 34th Regiment, Illinois Volunteers in Kentucky and Tennessee.

Kirk's papers consist of personal and professional correspondence together with Civil War letters to, from, and about Kirk; legal documents; clippings; and other miscellany. There is also his wife Eliza Cameron Kirk's incoming and outgoing correspondence, 1862–1868, and later as Mrs. Charles A. Thomas, 1889–1897.

The remainder of the collection is made up of miscellaneous letters and documents of several members of the Kirk family, 1688–1870, including a Ruth Kirk Price commonplace book, begun 1809.

Gift of Mrs. Andrew B. Foster, 1973.

2006

Maxcy family.   Letters, (1826–1850) 1895.   (85 items.)

Virgil Maxcy was solicitor of the United States Treasury, 1830–1837, diplomat, 1837–1842. These letters consist primarily of correspondence between Mary Galloway Maxcy, wife of Virgil Maxcy, and her daughters and her daughters Anne Sarah Maxcy Hughes and Mary Maxcy Markoe. There are personal letters of Virgil Maxcy and other members of the family, including letters, 1894–1895, from Joseph Jefferson, actor.

Gift of Edith C.F. Rivinus, 1969.

2007

Beale, Joseph Boggs, 1841–1926.   Papers, 1852–1882.   (40 items)

Mainly the diaries, 1857–1865, of Joseph Boggs Beale, Philadelphia artist, written while a student at Central High School, Philadelphia; while an instructor of drawing at Central High; and while serving with 33rd Pennsylvania Volunteer Reserves during the Civil War. Much of the diaries concern the interest of the family in religion, but they do provide some glimpses into his artistic development.

There are also family and professional letters to and from Beale, 1857–1882; and a few family photographs.

Gift of Arthur Colen, 1973.

2008

Hunn, Ezekiel, 3rd, 1841–1926.   Records, 1885–1925.   (26 v.)

Records of Ezekiel Hunn, III, Philadelphia lawyer, on his general, civil practice with James N. Stone, Jr. under the name of Hunn & Stone. The records consist of: letterbooks, 1892, 1906, 1915–1925; journal, 1885–1903; ledgers, 1885–1896; cashbooks, 1885–1895; blotter of rents collected, 1883–1914.

Gift of Katherine Hunn Karsner, 1973.

2009

**Wister, William, 1803–1881.　　Papers, 1790 (1831–1880), 1899.
(3 linear ft.)**

William Wister ran a cloth-printing business in Germantown. The Belfield Print Works, which Wister ran from 1833 to 1854, was destroyed by fire in 1839, but was eventually rebuilt.

The papers of William Wister consist primarily of bills, receipts, invoices, accounts for supplies and equipment of William Wister's printing business in Germantown. Some correspondence from clients include letters from Hoyt & Bogart, N.Y.; Henry Farnum; and David S. Brown, Philadelphia.

Gift of John Wister Wurts estate, 1973.

2010

Continental Hotel Company.　　Records, 1856–1900.　　(110 items.)

The Continental Hotel was the first building in Philadelphia built as a luxury hotel. It was designed by John A. McArthur. After several years of planning, $200,000 was subscribed for its erection in 1857 as the "Butler House." Renamed the Continental Hotel, it opened in 1860 at 9th and Chestnut streets.

The records include: plans; stockholder records; some construction records; a letterpress book, 1857–1897; stock certificate book, 1859–1895; paid coupon, 1860; 8% certificate books, 1860; dividend receipt book, 1878–1897; construction accounts with J. Struthers for masonry work and Matsinger Brothers for iron work; several payroll records; and other miscellaneous papers.

Gift of Philip M. Price, 1973.

2011

Logan, James, 1674–1751.　　Papers, 1670 (1734–1749).　　(30 items.)

These papers reflect James Logan's activities as agent for the Penn family, land speculator, and scholar. Letterbooks, 1734–1748, several of which are marked "friendship" or "business," include correspondence to Letitia Penn Aubrey, Samuel Blunston, Peter Collinson, John Fothergill, Josiah Martin, Thomas Penn, William Penn III, Richard Peters, John Reading, and Ralph Smith; also additional letterbook of single letters, on scientific subjects addressed to Johann Albrect Fabricus, Abraham Gronovius, Hugh Hones, Carl Linnaeus, Richard Mead, and Hans Sloane. Logan's scholarship is further represented by drafts of *The Duties of Man as they may be deduced from Nature,* [1736], and excerpts from Pietro Giannone, *Civil*

History of the Kingdom of Naples, as reported in Archibald Bower, *Historia Litteraria.* There are also [Joshua Francis Fisher's] abstracts from Logan's *Notes for and answer to George Keith,* 1699; *Of the Eseans,* n.d.; *Literary, philosophical and religious fragments,* n.d.; William Logan poem for Philadelphia, 1685.

Letters to Johann Albrect Fabricus, Abraham Gronovius, Hugh Hones, Carl Linnaeus, Richard Mead, and Hans Sloane mostly written in Latin.

Gift of Mrs. Daniel Coxe, 1970.

2012
Miscellaneous land title papers, 1653–1930.　(10 v.)

[DuPlessis, LeBarbier.] Real estate listing, 1792–1793. Describes property in and around Philadelphia and other Pennsylvania, New Jersey, Maryland, Delaware, Virginia, North Carolina, South Carolina, Kentucky, and Georgia lands. Gift of Agnes G. DuBarry. (1 v.)

Leaming, Aaron, 1715–1780. Surveys and draughts of land, 1765–1777. Leaming was a Cape May County, N.J., Loan Office commissioner, assemblyman, farmer, merchant, and surveyor. His surveys and draughts include extracts from Cape May County Loan Office records, 1733–1748, and proof of title to The Five Mile Beach. Purchased, 1975. (1 v.)

Mount Pleasant (Philadelphia, Pa.) Brief of title, 1684–1867. For tract of land in Northern Liberties on which Mount Pleasant was built. Gift of Frederic R. Kirkland, 1950. (1 v.)

New York (State). Land surveys, 1671–1681. Also land surveys for Pennsylvania and Delaware. Photostats from the New York State Library. (1 v.)

Pennsylvania surveys. Records of surveys with briefs of title, 1701 (1796–1804). Briefs of titles for land in Cambria, Clearfield, Cumberland, Lycoming, Northumberland, Northumberland, and Philadelphia Counties. With surveys in Delaware, New Jersey, and New York exemplifying the lands of the Drinker and Fisher families. (2 v.)

Philadelphia (Pa.). Board of Surveyors. Lot Surveys, [1855–1861]. Surveys of Germantown and Bristol, Philadelphia, made primarily by Jesse Lightfoot, surveyor, with occasional identification of lot owners. Some surveys copied from earlier plans. (1 v.)

Powel family. Briefs of title, 1768–1909. Briefs for Philadelphia and other Pennsylvania properties, mostly acquired by Samuel Powel, with some notations on active ground rents to 1909. (1 v.)

Rambo, Ormand. Abstracts of title, 1653–1930. For land at 20th and Pattison Avenue, Philadelphia. Typescript, [1941]. Gift of Ormand Rambo, 1942. (1 v.)

Tyson, William E., b. [1889]. Somerton Village digest of land records, 1681–1930. Compiled from country records, [1957–1969]. Gift of William E. Tyson, 1969. (1 v.)

2013
No entry.

2014
Wharton and Willing families.   Papers, 1669–1887.   (3 linear ft.)

The Whartons and Willings were two merchant families of Philadelphia. Thomas Wharton was a colonial merchant whose anti-British sentiments were compromised by his Quaker pacifism. His opposition to the Revolution caused him to be sent into exile during the war. Thomas Willing was a merchant, banker, legislator, and judge.

The bulk of Wharton and Willing papers concern the commercial and personal business of these two merchant families of Philadelphia, but there are a few political and personal papers. The earliest material, 1669–1751, consists of deeds, indentures, wills, and other documents on the Pennsylvania lands of various Philadelphians.

Thomas Wharton, Sr., papers, 1752–1782, forms the bulk of the collection. Wharton's deeds, bonds, powers of attorney, accounts, and letters touch on his commercial, legal, and philanthropic interests, and include correspondence during the exile, 1778–1778.

The principals of the Willing section, 1791–1887, are Thomas Willing; Thomas Mayne Willing, merchant and banker; the merchant firm of Willing and Francis; and Charles Willing, physician. Correspondence, legal papers, and accounts relate to mercantile concerns and family business, including the William Bingham estate, Willing lands in Allegheny County, Pa., New York, and elsewhere.

Gift of Frances L.B. Randolph, Ann B. Putnam, and Edward F. Beale, 1973, and purchased.

Finding aid available.

2015
Brown, Marjorie P.M.   Collection, 1763–1871.   (125 items.)

Personal and business papers of the Morris and several related Philadelphia families include: Margaret Emlen letters to Sarah Logan, 1768–1771; Jones family correspondence, especially letters of Benjamin Jones to Mary Howell Jones, 1803–1847; Margaret Emlen Howell household receipts and recipes, 1800–1810, and other Howell family manuscripts; Stephen Paschall, founder of Paschall's steel furnace, commonplace book and diary, ca. 1795–

1800; Deborah Morris family estate papers, 1763–1787; Henry Morris, iron manufacturer, diary on business and personal affairs, with a few business letters and accounts, 1862; [Stephen P.] Morris, [Thomas T.] Tasker and [Henry] Morris, an iron manufacturing company, order books, 1832–1838, and the firm's subsidiary Paschal Iron Works journals, 1841–1846.

Gift of Patricia Wells, 1973.

2016
Magdalen Society of Philadelphia.   Records, 1800–1921.   (31 v.)

These Magdalen Society of Philadelphia was a private charitable organization founded in 1800 by a group of Philadelphia men under the presidency of Bishop William White of the Protestant Episcopal Church and continuously governed by men until 1916. Its original purpose was to rescue women "fallen from a condition of innocence and virtue," but in 1849, the Managers, at the urging of George Williams, began to consider ways to expand the role of the Society to include educating the girls and women for jobs. Not until after the passage of the Pennsylvania Child Labor Law, 1916, was the society able to redirect its energies: it sold the Magdalen Home, its asylum, elected women to its Board, and appointed a woman director. The following year it embarked upon a program of visiting working children to urge them to return to school. In 1918 it changed its name to the White-Williams Foundation for Girls and, two years later, to the White-Williams Foundation.

The bulk of the records are for the society's asylum, purchased in 1807. They contain: minutes of the board of managers, 1800–1916; minutes of the annual meetings of the society, 1837–1916, including accounts of work done and letters from former Magdalens; minutes of the weekly visiting committee, 1878–1912, including personal information on the inmates and conditions at the home; matron's diaries of daily events at the home, 1829–1834, 1878–1917; ledger, 1832–1878; account books, 1871–1921; register of admissions and discharges, 1836–1917, including personal data and some follow-up reports concerning the women after their departure.

Gift of the White-Williams Foundation, 1973.

Records microfilmed and available at the Balch Institute.

Some published annual reports are bound in with managers' minutes, 1885–1916; the majority are available in the Historical Society's Library.

2017
Mother Bethel African Methodist Episcopal Church (Philadelphia, Pa.)   Records, 1822–1972.   (25 microfilm reels.)

Mother Bethel African Methodist Episcopal Church of Philadelphia, dedicated in 1793, was an outgrowth of the movement among Protestant blacks to organize into separate congregations. In 1787 a company of blacks in Philadelphia withdrew from the white dominated Methodist Church and under the leadership of Richard Allen built Bethel Church. In 1816 Bethel joined with 16 other congregations to form the African Methodist Episcopal Church with Allen as the first bishop.

The class system, which was the early system of the Methodist Church dividing the congregation into Classes, each with a layman as class leader, remained an important part of Bethel's organization late into the 19th century.

Part 1: General record books consists of three official church registers, 1865–1874, 1880–1895, 1907–1912. Included in the registers are historical records, class rolls, records of membership, office holders, baptisms, and marriages. The historical records of the first volume contain a transcription of Richard Allen's biography.

Part 2: Records of the board of trustees, the controllers and managers of the property of the church, including minutes, 1863–1894, 1910–1944; account books, 1832–1847, 1890–1903, 1909–1942.

Part 3: Records on the religious function of the church. This section contains the records of the corporation (a body embracing the entire membership), the official board, the Board of Stewards, the Quarterly Conference, the classes, and the Class leaders. Included in this part are: minutes, 1848–1849, 1876–1972; account books, 1846–1858, 1871–1901; Class rolls with records of contributions and disbursements, 1852–1854, 1872–1894.

Part 4: Records of special organizations and activities, including: minutes of the Union Benevolent Sons of Bethel, a burial society, 1826–1844; minutes of the United Daughters of Tapsico Society, a benevolent society offering aid to sick members, 1837–1847; minutes of the Preachers' Association, Philadelphia Conference, 1897–1901; minutes of the [Richard] Allen Christian Endeavor, 1902- 1910; minutes of the Ushers' Association, 1925–1941; minutes of church trials of members for breaches of church discipline, 1822–1835, 1838–1851, 1859–1865; Sunday School roll books, ca. 1860, 1934–1939; membership roll books, 1901, ca. 1916; and visitors' registration books, 1901–1970.

Part 5: Miscellany, including a Richard Allen bible, an early King James quarto, 1802.

Part 6: *The Christian Recorder,* the journal of the African Methodist Episcopal Church, 1854–1856, 1861–1902.

Gift of Mother Bethel Church, 1973.

Published finding aids by H.L. Wilson and A. H. Able, III, *The Holdings of Mother Bethel A.M.E. Church Historical Museum in Manuscript and Print.*

The originals of the Bethel Church records are located at the church's Historical Museum. Permission for microfilm copies must be secured from the Historical Commission, Mother Bethel A.M.E. Church, 6th & Lombard Streets, Philadelphia, PA 19106.

2018A

Morris, Anthony. **Family papers, 1781–1894.** **(300 items.)**

Papers of several residents of Bolton Farm, a Bristol estate, originally owned by the Pemberton family and passed onto the Morris family through marriage. There are a few James Pemberton estate papers. The majority of material relates to Pemberton's son-in-law Anthony Morris: various account books, 1793–1816; family letters, 1812–1817, 1825–1832, particularly from Louisa Pemberton Morris Chaderton; copybook of letters, 1813–1816, to James Monroe and with George W. Erving on Morris's unofficial diplomatic service in Spain; correspondence, 1817–1818, with John A. Morton on financial and personal matters; correspondence, 1827–1834, relating to his plan to establish an agricultural school at Bolton after the methods of Philipp Emanuel von Fellenberg. Additional papers, 1823–1894, consist of miscellaneous accounts, receipts, legal papers, some correspondence of James Pemberton Morris and Phineas Pemberton Morris, all on the farm operations and financing.

Gift of Mrs. John P. Gardiner, 1974.

2018B

Morris, Anthony. **Family papers, 1730–1888.** **(200 items.)**

Very miscellaneous papers of Anthony Morris, his son, James P. Morris, and grandson, Phineas P. Morris.

Anthony Morris papers, 1786–1859, include some correspondence, accounts, and 1813 memoranda relative to Morris's efforts to have Spain cede Florida to the United States. Also in this section are papers, 1767–1817, of Francis Nichols, who served with Morris during the Revolution. There is a small amount of correspondence, affidavits, and accounts on the battle of Quebec during which Nichols was captured; letters from his nephew Arthur St. C. Nichols, a merchant in Havanna; and estate correspondence, accounts, and other legal papers, Bird Wilson, executor.

The James P. Morris and Phineas P. Morris sections consist primarily of school notes with some additional legal and financial papers.

Finding aid available.

2019
**Fisher, Samuel Rowland, 1745–1834.   Papers, (1767–1792) 1856.
(12 v.)**

Diaries and account of Samuel Rowland Fisher, Philadelphia merchant, recording trips to England, 1767, 1783–1784; Ireland, 1768; Charleston, S.C., 1772; Pennsylvania, Maryland and Virginia, 1767; Rhode Island, 1792. Included are orders for British goods, 1767–1768; memorandum of expenses, 1768. Also in the collection are a diary, 1856, of Deborah Fisher Wharton.
Gift of William Wharton Smith, 1974.

2020
Leiper Railroad.   Collection, 1809–1972.   (75 items.)

The Leiper Railroad, the second railway to be constructed in the United States, was actually a tramway built in 1809 by Thomas Leiper, financier of Philadelphia, to transport stone from his quarries in eastern Delaware County. It operated until ca. 1830.
Maps and other materials on the location and operation of the Leiper Railroad.
Collected by Keith T. Postlewaite; gift of Mrs. Anna Postlewaite, 1974.

2021
Truxtun, Thomas, 1756–1822.   Correspondence, 1779–1822.   (100 items.)

Thomas Truxtun was a privateer during the American Revolution, a merchant ship commander, and United States naval officer.
Includes incoming and outgoing letters, 1779–1822, primarily on Truxtun's naval and political interests; and several printed circular letters, 1802–1808, on Truxtun's resignation in 1802 from the navy.
Typescript copies of 34 of the letters.
Gift of T. Truxtun Hare, 1971.
Finding aid available.

2022
No entry.

2023
Logan family.   Papers, 1698–1842.   (320 items.)

This small collection of Logan family papers includes: James Logan incoming correspondence and documents, 1698–1743, dealing with the administration of the province, the Penn-Baltimore boundary dispute, agriculture and business, and Logan's book orders; William Logan incoming correspondence, 1735–1775, including correspondence from such British horticulturalists as Thomas Binks and the two John Blackburnes as well as documents on his family, 1798–1810, n.d., several of which describe his personal diplomatic mission to France in 1798; Deborah Norris Logan family letters, 1790–1838; other family correspondence, 1785–1842. Also included is a memorandum, initialed by William Penn, of Colonel Robert Quary's complaints against the administration of Governor William Markham, n.d.

Gift of Mrs. Sydney L. Wright, 1974.

2024
No entry.

2025
Knepper brothers.   Letters, 1884 (1898–1900), 1907.   (100 items.)

Letters home of two brothers from Somerset, who were officers with the United States Navy. Chester M. Knepper letters, 1884, 1895–1900, 1917, were written while on a tour of duty in east Asia.

Orlo Knepper letters, 1892, 1898–1900, mainly relate to his service with George Dewey's Asiatic Squadron and include detailed observations on the Spanish defeat at Manila Bay, the United States occupation of the Philippine Islands, and the war between the U.S. and the Philippine "insurgents."

Gift of Henry C. Beerits, 1974.

2026
Ingersoll, R. Sturgis.   Collection, 1822–1917.   (16 v.)

The Bingham estate letterbooks, 1822–1848, 1856–1870, 1888–1917, were kept by successive trustees Thomas Mayne Willing, William Miller, J. Craig Miller, Henry G. Clay (Harry L. Albertson, "Secretary"). Other letterbooks concern Biddle family estate matters, 1827–1841, William Miller, trustee; S. Morris Waln & Company, Philadelphia shipping and commission merchants, 1879–1880, with foreign clients; Harry L. Albertson, 1887–1914, on administration of various estates and other legal business.

These volumes came to R. Sturgis Ingersoll as trustee of the William Bingham estate; gift of R. Sturgis Ingersoll and Boyd Lee Spahr, 1975.

2027
312th Field Artillery Association.   Minutes, 1927–1973.
(2 boxes.)

Minutes of a Philadelphia area veterans' social association open to members of the 312th Field Artillery who served in World War I.

Gift Mr. Bell, 1974.

2028

Fox family.   Papers, 1755 (1819–1910) 1964.   (ca. 850 items.)

The papers of the Fox family of Foxburg, Clarion County, cover four generations. The bulk of the collection consists of family correspondence between Joseph Mickle Fox; his wife, Hannah Emlen Fox; their son, Samuel Mickle Fox; and his wife, Mary Rodman Fisher Fox; William Logan Fisher of Philadelphia; William Logan Fisher Fox; and Joseph Mickle Fox [II]. Although mostly personal, the letters also touch on Joseph M. Fox [I] finances, management of Foxburg and other family lands, and the development of petroleum in western Pennsylvania. Additional papers include: Thomas Fisher diary, 1777–1778, for the Quaker exile in Virginia; Mary Rodman Fisher diary, 1852; Joseph M. Fox [II] diary, ca. 1885, of his campaign for Democratic nomination for Congress; indentures, deeds, wills, and other estate papers; views and photographs of Philadelphia, ca. 1800–1900; family photographs at Foxburg, ca. 1900; and miscellanea.

Anonymous gift in memory of William Logan Fox and Betty Carson Fox, 1974.

Finding aid available.

2029

Gruenberg, Frederick P., 1884–1976.   Papers, 1902–1970.
(6 linear ft.)

Frederick Paul Gruenberg came to Philadelphia in 1910 where he remained, interrupted only by a few years in Harrisburg, until his death in 1976.

These papers include Gruenberg's professional correspondence as an officer in a variety of civic, governmental, and banking organizations: Brown Brothers & Co., bankers, 1910–1913, head of foreign exchange department; Philadelphia Bureau of Municipal Research, 1913–1923, director from 1915; Bankers Bond and Mortgage Company, 1924–1931, treasurer; public service commissioner, 1931–1937, appointed by Governor Gifford Pinchot, who is among Gruenberg's correspondents; City Charter Committee of Philadelphia, 1938–1940, executive secretary; Office of Price Administration, 1942–1944, Philadelphia area rent director; Samuel Fels Fund, 1944–1958, director.

Gruenberg's personal correspondence consists of letters exchanged mostly with his wife, Bertha Sanford Gruenberg, his children, and other family members. Also included in the papers are: addresses and articles; diaries, 1909, 1956–1970, with daily memoranda of activities; clippings; news releases; birthday and anniversary greetings; and photographs.

Gift of Frederick P. Gruenberg, 1969, 1974.

2030

Warley Bascom Sons.   Business records, 1881 (1889–1923), 1970.
(ca. 75 items and 16 v.)

Warley Bascom Sons, specializing in general upholstering, interior decorations, and cabinet work, became one of the oldest and longest lived businesses owned and run by blacks in Philadelphia. Mattress-maker Warley Bascom, a freeman from Charleston, S.C., began the business ca. 1861; it continued under family management until 1974, managed successively by Warley Bascom, Jr., his wife, Josephine Davis Bascom, and their children William, Edgar, and Ethel Bascom Serjeant.

Included in the records are: order books, 1902–1923; customer list, 1907–1908; list of rental properties, 1898–1901, with lists of accounts receivable, 1897–1904; cashbook, 1944, 1953; payroll book, 1917–1922; bank books, 1889–1906; loose receipts, 1881–1882.

There are in addition a few miscellaneous family papers, including estate records.

Gift of Julia Serjeant Mitchell, 1974.

2031

Gibbon, John, 1827–1896.   Papers, 1845 (1862–1892).
(250 items.)

John Gibbon, born near Philadelphia, served as a Civil War brigadier general of volunteers in the Union army. He commanded troops at second Bull Run, Antietam, Fredericksburg, Gettysburg, the Wilderness, Spotsylvania, and other battles of the Army of the Potomac.

Following the Civil War, Gibbon became an officer in the regular army with duty mostly in the West.

The papers include Gibbon's letters, 1862–1865, to his wife, which report on the campaigns, particularly in Virginia. One letter concerns his role as one of the surrender commissioners at Appomattox. Although Gibbon's *Personal Recollections of the Civil War* (1928) were published, there are in these papers unpublished memoirs as well as articles *General John Buford, Lessons of the War,* and an manuscript copy of *The Army Under Pope,* by John C. Ropes (1881), and some correspondence relating to Pope.

His autobiographical accounts for the period following the Civil War cover his command of the attack on the Nez Perce Indians under Chief Joseph, 1877, and his peace enforcement during the anti-Chinese disturbances in Seattle, 1885.

Among other Gibbon papers are articles on the "dangerous" condition of the Army and the nation; *The Military in Schools and Colleges of America;*

account books, 1845–1847, as a military academy student; scrapbook covering his military career; and family photographs.

Gift of Mrs. Winthrop H. Battles, 1975.

2032

Ogden, Nicholas Gouverneur, 1776–1823.   **Correspondence, 1817–1823.**   **(86 items.)**

Incoming family correspondence of Nicholas Gouverneur Ogden while he, in partnership with John Jacob Astor, tended the Canton end of their Chinese trade business. The letters include news of the family, of business ventures, and economic and political developments in the United States.

Purchased, 1975.

2033

Paul family.   **Papers, 1709 (1783–1956).**   **(6 linear ft.)**

The Paul family was a merchant family of both Philadelphia and Belvidere, N.J.

Thomas Paul, the first generation to be represented here, was a merchant trading under the firm of [Cornelius] Comegys and Paul and successor names. In 1790 he purchased the Belvidere property where he established his residence and where he and following generations carried on the sale of town lots.

His son, Comegys Paul, returned to Philadelphia where he carried on a dry-goods trading business as [Benjamin] Cononge, Paul & Co. [James Ranten] and later as Comegys Paul & Co. [John T. and William Watson].

These papers consist of correspondence, accounts, and indentures which relate to the personal and business activities of the Paul family of Philadelphia and Belvidere, N.J.

The Thomas Paul papers, 1783–1798, consist of miscellaneous correspondence and records on his mercantile business, Belvidere, personal affairs, and his estate.

Comegys Paul's papers, 1810–1851, contain business correspondence and miscellaneous accounts to 1828. They also include his private correspondence from brothers and brothers-in-law largely on the management of the Belvidere property and other family affairs. There are also some Comegys Paul private accounts.

Among the letters of the John Rodman Paul branch of the family are: J. Rodman Paul's letters, 1823–1824, describing social life and touring activities while studying medicine in Paris; John Rodman Paul, Jr., letters, 1872, while touring Europe; and additional family correspondence, 1823–1902, which also includes letters from Elizabeth Duffield Paul, Margaret Neill Paul, and others. Henry Neill Paul letterpress books, 1858–1886, 1890–1899, contain letters on property in St. Paul, Minn., his other real estate holdings, Paul family estate business, letters written as officer of Manufacturers Land and Improvement Company, Gloucester Land Company, and Pennsylvania Company for Insurance on Lives and Granting Annuities; personal ledger, 1858–1859; and journal, 1879–1888. Memorial Missionary Society of Calvary Presbyterian Church minutes, 1870–1883, Mrs. Elizabeth Stadleman Paul, Secretary. Henry Neill Paul, Jr., lawyer, personal business, as well as bibliophilic and genealogical interests.

Another line of the Paul family is represented by Mary Pope Paul personal and family correspondence, 1868–1920, together with some correspondence of her son Augustus Russell Paul, 1900–1937, mainly on agricultural subjects.

Gift of Arthur Paul, 1975.

Finding aid available.

Genealogical materials transferred to the Genealogical Society of Pennsylvania.

2034
Kellner, Louise.   Diaries, 1889–1903.   (8 v.)

Diaries kept by Louise Kellner while a companion to Lydia T. Morris and her brother, John T. Morris, on their world travels: "Around the World," 1889–1890; "Egypt and the Nile," 1894–1896; "Winter Vacation—Italy," 1900; "A Trip to France and the Midnight Sun," (Scandinavia, Russia) 1903.

Gift of Mrs. Pauline L. Bowen, 1975.

2035
Cope family.   Estate papers, ca. 1838–1938.   (3 linear ft.)

Papers on the estates of Ruth Anna Cope, Jeremiah Brown, Anna S. Cope, Alfred Cope, and other members of the Cope family, including correspondence, accounts and legal papers.

Gift of Mrs. David Goddard, 1975.

2036
No entry.

2037
**Jones and Taylor family.   Papers, 1737 (1830–1919), 1925.
(9 linear ft.)**

Papers of the Jones and Taylor families, two related Philadelphia families. Benjamin Jones, merchant, iron manufacturer, land speculator, is represented by: incoming business correspondence and loose accounts, ca. 1831–1849, mainly dealing with land transactions; account books, with miscellaneous financial memoranda, 1809–1816, 1832–1839; estate papers; miscellanea. Andrew M. Jones, son of Benjamin Jones, merchant, is represented by papers, ca. 1829–1889, containing: incoming business correspondence and loose accounts; daily memoranda blotters, 1855, 1857; family letters; papers of several estates administered by Jones; letters, 1861–1866, from relatives with Union forces in Virginia and Tennessee. There is also a series of various Jones family letters, ca. 1821–1888.

Among the Taylor papers are family letters, 1843–1882, of Margaretta H. Jones Taylor, sister of Andrew M. Jones, and others. William Johnson Taylor [I], chemist and mineralogist, is represented by: pocket diaries, 1846, 1850–1863; miscellaneous account book, 1854; a few items of correspondence, 1861. The papers, ca. 1890–1925, of William Johnson Taylor [II], surgeon of Philadelphia, officer with the medical corps of the U.S. Army during World War I, include: medical records; notes and manuscript copies of speeches and articles by Johnson on medical topics; the originals and copies of (censored) World War I letters written to his family from hospitals on the western front in France; miscellanea.

Other papers include: Grubb family letters, 1812–1819; Buckley family letters and deeds, 1737–1831; Anna P. Buckley diary, 1854; Mrs. John Hewson's European diary, 1884; scrapbook; genealogical notes; miscellanea.

Gift of H. Newbold Taylor, 1975.

Finding aid available.

2038
Clubs and Association records, 1819–1932.   (65 v.)

Miscellaneous papers of community, fraternal, philanthropic, social, or veterans' organizations, including minutes, lists, dues, constitutions:

Ancient Order of Foresters of America. Court Good Will, 8340 (Philadelphia, Pa.) Minute book, 1893–1896. This was a social organization which paid small sick benefits to its members. Purchased, 1952. (1 v.)

The Apprentices Library Association of Carlisle (Cumberland County, Pa.) Minute book, 1831–1839. This was a literary society which founded a library for apprenticed and other youths. Contains constitution, by-laws, and library regulations. Purchased, 1949. (1 v.)

Army and Navy Club of Philadelphia (Pa.) Board of Directors minutes, (1926–1930) 1946. The Army and Navy Club of Philadelphia was an organization of World War I veterans to maintain past associations and encourage interest in national defense. Gift of Edgar S. Gardner, 1947. (1 v.)

Association of Cricket Clubs of Philadelphia (Pa.) Minute book, 1897–1941. The Association of Cricket Clubs of Philadelphia was formed to manage cricket in the Philadelphia area. Contains constitution and financial statements. Gift of James S. Ellison, Jr. 1959. (1 v.)

Bache Institute of the Central High School (Philadelphia, Pa.) Minute book, 1847–1848. The Bache Institute was organized in 1847 and later united with the Knights of the Round Table. Also contains constitution and by-laws. Purchased, 1963. (1 v.)

Bishop White Association of Philadelphia and Bucks County (Pa.) Minute book, 1862–1863. The Bishop White Association was an association of Protestant Episcopal clergymen organized for devotional purposes. Gift of E.H. Whitlock, 1956. (1 v.)

Booksellers Company of Philadelphia (Pa.) Minute book, 1802–1803. Contains attendance record to 1805; continued with anonymous female's reports on her readings and lectures attended, [1838]. Purchased, 1955. (1 v.)

Brotherhood of the Protestant Episcopal Hospital Mission (Philadelphia, Pa.) Minute book, 1878–1884. This group was organized for devotional, charitable, and social purposes. Contains some financial records. Purchased, 1952. (1 v.)

Bryn Mawr Polo Club (Bryn Mawr, Pa.) Minute book, 1911–1934. This polo club was chartered in 1898 and existed until 1935. Contains membership lists and financial statements. Gift of Mrs. Donald W. Darby, Jr., 1967. (1 v.)

The Charity Hospital (Philadelphia, Pa.) Medical Board minute book, (1857–1896) 1902. The Charity Hospital was incorporated in 1861 "for the relief of the sick poor." Gift of Dr. Justice Sinexon, 1940. (1 v.)

Citizens Committee of One Hundred (Philadelphia, Pa.) Records, 1880–1882. This was a municipal reform group led by disgruntled Republicans, Ellis D. Williams, Secretary. Contains minutes and letters. Gift of Justice Williams, 1948. (1 v.)

Citizens Temperance Union (Milton, Pa.) Executive Committee minutebook, 1874–1875. Contains newspaper clippings. Gift of the Genealogical Society of Pennsylvania, 1932. (1 v.)

Committee for Unemployment Relief (Philadelphia, Pa.) Records, 1930–1932. This was a private philanthropic organization which provided aid to Philadelphia's unemployed. The Committee was dissolved when private relief efforts were no longer adequate. The records include minutes, financial statements, and other papers. Gift of H. Gates Lloyd, 1950. (1 v.)

Democratic Douglas Arthur Association (Philadelphia, Pa.) Minute book, 1858–1860. This organization advocated the election of Stephen A. Douglas to President in 1860. Photocopy. Gift of the National Archives and Records Service, 1981. (1 v.)

Democratic Party. Philadelphia (Pa.). First Ward Executive Committee. Minute book, 1881–1890. Purchased, 1967. (1 v.)

Everett Literary Circle (Philadelphia, Pa.) Minute book, 1865–1868. This was a debating and literary society formerly known as Young Men's Aid and Debating Society. Purchased, 1952. (1 v.)

Falcon Barge Club of Philadelphia (Pa.) Records, 1834-[1841]. The Falcon Barge Club of Philadelphia is a rowing club. The records include the constitution and membership list. Gift of Felix Mininberg, 1952. (1 v.)

Fifth Young Women's Christian Temperance Union of Philadelphia (Pa.) Minutes, 1887–1891. Contains constitution and by-laws. (1 v.)

Friendly Society of the German Free Community (Philadelphia, Pa.) Records, 1855–1871. The records include summary statement of accounts, 1855–1865; continued with current accounts, 1866–1871, with lists of charter members and deceased members. In German. Gift of George Allen, 1956. (1 v.)

Friends of Bell and Everett (Philadelphia, Pa.) Minute book, 1860–1862. This was a political organization that later became known as the Constitutional Union Party. Gift of Mrs. Philip C. Herr, 1946. (1 v.)

Hancock Temperance B. Society of Moyamensing (Philadelphia, Pa.) Minute book, 1843–1848. This book record Treasurer's and Hall Committee reports, and other activities of the association. Gift of Ross Meeser, 1966. (1 v.)

Humane Fire Company (Philadelphia, Pa.) Minutes, 1819–1826. Purchased, 1959. (1 v.)

Independent Order of Sons of Malta. Minne-ha-ha Lodge, No. 1. (Philadelphia, Pa.) Minute book, 1861–1906. This was the last existing lodge of this social club which was organized in 1857 and dissolved in 1903. Gift of Edward Siter and M. Richards Mucklé, 1906. (1 v.)

Irving Literary Institute (Philadelphia, Pa.) Minute book, 1839–1845. This was a male debating society. Gift of John Rapson Curtis, 1958. (1 v.)

Junior Templars of Honor and Temperance. Endeavor Section No. 40 (Philadelphia, Pa.) Minute book, 1895–1897. Contains brief reports on proceedings. Gift of Mrs. Henry J. Ettenger, 1955. (1 v.)

Kensington Einjahrin Kranken Uterstutzungs Verein (Philadelphia, Pa.) Minute book, 1931–1939. This organization was formed to provide payment of sick benefits to its members. Gift of Lester Paul, 1963. (1 v.)

Centennial Exhibition. Women's Centennial Committee. Minute book, 18873–1874. Deals primarily with fund raising. Gift of Craig Wright Muckle, 1967. (1 v.)

Lafayette Ball. Manager's minutebook, 1824 . Includes guest list and cost estimate for ball in honor of Marquis de Lafayette's visit to Philadelphia Sept. 2–10, 1824. (1 v.)

Les Beaux Club (Philadelphia, Pa.) Minute books, 1904–1906. This was a Central High School student social club. Purchased, 1952. (1 v.)

Lippard, George, 1822–1854. *Order of the Brotherhood of the Union rules for installation ceremonies,* [1844]. Gift of J. Hawley Wilkers and Roger Butterfield, 1956. (1 v.)

National Guard of Pennsylvania. (Philadelphia, Pa.) Minutes, 1863. Purchased, 1930. (1 v.)

National Guard of Pennsylvania. Old Guard of "A" Company. First Regiment. Records, 1878–1880, 1893–1925. This was a fraternal association organized in 1878 in Philadelphia and reorganized in 1893. The records include: minutebook, 1878–1880, 1893–1925; dues and cash records, 1893–1925. Gift of Anna Janney DeArmond, 1969. (3 v.)

Native American Association of the Fourth Ward of Spring Garden (Philadelphia, Pa.) Records, [1844–1847]. Records include draft constitution, by-laws, signatures and addresses of members; continued as Edwin Bailey, miscellaneous accounts, [1844], 1856. Gift of Martin F. Meeser, 1904. (1 v.)

Northern Soup Society (Philadelphia, Pa.) Minutes, 1903–1920. The society was founded in 1817 and incorporated in 1839 to furnish soup, bread, and bathing facilities to the worthy poor in the Kensington area; its activities expanded to include a wide range of social activities. The minutes include reports from treasurers, auditors, and superintendents. Gift of Francis Bosworth, 1974. (1 v.)

Order of United States of America. New Jersey Camp No. 2 (Camden, N.J.) Minute book, 1849–1854. This was a patriotic organization. Gift of Henry T. Coates, 1894. (1 v.)

Pennsylvania Association of Surgeon Dentist. Constitution and by-laws, [1845], 1862, 1874. This professional association was organized in 1845 for professional and social intercourse. Gift of the Pennsylvania Association of Dental Surgeons, 1962. (1 v.)

Pennsylvania Society of New England (Philadelphia, Pa.) Membership records, 1899–1911. This was an association of Pennsylvanians with New England ancestors. Eleanor H.C. Dana maintained the records as corresponding secretary. (1 v.)

Periodical Publishers Association of America. Dinner program, 1907. Program for the fourth annual dinner, May 17, 1907, with some member autographs. Gift of Charles Francis Jenkins. (1 v.)

Philadelphia Business Progress Association (Philadelphia, Pa.) Papers, 1933. Papers for a special committee considering support of federally financed slum clearance program for Philadelphia, Pa. Gift of Jansen Haines, 1940. (1 v.)

Philadelphia Business Progress Association (Philadelphia, Pa.) Plan, 1928. Plan to develop the Philadelphia air-marine-rail terminal of the site of Hog Island, Philadelphia. (1 v.)

Philadelphia (Pa.). Chamber of Commerce. Tariff Committee. Scrapbook, 1820. The scrapbook contains letters, reports, and memorials requested and received from merchants of other cities in opposition to Congressional tariff bill. Also included is a memorial to Congress on the tariff by a Convention of delegates assembled in Philadelphia. Purchased, 1949. (1 v.)

Philadelphia (Pa.). Fire Department. Engine No. 4. Records, 1871–1880. Daily record of supplies, fires, and personnel records. Purchased, 1959. (1 v.)

Philadelphia Literary Association. Records, 1813. The records consist of constitution, by-laws, and membership list. Gift of Emma Troth, 1938. (1 v.)

Philadelphia Literary and Billiard Association. Records, [1857]. The records are primarily constitution and membership list of this social club; continued as a memoranda of "remarkable events, 1788–1857," of political, military, naval, scientific, and natural phenomena. Purchased, 1971. (1 v.)

Philomathean Association of Southwark (Philadelphia, Pa.) Constitution and by-laws, 1823. This was a literary association. (1 v.)

Philotasian Club (Philadelphia, Pa.) Minute book, 1914–1917. This was a social club of privileged older women organized in 1905. Purchased, 1952. (1 v.)

Phoenix Hose Company (Philadelphia, Pa.) Reports, 1865–1870. Reports of fires from the superintending director. Purchased, 1959. (1 v.)

The Round Table (Philadelphia, Pa.) Minute book, 1839–1841. This organization was a club of ladies and gentlemen for "Literary improvement . . . and the encouragement of single blessedness," the meetings of which were seemingly occasions for much merriment. Contains constitution and membership list. (1 v.)

Rumney Swan and Duck Shooting Company (Philadelphia, Pa.) Minutes, 1830–1834. Contains constitution and by-laws. Purchased, 1972. (1 v.)

Survivors of the Philadelphia Greys. Records, 1854 (1873–1910), 1919. This was a social organization formed in 1873 for an artillery company's former members. The records include articles of association, membership lists, minutes, and miscellaneous items. Gift of Claudia C. Briggs, 1958. (1 v.)

Union Beneficial Society of the County of Salem (Salem, N.J.) Minute book, 1832–1896. This organization provided financial aid and loans to its members for illness and funerals. The minutebook includes reports on income and disbursements. Purchased, 1958. (1 v.)

Union Volunteer Refreshment Saloon (Philadelphia, Pa.) Record and scrapbook, 1861–1865. Contains records of troops passing through Philadelphia, hospital admissions and deaths; Ladies Union Volunteer Refreshment Committee minutes, 1861–1865; cloth, tickets, envelopes, and other memorabilia. Gift of Arad Barrows' grandchildren, 1948. (1 v.)

United Bowemen of Philadelphia (Pa.) Records, 1828–1888. The records include: register/target books, 1828–1858; record book, 1828–1840, containing articles and members' "hits and value" records; minutebook, (1842–1859) 1888, of business meetings; miscellaneous items, 1852–1888. Gift of the United Bowmen of Philadelphia, 1888. (1 v.)

Washington's Birthday Celebration. Solicitation list, 1862. This was a target list of Center City Philadelphians for festivities planned by the Joint Committee of Philadelphia Councils. Gift of Mrs. S. Hamill Horne, 1945. (1 v.)

West Philadelphia Reading Society (Philadelphia, Pa.) Minute book, 1837–1843. This was an association for the intellectual improvement of its members and aid to the poor. Contains constitution and membership list. Gift of Edmund A. Bonnaffon, 1950. (1 v.)

Western Home for Poor Children of Philadelphia (Pa.) Minute book, 1858–1921, 1941. This home was founded in 1851 and incorporated in 1857 to shelter poor white Protestant orphan or half-orphan children. Includes charter and by-laws; assets statement for 1941 appended. Gift of Western Home for Poor Children, 1954. (1 v.)

White, John Brinton, b. 1840. Papers, (1877–1879) 1907. White was Philadelphia comptroller and treasurer of the memorial of the meeting of the descendants of Colonel Thomas White. The papers include circulars, letters, and accounts. Gift of William White, 1931. (1 v.)

Whitemarsh Valley Hunt Club (Flourtown, Pa.) Minute book, 1935–1954. Minutes for the Board of Governors meetings and members meetings with treasurers reports. Gift of John H.W. Ingersoll and Frederic L. Ballard, 1962. (1 v.)

Woman Suffrage Party of Logan (Philadelphia, Pa.) Minutes, 1915–1917. Gift of Jessie H. Murray, 1945. (1 v.)

Women's Christian Temperance Union of West Philadelphia (Pa.) Minutes, 1885–1898. Minutes for the executive committee meetings and regular meetings. Purchased, 1955. (3 v.)

Women's Farm and Garden Association (Philadelphia, Pa.) Register, 1875. Copy, alphabetized. (1 v.)

2039
Biddle, Nicholas, 1786–1844.   **Papers, 1776 (1799–1846) 1863.**
(650 items.)

Nicholas Biddle, litterateur and financier of Philadelphia, attended Princeton and served as: secretary to American Legation in Paris; editor of the *Port Folio;* member of the Pennsylvania state legislature; and president of the Bank of the United States. After leaving the Bank of the United States, Biddle lived as a retired gentleman at Andalusia, his country estate.

The bulk of the collection consists of incoming and outgoing correspondence, 1800–1844. The letters discuss personal affairs, politics, military developments, and economic matters, including the Bank of the United States. A letter dated April 19, 1839 explains Biddle's decision to retire from the bank. Additionally, there are manuscript copies of miscellaneous Biddle prose and verse dating from student days and from the period of association with the *Port Folio;* household account book, 1827, of Jane (Craig) Biddle, Nicholas' wife; and miscellanea.

Among the other papers are a few incoming and outgoing letters by several members of the Biddle family, including James Biddle, naval officer, 1813–1846; Charles J. Biddle, 1812–1828, 1863; and Craig Biddle, 1845–1862.

Gift of Nicholas Biddle Wainwright, 1976.

2040

**Second Baptist Church of Philadelphia.   Records, 1803–1972.
(40 linear ft.)**

Records of the Second Baptist Church of Philadelphia, organized 1803, representing religious, missionary, charitable and youth work.

General Records: outgoing correspondence, 1884–1966; incoming correspondence, 1861–1968; minutes of church meetings, 1832–1943; Board of Trustees minutes, 1839–1962; membership records, 1803–1911; correspondence on grants of dismission, 1857–1908; dismission records, 1897–1923; pew rolls and rent books, 1871–1908; guest book [register], n.d.; account books, 1884–1922; loose accounts, 1851–1972.

Religious Education: Sunday School Society minutes, 1832–1907; Sunday School registers and roll books, 1843–1931; Sunday School library records, 1879–1906; Adult Bible Class registers & superintendent's records, 1876–1900; Adult Bible Class minutes, 1923–1930; Lord's Day School records, including minutes, 1835–1969, roll books, 1847–1924, accounts, 1834–1967, miscellaneous.

Women's Activities: Women's Foreign Missionary Circle minutes, 1903–1919; Women's Home Mission Circle minutes, 1908–1937; Young Ladies Hope Dorcas Society minutes, 1840; Hope League treasurer's report, 1906–1912; King's Daughters minutes, rolls, and accounts, 1895–1949; Hope League and incoming correspondence and receipts, 1891–1956.

Special Activities: Hope Missionary Society records, ca. 1858–1901; Golden Promise Mission Band, collection accounts, 1899–1901; Volunteer Relief Society minutes, 1862–1867; Young Men's Association minutes, 1884–1888; Sheltering Arms roll and collection accounts, 1891–1895; Pastor's Aid Society account book, 1903–1907.

Other Records: Church construction records, 1873–1876, Addison Hutton, architect; Centennial records, 1902–1903; annual reports, legal records; broadsides; printed items; photographs; miscellaneous.
Gift of Stephen Karpiak, 1975.
Finding aid available.

2041
Moschzisker, Michael von.   **Fine Arts file, 1951 (1957–1962), 1976.** **(450 items.)**

Michael von Moschzisker was Chairman of the Philadelphia Redevelopment Authority from 1956 to 1962. His efforts resulted in a Redevelopment Authority contract clause requiring that 1 percent of construction cost be used for fine arts.
These files from his office relate to his campaign to make fine arts a part of urban redevelopment. The papers include correspondence, clippings, articles, memoranda. There are some additional papers *Arts in Architecture,* an unsuccessful project which was to have served as intermediary between artists and developers.
Gift of Michael von Moschzisker, 1967, 1974, 1976.

2042
Moschzisker, Michael von.   **Papers, 1954–1973.**   **(200 items.)**

The papers of Michael von Moschzisker, Philadelphia lawyer, on Richardson Dilworth, include: general correspondence, 1954–1973, mainly between Moschzisker and Dilworth; and correspondence and miscellaneous items on Moschzisker's activities on behalf of Dilworth during the campaigns to elect Dilworth mayor of Philadelphia, 1955 and 1959, and the campaign to elect him governor of Pennsylvania, 1962.

2043
Decatur family.   **Papers, 1792–1854.**   **(100 items.)**

Letters and documents primarily concerned with the claims of Priscilla Decatur McKnight Twiggs and her sisters on the estate of Stephen Decatur, their uncle. Also includes miscellaneous Susan Wheeler Decatur, Major Levi Twiggs, and McKnight family correspondence.
Gift of Mr. and Mrs. William F. Machold, 1976.
Finding aid available.

2044
No entry.

2045
Fairmount Park Art Association.   Archives, 1871–1972.
(56 linear ft.)

The Fairmount Park Art Association (F.P.A.A.) was chartered in 1872 with the original purpose for "adorning Fairmount Park with statues, busts, and other works of art" and came to include the promotion "of the beautiful in the City of Philadelphia, in its architecture, improvements and general plan."

These archives are the result of several different methods of record keeping and represent only the files of certain officers. Other records were presumably retained by the other principals.

General Correspondence: Secretary/Executive Secretary letterpress books, 1893–1896, 1898–1920, and loose correspondence, 1872–1933, 1972, composed of a chronological file and a topical file. This material relates to membership, meetings, finances and other general business as well as specific concerns and projects such as Benjamin Franklin Parkway, Carpenters Hall lot improvement, Japanese Temple—Gate, Sculpture in the Open Air Exhibit, Wilson Cary Swan Memorial Fountain, and Woodmere Art Gallery. These general files contain some minutes, contracts, clippings, bills, receipts, and photographs. Most of the correspondence relating to specific sculptures may be found in subsequent series.

Board of Trustees minutes, 1894–1973.

Treasurer's Office: correspondence, 1929–1940, 1948–1961; bills and receipts, 1871–1929, 1941–1965; bank statements, cancelled checks, ca. 1918-ca. 1932; scattered treasurers' reports and accountants' audits. Additional bills, receipts, and financial correspondence may be found in other series.

Standing Committees: Committee on City Planning correspondence, 1935–1951; Committee on Finances, Legacies, and Trusts correspondence and reports, 1937-1949; Committee on Location of Sculpture correspondence, 1937–1969; Committee on Works of Art correspondence and minutes, 1902–1914; Women's Committee of F.P.A.A. correspondence, 1958–1971, with some financial papers. Also included in this section are Charles J. Cohen letterpress books and correspondence on Cohen's activities with Committees on Auditing, Finances, Works of Art, and others.

Special Committees and Projects: Revision of Charter and By-laws, 1905–1908; Capt. John Ericsson Memorial, James A. Garfield Memorial, Ulysses S. Grant Memorial, H. Morris Harrison Memorial, Charles H. Howell Memorial, John F. Kennedy Plaza Fountain, William McKinley Memorial, Robert Morris Memorial, Ellen Phillips Samuel Memorial (including the three International Sculpture Exhibitions, 1933, 1940, 1949, held in conjunction with the Samuel Memorial, Shakespeare Memorial, Richard Smith Memorial). The above contain a variety of correspondence, minutes, accounts, and other papers on the projects.

Sculpture of A City: to commemorate its centennial, the F.P.A.A. published *Sculpture of a City* in 1974, a study of Philadelphia public sculpture. The research files compiled for the book, arranged according to sculptor, contain correspondence with the artist, correspondence of F.P.A.A. board members and others, minutes, contracts, *Sculpture of a City* research notes, letters, clippings, drafts of articles, photographs, and material relevant to the sculpture. Additional publication files include more correspondence, authors and photographers biographies, book outlines, contracts, photographs, and other business papers.

Miscellaneous records: scrapbooks, 1900–1926, annual reports, photographs, pamphlets.

Philadelphia Fountain Society Records, given to F.P.A.A., 1972: letterpress book, 1870–1871, 1902–1905; loose correspondence, 1883–1942, particularly concerning the Rebecca Darby Smith Fountain; minute books, 1869–1885, 1891–1916; bills and receipts, 1887–1941; and miscellaneous papers.

Deposited by Fairmount Park Art Association, 1975.

Finding aid available.

2046
No entry.

2047A
Wharton family.   Papers, 1778 (1813–1886) 1931.   (2 linear ft.)

Papers of the Whartons and related Philadelphia families. Wharton correspondence consists of incoming personal and professional letters, 1815–1869, of Thomas Isaac Wharton and his son Henry Wharton, lawyers; Arabella Griffith Wharton to her husband Thomas I.; and miscellaneous letters 1869–1931. Other Wharton papers include: Hannah Margaret Wharton diary, 1813–1824, including recollections of her childhood; legal papers including estate records and court cases; bills and receipts, 1819–1873, mainly of Henry Wharton; accounts of servants' wages, 1854–1855; Francis Wharton, son of Thomas I. Wharton, receipt book, 1852–1857; miscellany, including genealogical notes.

Related family papers include: Griffith family correspondence, 1815–1842, especially the letters of Mary Griffith, author and mother of Arabella

Griffith Wharton; Mary Griffith receipt book, 1825–1833; miscellaneous Griffith accounts, 1810–1845; Bayard family correspondence, 1854–1886, consisting principally of Florence Bayard letters from her father James Asheton Bayard, lawyer, and other family members; Mary Johnstone Brinley to her daughter Mary Gibbs Brinley, 1833; miscellaneous Rawle family papers, 1778, 1783; Rebecca Warner Rawle diary, 1808; Adolfo Carlos Munoz, architect and husband of Emily Wharton, incoming correspondence and miscellaneous papers 1891–1917, primarily on his activities during the Cuban rebellion against Spain and the Spanish-American War.

Purchased, 1976.

2047B
Wharton family.   Papers, 1742–1844.   (80 items)

Family letters, 1775–1783 and n.d., to Hannah Redwood, who later married Charles Wharton, mostly from her sister Sarah ("Sophia") Redwood Fisher, and other miscellaneous Wharton family letters and accounts, 1742–1837.

2048
Harrison family.   Papers, 1789 (1880–1964).   (4 linear ft.)

The bulk of the collection consists of the papers of Marie Louise Lemoine Harrison of Philadelphia. Included among her papers are personal and family correspondence, 1894–1964, including condolence letters on the death of her father Louis Rice Lemoine, 1926; appointment books, 1934–1935, 1938–1945; papers on her writing of religious books, especially manuscript notes and manuscript copies of several works; miscellanea. Her husband Charles Custis Harrison, Jr., and their children are also represented by family correspondence, 1898–1963.

There are some papers of the Lemoine family, chiefly of Mrs. Harrison's father Louis Rice Lemoine, President of the U.S. Cast Iron Pipe and Foundry County, St. Louis, Mo. His papers contain personal correspondence, 1869–1925, and business correspondence, board minutes, specifications, accounts, 1890–1926. There are also Ashton Lemoine accounts, 1906–1907, mainly on stock market transactions, and miscellaneous family correspondence and documents, 1789–1864. Among the miscellaneous papers are a Chuckwold Farm Stables book; scrapbooks; photographs; genealogical notes; newspaper clippings; printed items.

Gift of Mrs. John T. Nightingale, 1968.

Finding aid available.

2049

Coxe family.   **Papers, 1638 (1776–1879), 1897.**   (210 **linear ft.**)

The collection is broken into three major series of papers. They include the Tench Coxe section, 1638, 1776–1824, 1879; the Charles Sidney Coxe, Edward Sidney Coxe, and Alexander Sidney Coxe legal papers section, ca. 1810–1879; and Third Party Papers, ca. 1722–1815. The Tench Coxe Section is broken down further into four series: Volumes and printed materials; correspondence and general papers; Essays, addresses and resource material; and Bills and receipts.

In 1776 Tench Coxe began in the import-export business by joining his father's firm Coxe, Furman & Coxe. In 1780 he established his own house, entering into partnership in 1783 with Bostonian Nalbro Frazier. Coxe & Frazier was dissolved in 1790, after which government service became Tench Coxe's principal employment. A fervent supporter of the adoption of the Constitution, his increasing political involvement was especially concerned with patent legislation, funding of the national debt, the location of capital, and the effort to establish a National Manufactory. At first serving in the Federalist administration, Coxe was named assistant secretary of the treasury, 1790–1792, and commissioner of the revenue, 1792–1797. His sympathies moving toward the Republican Party, he spent from 1797 to 1800 engaged in party political activities and personal business, chiefly land speculation in Pennsylvania, New York, Maryland, North Carolina, and Virginia. By 1796 his personal finances were hopelessly complicated by debts and litigations from his own ventures and the bankruptcy of a partner Dr. Thomas Ruston. Nevertheless Coxe continued to retain and manage his property, from which his heirs would benefit greatly, until his death.

As a Republican, Coxe resumed his office-holding with his appointment as secretary of the Land Office of Pennsylvania, 1800–1801, collector of Revenue for Philadelphia, 1801–1802, supervisor of Revenue of Pennsylvania, 1802–1803, purveyor of public supplies, 1803–1812, and clerk of the Court of Quarter Sessions of Philadelphia, 1815–1818. Coxe is probably best known to both contemporaries and historians, as a writer. Throughout most of his life he published numerous pamphlets and contributed frequently to the press, writing on economic and political matters, foreign affairs, and sundry other subjects.

Volumes and printed material of Tench Coxe include: letterbooks, 1778–1819, deal chiefly with mercantile and real estate business matters, revenue letterbook, 1801–1802; letterbook, 1813–1816, concerning Coxe's difficulties in completing his accounts as purveyor of public supplies. Account books, 1772–1824 relate to Coxe's personal and official business finances and include daybooks, journals, ledgers, checkbooks, bank books, receipt books, land records, revenue records, and others. Additionally, there are Coxe's commercial records consisting of Coxe, Furman and Coxe letterbook, 1776–1779, and account books, 1776–1796; Coxe and Frazier letterbooks, 1784–1798, journals, 1783–1798, and other account books.

In this series also are: miscellaneous Coxe family volumes, 1810–1871, consisting of docket books and other legal records, estate records, and household accounts of Coxe's children, Alexander, Charles, Henry, and Mary Rebecca; Dr. Thomas Ruston and Mary Fisher Ruston account books, domestic account books, medical notes, 1762–1803; George Harrison's Office of Naval Agent letterbook, 1801–1806, journal, 1802, and personal journal, 1845, and ledger, 1842–1844; some account and letterbooks of other Coxe debtors, William Harrison, 1793–1799, and James McCalley, 1792–1797; Office of the collector of revenue letterbooks, 1791 (George Clymer), 1798–1800 (James Ash); and a final group of records, ca. 1759–1849, partly derived from business firms with which Coxe had dealings, partly from private individuals connected with him or his family, but much for which the provenance is undetermined.

Printed materials consist of: books; newspaper clippings, 1787–1885; pamphlets and booklets, 1767–1885, including pamphlets authored by Tench Coxe; circulars and form letters, 1783–1822; broadsides and broadsheets, 1782–1837; and miscellaneous.

Tench Coxe's incoming correspondence forms the bulk of the second series with a small body of outgoing correspondence, and a larger body of third party correspondence, all arranged together chronologically. Letters on all of the commercial, official, and personal subjects which concerned him are represented, usually in quantity: national economic policy, Coxe's writings and publications, land speculations and development, domestic and foreign commerce, the operations of his state and federal offices, politics and government, church, Philadelphia civic organizations, family matters. In addition to his business associates and family members, among his correspondents were James Madison, Thomas Jefferson, Alexander Hamilton, Benjamin Rush, John Dickinson, Joel Barlow, Pierce Butler, Aaron Burr, Albert Gallatin, John Jay, Robert Morris, Timothy Pickering, and Gouverneur Morris.

Interfiled with the correspondence are general papers: deeds, surveys and other land papers; ships' papers, insurance policies, invoices and other commercial pieces; tax records, licenses, and sundry revenue forms; notes and memoranda; financial accounts and calculations; calling cards and other personal memorabilia.

After his father's death, Charles S. Coxe, lawyer, judge, and executor of the family estate, became the principal recipient of correspondence in the

Coxe family papers. This remaining part of the series, 1824–1879, concerns management of the estate, family affairs, and personal business.

The bulk of the Essays, Addresses, and Resource Material series is made up of drafts and occasional fair copies of Tench Coxe's books (published and unpublished), pamphlets, and pieces for newspapers and periodicals. There is supplemental material such as manuscripts of other authors and excerpts of books. The series consists of writings on economic subjects, political topics, and miscellaneous and fragmentary material.

Tench Coxe's bills and receipts, the last series, filed in alphabetical order, relate to his personal expenses, to his business accounts, to his official duties, particularly his purchases as purveyor of public supplies, and to the accounts of persons for whom he acted as agent or trustee. Also included in this series are Tench Coxe's cancelled checks, 1783–1843.

The Charles Sidney Coxe, Edmund Sidney Coxe, Alexander Sidney Coxe Legal Papers section, ca. 1810–1879, includes: correspondence, financial papers, legal documents and memoranda of the attorney sons of Tench Coxe are primarily concerned with their law practices. Most correspondence and other papers of the three brothers which do not pertain directly to legal matters have been included in the Tench Coxe Section, Series II; however, some personal and family items do remain here. The papers of Charles Coxe, who served as deputy attorney general of Pennsylvania, and judge of District Court for Philadelphia, 1826–1841, are the most numerous, with lesser amounts for Edmund and Alexander.

The Third Party Papers, ca. 1722–1815, is filled with loose records supplementary to the volumes that appear in Section I. Dr. Thomas Ruston's papers, ca. 1722, 1785–1794, 1812, were seized by Coxe in an attempt to salvage something of the debt due to him after the Chester County, physician and land speculator went bankrupt. They relate to his business interests, especially land, to his writings, and to a small extent his medical education. There is correspondence, deeds, and other land papers, bills, receipts and other accounts, legal papers. Other of Coxe's debtors are represented by William Harrison correspondence, accounts, land paper, legal material, ca. 1790–1800; James McCalley accounts and other business papers, ca. 1785–1815; and Oliver Pollock miscellaneous papers, 1785–1790.

Gift of the Coxe family, 1964.

Tench Coxe section of collection available on microfilm through interlibrary loan.

West, Lucy Fisher, *Guide to the Microfilm of the Papers of Tench Coxe* (Philadelphia, Pa. : Historical Society of Pennsylvania, 1977)

2050

Chew family.   Papers, 1683–1896.   (183 linear ft.)

The arrangement of the collection follows both a generational and a chronological pattern. Family members have been grouped together according to generation, yet each individual's papers remain separate. The policy of ultimate use governs their position in the collection (the correspondence is filed according to recipient rather than by author). Emphasis has been placed on the Chew family itself with related families' papers forming small subgroups within the larger series. Papers of married couples have been sorted separately, but they are located together within the arrangement.

Originally, the papers were housed at Cliveden, the Chew family's country seat in Germantown. Built by Chief Justice Benjamin Chew between 1763 and 1767, the house served as the site for the Battle of Germantown on October 4, 1777. In 1778, Chew sold Cliveden to Blair McClenahan, but the family repurchased the property in 1797. Cliveden remained the Chew estate until 1972, when the family gave the house to the National Trust for Historic Preservation. Many family members lived at Cliveden for at least part of their lives; even those Chews who moved on to other places often returned to the house later to deposit their papers.

The collection reflects the family's interest in land speculation, particularly in western Pennsylvania and New Jersey; in the development of turnpikes, roads, mines, forges, and canals; and in local political affairs. Deeds, surveys, memoranda, administration agency accounts and correspondence, tax records, and correspondence from tenants make up a sizable part of the collection. Also of great import are the records of the several commissions appointed to resolve the Pennsylvania/Maryland boundary dispute and the records of the Mason/Dixon line commission, of which Chief Justice Benjamin Chew served as secretary. The Chew family members represented in the collection include: Samuel Chew, 1693–1744; his wife, Mary Chew, d. 1747; Benjamin Chew, 1722–1810; Elizabeth Oswald Chew; Samuel Chew, 1737–1809; Benjamin Chew, Jr., 1758–1844; Katherine Banning Chew, 1770–1855; Maria Chew; Henrietta Chew; Catherine Chew; Benjamin Chew III, 1793–1864; Samuel Chew, 1797–1815; Henry Banning Chew, 1800–1866; Elizabeth Ann Ralston Chew; William White Chew, 1803–1851; Anne Sophia Penn Chew, 1805–1892; Joseph Turner Chew, 1806–1835; Sarah Ann Kirker Chew; Anthony Banning Chew, 1809–1854; Samuel Chew, 1832–1887; Joseph Johnson; David Sands Brown; Mary Chew Wilcocks; Alexander Wilcocks; and Sir John Bridger.

Gift of the Chew family.

Finding aid available.

2051

West family. **Papers, 1810–1881.** **(70 items)**

James West letters, 1810–1811, 1813–1814, report on escapes and captures at sea, travel in Europe and some comments on European affairs. The rest of the material is miscellaneous West family estate papers.

Gift of Anne Simpson, 1978.

2053
Madeira, Edith, 1865–1951.   Papers, 1918–1919.   (150 items.)

Edith Madeira served as chief nurse with the American Red Cross Commission to Palestine, formed in 1918 "to look after the sickness and starvation of the civilian population in the occupied area of Palestine."

Papers of Edith Madeira consist of typescript copies of her letters, March, 1818-Feb., 1919, a *Report for Nursing Service,* and photographs. They chronicle the voyage to Jerusalem by way of Capetown, South Africa, wartime conditions in Palestine, and the work of the Red Cross Commission, including the organization of hospitals.

Gift of Mrs. Crawford Madeira, 1975.

2054
National Organization for Women. Philadelphia Chapter.
Archives, 1968–1977.   (4 linear ft.)

Incomplete archive of the Philadelphia Chapter of the National Organization for Women, including mostly incoming newsletters, circulars, publications from the National, Pennsylvania and Chapter offices. Annual files concern subjects such as child care, employment, abortion legislation, and media.

Gift of the Philadelphia Chapter, National Organization for Women, 1977.

Finding aid available.

2055
Kane, Florence Bayard, 1868–1943.   Papers, 1886–1943.
(12.75 linear ft.)

Florence Bayard Kane, member of the prominent Kane family of Pennsylvania, was a Philadelphia volunteer worker and much-travelled individual who briefly worked as a librarian and as a processor of manuscripts. She was a woman of many associations and activities, but with all a woman whose life was peripatetic and unfocussed.

The material consists of incoming and outgoing personal correspondence, papers from organizations to which Kane belonged or contributed, personal memorabilia and other miscellanea, and the manuscript writings of sister, Anne Francis (Nancy) Kane.

Florence Bayard Kane's outgoing correspondence consists primarily of letters, 1886–1895, to her mother, Mabel Bayard Kane Bird, and letters, 1899–1909, to members of her family while on various trips abroad. The latter include her reports on the Messina, Sicily, earthquake of December, 1908, and her role in rendering nursing assistance to the victims, for which the Italian Government awarded her a medal.

The bulk of the collection consists of incoming personal correspondence, 1886–1943, along with some draft replies by Kane. Principal correspondents are various family members, including several generations of siblings, cousins and nieces: her sisters, Jean Duval Leiper Kane Foulke, Elizabeth Bayard Kane Norris Rhein, Anne Francis (Nancy) Kane and her brother, J[ames] A[shton] Bayard Kane; her cousins, Eliza Middleton Kane Cope, with whom Kane often made her home, Francis Fisher Kane, Philadelphia lawyer and United States attorney for eastern Pennsylvania, 1913–1920, Elisha Kent Kane, prohibition advocate, and Helen Hamilton Shields Stockton; her nieces, Jean Kane Foulke DuPont and Florence Foulke Bird.

There are also letters from various friends, particularly: Langdon Elwyn Mitchell, playwright; Mary Moss, author and travelling companion of Florence Kane, who was with her at the time of the Sicilian earthquake; Maria Lansdale, with whom Kane often lived in Philadelphia; Etta de Vitti, Marchese de Vitti de Marco at whose home Kane often stayed while in Italy; Mary Sterrett Gittings, an old Baltimore, Md., friend; Emily Hobhouse, outspoken English opponent of the Boer War and pacifist in World War I; Margaret Munro Elder Dow, author and biographer of Elisha Kent Kane: Sarah Northcliff Cleghorne, author and poet. For Florence Kane's flirtation with a librarian's career the correspondence, 1897–1903, includes letters from Bryn Mawr College President M. Carey Thomas.

Letters to Florence at the time of the Messina earthquake, 1909, concern the supply and use of financial aid provided by her family and friends in the United States. Kane's interest in prison reform is evident from letters of penologist Thomas Mott Osborne, 1914–1918, and others. Miss Kane worked sporadically for many years organizing the papers of the Wister family, and Owen Wister, author, wrote her on this and other subjects, 1913–1935.

The miscellaneous section contains solicitations, acknowledgements, newsletters, and flyers of various conservation, philanthropic, civic, and international organizations; pamphlets, articles, clippings; collected poems and quotations, receipted bills, medical prescriptions, addresses; photographs.

Florence's sister, Anne Francis (Nancy) Kane, aspired to a literary career. Her death at age 24 was much lamented by family and friends, especially Langdon Elwyn Mitchell who was to become a noted playwright. A group of Nancy Kane's manuscripts are interspersed with Mitchell's translations and some writings.

Gift of Jean Kane Foulke DuPont, 1977.

2056
No entry.

2057
No entry.

2058
Elliot, Rebecca Ward, b. 1893.   Collection, ca. 1850-ca. 1930.
(3 linear ft.)

Rebecca Ward Elliot was a reporter for the *Philadelphia Public Ledger*.

Collection consists almost entirely of photographs of the family of Rebecca Ward Elliot, including her parents, grandparents, cousins. There is a large section of landscape photographs of Ellerly, the family home, and of Bermuda and Nassau where the family travelled often. There is one box of daguerreotypes, ambrotypes and tintypes, all portraits.

The remainder of the collection consists of miscellaneous correspondence, sketches and ephemera.

Gift of W.W. White, 1977.

Finding aid available.

2059
No entry.

2060
Jonathan Meredith Tannery.   Records, 1784–1800.   (2 linear ft.)

The business records of the Philadelphia tannery of Jonathan Meredith. They record the purchase of hides and barks, the operation of the tannery, the putting out of leather for currying, and sales. The volumes are in several hands. Of special interest is Meredith's "Waste Book for Tan Yard Accounts," 1786–1799, which records workmen's wages as well as purchases and sales. This is supplemented by hide accounts, 1784–1787, 1789–1794, 1798–1800, which show both quantities purchased and the sources of hides; bark accounts, 1793–1795; tannery yard books, indicating the bark used and the duration for each tanning lot, 1787–1796; "leather given out" for currying, 1785–1795; sales records, 1795–1797; miscellaneous accounts, 1785–1798.

Purchased, Dreer Fund, 1934.

2061
Renshaw, Richard.   Family papers, 1683 (1789–1865), 1911.
(225 items.)

These papers contain correspondence, wills, documents of Richard Renshaw and his family. Renshaw was justice of the peace for the District of Southwark, Philadelphia County, 1807–1835, and most of his incoming correspondence, 1789–1831, relates to this office. There are several personal letters from Caesar Augustus Rodney and a few of Renshaw's own letters. Alice Johnston Renshaw Neil's letters, ca. 1840's, to her brother give social notes from Philadelphia. There are wills, deeds, notes, accounts, and letters, 1790–1911, on the estates of the Johnston, Renshaw, and Neil families, particularly about coal lands in Northumberland County.

Gift of Mr. Richard Ludden and Mrs. Katherine Prew Ludden, 1979.

2062

Geary family.   Correspondence, 1859–1865.   (ca. 400 items.)

John White Geary, born in Westmoreland County, was a colonel in the Mexican War, first mayor of San Francisco, Calif., territorial governor of Kansas, a major general in the Union Army at the end of the Civil War, and governor of Pennsylvania, 1867–1873. He began his Civil War service as a colonel of the 28th Regiment, Pennsylvania Volunteers, at Harpers Ferry, and continuing with battles at Manassas and Leesburg. As brigadier general, Geary commanded troops with the Army of Virginia at Cedar Mountain (where he was wounded), with the Army of the Potomac at Chancellorsville and Gettysburg, with the Army of the Cumberland at Wauhatchie, Lookout Mountain, and Missionary Ridge. He remained with the Cumberland for the March to the Sea, his Corps, the 20th, being the first to enter Atlanta, and was appointed military governor in Savannah after its capture. In January, 1865, he was breveted major general and participated in the Carolinas campaign.

His letters, 1859–1865, to his second wife Mary (Mrs. Mary Church Henderson), include some pre-Civil War letters on family financial and legal concerns involving the Girard and James R. Logan estates, and on farm matters and politics. The bulk of the letters detail his Civil War military services. Geary's letters to his wife, reporting on these campaigns in detail, show clearly a general on the make, but they also increasingly reveal a horror of the death, destruction, and devastation around him. He expresses opinions on non-military matters as well: the Emancipation Proclamation, abolitionists, Copperheads, Abraham Lincoln's election and assassination, Pennsylvania politics, southern landscapes, people, and cities.

Geary's son, Lt. Edward R. Geary, served in the Civil War with his father. Edward's letters, 1861–1863, to his step-mother, provide another perspective on life in the Union army. Lt. Geary was killed at Wauhatchie.

Other letters to Mrs. John W. Geary, include those from her brother-in-law, Rev. Edward R. Geary, 1862–1864.

Gift of Col. Richard M. Ludlow, 1978–1979.

2063
Corporation for the Relief of Widows and Children of Clergymen in the Communion of the Protestant Episcopal Church in the Commonwealth of Pennsylvania. Records, 1769–1941.
(2.5 linear ft.)

This organization was founded in 1769 for the provision of annuities to the survivors of deceased clergy. During the Revolution the corporation was inactive, but resumed operations in 1784 with appropriate changes of title. In 1796 the Corporation resolved to separate into three independent organizations for New Jersey, New York, and Pennsylvania, although the formal division of funds was not accomplished for ten years.

Records include: minute books, 1769–1915, containing largely financial information; blotters, 1878–1894; cashbooks, 1894–1941; miscellaneous correspondence, financial, and other papers.

Gift of the Corporation for the Relief of Widows and Children, 1978.

2064
Fletcher Works (Philadelphia, Pa.) Records, 1890–1955.
(2.5 linear ft.)

Otto W. Schaum and his son Fletcher Schaum were directors and managers of the Fletcher Works, a Philadelphia manufacturer of machinery for the textile industry. The firm began in 1850 as Schaum & Uhlinger and became the Fletcher Works ca. 1920 because of a change of stock ownership in this closed corporation. The Schaums retained their interests in the firm. The firm was sold in 1955.

The records include Otto Schaum's foundry notebooks, 1890–1929, detailing the daily operations of the shop; annual financial statements of the firm, 1923–1955; records of cost estimates for orders and sales, 1920's-1946; and inventories of looms, 1952, and baten shop, 1953–1954. Of particular interest are the fairly extensive records of the firm's relations with its work force. Beginning with a 1945 job classification survey by the National Metal Trades Association, Fletcher Schaum's files reveal the company's efforts to adjust to unionization. Included are several time studies, 1946–1947, and a copy of the union contract with the International Moulders & Foundry Workers, Local #1, in 1948. There are additional wage surveys, 1951–1955, and information on employee retirement. Also included are papers containing correspondence with several Philadelphia banks on recapitalization in the 1920's and debt problems in 1930's and 1940's. Two personal account books of Otto Schaum, 1930–1947, a small group of Schaum family photographs and memorabilia complete the collection.

Gift of Mrs. Fletcher Schaum, 1978.

2065

Print Club (Philadelphia, Pa.)   Archives, 1915–1985.
(60 linear ft.)

Since its founding in 1915, the Print Club has achieved a national reputation and membership. Its purposes are to encourage the appreciation of prints and to provide audiences for the work of contemporary printmakers. The membership has always included both collectors and printmakers; many of the former from the Philadelphia area, the latter from across the United States and Canada. Since its incorporation in 1921 it has been governed by a board of governors, from which the officers are chosen, and has been administered by a full-time director. The club is located at 1614 Latimer Street, Philadelphia, a building it has occupied since 1919 and owned since 1927.

The Print Club's exhibition program includes annual juried shows, travelling exhibitions, and occasional retrospective exhibitions. In 1926 it mounted a Joseph Pennell retrospective. It showed the drawings of Brancusi, Modigliani, and Picasso in 1930, and a group of modern American printmakers in 1936. In the 1940's, the club conducted master classes under Stanley William Hayter and others. It has published editions of prints by such artists as Frasconi, Kaplan, Paone, Spruance and others. In the 1960's, the club began a program of print making demonstrations in the city's schools called "Prints in Progress." Until 1977, the club sold on consignment the works of many of its artist members. And, since 1940, the club has been contributing its purchase prize prints to the permanent collection of the Philadelphia Museum of Art.

The archives consist of five types of records: minutes of the board, 1921–1976; correspondence of the officers and director, 1916–1964; financial records, 1922–1972; consignment records, 1933–1964; and scrap books and published catalogues, 1926–1950.

Gift of the Print Club 1978–1986.

Finding aid available.

2066

Jordan, Thomas J., 1821–1895.   Civil War letters, 1861–1866.
(200 items.)

The letters of brevet brigadier general Thomas Jefferson Jordan, 9th Regiment, Pennsylvania Volunteers (also known as the Lochiel Cavalry) are mostly to his wife, Jane Jordan. The majority of Jordan's letters were written in Tennessee and Kentucky where the 9th was stationed for most of the war, and contain personal observations on the social and economic conditions of the region, as well as descriptions of the 9th's numerous skirmishes with the Confederate cavalry led by John Hunt Morgan and Nathan Bedford Forrest. Jordan's letters also record the role played by his regiment in the invasion of Georgia, Sherman's March to the Sea, and the Carolina campaigns. The battles at Thompson's Station, Tullahoma, Averasboro, and Bentonville are among the larger engagements described by Jordan.

A small portion of these letters describe Jordan's capture on July 9, 1862, his detention in the infamous Castle Thunder Prison in Richmond, Va., and his subsequent release as part of a prisoner exchange in December of the same year. There are also letters from various government officials to Jane Jordan, notifying her of Jordan's capture and informing her of the efforts being made on his behalf.

Gift of David L. Bacon, 1978.

2067
Poe, Philip Livingston, Mrs.   Collection, 1732–1876.   (50 items.)

Personal correspondence to various members of the Morris family, 1818, 1876, n.d.; elegies, many of which are transcriptions of those by Hannah Griffitts, and other miscellaneous transcribed pieces; business and legal papers, many dealing with land transactions of various members of the Shoemaker family in Philadelphia, Westmoreland, Bedford, and Northumberland Counties in Pennsylvania and Hawkins County, Tenn., 1732–1831.

Gift of Mrs. Philip Livingston Poe, 1978.

Finding aid available.

2068
Lowell, Charles Winthrop, 1834–1877.   Papers, 1860–1867.
(3 linear ft.)

Charles Winthrop Lowell is a ninth generation descendent of Percival Lowell, who was the first Lowell to emigrate to America, in 1639. He was born to Hon. Phillip Smith Lowell and Harriet Butler Lowell on November 20, 1834, in Farmingham, Maine. He graduated from Bowdoin College in 1859 and studied law with the Hon. Charles P. Chandler, whose daughter Mary Elizabeth he married in June of 1860. Their daughter, Mary Chandler Lowell, was born on January 18, 1864; her mother died six days later. He was a prominent lawyer in Maine and Louisiana and served as a colonel and as provost marshal general in the Civil War. At the close of the war he settled in New Orleans, La., was member and speaker of the Louisiana legislature and for several year was postmaster of New Orleans. He married, ca. 1879,

Sarah ("Sally") W. Huff of Salem, Va., but had no children from this marriage. He died October 5, 1877, in Foxcroft, Maine.

The papers of Charles W. Lowell consist mainly of materials collected by Lowell during his service as major of Company B, 80th Infantry Regiment, Corps D'Afrique. The collection contains correspondence, most of the later on military business; legal documents, which contain the records of court proceedings for which Lowell served as judge; bills and receipts; miscellaneous military inventories; military orders and circulars; and a section of miscellaneous documents.

Gift of Mrs. James Armentrout, Jr., 1977.

2069
Kelly, Edward Smith, d. 1915.   Collection, 1788–1920.
(4 linear ft.)

This collection is a miscellany of land papers, real estate account books, estate papers, and legal correspondence; presumably accumulated by Edward Smith Kelly, Philadelphia lawyer, during the course of his practice. Of special note are minute books of the Social Purity Alliance, 1886–1905, and several folders of Social Purity Alliance correspondence and newspaper clippings, 1898–1907. The collection also contains a Galilean Society minute book, 1815–1819.

A small portion of the collection is papers related to the career of Oswald Thompson, Philadelphia lawyer, judge and trustee of the University of Pennsylvania. The Thompson material includes a docket book, 1832–1851, letterpress books, 1839–1853, minute book of the Committee on the Department of Law at the University of Pennsylvania, 1857, with letters, 1859–1861, and estate papers. There are also letters from Andrew Gregg Curtin, Pennsylvania politician and governor, to the merchant firm of Hart, Cummings, and Hart, 1850–1861, on collection of debt claims.

2070
No entry.

2071
Markoe and Emlen families.   Correspondence, 1811–1876.
(85 items.)

Much of this miscellaneous family correspondence is to and between Hitty Markoe and her daughter Ellen, who married George Emlen in 1840; also Ellen Markoe Emlen recipe book.

Gift of Emily M.T. Fisher, 1979.

2072

Baylson, Isidore.   Papers, 1910 (1917–1919) 1928.   (200 items.)

Isidore Baylson, Philadelphia lawyer, served in World War I as an instructor at the Army Machine Gun School in France, joining the 5th Machine Gun Battalion just before the armistice.

Baylson's letters, 1917–1919, report on his military and recreational activities during the war and occupation of Germany. There is some military memorabilia, including training manuals, and miscellaneous papers from his civilian life.

Gift of Mrs. Isidore Baylson, 1978.

2073

Porter, Ruth Pearson Cook.   Letters, 1858–1866.   (150 items.)

Ruth Pearson Cook of Easton, personal letters, 1858–1866 and undated, to James Madison Porter (II) lawyer also of Easton, whom she married in 1863. Many of the letters are from Hackettstown, N.J.

Purchased, 1979.

2074

Union Volunteer Refreshment Saloon. (Philadelphia).   Telegrams, 1861–1864.   (400 items.)

Telegrams to Barzilai S. Brown and other officers of the Union Volunteer Refreshment Saloon giving troop departures for Philadelphia.

2075

Harrison Brothers and Company (Philadelphia, Pa.)   Account books, 1867–1893.   (5 v.)

Harrison Brothers and Company was a Philadelphia chemical and paint manufactory with offices and plant at 35th and Grey's Ferry Avenue. The firm survived until 1917, when it was absorbed by E.I. du Pont.

The journals and ledgers give the annual financial statements of the partners. Also included is an annual account stock book, 1873–1886.

2076

Philadelphia Typographical Union. #2.   Records, 1850–1967. (9 linear ft.)

The Philadelphia Typographical Union #2 was organized in 1850 to protect the interests of journeymen printers. Activities of the Union include: apprenticeship program begun in 1857, National Fund established in 1867 to compensate striking workmen, Union Employment Office and Reading Room created in 1879; various boycott, management and financial committees; child care programs begun in 1943; New Processes Training Center of P.T.U. opened in 1957; political education groups (Labor League for Political Education organized in 1948 and joined with CIO's Political Action Committee in 1956 to form Committee on Public Education (COPE).

The records include: constitution with member lists; regular and special meeting minutes, 1853–1967; executive committee minutebook, 1901–1905; business committee minutebook, 1850–1861; membership book, 1854–1865; and miscellaneous records.

Union regular and special meeting minutes reveal support of factory, wage and labor laws and revision of labor laws, 1884–1904, 1927–1937; International Copyright Laws, 1868, 1886; High Tariff Laws, 1882, 1894; Immigration Restriction, 1902; A.F.L.-C.I.O. merger, 1939. Minutes also show opposition to Taft-Hartley and N.L.R.B.

Deposited by the Typographical Union #2, 1978.

2077
Lewis family.   Papers, 1807–1920.   (4 linear ft.)

The bulk of this collection is highly miscellaneous Farmers' and Mechanics' Bank papers that were apparently retained by Howard W. Lewis who was the bank's last president and liquidating agent. The Farmers' and Mechanics' Bank, Philadelphia, began operations in 1807 and was merged with Philadelphia National Bank in 1918. There are extracts of minutes evidently prepared for the bank's centennial, some correspondence, and some financial papers.

Family papers include Howard W. Lewis letterpress books, 1897–1918, which concern philanthropic and social institutions with which he was associated, estates for which he was executor, and his own personal business affairs. Mabel Potter Lewis letters, memoranda, reports, flyers, memorabilia, 1917–1920, on the Woman's Land Army of America which she served as a board member. There are a few items of S. Weir Lewis, father of Howard Lewis: personal ledger, 1847–1888, and accounts for estates of James M. Barclay, Hannah Ellmaker, Nancy Read.

Gift of Howard W. Lewis, 1939–1946.

2078
Pennsylvania Volunteers. 28th Regiment.   Papers, 1861–1863. (180 items.)

Special and general orders with other miscellaneous papers.

2079

Wood, Richard.   Diaries, 1801–1802, 1809–1821.   (14 v.)

Richard Wood, a Quaker merchant and farmer of Greenwich, Cumberland County, N.J., owned and successfully farmed large tracts of land in the Stow Creek/Greenwich area. He also successfully operated a large general store, known after 1785 as Wood and Bacon Store.

His diaries contain daily memoranda depicting primarily the farm routine of planting and harvesting, buying, selling and butchering livestock, tending woodlots and orchards, and dealing with farm tenants and farm hands; also the semi-weekly routine of attendance at Quaker meetings, business and social trips to Philadelphia; and social visits exchanged with neighbors and relatives. On opposite pages from the diary entries are Wood's notes on his readings, historical and religious, and his philosophical meditations.

Gift of Dr. Emlen Wood, 1938.

2080

C. Schrack and Company (Philadelphia, Pa.)   Records, 1823–1933. (250 v.)

C. Schrack & Co., manufacturers and merchants of varnish and paint, was founded ca. 1820 by Christian Schrack. At his death in 1854, the business was continued by Joseph Stulb, who was succeeded in 1898 by his sons Edwin H. Stulb and Joseph Stulb, Jr. Edwin became the sole owner in 1911 and was in turn succeeded by his sons Edwin H. Stulb, Jr., and Joseph Reichert Stulb in 1920.

The C. Schrack & Co. records consist of: daybooks, 1823–1853; sales books, 1853–1890; order books, 1853–1907; debit journals, 1853–1920; ledgers, 1827–1902; petty ledgers, 1829–1911; cashbooks, 1845–1933; stock books, 1841–1920; receipt books, 1827–1902; letterbooks, 1849–1915; and other miscellaneous account books.

Finding aid available.

2081

Magee, James Francis, Jr.   Chess Albums, (1917–1919) 1951. (3 v.)

These volumes were presented to James Francis Magee, Jr., in recognition of his service to the Good Companion Chess Problem Club (International), particularly his work as club secretary and editor of the club's monthly publication *Our Folder*. The first volume, compiled by the presenters, consists of congratulatory letters, 1918, from club members throughout the world, including Edward A. Coswell, John Carey Gardiner, Frank Janet, Murray Marble, Alain C. White. The other two volumes are scrapbooks filled by Magee himself containing letters, photographs, newsletters, and clippings relating to chess.

2082
Scrapbooks, Autograph albums, Commonplace books, 1796–1957.
(89 v.)

Benner, Catherine A. Autograph album, 1869 (1883–1886). Autographs mostly from Cutler, Ill. with some from Philadelphia. (1 v.)

Carr, Franklin, b. 1846. Scrapbook, 1889 (1892–1915). Carr was a Philadelphia converted burglar and Methodist Episcopal evangelist. Contains clippings, programs, letters of recommendation relating to Carr's lectures on his conversion. (1 v.)

Conner, Philip Syng Physick, 1837–1910. Scrapbook, 1884–1900. Conner was a Philadelphia genealogist and author. Scrapbook of materials collected in defense of actions of his father Commodore David Conner, Commander of the Home Squadron, at the 1847 combined Army/Navy operation at Vera Cruz. Included is Philip Syng Physick Conner's correspondence with naval officers, his 1897 article, "The Castle of San Juan de Ulloa, and the Topsy Turvyists," and a copy of Admiral William G. Temple's 1852 memoir on the Vera Cruz landing. Gift of Mrs. P.S.P. Conner, 1914. (1 v.)

Davis, ? Recipe book, [1861]. (1 v.)

Fairchild, George H., b. 1887. Album, 1950, 1956–1957. Fairchild was Assistant Librarian at the Historical Society of Pennsylvania. This album is honoring the 50th year of service to the Historical Society; with some letters on the occasion of his retirement in 1956. (1 v.)

Foreman, George Albright. Scrapbook, 1918, 1939–1947. Foreman was a Philadelphia Transit Company conductor, motorman, and depot dispatcher. This scrapbook relates to his service for the transit company and contains clippings, photographs, and memorabilia. Gift of George A. Foreman, 1950. (1 v.)

Foulkrod, John C. Scrapbook, [1872–1915]. Foulkrod was a clerk, conveyancer, and volunteer fireman. The scrapbook contains clippings, photographs, invitations, broadsides, and other memorabilia of the Philadelphia Volunteer Fire Department, Volunteer Fireman's Association of Philadelphia, and Fireman's Active Association. Gift of Mrs. F. Foulkrod, 1927. (1 v.)

Gardiner, Susan H. "The Village Rambler or a Collection of Pathetic and Rurall Poetry," [1817–1821]. (1 v.)

Garrigues, Mary B. Commonplace book, 1812–1815. Mainly of poems and clever ditties, with some memoranda and arithmetic problems. (1 v.)

"General Instructions of a Mother to a Daughter for her Conduct in Life," and "Advice and Caution to Women," [1790]. (1 v.)

Henry, Alexander, 1850–1925. Testimonial, 1905. Alexander Henry was a Presbyterian clergyman. This testimonial comes from his congregation of the Hermon Church in Germantown, upon his resignation as pastor. Gift of Christine Henry Wainwright, 1959. (1 v.)

Hicks, Isaac, 1748–1836. Miscellaneous papers, 1768–1833. Isaac Hicks was a Newtown, Bucks County, surveyor and justice of the peace. These papers include vendue book, 1813–1818, for the estate of Dr. James Tate, and surveying notes, 1768–1833. Photostats; originals of the surveying notes in possession of J. Stanley Lee. Gift of the Genealogical Society of Pennsylvania, 1953. (1 v.)

Historical Society of Pennsylvania. Scrapbook, 1865. Sermons and resolutions on the death of Abraham Lincoln. Collected by the Historical Society of Pennsylvania. (1 v.)

Kayne, John, d. 1909. "Eulogy of Thomas Paine," 1896. John Kayne was a Philadelphia physicians. (1 v.)

Keen, William W. Autograph scrapbook, 1836–1863. Gift of W.W. Keen, 1918. (1 v.)

Kinsey, Thomas P. Recipe book, 1882. Contains recipes for health, toilet, household, garden, and other needs. (1 v.)

Klinger, Johann Berhard. Passport, 1826. Passport from Ludwigsburg, Germany, to New York, N.Y.; continued as miscellaneous accounts, notes and recipes, 1826–1831. (1 v.)

Kremer, James B. Scrapbook, 1889–1893. Kremer was a Carlise agent of the Liverpool and London Globe Insurance Company and Secretary of Flood Relief Commission of Pennsylvania. The scrapbook contains newspaper clippings and letters concerning the work of the Commission following the Johnstown Flood and the controversy over the distribution of relief. Purchased, 1973. (1 v.)

Lascelles, Harold. "The Sons of Zarah : A Lia Fail Story. Founded upon Ancient History and Mythology," n.d. Lascelles was a Winter Park, Fla., retired Episcopalian minister. This work traces the lost tribes of Israel to the Royal House of Britain. Typescript. Gift of Harold Lascelles, 1954. (1 v.)

Lee, Ellis. Commonplace book, 1817–1824, n.d. Contains poem and extracts from Quaker writings. (4 v.)

Lloyd, Anabella W. Williams and Shoemaker family autograph album, 1812–1886, n.d. Gift of Mary W. Shoemaker. (1 v.)

Lukens, Ambler Wilson. Genealogical notes on the Lukens family. (1 v.)

Marsh, Anna. Autograph album and commonplace book, 1823–1828. Contains poems from Concord School, Willow Grove. Gift of Anna M. Peters estate, 1938. (1 v.)

Matlack, Rachel S. Autograph album, 1833–1852. Contains mainly verses. (1 v.)

May, Edyth W. Autograph album, 1898–1900. Contains signatures of politicians and other prominent persons. Bequest of Anna E. Wynn, 1948. (1 v.)

McAllister, John, 1786–1877. Scrapbook, 1854–1865. McAllister was a Philadelphia optician. This scrapbook concerns Pennsylvania College Medical Department and contains clippings, letters, and other materials collected when McAllister was a trustee. (1 v.)

McCauley, Charles A.H. Scrapbook, 1898–1901. McCauley was a Quartermaster in the U.S. Army. The scrapbook contains letters and memorabilia concerning McCauley's efforts for promotion. Gift of Edward D. McCauley, 1970. (1 v.)

McDowell, Georgine. Commonplace book of poems. (1 v.)

Mifflin, Elizabeth, 1797–1885. Scrapbook, 1820 (1864), 1882. Contains letters, autographs, memorabilia mainly relating to her compilation of autographs of bishops and other eminent men for the Central Fair. Gift of J.E. Fields, 1960. (1 v.)

Moore, Thomas. Commonplace book, 1829–1832. Contains poems, extracts, and translations. Presented to Cecilia Sanderson, 1939. Gift of the Wilbur Collection, Bailey Library, University of Vermont, 1970. (1 v.)

Morris, Catherine. Commonplace book, 1816. Gift of Mrs. William Jenks Wright, 1964. (2 v.)

Newspaper extracts, [1841]. (1 v.)

Norris, Charles Camblos. Memorandum, [1948]. Morris was a Philadelphia physician. This memorandum relates to the history of the Norris family dish presented to the Historical Society of Pennsylvania in 1948. Gift of Charmes Camblos Norris. (1 v.)

Notebook, 1829–1833, n.d. Contains clippings, pamphlets, and memoranda relating to transportation, commerce, and other topics. (1 v.)

Recipe book, 1817, 1837, n.d. Purchased, Gratz Fund, 1949. (1 v.)

Parke, James Pemberton,1783-[1859]. Testimonial, [1812]. Parke was a Philadelphia bookseller and stationer. This testimonial is to his grandfather James Pemberton, Philadelphia Quaker merchant and philanthropist, giving an account of Pemberton's life and death in the context of his Quaker faith. Gift of Henry Pemberton, 1975. (1 v.)

Pennington, Hyland Robert. "The Pennington family," 1859. Genealogical and historical notes. Purchased, 1958. (1 v.)

Pennsylvania Academy of Fine Arts. Scrapbook, 1845. Contains clippings and souvenirs related to the Academy fire of June, 1845, and subsequent ladies fund raising bazaar of October, 1845. Gift of Mrs. William B. Whelan, 1951. (1 v.)

Penrose, Charles Bingham, 1798–1857. Legal case notes, [1844–1857]. Penrose was a Philadelphia lawyer. (1 v.)

Peterson, Henry, 1818–1891. Works, 1876–1891. Peterson was a Philadelphia editor-publisher and poet. His works include: "Becky Sharp, A Tragedy . . . (dramatized from Thackery's *Vanity Fair*), copyrighted 1889; "Columbus, A Drama in Prose," copyrighted 1889, published, 1893; "Deus in Natura, and other Poems and Verses," 1888–1891. Purchased, 1940. (3 v.)

Porter, Josephine, 1837–1896. Autograph album, 1852 (1856–1857). Gift of Porter J. Cope, 1942. (1 v.)

Porter, Rebecca, 1810–1885. Autograph album, 1830–1833. Gift of Porter J. Cope, 1942. (1 v.)

Potts, Sarah P., 1774–1851. Commonplace book, [1809–1847]. Sarah Potts was a Pottstown Quaker. Her commonplace book contains extracts of religious poems and prose. Bequest of M.A. Leach, 1946. (1 v.)

Randolph, Jacob. *Memoir of the Life and Character of Philip Syng Physick*, (Philadelphia, Pa. : T.K. & P.G. Collins), 1829. Illustrated by Ferdinand J. Dreer, 1870. Purchased, 1982. (1 v.)

Richardson, Elizabeth, b. 1788. Commonplace book, [1830]. Elizabeth Richardson was a Philadelphia Quaker. Her commonplace book contains extracts from the writings of George Fox and other Quakers; also "Notes of the Roman Empire" from Edinburgh Encyclopedia. (1 v.)

Robins, Edward. Autograph album, (1874–1877) 1881. Kept while a student at Central School, Middleton, Conn. Gift of Mrs. Edward Robins, 1969. (1 v.)

Rush, Richard Henry, [1824]-1893. Copy book, [1840]. Contains philosophical selections. Gift of Dr. Solomon Solis-Cohen estate. (1 v.)

Sharpless, Jacob, 1791–1863. Commonplace book, 1814. Sharpless was a Downingtown physician. His commonplace book contains religious and philosophical writings. (1 v.)

Shoemaker, J. Autograph album, 1861–1891. Gift of Alice and Marjorie Shoemaker, 1971. (1 v.)

Shoemaker, Rebecca Warner Rawle, 1730–1819. Pocket notebook, 1796–1801. Contains miscellaneous notes on housekeeping, family moves and gatherings, and other events. (1 v.)

Shoemaker family. Autograph scrapbook, 1822–1874. Gift of Mary W. Shoemaker, 1936. (1 v.)

Smith, Anne Amelia. Autograph album, [1832–1855]. (1 v.)

Smith, Joseph P. Lecture, 1860 : before the Philomatheon Lodge. Describing Mediterranean cruise aboard the U.S. frigate Congress, 1855–1858. Gift of Genealogical Society of Pennsylvania, 1952. (1 v.)

Smith, Mary C. Autograph album, 1823–1825. (1 v.)

Smith, S. Decatur. Plays, 1884–1902. Smith was a Philadelphia ironfounder. His plays include: "A Fish in the Water" (from the Spanish; "Marion Grace . . . " adapted from French; "A Pilgrim. By one of them;" and "Mistress Gwyn." (4 v.)

Smith, Sidney Vanuxem. Autograph scrapbook, [1851]. Contains signatures of 18th-century Philadelphians. Gift of Sidney V. Smith, 1851. (1 v.)

Smith, William Rudolph, 1787–1868. Poems, [1814–1853]. Smith was a Pennsylvania lawyer, legislator, and major-general in state militia. He was U.S. Commissioner to the Chippewa Indians of Upper Mississippi and Wisconsin adjutant general, lawyer, attorney general, and president of the State Historical Society. (1 v.)

Sprague, William Buell, 1795–1876. Collection, 1799–1872. The collection consists of autograph sermons and speeches of Joseph Steven Buckminster, 1799–1809, John Quincy Adams, 1839, Edward Everett, 1848–1857, and Jared Sparks, 1849, and an autograph album, 1872, of members of the 42nd U.S. Congress. Gift of the Free Library of Philadelphia, 1946. (2 v.)

Sutton, Henry, 1808–1876. Sermons, 1846–1847, n.d. Sutton was a Methodist Episcopal itinerant minister traveling through Pennsylvania, Delaware, and Maryland. Gift of Estate of Isaac C. Sutton, 1967. (1 v.)

Sydney. Poems, 1814–1817. Some of these poems were published in the *Port Folio* under the name of "Quevado." (1 v.)

Taylor, Rebecca F. Autograph album, (1823–1826) 1833. Gift of Mrs. Caryl Roberts, 1959. (1 v.)

Thayer, Russell, 1853–1933. Scrapbook, [1874–1933]. Thayer was a Philadelphia civil engineer and balloon inventor. His scrapbook contains news clippings touching upon Thayer's career as superintendent of Fairmount Park, Brigadier General in the National Guard, and exponent of dirigible balloons for war purposes. Gift of Edmund Thayer, 1973. (1 v.)

[Townsend family]. Scrapbook, 1859 (1880–1882), 1945. Contains clippings of poems, prose, and obituaries. (1 v.)

Townsend, John P. Commonplace book, [1741]. Contains Quaker writings and testimonials. Gift of William M. Bartram, 1891. (1 v.)

Travis, Charles, 1882–1941. Autograph album, 1888–1892. Autographs of family members. Gift of Helen Dryden, 1959. (1 v.)

Union officers. Autograph album, 1863–1864. Autographs of Union soldiers imprisoned at Libby Prison, Richmond, Va., including rank, regiment, and home address. Gift of Mrs. Hampton L. Carson, 1905. (1 v.)

Waln, Sarah, 1746–1825. Recipe book, [1800]. Contains recipes for health and household needs. Purchased, 1943. (1 v.)

Ward, John M.E., d. 1940. Testimonial album, 1911, 1933, 1938. Ward as a Philadelphia organist. Testimonial from the Church Council of St. Mark's Evangelical Lutheran Church for anniversaries as organist and musical director. (1 v.)

Warner, Hannah F. Autograph book, 1832–1837, 1841. (1 v.)

Welsh, Maurice. Pocket notebook, 1772–1811. Contains mostly family birth and marriage dates. (1 v.)

Wetherill, Rebecca, 1819–1908. Scrapbook, [1890–1908]. The scrapbook contains clippings, photographs, programs, and other memorabilia relating to the Wetherill events; includes some late additions by Marion Walton Putnam. Gift of Marion Walton Putnam, 1964. (1 v.)

Widdifield, Anna M. Commonplace book, 1852-[1861]. Mainly of poems. (1 v.)

Williams, Eliza W. Pusey. Autograph album, 1841–1848. Poems by family and friends including author Bayard Taylor. Gift of Leonard Denis, 1963. (1 v.)

Williams, Julia Rush, 1792–1860. Commonplace book, [1808]-1812 and notebook, 1816. Contains poems and prose, including some original pieces, original prayers and personal expense accounts. (2 v.)

Wilson, Joseph Lapsley, d. 1928. Scrapbook, 1874–1881. Concerns Wilson's participation in Republican politics through membership in the Union League and the National Republican League. Gift of Caroline Alice Smith Estate, 1953. (1 v.)

Wright, Elizabeth P. Commonplace book, 1823–1824. (1 v.)

Yarnall, Rebecca, 1786–1859. Autograph album, 1801–1802, and commonplace books, [1805]. Kept while attending Westtown Boarding School. Gift of Frances Richardson, 1940. (3 v.)

Yerkes, John Keith, 1817–1894. Scrapbook, [1839–1856]. Contains newspaper clippings of poems, anecdotes and literary passages, many from the *Village Record* of West Chester. The clippings are mounted over an anonymous general store ledger, [1817]. [Gift of W. Austin Yerkes.] (1 v.)

2083

Museum Council of Philadelphia.   **Records, (1939–1976) 1978. (6 linear ft.)**

The Museum Council of Philadelphia was organized in 1939, as Philadelphia Council of Museums, and incorporated in 1975 to provide an association of the city's cultural, historical, and scientific museums for promoting their resources and encouraging cooperation between them.

Special, regular and luncheon meetings, 1939–1976, 1978; general correspondence, 1939–1976; files relating to special programs; some financial records, 1947–1976; membership lists, directories, calendars, and other literature of the council; miscellanea.

Gift of Museum Council of Philadelphia.

2084

Crothers family.   Papers, 1753–1935.   (600 items.)

These are the papers of Stevenson Crothers of Springfield Township, Montgomery County, his parents, grandparents, and all sorts of ancestors and in-laws, nearly all of whom were Philadelphians. There are letters of various family members reporting from vacation spots and European tours, and on family business. Stevenson Crothers incoming correspondence, 1882–1931, includes letters from his wife Alice Poultney Morris Crothers and his sister Mary Bartow Cooke Crothers Dulles. Among other small groups are letters of William S. Crothers, [II], 1839–1885, and Rachel Dawson Morris, 1890–1891.

The papers also include account books of several merchants in the family: Thomas Bartow, [II], (N.Y.) ledger, 1759, with receipt book, 1760–1766, and Thomas Bartow, [I], estate records, 1781–1793; Daniel Benezet cashbooks, 1759–1763, 1771–1779; William S. Crothers, [I], ledger, 1810–1829 and 1819–1821, merchandise book, 1819–1828, receipt book, 1825–1829; William S. Crothers, [II], cashbook, 1848–1875. There are additional estate account books, financial memoranda, wills, and inventories, especially the William S. Crothers, [II], estate, 1887–1922. In the miscellaneous papers is material on "Roslyn Heights" in Montgomery County and properties in Philadelphia and concerning genealogical interests.

Gift of George C. Bland, 1977.

2085

Dimock, John H., b. 1815.   Papers, (1833–1846) 1898.
(70 items.)

John H. Dimock was a Montrose lawyer who later became a land speculator in the West.

These papers contain his incoming correspondence primarily as a young man in Harrisburg, under the care of a cousin and brother both of whom served in the state legislature. The letters are from family and friends reporting on local politics and doings. There are some legal papers for land transactions in Wisconsin.

2086

Bosworth, Francis. **Papers, 1934–1956.** **(400 items.)**

Francis Bosworth was long involved with the theatre and the arts. He worked with the Federal Theatre Project, established under the Works Progress Administration in 1935. Bosworth acted as director of the Play Bureau which reviewed scripts offered by American authors. He remained associated with the Theatre Project until 1938.

Included are scripts of plays and Bosworth's personal copies of correspondence, memoranda, conference reports, manuals and other publications of the Federal Theatre Project. There are also letters and reports, 1940–1942, on the Community Arts Workshop, sponsored by the American Friends Service Committee; carbon copies of letters, 1943, to Everett McCarter who was stationed in Iceland, reporting stateside events and personal activities in New York City, and his opinions on the war; correspondence and progress reports, 1948–1951, on his ward, John Rybczyk; and Bosworth's own letters, 1955, sent while traveling in North Africa, Europe and the Middle East.

Gift of Francis Bosworth, 1976.

2087

Roberts family. **Papers, 1684–1897.** **(250 items.)**

Papers of the Roberts family follow the succession of proprietors of Pencoyd, the family estate in what is now Bala Cynwyd. Although the majority of the material consists of marriage certificates, bonds, inventories, school exercise books, wills, memorial albums, and miscellaneous documents, there are also several diaries and other papers that provide accounts of farm life, professional pursuits, and personal activities of family members.

The earliest is Algernon Roberts's diary, 1776, describing scenes and living conditions during his march from Philadelphia to Elizabeth, N.J., with a Company of Associators. Algernon was responsible for expanding Pencoyd into a thriving dairy farm, and there are some butter sales and other farm financial papers, 1796–1824, during his and his son Isaac Warner Roberts's ownership. A more detailed view of farm life can be gleaned from diaries, 1847–1869, begun by the next heir, George Brooke Roberts, during his school vacations at home, but continued by his mother, Rosalinda Brooke Roberts, who managed Pencoyd as a tenant farm for 20 years. The diaries record farm work, building projects, visitors and visiting.

Although the children of Rosalinda continued to own and be closely interested in Pencoyd, they took up other careers. Algernon, [II], who would later found Pencoyd Iron Works, began by working for a hardware firm in Philadelphia. His diary, 1847–1848, records his life in the city and his visits to Pencoyd. Algernon Roberts's private account books, 1849–1868, note expenses and income derived from estate and business.

George Brooke Roberts started as an engineer on various railroad lines throughout Pennsylvania, and his diary, 1851–1857, gives an account of this period. In 1880 he became president of the Pennsylvania Railroad and remained in that position until his death in 1897. A letterpress book, 1883–1885, concerns personal, farm, and railroad business; a farm diary, 1886–1896, reports on building and other projects; personal account books, 1865–1868, 1878–1885, give farm, household, and private business finances. Additional volumes include Pennsylvania Railroad anniversary scrapbook, obituary scrapbooks, memorial albums.

There are some miscellaneous documents of the Warner family, into which Algernon, [I], married in 1781.

2088
Philadelphia (Pa.). Public School.   Records, 1830–1906.   (15 v.)

Registers, roll books, school directors' minute book, for various kindergarten, primary, secondary and grammar schools in Southwark, Moyamensing, Society Hill and Northern Liberties. Information contained in the various records include: pupils' names, ages, whether vaccinated; parent's names, addresses and occupations; teacher's comments including explanations of student absences and departures; visiting school directors' reports with attendance and other figures; notes on text book and supply purchases. Schools specified by name are Moyamensing Boys' School, Ringgold Boys' Grammar School, Madison [Primary and Secondary] School for boys and girls, Primary School No. 3 (Fourth Section) for boys and girls. There is also an account of text books and supplies furnished Chatham Primary School, London Grove District, Chester County.

Purchased, 1966.

2089
Philadelphia Award.   Records, 1921–1974.   (3 linear ft.)

The Philadelphia Award, established by Edward William Bok in 1921, is presented annually in recognition of outstanding service to the community.

Most of the records consist of files for recipients, containing nominating letters, biographical material, newspaper clippings, guest lists. There are also incomplete files of presentation addresses, 1921–1966, nominee files, 1955–1967, trustee correspondence and financial papers, 1941–1968.

Gift of Board of Trustees, The Philadelphia Award.

2090
Rickabaugh, Adam. Account books, 1840–1843. (8 v.)

Adam Rickabaugh took over the Philadelphia flour merchant business of Beaver and Company in September, 1841.

The account books, 1840–1843, are: daybooks; ledgers; receipt book. There are also George Rickabaugh account memoranda for livestock, 1843.

Gift of Chester County Historical Society, 1967.

2091
Coxe, Daniel William, 1769–1852. Papers, 1793–1868. (4.5 linear ft.)

Daniel William Coxe was a Philadelphia merchant who turned to speculation in Spanish Grant lands. In 1793 he formed a mercantile partnership with Daniel Clark of New Orleans, La., and in 1801 they joined forces with Beverly Chew and Richard Relf, also New Orleans merchants. In 1803 Clark began extensive purchases of land in Louisiana, West Florida, and elsewhere on behalf of himself and Coxe. By 1811, with all partners heavily in debt, they liquidated their connections, but because of Clark's death, the final settlement of accounts was not made until 1819. Coxe's primary occupation would be the confirmation of his claims to the southern property, particularly the large Louisiana tract on the Ouachita River, the "Maison Rouge Grant." To this end, he made repeated applications to the federal government and was involved in continuous litigation with squatters and heirs of former owners who challenged his title.

These papers include a general correspondence file, 1793–1851, and additional letters, legal and financial documents and memoranda on specific aspects of his business affairs. The greater part of Coxe's correspondence was with his agents and lawyers about the Maison Rouge and West Florida lands. Other correspondents were: Daniel Clark on commercial and land business, with some mention of James Wilkinson's adventures; Chew and Relf on trade and settlement of Clark's estate; Richard S. Coxe, Daniel's nephew and Washington lawyer, as well as other prominent attorneys among whom were Daniel Webster, 1827–1829, and Horace Binney, 1820–1845; various members of Congress; A.P. Merrill, 1833–1841, Cashier of Agricultural Bank of Mississippi, Natchez, concerning Coxe's shares in that bank and banking affairs in general.

There are small series of papers on particular subjects: Clark, Chew and Relf; Mason Rouge Grant; West Florida lands; Teche River, Attakapos, La., lands; Barthelemy Bosque heirs' claim on the 1807 cargo of the Comet; Coxe's memorials to Congress and annotated copies of Congressional bills, reports, and other documents; personal bills, 1793–1809; Bloomsbury, Burlington, County, N.J., lands, 1800–1812; Nalbro Frazier estate; Daniel Coxe estate papers, 1852- 1868; pamphlets, bills, newspapers, clippings.

Gift of Tench C. Coxe, Jr., 1979.

2092
No entry.

2093
William Amer Company (Philadelphia, Pa.)   **Records, 1836–1953.**
(15 linear ft.)

William Amer Company, a Philadelphia tannery, was founded in 1832 and specialized in kid and later kangaroo leathers. In 1978 they ceased tanning operations; the firm continues operation as an importer of shoe findings.

Cashbooks, 1844–1845, 1898–1907, 1912–1953; entry of goods received and shipments out, 1918–1953; lot records, 1918–1934; Christmas Savings Fund, 1917–1934; daybooks, 1842–1846, (Amer and Fritz, 1840–1858), 1906–1909; journals, 1836–1841, 1896–1950; ledgers, 1836–1843, 1905–1909; and miscellaneous records.

Gift of William Amer Company, 1978.

2094
Fisher family.   **Papers, 1761–1868.**   **(15 linear ft.)**

Miers Fisher was admitted to the Philadelphia bar in 1769 and retired some 24 years later, moving to his Fox Chase estate "Ury." He and other members of his family were among the Quakers exiled in Virginia during the Revolution. He was elected a member of the Pennsylvania Assembly, 1791–1792, and was a counselor for the Pennsylvania Abolition Society.

The Fisher family papers center on Miers Fisher, with smaller sections of Jabez Maude Fisher, a brother, and other branches.

The Miers Fisher section of the papers consists largely of incoming and outgoing correspondence and documents following Fisher's retirement from his law practice in 1793. It concerns family affairs and Miers Fisher's activities as agent for foreigners with business in Pennsylvania, but touches on other aspects of his life. Major family correspondents are: son Miers Fisher, Jr., 1797–1813, mostly letters from are Miers, Sr. while Miers, Jr. was running a mercantile business in St. Petersburg, Russia; son Redwood Fisher, 1797–1825, 1848–1850, which includes letters from his father exhorting the boy to improve himself; brother Samuel Rowland Fisher, 1792–1817, with letters to Miers on family and some on business; wife, Sarah Redwood

Fisher, 1777–1819, mostly letters from Miers reporting on trips away from home; brother Thomas Fisher, 1774–1806, on family affairs and a lot of sickness; son Thomas Fisher, Jr., 1791–1896, mostly letters from his father and other relatives while Thomas was apprenticed to a Baltimore, Md., merchant; nephew Joshua Gilpin, 1792–1796, with personal notes and reports on British manufacturing, technology, public affairs. There are additional letters from miscellaneous Fishers, Gilpins and Redwoods.

Other correspondents of Miers Fisher, writing from England, are: Maria Ann Dupont Aublay, 1792–1818, on the estate of her brother Francis LeClerc Dupont and including personal news; Robert Barclay, 1775–1817, on trade, public events, and personal matters; James Delancey, 1784–1794, on the estate of William Allen; Jacob Duché, 1786–1793, on his American lands, with some mention of spiritual concerns; William Fisher, 1798–1819, about Tobyhanna and other real estate in Northampton and Wayne Counties; Elizabeth Galloway Roberts, 1804–1812, on her estate. There is also general correspondence, miscellaneous land and legal papers, and a draft of a portion of the *Journal of the Transactions of the Exiles.*

Miers Fisher's brother Jabez Maude Fisher went to England in 1775 and died there in 1779. Letters, 1774–1779, are primarily from his friends and acquaintances in England, with some letters from home. The correspondence is personal with frequent mention of the state of affairs between England and the colonies, with later letters being more concerned with commerce. Among the correspondents are Joseph Guerney and Robert Ormston.

There are some very general letters, 1820–1865, to Jabez Maude Fisher, [II], Miers Fisher's son.

Miers Fisher's daughter Lydia married Benjamin Warner, Philadelphia bookseller. Warner family papers include: Benjamin Warner incoming letters, 1810–1817; and Benjamin Warner's letters, 1815–1821, to Lydia while on business trips through Pittsburgh, Cincinnati, Lexington, Ky., Richmond. Benjamin died in 1821, and apparently his brother Joseph assumed paternal responsibilities for the children. There are several letters to Joseph from the nieces and nephews, particularly from John Warner, 1849–1851, while trying to establish himself in Pottsville. Joseph Warner's receipt book, 1830–1859, is largely for rent and taxes. There is Redwood Fisher Warner correspondence, 1830–1868, primarily school age letters from siblings and 1867 family news from sister Sarah Warner Lewis while "Red" and his wife are in Europe. Other items associated with Redwood Fisher related items are sister-in-law Jane Johnson receipt book, 1840–1884, for general expenses, and Ella I. Yardley estate accounts, 1870–1889, Joseph W. Johnson, Jr., and Redwood F. Warner, trustees of Mary S. Yardley.

Finally, there is general correspondence, 1801–1829, of William Redwood and William Redwood, Jr., merchants.

Gift of Franklin C. Wood, 1980.
Finding aid available.

2095
League of Women Voters of Pennsylvania. **Records, 1867**
(1959–1977) 1980. **(81 linear ft.)**

The League of Women Voters of Pennsylvania was established in 1920, a successor organization to the Pennsylvania Woman Suffrage Association, with the purpose of providing "education to increase the effectiveness of women voters and to further better government." In biennial conventions the Pennsylvania League established its "Program," the issues selected for study, decision and action. State Programs have been concerned with constitution reform, legislative apportionment, election laws, education, welfare, environment, city and town planning.

The files here are primarily records for the 1960's and 1970's, although there is some earlier material. They consist almost entirely of minutes, newsletters, reports, and memorabilia, with little correspondence. A third of the material comes from local leagues, which are the basic units of the national/state/local organization.

Series include: State board and agenda minutes, 1920–1973; state and local annual reports, 1957–1973; miscellaneous organizational material and correspondence, 1957–1973; treasurer's reports and other financial records, 1933–1977; local league reports, 1923–1977; mailings, 1959–1974; state league convention minutes and reports, 1939–1977; mailings, 1959–1974; political material, 1920–1976, much on reform of the state constitution; educational material, 1972, particularly on the Education Fund, which was a non-profit trust established in 1970 for educating the public on government; Time for Action, 1969–1976, a program to involve local leagues in state legislative issues; Pennsylvania Assess Coal Today, 1977, a study on potential uses and environmental impact of coal on the state; local government and community projects, 1957–1978; environmental projects, 1958–1978; national issues, 1946–1971; state issues, 1934–1976; scrapbooks, 1951–1969. There is some miscellaneous material on the suffrage movement, including photographs of the 1915 Women's Liberty Bell Tour in support of the vote.

Gift of the League of Women Voters of Pennsylvania, 1980.

2096
Wright, Sydney L., 1852–1927. **Family papers, 1752–1928.**
(14 linear ft.)

The collection is in seven sections, arranged chronologically by generation: Logan, Fisher; Fisher, Ellicott, and Wright; William Redwood Wright;

and a miscellaneous section that may contain materials belonging to more than one generation.

Through descent and marriage, the Wright family is connected with the Fisher and Logan families of Philadelphia. William Redwood Wright, the oldest child of Henrietta Hoskins Price Wright and Robert Kemp Wright, was born in 1846, attended the Germantown Academy, and joined Rush's Lancers, the sixth Pennsylvania Cavalry, during the Civil War. He left service as a Captain and joined the firm of Peter Wright's Sons, merchants, in New York City and his uncle's firm. In 1873, he moved to Philadelphia, continuing on in the same business, and married Letitia Ellicott Carpenter in 1882. He became involved in city politics as a Democrat, was a presidential elector in 1888 and 1892, and filled an unexpired term as Philadelphia City Treasurer from June, 1891, to January, 1892. For the rest of his life, William Redwood Wright worked as a banker and broker in a variety of businesses, both independently and with family members, mainly his brother Sydney Longstreth Wright, and his brother-in-law Robert Glendinning.

Letitia Ellicott Carpenter Wright, wife of William Redwood Wright, was a Colonial Dame of America and helped plan and plant the Stenton garden. She was friends with Helen Tower whose husband, Mr. Charlemagne Tower, was a diplomat in the foreign service, at one time United States ambassador to France.

The first section consists of William Logan's business ledger, 1752–1755, and Thomas Fisher's personal ledger, 1806–1813.

There is correspondence, financial papers, and miscellanea, 1823–1895 for Thomas Rodman Fisher, his wife Letitia Ellicott Fisher, her mother Sara Ellicott, William Redwood Wright's mother Henrietta Hoskins Price, and his uncle William Redwood Price; account books and scrapbooks of Thomas Rodman Fisher and Ellicott Fisher; and a remedy book of Letitia Ellicott Fisher. The correspondence is primarily between family members.

For William Redwood Wright there is correspondence, 1870–1914, touching on his involvement in Philadelphia politics and clubs, and on his business matters; receipts and accounts; business papers, scrapbooks, invitations and miscellanea.

There is correspondence, property and financial papers, and miscellanea for Letitia E.C. Wright.

George W. Carpenter traveled abroad extensively after his first marriage and acquired a large circle of European friends. The correspondence with these friends constitutes a large portion of this section, as does other personal correspondence. There are also a scrapbook, and a receipt book from the Wright Pike Company.

The sixth section includes the correspondence of William Redwood Wright's generation. These include the correspondence, business, and financial papers of Ellicott Fisher, Harvey Fisher, Sydney Longstreth Wright, Mary Rodman Fisher Carpenter, Sydney George Fisher, Charles Graff Wright, William Logan Fisher, Robert Kemp Wright, Jr., and Emlen Newbold Carpenter. There is some miscellaneous family correspondence.

The last section of papers includes a small autograph collection assembled by George W. Carpenter with signatures from prominent American and European figures. There are also photographs, maps, land papers, genealogical material, train car brake diagrams, and copies of newspaper clippings and pamphlets.

Pamphlets have been transferred to the Library.

The collection was retained by the Wright family of Jamestown, R.I.; gift of Mrs. Catherine Morris Wright, 1977.

Finding aid available.

2097
No entry.

2098
Boyd, David Knickerbacker, 1872–1944.   **Papers (1893–1952) 1977.** (200 items.)

David Knickerbacker Boyd was a prominent Philadelphia architect credited with being one of the original advocates of the setback principle in architecture. He was active in many business, civic, and professional organizations on local, state and national levels.

This small and random group of papers includes correspondence, speeches, articles, clippings, and other material on his interests, particularly: Structural Services Bureau, 1920–1929; American Construction Council, 1922–1924, 1927, including correspondence with Franklin D. Roosevelt who was President of the Council; Independence Hall Association, 1942–1952, 1977; Boyd's report, prepared for the Russell Sage Foundation, on the Building and Construction Industry, 1937–1938. There are also scrapbooks related to the Structural Service Bureau, building codes, city planning, exhibitions, industrial relations, building congresses, and American Institute of Architects conventions; Report of the Parking Committee, 1952; personal copies of the Journal of American Institute of Architects, and some photographs of houses designed by Boyd.

Gift of Lysbeth Borie and Barbara Murdoch, 1977.

2099

**Literary Fellowship of Philadelphia.   Correspondence, 1947–1979.
(950 items.)**

The Fellowship was established to provide an opportunity for a small group of scholars to met informally at dinner three to four times a year to present and discuss papers about literature. It was founded by W. Otto Sypherd and Robert E. Spiller.

The correspondence is to and from W. Otto Sypherd and Robert E. Spiller and their successors as organizers.

Gift of John A. Lester, Jr., 1979, and Robert E. Spiller, 1981.

2100

**Pennypacker, Galusha, 1844–1916.   Military papers, 1863–1881.
(100 items.)**

Galusha Pennypacker was a career soldier from Chester County.

These papers consist primarily of copies of military documents on his service as brigadier and brevet major-general with the 97th Pennsylvania Volunteers, 1863–1865; brevet appointments, 1865, 1867–1868; disability and leaves of absence, 1865–1867, 1871–1872, 1876; appointment to the 34th Infantry, 1866–1868; and service in the Mississippi, Tennessee, and Louisiana Reconstruction administration, 1867–1876, and the frontier, 1877–1881.

2101

Thompson, Eleanor.   Papers, 1858–1978.   (249 items.)

Miscellanea from the files of Eleanor Thompson, including: materials from research on Amelia Bloomer, 1858–1951; souvenirs of the Women's Rights Centennial Conference in Seneca Falls, N.Y., 1948; materials on the Chester County Revolutionary War Depredations Project of the Women's University Club, including an index of claims by name and by township.

Gift, 1981

2102

Shober, John A.H.   Collection, 1688–1903.   (70 items.)

A collection of miscellaneous letters and legal papers, mostly relating to Anthony J. Morris and to James Pemberton, but also including items of or on Benedict Arnold, William Shippen, Pemberton S. Hutchinson, and others.

Gift of John A.H. Shober, 1981.

2103
No entry.

2104
No entry.

2105
Knerr, Horace C.   **Papers, 1909–1924.**   **(82 items.)**

Incoming letters to Horace C. Knerr and his mother, Mrs. C.B. Knerr, of Primos and Philadelphia, from Anita Wilson Howe and Annie E. (Wilson) Howe, Woodrow Wilson's niece and nephew, respectively. The letters outline their friendship and reflect Anita Wilson Howe's life while a member of the Wilson household and while pursuing her vocal studies in New York and Paris. The collection also includes a photograph of Anita Wilson Howe and two photographs of her children.

Gift of Roseann Knerr Hough, 1980.

2106
No entry.

2107
Weidman family.   **Papers, 1737–1915.**   **(300 items.)**

These papers shed light on the Weidman family and other families in Lebanon and Dauphin counties, including Hoke, Lineaweaver, and Mitchell. The papers include items on land transactions in Lancaster, Dauphin, and Lebanon counties, papers from the law offices of Jacob Barge Weidman and his son John Weidman, and a few items on Grant, Mason, and Morris Weidman.

Materials include surveys and warrants for surveys, receipts, copies of land office records, indentures and bonds, notes for cases handled by the Weidmans (including that of the German Lutheran Congregation of Lebanon versus Jonathan Ruthrauff, 1844), miscellaneous genealogical materials assembled by the later Weidmans, and correspondence. There is also a small group consisting of Grant Weidman's school papers, 1849–1850. A third section includes all undated material, divided into legal papers; accounts; speeches, essays, and poems; and genealogical materials.

Gift of Emilie Mitchell Gibbs, 1980.

2108

No entry.

2109

No entry.

2110

Greene, Le Roy Vincent, 1908-   **Papers, 1931–1959.**
(7.5 linear ft.)

Le Roy Vincent Greene came to Philadelphia, from Los Angeles, Cal., in 1931, joining the staff of the Philadelphia *Public Ledger* as a public reporter. He became involved in politics and in the military.

The collection includes newspaper and magazine articles written by Greene, incoming and outgoing professional and personal correspondence, unpublished manuscripts and speech materials, invitations, clippings, maps and charts, photographs and miscellanea.

The papers have been divided into seven parts of related materials. Part one is made up of material from his years as a newspaper reporter for the Philadelphia *Public Ledger,* the Philadelphia *Evening Public Ledger,* and the Philadelphia *Daily News,* 1931–1939. This material is mostly clippings of his articles. Part two contains material when Greene was public secretary to Governor Arthur James, 1939–1943. This reflects his duties in Governor James' office. Part three consists of material from Greene's military career, both active and reserve service, 1934–1952. The material traces his career with the 79th Division. Part four, the largest part of his papers, contains materials from his active involvement in Pennsylvania and national Republican politics including his role as secretary to the chairman of the Republican National Committee for the 1952 and 1956 national campaigns, and as public secretary of Senator Edward Martin of Pennsylvania, 1947–1959. The material includes publicity reports and campaign strategy. Part five is made up of personal miscellaneous ephemera. Part six consists of maps and charts collected by Greene, ca. 1926–1957, from his travels overseas, military and political involvement. Part seven is made up of photoprints, documenting his later political activity, including many of General Eisenhower.

Published materials have been transferred to the Library. Military and Political Campaign memorabilia have been transferred to the Museum.

Gift of Le Roy Vincent Greene, Jr., 1966.

2111
No entry.

2112
Neagle, John, ca. 1796–1866.   Papers, 1824–1861.   (4 v.)

The papers of John Neagle, Philadelphia artist include: student note-book, 1824; notes from the writings of famous artists, comments on the work of Thomas Sully, and conclusions on his own experiments in shading; blotter, 1825–1852; financial and personal diary, with notes on "Pat Lyon the Blacksmith," his courtship with Mary Chester Sully, family matters, and personal affairs; memoranda of articles loaned by J. Neagle, 1827–1861: a record of the books, paintings, engravings, and cash lent to other artists and engravers; and cashbook, 1832–1842: household and business accounts.

Purchased from Southeby's with funds from the Gratz Purchase fund and the Barra Foundation, 1984.

2113
Leonard, Edith Lincoln.   Collection, 1916 (1942–1945).
(ca. 100 items)

One letter, dated July 23, 1916, from L.P. Wood to J.B. Leonard com-ments on Naval action at the close of World War I. The remainder of the collection is correspondence addressed to Edith Lincoln Leonard, a school teacher during World War II. The correspondents include: Phil Huffman, Alan Grout, Dick Thomas, J.P. Danton, George Dawson Perry, and Warner Bunden. The letters discuss life in the service from training camp through to the end of the men's service. Some topics include: censorship, active duty in the Army, Naval Air Combat Intelligence, west coast and Pacific assign-ments, the Zoot Suit Riots, Marine life, and Navy life.

Gift of Miss Edith Lincoln Leonard, 1982.

2114
Franklin and Company.   Journals, 1861–1873.   (11 v.)

Journals of Franklin and Company, Philadelphia wagon and cart in-dustry. Meteorological reports are also listed.

Purchased from Bookworm and Silverfish, 1985.

2115
Hubbel, Horatio, d. 1875.   Papers, 1844–1871.   (ca. 100 items)

Horatio Hubbel served in the War with Mexico and as brigadier general during the riots of 1844 in Philadelphia. He was responsible, along with John Henry Sherburne, for originating the plans for a transatlantic cable.

These papers cover both Hubbel's military service and his involvement with the implementation of the transatlantic cable.

Gift of Mr. William H. Baker, Jr., 1980.

2116
Lee, Wallace Rogers, 1879-   Papers, 1908–1910.   (7 v.)

Wallace Rodgers Lee was the Technical Representative for Baldwin Locomotive Works in South America.

Letterpress books, 1908–1910, and notebooks, dealing specifically with the Baldwin Locomotive Works in South America.

Gift of Mr. John Foster, 1980.

2117A
Knight, Bernando Hoff, 1889–1964.   Papers, 1927–1937.
(ca. 600 items)

Correspondence, reports, memoranda, notes, and newspaper clippings on the Port of Philadelphia and the costs of all charges for rates, wharfage, handling, and storage with respect to carriers subject to the Interstate Commerce Act.

Transferred from the Genealogical Society of Pennsylvania, 1978.

2117B
Knight, Bernando Hoff, 1889–1964.   Papers, 1700–1930.
(300 items.)

Correspondence between B. Hoff Knight and C.E. Smart on Smart's book *Makers of Surveying Instruments in America Since 1700.*

2117C
Knight, Bernando Hoff, 1889–1964.   Collection, n.d.
(200 items.)

Manuscript and typed notes on Philadelphia monuments. Arranged alphabetically by geographical location.

Gift of Maria Knight, 1970.

2118
Philadelphia Classical Club.   **Records, 1985–1962.**   **(2 linear ft.)**

The Philadelphia Classical Club was organized in 1895. Membership was open, upon nomination, to all Classics teachers in the Philadelphia vicinity. Members met twice a month at the home of one of the members in order to give and listen to papers of the classics. The host was responsible for arranging the evening's lecture.

Minutes, 1895–1956 (include summaries of papers given as well as general business); financial papers, 1950–1962; Annual Dinner information; correspondence of Raymond T. Ohl, secretary; and papers relating to the Elmer S. Gerhard fund for the commemorative cigar box that was to be presented in appreciation for his dedication to the club.

Gift of Robert S.A. Palmer, 1982.

2119
Figner Collection, 1947–1961.   **(200 items.)**

Draft fragment and typescript of *History of Colonial Churches* and miscellaneous correspondence on church research and membership to the Virginia Historical Society and *First Families of Virginia*.

Gift of Mrs. A.W. Figner.

2120
Trotter, Kenneth.   **Collection, 1920–1940.**   **(ca. 300 items.)**

Miscellaneous theatre programs, ticket stubs and playbills.
Gift of Kenneth Trotter, 1981.

2121
No entry.

2122
Stuart, Edwin Sydney, 1853–1920.   **Papers, 1886–1905.**
(2 linear ft.)

Edwin Sydney Stuart was very active in the Republican Party and Pennsylvania politics. He served as a Philadelphia select councilman, delegate to the Republican national conventions, mayor of Philadelphia, 1891–1895, and governor of Pennsylvania, 1907–1911. His business interests included bookselling with Leary's Bookstore (later renamed Leary, Stuart, and Co.), and then directing Bell Telephone Company of Pennsylvania.

The bulk of the collection is correspondence, 1886–1905. Some of this material is on Stuart's business, Leary's Bookstore; the majority, however, covers his political activities as a member of Republican organizations, as a select councilman, and as mayor of Philadelphia. Some of the issues are: Stalwart Republicanism, powers of favorable press, city improvements, especially street pavements, and political loyalty over business qualifications. John Wanamaker, Matthew Quay, and Simon Cameron are among Stuart's influential constituents.

Business and political papers comprise a small part of the collection. Invoices, receipts, and insurance information of Leary, Stuart and Co. may be found among the business papers. More significant are the political papers which include endorsements for the mayoralty in support of Stuart. One endorsement comes from " a group of colored voters from West Philadelphia calling themselves the Edwin S. Stuart Club." Invitations and announcements for various social functions complete the collection.

Gift of Mr. Edward Krimmel, 1981.

Finding aid available.

2123

Irwin, John.   Papers, 1778–1820.   (ca. 175 items.)

John Irwin was deputy commissary general of issues for the Western District for the United States in 1781 and appointed judge in the Court of Common Pleas for Westmoreland County in 1795.

Most of this collection is correspondence on his retirement as a soldier of the Revolutionary War, as a land agent in Western Pennsylvania, and the politics of the day, taxes, war and constitutional power.

Two Nicholas Scull Surveys (1 copy) for Bucks County included.

Gift of Mr. Edward Scull, 1982.

2124

Knerr, M.W.   Papers, n.d.   (6 v.)

Notebooks of his studies at the Medico-chirurgical College of Philadelphia.

2125

Potts, William John.   Papers, 1795–18—.
(8 v. and ca. 300 items.)

These papers consist largely of the correspondence and papers of William John Potts. The topics include, some studies by Potts on: allegories, superstitions, American Indians, and Indian vocabulary, and chemistry. One of Pott's hobbies was collecting bookplates. Some correspondence relates to this activity; the bookplates he collected are also part of the collection.

In addition to Pott's correspondence, there are five letters, 1795, written by Mary Grew, one of Pott's ancestors. There are also diaries filled with religious reflection by Mary Grew, 1795–1834.

The other volumes in the collection are: nineteenth century notebook with construction, numerical, and miscellaneous notes; journal with entries for various Grew family members which includes accounts and recipes, 1821–1822, 1855; and docket book, 1772. Family members included in this collection are: Ann Grew, Charles Grew, Mary Grew, John Grew, Sarah P. Grew, Robert B. Potts, Sallie Hughes Potts, and Sarah P. Potts.

Transferred from the Genealogical Society of Pennsylvania, 1983.

2126
Cox family.   Papers, 1824–1859.   (106 items.)

Letters written from various locations in Europe to family members and friends in Philadelphia and Easton. The majority of the letters were written by Elizabeth Baynton Cox and her husband, William S. Cox and describe their life in Europe. Recipients include: Hannah Churchman, Mrs. John Markoe, Mrs. William Camac and E.B. Cox's sisters.

Gift of Miss Alice L.C. Dodge, 1981.

Finding aid available.

2127
**Philadelphia City Missionary and Church Extension Society.
Records, 1849–1924.   (3 v.)**

The Philadelphia City Missionary and Church Extension Society was founded in 1821 and was originally called the Missionary Society of the Methodist Episcopal Church. It had both foreign and domestic missionary objectives.

Minute books and reports to the executive committee.

Gift of Mrs. Wayne R. Campbell and Mrs. John R. Richards, 1983.

2128
**William H. Vanderherchen (Philadelphia, Pa.)   Papers, 1937–1965.
(3 v. of photoprints, 70 items.)**

William H. Vanderherchen was a tent and catering supply company.

The papers include: patents, trademarks and agreements, and three volumes of photographs, with information on various jobs including weddings, clubs and societies, balls and other functions such as the Ice Capades.

Gift of Joanne V. Fulcony, 1981.

2129
Cobbett, William, 1763–1835.   Papers, 1792–1835.
(ca. 500 items.)

William Cobbett emigrated to Philadelphia in 1792. He taught English to French refugees. He became very active in bookselling and publishing and eventually, as a pamphleteer, became a factor in American politics. In 1796, he began *The Censor,* a monthly publication; it was replaced in 1797 by *Porcupine's Gazette,* which ran until 1799. He was a Royalist who sided with the Federalist in American politics.

In 1797 he was sued for libel by Dr. Benjamin Rush. Cobbett took issue with Rush's treatment of Yellow Fever by bleeding. Cobbett contended that the bleeding caused more deaths of those stricken by the epidemic than cured. Rush won the lawsuit and was awarded $5,000.

Cobbett removed to England in 1800, where he renewed his bookselling and publishing interests and became quite active in English politics.

These typescripts of William Cobbett's correspondence are to both social acquaintances and business associates. They discuss primarily English, French, and American politics and his interests in the bookselling and publishing trade. Correspondents include: Charles Dickens, T.C. Hansard, Henry Hunt, James Mathieu, John Nichols, Daniel O'Connell, William Palmer, and Sir Charles Wolseley.

Gift of Haverford College Library, 1981.

2130
Cook, Lewis D.   Collection, 1790–1922.   (ca. 100 items and 1 v.)

Miscellaneous family papers of the Tingey and Craven family. Correspondence between family members discuss: family life, religious thought, health, advice for a travelling daughter, careers of family members (in the Coast Guard, Navy, Railroad and the Croton Aqueduct Company), and various estate settlements.

Gift, date unknown.

2131
Postlethwaite, Samuel.   Papers, 1778–1795.   (35 items.)

Correspondence to and miscellaneous military papers of Samuel Postlethwaite primarily on the distribution of provisions during the Revolution.

2132
Fitzgerald family.   Papers, 1888–1954.   (10 v., ca. 400 items.)

Personal and business papers for Emma J. Fitzgerald, Emma H. Fitzgerald, and Edward Fitzgerald on real estate rentals and sales. Some of the property includes homes on Dudley Street, Tenth Street, Ogden Street, Eleventh Street, Geritt Street, and Alder Street in Philadelphia.

Gift of Mrs. Barbara Haig, 1982–1984.

Finding aid available.

2133
Kranzel, Isadore, 1932-   Papers, 1967–1982.   (ca. 1,000 items.)

Isadore Kranzel of Philadelphia served as assistant city solicitor and as a justice on the Supreme Court for Pennsylvania. He has been very active in civic and political affairs in Philadelphia.

Most of the correspondence deals with either solicitations or thank you letters for political endorsements and/or financial contributions. Some of the correspondents are: Arlen Specter, Milton Shapp, Wilson Goode, William Green, Donald Wagner, Louis Hill, Charles Bowser, Joseph Clark, William Grey, III, William Klenk, Ed Rendell, Ernest Kline, George X. Schwartz, Bill Ewing, Ray Lederer, Robert O'Donnell, and other political aspirants.

The remainder of the papers include: memorandum, papers pertaining to the Philadelphia Committee on City Policy, miscellaneous political and civic papers, reports, speeches, notes, newspaper reprints, political flyers, and invitations to political fundraisers.

Gift of Isadore Kranzel, 1982.

Finding aid available.

2134
Thompson, William B.   Papers, 1733–1817.   (ca. 250 items.)

Family correspondence and business papers of the William Thompson family. Included are a diary belonging to Mary B. Thompson while in Liverpool and a letterbook of correspondence written also while in Liverpool.

2135
Thompson, William.   Collection, 1855–1907.   (ca. 250 items.)

Dr. William Thompson served as assistant surgeon general during the Civil War and Head of Douglass Hospital.

Correspondence relating to his career as assistant surgeon general and as Head of Douglass Hospital. Other papers include an account of the Potomac Campaign by Carlos Carvallo, medical notations, and invitations and appointments to various medical societies.

2136
National League for Woman's Service.   **Records, 1917–1920.**
(ca. 1,000 items.)

The National League for Woman's Services was the result of a study done by Grace Parker in 1916 on the work of British women during World War I. After completing her observations, she returned to the United States to organize the American version of what she saw. The League was organized in Washington, D.C., 1917, "with the object of establishing through the country, state branches to maintain a Bureau of Registration and Information, under which Bureau organizations may enroll, to be called upon for service by the Government in case of need." The League called for women to enlist their talents such as sewing, skilled labor, and arsenal work as appropriate to each committee. Some of the committees include: War Hospital Library committee, Comfort Kit committee (sending sweaters, socks and other home made items), Musical Records and Games committee, Canteen committee, Membership committee, Belgian Relief committee, French War Relief committee, British committee.

Minutes, 1917–1920 reporting on provisions sent to soldiers, American Red Cross medical volunteer service, instructions to civilians and soldiers, Liberty Loan and Victory Loan Campaigns, and other fund raising efforts; membership lists; Liberty Loan Campaign information; and printed materials on the roles played by the National League and its activities (including the responsibilities of each committee) as well as information on League for Woman's Service outside the United States.

The individuals most mentioned throughout the records in connection with the National League are: Mrs. J. Bailey Browder, Mrs. John C. Groome, Mrs. J. Willis Martin, Mrs. Thomas Robins, Miss Sarah Bache Hodge, Mrs. Alexander Van Rensselaer, Mrs. E. T. Stotesbury, Mrs. Horace Brock, Mrs. S.P. Snowden, Mrs. Alan Harris, Mrs. George Dallas Dixon, Mrs. James Starr, Jr., Mrs. Nathaniel Seaver Keay, Miss McInnes, Mrs. Mary Gallagher, Mrs. J. Claude Bedford, Mrs. Bayard Henry, Mrs. Charles Lea, and others.

Gift of the National Society of Colonial Dames in the Commonwealth of Pennsylvania.

Finding aid available.

2137
Lewis, Dora Kelly, b. 1862.   **Correspondence, 1884–1921.**
(200 items.)

Dora Kelly Lewis served actively in the Suffrage movement. She became an executive member of the National Women's Party in 1913. She served as the chairman of finance in 1918 and as the national treasurer in 1919. In 1920, she headed the ratification committee.

The correspondence of Dora Kelly Lewis consists of encouraging and endearing letters from her husband, Larwence Lewis, 1884–1903, reporting on his legal practice and commenting on Dora's suffragette activities. The letters, 1914–1921, are, for the most part, from Dora to her children, some, from prison, reassuring her family that her actions were not illegal, and to her mother. There are a few typed, diary pages. These letters document her efforts in gaining franchise for women.

Gift of Dora Kelly Lewis descendants, 1986.

2138
American Association of University Women. Pennsylvania Division. Philadelphia Branch.   Archives, 1923–1984.   (24 linear ft.)

The American Association of University Women incorporated in 1899 "for the purpose of uniting alumnae of different institutions for practical educational work, for the collection and publication of statistical and other information concerning education, and in general for the maintenance of high standards of education." Membership is open to women holding approved degrees from institutions accepted by the association. The Philadelphia Branch, also known as the College Club of Philadelphia, was recognized by the association in 1886.

Minutes and correspondence of various committees within the A.A.U.W. including: the executive board, membership, admissions, art, bi-centennial, civic house, legislative, reorganization/relocation, fellowship, social and economic issues, status of women, steering and tea committees. Statements, tax related materials, personnel records, time sheets, journals, ledgers, cashbooks, and bank account books give information on the financial aspects of the organization. The remaining part of the archives is devoted to conferences, publicity, and printed materials and include: press releases, publicity calendars, clippings, the *Bulletin,* and general director's letters.

Represented in the collection are: Eleanore Harris Albany, Marie Jeanette Osgood Aydelotte, Sarah Ann Pithouse Becker, Anna F. Davies, Mildred Fairchild, Bertha Sanford Greenberg, Lucy Biddle Lewis, Ellen Moore, May A. Naylor, Mildred Scott Olmsted, Kelly Roes, Edith Wilder Scott, Fay Mary MacCracken Stockwell, Katherine Tucker, and Lucy Langdon Wilson. 67

Gift of the A.A.U.W.

Finding aid available.

2139–2145
No entry.

2146
Biddle family.   Papers, 1688–1883.   (33 linear ft.)

The Biddle family papers include the papers of Charles Biddle, William S. Biddle, Nicholas Biddle, Charles J. Biddle, and Craig Biddle.

The papers for Charles Biddle deal primarily with his land investments with Isaac Meason. These papers include patents, and correspondence concerned with Western land speculation. Papers for his sons Edward and Richard are also among his papers.

The papers for William S. Biddle, son of Charles and Hannah Shepard Biddle, include: correspondence, 1805–1835; real estate papers dealing with a lot on Race Street; legal papers concerning the settlement of various family member's estates; and miscellaneous printed material.

The correspondence,1800–1844, 1849, 1863, n.d., for Nicholas Biddle discusses local and national politics, private investments, and private matters such as grape cultivation at Andalusia. Correspondents include: A.J. Dallas and Edward Coles on banking; Robert and John Oliver on the Craig estate; R.L. Colt on the Bank of the United States and land speculation; Thomas Biddle as land agent for Nicholas Biddle; B. DeHaert on Salt Spring, Montrose; James Monroe; Davey Crockett, on the bank question and Crockett's election; Daniel Webster; Henry Clay; George M. Dallas, William M. Meredith, John Read, E.R. Biddle, George M. Edwards, William Rawle, T.S. Taylor, and Henry Drinker on the Bank of the United States; Jno. McKinney and Henry D. Rogers on the Buffalo Furnace; and Thaddeus Stevens, on his relationship with the Court.

The remainder of Nicholas Biddle's papers include: diaries on his travels in Europe; legal papers primarily for the Craig family and other family members; investment papers; Bank of the United States papers including his defense; receipted bills; commonplace books; and miscellaneous items.

Correspondence, 1816, 1827, 1831–1873, 1882, 1883, n.d. represents the bulk of papers for Charles J. Biddle, son of Nicholas Biddle, There is a separate group of correspondence between Charles J. Biddle and his wife Emma Biddle of both personal and political nature, most of which discuss his experience in the House of Representatives. Topics in the chronological correspondence include his military and political careers, and his investments and various legal trusts. Correspondents include: John Cadwalader on legal matters; Roswell L. Colt on salt works and land purchasing; A.B. Reed on the Craig/McMurtrie lands; James Biddle, Thomas White, G.M. Dallas, and Henry Drinker all on the Mexican War; C.J. Ingersoll, Craig

Biddle, Simon Cameron, William Seward, and James Buchanan all on political and military matters during the Civil War; George W. Woodward on
Woodward's run for governor and other matters concerning the Democratic
party; and Benjamin Rush on the Alabama claims.

Legal papers, real estate papers, financial papers and miscellaneous papers including his literary pursuits finish out the Charles J. Biddle papers.

The final series of papers belongs to Craig Biddle, youngest son of
Nicholas Biddle. His papers include legal and miscellaneous papers and
receipts. There is also an indexed volume of Biddle and Craig family letters,
1787–1825.

Gift of Charles and James Biddle, 1978.

Finding aid available.

2147–2167
No entry.

2168
Nauman Family.   Papers, 1836–1865.   (1 linear ft.)

George Nauman was an officer with the United States Army. His son
George, was a Lancaster lawyer. Anne Nauman lived in St. Augustine, Fla.,
and in Lancaster during the Civil War.

Papers primarily consist of Anne Nauman's incoming correspondence
and include letters from her father George Nauman. There are also letters
from various school friends and relatives in St. Augustine and some miscellaneous documents on the family.

Gift of John H. Eberman, 1987.

2169
Coates family.   Papers, (1763–1789) (1832–1915).   (30 items.)

Papers for various members of the Coates family, a prominent Philadelphia family including: Samuel Coates, Philadelphia merchant, Beulah
Coates, Mary Coates, and Sarah Coates. Much of the collection documents
their activity as members of or officers for the following benevolent societies:
the Female Society of Philadelphia for the Relief and Employment of the
Poor (operated a House of Industry where women sewed garments in exchange for food and childcare), the Sewing Society (private group concerned
with sewing clothing for the poor), the Temporary Home Association (established in 1849 to provide a transient boarding house for women looking
for work, also for children of employable age), and the Union Benevolent
Association (established in 1830 to provide donations of coal, groceries,
provisions, clothing, furniture for the "worthy" poor).

Gift of Elizabeth Coates.

2170
Beatty family. **Papers, 1768–1816.** **(.5 linear ft.)**

Correspondence between: Charles Clinton Beatty, Presbyterian minister; John Beatty, revolutionary soldier and New Jersey politician; Reading; physician; Erkuries Beatty, revolutionary soldier; and William Beatty, soldier and merchant.

Gift of Laird U. Park, Jr., 1987.

INDEX

INDEX

INDEX

INDEX

INDEX

INDEX

INDEX

INDEX

INDEX

INDEX

INDEX

Bruce, David. 129
Brumbaugh, Martin Grove. 1551
Brustar, Henry. 1976
Bryan, George, 1731–1791. 22, 90, 190, 193, 225, 250, 429, 888, 1429
Bryan, William Jennings, 1860–1925. 121, 175, 1381, 1541, 1616
Bryn Mawr College. 2055, 2120
Bryant, William Cullen. 1381
Bryn Mawr Polo Club (Bryn Mawr, Pa.) 2038
Buchanan, Alexander, d.1913. 1872
Buchanan and Dunlap. 1692
Buchanan and McGill. 2001
Buchanan Fund. 93
Buchanan, Harriet, 1794–1838. 92
Buchanan, James, 1791–1868. 23, 91, 92, 93, 151, 164, 193, 199, 238, 252, 266, 365, 447, 512, 517, 586, 831, 1454, 1676, 1743A
Buchanan, Roberdeau, 1839–1916, collector. 94
Buck, Charles N., 1775–1851. 95
Buck, Hammitt, Apple, and Company. 820
Buck, Jacob E., 1801–1880. 96
Buck, Pearl S. (Pearl Syndenstricker), 1892–1973. 1679
Buck, William J., b. 1825. 849
Buckingham, John Sheffield, Duke of, 1648–1720 or 21. 97
Buckley, Annie Morris, b.1835. 2000C
Buckley, D. Penrose, d. 1862. 1775
Buckley, Daniel. 595B
Buckley family. 2037
Buckley, William. 403
Buckner, Simon B. 175
Bucks County (Pa.) 3, 18, 22, 32, 96, 98, 175, 186, 281, 316, 454, 485, 488, 649, 697, 779, 805, 950, 1624, 2123–Census. 777–History. 1837
Buckshot War, 1838. 510
Buckstone, John Baldwin, 1802–1879. 2001
Budd, John. 316
Buenos Aires (Argentina). 512
Buffalo Furnace Company. 1801, 2146
Buffington, Jonathan. 150
Buffington, Lee H. 99
Buffington, Peter. 150
Buford, John, 1826–1863. 2031
Buford, Napoleon B., 1807–1883. 121
Building and Loan Association books, 1871–1909. 1418

Building and loan associations–Pennsylvania–Philadelphia. 1418
Building 104, 108, 1540
Bull, Edward. 1802
Bull, Eliza. 1802
Bull family. 100
Bull, James, 1817–1904. 101
Bull, Levi, 1780–1859. 100
Bull, Mary Brandford, 1699–1771. 1447
Bull, Ole, 1810–1880. 592
Bull Run, 1st Battle, 1861. 1546
Bull Run, 2d Battle of, 1862. 1910, 2031
Bull, Thomas, 1744–1837. 973
Bulletin. 2138
Bullit, John. 22
Bulley, Robert. 708B
Bulwer-Lytton, Edward. 22
Bumstead, Jeremiah, b. 1678. 703
Bumstead, Sarah, b. 1676. 703
Bunden, Warren. 2113
Bundock, Mary. 337
Bunel, Joseph R.E. 1811
Bunel, Marie F.M. 1811
Bunne, James. 808
Bunner, Sarah. 1628
Bunting-Nicholson Manuscripts, 1684–1850. 102
Bunting, Samuel, d. 1724. 102
Bunting, Samuel J., 1889–1959. 1948
Bunting, William M. 1539
Burbank, Luther. 22
Burd, Edward, 1751–1833. 22, 103, 108, 595B, 740, 778
Burd, Edward Shippen, 1779–1848. 22, 104, 105, 108, 347, 595
Burd, Eliza H., 1793–1860. 104
Burd family. 595C, 1174, 1494, 2001
Burd, James, 1726–1793. 454, 595, 595C
Burd Orphan Asylum. 104
Burd, Sarah Shippen, 1731–1784. 595C
Burd, Sarah. 595, 595B
Bureau of Municipal Research (Philadelphia, Pa.) 2029
Bureau of Unemployment Relief. 1585
Burgoyne, John, Sir, 1739–1785. 145
Burke, Thomas, 1747 (ca.)-1783. 455
Burkhardt, John, 1893–1969. 1880
Burleigh, Charles Calistus, 1810–1878. 10
Burlington, (N.J.) 129, 143, 154, 301, 450, 607, 698, 1450–Climate. 1249

INDEX

Buxton, Thomas Folwell, Sir, 1786–1845. 189
Buzby, John Burrows. 1987
Byberry School (Philadelphia, Pa.) 1654
Byers, James. 466
Byers, William Vincent. 840
Byrd, William, 1674–1744. 36
Byron, George Gordon (Lord Byron). 193
C. Schrack and Company. 2080
Cab and omnibus service. 820
Cabinet-workers–Pennsylvania–Philadelphia. 1215
Cabinet-workers. 1951
Cadbury, Elizabeth Head. 692
Cadbury, Richard, 1825–1897 2001
Cadwalader, Charles Evert, 1839–1907. 1454
Cadwalader family. 1454
Cadwalader, George, 1806–1879. 1454, 1462, 1976
Cadwalader, John, 1742–1786. 111, 225, 250, 973, 1041, 1454
Cadwalader, John, 1805–1879. 91, 1235, 1454
Cadwalader, John, 1843–1925. 1454
Cadwalader, Thomas, 1779–1841. 973, 1454
Caesar, Julius. 576
Calcutta (India) 154–Description. 1582
Caldwell and Ewing. 1982
Caldwell family. 1863
Caldwell, Charles. 108
Caldwell, David. 1962
Caldwell, Robert S. 1982
Calfe, John. 957, 1995
Calhoun, Alexander. 36
Calhoun, Benjamin C. 112
Calhoun, John C. (John Caldwell), 1782–1850. 94, 151, 238, 250, 380, 447, 466, 512, 517, 645, 1812, 1978
Calico-printing. 582, 1586
California 101, 108, 226, 558, 1425–Description and travel. 101, 728,–Gold discoveries. 158, 1425, 1509–History. 1311
Callender, William. 1123
Calligraphy–Copy-books. 311
Callowhill, Hannah. 485
Callowhill Market (Philadelphia, Pa.) 967
Calvert, Charles, Lord Baltimore, 1637–1715. 111, 183, 485, 655, 1333, 1455
Calvert County (Md.) 176
Calvin, Samuel, 1811–1890. 1732
Camac, Mrs. William. 2126
Camac, William Masters, 1802–1842. 1420

Cambria County (Pa.) 176
Cambridge (Mass.) 973
Camden (N.J.) 781, 1101, 1540, 1546, 1855–Bridges. 1258
Camden and Gloucester Poll books, 1856. 781
Camden, Charles Pratt, Earl, 1714–1794. 603
Cameron, John, d. 1770. 1625A
Cameron, Margaret. 1616
Cameron, Simon, 1799–1889. 91, 121, 151, 250, 266, 557, 645, 1151, 1616, 1732, 1868, 2122, 2146
Cammerhoff, John Christopher Frederick, 1721–1751. 782
Camp Brandywine (Pa.) 1093
Camp Dupont (Pa.) 1093
Camp Marcus Hook (Philadelphia, Pa.) 1332
Campbell, Francis Duncan, 1845–1864. 113
Campbell, Hugh G., 1760–1825. 331
Campbell, Mary 2001
Campbell, James Hepburn, 1820–1895. 113
Campbell, John, 114
Campbell, John H. 988
Campbell, Samuel, 1763?–1836. 114
Campbell, Thomas 2001
Camps (Military). 1332
Canada and the Continental Congress, 1850. 178
Canada 39, 116, 178, 262, 511, 512, 590–History–Rebellion, 1837–1838. 250–War of 1812–Campaigns. 482, 817, 1058
Canadian Invasion, 1775–1776. 280, 2018B
Canal boats. 108
Canals 160, 600, 728, 2001–Cost of construction. 167, 644, 813–Design and construction. 84, 303–Pennsylvania 2, 632, 1216, 1328, 1988A, 1988B, 2050–Philadelphia. 2001- Statistics. 127
Canal companies. 722, 1148, 1328, 1339
Canby, Thomas. 1021
Canedo, Juan de. 512
Canfield, D.B. 939
Canoes. 317
Canonge, Benjamin. 2033
Canteens (War-time, emergency, etc.). 1479)1534
Canton (China) 108, 734–Commerce. 184, 622–Travel and description. 1878
Cantwells Bridge (Del.) 108
Cape May (N.J.) 322, 359, 622

INDEX

INDEX

INDEX

INDEX

INDEX

INDEX

INDEX

INDEX

INDEX

INDEX

INDEX

INDEX

INDEX

INDEX

INDEX

INDEX

INDEX

Fire in art. 580

Fire Insurance Company of Philadelphia County. 839

Firemen's Active Association of Philadelphia. 1548

Fireplaces. 813

First African Presbyterian Church (Philadelphia, Pa.) 8

First American movement west, 1750–1850. 840

First Bank of the United States. 1692

First Congregational Society of Unitarian Christians (Philadelphia, Pa.) 707

First Female Beneficial Society of Philadelphia (Philadelphia, Pa.) 756

First Independent Church (Philadelphia, Pa.) Youth's Missionary Society. 788

First Presbyterian Church (Philadelphia, Pa.) Building Committee. 788

First Reformed Dutch Church (Philadelphia, Pa.) 1518

First Troop Philadelphia City Cavalry. 1934B, 1973

First Universalist Church (Philadelphia, Pa.) 680

Fish, Asa Israel, 1820–1879. 1987

Fish, Hamilton, 1808–1893. 645

Fish trade. 108, 243, 499, 595, 1982

Fishbourne, Benjamin. 973

Fisher, Ann Eliza George, 1785–1821. 1850B

Fisher Anna Wells. 759

Fisher, Elizabeth Ingersoll, 1815–1872. 1850A, 1850B

Fisher, Elizabeth Rhoads, 1770–1796. 1955

Fisher, Ellicott, 1840–1908. 2096

Fisher family. 382, 692, 1462, 1955, 2094

Fisher, Howell Tracy, Mrs., collector. 206

Fisher, J. Sydney. 1976

Fisher, Jabez Maude, 1801–1876. 2094

Fisher, James C. 708, 1148, 1757 1735

Fisher, John. 1404

Fisher, Johannes. 1987

Fisher, Joshua. 1864

Fisher, Joshua, 1707–1783. 225, 2001

Fisher, Joshua Francis, 1807–1873. 485, 1858, 2011

Fisher, Letitia Ellicott, d. 1881. 2096

Fisher, Martin. 2117B

Fisher, Michael C. 206

Fisher, Miers, 1748–1819. 207, 2001, 2094

Fisher, Miers, 1786–1813. 2094

Fisher, Miers. 108, 1375

Fisher, Redwood, 1782–1856. 2094

Fisher, Samuel Rowland, 1745–1834. 586, 2001, 2019, 2094

Fisher, Samuel W. 1955

Fisher, Samuel. 108, 1375, 2001

Fisher, Sarah Logan, 1751–1796. 1923, 1995, 2015

Fisher, Sarah Redwood, 1759–1847. 2047B, 2094

Fisher, Sidney. 225

Fisher, Sidney George, 1809–1871. 1462, 1850A, 1850B

Fisher, Sydney George, 1856–1927. 1850B, 2096

Fisher, Thomas, 1741–1810. 108, 238, 379, 1923, 2001, 2028, 2094, 2096

Fisher, Thomas Rodman, 1803–1861. 2009, 2096

Fisher, William. 193

Fisher, William Logan, 1701–1862. 1858, 2028

Fisher, William Logan, 1832–1858. 2096

Fisheries 1526–Nova Scotia. 243– Pennsylvania–Philadelphia. 499

Fishing nets industry. 719

Fiske, Anne. 1962

Fitch, John, 1743–1798. 90, 208

Fithian, Enoch. 841

Fitler, Elvina, fl. 1865–1874 2001

Fitz Randolph-Snowden Genealogy, 1695–1832. 209

Fitzgerald, Edward, d. 1929. 2132

Fitzgerald, Emma H. 2132

Fitzgerald, Emma J. 2132

Fitzgerald, F. Scott (Francis Scott), 1896–1940. 1679

Fitzgerald family. 2132

Fitzgerald, Thomas. 842

Fitzsimons, Thomas, 1741–1811. 1041, 1141, 1183, 1242, 1744, 1791, 2001

Fitzwater, Jacob. 1540

Fitzwater, John. 1540

Five O'Clock Club (Philadelphia, Pa.) 1541

Flagg, John Foster Brewster. 1425

Flagg, Josiah Foster, 1828–1903. 1425

Flagg, Thomas. 58

Flags–United States. 1519

Flanders, Benjamin F., 1816–1896. 121

Flat Bush (N.Y.) 8

INDEX

INDEX

INDEX

INDEX

INDEX

INDEX

INDEX

INDEX

INDEX

INDEX

INDEX

INDEX

INDEX

INDEX

INDEX

INDEX

INDEX

INDEX

INDEX

INDEX

INDEX

INDEX

INDEX

INDEX

INDEX

INDEX

INDEX

INDEX

INDEX

INDEX

INDEX

INDEX

INDEX

INDEX

INDEX

INDEX

INDEX

INDEX

INDEX

INDEX

INDEX

INDEX

INDEX

INDEX

INDEX

INDEX

INDEX

INDEX

INDEX

INDEX

INDEX

INDEX

INDEX

INDEX

INDEX

INDEX

INDEX